David S. McDougall
Ga. Tech Box 33269
Spring '69

Economic Analysis

For Engineering and Managerial Decision-Making

Economic Analysis

For Engineering and Managerial Decision-Making

NORMAN N. BARISH, *Professor of Management Engineering*
Chairman of the Department of Industrial Engineering and Operations
Research, New York University

1962   **McGraw-Hill Book Company**

New York   San Francisco   Toronto   London

ECONOMIC ANALYSIS

Preface

Making decisions is the key function in engineering and business activity. Most of the engineering and management decisions made in industry are or should be based upon economic analyses.

This book is directed to persons who are concerned with these economic analyses and aims to present the basic reasoning and methodology of various disciplines which are important in decision-making. It is designed to be practical rather than theoretical. It is technique-oriented. Mathematical symbolism is kept as simple as possible and derivations or proofs are presented only if they are simple and will illuminate the subject matter.

The book has been planned as a college text for students of engineering, business, and economics for use in half-year or full-year courses which frequently bear such titles as engineering economy; managerial, industrial, or business economics; or business analysis. It has also been designed to be useful to operating executives and staff personnel. It can serve both groups as a reference book on the economic aspects of business decision-making.

Although no specified background or courses are prerequisite for its use, it is anticipated that many students using this book will have completed courses in such subjects as accounting, economics and management, and probability and statistics. However, relevant aspects of all these subjects are presented in problem-oriented introductions throughout the text. Readers with no background in some of these areas should therefore be able to follow most of the text presentation. The Bibliography presents supplementary readings useful for those who desire further background in some of these areas. (In a few places, a knowledge of the calculus would be helpful, but the text can be readily followed omitting the mathematical derivations.)

The book is arranged to permit maximum flexibility in the choice of material and in the sequence of class presentation and to provide for its use in classes with students of different backgrounds. Sufficient material is included for courses and course sequences of varying length. Each section and chapter has been made as self-sufficient as possible.

1. Chapters 3 to 12 and 17 cover the fundamental material on project and equipment evaluation traditionally included in courses in engineering economy.
2. Chapters 18 and 19 are an extension of the traditional material on decision-making under certainty to minimum-cost and maximum-profit determinations.
3. Chapters 13 to 16 cover the managerial economic problems of capital budgeting.
4. Chapters 20 to 27 examine the subject of risk, uncertainty, and intangibles in economic analysis. For those who desire to omit most of the material on probability and statistical techniques, the course coverage may be restricted to Chapters 20 and 27.
5. Chapters 28 to 35 are concerned with elements of economic measurement and analysis and with the managerial economic problems of forecasting sales, costs, and profits.

Each of these groups (and sections of them) may be included in or excluded from course coverage depending upon the objectives of the course and the background of the student.

I am grateful to the many business organizations and executives with whom I have been associated and who have contributed directly and indirectly to whatever value this book may have as well as to those who have permitted me to use illustrations included in this book. I am indebted to Professor Sir Ronald A. Fisher, F.R.S., Cambridge, and to Dr. Frank Yates, F.R.S., Rothamsted, also to Messrs. Oliver & Boyd, Ltd., Edinburgh, for permission to reprint Table 19 in the Appendix from their book *Statistical Tables for Biological, Agricultural and Medical Research*, and to Stephen T. Heinaman and the Armstrong Cork Company for permission to reproduce forms for evaluating capital expenditures. I am particularly grateful to Miss Justine L. Schmalzl for her capable and invaluable assistance in the preparation of text, tables, and charts. I am indebted to Norbert Hauser for reading the entire manuscript and offering helpful comments. I wish to thank Professors Eugene D. Homer, Arthur Lesser, Jr., and Wallace J. Richardson as well as Messrs. Harold Greenberg and Irwin Greenberg for reading and commenting on various sections of the book and Miss Betty Kiernan for typing the manuscript.

Norman N. Barish

Contents

PART ONE

Engineering and Business Decision-making

1 Introduction

Economic analysis for engineering and management decision-making encompasses the rational, scientific methods of analysis which are available to engineers and staff management personnel. This volume emphasizes the quantitative aspects of decision-making because they are most amenable to scientific treatment.

The success of an enterprise depends upon how effectively the managers and engineers do the following:

1. Decide what needs to be done and how and when
2. Administer the persons and groups in the enterprise who will carry out the decisions

We are concerned in this book with the first of these tasks, with the decisions which the engineers and managers of business enterprises and other organizations must recommend and make.

Engineering and Managerial Economic Decisions. The methods of analysis considered in this book are applicable to a large variety of engineering and economic decisions. For example: What should be the economic objective of the enterprise? its scope? its policies? its organizational structure? its systems? its strategies? its pricing procedures? What are the best sizes, numbers, and locations of servicing facilities for repairing the company's products? Should a fleet of delivery trucks be leased or bought?

Which research projects should be undertaken and how much should be invested in each? Which alternative engineering design should be chosen? Should production planning be performed manually or by means of a high-speed digital computer? If a computer system is desirable, which of the available computers should be chosen?

Is centralized or decentralized control of inventories more desirable? Should larger quantities of raw materials and parts be purchased at one time? Should a larger safety stock of finished goods be maintained? How many finished-goods warehouses should be constructed and where should they be located?

How large should the capital budget of the company be? Which investment proposals should be included? Should a proposed new venture be established? Should plant capacity be expanded? If yes, how much excess capacity should be built now to meet future anticipated needs? Should

3

new labor-saving automation equipment be purchased? If yes, which of the competing types should be chosen?

These are just a few of the types of questions which are amenable to solution by the analytic methods discussed in this book. The analyses and evaluations to reach decisions on these questions can be very simple or very sophisticated. How well these analyses and evaluations are made will affect the future welfare of the business and will determine the quality of the engineering design.

This discussion of problems requiring decisions has been stated in terms which are applicable to business enterprises. However, many of these same questions and the methods of analysis and evaluation apply equally to activities in government and nonprofit organizations.

Uneconomic "Modern" Decisions. Many computer systems have been adopted by company managements in recent years based upon evaluation studies which indicated that tangible costs would be reduced, or remain the same, or just increase slightly. The incentive behind the adoption of some of these systems has been the desire of company executives to have the "most modern, advanced data-processing system." There are numerous explanations for the errors of evaluation which have been made in many of these cases and many of these will be discussed later. However, it will be useful to review two factors briefly.

Many of the problems and complications of actual operation are not envisioned by the systems planners prior to the installation of the computer system. Why? Sometimes equipment used in the system does not perform to design specifications. In other cases, the people familiar with the machine capabilities are not familiar enough with procedural requirements and the people who know the procedural requirements do not know the machine capabilities.

Another factor in some cases is that, with the use of some of the modern data-processing and electronic equipment, the incremental costs of producing reports are low and the ability of the equipment to produce these reports swiftly is high. Under these conditions, reports of limited usefulness have sometimes proliferated because they have been easily available from data already coded and stored in readily usable form. The natural tendency to increase the number of reports is encouraged by the great effectiveness of this new equipment. The result is the continuance on a regular basis of reports with limited or no usefulness or only a one-time usefulness.

These uneconomic "modern" decisions illustrate three points:

1. Decisions made on the basis of modernity, progressiveness, rules of thumb, and hunch can be uneconomic.

2. Engineering and economic analyses for decision-making should be entrusted only to qualified analysts who are aware of both the system requirements and the machine capabilities.

3. Administrative performance after decisions have been reached can alter the relative economy of operations. Effective managerial control is usually essential to insure that anticipated cost savings are obtained and that anticipated economic advantages are achieved.

Economic Evaluation of Existing Company Policies. Many companies have over the years developed policies in various areas of their operations which function as guideposts for decision-making. Some of these policies were valid when they were first established years ago but have lost their validity because of changed conditions. Others were never good policies and were continued because their economic implications were never carefully estimated.

Examples of the former type of policies are these: maintain a complete line of products to meet customer requirements (valid when the product line was relatively small); make all appointments to supervisory and managerial positions by promotion (valid when the organization was small and specialized technical or managerial skills were not required).

Examples of the latter types of policies are these: maintain inventory levels on all items so as never to be out of stock (usually unachievable, resulting in uneconomically high inventory levels); maintain employment at stable levels, smoothing out all seasonal and cyclical demand fluctuations by varying the stock level (absolute stability of employment is not always economically justifiable).

The economic effects of all company policies on current and future operations should be periodically evaluated to ascertain whether the policies should be continued or amended.

Rational Objectives. Successful economic decision-making may involve very simple procedures in one case and very complex, technical ones in another. However, some basic elements are common to all economic analyses.

A first, and crucial, step in any economic evaluation is a logical statement of the objectives to be achieved. When the relative importance of these objectives has been determined, they will furnish the basis for establishing the criteria for the desirability of alternative proposals. A rational set of objectives is therefore of pivotal importance in engineering and economic decision-making.

Data Collection. It is necessary to collect data on the environment in which the various alternative proposals will operate. These data are of three types: quantitative data based on observations which describe organizational, financial, procedural, physical, and operational relationships and flows; qualitative data based on observations which describe these relationships and flows; and data based upon the opinions, intuition, and personal judgment of experts with experience. These types of data have been presented in descending order of general usefulness in economic analysis. Quantitative data are most amenable to scientific analysis.

Qualitative data do not usually permit as rigorous analytic manipulation nor as definite a conclusion. Data based on personal opinions have been frequently found to be unconsciously biased and unreliable for many reasons, some of which can be explained by statistical probability and psychology.

A critical approach is necessary in gathering data. The engineering and economic analyst must always be silently critical and skeptical of all alleged facts. A statement is considered suspect until it is proved true. A well-executed analysis will not be worth the paper it is written on if it is based on incorrect or incomplete data.

The problem of obtaining correct data is complicated because there may be a number of different answers to the same question, for example, how is a certain activity performed?

1. The way the supervisor thinks it is done
2. The way the employee thinks the supervisor wants it done
3. The way the supervisor tells the employee to do it
4. The way the instruction manual says it should be done
5. The way it is actually done

People mislead not only from malicious intent: they sometimes are misinformed themselves; they sometimes do not desire to admit their ignorance and therefore guess at the answer. Written information may be incorrect because it is out of date. The only answer to the accuracy problem is to double-check all crucial information by actual observation whenever possible.

Determining the Alternatives. When engineering and business decisions are made logically, they always involve an evaluation of alternative courses of action. As much as possible, all alternative courses of action should be considered and evaluated. Otherwise, the evaluation may suggest an alternative as optimum which is only the best among those alternatives considered, but is not the best of all possible ones. The best decision may then be missed.

Alternative courses of action are determined at all levels in an organization by operating and supervisory as well as staff research and engineering personnel. Alternatives for accomplishing the objectives of the study also suggest themselves to an analyst at the same time as the data are being gathered, analyzed, and evaluated. Not only should alternatives be considered which are available with existing technology, but, in some cases, it may be feasible to consider the research and development of new technology or the modification of existing facilities. All these alternatives should be systematically listed so that they will receive mature consideration before any are discarded.

It is important that alternative possibilities be considered separately as well as in combination with each other. This should reduce a source of error in economic evaluations which has in the past crept into the economic justification for computer installations. Let us suppose that there is a noncomputer system for performing a task which is better than the presently used noncomputer system. Then, logically, the economy of the computer system should be compared with this better noncomputer method as well as with any other possible alternatives. The study preliminary to a computer application will frequently disclose possibilities for major systems improvements and savings which are not necessarily tied to use of the computer. The alternative of a computer installation should not be credited with these savings.

Decision-making Costs. For many engineering and business decisions, dollar income and costs provide convenient measures for summarizing the potential future performance of alternative courses of action. However, costs as determined by the usual accounting systems, which are designed to measure past occurrences rather than future prospects, are not always suitable for decision-making purposes. We must therefore examine how accounting costs have been determined before using them in economic analysis. The handling of depreciation, interest, profits, and income taxes in economy analyses must receive careful consideration. Potential pitfalls from using sunk (past) costs to estimate future expected cost should be avoided.

Evaluating Investment Proposals. When all the significant effects of an investment proposal can be estimated in dollars, a tangible analysis of the worth of the proposal can be made. Annual-cost comparisons are the most commonly used and are easily understood in industry because the format is analogous (but only in some respects) to a forecasted profit and loss statement. Present-worth and premium-worth calculations are useful for comparisons of certain kinds of long-term investment proposals. Rate-of-return determinations provide a measure of profitability which is quite universal in its applicability to all kinds of investment proposals. Rate-of-return evaluation is especially useful in overall capital-budgeting procedures. Equal-cost determinations are helpful when we are uncertain about the correct value to use for one important factor in our dollar analysis. They are also useful for evaluating the sensitivity of a decision to changes in the expected value of one important factor. Payout determinations are especially valuable when a business is short of capital funds and desires to make investments in which the funds will be recovered rapidly.

Capital management represents a central decision-making function in the enterprise. What are the investment opportunities in the firm? What are the sources of capital funds? Which investment opportunities should be undertaken and which sources of funds utilized to finance these investments to promote the profitability and long-range growth of the enterprise? Capital-budgeting procedures should be designed to provide rational answers to these questions.

Minimum Costs or Maximum Profits. Many decisions which involve the choice of the size or the amount of an activity or a facility may be handled by determining the size or amount which will result in a minimum-cost point. Other decisions involving the allocation of limited resources may be determined by programming these resources to achieve a minimum-cost or maximum-profit objective.

Risk, Uncertainty, and Intangibles. We can classify engineering and business decisions as to whether the conditions under which the decision is made are certain, risky, uncertain (partial or complete), or both risky and uncertain. Risk exists when each alternative will lead to one of a set of possible outcomes and there is a known probability of each outcome. Uncertainty exists when the probabilities of these outcomes are completely or partially unknown. For example, if one alternative is to install an automatic-control device to correct a quality defect and if there is a known probability that such a device will correct this trouble only one time in 10, the conditions are risky. If the probability that it will correct the defect is unknown or only partially known, the conditions are uncertain as well as risky.

In actual fact, all economic analyses are made under conditions of risk and uncertainty to varying degrees. Evaluations of the relative desirability of alternatives require estimates of present conditions as well as forecasts of future events, which involve risks and uncertainties. Yet none of the methods of analysis thus far mentioned explicitly take account of risk and uncertainty.

To take account of risk explicitly, we need to apply theories of statistics, probability, probability distributions, sampling, and confidence limits.

When the data describing important environmental relationships are not available, experimentation may be desirable to obtain required quantitative data. Unfortunately, it is frequently difficult and prohibitively expensive to arrange many of the types of experiments required in economic analysis. The use of models and Monte Carlo simulations of actual operating conditions can sometimes be helpful in developing data. Monte Carlo techniques may be helpful with models of situations in which risk is present. Analytic queuing models can be useful in waiting-time problems.

When we cannot measure the risks and uncertainty in an economic analysis, they become intangible factors in the evaluation. In addition, there may be significant factors involved in the decision which cannot be quantified into dollars or another common denominator. It may be very difficult to devise adequate, scientific methods for evaluating these intangibles.

Economic and Business Forecasting. All the decisions we have been discussing affect future events. Therefore, no mathematical calculation, however sophisticated, erudite, and accurate, can be better than the validity and reliability of the forecasted data used in the analysis. The forecasted revenues and costs will depend upon the future state of the company, the industry or industries, and the economy. To assist in this forecasting, it is helpful to have an understanding of the economics of the firm and its relationship to other firms in the same, competing, and complementary industries. Time-series and correlation analysis are useful tools for the econometric task of measuring the nature of the demand for various products and services as well as forecasting future values for various factors. Index numbers and other measures of the economy are helpful in forecasting future economic activity and sales of a company's product.

Available methods of forecasting future requirements for the goods and services of a company are varied, but they are all fraught with large possibilities for error. It is well to use as many different independent approaches as possible to check one against the other in an attempt to discover the sources of any mistakes.

If we have developed a forecast of sales and can determine how our costs will vary in the short run with changes in output rate, we can forecast our short-run profits. We can also use this short-run revenue-cost comparison (break-even analysis) to determine how various policy decisions will affect our profits. In the long run a company can vary other factors in addition to output rate. The long-run cost function shows the average cost of producing a product or service, assuming that the correct size of facility has been chosen, and is useful for making facility-size-and-location decisions.

Cost of Data Gathering, Analysis, and Evaluation. We are confronted with the problem of making a decision on how much cost and effort it is economical to spend to make the economic decision. Data gathering, analysis, and evaluation are expensive. It is not economic to attempt to collect all the information which might be pertinent to an optimum solution and make all of the analyses and evaluations of all the alternatives which may conceivably yield useful results.

What are some of the factors which will determine the amount of data gathering, analysis, and evaluation which is desirable?

A decision on whether or not to research, develop, manufacture, and market a proposed new line of products may or may not be more important to the future welfare of the business than a decision on a proposed change in the product-warranty policy. Other things being equal, a decision on whether or not to invest $500 in laborsaving equipment which will yield a prospective return of 20 per cent is not as crucial as whether or not to invest $500,000 in laborsaving equipment which will yield the same prospective rate of return. Obviously, more time and money should be spent on those decisions which are more important in promoting the prime objectives of the organization.

Even though the correctness of a decision may be very important in determining the future performance of the organization, it still may not be desirable to spend a large amount of time and money collecting and analyzing data if variations in the values of the variable being studied do not produce significant differences in total costs, profits, or other decision criteria. Other things being equal, more time and effort should be expended in determining economic purchasing quantities when a 10 per cent error in estimating the optimum quantity will produce a 1 per cent increase in total costs than when it will produce only a 0.1 per cent increase.

The uneconomic collection of detailed, accurate data and the use of refined analyses should be avoided when rough approximations will do the job effectively enough.

Economic Progress and Economy Analysis. Economic and business progress in the United States or elsewhere is not the automatic result of the functioning of a superior economic system. Nor does it occur automatically because of the presence of abundant natural and human resources. Rather, the economic system encourages the kind of individual initiative and business and engineering decision-making which promotes growth in the whole economy.

Our concern in this volume is more with decision-making at the enterprise, organization, and individual-person level rather than with the whole economy. However, when the aggregate of the many individual engineering, business, and governmental decisions in the economy is economic, then the productivity of our entire nation rises.

Our high standard of living and productivity and the strength of our economy and national defense are related both to the skill, ingenuity, initiative, and inventiveness of our business leaders as well as our research scientists and engineers. To meet our civilian and military needs our research scientists and engineers develop new and improved products and new methods of producing these products more efficiently. However, business leaders must make the correct decisions to invest in those research undertakings and facility expansions which will prove economic and advance our national well-being or the work of the scientist and engineer will be unproductive.

A major factor in increasing labor productivity has been the development of inanimate sources of energy (wind, water, and fuel) for performing industrial tasks. Table 1-1 summarizes work output by sources of energy from 1850 to 1950. These figures indicate that 10 years prior to the Civil War human workers provided 12.6 per cent of work output, work animals 52.4 per cent, and inanimate sources 35.0 per cent. By 1880, human workers were providing 9.4 per cent, work animals 37.1 per cent, and inanimate sources 53.5 per cent. By 1910, human workers were providing 3.0 per cent, work animals 10.9 per cent, and inanimate sources 86.1 per cent. The 1910 period was also the heyday of the horse, with

Table 1-1. Estimated Work Output, by Source of Energy, 1850 to 1950

	Billions of horsepower-hours	Percentage of horsepower-hours from each source		
		Human workers	Work animals	Inanimate*
1850	10.3	12.6	52.4	35.0
1860	15.4	11.8	49.7	38.5
1870	19.0	11.1	44.2	44.7
1880	29.9	9.4	37.1	53.5
1890	48.2	7.3	29.9	62.8
1900	78.5	5.3	21.5	73.2
1910	165.7	3.0	10.9	86.1
1920	288.4	1.8	5.3	92.9
1930	440.3	1.2	2.2	96.6
1940	497.4	1.1	1.4	97.5
1950	674.9	0.9	0.6	98.5

* Wind, water, and fuel.

SOURCE: Based on data in J. F. Dewhurst and Associates, *America's Needs and Resources*, The Twentieth Century Fund, Inc., New York, 1955, p. 1416.

24 million horses and mules at work compared to 37 million human beings. By 1930, human workers were providing 1.2 per cent, work animals 2.2 per cent, and inanimate sources 96.6 per cent. By 1950, only 0.9 per cent of work output was provided by human beings, and only 0.6 per cent by work animals; the remaining 98.5 per cent came from inanimate sources. Small as they are, even these percentages of work output from human beings and work animals will decrease in the future with further improvement and expansion of power production facilities and engineering advances in the use of new fuels, such as atomic energy.

Our nation's ability to produce work energy increased more than 60 times between 1850 and 1950, and about 8 times between 1900 and 1950. This development of economical inanimate energy sources was accomplished by American industry with the combined efforts of engineers and scientists. It made possible remarkable increases in American labor productivity over the past century.

Thus, the average worker today produces more than three times as much in a 40-hr week as his grandparents did in a 70-hr week one hundred years ago. This sixfold increase in productivity was achieved at an ever accelerating tempo, correspondent to the development of engineering and technology. During the second half of the nineteenth century, productivity almost doubled; since 1900 it has almost trebled. Moreover, the rate of increase during the past decade and a half has been greater than in any previous period.

The key factors in this progress are the incentives for innovation which a free competitive economy provides and the ability of engineers and managers to make economic decisions so that our productive resources are constantly being channeled into those businesses and activities where they can be most effectively used.

With the increasing complexity of our industrial technology, economic decision-making is becoming more difficult at the same time that it is becoming more critical. Business decisions frequently involve investments which must be planned and executed many years before the expected returns will be realized. Moreover, the scale of the investments in research and capital assets which are required for our expanding economy grows larger and larger as new technologies develop. All indications point to increasingly rapid technological advances in the future which will make these decision-making functions even more difficult as well as more critical.

Brief mention of some of the new technology which is developing, and will in the future develop still further, is perhaps of some value in attempting to evaluate economic decision-making problems of the future. Automation is, and will continue to grow as, an important factor in our economy. Further developments in electronics, machine design, and materials-handling and -transfer mechanisms will enable us to continue our rapid progress in the use of automation in industry. Electronic computers will be further improved to extend their usefulness to new industrial-control and information-processing and -transfer functions. Inventions in micro-electronics are opening up a vast development of new devices. Industrial use of television equipment for control and communication will be developed. Ultrasonic devices are being developed for detection and other industrial purposes. In the field of transportation, developments in our future modes of travel will no doubt be spectacular. Jet-powered planes will continue to cut air travel time drastically. The problem of space travel will be conquered within the next few years. New petrochemicals, new metals (such as titanium and zirconium), new plastics, new dyes and insecticides will come into common use. Biochemists will develop new drugs to keep us healthier longer. Synthetic-fiber research will continue to develop textiles with improved properties for clothing and industrial use. Methods of food preservation will continue to improve. Some of the more revolutionary methods of the future will undoubtedly use a form of cold sterilization with cathode rays or atomic radiation. Advances in harnessing atomic energy will open many vistas in numerous fields, including, of course, power generation. Methods of generating power economically from the sun, the tides, and the ocean will also be developed and perfected.

These new technological advances will create additional complexities in our economy and will create new challenges to our ability to make economic engineering and business decisions. The scale of investments in research and capital assets will continue to grow, and rational decision-making will require even longer-range forecasts of rapidly changing conditions.

Our future economic progress depends not only on our ability to continue to improve our decision-making techniques but also on our ability to maintain an environment which will encourage initiative and innovation. Businesses should feel that they must continue to innovate or fall by the wayside. The more we safeguard uneconomic positions of companies and individuals in our economy by legislation, union contract, management agreement, etc., the more we encourage passive attitudes and discourage the kinds of activity and decision-making which promote technological progress and increased productivity. We need a competitive economy which, with due regard for the welfare of all its citizens, creates the incentives for effective utilization of our nation's resources and does not promote the use of our resources by inefficient producers or for purposes which are no longer desired by consumers choosing in a free market.

2 Objectives and Criteria for Engineering and Business Decisions

The major objective of most businesses is to make profits by selling products, designs, or services which have been created or purchased by the business.

Maximizing Profits. The reasoning in this book is based largely on the assumption that a business firm has the primary motive of maximizing its profits—that is, having the largest excess of income over expenses. By and large, businessmen will try to make as much money as possible. This does not mean that nonpecuniary motives do not also enter into many business decisions. Nor does it mean that a businessman will or should always choose the alternative of maximizing immediate profits as against providing for the long-run position and profits of the company. A reasonable, if oversimplified, statement of the situation is as follows:

1. Business decisions are usually made with an eye to their effects on profits.

2. Profits in the long run are considered as well as the immediate returns. With this in mind, profits may be held to what is considered respectable levels to promote better public and labor relations.

3. The businessman's concept of his public-service and social responsibilities will frequently play a part in his decisions.

This oversimplified statement does not ignore the nonfinancial economic motivations of competitive enterprises. It considers profits as a means of furthering the achievement of these other goals. Examples of these nonfinancial economic motivations—which are, of course, related to long-run profits—are

To produce goods and/or services at low cost and as required by the economy

To provide economically useful employment

To promote survival of the enterprise—the self-preservation motive as applied to a business organization

All these goals depend upon profits as the means of achievement in a free, competitive economy.

Maximizing profits is, thus, the major objective of a business. The managers of a business, however, will sometimes say that they are interested in earning reasonable profits rather than maximum profits. This has become more prevalent as the management of enterprises has become separated from the ownership.

The term "reasonable profit" has different meanings to different people. One meaning may be a large enough profit to support a given dividend rate. Another may be large enough profits to attract additional capital at reasonable rates for expansion purposes. Another may be determined by management's desire to limit profits in the short run in order to maximize them in the long run by not encouraging competition, congressional investigations, or bad public, customer, or labor relations. (Labor unions are more likely to press for higher wages when profits are unusually high.)

Management will sometimes prefer to forgo potentially profitable investments so as not to endanger its future control of the business. For example, a potentially profitable investment may require outside financing. If this financing is through the sale of additional stock, the interest of the stockholders favorable to the present management may be diluted. If financing is through the sale of bonds, restrictions may be placed on management's operations until the bonds are retired. In addition to the question of financing, a new potentially profitable project may entail a small risk of failure which could endanger management's future position in the business.

Although the profit objective is primary in most businesses, other considerations may assume importance as auxiliary objectives. These auxiliary objectives, which may change as conditions change, constitute the rationale by which the management plans to develop profitable operations. They are usually designed to maximize profits in the long run.

Objectives of Nonprofit Enterprises. The objectives of nonprofit enterprises—such as governmental units, educational institutions, charitable institutions, foundations, etc.—differ from business enterprises in many respects. These differences require variations in approaches and methodology when evaluating proposals for alternative courses of action.

The objectives of nonprofit enterprises tend to be more intangible and subjective than the objectives of business enterprises. A government agency may have as one of its objectives the promotion of the balanced development of the economy. This goal can have many meanings and is difficult to measure. Another agency may have as one of its objectives the promotion of adequate flood control. The risk of floods cannot be reduced to zero. How small does the probability of a flood have to be made before flood control is considered adequate?

The objectives of an educational foundation may be to promote the quality of graduate study and research in the biological sciences. What are the measures of quality of graduate study and research? How do we establish subobjectives and subcriteria to evaluate alternative possibilities for raising this quality level?

Objectives and Systems. We may think of all of the segments of the enterprise—all the offices, factories, laboratories, warehouses, transportation facilities, etc.—as parts of one large system to accomplish the basic objectives of the enterprise. We may then conceive of the design and evaluation problem as one of establishing the optimum system to achieve these objectives.

The scope of this one system is so vast and the complexity of attempting to handle all of the interactions within the system so great that it is not practical to attempt the design of an optimum system starting with so vast a project. Moreover, it is not possible in an organization of any size to have one person or group examine all alternative courses of action and decide upon the optimum choices, giving consideration to all previous and potential future decisions. It is, therefore, necessary to subdivide the systems into subsystems, each of which has subobjectives which are to be optimized. (This process is frequently called suboptimization.) Of course, these subobjectives must be chosen with care so that the achievement of these objectives is the optimum manner of achieving the prime objectives of the enterprise.

The subobjectives, when properly weighted for relative importance, become the subcriteria which are used to evaluate the alternative subsystems in the attempt to insure that optimum subsystems are chosen.

The establishment of subobjectives and suboptima divides systems design and decision-making problems into manageable chunks. It also makes it possible to decentralize those aspects of the decision-making process which can best be performed close to the operating level by the people who have the greatest knowledge of the details. It thereby has an advantageous effect on the motivation of the people who participate in this decision-making responsibility.

Figure 2-1 illustrates how the optimizing decisions in a capital budgetary program are delegated by a suboptimizing procedure to lower-level units in the organization.

Systems and Subsystems. The term "system" is used here to include the general policies adopted by management to achieve its objectives as well as the more detailed operating systems and procedures.

The boundaries of a system must be defined in each case and may be large or small depending on what suits our purposes best. Every system can be considered a subsystem of a larger system. Thus, the enterprise as a system could be considered a subsystem of the United States business system. The United States business system could be considered a subsystem of the Northern Hemisphere business system. And so on.

We will, therefore, use the term system and subsystem interchangeably in this book, using the term subsystem primarily when we are discussing the subsystem in its relationship to a larger system of which it is a part. We may speak of an inventory-control system at one time and later refer

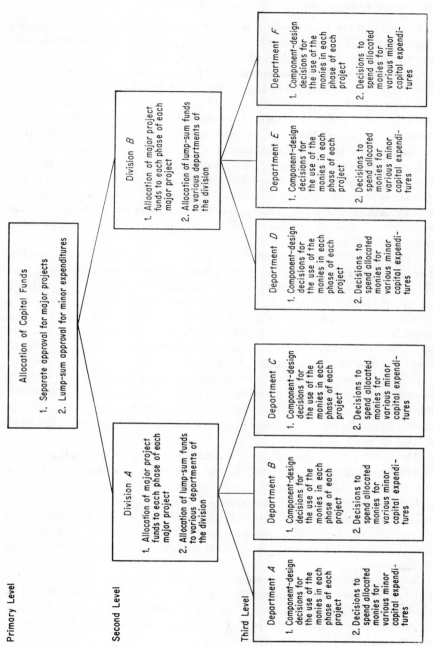

Figure 2-1. Suboptimization of capital-investment decisions.

to the inventory-control subsystem of the enterprise-control system. We may speak of the economical order-quantity system or of the economical order-quantity subsubsystem of the inventory-control subsystem.

Consistency of Subobjectives with Objectives. Serious problems may arise in designing suboptimal subsystems and in making suboptimal decisions when the subobjectives are not consistent with the over-all objectives of the entire enterprise or organizational unit. This can cause error in decision-making and the greater the degree of suboptimization, the greater are the potential difficulties with these problems.

Higher inventory-turnover rate, for example, may appear to be a logical subobjective in an inventory-control system. However, this objective is not in itself consistent with an enterprise objective of maximizing profits. A high turnover rate may result in higher costs, because of the necessity of shorter production lots, and in poorer customer service, because of the greater frequency of running out of stock.

High reliability in a computer may appear to be a logical subobjective. The subobjective, however, may be inconsistent with an objective of high accuracy in the entire clerical system. Thus, a computation system using an electronic computer with, say, 85 per cent reliability may give much greater clerical accuracy in the whole system at lower cost than a system using a mechanical desk calculator with, say, 98 per cent reliability because operator errors in the computer-oriented system may be much lower than in the desk-calculator-oriented system.

It may, therefore, be desirable for persons who are attempting to make decisions based upon subobjectives to examine how these subobjectives relate to the achievement of the over-all objectives, even though the authority of the decision-maker or decision-making group does not extend to this broader scope.

The greater the degree of suboptimization, the easier the manageability of the systems design, but the greater the risks of error in evaluation because of potential inconsistency in subobjectives.

Interdependence of Subsystems. As much as possible, the boundaries of subsystems should be established so that they are as independent as possible of the other subsystems making up the larger system. As a practical matter, however, all subsystems are interdependent to varying degrees.

We, therefore, cannot assume that each subsystem is an insulated entity. We must determine which related subsystems may be affected by changes in the subsystem being studied. The objectives of our subsystem must then be expanded or adjusted to take into account interdependence, which can affect the achievement of the objectives of the larger parent system and of the enterprise.

For example, the establishment of an optimum subsystem for order picking, packing, and shipping should take into account this subsystem's

not be readily estimated in dollars. The quantitative effect on profit cannot then be forecast. The significant consequences which cannot be quantitatively estimated are called intangibles.

The differences between tangible and intangible factors are related to the ease and accuracy with which the past and prospective performance in achieving objectives can be evaluated in dollars. Where this evaluation in dollars can be made easily and accurately, the objective or criterion is considered tangible. Where it is extremely difficult or impossible to make this dollar evaluation—or where it is not worth the effort and expense—the objective or criterion is considered intangible.

The distinction between tangible and intangible factors is one of degree. No factor can be evaluated in dollars of cost and revenue so that it is or can be considered perfectly accurate. There is no such thing as perfect accuracy in determining even present costs. When we speak of future costs, which we must do in any economic evaluation, it is impossible, even with a great deal of work, to get anything but approximate estimates. Even the most tangible elements have intangible elements of uncertainty.

With enough time, effort, and cost, estimates of future revenue and expense can always be made with varying degrees of accuracy and possible judgmental bias. Thus, all intangible elements can be made tangible, up to a point, depending upon the amount of effort and expense worth putting into this process and the amount of inaccuracy and uncertainty one is willing to permit.

Deciding whether to consider a criterion tangible or intangible becomes an economic decision. It involves the economics of making economic evaluations of systems alternatives. How much money and effort is it economic to spend to make intangible criteria tangible?

Tangible and Intangible Consequences in Nonprofit Enterprise. When we are dealing with nonprofit enterprise and governmental operations, we may modify the distinction between tangible and intangible objectives. When the major criterion is not profit, we may find it convenient to use some common denominator other than dollars to measure quantitatively the degree to which each alternative furthers our objectives.

Thus, in military proposals, a measure of destructiveness may be the governing common denominator for evaluating the relative worth of proposals. Destructiveness per dollar could then be a measurable tangible criterion. However, it may not be a good criterion. For example, we may find that a machine gun gives the highest destructiveness per dollar but there is an upper limit to the total amount of destructiveness that can be obtained by machine guns. Total destructiveness may be a better criterion, but the factor of cost cannot be completely ignored. Dollars of cost may become an intangible criterion in this case.

Intangibles in the Design of Management Systems. Many intangible factors are involved in the design of management systems. It may be helpful to consider some of these briefly as examples of the kind of intangibles which must be evaluated in making many engineering and business decisions.

Personnel Motivation. Some systems alternatives will affect the performance motivation of operating personnel. Good personnel motivation is frequently a significant intangible criterion which should be carefully evaluated.

The design of the system should take into account the problem of motivating the supervisor and worker as well as the physical limitations of coordination and information transfer from person to person or group to group. It becomes increasingly difficult for management to give an employee a substantial feeling of accomplishment in performing his job effectively when accomplishment is too dependent on other groups in the organization. The larger the span of the operation—the more successive, related steps performed by one person or group of persons—the more likely the supervisor and worker will visualize the results of their efforts in a better product or service. They will then have a better sense of responsibility and control and will have greater motivation to perform effectively. These considerations call for enlargement of the scope of individual jobs and departments. Enlargement of organizational and job responsibilities will frequently result in departments and jobs which are creating measurable results in competition with each other. This measure of results in competition is valuable in motivating better performance.

This consideration, however, will sometimes result in a decrease in the specialized effort or in specialization by skill.

It is sometimes possible to obtain greater clerical efficiency by establishing procedures which require organizational reorientation of functions in the organization. Thus, new electronic computer equipment has frequently created pressures for centralization of office and control operations. Because such equipment is relatively expensive, a large volume of transactions is often required before replacing current methods economically. There is thus a tendency to gain the clerical efficiency which these machines make possible by concentrating a large volume of the transactions in a centralized location. Under these circumstances, the economic evaluation will frequently disclose substantial tangible savings.

It is important under these circumstances to evaluate the intangible factors carefully. The many benefits of decentralized operation in which each administrator has authority over all the functions in his area of responsibility must be carefully weighed against the advantages of clerical efficiency. We are all aware of the strong performance motivations which can be developed under a well-designed decentralized organization plan as well as the usefulness of this type of organization in testing and developing administrative talent. These intangible factors should receive due weight in the systems evaluation. With proper ingenuity, systems can be developed which will allow utilization of these computers to the fullest advantages without sacrificing some of the advantages of decentralized operations.

Accuracy. Accuracy in a system may be a tangible or an intangible factor or both. Much depends upon the degree of difficulty in estimating quantitatively the level of accuracy under each alternative and the dollar effect of inaccuracy.

In most cases, of course, it is not necessary to estimate the absolute value of these quantities but only the changes which will be brought about by possible adoption of one of the alternative systems. For example, suppose we were considering the alternative of substituting a machine data-processing operation for a current manual operation. Then the accuracy of our results would depend upon three factors: (1) accuracy of the input data, (2) errors made by the machines, and (3) ability of the machines to discover errors.

The accuracy of the input data would not vary in many cases whether or not machines were substituted for the manual operation. Therefore, the accuracy of the input data is of no significance in this study, except in so far as it may affect errors made by the machines or the ability of the machines to discover errors.

Now we know that machines, in general, have no positive effect on the accuracy of the input data. Where manual transcriptions are eliminated, accuracy may improve. (However, changes in input accuracy may occur because of related systems changes, such as in coding and in job organization.)

On the second aspect, errors made by the machines themselves are usually considerably less, by a very large margin, than those made by human beings performing the operations manually.

On the third aspect, the ability of the machines to discover errors, the machines can usually be designed to have an ability considerably superior to human beings in the discovering of machine errors in processing data. Self-checking devices can be built into the equipment and the programming to provide almost all the accuracy which can be desired. Questions of economy determine how far it is desirable to go in this direction.

However, when it comes to discovering errors in the input data, the machine has very limited abilities. It can only catch errors which result in unacceptable input data. A person's ability to catch input errors in a manual routine varies widely, depending upon the person, the kind and magnitude of the errors, and the nature of the clerical routine. A person can exercise judgment. A machine can only follow instructions.

Where the dollar effects of these errors can be estimated with reasonable accuracy and effort, the accuracy criterion can be considered tangible. Where this cannot be done, accuracy must be considered an intangible and its evaluation is more complicated.

Flexibility and Sensitivity of System. The ability of a management system to handle unusual situations, to withstand change, and to adapt itself to the normally changing demands of the organization can be both a tangible and an intangible factor. How easily and expeditiously does the system handle extraordinary situations? Is the discovery and correction of errors complicated?

How about the sensitivity of the various alternatives to changes in operating conditions? How well will the alternative systems adjust to changes in the level of accuracy of the input data? How well will they operate with changes in the abilities of the employees? How catastrophic will mistakes in employee selection be? These criteria will be significant as factors in decision-making in some cases and are frequently intangible.

We sometimes have the problem of choosing between the highly generalized, flexible, permanent, but ineffective procedure and the temporary, highly efficient, specialized, but inflexible one. Of course, we also have other alternatives falling anywhere between these two extremes.

Some of these considerations are important factors in the selection of various types of mechanical and electronic equipment. Many transactions must be handled as exceptions on a manual basis with certain kinds of equipment. The costs of this manual handling can usually be estimated and treated as a tangible factor.

Cash Requirements. For alternatives involving a capital investment, the cash requirements of the investment may be an intangible element. This criterion is different from the question of the rate of return on the investment. It means the availability of funds regardless of the desirability of the investment. If a systems alternative requires expenditure of funds which it is known will not be available, then this is neither a tangible nor an intangible factor, but requires the elimination of the systems alternative, at least until the funds become available. If, however, there is the possibility that funds will be available, but the total of these funds available for all types of use in the organization is limited, then this becomes an intangible factor operating against the projects requiring the larger amounts of capital-investment funds. Of course, if funds are available for all sufficiently profitable purposes, then the cash requirements are not a factor at all.

Time Cycles. A short time cycle is an objective which is common to many systems. These may be design-time requirements, manufacturing-time cycles, time for reply to customer inquiries, time between receipt of orders and delivery to customer, promptness of repair service, timeliness of control reports. In some cases, current and prospective performance in meeting these objectives can be estimated in terms of dollars of cost or revenue charge. In others, time cycles are intangible criteria because it is not economic to make these dollar estimates.

Effectiveness of Control. Some systems alternatives may provide for tighter or more effective control over some activities in the organization. How valuable is this extra control?

If it is control of cash funds to reduce the risk of pilferage or other loss, it may be possible to estimate statistically the expected losses under the various systems alternatives. This aspect would then be tangible. (An intangible aspect may be the good or poor effects of this control on employee morale.)

In considering the extent of control over the operations of the enterprise, ability to estimate expected losses and gains statistically decreases. Effectiveness of control becomes a more intangible criterion.

These are just a few of the kinds of intangible factors which must be evaluated for effective business systems decision-making. Effectiveness of supervision, employee morale, ease of communications, and prestige are other intangible factors. Still others are discussed in various sections of this book.

Objectives to Be Retained. In establishing our objectives, we must be certain that all significant consequences are included or we may not choose the optimal alternative. Our objectives, which determine the criteria for our decisions, should include present advantages we want to retain as well as possible disadvantages we want to avoid.

To illustrate this point, there is the classic story about washing and rinsing mess kits in the Army. The analyst had for his objective the elimination of waiting lines. The original arrangement was one wash tub and three rinse tubs. This resulted in long waiting lines at the wash tub because it took several times as long for each soldier to wash as to rinse. By switching to three wash tubs and one rinse tub, it was possible to eliminate the waiting line in the washing operation. When this was done, a large percentage of the outfit became ill with digestive disorders because of the increase in the bacteria count in the single rinse tub. The analyst had neglected to consider an important objective which was desirable to retain, namely, keeping the bacteria count down below the critical point at which it would cause illness.

Evaluation Criteria. Any attempt to use the objectives of the entire enterprise as the criteria for evaluating alternative proposals will usually encounter two monumental difficulties.

1. The objectives in themselves do not provide a guide to choosing the optimum alternative because they cannot all be achieved completely by any one alternative. It is, therefore, necessary to establish a scale of relative importance of each objective to make them useful as criteria. Thus, we cannot have the lowest cost, the highest quality, and the fastest delivery service all at the same time. The optimum combination in some cases may involve highest quality, but not lowest cost and fastest delivery.

In other cases, it may involve lowest cost and not highest quality and fastest delivery. In others, the best combination may be neither lowest cost, nor highest quality, nor fastest delivery.

2. Because of the unwieldiness and complexity of attempting to design large-scale management systems, most management proposals deal with subsystems which must, therefore, be evaluated by means of subcriteria. This suboptimization procedure is necessary to simplify the design and evaluation task, but, as mentioned previously, it presents some dangers of misevaluation when the subobjectives are not consistent with the objectives of the entire system or are interdependent or are not mutually consistent.

Establishing the Evaluation Criteria. How do we establish the criteria to evaluate the relative desirability of alternative designs or courses of action? By first determining the importance of each of the objectives. These objectives, weighted according to importance, then become the measure against which the effectiveness of each of the alternatives is measured.

If all the objectives are tangible, the economic evaluation is usually much simplified. A dollar analysis can then be made of all the factors. This is accomplished by making revenue-cost comparisons or rate-of-return determinations, as discussed in the chapters of Part Three. The relative dollar values automatically weight the various objectives.

Dollar comparisons are also the key to solving the economy problem when the intangible factors are relatively unimportant. Even if intangible factors are relatively important, dollar comparisons may be used if there is little difference in the effectiveness of the various alternatives in accomplishing the intangible objectives.

In reviewing our desired objectives to establish the criteria which we will use to determine the relative desirability of the alternatives, we should carefully examine the listing to see if we cannot simplify them without losing any effectiveness in our evaluation. We should attempt to make the criteria distinct (one not implying the other), mutually independent, not contradictory, and additive. As much as possible, we should attempt to state our objectives and criteria so that greater fulfillment of each criterion will add to the value of the alternative regardless of the values of the other criteria.

For example, let us consider the objective of increasing the net profits of the company and the objective of reducing production costs. If reduced production costs are desired to increase net profits, then reduced production costs are a redundant objective and can be eliminated, since they are a method of getting increased profits. Assume that a third objective is increased share of the national market. Here again, if the sole purpose of the increased share of the national market is to increase net profits, then this objective can also be eliminated as redundant. However, if the company is interested in increasing its share of the national market regardless of whether it increases its profits and, perhaps, even if within certain limits it reduces its profits, then this objective should be retained for use as a criterion in evaluating the alternatives.

In evaluating alternatives, we can sometimes save a considerable amount of effort by eliminating from consideration those objectives and criteria which are unaffected by any of the alternatives. Thus, if the delivery-time cycles would be the same under all of the alternatives proposed for a warehousing operation, shortening of time cycles can be eliminated as a criterion in this consideration. Reduced spoilage may also be eliminated as an objective in the evaluation if none of the alternatives will have any effect on the spoilage rate.

PROBLEMS

1. It has been suggested that an organization be evaluated in terms of (a) the degree to which it is productive, profitable, self-maintaining, and so forth; (b) the degree to which it is of value to its members; and (c) the degree to which it and its members are of value to society.[1] To what extent do you think that these criteria are at variance with long-run profit as a criterion for decision-making? Explain your answer.

2. The objectives of Johnson and Johnson, a major manufacturer of surgical supplies and related items, have been stated by the company as follows:

We believe that our first responsibility is to our customers. Our products must always be good, and we must strive to make them better at lower costs. Our orders must be promptly and accurately filled. Our dealers must make a fair profit.

Our second responsibility is to those who work with us—the men and women in our factories and offices. They must have a sense of security in their jobs. Wages must be fair and adequate, management just, hours short, and working conditions clean and orderly. Workers should have an organized system for suggestions and complaints. Foremen and department heads must be qualified and fair-minded. There must be opportunity for advancement—for those qualified. And each person must be considered an individual, standing on his own dignity and merit.

Our third responsibility is to our management. Our executives must be persons of talent, education, experience, and ability. They must be persons of common sense and full understanding.

Our fourth responsibility is to the communities in which we live. We must be a good citizen—support good works and charity and bear our fair share of taxes. We must maintain in good order the property we are privileged to use.

[1] B. M. Bass, "Ultimate Criteria of Organizational Worth," *Personnel Psychology*, vol. 5, no. 3, Autumn, 1952.

We must participate in promotion of civic improvement, health, education and good government and acquaint the community with our activities.

Our fifth and last responsibility is to our stockholders. Business must make a sound profit. Reserves must be created, research must be carried on, adventurous programs developed, and mistakes made and paid for. Bad times must be provided for, high taxes paid, new machines purchased, new factories built, new products launched, and new sales plans developed. We must experiment with new ideas. When these things have been done, the stockholder should receive a fair return. We are determined with the help of God's grace to fulfill these obligations to the best of our ability.

Reconcile the foregoing statement with the statement in the text that a business firm has the primary motive of maximizing its profits.

3. Using your college or company as an example, describe (a) the scope of the system, (b) its objectives, (c) suboptimization to accomplish these objectives.

4. Which portions, if any, of the objectives of the college or company stated in problem 3 are tangible and which are intangible? Explain your reasoning in each case.

5. How would you recommend that a company test the rationality of its objectives?

6. How would you recommend that a company test for consistency of the subobjectives of the various units in its organization?

7. Suggest criteria for the following decisions and state which you consider tangible and which intangible, giving the reasons for your tangibility classifications: (a) To buy or not to buy a Multilith machine to duplicate sales-promotion material presently prepared by an outside service, (b) To present or not to present a lecture series on "the responsibilities of business to support education."

PART TWO

Costs

3 The Costs of Operating an Enterprise

How much did it cost to run the business last month or last year? How much did it cost to manufacture product Z? Did product Z make a profit? Did the business make a profit? How much would be saved by eliminating product Y? How much additional cost will be incurred if operations are increased by 10 per cent? Will it be cheaper to make or buy component M? Should facility A be scrapped? Should the product line be expanded by manufacturing a new product W? These are a few of the questions which an adequate accounting and cost system should assist in answering.

A cost accounting system should provide information required for making decisions. These decisions include :

1. The establishment of objectives, policies, and plans on a logical basis

2. The continual direction and evaluation of operations in conformance with these plans, policies, and objectives

The accounting system should also enable management to conform with tax, financial, and legal requirements.

Costs and Expenses. The terms "costs" and "expenses" will be used interchangeably and, for our purposes, they are synonymous. The noted economist Alfred Marshall defined the terms very adequately: "The sums of money that have to be paid for these efforts and sacrifices will be called either its money cost of production, or, for shortness, its expenses of production; they are the prices which have to be paid in order to call forth an adequate supply of the efforts and waitings that are required for making it; or, in other words, they are its supply price."[1]

Operating, or Profit and Loss, Statement. Without attempting to review the detailed bases and philosophy of financial accounting procedures, it would be helpful to familiarize ourselves with the most common financial document, the operating, or profit and loss, statement. This document summarizes the costs of operating a business and compares the enterprise's costs with revenues or income.

The operating or profit and loss statement of an enterprise (also called statement of income and expenses) normally indicates the gross profit,

[1] Alfred Marshall, *Principles of Economics*, Macmillan & Co., Ltd., London, 1916, p. 339.

net operating profit, and net profit resulting from operations during that period. The format of the profit and loss statement for a manufacturing company is illustrated in Table 3-1.

The format of the profit and loss statement is essentially the same for both manufacturing and merchandising companies. In a manufacturing company, the cost of goods manufactured is substituted for the cost of

Table **3-1. The Schabe Corporation**
Profit and Loss Statement for Year Ending September 30, 1960

Gross sales			$5,000,000
Less, Returns and allowances			150,000
Net sales			$4,850,000
Less, Cost of goods sold:			
Finished-goods inventory, October 1, 1959	$ 260,000		
Cost of goods manufactured (Schedule A)	2,950,000	$3,210,000	
Less, Finished-goods inventory, September 30, 1960		310,000	2,900,000
Gross profit			$1,950,000
Operating expenses:			
Selling expenses:			
Sales salaries and commissions	$ 390,000		
Sales office	40,000		
Shipping	60,000		
Advertising	75,000		
Depreciation of sales equipment	10,000		
Social security and other sales department taxes	5,000		
Other selling expenses	20,000	$ 600,000	
Provision for doubtful accounts		10,000	
General and administrative expenses:			
Officer salaries	$ 210,000		
Office salaries	250,000		
Insurance	15,000		
Depreciation (general and admin. facilities)	10,000		
Taxes	20,000		
Stationery, postage, telephone, etc	25,000		
Other general and administrative expenses	30,000	560,000	
Total operating expenses			1,170,000
Net operating profit			$ 780,000
Other income:			
Income from investments	$ 8,000		
Interest on notes receivable, etc	3,000	$ 11,000	
Other expense:			
Interest on bonded debt	$ 94,000		
Interest on notes payable, etc	38,000	132,000	
Net nonoperating income			−121,000
Net profit before income taxes			$ 659,000
Estimated income taxes			342,680
Net profit after income taxes			$ 316,320

goods purchased. The cost of goods manufactured must be separately calculated from an analysis of factory labor, material, and indirect expenses, as illustrated later.

The gross profit is obtained by subtracting from net sales (gross sales less sales returns, discounts, and allowances) the cost of goods sold. For a manufacturing enterprise, the cost of goods sold includes direct labor, direct material, and factory expenses to produce the items sold during the period. For a merchandising firm, the cost of sales includes the cost of purchasing and obtaining the items sold during the period.

The net operating profit is obtained by subtracting operating expenses, consisting of selling, administrative, and general expenses, from the gross profit. The types of expenses in these categories of operating expenses are illustrated in Table 3-1.

Nonoperating income, such as income from investments, is reduced by the amount of nonoperating expense, such as interest on debt, and is then added to net operating profit to obtain net profit before income taxes.

Subtracting estimated income taxes from this net profit gives the net profit after income taxes.

Sales. Gross sales are the total of the selling prices of all goods and services sold during the period covered by the statement. Orders do not become sales until the goods have been delivered, or the services rendered, and billed. Sometimes, the gross sales total is broken down into two categories, cash sales and credit sales, which makes possible determination of the average collection period.

Sales returns, discounts, and allowances comprise deductions from the billed price which have been allowed by the company for various reasons. Returns because of defects, misrepresentation, or any other source of customer dissatisfaction may significantly reduce gross sales. Discounts for prompt payment of bills and for purchases in quantity are frequently allowed.

Determination of Cost of Goods Sold. The cost of goods sold consists of the net cost of acquiring or producing the articles sold by the business during the period. If the company does not keep some kind of perpetual-inventory records (a complete record of what goes in and out of its stores and warehouses in order to know at all times what is there), the cost of goods sold cannot be determined without the taking of complete physical inventories at the end of each period.

In a *merchandising* concern after the inventory has been priced and valued, the cost of goods available for sale is determined by taking the value of the inventory at the beginning of the period and adding the total value of all inventory purchased during the period to give the total inventory available for sale during the period. If the value of the inventory at the end of the period is subtracted from this total available for sale during the period, the cost of goods sold during the period is obtained.

In a *manufacturing* concern, the cost of goods manufactured and sold is determined in a manner similar to that for a merchandising company. However, a calculation of the cost of goods manufactured and delivered to finished-goods inventory must be made so that it can be added to finished-goods inventory at the beginning of the period to obtain the total available for sale during the period. Then, subtracting the value of the finished-goods inventory at the end of the period from this total available for sale during the period, we obtain the cost of goods sold during the period.

Cost of Goods Manufactured. The calculation of the cost of goods manufactured is illustrated for the Schabe Corporation in Schedule A of Table 3-2.

Table **3-2. The Schabe Corporation**
Schedule A
Cost of Goods Manufactured—Year Ending September 30, 1960

Direct labor			$ 410,000
Direct material:			
Inventory, October 1, 1959		$ 235,000	
Purchases (less returns)		1,875,000	
Transportation cost of purchases		40,000	
Total material available		2,150,000	
Less, Inventory, September 30, 1960		200,000	
Material used			1,950,000
Factory expense:			
Indirect factory labor		$ 110,000	
Factory supplies		85,000	
Maintenance and repairs		115,000	
Heat, light, and power		65,000	
Depreciation of factory facilities		130,000	
Property taxes		70,000	
Social security taxes		20,000	
Insurance		25,000	
Other factory expense		10,000	630,000
Total factory costs			$2,990,000
Change in work-in-process inventory:			
Work-in-process inventory, October 1, 1959		$ 100,000	
Less, Work-in-process inventory, September 30, 1960		140,000	−40,000
Cost of goods manufactured and delivered to finished-goods inventory			$2,950,000

The total factory cost during the period is calculated by adding together the direct labor, direct material, and factory expense incurred during the period to obtain total factory costs. Then this factory cost is adjusted to take into account that some of this factory cost may have gone into the production of work-in-process inventory (items of products which are incomplete at the end of the period and, therefore, not yet delivered into the finished-goods inventory).

If there has been no change in the work-in-process inventory since the beginning of the period, then no adjustment is necessary because it means that the same dollar value of factory cost is tied up in work-in-process inventory as at the beginning of the period. However, if, as in the example of the Schabe Corporation, the work-in-process inventory at the end of the year is $40,000 larger than at the beginning of the year period, then $40,000 of the total factory cost of $2,990,000 went into building up the work-in-process inventory and only $2,950,000 was delivered to finished-goods inventory. Conversely, if the work-in-process inventory had decreased in value since the beginning of the period, it would mean that deliveries to finished-goods inventory were greater than the total factory cost for the period by the amount of the decrease.

Computation of the direct-material-cost portion of the total factory cost is accomplished in this example by determining total material available for use by adding together the inventory at the beginning of the period, all direct-material purchases during the period (less returns), and the cost of transporting the purchased items to the plant. Subtracting the amount of purchased-material inventory available at the end of the period from this total available figure gives the direct-material usage.

Direct labor is all labor cost which is directly assigned to a particular product, process, or job. Similarly, direct material is all material cost which is directly assigned to a particular product, process, or job. When it is difficult or too expensive to segregate some of these labor or material costs, they are not directly assigned (charged). They are then considered factory expense.

Factory expense, often called factory burden or overhead, thus consists of all factory operating costs not considered direct costs. It commonly contains such items as indirect factory labor (supervision, tool attendants, material handlers, stock clerks, etc.), employee vacation pay and fringe benefits, factory supplies (stationery, oil, grease, files, brooms, belting, etc.), maintenance, depreciation, repairs, insurance, and taxes for machinery, tools, and factory buildings, as well as heat, light, power, and other miscellaneous items required for factory operation.

Valuing Inventory Withdrawals. In the illustrative example of the Schabe Corporation, the determination of the cost of goods sold was made using the values of physical inventories at the beginning and the end of the period as well as the dollar value of purchases. The problem of valuing (costing) these physical inventories is somewhat complicated by the fact that different prices are paid for various lots of the same material over a period of time. What price do we use in valuing the inventories?

We could work on the basis that the oldest material is withdrawn first. In this case, the inventory is valued at the most recent prices for the quantities in inventory. In effect, the cost of goods manufactured is thus charged with the older material which was in inventory at the beginning of the period. This method is called FIFO, first in–first out. In times of changing prices, this method gives a more realistic inventory value on the balance sheet of a company (a value more closely approximating replacement cost). However, the cost of inventory consumed in manufacture as shown on the profit and loss statement is valued at older prices and is, therefore, less realistic.

Thus, in a period of rising prices, FIFO will tend to give lower material costs of goods manufactured than current prices would justify. As a result higher profits would be shown and, incidentally, higher income tax charges would be assessed for the given year. The reverse situation would be true in a period of declining prices.

We could consider that we maintain a reservoir of material in inventory which is a permanent investment to stay in business. In this case, this investment in our inventory reservoir is valued at the original (oldest) costs. In effect, the cost of goods manufactured is charged at the price of the more recent acquisitions. This method is called LIFO, last in–first out. In times of changing prices, this method gives a more realistic cost for the current cost of goods manufactured as shown on the profit and loss statement (a cost more closely approximating replacement cost). However, the inventory shown on the balance sheet is valued at older prices and is, therefore, less realistic.

Thus, in a period of rising prices, LIFO will tend to give higher costs of goods manufactured and lower reported profits and, incidentally, lower income tax charges for the given year than would FIFO. LIFO will also tend to understate inventory values on the balance sheet of the company. The reverse situation would be true in a period of declining prices.

We could decide that we should predetermine a standard cost for each item using a careful analysis, not only of the prices and costs which we have been paying in the immediate past, but, more importantly, of the prices and costs we should be paying in the current period based upon engineering and market studies.

Use of standard costs for valuing inventory withdrawals can be of great assistance in controlling material costs by providing a basis for comparing actual item costs with a predetermined standard. It can also reduce the amount of clerical record-keeping because only the one predetermined standard cost need be considered for each inventory item.

When perpetual-inventory records are kept as part of the accounting system, the computation of material cost of goods manufactured is done on a continuing basis every time material is used. In the case of a job-order shop, each withdrawal of material or parts from the stockrooms for use on a production job is charged to the job and the inventory account credited (relieved of the charge). In the case of a process cost accounting system, each withdrawal of material or parts is charged to a department

or process. In both cases, each sale of finished goods is charged to cost of sales and the finished-goods inventory account is credited.

Many considerations which are beyond the scope of this book enter into the determination of the best method for any particular company to value its inventories and inventory withdrawals. Income taxes are an important factor in this choice.

Allocation of Indirect and Common Costs. We have mentioned the manner in which direct-labor and direct-material costs can be segregated and charged to each job, process, or product. We have not discussed how the indirect labor and material and other factory expenses can be allocated to the various products.

These overhead costs are ordinarily allocated to products by means of an overhead rate. An overhead rate is determined by dividing the estimated overhead cost to be allocated by the estimated size of the allocation base for a given period.

For example, let us suppose that direct-labor cost is the allocation base. It is estimated that during the coming year $500,000 will be spent on direct labor and that indirect costs will total $600,000. The overhead rate would be

$$\frac{\text{Estimated indirect costs}}{\text{Estimated direct-labor costs}} = \frac{\$600,000}{\$500,000} = 120\%$$

Then, for each dollar of direct-labor cost, $1.20 of indirect cost will be charged. A product with $6.00 of direct labor will be charged with $7.20 (120 per cent of $6.00) of overhead expense in addition to its direct-labor and direct-material costs to compute its factory cost.

A basis for allocation (direct-labor cost in the example just cited) should provide for the charging of indirect costs, in the correct proportions, to those jobs, processes, and products which are responsible for them. In addition, for routine accounting application, the basis must be easily measured and simple to apply in order to keep clerical costs low.

Separate overhead rates may be established for different departments or groups of departments in a plant (each such department or group of departments is called a cost center). Separate cost centers are appropriate when the size, character, and relationship of the overhead costs vary substantially between the cost centers.

If two cost centers were established in the company of the previous example, the two overhead rates might be as follows:

Cost Center A:

$$\frac{\text{Estimated indirect costs}}{\text{Estimated direct-labor costs}} = \frac{\$300,000}{\$200,000} = 150\%$$

Cost Center B:

$$\frac{\text{Estimated indirect costs}}{\text{Estimated direct-labor costs}} = \frac{\$300,000}{\$300,000} = 100\%$$

The product with $6.00 direct-labor cost previously mentioned had $4.00 of it in Cost Center A and $2.00 of it in Cost Center B. Total overhead charge using the more accurate breakdown into separate overhead rates by cost center is $8.00 (150% of $4.00 plus 100% of $2.00) instead of $7.20.

When the cost characteristics of departments vary significantly, it is sometimes appropriate to use different bases for allocating overhead in various cost centers in the same plant. Thus, a center may use direct-labor cost, another direct-labor-hours, another machine-hours, and another weight of product.

For accounting purposes, overhead costs should be allocated among products on the basis of factors which fluctuate with the costs of the products. Thus, the appropriate bases for allocating overhead will vary from plant to plant.

The most commonly used basis for allocating overhead is direct-labor cost, which was used in the previous illustration. Its great popularity is undoubtedly due in large measure to its clerical simplicity as well as to the fact that many overhead costs, such as supervision, personnel costs, fringe benefits, etc., vary in a manner roughly proportional to direct-labor cost. It is thus most suitable when the costs associated with equipment and machinery are relatively low as compared with labor costs.

A direct-labor-hour is sometimes a more appropriate basis than a direct-labor dollar when hourly wage rates among direct-labor employees vary widely. A simple example will illustrate this kind of situation. Highly skilled employees working with relatively simple tools receive high hourly wage rates, and employees of lower skill receive low hourly wage rates but work with highly automatic, complex, and expensive equipment. The direct-labor-hour basis will allocate more overhead cost to the products using the more expensive equipment than will a direct-labor-cost basis. This is probably appropriate in this case because the machine costs will undoubtedly constitute a large percentage of the indirect costs.

Where there is a relationship between the amount of material cost of the products and the amount of indirect cost, material cost may be an appropriate basis for allocating overhead costs. Of course, if the more expensive materials are not responsible for more overhead costs than the cheaper ones, this will not be an appropriate basis.

In some cases, weight of an input material or of the product may be a practicable basis for the allocation if it will result in an equitable distribution of the overhead costs.

When some of the overhead costs are related to material cost and some to direct-labor cost, the sum of the direct-labor and direct-material cost (called prime cost) may prove to be an appropriate basis.

When a unit of product measure, such as number of TV receivers in the case of an electronics manufacturer, is appropriate and possible, it can provide a simple basis for allocating overhead. However, this is rarely the case in plants producing a wide variety of items.

A machine-hour basis is particularly appropriate where a large portion of the overhead costs are associated with machinery, such as power, maintenance and repair, rent, depreciation charges, taxes, insurance, etc. In these cases, it will generally give the most useful results for most accounting purposes. This method is becoming increasingly important with the advent of automation, which has a tendency to cause increases in machine-associated overhead costs and decreases in direct labor. However, numerous cost centers must usually be set up for each machine or group of similar machines and the clerical costs for this method are sometimes high.

It is sometimes logical and desirable to allocate one group of overhead costs on one basis and another group of overhead costs on a different basis in the same cost center. Thus, depreciation, maintenance, repairs, power, and rent may be allocated on a machine-hour basis and all other overhead expenses on a direct-labor-hour basis.

The more complex schemes for allocating overhead are rarely found to be practicable and desirable over long periods of time because of their added clerical costs.

In general, accounting allocations of overhead are not valid for decision-making purposes without further analysis and refinement. In most cases, the individual items of overhead cost which will vary with the alternative decisions must be separately ascertained. Costs under each alternative would then be estimated by observing the patterns of their variability as well as by such engineering analysis as is appropriate.

Assignment or allocation of common nonmanufacturing costs to products presents problems of arbitrary methodology similar to those associated with factory-overhead allocations. Here too, accounting allocations are not generally valid for decision-making purposes. Usually opportunity or alternative costs must be estimated for those common costs which will change with the alternatives being considered.

Other Period Effects. A profit and loss statement is designed to summarize costs, revenues, and profits exclusively for the period under consideration.

Nevertheless, the cost of sales for any given period of time is dependent on some operations which were performed in previous periods. In the manufacturing enterprise, some of the items sold in one period were produced in previous periods, and their costs depend on the efficiency of production during these previous periods. In the merchandising and manufacturing enterprise, the gross profit depends in part on how well the purchasing and advertising functions were performed in previous periods.

Dependence of the enterprise's profits upon operations in previous periods is not confined to this financial overlap in the cost of sales. Thus, the reputation of a firm and its products is important to its successful operations. This reputation depends upon past performance.

Some current costs involve activities the benefits of which will be derived in large part in future periods. Arguments may even be made to charge some of these costs against income in future periods. This is known as capitalizing these costs. For example, the extent and quality of current advertising and promotion affect sales and profits in future periods. This is especially true when new products are being promoted or new sales territories are being developed. Much research effort could also fall into this category (and, at one time, income tax regulations required that many of these costs be capitalized).

PROBLEMS

1. A small retailing corporation, which has neglected to keep a formal set of books, desires to prepare a profit and loss statement for the year ending December 31, 1960. All sales were for cash and the cash register showed sales totaling $428,000. Returns totaled $18,000. All payments were by check. Analysis of checkbook stubs showed the following payments:

Advertising	$ 26,000
Insurance	2,100
Interest expense	4,000
Light, heat, fuel	18,900
Merchandise	236,000
Payroll and other business taxes	13,000
Rent	21,000
Salaries and wages	79,000
Telephone and telegraph	4,500
Freight charges on purchases	5,000

The following payments included in the analysis of 1960 payments were for items used or expended in 1959:

Advertising	$ 12,500
Light, heat, and fuel	2,000
Merchandise	Not analyzed
Payroll and other business taxes	400
Salaries and wages	2,200
Telephone and telegraph	700

Some of the monies paid in 1960 represented services not fully received or supplies not fully used or expended:

Advertising	$2,500
Insurance	900
Light, heat, and fuel	3,000
Merchandise	Not analyzed
Rent	2,800

Items in the following categories were received in 1960, but had not been paid as of December 31, 1960. (Some had been billed, but not paid and some had been neither billed nor paid.):

Advertising...................... $4,000
Light, heat, and fuel............. 6,500
Merchandise.................... Not analyzed
Telephone and telegraph..........   300

Inventories totaled $89,000 valued at cost on December 31, 1959. They totaled $96,000 on December 31, 1960.

a. Prepare a profit and loss statement for this corporation for the year ending December 31, 1960, placing sales, general, and administrative expenses in one category.

b. What kind of expense may have been inadvertently omitted from this profit and loss statement?

2. The total overhead cost incurred by a factory producing screw-machine products last year was $800,000, of which $400,000 was assigned to an automated screw-machine center which ran for 200,000 machine-hours. Direct-material consumption during that period was $725,000; direct labor, totaling 150,000 man-hours, cost $300,000.

A new product is estimated to require 25 cents worth of direct material, 6 minutes of direct labor, and 10 minutes of screw-machine time per unit. This same product can be produced manually, requiring one hour of direct labor.

a. Estimate the factory cost per unit of this new product (1) machine-made and (2) handmade. For each case, allocate the overhead by each of the following methods: (*a*) direct-labor cost, (*b*) direct-labor-hours, (*c*) direct-material cost, (*d*) prime cost, (*e*) machine-hours.

b. Which estimates are realistic? What additional information would be useful to answer this question?

3. The Carlin Corporation manufactures electrical components. During the three-month period ending March 31, 1961, it incurred the following expenses in its factory:

Depreciation... $ 10,000
Insurance...   3,000
Labor—direct.. 100,000
Labor—indirect..   70,000
Maintenance and repairs...............................   15,000
Materials—direct (invoice cost)....................... 380,000
Materials—indirect (invoice cost).....................   45,000
Miscellaneous items...................................   30,000
Supplies..   60,000
Taxes (social security and property)..................   30,000
Transportation costs of direct-materials purchases....   20,000
Transportation costs of indirect-materials purchases..   2,000
Utilities...   40,000

Inventories as of December 31, 1960, were:

Finished goods.. $480,000
Raw materials... 365,000
Work in process....................................... 170,000

Inventories as of March 31, 1961, were:

Finished goods...	$535,000
Raw materials...	340,000
Work in process.......................................	160,000

Prepare a schedule of cost of goods manufactured during the three-month period ending March 31, 1961.

4. The Arco Company started to use a new chemical compound in its manufacturing processes in April, 1960. The following purchases were received during 1960:

Date of receipt	Number of pounds	Price per pound
April 12	4,000	$0.38
May 17	2,000	0.37
August 28	2,000	0.40
September 20	4,000	0.41

The following withdrawals and use of this compound were made in 1960:

Date of withdrawal from stockroom	Number of pounds
May 10	2,000
July 27	1,000
August 22	1,500
November 1	1,000
November 29	3,000

Determine the cost of this compound during 1960 and the value of the inventory remaining as of December 31, 1960, using (a) FIFO, (b) LIFO. Which is the more realistic inventory valuation? Which are the more realistic figures for the cost of compound consumed during 1960?

4 Cost Concepts for Decision-making

Costs such as are recorded for financial statements may not be suitable for the decision-making purposes with which we are concerned. The relevant types of costs which are suitable for different decision-making problems will vary. It will be valuable to consider briefly here some of the different types of cost concepts which are useful under certain conditions. This discussion of cost concepts will disclose that:

1. Unadjusted conventional accounting costs are frequently inappropriate for many types of decisions.

2. Different types of cost estimates and cost concepts are appropriate for various management decisions.

3. For decision-making purposes, we are usually interested in future costs, not past or present costs. Of course, accounting records of past costs may be useful in providing basic information to assist in estimating future costs.

4. Accounting data must frequently be supplemented by statistical, economic, and engineering data as well as good judgment and mature analysis to arrive at the most valid cost estimates.

Future Costs. Managerial decisions usually involve a forecast of what will occur in the future. Among other factors, whether or not to buy a new facility should be based on estimates of *future* operating costs of the proposed facility. The price charged for our product should depend upon estimated *future* costs of production and distribution as well as other market supply-and-demand considerations. If we make these decisions using past or current costs without attempting to forecast what future costs will be, we are automatically saying that the future will be the same as the past or present. If in our best judgment there will be no change in the future, then this procedure is satisfactory.

Traceable Costs. Traceable costs are costs which can be identified with a given product, operation, or service. Costs which are not traceable are called common costs.

Traceable material costs are not necessarily visible in the final product, for example, a polishing material or a chemical reagent which is consumed in a processing operation.

Electric power could be a traceable cost if the production process was

43

such that it could be metered so that usage could be identified by product, operation, or service. This can usually be done, although it is not usually desirable or economical to do it.

Common Costs. Common costs cannot be identified with a given output of products, operations, or services.

Products having common costs are sometimes categorized on the basis of the relationship which exists between their production and costs. When the outputs are directly related to the common-cost expenditure so that an increase in the common-cost expenditure results in an increase in all of the outputs, a joint product relationship is said to exist and the common cost is known as a joint cost. Thus, cattle is a joint cost of the production of beef and leather, and crude petroleum is a joint cost of gasoline, fuel oil, etc.

These examples of joint costs point up two different conditions: in the first case, the relative output of the joint products, beef and hides, is fixed and cannot be varied; in the second case, the relative proportions can be varied within limits, so that an increased output of one, say gasoline, can be made at the expense of fuel oil, within limits.

When the outputs are related to the common cost or costs such that an increase in the output of one product can only be made if the output of one or more other products is reduced, then an alternative product relationship exists. An alternative product relationship is usually the result of limited facilities to handle the size and kind of production required in the immediate future.

Direct and Indirect (Overhead) Costs. Direct costs are those traceable costs which are economically feasible and desirable to segregate and charge to products, operations, or services. Indirect costs consist of all common costs as well as those traceable costs which are not segregated and charged directly. The distinction between direct-labor-and-material costs and indirect costs is based on the method of charging the costs to the items produced.

Direct labor consists of all types of traceable labor costs which are charged directly to the products, operations, or services being produced. For example, it is usually possible to charge the time of a machine operator directly to each job on which he works by means of time tickets which specify the exact time spent on the jobs. However, it is usually not practical or economically desirable to charge the time of a tool room attendant directly to each job handled by the shop. For this reason, the machine operator's time is normally classified as direct labor and the tool room attendant as indirect labor. Indirect charges (frequently called overhead) are then allocated to each job, using methods previously discussed.

This same distinction also applies to direct- and indirect-material costs. Direct materials consist of traceable material costs which can be conveniently charged directly to the job or product. In the manufacture of a radio set, for example, the cost of sheet steel for the chassis would normally be a direct-material cost because it is economically feasible to charge the cost of this steel directly to the job in which it is used by means of a stores requisition charge ticket which is issued when the material is moved from the storeroom to the fabrication floor. The stores requisition specifies the job on which the metal will be used. When grease and oil for the machine tools are withdrawn from the storeroom, it is not usually practicable to specify the jobs on which the machines will be used when the grease and oil are consumed. To charge these materials directly to the job, it would be necessary to determine grease and oil usage each time the machine is operated. Because it is not generally economical to do this, grease and oil for lubrication purposes are usually considered indirect materials and their costs are charged to the various jobs by allocation methods. For similar reasons, electric power is usually an indirect cost.

Other things being equal, the larger the proportion of the traceable costs which can be charged on a direct basis, the more accurate will be the record of production costs of each job or product. It is, therefore, desirable to charge as much traceable labor and material directly as is possible without increasing accounting costs too greatly. If the tool room attendant works continuously on one job for a considerable period of time, then on another job for another period of time, and so on, it may be practical and desirable to charge his time as direct labor. However, if he switches continually from job to job, it may cost more in paper work than it is worth to segregate his costs on a direct basis.

Alternative or Opportunity Costs. Alternative or opportunity costs represent the cost of an opportunity which is forgone because limited resources are used in the chosen alternative and, therefore, cannot be disposed of or used for other possible income-producing or expense-reducing alternatives. Opportunity costs are not recorded in the books of account and may be distinguished from costs which are determined by the amount of current or past payments.

In considering whether or not to replace a piece of fully depreciated equipment by a newly developed machine, an opportunity cost should be assessed against the alternative of keeping the old machine. This cost should be based upon the difference between the amount of money which can be obtained for the old equipment now and its prospective future salvage value if it is kept in service for one or more additional years.

The interest cost chargeable to a proposed capital-investment proposal is not the amount which is paid on the borrowed money. The proper interest cost is the opportunity cost: how much income is forgone or expense incurred because the money is invested in this proposal instead of other available investments.

When equity or ownership rather than borrowed money is used in a proposed project, the interest cost is an opportunity cost in terms of sacrificed income or earnings although no cash outlay is made for interest payments. Alternative investment of the ownership money would yield a return which is forgone if the money is used in the proposed project. If the best available alternatives will give returns of around 10 per cent, then a 10 per cent interest rate might be appropriate in computing the opportunity interest cost for the proposed project.

If a proposal involves the use of company-owned space which is presently vacant, the opportunity cost chargeable to the proposal for the use of this space depends upon the income or savings which other possible uses of the space may bring to the company.

Where common costs are involved in an alternative products relationship, so that an increase in the production of one item requires a decrease in the output of one or more other products, a comparison of opportunity costs is frequently most logical.

Considerations of alternative or opportunity cost always require that the company investigate other alternative uses of one or more of its limited resources to ascertain the magnitude of these costs.

Sunk Costs. Sunk costs are past costs which cannot be charged to any of the alternatives being considered. They are, therefore, irrelevant to the consideration of alternative courses of action.

If a machine costing $1,000,000 was purchased last year and management is presently considering its replacement by another machine, the $1,000,000 cost last year is a sunk cost and is irrelevant to the decisions of whether or not to replace. The relevant cost for this machine is its opportunity cost, the amount of value which is lost because the machine is not being applied in its best alternative use. If this best other use were resale, then the opportunity cost would be its resale price.

Book Costs. Book costs are costs which do not involve current payments of cash or increase of liability because they represent the amortization of past expenditures for items of lengthy durability (several years). Depreciation and depletion charges for the use of fixed assets are the most common examples of book costs.

The significance of book costs lies primarily in their effects on the firm's cash position and income tax liability. These will be discussed in later chapters.

Cash Costs, Cash Income, and Cash Flow. The profitability of a business operation depends upon its cash flow.

Costs which involve payments of cash or increase of liability are called cash costs to distinguish them from all noncash (book) costs. Cash costs affect the cash or liability position of the company whereas book costs do not. Income which is earned and collected in cash or results in an increase in collectible accounts or notes receivable is called cash income. Cash costs which are saved by the adoption of an alternative are the equivalent of cash income. Cash income and cash costs result in cash flows of specified magnitudes at specified times. As will be illustrated later, the profitability of an investment is dependent upon the cash flow: the amount and timing of the cash income and cash costs produced by the investment.

Replacement Costs. Assets are valued on the books of a company at the price originally paid for them, less, in the case of deteriorating or wasting assets, accumulated depreciation or depletion charges. Original cost is rarely a valid basis for making most kinds of management decisions. In making decisions on pricing, for example, the relevant cost factor in the decision is replacement cost, the price which will have to be paid to replace the material, labor, and equipment, rather than the historical original cost which is used in the accounting records of the firm.

Postponable Costs. Certain kinds of costs, such as wages and direct materials, are unavoidable and cannot be postponed. Other costs, such as certain types of maintenance, are usually postponable in that they may be reduced or eliminated during a period of declining business profits, although not necessarily declining volume.

Incremental Costs. Incremental costs are the added costs of increasing the volume of business output from one level to another. They are the valid costs to be considered when the alternatives involve a choice of different levels of future activity.

In using incremental costs, care must be taken to be certain that long-run as well as short-run costs are considered if the alternative will last into the long run. Thus, the incremental cost of using currently idle or partially idle facilities may be zero in the short run, but if the facilities will be required for other uses before the alternative use is completed, or if the useful life of the facilities will not be as long as the alternative use, then the zero short-run incremental costs give incorrect results. Long-run incremental costs should be used.

Marginal Costs. Marginal costs are the costs of one additional unit of production, activity, or service. Marginal costs are the incremental costs of increasing the volume of business output one unit. The significance of marginal costs will be discussed in some detail in Chapter 28, in which is presented a review of the relationships between a firm's production and its markets and how these relationships affect economic decisions.

Escapable Costs. When a reduction or elimination of business activity will result in certain costs being eliminated (with perhaps others increased), the net reduction in costs is considered escapable costs. Escapable costs are related to declines in activity in a manner similar to the way incremental costs are related to increases in business activity. The escapable cost when a business activity is decreased from Q_2 to Q_1 is frequently smaller than the incremental cost which originally resulted when the volume was expanded from Q_1 to Q_2. (It is usually a more difficult management task to reduce labor and other costs and commitments during a contraction than to increase them during an expansion.) It is important in estimating net escapable costs that the amount of eliminated costs be reduced by the amount of any additional costs which will be incurred in related activities as a result of the change.

Controllable and Reducible Costs. Controllability of costs is used primarily in establishing the managerial level at which the costs are controlled. Of course, in the long run all costs are controllable at some level. Those which are not controllable at the lower operating levels are subject to managerial control at some higher levels.

Reducibility, as distinguished from controllability, refers to the ease with which a cost can be reduced or eliminated. It is not related to the level of control. Some costs, such as institutional advertising, executive salaries, etc., which are uncontrollable at the lower operating levels are, nevertheless, reducible costs. Other costs, such as some types of manufacturing supplies (oil, grease, cleaning supplies, etc.), may be controllable at the lowest operating levels, but may not be reducible.

PROBLEMS

1. Are the following two statements contradictory? Explain your answer. Statement 1: Forecasting a continuation of past or current costs or cost trends will usually give a more accurate estimate of future costs than any other simple method. Statement 2: Using past costs as the basis for economy decisions is poor practice which will cause inaccurate decision-making.

2. A company is considering the manufacture of a proposed new product. The new product-manufacturing facilities would occupy space which is currently not used for any purpose and no other immediate use is foreseen for this space. What would be the opportunity cost of this space?

3. Give three examples of each type of costs listed below and, in each case, justify briefly your characterization of the example: (*a*) traceable costs, (*b*) common costs, (*c*) sunk costs, (*d*) incremental costs, (*e*) marginal costs.

4. Briefly describe how you would make an economic evaluation of whether or not to charge the material handlers and movers in a factory directly or indirectly?

5. Explain by example the difference between book costs and sunk costs.

5   Interest and the Time Value of Money

Why must interest be considered in many economy studies? Interest, from the point of view of the business enterprise or the individual, can be considered as a rental for the use of money. If you have saved some money and I would like to borrow it from you to use in my business, you will agree to lend or rent it to me only if I agree to pay you interest for the use of the money. If I were not willing to pay you a rental (interest) for the use of your money, there would be no incentive for you to lend me the money and your incentive to save money would be reduced.

If you were to place $1,000 in an insured savings bank account paying 4 per cent interest compounded annually, at the end of 10 years you would have $1,480 in the account, assuming you made no further deposits or withdrawals. You would thus not be willing to give me $1,000 in return for a promise to give you $1,000 ten years from now. You would consider that the equivalent value of a present sum of $1,000 ten years from now is $1,480 at 4 per cent interest. You would also consider that you should possibly receive more than a 4 per cent return if you lend the money to me rather than deposit it in an insured savings bank account because of the possibly greater risks involved in an uninsured loan. You may therefore consider that you should receive a 5 per cent return on the $1,000 you lend me. At 5 per cent interest, the equivalent value of a present sum of $1,000 ten years from now is $1,629.

The values of sums of money at different points in time depend upon the interest rate and the time spans. A sum of money today is not equivalent to the same sum ten years later unless interest were assumed at the unrealistic rate of zero. We shall consider in this chapter the methods of calculating these equivalent values of money at different points in time.

Simple Interest. If I lend you $100 for three years at 5 per cent interest payable annually, you will pay me $5 at the end of each of three years, or a total of $15, in addition to returning the principal sum of $100 at the end of the three years.

Simple interest on any investment is computed by multiplying the present investment by the interest rate per period (in this case per year) by the number of periods (in this case years). If we let

> P = sum of money at a time designated as the present
> i = interest rate per interest period
> n = number of interest periods

Then, the simple-interest charge equals Pin.

In the example previously cited, simple interest for the three-year period equals ($100)(0.05)(3), or $15.

Compound Interest. If, in the previous example, I lent you the $100 with the understanding that you would credit me with interest at 5 per cent each year, but would retain the interest until the termination of the loan at the end of three years, paying me interest on the interest you retained, the process is called compounding interest. This is similar to depositing money in a savings bank account and letting the interest accumulate in the account so that interest is earned on the interest.

An arithmetic calculation of the amount that I should receive at the end of three years is shown below.

Year	Principal amount at beginning of year (A)	Interest earned during year at 5% interest (B)	Total amount at end of year (A) + (B)
1	$100.00	$100.00(0.05) = $5.00	$105.00
2	105.00	105.00(0.05) = 5.25	110.25
3	110.25	110.25(0.05) = 5.51	115.76

When you pay me $115.76 at the end of three years, $0.76 of the sum is interest on the interest which you retained until the end of the loan period. Another way of looking at these calculations is that $100.00 today is equivalent to $115.76 three years later, calculating interest at 5 per cent.

Let us designate S as the future sum which is equivalent to present sum P. Thus, S is a sum of money n interest periods from the present which is equivalent to P with interest rate i. We can develop a compound-interest formula to compute S.

Year	Principal amount at beginning of year (A)	Interest earned during year (B)	Total amount at end of year (A) + (B)
1	P	Pi	$P + Pi = P(1 + i)$
2	$P(1 + i)$	$P(1 + i)i$	$P(1 + i) + P(1 + i)i = P(1 + i)(1 + i) = P(1 + i)^2$
3	$P(1 + i)^2$	$P(1 + i)^2 i$	$P(1 + i)^2 + P(1 + i)^2 i = P(1 + i)^2(1 + i) = P(1 + i)^3$
.	.	.	.
.	.	.	
.	.	.	.
n	$P(1 + i)^{n-1}$	$P(1 + i)^{n-1}i$	$P(1 + i)^{n-1} + P(1 + i)^{n-1}i = P(1 + i)^{n-1}(1 + i) = P(1 + i)^n$

Thus, the total amount S, at the end of year n, equals $P(1 + i)^n$.

The formula $S = P(1 + i)^n$ was developed using interest compounded annually, so that n equaled the number of years and i the annual interest rate. If interest is compounded more frequently, then n will be equal to the number of periods of compounding and i will be equal to the rate per interest period, not the nominal rate per year.

Let us consider how much $100 would be worth in five years at 4 per cent interest compounded semiannually. In this case, $n = 10$ half-year periods and $i = 0.02$, or 2 per cent per half-year period. Using our formula, the solution would be

$$S = P(1 + i)^n$$
$$S = \$100(1 + 0.02)^{10}$$
$$S = \$121.90$$

Present Worth. If I desire to receive $100 three years from now, how much money must I invest now if the money will earn 5 per cent interest? Another way of asking this same question is: What is the present worth of $100 three years from now, with interest at 5 per cent?

This question can be answered using the compound-interest formula, $S = P(1 + i)^n$. In this case, P is the unknown quantity and S is the $100 which I desire to receive three years hence. Solving, $S = P(1 + i)^n$ for P,

$$P = S\left(\frac{1}{1 + i}\right)^n$$

To answer the original question,

$$P = S\left(\frac{1}{1 + i}\right)^n$$
$$P = \$100\left(\frac{1}{1 + 0.05}\right)^3$$
$$P = \$86.38$$

Uniform-series Payments. If I deposit $100 at the end of each year for four years in a savings bank account which earns interest at the rate of 4 per cent annually and make no withdrawals during the period, how much money will I have in the account at the end of the four years?

The $100 deposited at the end of the fourth year will earn no interest and will, therefore, contribute only $100 to the total in the account. The $100 deposited at the end of the third year will earn interest for one year and will, therefore, contribute $100(1 + 0.04)$. The $100 deposited at the end of the second year will earn interest for two years and will, therefore, contribute $\$100(1 + 0.04)^2$. The $100 deposited at the end of the first year will earn interest for three years and will, therefore, contribute $\$100(1 + 0.04)^3$. The total in the account at the end of the four years will be $100 + 100(1 + 0.04) + 100(1 + 0.04)^2 + 100(1 + 0.04)^3$.

Solving, we find

$$S = \$100[1 + (1 + 0.04) + (1 + 0.04)^2 + (1 + 0.04)^3]$$
$$= \$424.60$$

These calculations can be graphically represented by a simple line diagram to show the time relationships, as follows:

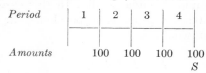

In this problem, we desire to determine the value of S which will be equal to the compound amounts of the four $100 payments. Using our compound-interest formula for the value of each $100 payment at the end of period 4 gives us the previously stated formulation.

Formula for Compound Amount in Fund. Let us say that R = a single end-of-period payment and let us expand our definition of S so that it is a sum of money n interest periods from the present which is equivalent either to P with interest rate i or to a uniform series of end-of-period payments, R, with interest rate i.

We want to derive a formula for the value of a fund in which R dollars are deposited at the end of each period for n periods and in which all monies in the fund earn interest at a rate of i. Graphically, we can represent the model as follows:

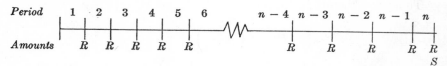

We want to find that value of S which will be equivalent to all of the n end-of-period R's at interest rate i.

The R dollars deposited at the end of the nth period earn no interest and, therefore, contribute R dollars to the fund. The R dollars deposited at the end of the $(n - 1)$ period earn interest for 1 year and will, therefore, contribute $R(1 + i)$ dollars to the fund. The R dollars deposited at the end of the $(n - 2)$ period earn interest for 2 years and will, therefore contribute $R(1 + i)^2$. These years of earned interest in the contributions will continue to increase in this manner, and the R deposited at the end of the first period will have earned interest for $(n - 1)$ periods. The total in the fund S is, thus, equal to $R + R(1 + i) + R(1 + i)^2 + R(1 + i)^3 + R(1 + i)^4 + \cdots + R(1 + i)^{n-2} + R(1 + i)^{n-1}$. Factoring out R, we obtain

$$S = R[1 + (1 + i) + (1 + i)^2 + \cdots + (1 + i)^{n-2} + (1 + i)^{n-1}] \quad (1)$$

If we multiply both sides of this equation by $(1 + i)$, we obtain

$$(1 + i)S = R[(1 + i) + (1 + i)^2 + (1 + i)^3 + \cdots + (1 + i)^{n-1} + (1 + i)^n] \quad (2)$$

If we now subtract equation (1) from (2), we obtain

$$
\begin{aligned}
(1 + i)S - S &= R[(1 + i) + (1 + i)^2 + (1 + i)^3 + \cdots \\
&\quad + (1 + i)^{n-1} + (1 + i)^n] - R[1 + (1 + i) \\
&\quad + (1 + i)^2 + \cdots + (1 + i)^{n-2} + (1 + i)^{n-1}] \\
iS &= R[(1 + i)^n - 1] \\
S &= R\left[\frac{(1 + i)^n - 1}{i}\right]
\end{aligned}
$$

This formula enables us to compute the compound amount of a uniform periodic series. Using it to verify the value of S in the immediately preceding illustration, we obtain

$$S = \$100\left[\frac{(1 + 0.04)^4 - 1}{0.04}\right] = \$424.60$$

Sinking-fund Deposit. I desire to deposit a uniform sum at the end of each year for the next 10 years to provide a sum of $5,000 at the end of the 10-year period for my son's education. If the fund will earn a 4 per cent return on its monies, how much should I deposit at the end of each year? (This type of fund is frequently called a sinking fund.)

To answer this question, let us take the previously developed formula for the compound amount of a uniform series and solve for R, the end-of-period deposit.

$$S = R\left[\frac{(1 + i)^n - 1}{i}\right]$$
$$R = S\left[\frac{i}{(1 + i)^n - 1}\right]$$

Then, to answer my question

$$R = \$5,000\left[\frac{0.04}{(1 + 0.04)^{10} - 1}\right]$$
$$R = \$416.45$$

Capital Recovery. If I lend you $10,000 with the understanding that you will repay this principal sum, including interest at 4 per cent on all unpaid balances, in uniform annual payments, how much should you pay me at the end of each year for five years?

Let us refer to our previous formula for end-of-period payments, R.

$$R = S\left[\frac{i}{(1 + i)^n - 1}\right]$$

and since $S = P(1 + i)^n$

$$R = P(1 + i)^n \left[\frac{i}{(1 + i)^n - 1}\right]$$

$$R = P\left[\frac{i(1 + i)^n}{(1 + i)^n - 1}\right]$$

To answer our original question,

$$R = \$10{,}000\left[\frac{0.04(1 + 0.04)^5}{(1 + 0.04)^5 - 1}\right]$$

$$R = \$2{,}246.30$$

Present Value of a Uniform Series. How much should you be willing to pay me now for my agreement to pay you \$100 at the end of each year for six years if you desire 6 per cent return on the payment you make? (In other words, you would like to receive your principal plus 6 per cent interest on unpaid balances.)

Referring to our previous formula for capital recovery,

$$R = P\left[\frac{i(1 + i)^n}{(1 + i)^n - 1}\right]$$

Let us solve for P:

$$P = R\left[\frac{(1 + i)^n - 1}{i(1 + i)^n}\right]$$

To answer our question,

$$P = \$100\left[\frac{(1 + 0.06)^6 - 1}{0.06(1 + 0.06)^6}\right]$$

$$P = \$491.70$$

Interest Tables. To evaluate numerically the terms with exponents in the answers to our previous questions required the use of logarithms or a calculator or slide rule and is somewhat tedious. To facilitate the solution of interest calculation problems, tables such as those in the Appendix of this book are convenient. These give values for each of the following six interest factors.

Factor name	*Formula*	*Abbreviation*
Single-payment compound-amount factor	$(1 + i)^n$	SPCA $i =$ $n =$
Single-payment present-worth factor	$\dfrac{1}{(1 + i)^n}$	SPPW $i =$ $n =$
Uniform-series compound-amount factor	$\dfrac{(1 + i)^n - 1}{i}$	USCA $i =$ $n =$

Factor name	Formula	Abbreviation
Sinking-fund-payment factor	$\dfrac{i}{(1+i)^n - 1}$	SFP $i =$ $n =$
Capital-recovery factor	$\dfrac{i(1+i)^n}{(1+i)^n - 1}$	CR $i =$ $n =$
Uniform-series present-worth factor	$\dfrac{(1+i)^n - 1}{i(1+i)^n}$	USPW $i =$ $n =$

The values of these factors are computed for the following interest rates: $\frac{1}{2}\%$, 1%, 2%, 3%, 4%, 5%, 6%, 8%, 10%, 12%, 15%, 20%, 25%, 30%, 40%, and 50%. We shall use these interest tables in the solution of most problems in this book requiring the use of the interest formula.

When the values of interest factors are desired for interest rates for which tables are not available, approximations of the desired values can be obtained by linear interpolation between the values for available interest rates on each side of the desired rate. For most of the types of economy calculations with which we are concerned, such approximate solutions are adequate and can obviate the necessity for the more arduous calculations using the formula.

Interest Charts. Six charts of interest factors are presented in the Appendix to this book:

1. Single-payment compound amount
2. Single-payment present worth
3. Uniform-series compound amount
4. Sinking-fund payment
5. Capital recovery
6. Uniform-series present worth

For many purposes, these charts are more convenient to use than the interest tables. The accuracy obtained by reading values off these charts is sufficient for most economy calculations. The charts are especially suitable for use in calculations in which we are desirous of determining an interest rate. Their use may be illustrated with several examples.

You offer me $800 five years from now if I will give you $500 now. What rate of return is the $500 loan earning?

$$\$800 = \$500 \begin{pmatrix} \text{SPCA} \\ i = ? \\ n = 5 \end{pmatrix}$$

$$\begin{pmatrix} \text{SPCA} \\ i = ? \\ n = 5 \end{pmatrix} = \tfrac{800}{500} = 1.60$$

Turning to Chart 1, we start at the $n = 5$ value on the horizontal axis. We then move up to the 1.6 value on the vertical axis. An SPCA of 1.6 is obtained between $i = 8$ and $i = 10$ per cent, or approximately 9.8 per cent.

By spending $1,000 now on a new machine, you will save $150 a year for 10 years, which is the life of the machine. The machine will have no salvage value. What rate of return will this $1,000 investment give you?

Saving $150 a year in costs is the equivalent of receiving $150 a year. The problem is one of finding the interest rate which will make $150 a year for 10 years equivalent to $1,000 now.

$$\$150 = \$1,000 \left(\begin{array}{c} \text{CR} \\ i = ? \\ n = 10 \end{array} \right)$$

$$\left(\begin{array}{c} \text{CR} \\ i = ? \\ n = 10 \end{array} \right) = 0.15$$

Referring to Chart 5, we find that the interest rate for a CR of 0.15 with $n = 10$ is approximately 8 per cent.

In how many years will money triple in value if it can be continually reinvested at the various interest rates shown on the charts?

Turning to Chart 1, we read across the SPCA = 3 line and find the values of n where each interest line crosses the SPCA = 3 horizontal line. Thus, the $i = 50$ per cent line crosses the $n = 3$ line at 2.7 years. This means that $\left(\begin{array}{c} \text{SPCA} \\ i = 50\% \\ n = 2.7 \end{array} \right) = 3$. At 50 per cent interest, money will triple in 2.7 years. Continuing across the SPCA = 3 horizontal line, we obtain the results shown in Table 5-1.

Table 5-1. **Number of Years to Triple Investment at Various Interest Rates**

Interest rate	Approximate number of years to triple investment	Interest rate	Approximate number of years to triple investment
50%	2.7	10%	11.6
40	3.2	8	14.2
30	4.2	6	18.9
25	4.9	5	22.5
20	6.0	4	28.0
15	7.9	3	37.5
12	9.7	2	56.0

If $500 is deposited in a fund at the end of each year for 20 years, what rate of interest must the fund earn if the fund is to amount to $25,000 at the end of the 20-year period?

$$\$25,000 = \$500 \left(\begin{array}{c} \text{USCA} \\ i = ? \\ n = 20 \end{array} \right)$$

$$\left(\begin{array}{c} \text{USCA} \\ i = ? \\ n = 20 \end{array} \right) = \$50$$

On Chart 3, for $n = 20$, the USCA of 50 lies between $i = 8$ per cent and $i = 10$ per cent, or approximately 8.8 per cent.

Relationship between Interest Factors. It is interesting and useful to note the following relationships between the interest factors just discussed.

There are three sets of reciprocal factor values:

1. Single-payment compound amount and single-payment present worth
2. Uniform-series compound amount and sinking-fund payment
3. Capital recovery and uniform-series present worth

We can check these reciprocal relationships by noting the values of these factors in the interest tables if $i = 10\%$, $n = 5$:

1. $1.611 = \frac{1}{0.6209}$
2. $6.105 = \frac{1}{0.16380}$
3. $0.26380 = \frac{1}{3.791}$

The uniform-series present-worth factor is equal to the sum of the single-payment present-worth factors from year 1 to year n. Also, the uniform-series compound-amount factor is equal to one (1.0) plus the sum of the single-payment compound-amount factors from year 1 to year $(n - 1)$. (Note that in this latter case we add one (1.0) to the single payments up to year $(n - 1)$ because the last payment does not earn interest since it is deposited at the same time as the fund value is determined.)

We can check these with the table values for $i = 10\%$, $n = 5$.

$$0.9091 + 0.8264 + 0.7513 + 0.6830 + 0.6209 = 3.791$$
$$1.000 + 1.100 + 1.210 + 1.331 + 1.464 = 6.105$$

Our previously developed formula for the capital-recovery factor was

$$\frac{i(1 + i)^n}{(1 + i)^n - 1}$$

Let us add and subtract i in the numerator:

$$\frac{i + i(1 + i)^n - i}{(1 + i)^n - 1} = \frac{i + i[(1 + i)^n - 1]}{(1 + i)^n - 1} = \frac{i}{(1 + i)^n - 1} + i$$

We previously noted that $\frac{i}{(1 + i)^n - 1}$ is the sinking-fund-payment factor. Thus, the capital-recovery factor is equal to the sinking-fund-payment factor plus the interest rate. Checking in the interest tables for $i = 10$ per cent, $n = 5$, we find that $0.26380 = 0.16380 + 0.10000$.

Perpetual Endowment. If you give a corporation \$1,000 in return for which the corporation agrees to pay you and your heirs 4 per cent interest at the end of each year forever, never returning the \$1,000, how much should you receive each year? The answer is, obviously,

$$R = Pi$$
$$R = \$1,000(0.04) = \$40$$

Since the original investment is never repaid, all that is paid is simple interest on the $1,000.

Capitalized Cost. If a corporation promises to pay you and your heirs $100 a year forever, how much should you be willing to pay for this promise if you desire a return of 5 per cent on your money? This is just the reverse of the previous example of perpetual endowment. Thus,

$$R = Pi$$

Solving for P,

$$P = \frac{R}{i} = R\left(\frac{1}{i}\right)$$

$$P = \$100 \left(\frac{1}{0.05}\right) = \$2,000$$

If you pay $2,000, you will be obtaining a 5 per cent return on your money.

This calculation represents the present worth of a uniform series of payments for an infinite number of years. Thus, $(1/i)$ represents the uniform-series present-worth factor with the number of payments (n) equal to infinity. (The limiting value of the uniform-series present-worth factor, $\left[\dfrac{(1 + i)^n - 1}{i(1 + i)^n}\right]$, as n approaches infinity is $1/i$.) This procedure for finding the present worth of an infinite series of payments is frequently called capitalization of the payments.

Nominal and Effective Interest Rates. Interest rates are usually quoted as nominal interest rates. Thus, interest at 6 per cent means 6 per cent compounded annually unless otherwise specified. Interest at 6 per cent compounded semiannually means that 3 per cent interest is credited or charged every half year. The nominal interest rate is still 6 per cent, but the effective annual rate is greater because half of the 6 per cent interest is received at the end of six months instead of at the end of the year. Interest must, therefore, be compounded on this interest to obtain the effective rate.

Thus, at the end of the first six-month period, the amount of principal has grown to $(1 + i)$ or 1.03 (i is the interest per six-month period, or 0.03) times the amount at the beginning. At the end of the second period the $(1 + i)P$, or $(1.03)P$, has grown to $(1 + i)^2 P$ or $(1.03)^2 P$. Therefore, the effective interest rate per year of 6 per cent compounded semiannually is $(1 + i)^K - 1 = (1.03)^2 - 1 = 1.0609 - 1 = 0.0609$, or 6.09 per cent, where K is the number of times per year the interest is compounded.

Similarly, a nominal interest rate of 6 per cent compounded quarterly means $1\frac{1}{2}$ per cent interest every three months and is an effective annual interest rate of $(1 + i)^K - 1 = (1.015)^4 - 1 = 1.0614 - 1 = 0.0614$, or 6.14 per cent.

Calculating Equivalencies. Using the interest formula and tables, we can readily calculate the equivalent values of various sums of money at different points in time, depending upon the interest rate used.

For example, at 6 per cent interest compounded semiannually $5,000 today is equivalent to

1. How much money 5 years from now?

$$S = P \left(\begin{array}{c} \text{SPCA} \\ i = 3\% \\ n = 10 \end{array} \right) = \$5,000(1.344) = \$6,720$$

2. How much money at the end of each six-month period for five years?

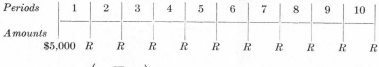

$$R = P \left(\begin{array}{c} \text{CR} \\ i = 3\% \\ n = 10 \end{array} \right) = \$5,000(0.11723) = \$586.15$$

3. How much simple interest every six months if the $5,000 is to be returned at the end of five years?

Simple interest every six months $= Pi = \$5,000(0.03) = \$150.00$

4. How much simple interest every year if the $5,000 is to be returned at the end of five years?

Effective annual interest rate $= (1 + i)^K - 1 = (1 + 0.03)^2 - 1$
$$= 0.0609, \text{ or } 6.09 \text{ per cent}$$
Simple interest every year $= \$5,000(0.0609) = \$304.50$

5. How much money each year if $1,000 of principal plus interest on the unpaid balance is paid at the end of each year for five years?

Year	Unpaid balance at beginning of year	Interest for year at 6.09% effective rate	Total yearly payment ($1,000 plus interest for year)
1	$5,000	$304.50	$1,304.50
2	4,000	243.60	1,243.60
3	3,000	182.70	1,182.70
4	2,000	121.80	1,121.80
5	1,000	60.90	1,060.90

Each of the answers to the preceding five questions is equivalent to $5,000 today at 6 per cent interest compounded semiannually, and each is equivalent to every other. The five represent possible ways of repaying a loan of $5,000 at 6 per cent compounded semiannually. Because the $5,000 is repaid more rapidly in some cases than in others, the total dollars paid will vary. Thus, the total dollars are (1) \$6,720.00; (2) \$5,861.50; (3)\$6,500.00; (4) \$6,522.50; and (5) \$5,913.50. Where the total dollars are lowest, the money is repaid at the earliest date and can be used or invested in uses which will yield interest or other returns.

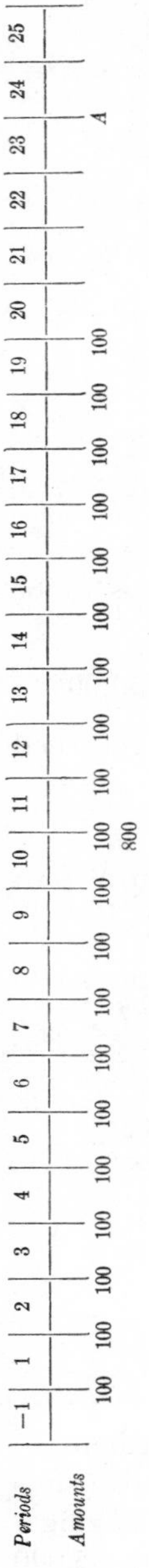

Adjusting Nomenclature of Payment Timing to Conform to Model. In some cases, the statement of the problem may not conform to the assumptions built into our interest-formula models. However, the form of the problem can frequently be adjusted to provide for the easier solution using interest tables rather than going through the more laborious construction of new formulas.

For example, I propose to sign an agreement to deposit \$100 at the *beginning* of this year and each year from now on for the next 19 years (20 payments). I propose to withdraw \$800 at the *end* of the 10th year and the remainder I will receive at the *beginning* of the 24th year. How much will I receive at the *beginning* of the 24th year, with interest at 4 per cent?

Let us draw a diagram, as shown to the left, indicating the timing of payments and receipts. (The end of any year is the same point in time as the beginning of the next year.)

To find A, the amount to be withdrawn at the beginning of the 24th year, we must write an equivalence equation: the 24 \$100 payments equal the 2 withdrawals, \$800 and A, taking interest into account. To do this, we must find the worth of each of these sums at one point in time and set up the equivalence equation.

One point in time which we can use is one year before period one (the beginning of year −1). We choose this point because then we have a series of 20 end-of-period payments of \$100, considering that the first payment is at the end of a −1 period rather than at the beginning of the first period. Correspondingly, the second payment is at the end of period 1 rather than the beginning of period 2.

$$\$100\begin{pmatrix}\text{USPW}\\ i = 4\%\\ n = 20\end{pmatrix} = \$800\begin{pmatrix}\text{SPPW}\\ i = 4\%\\ n = 11\end{pmatrix} + A\begin{pmatrix}\text{SPPW}\\ i = 4\%\\ n = 24\end{pmatrix}$$

$$\$100(13.590) = \$800(0.6496) + A(0.3901)$$

$$A = \$2,151.55$$

If we used the end of the 19th or the beginning of the 20th year as the point in time for writing the equivalence equation, the value of the $100 annual deposit at the end of the 19th year is determined by multiplying $100 by USCA with n equal to 20 because the first deposit of $100 is made at the end of the -1 period. The value of the $800 payment which is received at the end of the 10th year is multiplied by the SPCA with n equal to 9 because the end of the 19th year is 9 periods later than the 10th year. The value of the unknown payment A at the end of the 23d year is multiplied by SPPW with n equal to 4 because this payment is made 4 years after the end of the 19th year. Thus,

$$\$100 \begin{pmatrix} \text{USCA} \\ i = 4\% \\ n = 20 \end{pmatrix} = \$800 \begin{pmatrix} \text{SPCA} \\ i = 4\% \\ n = 9 \end{pmatrix} + A \begin{pmatrix} \text{SPPW} \\ i = 4\% \\ n = 4 \end{pmatrix}$$
$$\$100(29.778) = \$800(1.423) + A(0.8548)$$
$$A = \$2,151.84$$

If we used the end of the 23d or the beginning of the 24th year,

$$\$100 \begin{pmatrix} \text{USCA} \\ i = 4\% \\ n = 20 \end{pmatrix} \begin{pmatrix} \text{SPCA} \\ i = 4\% \\ n = 4 \end{pmatrix} = \$800 \begin{pmatrix} \text{SPCA} \\ i = 4\% \\ n = 13 \end{pmatrix} + A$$
$$\$100(29.778)(1.17) = \$800(1.665) + A$$
$$A = \$2,152.03$$

If we used the end of the 10th or the beginning of the 11th year,

$$\$100 \begin{pmatrix} \text{USPW} \\ i = 4\% \\ n = 20 \end{pmatrix} \begin{pmatrix} \text{SPCA} \\ i = 4\% \\ n = 11 \end{pmatrix} = \$800 + A \begin{pmatrix} \text{SPPW} \\ i = 4\% \\ n = 13 \end{pmatrix}$$
$$\$100(13.590)(1.539) = \$800 + A(0.6006)$$
$$A = \$2,150.35$$

Or we could write for this same point in time,

$$\$100 \begin{pmatrix} \text{USCA} \\ i = 4\% \\ n = 11 \end{pmatrix} + \$100 \begin{pmatrix} \text{USPW} \\ i = 4\% \\ n = 9 \end{pmatrix} = \$800 + A \begin{pmatrix} \text{SPPW} \\ i = 4\% \\ n = 13 \end{pmatrix}$$
$$\$100(13.486) + \$100(7.435) = \$800 + A(0.6006)$$
$$A = \$2,151.34$$

Or we could write for this same point in time,

$$\$100 \begin{pmatrix} \text{USCA} \\ i = 4\% \\ n = 20 \end{pmatrix} \begin{pmatrix} \text{SPPW} \\ i = 4\% \\ n = 9 \end{pmatrix} = \$800 + A \begin{pmatrix} \text{SPPW} \\ i = 4\% \\ n = 13 \end{pmatrix}$$
$$\$100(29.778)(0.7026) = \$800 + A(0.6006)$$
$$A = \$2,151.51$$

As you can see, there are numerous ways of arriving at this answer. And there are even more possible ways. Each of the methods will give us exactly the same answer if the interest factor values and calculations are carried to enough significant figures. In our examples, the minor variations in the answers are due to the rounding off in the factor values and calculations.

Precision of Interest Calculations. We shall see that for most purposes in engineering and managerial economy, a high degree of precision in making interest calculations is not required. Most economy decisions are based upon forecasts of future costs and future demands. They are thus subject to estimating errors of varying dimensions. There is, therefore, little point in carrying out interest calculations to a large number of significant figures. It is also not usually necessary in economy studies to worry about differences in compounding interest annually rather than semiannually or quarterly, although such differences could be very important in banking and finance.

Continuous Compounding. In the operation of my business, I am receiving and disbursing money continuously. The profits I make are not taken out of the business, except when I make dividend payments. The profits are being continuously reinvested in the business. There is thus logic in considering that the funds invested in a business should be continuously compounded, that the rate of interest or profit growth should be continuous (proportional to the amount of total principal and interest at each instant).

To find the effective interest rate under continuous compounding, we start with the same formula as before:

$$\text{Effective interest rate} = (1 + i)^K - 1$$

If we let I equal the nominal interest rate,

$$\left(1 + \frac{I}{K}\right)^K - 1 = \left[\left(1 + \frac{1}{K/I}\right)^{K/I}\right]^I - 1$$

Continuous compounding means letting K, the number of times the interest is compounded, get infinitely large. As K gets infinitely large, the limiting value of $\left(1 + \dfrac{1}{K/I}\right)^{K/I}$ equals e, which is the base of the Naperian or natural logarithms and equals 2.71828.

Our effective rate of interest when it is compounded continuously thus becomes

$$e^I - 1$$

For a nominal interest rate of 6 per cent compounded continuously,

$$\text{Effective interest rate} = e^{0.06} - 1$$

Using logarithms, we find that this effective rate is 0.06184, or 6.184 per cent. There is a difference of about 3 per cent in the effective interest rate between annual and continuous compounding. Table 5-2 summarizes the increases in the effective interest rates for a nominal interest rate of 6 per cent as we increase the frequency of compounding.

Table 5-2. **Effective Interest Rates Using a Nominal 6 Per Cent Rate**

Compounded	*Effective rate*
Annually.................	6.000%
Semiannually............	6.090
Quarterly...............	6.136
Bimonthly..............	6.152
Monthly................	6.168
Semimonthly...........	6.176
Daily..................	6.183
Continuously...........	6.184

In the types of applied economic evaluation with which we are concerned in this book, the theoretical accuracy to be obtained by any continuous compounding is usually not significant. In determining prospective rates of return on proposed investments by techniques such as the forecasted-cash-flow method described in Chapter 11, it is theoretically more accurate to use continuous compounding for funds which are flowing continuously. As a practical matter, however, this refinement is not worth bothering about, considering the risk and uncertainties in the revenue and cost forecasts, the relative crudeness of our tools for evaluating the intangible factors in capital-investment decisions, and the large amount of judgment involved in the determination of what is an acceptable rate of return in capital-budget decision-making. (In some theoretical studies, it is convenient to use continuous compounding because it is well adapted for some mathematical manipulations.)

Continuous-compounding Interest Formula. Occasionally there may arise instances where it may be appropriate to use continuous compounding and where the additional theoretical accuracy of continuous compounding as applied to the problem being decided will be significant. When the decision-maker is accustomed to thinking in terms of continuous compounding, it certainly does not hurt to use continuous-compound-interest formulas.

Based upon our previous discussion, substituting in our standard single-payment present-worth formula I/K for i, we can write

$$P = S\left[\frac{1}{\left(1 + \dfrac{I}{K}\right)^{KN}}\right] = S\frac{1}{\left[\left(1 + \dfrac{1}{K/I}\right)^{K/I}\right]^{IN}} = S\frac{1}{e^{IN}} = S(e^{-IN})$$

Our single-payment present-worth factor for continuous compounding thus equals e^{-IN}, where e equals 2.71828, I is the nominal annual interest rate, and N is the number of years. For example, the present value at 15 per cent interest compounded continuously of a payment of $2,000 which will be required 10 years from now is equal to

$$\$2,000(e^{-IN}) = \$2,000[e^{-0.15(10)}] = \$446$$

The effective annual rate of interest in this case is

$$e^I - 1 = e^{0.15} - 1 = 0.1618$$

Continuous compounding at 15 per cent is thus equivalent to 16.2 per cent with annual compounding. In performing interest calculations, there is then no real advantage to using continuous compounding. We can determine the annual effective equivalent interest rate; we can then use the single-payment compound-amount factor with annual compounding; and we shall obtain the same result.

Uniform Continuous Payment or Receipt and Continuous Compounding. We may be receiving or paying sums of money on a relatively uniform basis throughout a period of time. We do not desire to make the approximating and simplifying assumption that the payments are concentrated at one point in the period.

For example, I shall receive an income of $10,000 at a continuous uniform rate over the next year. What is the present value of this money at 15 per cent interest compounded continuously?

Let us first derive a formula for the present worth of $1 received at a continuous uniform rate spread over an entire year. We can use the uniform-series present-worth formula for this purpose:

$$P = R \frac{(1 + i)^n - 1}{i(1 + i)^n}$$

Using K to indicate the number of receipts, the size of each uniform receipt during the year is $R = 1/K$. In addition, $i = I/K$, $n = K$, and

$$P = \frac{1}{K} \frac{[1 + (I/K)]^K - 1}{(I/K)[1 + (I/K)]^K} = \frac{[1 + (I/K)]^K - 1}{I[1 + (I/K)]^K}$$

K approaches infinity for continuous receipt and compounding. We previously showed that as K approaches infinity, $[1 + (I/K)]^K = e^I$. Therefore, when K approaches infinity,

$$P = \frac{e^I - 1}{Ie^I}$$

The present worth of my next year's income of $10,000 is 10,000 times the present worth of $1.

$$P = \$10,000 \left(\frac{e^I - 1}{Ie^I} \right) = \$10,000 \left(\frac{e^{0.15} - 1}{0.15e^{0.15}} \right)$$

Using logarithms, we find the answer: $10,000(0.9284) = $9,284.

Thus, $9,284 is the present worth at the beginning of the year of $10,000 uniformly received or paid throughout the year at a 15 per cent nominal interest rate compounded continuously or a 16.2 per cent effective annual interest rate.

$\dfrac{e^I - 1}{Ie^I}$ is a continuous-payment present-worth factor. It represents the worth at the beginning of the year of $1 which is uniformly distributed over the year. I is a nominal interest rate which is compounded continuously.

Uniform Continuous Payment or Receipt—Effective Annual Compounding. We would like to know the present value of the $10,000 received at a continuous uniform rate over the next year with effective annual interest at 15 per cent.

We can solve this problem using the same formula as in the immediately preceding problem, provided that we first find the nominal interest rate, I, whose effective rate is equal to 15 per cent.

$$\text{Effective rate} = e^I - 1$$
$$0.15 = e^I - 1$$
$$e^I = 1.15$$
$$I = 0.1398$$

Then

$$P = \$10,000 \left(\frac{e^I - 1}{Ie^I} \right) = \$10,000 \left(\frac{e^{0.1398} - 1}{0.1398 e^{0.1398}} \right)$$
$$= \$10,000(0.9333) = \$9,333$$

For those occasions when its use is desired, it would be convenient to tabulate the values of the present worth at the beginning of the year of a uniform continuous payment at the rate of $1 per year throughout the year. This is done in Table 5-3 for various effective interest rates. We shall call these factors the uniform continuous-payment present-worth factors, abbreviated UCPPW.

Table 5-3. **Uniform Continuous-payment Present-worth Factors (UCPPW)**
Present Worth at Beginning of Year of Uniform Continuous Payment at Rate of $1 per Year throughout Year

Effective annual interest rate i	UCPPW factor	Effective annual interest rate i	UCPPW factor
$\frac{1}{2}\%$	0.9957	10%	0.9538
1	0.9950	12	0.9454
2	0.9902	15	0.9333
3	0.9854	20	0.9141
4	0.9806	25	0.8963
5	0.9760	30	0.8796
6	0.9714	40	0.8491
8	0.9625	50	0.8221

Example 1. We desire to determine the worth at the beginning of 1962 of a uniform continuous receipt during 1968 of $5,000 using an effective annual interest rate of 6 per cent. Using Table 5-3, we determine the worth at the beginning of 1968 as $5,000 $\left(\begin{smallmatrix} \text{UCPPW} \\ i = 6\% \end{smallmatrix} \right)$ = $5,000(0.9714) = $4,857. To determine the worth of this $4,857 at the beginning of 1962, we compute

$$\$4,857 \left(\begin{smallmatrix} \text{SPPW} \\ i = 6\% \\ n = 5 \end{smallmatrix} \right) = \$4,857(0.7473) = \$3,630$$

Example 2. Mr. Brown anticipates that a new machine he plans to purchase will save him $8,000 per year in operating costs uniformly distributed throughout the expected life of 15 years. Using an effective annual interest rate of 10 per cent, what is the present value of these prospective future cost savings?

In most practical problems, we would assume that the $8,000 per year is concentrated at the end of each year. The solution would be $8,000 $\left(\begin{smallmatrix} \text{USPW} \\ i = 10\% \\ n = 15 \end{smallmatrix} \right)$ = $8,000(7.606) = $60,848. This method is sufficiently accurate considering the usual reliability of the cost estimates in these types of studies. However, in this case it is desired to take explicit account of the fact that the funds are to be received uniformly over the years. The first step is to calculate the worth of each year's receipts at the beginning of each year: $8,000 $\left(\begin{smallmatrix} \text{UCPPW} \\ i = 10\% \end{smallmatrix} \right)$ = $8,000(0.9538) = $7,630. Thus, the $8,000 per year uniformly distributed over the 15-year period is equivalent to $7,630 at the beginning of each year. Making R = $7,630, this series of receipts is illustrated below in our standard format for receipts at specific points in time.

1	2	3	4	5	6	7	8	9	10	11	12	13	14	15
R	R	R	R	R	R	R	R	R	R	R	R	R	R	R

The worth at the beginning of year 1 of these R = $7,630 payments is

$$\$7,630 \left[1 + \left(\begin{smallmatrix} \text{USPW} \\ i = 10\% \\ n = 14 \end{smallmatrix} \right) \right] = \$7,630(1 + 7.367) = \$63,840.$$

Table 5-3 can thus be used to convert readily any regular single-payment or uniform-series factors to permit the exact solution of all problems in which uniform continuous payments and receipts occur.

Interest Calculations for Uniform Gradient. You have undertaken to assist in providing for the education of a nephew and have committed yourself to contribute $400 one year from now, $500 two years from now,

$600 three years from now, and $700 four years from now. Because you have a relatively fixed annual income, you would prefer to contribute a uniform sum at the end of each of the four years rather than the uniformly increasing amount. You ask me if I would be agreeable to make the uniformly increasing payments at the end of each of the four years providing you gave me a uniform sum each year. Since in the early years you would be giving me more than the payments I would be making, I would be expected to pay interest at 6 per cent on the excess during those years. How much should you pay me each year?

One way of solving this problem is to calculate the equivalent sum you would have to pay me if I made all of the payments and you repaid me a lump sum at the end of the fourth year with interest at 6 per cent. We could then calculate the uniform annual amount which would result in this lump sum at 6 per cent interest.

The diagrammatic representation of the time values for calculating S is shown in Figure 5-1.

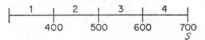

Figure 5-1. Diagrammatic representation of uniform-gradient problem.

$$S = \$400 \left(\begin{array}{c} \text{SPCA} \\ i = 6\% \\ n = 3 \end{array}\right) + \$500 \left(\begin{array}{c} \text{SPCA} \\ i = 6\% \\ n = 2 \end{array}\right) + \$600 \left(\begin{array}{c} \text{SPCA} \\ i = 6\% \\ n = 1 \end{array}\right) + \$700$$

$$= \$400(1.191) + \$500(1.124) + \$600(1.060) + \$700 = \$2,374.40$$

The uniform end-of-year payments to me should, therefore, be

$$R = \$2,374.40 \left(\begin{array}{c} \text{SFP} \\ i = 6\% \\ n = 4 \end{array}\right)$$

$$= \$2,374.40(0.22859) = \$543$$

Uniform-gradient Formulas. When problems involving a uniform gradient extend over a substantial number of years, it is sometimes desirable to use a special formula and tables to convert the uniform-gradient series to a uniform-annual series in one calculation rather than the single-payment summation just illustrated. We will develop our formula based upon the uniform-gradient model shown in Figure 5-2.

Figure 5-2. Diagrammatic representation of time values in a uniform gradient.

Using this model, we want to determine at interest rate i the equivalent compound amount at the end of the nth period of the uniformly increasing gradient series extending for n periods with a payment of zero at the end of the first period, g at the end of the second period, $2g$ at the end of the third, continuing to $(n - 2)g$ at the end of the $(n - 1)$ period and $(n - 1)g$ at the end of the nth period. We will then convert this compound amount to an equivalent uniform series using the sinking-fund-payment formula.

Taking the compound amount at the end of the nth period of each single payment, we obtain

$$S = (n - 1)g + (n - 2)g(1 + i) + (n - 3)g(1 + i)^2 + \cdots$$
$$+ 2g(1 + i)^{n-3} + g(1 + i)^{n-2}$$

Factoring out g,

$$S = g[(n - 1) + (n - 2)(1 + i) + (n - 3)(1 + i)^2 + \cdots$$
$$+ 2(1 + i)^{n-3} + (1 + i)^{n-2}] \quad (1)$$

Multiplying both sides of the equation by $(1 + i)$,

$$(1 + i)S = g[(n - 1)(1 + i) + (n - 2)(1 + i)^2 + (n - 3)(1 + i)^3$$
$$+ \cdots + 2(1 + i)^{n-2} + (1 + i)^{n-1}] \quad (2)$$

Subtracting equation (1) from equation (2),

$$(1 + i)S - S = g[(n - 1)(1 + i) + (n - 2)(1 + i)^2$$
$$+ (n - 3)(1 + i)^3 + \cdots + 2(1 + i)^{n-2}$$
$$+ (1 + i)^{n-1}] - g[(n - 1) + (n - 2)(1 + i)$$
$$+ (n - 3)(1 + i)^2 + \cdots + 2(1 + i)^{n-3}$$
$$+ (1 + i)^{n-2}]$$
$$iS = g[(1 + i) + (1 + i)^2 + (1 + i)^3 + \cdots + (1 + i)^{n-2}$$
$$+ (1 + i)^{n-1} - (n - 1)]$$

Rearranging the last term,

$$iS = g[1 + (1 + i) + (1 + i)^2 + (1 + i)^3 + \cdots + (1 + i)^{n-2}$$
$$+ (1 + i)^{n-1}] - ng$$

The term in brackets is the uniform-series compound-amount factor, which we have previously shown is equal to $\left[\dfrac{(1 + i)^n - 1}{i}\right]$.

$$iS = g\left[\frac{(1 + i)^n - 1}{i}\right] - ng$$
$$S = \frac{g}{i}\left[\frac{(1 + i)^n - 1}{i}\right] - \frac{ng}{i}$$

To find the uniform-series equivalent, we multiply S by the sinking-fund-payment factor.

$$R = \left[\frac{i}{(1 + i)^n - 1}\right]\left[\frac{g}{i}\left(\frac{(1 + i)^n - 1}{i}\right) - \frac{ng}{i}\right]$$
$$R = \frac{g}{i} - \frac{ng}{i}\left[\frac{i}{(1 + i)^n - 1}\right] = g\left[\frac{1}{i} - \frac{n}{(1 + i)^n - 1}\right]$$

The term $\left[\dfrac{1}{i} - \dfrac{n}{(1 + i)^n - 1}\right]$, the uniform-gradient conversion factor (represented by the letters UGC), is used to convert the gradient series to a uniform series.

Uniform-gradient Table. In the Appendix to this book are tabulated values of the uniform-gradient conversion factor for various values of i and n.

Let us use this table to solve the illustrative gradient problem we discussed just prior to developing the formula for the conversion factor. We desire to compute the uniform-series equivalent of the gradient series starting with $400 one year from now, $500 two years from now, $600 three years from now, and $700 four years from now.

Our uniform-gradient-factor model has zero payment at the end of the first year, g at the end of the second, etc. We therefore divide the gradient series into two parts: a uniform series of $400 per year for four years and a uniform gradient with a gradient (g) of $100 for four years. The uniform-series equivalent of these two series is

$$R = \$400 + \$100 \begin{pmatrix} \text{UGC} \\ i = 6\% \\ n = 4 \end{pmatrix}$$
$$= \$400 + \$100(1.43) = \$543$$

This answer agrees with our previous calculation.

It is apparent that the present worth of a uniform-gradient series can be readily determined from the uniform-series equivalent by using the appropriate USPW factor.

Uniformly Decreasing Gradient. The uniform-gradient table can also be used for determining the uniform-series equivalent of a uniformly decreasing series. Let us determine the uniform-series equivalent at 10 per cent interest of an income which is given in Table 5-4.

Table 5-4. **Uniformly Decreasing Income**

End of year	Amount
1	$5,000
2	4,600
3	4,200
4	3,800
5	3,400
6	3,000
7	2,600
8	2,200

We can consider this decreasing series to consist of a uniform series of $5,000 from which is subtracted a uniformly increasing gradient series of

$400 per year. The equivalent uniform series then becomes

$$R = \$5,000 - \$400 \left(\begin{array}{c} \text{UGC} \\ i = 10\% \\ n = 8 \end{array} \right)$$

$$= \$5,000 - \$400(3.00) = \$3,800$$

Of course, this could also be computed by calculating the present worths of each payment.

PROBLEMS

1. What is the simple interest which will be paid on a loan of $3,000 over a four-year period if the interest rate is 5 per cent payable annually?

2. Smith borrowed $1,000 from Jones for a five-year period, promising to make a payment of 6 per cent interest at the end of each year. List the payments Jones will receive.

3. If the agreement in problem 2 is changed so that Smith is to make only one lump-sum payment of principal and interest at the end of the five-year period, how much should Jones receive at that time?

4. How much will $5,000 be worth in 10 years if interest is accrued at the rate of 4 per cent compounded semiannually?

5. At 5 per cent interest, what is the present worth of an inheritance of $100,000 to be received fifteen years from now?

6. What is the present worth of a $5,000 expenditure which I expect to incur in four years, using interest at 10 per cent?

7. Joe Barnes will require $10,000 fifteen years from now. How much must be invested today if the money will earn 5 per cent per annum?

8. If Clark deposits $100 a year in a fund earning 5 per cent interest, how much will have accumulated by the end of the 15th year?

9. At the end of each year $500 is deposited in a fund which earns 6 per cent compounded semiannually. How much will be in the fund at the end of 20 years?

10. What is the present worth of a promise to pay $100 at the end of each of the next 10 years if interest is computed at 8 per cent?

11. A machine will save $4,000 a year in operating costs for the next 10 years. Using interest at 12 per cent, what is the present worth of these savings?

12. I must repay a $15,000 interest-free loan six years from now. What uniform sum must I deposit at the end of each of the next six years in a fund earning 4 per cent interest to have the $15,000 available as required?

13. The Arco Company borrowed $100,000 at 6 per cent interest which it must repay in equal end-of-year amounts (covering both principal and interest) over the next eight years. How much must the company pay at the end of each year?

14. Using B equal to a single beginning-of-period payment instead of R equal to a single end-of-period payment and keeping the definitions of i, P, S, and n the same as in the text, derive formulas for the following factors: (a) uniform-series compound-amount, (b) uniform-series present-worth, (c) capital-recovery, (d) sinking-fund-payment.

15. How long will it take money to double at 5 per cent interest?

16. At what interest rate must a man invest $79.50 a year in order to have a balance of $1,000 after his tenth payment?

17. The sinking-fund-payment factor for $i = 5\frac{1}{2}\%$, $n = 4$ is 0.2303. For the same i and n, find the (a) uniform-series compound-amount factor, (b) uniform-series present-worth factor, (c) capital-recovery factor.

18. The single-payment compound-amount factor for $i = 6.146\%$, $n = 5$ is 1.3475. For the same i and n, find the (a) single-payment present-worth factor, (b) uniform-series compound-amount factor, (c) uniform-series present-worth factor, (d) capital-recovery factor, (e) sinking-fund-payment factor.

19. What is the capitalized cost of a $3,000 annual payment, using interest at 4 per cent?

20. A philanthropist wishes to provide a university with an income of $800 per year forever. If the university can invest his money at 4 per cent, what sum must he donate to provide this income?

21. If interest is compounded monthly, and the annual nominal interest rate is 12 per cent, determine the amount necessary to repay a $100 loan within two years (a) in equal monthly installments, (b) in a lump sum at the end of two years.

22. What is the effective annual interest rate if 3 per cent interest is compounded monthly?

23. You invest $1,000 at 4 per cent interest, compounded annually. Determine your balance at the end of 10 years (a) if you make no further deposits or withdrawals; (b) if you deposit $30 at the end of each year, including the tenth; (c) if you withdraw $30 at the end of each year, including the tenth.

24. A man has the following debts outstanding: (a) 10 annual mortgage payments of $1,000, (b) 12 monthly payments of $100 on his automobile, (c) a bill for $2,000 due in two years, (d) a bill for $1,000 due today. Using an annual interest rate of 12 per cent (nominal rate on the automobile loan and effective rate on all other debts), determine the annual amount necessary to retire the entire debt in 15 years.

25. A man arranges to repay a $1,000 loan in 15 equal annual installments. Interest is 4 per cent. After his tenth payment, he wishes to pay the balance in a lump sum. Assuming he can do this without an additional penalty premium, how much does he owe?

26. What uniform sum must I deposit in a fund on my son's 8th through 22d birthdays if he is to receive $2,000 per year on his 18th through 22d birthdays? The fund will earn 5 per cent per annum.

27. A man arranges to repay a 6 per cent $1,000 loan in 10 equal annual installments. After his sixth payment, he borrows another $1,000, also at 6 per cent, with the following understanding: he is to pay nothing for the next two years and then repay the balance of the first loan plus the entire second loan in 8 equal annual installments starting at the end of the third year. What will this annual payment be?

28. What is the present worth of $4,000 end-of-year payments for 20 years at 15 per cent compounded (*a*) annually and (*b*) continuously?

29. What will be the value in 20 years of a $10,000 investment earning a 12 per cent return compounded (*a*) annually and (*b*) continuously?

30. You are considering the purchase of a machine which will give you an annual return of $1,000 a year for 20 years. The return will be received uniformly and continuously over the years. How much can you pay for the machine and still obtain at least a 10 per cent effective annual return on your investment in the machine? (Solve by determining the present worth of the prospective continuous uniform receipts for 20 years at 10 per cent effective annual interest.)

31. A bridge is expected to have maintenance and repair expenses of $2,000 in the first year. It is anticipated that these expenses will increase $500 per year each year thereafter during the bridge's expected life of 50 years. What is the present worth of these expenses for the 50-year life of the bridge using interest at 4 per cent?

32. Mr. Redd has received an income contract which provides for 25 decreasing annual payments to himself, starting with $1,000 at the end of the first year and decreasing at the rate of $20 per year each year. Thus his last receipt, at the end of the 25th year, will be $520. Using interest at 6 per cent, compute the uniform annual equivalent of these 25 payments.

6 Depreciation

Many types of industrial assets decrease in utility and value with use and with the passage of time. Machines and facilities are eventually replaced, relegated to subsidiary uses, or retired as their utility is decreased and their services are no longer required. This process is called depreciation.

A form of depreciation, called depletion, occurs when natural resources, such as coal mines, oil wells, copper mines, timberlands, etc., are exhausted or consumed.

Purposes of Depreciation Technique. The process of depreciation results in a consumption of the values in depreciable capital investments. Depreciation technique, which comprises the methodology for accounting for this consumption, has three principal purposes:

1. To provide for the proper charging of depreciation to the operating expenses of an enterprise, so that profit portrayals will reflect capital-consumption costs

2. To provide for recovery of capital-consumption costs

3. To provide for proper recording of depreciable assets in the accounts of the company (This recording bears no necessary relation to the real worth of the asset.)[1]

These purposes are all interrelated. This chapter will be devoted primarily to the first of these purposes, the charging of depreciation costs to operating expenses. Other sections of this volume are devoted to aspects of the other two purposes.

Factors Producing Capital Consumption and Retirement of Assets. Some of the many reasons for capital consumption and the resulting depreciation are summarized here. Many factors combine in varying proportions in each case to bring about a total situation in which it is economically desirable to retire or replace an asset.

---

[1] Because depreciation-accounting procedures for determining book values result in figures which bear no relationship to real value, the American Institute of Accountants considers depreciation a process of allocation of costs, not of valuation. The term "depreciation" is also used with different meanings in the valuation of assets by appraisal.

1. *Physical deterioration of the equipment.* Such deterioration occurs because of the wear and tear resulting from usage, because of the action of physical and organic elements, and because of accidental damage. These all contribute to rising maintenance costs, which may make replacement worthwhile.

Old equipment cannot produce the same high-quality product as new facilities. Equipment gets worn to the point where it cannot give the same quality of service it has previously given. A machine's precision of performance declines as the years pass, and it must then be used for less exacting work.

Because of the deterioration of equipment with age, it sometimes cannot be used as intensively as when it is relatively new.

Accidental physical damage to facilities by such calamities as fire, flood, windstorm, etc., may require immediate replacement or may accelerate replacement.

2. *New production or service requirements.* The service requirements of equipment may be increased beyond its capacity. These increased requirements may be in the nature of higher quality standards or larger required capacities. Thus, a telephone switchboard may prove to have inadequate capacity because of the expansion of the business and the increased number of telephone extensions required.

3. *Development of improved facilities.* Improved equipment or processes are discovered which will perform the same operation more cheaply. A new process may give a higher-quality product. Or, the improved facility may give both higher quality and lower costs. In some cases, improved safety of the newer equipment may be a deciding factor in replacement.

4. *Obsolescence of facilities by technological advances.* The service performed by the machine is no longer required. Thus, much equipment required for the construction of the large reciprocating steam engines used in power plant installations was made obsolete by development of the steam turbine. The obsolete equipment was then no longer required for its original service.

Depreciation Cost. The total dollars which it is desired to recover over the life of a depreciable asset are equal to the cost less the prospective salvage value at the time of retirement. The cost includes the price of the item, plus transportation charges to site, plus installation charges, plus costs to prepare the item for operation. The salvage value is equal to the estimated resale value at the time of retirement minus any costs of removing the item or making the sale.

Consider an item costing $5,000 with a prospective resale value at the end of its economic life of $1,000 and a removal cost of $400. This item would have a salvage value of $1,000 minus $400, or $600. It would have a depreciation cost of $5,000 minus $600, or $4,400.

Life of a Depreciable Asset. The life of a depreciating or depleting asset is dependent upon numerous factors, many of which were mentioned earlier in this chapter. Forecasting this life is a difficult task. Some of the economic background for making these forecasts is discussed in Chapter 17.

The amount of income tax paid in any year is dependent upon the amount of profits earned. This is affected by the rate at which depreciation is applied and, therefore, by the estimated life of the asset. The Bureau of Internal Revenue is concerned about the estimates of life used by taxpayers in their depreciation accounting. Its regulations provide that the lives used for computing depreciation charges for income tax determinations should correspond to the expected useful life of the assets. Bulletin F, revised January, 1942, of the Bureau of Internal Revenue provides statements of policy on estimating average useful lives and depreciation rates and also presents estimates of average useful lives for thousands of assets.

A reasonable rate for depreciation is dependent not only on the prospective useful life of the property when acquired, but also on the particular conditions under which the property is used as reflected in the taxpayer's operating policy and the accounting policy followed with respect to repairs, maintenance, replacements, charges to the capital-asset account and to the depreciation reserve. If the useful life of the various assets shown hereafter could be determined precisely, which cannot be done, there still could not be established standard rates of depreciation unless there existed standard methods of operation and of accounting from which there could be no deviation.

Being based on the usual experience of property owners, the probable useful lives shown herein for each kind or class of assets are predicated on a reasonable expense policy as to the cost of repairs and maintenance. Therefore, in the determination of the depreciation allowance in each case, due consideration should be given the maintenance and replacement policy of the taxpayer and the accounting practice regarding the same.

The estimates of useful life set forth herein are for new properties only. In applying them, consideration should be given to salvage values, to that portion of the service life already expired, and to that portion of the cost previously recovered or recoverable through prior depreciation deductions or other allowances.

It has been found that normal obsolescence is a very important factor in determining the useful life of property. The estimated useful lives shown herein include an allowance for normal obsolescence, but do not contain any provision for extraordinary obsolescence, such as is occasioned by revolutionary inventions, abnormal growth or development, radical economic changes, or other unpredictable factors which may force the retirement or other disposition of property prior to the termination of its normal useful life.

When the average useful life of an asset is shorter or longer than suggested in this listing, the actual average values should be used. However, the burden of proof on using shorter lives falls on the taxpayer. For this

Table 6-1. Motor and Other Vehicles

Motor vehicles included in this classification are those used by commercial enterprises other than public utility and construction. Lives considered reasonable are indicated below:

	Years		Years
Automobiles:		Trucks:	
Passenger...............	5	Outside use—	
Salesman................	3	Electric..............	10
Horse-drawn vehicles.......	8	Gas, light.............	4
Motorcycles...............	4	Medium..........	6
Tractors..................	6	Heavy...........	8
Trailers..................	6	Inside use..............	15

SOURCE: Bureau of Internal Revenue, Bulletin F, January, 1942.

Table 6-2. Office Equipment

A composite life of about 15 years has been found applicable to office equipment. Where the equipment is segregated into groups, the following lives are recognized:

	Years
Safes.....................................	50
Furniture, fixtures, and filing cases...........	20
Mechanical equipment.....................	8

Item lives are given in the following list:

	Average useful life (years)		Average useful life (years)
Adding machines..............	10	Duplicating machines.........	10
Addressing and mailing machines	15	Fans, electric.................	10
Billing machines.............	8	Folding and sealing machines..	10
Binders, loose-leaf.............	20	Helmets, rescue..............	6
Blueprinting machines.........	15	Hospital equipment...........	15
Bookkeeping machines.........	8	Lamps, desk and floor........	10
Cabinets and files.............	15	Linoleum....................	8
Calculators...................	10	Lockers.....................	25
Call system and annunciators..	14	Lunchroom equipment.........	15
Cases:		Mirrors.....................	20
Book.....................	20	Money machines..............	10
Display...................	20	Numbering machines..........	10
Chairs:		Photographing machines.......	16
Bentwood.................	5	Pneumatic-tube systems.......	20
Heavy....................	16	Racks and stands.............	15
Check perforators.............	10	Rugs, carpets, and mats.......	10
Check writers................	8	Safes and vaults..............	50
Cleaners, electric vacuum......	6	Scales, counter and mail.......	10
Clocks:		Settees.....................	13
Time.....................	15	Shades, window..............	10
Time-stamping.............	10	Signs, board.................	10
Wall.....................	20	Tables......................	15
Coolers, water...............	10	Typewriter..................	5
Desks.......................	20	Wardrobes..................	20
Dictation machines...........	6		

SOURCE: Bureau of Internal Revenue, Bulletin F, January, 1942.

reason, depreciation rates for income tax purposes tend to follow Bulletin F rates.

In the Bulletin F compilations, useful lives for composite accounts as well as group accounts are presented in many cases. Two examples from this bulletin are quoted in Tables 6-1 and 6-2.

Accounting for Depreciation Cost. When we purchase a depreciable asset, we increase our fixed assets by the cost value of the asset, say a $200,000 building, and either

1. Decrease the value of some other asset, such as cash (if we pay cash), by $200,000; or

2. Increase the value of some liability by $200,000, such as accounts payable (if we do not pay immediately) or notes payable (if we give a promissory note in payment) or mortgage bonds payable (if we finance the payment by issuing mortgage bonds); or

3. Combine some of (1) and (2).

This purchase transaction neither increases nor decreases the net worth of the business.

Each year's depreciation is charged as a cost of operations and credited to an allowance for depreciation account (sometimes also called reserve for depreciation or accumulated depreciation). This credit is accumulated as long as the asset is maintained on the books of the company. The account is used to decrease the book value of the depreciated asset. It does not represent a reservoir of cash or any other asset.

Thus, if the $200,000 building were purchased at the beginning of the year, the depreciation charge would be $5,000 ($200,000 divided by 40 years) per year. At the end of the first year, the asset would be shown on the statement of the company as follows:

Building............................ $200,000
Less, Allowance for depreciation........... 5,000 $195,000

The original cost of the building minus the allowance for depreciation (accumulated depreciation) is its *book value*.

Assets Acquired during Year. Depreciation is generally figured on an annual basis which conforms to the fiscal year of the company. Assets, however, may be purchased at any time during the year. Therefore, the depreciation charge for the first year of an asset's life will depend upon the purchase date. The depreciation for this first year can be calculated in either of the following ways:

1. For simplicity, the depreciation on all of the assets acquired during the year can be figured at one-half a year's rate. (This is based on the assumption that some assets are purchased near the beginning of the period and some near the end, averaging about one-half a year for all the assets.)

2. A more exact method would be to count the months from the time the asset was purchased to the end of the fiscal year and divide by 12 to determine the portion of the full year's charge for this first year. (To avoid fractional months, the month is counted if the asset is acquired during the first 15 days of the month; otherwise the month is disregarded.)

Alternative Methods of Computing Depreciation. Many of the factors which depreciate the value of an asset are functions of time. Others are functions of use or activity. And some are functions of both time and use.

Depreciation factors most closely related to the passage of time are obsolescence, the development of more efficient equipment or equipment capable of higher-quality production, deterioration from action of physical elements, and inability to handle higher service requirements.

Depreciation factors most closely related to activity and usage are wear and tear and their effects on the ability to produce at various quality levels. Sometimes, a machine may have greater probabilities of accidental damage when its rate of usage is higher.

For many assets, usage is not the critical factor in determining depreciated value. Even in most cases where it is, time is usually a good enough measure of usage when the rate of usage is relatively constant.

When the usage of a facility is at a relatively constant rate from year to year, then time and usage are equivalent as bases for allocating depreciation and will give the same results. Consider a machine costing $5,000 capable of producing 500,000 units in its lifetime. Production is uniform at 50,000 units per year. Expected life is 10 years. Zero salvage value is anticipated. Production rate per year does not vary.

Time depreciation on a straight-line basis:

$$\text{Annual charge} = \frac{\$5,000}{10} = \$500$$

Constant-unit-use charge basis:

$$\text{Unit depreciation charge} = \frac{\$5,000}{500,000} = \$0.01 \text{ per unit}$$

$$\text{Annual charge} = (50,000 \text{ units per year})(\$0.01 \text{ per unit}) = \$500$$

For some assets, especially when usage is at a relatively high rate, wear and tear usage factors may be more critical in determining life than the passage of time. Thus, the life of an aircraft engine is more a function of number of flight hours than passage of time. This is because such factors as wear and tear are more important than such factors as obsolescence and new technology in determining the value of future services obtainable from the engine, assuming that it is used a reasonable number of hours per year. Also, there are likely to be large variations in the amount of usage different engines receive.

The methods for computing depreciation discussed in this chapter are as follows:

1. As function of time
    a. Straight-line
    b. Declining-balance
    c. Sum-of-digits
    d. Straight-line with rate changes
    e. Sinking-fund
2. As a function of activity or use
    a. Constant-unit-use charge
    b. Straight-line modified by use factor
    c. Declining-unit-use charge
3. Combination of time and use methods

Straight-line Depreciation. The simplest method of computing depreciation as a function of time—and the most commonly used method of charging depreciation—is the straight-line method. In this case, the cost less the prospective salvage value is divided by the number of years of expected life to obtain the annual depreciation charge. If we let

P = cost of asset

L = salvage value

N = number of years of expected life

Annual depreciation charge = $\dfrac{P - L}{N}$

Rate of depreciation[1] = $\dfrac{1}{N}$

Book value at end of Uth year = $P - \left(\dfrac{P - L}{N}\right)(U)$

Consider machine A costing $8,000 installed with an estimated salvage value of $500 at the end of 8 years.

Annual depreciation charge = $\dfrac{P - L}{N} = \dfrac{\$8,000 - \$500}{8}$

$= \$937.50$ per year

Rate of depreciation = $\dfrac{1}{N} = \dfrac{1}{8} = 0.125$, or 12.5%

---

[1] Rate of straight-line depreciation is sometimes computed as $\dfrac{1 - L/P}{N}$. The annual depreciation charge is the same in this case, but it is computed by multiplying the total cost P, rather than $(P - L)$, by the rate.

Book value at end of 5th year $= P - \left(\dfrac{P-L}{N}\right)(U)$

$$= \$8,000 - \left(\dfrac{\$8,000 - \$500}{8}\right)(5)$$

$$= \$3,312.50$$

Next, consider machine B costing \$10,000 installed with an expected life of 5 years and with a zero expected salvage value. (The expected resale value at the end of its life would just about equal the dismantling cost.)

Annual depreciation charge $= \dfrac{P}{N} = \dfrac{\$10,000}{5} = \$2,000$ per year

Rate of depreciation $= \dfrac{1}{N} = \dfrac{1}{5} = 0.20$, or 20%

Book value at end of 2d year $= P - \left(\dfrac{P}{N}\right)(U)$

$$= \$10,000 - \left(\dfrac{\$10,000}{5}\right)(2) = \$6,000$$

Declining-balance Depreciation. The declining-balance method provides larger depreciation charges in the early years, sometimes called accelerated depreciation or fast write-off. The annual depreciation charge is calculated by taking a constant percentage of the declining undepreciated balance. This method will never depreciate the entire cost of an asset, but requires an explicit or implicit salvage value of a significant size. If the salvage value is too small, the constant percentage becomes ridiculously high.

There are two approaches to this method. In the first approach, we estimate the salvage value and then compute the fixed percentage rate. This approach is rarely used because the percentage rate varies with the salvage value and bears no real relationship to the way the asset is actually depreciating. In the second approach, we decide on a constant percentage rate, which then fixes the unrecovered cost at the end of the asset's life. (This may be more or less than the estimated salvage.)

Depreciation Rate Fixed by Salvage Value. Letting D represent the constant depreciation rate,

$$D = 1 - \left(\dfrac{L}{P}\right)^{1/N}$$

Book value at end of Uth year $= P(1 - D)^U = P\left(\dfrac{L}{P}\right)^{U/N}$

For machine A:

$$D = 1 - \left(\frac{L}{P}\right)^{1/N} = 1 - \left(\frac{500}{8,000}\right)^{\frac{1}{8}} = 0.293, \text{ or } 29.3\%$$

Book value at end of 5th year $= P\left(\frac{L}{P}\right)^{U/N} = P\left(\frac{500}{8,000}\right)^{\frac{5}{8}} = \$1,413$

This agrees with the tabular presentation of the undepreciated balance as shown in Table 6-3.

Table 6-3. **Declining-balance Depreciation, Machine A**

Year	Undepreciated balance at beginning of year	Depreciation charge
1	$8,000	$2,344
2	5,656	1,657
3	3,999	1,172
4	2,827	828
5	1,999	586
6	1,413	414
7	999	293
8	706	206
Total	. . . . . .	$7,500

For machine B: This method cannot be used unless a salvage value is assumed.

Depreciation Rate Predetermined. An undepreciated portion of the original cost of the asset, which may be more or less than the salvage value, will remain as the undepreciated balance at the end of the estimated life. For new assets having a life of at least three years and the use of which commenced after December 31, 1953, the 1954 Income Tax Code, currently in force (1961), permits use of the declining-balance method with a rate equal to 200 per cent of the straight-line depreciation rate. For assets acquired earlier, the rate may not exceed 150 per cent of the straight-line rate.

For machine A:

Straight-line depreciation rate $= 12.5\%$
Allowable declining-balance rate for income tax purposes
$$= 2(12.5\%) = 25\%$$

Solving for the undepreciated cost at the end of eight years,

$$D = 1 - \left(\frac{L}{P}\right)^{1/N}$$

$$0.25 = 1 - \left(\frac{L}{\$8,000}\right)^{\frac{1}{8}}$$

$$L = \$800$$

The asset will have an undepreciated book value of $800 at the end of eight years, although its expected salvage value is only $500. This agrees with Table 6-4, showing an undepreciated balance of $800 at the end of eight years.

Table 6-4. **Declining-balance Depreciation, Machine A**

Year	Undepreciated balance at beginning of year	Depreciation charge
1	$8,000	$2,000
2	6,000	1,500
3	4,500	1,125
4	3,375	844
5	2,531	633
6	1,898	475
7	1,423	356
8	1,067	267
Total	......	$7,200

If at the end of the eight years the asset has no salvage value and the machine is abandoned at that time, the income tax laws permit a write-off of the $800 book value as a loss. Alternatively, the depreciation of the undepreciated balance could be shifted to straight-line depreciation at any time for the remaining life of the asset. If this were done at the end of the fifth year, the depreciation charge for the remaining three years of life would be $633 per year, with no book value at the end.

For machine B: This method cannot be used unless a salvage value is assumed.

Sum-of-digits Depreciation. Another method of providing for depreciation charges which are larger in the early years and smaller in the later years is the sum-of-digits method. This method, which is permitted by the current (1961) tax regulations, does not require a salvage value, as does the declining-balance method. It is more easily explained by example.

For machine A: First add the years' digits:

$$
\begin{array}{r}
8 \\
7 \\
6 \\
5 \\
4 \\
3 \\
2 \\
\underline{1} \\
36
\end{array}
$$

(The sum of digits is always equal to $(N)(N+1)/2$. Thus, in this example, $(8)(9)/2 = 36$.) Then each year's depreciation charge is calculated as shown in Table 6-5.

Table 6-5. Sum-of-digits Depreciation, Machine A

Year	Calculation of depreciation charge
1	$\frac{8}{36} (P - L) = \frac{8}{36} (\$7,500) = \$1,667$
2	$\frac{7}{36} (P - L) = \frac{7}{36} (\$7,500) = 1,458$
3	$\frac{6}{36} (P - L) = \frac{6}{36} (\$7,500) = 1,250$
4	$\frac{5}{36} (P - L) = \frac{5}{36} (\$7,500) = 1,042$
5	$\frac{4}{36} (P - L) = \frac{4}{36} (\$7,500) = 833$
6	$\frac{3}{36} (P - L) = \frac{3}{36} (\$7,500) = 625$
7	$\frac{2}{36} (P - L) = \frac{2}{36} (\$7,500) = 417$
8	$\frac{1}{36} (P - L) = \frac{1}{36} (\$7,500) = 208$
	Total = \$7,500

The same results can be obtained by applying fractions, with the denominator representing the remaining life of the sum-of-digits, to the undepreciated portion of the asset cost as shown in Table 6-6.

Table 6-6. Sum-of-digits Depreciation, Machine A

Year	Calculation of depreciation charge
1	$\frac{8}{36} (\$7,500) = \$1,667$
2	$\frac{7}{28} (\$5,833) = 1,458$
3	$\frac{6}{21} (\$4,375) = 1,250$
4	$\frac{5}{15} (\$3,125) = 1,042$
5	$\frac{4}{10} (\$2,083) = 833$
6	$\frac{3}{6} (\$1,250) = 625$
7	$\frac{2}{3} (\$625) = 417$
8	$\frac{1}{1} (\$208) = 208$
	Total = \$7,500

This remaining-life-calculation approach is usually simpler for group depreciation than the first approach, especially when fractional years must be used.

For machine B: The sum-of-digits depreciation calculation for machine B is shown in Table 6-7.

Table 6-7. Sum-of-digits Depreciation, Machine B

Year	Calculation of depreciation charge
1	$\frac{5}{15} (P) = \frac{5}{15} (\$10,000) = \$ 3,333$
2	$\frac{4}{15} (P) = \frac{4}{15} (\$10,000) = 2,667$
3	$\frac{3}{15} (P) = \frac{3}{15} (\$10,000) = 2,000$
4	$\frac{2}{15} (P) = \frac{2}{15} (\$10,000) = 1,333$
5	$\frac{1}{15} (P) = \frac{1}{15} (\$10,000) = 667$
	Total = \$10,000

Straight-line Depreciation with Rate Changes. Another method of obtaining a higher or a lower rate of depreciation in the early years as compared with the later ones is to use two different straight-line rates of depreciation during the life of the asset.

For example, two-thirds of the depreciating value of machine A may be depreciated in one-half its life.

$$\text{First 4 years, annual charge} = \frac{2/3(P - L)}{N/2} = \frac{2/3(\$7,500)}{8/2} = \$1,250$$

$$\text{Second 4 years, annual charge} = \frac{1/3(P - L)}{N/2} = \frac{1/3(\$7,500)}{8/2} = \$625$$

$$\text{Total depreciation (first 4 years)} = 4(\$1,250) = \$5,000$$
$$\text{Total depreciation (last 4 years)} = 4(\$625) = \$2,500$$
$$\text{Total} = \$7,500$$

Sinking-fund Depreciation. The sinking-fund method of computing depreciation as a function of time is a rarely used system because charges computed by this method are seldom descriptive of the actual situation. The charges under this system are smallest in the early years and largest in the later years, sometimes called slow write-off. It may be an appropriate method when actual depreciation occurs more slowly in the early years and more rapidly as the years progress.

Sinking-fund depreciation accounting is based upon the concept that the depreciation recoveries each year are placed in a sinking fund. The monies placed in this sinking fund earn interest which accumulates in the fund. The annual amount to be deposited in the fund so that the depreciable cost of the asset $(P - L)$ is accumulated in N years is obviously dependent on the interest return, i, that this fund will earn. It is equal to $(P - L)\begin{pmatrix} \text{SFP} \\ i = ? \\ n = N \end{pmatrix}$.

It would be unusual for a business actually to set up a sinking fund in which it deposited its depreciation recoveries. A progressive business has many internal requirements for capital which can earn much higher returns than a sinking fund. In many cases, the business itself is borrowing money externally at higher interest rates to finance its operations. The recoveries from depreciation charges are, therefore, kept invested in the business.

The sinking fund is thus fictitious. The business must pay interest on the balance in the fictitious fund each year in the form of an added depreciation charge. The interest charge increases each year as the fictitious fund builds up with depreciation charges. The depreciation charges are thus smaller in early years and larger in later ones.

$$\text{Depreciation charge in } U\text{th year} = (P - L)\begin{pmatrix} \text{SFP} \\ i = ? \\ n = N \end{pmatrix}\begin{pmatrix} \text{SPCA} \\ i = ? \\ n = U - 1 \end{pmatrix}$$

Accumulated depreciation at end of Uth year

$$= (P - L) \begin{pmatrix} \text{SFP} \\ i = ? \\ n = N \end{pmatrix} \begin{pmatrix} \text{USCA} \\ i = ? \\ n = U \end{pmatrix}$$

Book value at end of Uth year $= P - (P - L) \begin{pmatrix} \text{SFP} \\ i = ? \\ n = N \end{pmatrix} \begin{pmatrix} \text{USCA} \\ i = ? \\ n = U \end{pmatrix}$

If an interest rate of zero is used in the above formulations, sinking-fund depreciation becomes straight-line depreciation. As the assumed interest rate of the fictitious fund is increased, the sizes of the charges become smaller in the early years, and larger in the later years. To illustrate, the sinking-fund depreciation charges for machine A at 4 per cent interest are shown in Table 6-8, and at 10 per cent interest in Table 6-9.

Table **6-8. Sinking-fund Depreciation,**
(4 Per Cent Interest), Machine A

Year	Depreciation charge
1	$ 814
2	847
3	880
4	916
5	952
6	990
7	1,030
8	1,071
Total	$7,500

Table **6-9. Sinking-fund Depreciation,**
(10 Per Cent Interest), Machine A

Year	Depreciation charge
1	$ 656
2	721
3	794
4	873
5	960
6	1,056
7	1,162
8	1,278
Total	$7,500

Activity or Use Depreciation. When the life of an asset is more a function of activity or use than of time, the appropriate means of depreciating the asset value may be the number of items produced by the asset or the number of hours of service.

The Bureau of Internal Revenue's Bulletin F states that the unit-of-production method (of which this is a variant)

must be confined to those items in the property account whose useful lives are determined by the factors of wear and tear or where the extent of use or the rate of production measures the rate of exhaustion of the property . . . . For most property it is not possible to obtain this information with any degree of accuracy and, therefore, the method is not considered an acceptable one for general application to the machinery account of industrial concerns, or to the property of those companies exploiting a natural resource with reserves sufficient to extend operations beyond the physical life of the original plant.

Constant-unit-use Charge. The depreciation charge is on a constant-unit-use charge basis when all units are charged at the same rate. Thus, machine A has a capacity of producing an estimated 1,200,000 lb of product during its life.

$$\text{Depreciation rate} = \frac{P - L}{\text{lifetime capacity}} = \frac{\$8,000 - \$500}{1,200,000}$$
$$= \$0.00625 \text{ per pound}$$

Table 6-10 summarizes the depreciation calculations for machine A.

Table **6-10. Depreciation Using a Constant-unit-use Charge, Machine A**

Year	Actual production (lb)	Depreciation charge	Undepreciated value at end of year
1	150,000	$ 937.50	$7,062.50
2	120,000	750.00	6,312.50
3	165,000	1,031.25	5,281.25
4	140,000	875.00	4,406.25
5	170,000	1,062.50	3,343.75
6	175,000	1,093.75	2,250.00
7	145,000	906.25	1,343.75
8	135,000	843.75	500.00
Total	1,200,000	$7,500.00	

Straight-line Modified by Usage Factor. Another way of taking usage into account in depreciating an asset is to adjust a normal annual straight-line depreciation charge by a factor determined by the ratio of actual production to normal production. This method can give the same results as the constant-unit-use charge method.

Calculations for machine A are as follows:

Normal annual straight-line depreciation charge

$$= \frac{P - L}{N} = \frac{\$8,000 - \$500}{8} = \$937.50$$

$$\text{Normal production per year} = \frac{1,200,000}{8} = 150,000 \text{ lb per year}$$

$$\text{Depreciation charge} = \frac{\text{actual production}}{\text{normal production}} \text{ (normal charge)}$$

The annual depreciation calculations using this method are summarized in Table 6-11.

Table 6-11. Straight-line Depreciation Modified by Usage Factor, Machine A

Year	Actual production (lb)	$\left(\dfrac{\text{Actual production}}{\text{Normal production}}\right)$	Depreciation charge	Undepreciated value at end of year
1	150,000	150,000/150,000	$ 937.50	$7,062.50
2	120,000	120,000/150,000	750.00	6,312.50
3	165,000	165,000/150,000	1,031.25	5,281.25
4	140,000	140,000/150,000	875.00	4,406.25
5	170,000	170,000/150,000	1,062.50	3,343.75
6	175,000	175,000/150,000	1,093.75	2,250.00
7	145,000	145,000/150,000	906.25	1,343.75
8	135,000	135,000/150,000	843.75	500.00
Total	1,200,000		$7,500.00	

Declining-unit-use Charge. When a machine is older, its production may be less valuable because of poorer quality or reduced demand for the product. A use charge on a declining-unit basis may then be appropriate, the earlier units of production being charged at a higher rate than later units produced when the machine is older.

For example, machine A's output life capacity of 1,200,000 pounds will be divided into three groups of 400,000 pounds: the first group will be charged at three times the rate of the last group and the second group twice the rate of the last group.

$$\text{First group } 3(400,000) \ = \ 1,200,000$$
$$\text{Second group } 2(400,000) = \ \ \ 800,000$$
$$\text{Third group } 1(400,000) \ = \ \ \ 400,000$$
$$\text{Total} \qquad\qquad\qquad = \ 2,400,000 \text{ depreciation units}$$

$$\text{Depreciation rate} = \frac{P - L}{\text{depreciation units}} = \frac{\$8,000 - \$500}{2,400,000}$$
$$= \$0.003125 \text{ per unit}$$

The annual depreciation calculations using this method are summarized in Table 6-12.

Combination of Time and Usage Depreciation. If it is possible to estimate the percentage of depreciation of an asset which is a function of time and the percentage which is a function of usage, then a combination of some of the previously illustrated methods may be used.

For example, if the depreciation of a machine is judged to be caused

Table 6-12. Depreciation by Declining-unit-use-charge
Method, Machine A

Year	Actual production (lb)	Depreciation units	Depreciation charge	Undepreciated value at end of year
1	150,000	450,000	$1,406.25	$6,593.75
2	120,000	360,000	1,125.00	5,468.75
3	165,000	460,000	1,437.50	4,031.25
4	140,000	280,000	875.00	3,156.25
5	170,000	340,000	1,062.50	2,093.75
6	175,000	230,000	718.75	1,375.00
7	145,000	145,000	453.13	921.87
8	135,000	135,000	421.87	500.00
Total	1,200,000	2,400,000	$7,500.00	

60 per cent by usage and 40 per cent by the passage of time, the depreciation formula for the charge in a given year may be:

$$0.60 \left(\frac{P - L}{N} \right) \left(\frac{\text{actual production}}{\text{normal production}} \right) + 0.40 \left(\frac{P - L}{N} \right)$$

Group and Composite versus Individual-item Depreciation.
Instead of computing depreciation charges for each item asset as we have discussed up to the present, a company may combine assets and calculate depreciation on these combinations. Instead of keeping separate account records on each asset, one combined account record is kept for each group or composite. There are two types of combinations:

1. Combinations of homogenous assets which are depreciated as a *group*

2. Combinations of nonhomogenous assets which are depreciated under a *composite* rate

Thus, there may be group depreciation for adding machines in the company offices or composite depreciation for all office equipment or certain categories of office equipment. Tables in Bulletin F of the Bureau of Internal Revenue (see Tables 6-1 and 6-2) give suggested lives for individual items, such as adding machines, which may be grouped as well as for composite combinations of nonhomogenous assets, such as office equipment or mechanical office equipment.

For group depreciation, the same average useful lives are used as for item depreciation. For composite depreciation, item-depreciation charges must be averaged depending upon the composition of the combination of assets.

Since average lives are used, some assets will last longer than the average and some will be retired before the average life is reached. In item depreciation, when an asset is retired before the average life is reached, the book value will normally be greater than the salvage value. The difference will be taken as a book loss, and the book asset values will be reduced accordingly. Depreciation charges are never charged on any asset after its average life has been reached even though it continues to be used because the depreciable investment has been recovered by then.

In group and composite depreciation, when an item is retired before its average or expected life, no loss or deduction in asset values is taken because, if the average life is correct, other items in the group will be in service longer than the average and depreciation is charged for them as long as they are in service after the average life has been passed. The extra depreciation on the longer-than-average-life ones makes up for the underdepreciation on the shorter-lived ones. Of course, if the estimated average life is faulty, it can be adjusted when this is recognized and a loss or gain adjustment in asset value will result. There is also a possible adjustment when the last of the assets are retired if the average life is somewhat different from that originally estimated.

Depletion. When oil is removed from a well, coal or copper from a mine, timber from forest holdings, stone or sand from a quarry, an exhaustible natural resource is being depleted. Depletion bears the same relationship to exhaustible natural resource assets that depreciation does to depreciable facilities.

Cost depletion charges are similar to those depreciation charges which are computed on an activity or usage basis rather than a time basis. The formula for determining this charge is to divide the cost of acquiring the natural resource by the number of units (tons of metal, barrels of oil, etc.) of recoverable asset which is estimated to be in the property.

A mine was purchased for $200,000 and was estimated to hold 80,000 tons of metal. The cost depletion rate is $200,000/80,000 = $2.50 per ton. During the first year, 6,000 tons are extracted. The depletion cost charge is therefore 6,000($2.50) = $15,000. During the second year, as a result of the operations in the mine, the estimate of the amount of metal remaining in the mine is reduced from 74,000 to 60,000 tons. The cost depletion rate is, therefore, adjusted as follows:

$$\frac{\text{Remaining unrecovered cost}}{\text{Estimated remaining resource}} = \frac{\$200,000 - \$15,000}{60,000} = \$3.083 \text{ per ton}$$

Similarly, if the estimated remaining resource were higher than the original estimate, the depletion rate would be lowered to distribute the remaining unrecovered cost. As in the case of cost depreciation, the total recovered cost depletion charges may not exceed the total cost of the resource.

The United States income tax laws, however, provide an optional special method of computing depletion charges for oil and gas wells and all mineral deposits. When this special method is used, cumulative depletion charges may exceed costs without limitation. This special method provides that a flat percentage of the gross income from the property may be taken as a depletion deduction from income, with the proviso that this deduction may not exceed 50 per cent of the taxable net income from the property computed without a depletion charge.

The 1954 Income Tax Code provides the following depletion rates to be applied to the gross income from the property under this optional special method: Oil and gas wells, $27\frac{1}{2}$ per cent; coal, 10 per cent; various metals, minerals, and sands, 23 per cent, 15 per cent, 10 per cent, and 5 per cent, as shown in detailed listing under Section 613 (b) of the code.

Depreciation Accounting and the Economy Analysis. One of the problems which frequently plagues attempts at logical economy analysis is a confusion of the relationship between replacement decisions and accounting for depreciation. Depreciation accounting follows an historical approach. Among other things, it is a device to recover the cost of a depreciating investment in equipment by charging that cost to production expense over the life of the equipment. The economy-analysis approach is an attempt to forecast the future and decide which of the available alternative investments looks most favorable.

The method of accounting for depreciation will affect the profit and loss statement of a company. For example, when the sum-of-digits method is used, a larger percentage of the depreciable cost is charged in the early years of the investment than when the straight-line method is used. The profits during these early years will, therefore, appear smaller. Of course, profits in the later years will appear higher.

This difference in depreciation accounting and the corresponding shifting in the timing of its effects on profit would not have any effect on the relative economy of the investment were it not for income taxes. In an economy study, we are interested in the total cash return from an investment each year. This total cash return is the same regardless of accounting methods. The pattern in which depreciation charges are made does not change the rate of return on the investment (assuming no income taxes for the moment).

This is illustrated by the data in Table 6-13. I invest $300,000 in an asset which has no value after five years. My total cash income over and above cash expenses is $100,000 each year. Table 6-13 shows that my profit after allocating depreciation cost will be $40,000 each year if I use straight-line depreciation, but will vary from $0 in year 1 to $80,000 in year 5 if I use sum-of-digits depreciation. However, in both cases, my cash return is still $100,000 each year, the depreciation charges being noncash allocations of the $300,000 investment cost. I receive $100,000 in cash each year just as if it were a loan repayment.

Therefore, the rate of return on my $300,000 investment is determined to be approximately 20 per cent by computing

$$\left(\begin{matrix} \text{CR} \\ i = ? \\ n = 5 \end{matrix}\right) = \frac{R}{P} = \frac{\$100,000}{\$300,000} = 0.3333$$

and using the capital-recovery chart of the Appendix. This is the return a man would make if he loaned me $300,000 and I paid him $100,000 a year for five years in repayment of the principal of the loan and interest at 20 per cent.

Table 6-13. **Comparison of Annual Profits Using Straight-line and Sum-of-digits Depreciation Methods**

Year	Cash return	Straight-line depreciation		Sum-of-digits depreciation	
		Depreciation charge	Profit	Depreciation charge	Profit
1	$100,000	$60,000	$40,000	$100,000	$ 0
2	100,000	60,000	40,000	80,000	20,000
3	100,000	60,000	40,000	60,000	40,000
4	100,000	60,000	40,000	40,000	60,000
5	100,000	60,000	40,000	20,000	80,000

Effect of Income Taxes. All this neglects income taxes. When we consider income taxes, there is a difference in rates of return in these two cases. When the cash return is through a depreciation charge, there is no income tax on it. When it is through profits, there is an income tax. Let us use a 52 per cent Federal income tax rate, assuming no state or local income tax, to illustrate the effect of income taxes on the rates of return.

Table 6-14 illustrates what happens when we use straight-line depreciation. (The after-tax-return column is computed by subtracting the "52% income tax" column from the "before-tax return" column.) The 52 per cent income tax is applied on the profits (cash return less depreciation charge) of $40,000 each year. This reduces our after-tax return by $20,800 to $79,200 per year for five years. This represents approximately a 10 per cent return on the $300,000 investment.

When we use sum-of-digits depreciation, the situation illustrated in Table 6-15 occurs. The depreciation charge of $100,000 during the first year results in no profits or income taxes that year, so that we obtain a $100,000 return after taxes. As the depreciation charge decreases each year, the income taxes increase, decreasing the after-tax return. This results in a 11.1 per cent return on our $300,000 investment, approximately 1.1 per cent more than when straight-line depreciation was used.

The rate of return is higher in this second case even though the total of the after-tax return over the five-year period is the same as in the first

Table 6-14. **Annual After-tax Returns Using Straight-line Depreciation**

| Year | Straight-line depreciation | | Before-tax profit | 52% Income tax | After-tax return |
	Before-tax return	Depreciation charge			
1	$100,000	$60,000	$40,000	$20,800	$79,200
2	100,000	60,000	40,000	20,800	79,200
3	100,000	60,000	40,000	20,800	79,200
4	100,000	60,000	40,000	20,800	79,200
5	100,000	60,000	40,000	20,800	79,200

case. In the second case, however, the early-year returns are larger. The average unreturned investment is, therefore, smaller. With a smaller average investment outstanding and the same total after-tax returns, a larger rate of return results.

Table 6-15. **Annual After-tax Returns Using Sum-of-digits Depreciation**

| Year | Before-tax return | Sum-of-digits depreciation | | 52% Income tax | After-tax return |
		Depreciation charge	Before-tax profit		
1	$100,000	$100,000	$ 0	$ 0	$100,000
2	100,000	80,000	20,000	10,400	89,600
3	100,000	60,000	40,000	20,800	79,200
4	100,000	40,000	60,000	31,200	68,800
5	100,000	20,000	80,000	41,600	58,400

Depreciation Accounting and Availability of Capital Funds. Depreciation policy may influence the availability of funds to purchase new facilities. Thus, depreciation methods which recover the cost of facilities in a short period of time or concentrate the bulk of cost recovery in the early years of the life of the equipment will provide funds for reinvestment in additional assets sooner (assuming that the costs are actually earned) than systems which spread the charges over a longer life.

A numerical example will illustrate this relationship and demonstrate how depreciation policy can affect the availability of cash to make facility purchases. If a $100,000 facility is depreciated on a straight-line basis with 20 years estimated life instead of a 10-year life, the amount of cash available for replacement purposes is reduced if profits are distributed each year. Profits will be higher during the first 10 years by $5,000 per year: on a 10-year life, the depreciation cost equals $100,000 divided by 10, or $10,000 per year; on a 20-year life, the depreciation cost is charged on the books of the company at $100,000 divided by 20, or $5,000 per year; the cost of production is thus charged $5,000 per year less on a

20-year life. If the profits are distributed each year, the actual assets of the enterprise at the end of 10 years will be $50,000 lower when the 20-year life is used because paper profits totaling $50,000 more were distributed to the owners of the business.

Replacement-value Depreciation. One of the purposes of depreciation accounting is to provide for the recovery of capital consumption costs to enable the company to replace its assets. The cash for the recovery of the capital investment comes from the sales of the product or service and not from the depreciation charge. However, because of income taxes, the size of the depreciation charge indirectly affects this recovery.

In addition, the ability of a company to replace its capital assets may be greatly influenced by the size of its reported profits, and these are affected by depreciation methods. The prices charged by some companies are regulated by public utility commissions, or other government agencies, and these prices are based upon earning a fair profit on investment. Labor demands for higher wages are based, to some extent, on ability to pay. Higher reported earnings tend to result in higher dividend payments.

If the depreciation methods used by a company understate the total amount of depreciation, then this recovery of capital by the company may be threatened. With the advent of inflation following World War II, increased attention has been focused on the problems created when depreciated dollars will not replace the asset being consumed.

It is, therefore, advocated by some that depreciation accounting should be performed in terms of the current dollar equivalent of the capital invested rather than initial costs. These proposals involve adjusting depreciation charges each year by means of an index number, to eliminate the effects of general monetary inflation. A general price index, such as the wholesale price index, may be used to convert the depreciation charges each year to a dollar equivalent in that year's currency. For example, an asset with a 20-year life is purchased in 1950 for $200,000 and is depreciated on a straight-line basis. The unadjusted depreciation charge for 1965 would be $10,000. If the wholesale price index has increased by 45 per cent from 1950 to 1965, then the depreciation charge for 1965 would be 145 per cent of $10,000, or $14,500 instead of $10,000.

This system is based on the logic that we are attempting to recover dollars of equivalent purchasing power. If, instead, our rationale were that we desire to recover the replacement value of the equipment, then we could use an index of equipment prices rather than the wholesale price index, to adjust the depreciation charge.

The problem of measuring and adjusting costs for changes in the value of the dollar is not confined to this one item, but is a general one which affects many income and expense items as well as many assets and liabilities of the business. It has many ramifications which have not been touched upon here. Should adjusted depreciation charges be allowed for income tax purposes? Should they be allowed in the establishment of public utility rates? If their use became universal, how would these and other adjustments to take account of dollar value changes affect the general economy and business cycles?

PROBLEMS

1. Describe the most important factors responsible for the retirement of (a) passenger automobiles, (b) motor trucks, (c) reciprocating steam engines, (d) electronic computers, (e) automatic screw machines.

2. A machine is purchased on January 1, 1960, for $4,200. Delivery charges are $200 and installation costs $600. Expected useful life of the equipment is 6 years, at which time it is anticipated that it can be dismantled at a cost of $200 and sold for $1,000. Compute the depreciation charge for the 4th year by each of the following depreciation methods: (a) straight-line, (b) declining-balance, (c) declining-balance at twice straight-line rate, (d) sum-of-digits, (e) straight-line with rates which will recover 1.5 times as much during the first half of the life as during the second half, (f) sinking-fund, using 6 per cent interest.

3. What is the book value of the machine at the end of the 4th year using each of the depreciation methods in problem 2?

4. It is estimated that the machine of problem 2 has a capacity to produce 12,000 hours of production. Compute the depreciation charge for the 4th year, in which it produced 3,000 hours of work, by each of the following methods. (a) constant-unit-use charge, (b) straight-line modified by usage factor, (c) declining-unit-use charge, charging the first half of the expected total production at 1.5 times the rate for the second half (The machine was used for a total of 2,000 hours in the first 3 years.), (d) combination of 70 per cent time and 30 per cent usage.

5. What is the book value of the machine at the end of the 4th year using each of the depreciation methods in problem 4?

6. Stipulate a type of machine and situation in which it would be desirable to use each of the methods of problems 2 and 4.

7. A mine, acquired at a cost of $1,000,000, is estimated to have 400,000 tons of recoverable ore. The ore currently sells for $40 per ton. Compute the depletion charge per ton based on (a) the cost of the mine, (b) the depletion rate of 15 per cent of gross income permitted by income tax laws.

8. Why do companies generally prefer to depreciate their equipment more rapidly than permitted by income tax laws even though it results in the appearance of lower profits on their profit and loss statements in the early years?

9. Do you consider it logical to use replacement cost rather than original cost as the basis for charging depreciation? Consider the three principal purposes of depreciation mentioned in the text in discussing this question.

7 Profits, Interest, and Return on Investment

What is the nature of profit and interest? How are profits measured? What is a fair rate of profit? What rate of return should be used in economy calculations? These are pertinent questions in economic analysis and business decision-making which will be considered in this chapter.

Interest is paid for the use of borrowed money. Profit is paid for the use of ownership money. Both interest and profit are expenses to a business enterprise. A company does not pay income tax on the money it earns to cover interest payments. However, it does pay income tax on all profits whether paid to the owners or reinvested in the business to finance expansion.

Interest and profit are income to the persons who receive them. Just as salaries and wages are income to the employee, interest is income to the person who permits other people to use his money and profit is income to the owners of the enterprise.

Both interest and profits thus represent returns to investors. Thus, interest is return to a lender and profit is return to an owner. The term "rate of return" may refer to the interest or profit rate which the lender or owner receives on his investment; it may also refer to the rate which the business earns on its investment of the lenders' and owners' funds to procure facilities and operate the enterprise.

The reason it is necessary to have an interest expense to obtain the use of other people's money is essentially simple. It is necessary to pay people to induce them to save money and lend it to other people or businesses rather than spend it or keep the money themselves (hoard it). Because money can be invested in assets which will reduce costs or create revenue, businesses can afford and desire to pay an interest charge to obtain the use of the money.

The nature and causes of profits cannot be explained as simply as we have just explained interest. Concepts of the nature of profits and what is included in profit vary. Everyone agrees that profit is the income which remains after costs are subtracted, but accountants, economists, and engineers disagree on what is included in the costs which are subtracted.

95

Profit Theories. Concepts of the nature of profits in business enterprises can be categorized into four groups: entrepreneurial-compensation theories, risk-bearing theories, friction-and-monopolistic-imperfection theories; and innovation theories.

Entrepreneurial-compensation Theories. These theories state that profits are the reward to the entrepreneur who successfully creates, plans, organizes, and manages the enterprise. These theories had credence when businesses were generally owner-managed. They have lost acceptance in the twentieth century. In the modern large corporations, the ownership function has been separated from the management function. Management is paid a salary which is not usually considered a part of profits.

Risk-bearing Theories. According to these theories, the owners of a business receive profits because they bear the principal financial risks of loss should the business lose money. Thus, other things being equal, the price-earnings ratio of the stocks of conservative companies where the risks are relatively low is usually higher than those of more speculative companies where the risks are relatively higher.

Friction-and-monopolistic-imperfection Theories. These theories view profits as resulting from imperfections in the adjustments of the economy to change through the operation of free markets and the frictionless flow of resources. If the markets were perfect and flow of resources frictionless, adjustments to changes which disturbed a business equilibrium would take place smoothly and rapidly and a new equilibrium would be quickly formed.

In an equilibrium state, businesses make only normal profits, which are considered the opportunity costs of the owner's financial investment in the business. Real profits are surpluses over and above this normal profit. These surpluses may occur because competitive forces do not operate freely in a market (e.g., new firms are not permitted to enter to increase the supply of a product); or because the business community cannot adjust immediately to changes in production costs and market demands.

Innovation Theories. These theories maintain that profits result from innovation, the adaptation of new ideas, inventions, methods, materials, and managerial techniques to produce a new product, expand sales of existing products, or produce at lower costs. Planning staffs, research and engineering groups, advertising and promotion departments all direct their activities to achieve innovations which will produce profits.

Based on this theory, innovations follow a cyclical pattern. An equilibrium situation, in which the businesses are making only normal profits, is disturbed by an innovation. The innovating firm reaps extraordinary profits, and others, therefore, try to adopt the same or similar innovation to obtain some of these profits. As a result of this adoption of the innovation by others, the economic (extraordinary) profits disappear and a new equilibrium develops in which the businesses are making only normal profits.

Because many innovations are interrelated, are taking place continuously, and overlap each other, equilibrium conditions are practically never actually reached. The equilibrium situation is the theoretically stable position toward which the businesses tend to move. They rarely reach it because the business world is dynamic and additional changes are usually made before equilibrium is ever reached.

Measurement of Profits. Our previous discussion of profit theories pointed up several differences between accounting practice and economic concepts of what items are included in costs as opposed to profits.

When the ownership function is separate from the management function, management is paid a salary. When the same persons own and manage a business, two possible types of errors in accounting measurement of profits may occur. The owners may not pay themselves salaries large enough to cover fully the management function they perform. Accounting profits will then overstate true profits by the amounts the owners refrained from including as salaries to themselves. Or they may pay themselves more than the proper wages of management. Accounting profits will then understate true profits by the amount of excess in the salary payments.

Accounting practice does not provide for charging the business for the cost of the equity capital which the owner invests in the business. Economic theory of profits would require that profits be reduced by a charge for the normal profit or interest cost on the owner's investment.

Accounting versus Engineering and Economic Approach. Aside from these differences in concept of what should be included in the costs which are subtracted from revenues to obtain profits, there is a basic difference in the approach of the accountant on the one hand and the economist and engineer on the other to determination of value.

In order to be objective, factual, and, in some instances, legal, the public accountant must have his reports based on historically verifiable data, with a minimum of speculation on the future. He, thus, is concerned primarily with sunk costs and past revenues. When he does speculate on the future, it is typically in a conservative direction: he includes only relatively certain future revenues, such as accounts and notes receivable; but includes possible, but less certain, future expenses, such as contingency reserves. This point of view is necessary for the public certification role of accounting.

The engineer and economist, however, are primarily interested in the present and the future. Knowledge of the past is, of course, helpful, but only in so far as it assists in understanding the present and forecasting the future.

From an engineering and economic point of view, the value of the assets of a business should not be based on their costs but on the present worth of the future streams of income which these assets will bring to the business. This is a theoretical concept which cannot be put into practice in the preparation of balance sheets and operating statements because it requires forecasts of future technology, markets, income, production processes, costs, prices, etc., which are not attainable with sufficient accuracy. The concept is useful, however, in defining a logical approach to the valuation of assets and the determination of profits even if it cannot be directly applied in most cases.

Before making an investment, we forecast the future revenues and costs and compute a prospective rate of return. During the life of the asset, we can reestimate our prospective rate of return with the new knowledge we have gained from our experience with the project. We can also compute apparent rates of return at the end of each year by dividing the return each year by the amount of the remaining unrecovered investment at the beginning of the year. But it is only after the asset or business has been sold that we can finally compute what the actual return has been on our investment. Illustrations of the calculation of prospective, apparent, and actual rates of return are presented in Chapter 11.

Nevertheless, we desire to know periodically how our business and investments are making out. To prepare periodic statements of profit and loss, we must allocate costs and revenues to the periods covered by our operating statement. The necessity for allocations causes many problems of profit measurement. We shall discuss three aspects of these problems: depreciation accounting, inventory costing, and unaccounted-value changes.

Depreciation. The accounting approach to depreciation was presented in Chapter 6. The cost of the asset is allocated by making a depreciation-expense charge each year over its useful life.

From the engineering and economic viewpoints, the opportunity- and replacement-cost concepts are more pertinent than the accounting concept of original-cost recovery. These concepts consider the opportunity cost of using the asset and the replacement cost of the usage during the period.

The opportunity cost of an asset is the benefit that was forgone because the asset was not employed in the most profitable alternative available use. The most profitable alternative to employing a machine in the manufacture of a product is usually to sell the machine. Therefore, the opportunity cost of using a machine for one year is the difference between the sale price of the machine at the beginning of the year and the sale price at the end of the year when it is one year older.

The replacement cost of the usage during the period is the amount of additional money needed to procure another asset at the end of the period which will have the same earning power as the original asset had at the beginning of the period. It is equal to the cost of the replacement asset minus the sale price of the original asset at the end of the period. Changes in the level of prices will raise the replacement cost of the usage during periods of inflation, and lower the replacement cost of the usage during a period of declining prices.

Valuing and Costing Inventory. We noted in Chapter 3 that the FIFO method of computing inventory costs charges manufacturing cost with the first or oldest purchases and values the remaining inventory at the most recent prices. LIFO charges manufacturing cost with the last or newest purchases, and values the remaining inventory at the cost of the older purchases.

FIFO will tend to give more realistic book-asset values than LIFO because the later-priced items are the ones which remain in the inventory. However, it will show unrealistically high profits during inflationary periods and unrealistically low profits during deflationary periods.

LIFO will give less realistic asset values than FIFO, showing lower asset values during inflationary periods and higher values during deflationary periods. However, the inventory costs of manufacturing with LIFO will tend to be more realistic than FIFO because manufacturing costs are charged with the prices of the more recent acquisitions.

Nevertheless, if a company's inventories are depleted and the company has been using LIFO for many years during which prices were increasing, it will show unrealistically high profits. The inventory which is being used up in this case will be priced at the lower prices of many years ago.

On the other hand, if prices declined after a company adopted LIFO, the cost of manufacturing would be charged only at the lower prices. However, the accountants would not carry the inventory asset on the books at the higher first-in cost if it is above the market price (under the accounting rule of cost-or-market value, whichever is lower). They would, therefore, reduce the asset value of the inventory by charging an inventory loss to the operations of the period.

None of these accounting methods will produce realistic measures of profit because we are measuring and mixing costs with dollars of different values at different times and mixing them with revenue dollars of different values.

Unaccounted-value Changes in Assets and Liabilities. There are many changes in the values of assets and liabilities of an enterprise which are not recorded on the books of the company at the time of their occurrence. The periodic profits and net worth of the enterprise are misstated when this occurs.

Research expenditures which are charged to expense may be creating intangible assets which are part of the capital value of the enterprise. Advertising-program expenditures may be creating good will, brand loyalties, and opening up markets which will yield future revenue. Executive-development programs may build up assets of trained personnel. Assets of this kind are usually not recorded on the books of the company. To this extent, profits are understated.

The unrecorded effects of inflation on fixed assets and inventory values was previously discussed. During periods of inflation, conventional accounting practice relating to depreciation and inventories results in an overstatement of business profits. When costs do not include high enough depreciation charges to cover replacement of the assets which are being used up and when, through valuation at the higher recent prices when using FIFO accounting, increases are made in the dollar value of an inventory which is physically the same size, we are creating paper profits, subject to income taxes, without increasing the actual assets in the enterprise. Also, the real value of cash, accounts receivable, and notes receivable is diluted by the inflation.

New technology may make certain machinery obsolete for current purposes, even though it is retained for stand-by use. The machinery will nevertheless usually be retained on the books at full depreciated value and continue to be depreciated as if its value had not been suddenly reduced by the new innovation. The costs of the later period will, therefore, be overcharged for depreciation expense.

Fair Rate of Profit. What is a fair rate of profit?

This question may have significance in economy studies because, as mentioned previously, the immediate goal of an enterprise may sometimes be perceived by its managers as earning a fair rather than a maximum profit. Of course, to earn a fair profit in a competitive environment will usually require that management attempt to maximize long-run profit opportunities.

We shall discuss here the nature of the standards which can be applied to ascertain what may be a fair rate of profit for a business. Before considering the possible approaches to this problem, we must decide on our measure of profits. Using the amount of profit dollars as a measure would thwart comparisons of companies of varying size. A ratio is, therefore, customarily used.

The two most commonly used ratios are profits as a percentage of sales and profits as a percentage of capital investment. Profits as a percentage of sales will vary more widely from company to company and industry to industry because the ratios of sales to capital investment may be so different. A company may do very little conversion on an expensive raw material or product. It may then have high sales dollars even though it does very little work on the materials it purchases. Its investment in facilities may, therefore, be small. It may, thus, handle a large volume of sales with a low percentage profit on each dollar of sales and yet make an unusually large profit as a percentage of capital investment. Thus, profits as a percentage of capital investment are usually more meaningful than as a percentage of sales, especially for interindustry comparisons.

Various criteria, such as the following, can be used for measuring the adequacy of the firm's rate of profit and determining what may be a fair rate:

1. Rate necessary to attract equity capital
2. Rate required to maintain usual market-price relationship
3. Rate earned by other companies
4. Historical earnings rates
5. Rate necessary to finance growth from internal sources

Profit Rate to Attract Equity Capital. This is the rate of profit which will support a high enough average level of prices for its common stock so that it can sell new shares at a price which will not dilute the ownership of the current stockholders. This profit standard is based on the thesis that a company should earn enough to be able to obtain from the public needed equity capital for expansion. To apply this criterion, the per share value of the common stockholders' equity in the company is compared with the market price of the common stock. (Book values will frequently have to be adjusted for current prices and values when this evaluation is made.)

Profit Rate to Maintain Market-price Relationship. This is a rate of profit which is determined by the consensus of the securities market. It is that profit rate which will enable the price of the firm's securities to keep their usual historical relationship to the securities of other firms. This approach hypothesizes the continuation of past price relationships. The average ratio of the price of the company's stock to that of a composite index of stock prices over the past dozen years may be used as a means of measuring the adequacy of the current value of this ratio.

Profit Rate Earned by Other Companies. This involves a comparison of the rate of profit with the rates earned by other companies in the same industry to ascertain a relationship with concerns operating under similar conditions. Comparison with firms in different industries may also be made to ascertain the adequacy of the rates earned by companies in the given industry.

Historical Profit Rate of Company and/or Industry. This establishes an historical basis for what may be considered a normal profit rate for the company by examining how the profit rate has varied over the years. The average profit rates during what is considered normal times may be called the fair rate of profit. This historical analysis may also be done on an industry-wide basis to obtain an industry-wide normal profit rate.

Profit Rate to Finance Growth Internally. This is the rate of profit which will enable the company to finance its planned expansion from internal sources (retained profits and depreciation) without recourse to the sale of common stock or borrowing. This measure is subjective. The growth plans of the company will be an important factor in determining these requirements for capital funds.

Opinions of Profit Rate. A consideration of opinions of profit rate covers the opinions of different segments of the population as well as the public as a whole.

1. The attitude of labor to varying profit rates is hard to predict, but high rates tend to increase wage demands by labor.

2. The amount of new competition which will enter an industry under various profit conditions is also hard to predict, since it depends upon the opinions of the investing and entrepreneurial segments of the population.

3. The public as a whole has popular concepts of what constitutes a fair profit and these concepts change from time to time. These public attitudes determine legislative, executive, and judicial action by the government in such fields as antitrust and labor legislation, the renegotiation of profits on government contracts, the regulation of pricing and other industrial practices.

Choosing Rate of Return for Economy Calculations. What rate of return should a company require on prospective investments? What rate of return should be used for interest calculations in economy studies? It should include the following elements:

1. A basic charge for the use of money: This is the rate for a conservative loan, such as a United States Government bond, which has little risk. It may be considered the interest charge for a riskless loan. This rate will vary and will depend upon the demand and supply of funds in the money market at the time. Figure 7-1 shows how interest rates on

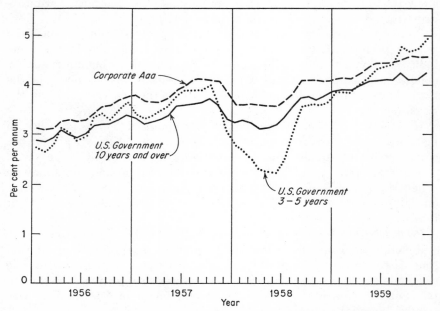

Figure 7-1. Bond yields. SOURCE: Board of Governors of the Federal Reserve System, Treasury Department, and Moody's Investors Service.

United States Government bonds and top-quality (low-risk) corporate bonds varied from 1956 through 1959.

2. A charge to cover risk: The amount of this charge should be higher as the risk of the investment increases. There are many factors affecting risk of loss. These are discussed in later chapters. Each investment proposal must be carefully analyzed to evaluate the level of risk.

3. A charge to cover opportunity costs of the funds: The greater the opportunities for profitable investment of funds in high-return projects, the higher should be this charge. Capital-budgeting procedures discussed later provide a means of determining these opportunity costs.

The choice of the rate of return to be used in an economy calculation is governed by the desire to maximize profits in the long run. Capital-management procedures discussed in Part Four of this volume are directed toward this goal.

PROBLEMS

1. State which of the four groups of profit theories presented in the text best explains the profits and losses in the following situations and discuss the reasons for each choice: (a) a farmer's profits and losses, (b) a drug manufacturer's profits on a new antibiotic, (c) a retail liquor store's profits and losses, (d) an oil company's profits on discovery of new fields, (e) an oil company's losses because of low prices caused by large production from newly discovered fields, (f) an oil company's losses because of state expropriation of properties, (g) a regulated public utility's profits, (h) a railroad's continued losses over the years, (i) an electronic computer manufacturer's profits and losses.

2. Five criteria for measuring the adequacy of a firm's rate of profit were presented in the text. Which of these do you consider most important? Explain your answer.

3. Determine the profits made by each of the following companies during the past fiscal year. State whether the profits were fair in your opinion and explain your reasoning: (a) General Motors, (b) Sears-Roebuck, (c) Glenn L. Martin, (d) International Business Machines, (e) American Telephone and Telegraph, (f) U.S. Steel, (g) any local company.

4. Do you think it is logical that a more successful, profitable company should require a higher return before investing in a piece of laborsaving equipment (and therefore be less likely to purchase the equipment) than its less successful competitor? Explain.

5. Referring to Figure 7-1 in the text, (a) why should interest rates on corporate bonds (which are usually 10 years and over) always be higher than the rates on U.S. Government 10-years-and-over bonds? (b) Why do interest rates on U.S. Government 3-to-5-year bonds fluctuate above and below the U.S. Government 10-years-and-over bonds?

8 Income Taxes

Income taxes constitute an important factor in evaluating the economy of alternative courses of action. Like all taxes, they are disbursements. They will receive special attention here because income tax liability can result in large increases and decreases in the profitableness of various proposals. Income tax considerations may be the key factor in determining certain economy decisions.

We will not attempt to consider all the ramifications of income tax laws and regulations in this discussion. Many volumes have been written on this subject without exhausting it. We will present the principal aspects of current federal income tax rules. Knowledge of these rules is essential in making logical decisions in many economy problems.

These rules are subject to change, of course. Changes in the income tax treatment of depreciation are constantly being proposed, and Congress and its committees consider such proposals at frequent intervals. The fact that changes are made periodically can add to the uncertainties of decision-making. Thus, the March 7, 1960, *Wall Street Journal* notes that the "House Ways and Means Committee today begins consideration of the Treasury's proposal to tax gains from the sale of depreciable property as regular income rather than as capital gains."

Individual Income Taxes. Every citizen or resident of the United States who had $600 or more gross income ($1,200 if 65 years of age or over) in the previous calendar year must file an income tax return. Gross income consists of income from all sources: salaries, net income from a business or profession (after deducting expenses), royalties, stock dividends, interest, rental income, income from pensions, profits on sale of capital assets, stock and bonds, etc. The only income excluded from adjusted gross income are specified items, such as interest from certain state and municipal bonds, life insurance proceeds, social security benefits, etc.

The individual's income tax liability, however, is not based on gross income. It is based on net taxable income which is computed by subtracting deductions and exemptions from gross income.

Deductions are allowed for contributions to nonprofit religious, educational, scientific, literary, etc., organizations whose activities conform to certain specified criteria. This deduction for contributions is limited to

20 per cent of gross income plus an extra 10 per cent if contributed to certain types of organizations (churches, certain educational, hospital and medical research institutions, etc.). Deductions are also allowed for interest paid on personal debts; most nonfederal taxes; medical and dental expenses above specified amounts and subject to limitations; casualty losses and thefts; expenses for education for specified purposes; certain types of expenses which are ordinary and necessary for an employee or for the production or collection of income; as well as other expenses permitted by the income tax law. In lieu of these specific deductions, a taxpayer may elect to take a flat 10 per cent of his gross income as a deduction or $1,000 whichever is less. This flat deduction is limited to $500 each when husband and wife file separate returns.

Each exemption permits a $600 deduction when computing net taxable income. One exemption is allowed for the taxpayer and one for each dependent, with additional exemptions if the taxpayer or his spouse are over 65 or are blind.

In 1960, net taxable income was taxed at the rates shown in Tables 8-1 to 8-3. Table 8-1 shows the rates for married persons who file joint returns (combining husband's and wife's income and deductions) and,

Table 8-1. Married Taxpayers Filing Joint Returns and Certain Widows and Widowers

Net taxable income	Amount of tax
Not over $4,000	20% of net taxable income
Over— But not over—	of excess over—
$ 4,000-$ 8,000	$ 800, plus 22%-$ 4,000
8,000- 12,000	1,680, plus 26%- 8,000
12,000- 16,000	2,720, plus 30%- 12,000
16,000- 20,000	3,920, plus 34%- 16,000
20,000- 24,000	5,280, plus 38%- 20,000
24,000- 28,000	6,800, plus 43%- 24,000
28,000- 32,000	8,520, plus 47%- 28,000
32,000- 36,000	10,400, plus 50%- 32,000
36,000- 40,000	12,400, plus 53%- 36,000
40,000- 44,000	14,520, plus 56%- 40,000
44,000- 52,000	16,760, plus 59%- 44,000
52,000- 64,000	21,480, plus 62%- 52,000
64,000- 76,000	28,920, plus 65%- 64,000
76,000- 88,000	36,720, plus 69%- 76,000
88,000- 100,000	45,000, plus 72%- 88,000
100,000- 120,000	53,640, plus 75%- 100,000
120,000- 140,000	68,640, plus 78%- 120,000
140,000- 160,000	84,240, plus 81%- 140,000
160,000- 180,000	100,440, plus 84%- 160,000
180,000- 200,000	117,240, plus 87%- 180,000
200,000- 300,000	134,640, plus 89%- 200,000
300,000- 400,000	223,640, plus 90%- 300,000
400,000	313,640, plus 91%- 400,000

106   COSTS

under certain conditions, widows and widowers whose spouse died during either of the two preceding taxable years. Table 8-2 shows rates for unmarried or legally separated persons who qualify as head of household by furnishing over half the cost of maintaining, as their home, a household for certain specified dependents or close relatives. Table 8-3 shows rates for all other single persons and married persons who file separate returns.

Table 8-2. **Unmarried (or Legally Separated) Taxpayers Who Qualify as Head of Household**

Net taxable income	Amount of tax
Not over $2,000	20% of net taxable income
Over— But not over —	of excess over—
$ 2,000–$ 4,000	$ 400, plus 21%–$ 2,000
4,000– 6,000	820, plus 24%– 4,000
6,000– 8,000	1,300, plus 26%– 6,000
8,000– 10,000	1,820, plus 30%– 8,000
10,000– 12,000	2,420, plus 32%– 10,000
12,000– 14,000	3,060, plus 36%– 12,000
14,000– 16,000	3,780, plus 39%– 14,000
16,000– 18,000	4,560, plus 42%– 16,000
18,000– 20,000	5,400, plus 43%– 18,000
20,000– 22,000	6,260, plus 47%– 20,000
22,000– 24,000	7,200, plus 49%– 22,000
24,000– 28,000	8,180, plus 52%– 24,000
28,000– 32,000	10,260, plus 54%– 28,000
32,000– 38,000	12,420, plus 58%– 32,000
38,000– 44,000	15,900, plus 62%– 38,000
44,000– 50,000	19,620, plus 66%– 44,000
50,000– 60,000	23,580, plus 68%– 50,000
60,000– 70,000	30,380, plus 71%– 60,000
70,000– 80,000	37,480, plus 74%– 70,000
80,000– 90,000	44,880, plus 76%– 80,000
90,000– 100,000	52,480, plus 80%– 90,000
100,000– 150,000	60,480, plus 83%– 100,000
150,000– 200,000	101,980, plus 87%– 150,000
200,000– 300,000	145,480, plus 90%– 200,000
300,000	235,480, plus 91%– 300,000

Table 8-1 when used by married taxpayers filing joint returns provides, in effect, for "splitting income" between husband and wife. The tax is twice what it would be if the total income of both is equally divided and the rates computed for single persons in Table 8-3. Married persons may choose to file one joint return and use Table 8-1 or file separate returns and use Table 8-3.

For persons whose income consists almost entirely of salaries and wages and no more than $200 of interest and dividends, the Internal Revenue Service provides simplified tables. The income tax in these tables is based on total income and the number of exemptions to which the taxpayer is entitled. (The tables make allowance for the standard exemption.) Persons in this category whose income is less than $5,000 may elect to have the Internal Revenue Service compute their tax for them.

Table 8-3. **Single Taxpayers Who Do Not Qualify for Rates in Tables 8-1 and 8-2 and Married Persons Filing Separate Returns**

Net taxable income Not over $2,000 Over— But not over—	Amount of tax 20% of net taxable income of excess over—
$ 2,000–$ 4,000	$ 400, plus 22%–$ 2,000
4,000– 6,000	840, plus 26%– 4,000
6,000– 8,000	1,360, plus 30%– 6,000
8,000– 10,000	1,960, plus 34%– 8,000
10,000– 12,000	2,640, plus 38%– 10,000
12,000– 14,000	3,400, plus 43%– 12,000
14,000– 16,000	4,260, plus 47%– 14,000
16,000– 18,000	5,200, plus 50%– 16,000
18,000– 20,000	6,200, plus 53%– 18,000
20,000– 22,000	7,260, plus 56%– 20,000
22,000– 26,000	8,380, plus 59%– 22,000
26,000– 32,000	10,740, plus 62%– 26,000
32,000– 38,000	14,460, plus 65%– 32,000
38,000– 44,000	18,360, plus 69%– 38,000
44,000– 50,000	22,500, plus 72%– 44,000
50,000– 60,000	26,820, plus 75%– 50,000
60,000– 70,000	34,320, plus 78%– 60,000
70,000– 80,000	42,120, plus 81%– 70,000
80,000– 90,000	50,220, plus 84%– 80,000
90,000– 100,000	58,620, plus 87%– 90,000
100,000– 150,000	67,320, plus 89%– 100,000
150,000– 200,000	111,820, plus 90%– 150,000
200,000	156,820, plus 91%– 200,000

Corporation Income Taxes. The Federal corporation income tax rates for 1960 are shown in Table 8-4. The table shows that corporations pay 52 per cent on all net taxable income above $25,000, unless it is a consolidated return in which case this percentage is 54 per cent.

Table 8-4. **1960 Federal Corporation Income Tax Rates**

On all net taxable income.......................... 30%
On net taxable income over $25,000................ 22%
Special additional tax on consolidated returns........ 2% of consolidated net taxable income, except of regulated public utilities and Western Hemisphere trade corporations

Corporations with one or more subsidiary corporations may find it desirable to file consolidated returns when the regulations permit it. Otherwise, when the subsidiary corporation's income is distributed as dividends to the parent corporation, the parent corporation will have to pay an income tax on the dividend even though the subsidiary corporation already has paid. The parent corporation would, in this latter case, be allowed a special deduction of 85 per cent of all dividends received from a domestic corporation subject to income tax. This means that the total corporate income tax rate on the subsidiary's distributed net taxable earning over $25,000 would be 55.744 per cent, computed as follows:

100.000%	Subsidiary corporation net taxable income
52.000%	52% federal income tax on subsidiary corporation earnings over $25,000
48.000%	Available to subsidiary corporation for dividends
40.800%	85% deduction for dividends from income-tax-paying corporation
7.200%	Subject to parent corporation income tax
3.744%	52% federal income tax on parent corporation earnings over $25,000
52.000%	Income tax paid by subsidiary corporation (line 2 above)
55.744%	Total income tax on subsidiary corporation earnings over $25,000

Operating-loss Carry-back and Carry-forward. When a business loses money in any year, it may carry this loss back three preceding years and forward for the five succeeding years. This loss carry-back and carry-forward regulation has been in effect since 1953. By applying the loss against profits in these other years, the Federal income taxes in these preceding or succeeding years will be reduced.

Capital Gains and Losses. When certain types of property, called capital assets in income tax regulations, are sold for more or less than their cost, a capital gain or loss occurs. Capital assets include such items as personal residences, automobiles, nondepreciable assets, stocks, bonds, securities, etc. For income tax purposes, capital assets do not include business real estate or any depreciable business property although the law provides for special favorable treatment of these items similar to the treatment for capital assets. Not considered as capital assets and also not entitled to special treatment is property which is held for sale to customers in the ordinary course of business and property such as copyrights or literary, artistic, or musical compositions which are owned by their creators or by a person who acquired them by gift.

Long- and Short-term Gains and Losses. Capital gains and losses are classified as short-term gains or losses if the assets were owned for six months or less prior to sale and as long-term gains or losses if the assets were owned for more than six months.

Long-term capital gains are given special favorable capital-gains tax treatment. Short-term capital gains are treated as ordinary income. Capital losses (both long-term and short-term) are given less favorable tax treatment than are ordinary losses.

Long-term capital gains and losses are combined to obtain a net long-term capital gain or loss. Short-term capital gains and losses are similarly combined to obtain a net short-term capital gain or loss. The possible results in any business year are summarized in Table 8-5.

Table 8-5. Tax Treatment of Capital Gains and Losses

Combined long-term transactions	Combined short-term transactions	Net result	Tax treatment		
			Capital gain	Capital loss	Ordinary income
Long-term capital gain	None	Long-term capital gain	X		
	Short-term capital gain	Long-term capital gain and Short-term capital gain	X		X
	Short-term capital loss	Net long-term capital gain or Net short-term capital loss	X	X	
Long-term capital loss	None	Long-term capital loss		X	
	Short-term capital gain	Net long-term capital loss or Net short-term capital gain		X	X
	Short-term capital loss	Long-term capital loss and Short-term capital loss		X X	
None	Short-term capital gain	Short-term capital gain			X
	Short-term capital loss	Short-term capital loss		X	

Tax Computation of Capital Gains. For both individuals and corporations, the maximum tax on the net long-term capital gain (less any net short-term capital loss) is 25 per cent.

Individuals may choose an alternative treatment of including only one-half of the net long-term capital gain (less any net short-term capital loss) in gross income and then use regular tax rates. In effect, this reduces the tax on these gains to one-half the regular rates. Depending upon the income tax bracket, this may be more or less advantageous than electing the flat 25 per cent tax.

For single taxpayers, Table 8-3 shows that when net taxable income, including one-half of net long-term capital gains (less any short-term capital losses) exceeds $18,000, it is frequently preferable to use the 25 per cent tax alternative. Thus, a single individual with net taxable income of $12,000, before a long-term capital gain of $1,000, should choose the alternative of one-half regular rates. He would pay only one-half of 43 per cent of $1,000, or $215 on the capital gain, or only $21\frac{1}{2}$ per cent. For net taxable income between $16,000 and 18,000, either method will give a 25 per cent tax on the $1,000.

Tax Treatment of Capital Losses. For corporations, short-term and long-term capital losses are deductible only to the extent that they offset short-term and long-term capital gains. When total capital losses exceed total capital gains in any tax year, the excess capital loss may be carried forward into the next five years. This means that, until it has been absorbed, the excess loss can be used to offset any capital gains during the next five years.

The above provisions also apply to individual taxpayers who have capital losses exceeding capital gains with one exception. During any year, up to $1,000 of excess capital loss may be used as a deduction from taxable income. Any excess above the $1,000 may be carried forward into the next five years. When capital assets (such as residences and automobiles) are devoted to personal use, rather than being held for the production of income, losses on sale cannot be used to reduce taxable income, although gains on sale are treated as capital gains.

For both individuals and corporations, capital losses thus have much more limited deductibility than ordinary business losses. Ordinary business losses can be offset against taxable income without limit.

Business Real Estate and Depreciable Property. Business real estate and depreciable business property are not considered capital assets under income tax law. However, if long-term gains on these and certain other specified assets exceed losses, the gains and losses are treated exactly as if they were capital assets. However, if the losses exceed the gains, the gains and losses are treated as if they were not capital assets. Thus, when gains exceed losses, the capital-gains benefit is provided. When losses exceed gains, the ordinary-income-loss benefit is provided.

Incremental Tax Rate. In most economy decisions, we are concerned with the amount that income taxes will reduce prospective additional net ordinary-income receipts if a proposed alternative is adopted. Consider a married person who files a joint return and is currently paying a 59 per cent income tax on the last additional dollars he receives. He is planning to make an investment which will give him a prospective return of $1,500 per year. This additional income will raise his net taxable income from $46,000 to $47,500. His net return after Federal taxes will be only 41 per cent of $1,500, or $615.

This 59 per cent tax rate is the incremental tax rate on ordinary income. It is the rate at which the next increment of income will be taxed. It differs from the average tax rate. In this person's case, his average tax rate on net taxable income is his current tax bill of $17,940 divided by his net taxable income of $46,000, or 39 per cent. This average rate has no relevance to most economy problems.

For most corporations earning $25,000 or more, the incremental Federal tax rate on ordinary income is 52 per cent. When a corporation has one or more subsidiaries and files a consolidated return, 2 per cent is added to bring the incremental rate to 54 per cent.

Double Taxation of Corporate Income. Dividends are paid by corporations out of earnings. These earnings have already been reduced by the corporate income tax. The individual taxpayer who receives dividends must also report these same earnings and pay a second income tax on them except for the exclusion discussed below. The rate at which this second tax is imposed depends on the total taxable income of the individual.

The first $50 of dividends received each year from taxable domestic corporations is currently (1961) excluded from an individual's gross taxable income and, therefore, not subject to income tax. In addition, an individual may reduce his income tax liability by an amount equal to 4 per cent of the dividends he received from taxable domestic corporations (after deducting the first $50).

With the exception of the $50 exclusion and the 4 per cent tax credit on dividends received, when corporate earnings are distributed to stockholders, they are subject to a second taxation. This may be considered a serious disadvantage of the corporate business structure over the unincorporated firm, especially if the ownership is limited to relatively few persons. However, under some circumstances, the corporate business may be a means of postponing income taxes and perhaps eventually reducing them.

Consider the case when the income of the corporation's owners places them in the top tax rate brackets. The tax paid on corporate earnings is considerably less than would be paid if the business were unincorporated. If these earnings are retained in the business (and possibly used for expansion or other needs), no tax is paid except the corporate tax. If the business is sold, the sellers will be taxed on the profits from the sale of the business a maximum of 25 per cent as a capital gain. This may be considerably below the tax the individuals would pay on ordinary income.

Accumulated-earnings Tax. The accumulated-earnings tax in the 1954 Income Tax Code, Section 531 (replacing the former Section 102 surtax on improper accumulations), is designed to discourage the retention of earnings beyond the needs of the business in order to avoid paying income taxes. It applies to a corporation which accumulates earnings instead of distributing them to stockholders to avoid individual income taxes.

A company is judged to be attempting to avoid income taxes for its stockholders and is, therefore, subject to this surtax when its earnings are permitted to accumulate beyond its reasonable present or anticipated needs. Funds retained to finance expansion programs, to provide working capital, to retire indebtedness when it comes due are examples of reasonable accumulations. Investing funds in stocks and bonds when not related to the business may not be a reasonable accumulation.

The surtax rate on "improper" accumulations is $27\frac{1}{2}$ per cent on the first $100,000 of accumulated taxable income and $38\frac{1}{2}$ per cent on the remainder. Accumulated taxable income is computed using a relatively complicated formula in which the retained earnings are subject to various allowed deductions. This surtax can be a very severe penalty. It must, therefore, be considered seriously when expansion plans and dividend policies are established, especially in companies with a small number of stockholders.

State and Local Government Income Taxes. A large majority of the states also tax individual and corporate income. Some local communities have income taxes. These taxes are allowable deductions in computing net income for the Federal tax. The Federal tax is allowed as a deduction in computing the state tax in only a few states.

The income taxes in the various states follow diverse patterns and schedules. It would, therefore, not be practical to describe them in this volume. We shall, therefore, consider only Federal income taxes in our examples of how income taxes affect economic decisions. In actual practice, the applicable state or local taxes should be added to the Federal on a net basis. The state or local tax liability should be reduced by the amount by which the Federal tax is reduced because of the deductibility of the state or local tax. Where state or local taxes allow deductions for Federal taxes, the Federal tax liability should be correspondingly reduced.

For example, a corporation paying 52 per cent on its incremental net taxable income also pays a 5 per cent state income tax on its incremental income. The total tax rate on incremental income is not 57 per cent (52 plus 5 per cent) because the Federal tax is reduced by the allowance of the state tax as an expense, reducing taxable income subject to the Federal tax. A $1,000 increase in state income taxes costs the corporation only $480 because its Federal income tax is reduced by $520 (52 per cent of $1,000). The total tax rate of 57 per cent is reduced by the 52 per cent of 5 per cent which is saved on the Federal income tax. The rate, therefore, becomes 54.4 per cent (57 minus 2.6 per cent).

PROBLEMS

1. Brown is unmarried and had the following income in 1960: salary, $30,000; stock dividends, $1,600; tax-exempt municipal-bond interest, $300; contributions to deductible religious and educational institutions, $4,800; interest on

personal debts, $400; state and other deductible taxes, $1,200; other deductible expenses, such as dues to professional societies, $500. Brown has no dependents. Determine his income tax.

2. Jones is married and has four dependents (wife and three children). He has the same income and deductions as Brown in problem 1. His wife has an independent net taxable income of $18,000 in 1960, with no dividend income and before taking any $600 deductions for exemptions. Determine Mr. and Mrs. Jones' total income tax for 1960. Should they file separate returns or one joint return?

3. Harris has exactly the same income in 1960 as Brown of problem 1, but in addition has long-term capital gains, $15,000; long-term capital losses, $1,000; short-term capital gains, $600; short-term capital losses, $2,500. Determine Harris's income tax.

4. Brown, Jones, and Harris of problems 1, 2, and 3 are each considering the same investment which is expected to yield $5,000 per year. What is the prospective annual return, after Federal income taxes, to each of them?

5. (a) The Mallo Corporation had net taxable income from operations in 1960 of $680,000. In addition, it incurred a loss on the sale of machinery for $80,000 which had a book value of $220,000. Calculate the corporation's income tax for 1960.

   (b) The corporation is considering the investment of $100,000 in nondepreciating inventories for a new project which, if successful, will produce added annual income of $50,000 for the next eight years. It is anticipated that the income of the corporation from its current operations will remain approximately the same as in 1960 during the period and that income tax rates will remain the same. If the project is successful, what will be the additional annual income from this investment after taxes?

   (c) If the project is unsuccessful and produces a loss of $75,000 in the first year, what will be the net loss after taxes from this project during this first year?

   (d) If the project is liquidated at the beginning of the second year to stop further operating losses and the inventories are sold at a book-value loss of $80,000, what will be the net loss after taxes from this project during the second year?

6. (a) The Standard Manufacturing Corporation had net income of $3,650,000 during 1960 as follows:

Operating profit	$2,800,000
Dividends from subsidiary corporation (National Manufacturing Corp.)	850,000
Total net income	$3,650,000

Determine the income tax which the corporation will be required to pay.

   (b) The company is considering the advisability of filing a consolidated return for Standard and National. National had net taxable income of $1,800,000 during 1960. Compare the total income tax of the two corporations using and not using consolidated returns.

7. Joseph Moore is the sole owner of Moore Corporation, in which he has personally invested $400,000. He has net taxable personal income of $500,000 per year from sources other than Moore Corporation. Joseph Moore has been offered $5,000,000 for the business, which he considers a fair price, but he

decides not to sell. Moore Corporation shows an annual net profit of $2,000,-000 before income taxes. There are no state or local income taxes.

(a) What is the net profit after income taxes of Moore Corporation?

(b) If Moore Corporation distributes these profits as dividends, how much of the $2,000,000 will Joseph Moore retain after taxes? What has been the effective tax rate on the $2,000,000 profit?

8. (a) If the Moore Corporation of problem 7 distributes no dividends, but keeps all its profits in the business and this is judged by the Internal Revenue Bureau to be an improper accumulation of $950,000 beyond the reasonable needs of the business, what surtax penalty will the company have to pay?

(b) If the annual net profit after the surtax penalty is now distributed as a dividend, how much of the $2,000,000 pretax profits of Moore Corporation will Joseph Moore retain? What has been the effective tax rate on the $2,000,000 profit?

9. Joseph Moore of problem 7 decides to use the profits of the Moore Corporation to expand and diversify the corporation's activities. He embarks on a 5-year expansion program which requires the investment of the amount of the net annual earnings after taxes, approximately $950,000 per year. The corporation, therefore pays no dividends during this period. At the end of the five years, Joseph Moore sells the business for $9,750,000. This amount is only equal to the $5,000,000 which Moore could have received for the business five years ago plus the $4,750,000 of profits after taxes which were retained in the business since that time. It is considerably less than the business is worth in Joseph Moore's estimation.

(a) How much income tax will Joseph Moore pay on the extra $4,750,000 which he received when selling the business now rather than five years ago?

(b) What is the total income tax Joseph Moore would have paid on the $4,750,000 ($950,000 per year over the five-year period) if the expansion program had not been undertaken, and if instead the $950,000 per year had been paid to him as dividends each year?

10. The legislature of a state with no income tax is considering the establishment of a flat 4 per cent tax on the net income, after deduction of the Federal income tax, of all corporations doing business in the state. The Federal income tax will, of course, be computed on net income after deduction of the state income tax.

(a) What will be the effective Federal and state tax rates on taxable net income over $25,000 for a corporation which is not filing a consolidated return?

(b) What is the incremental tax cost to corporations if the new state income tax is adopted?

PART THREE

Methods for Tangible Evaluation
of Alternatives

9   Annual-cost Comparisons

The use of annual-cost comparisons as a basis for economy decisions fits in with the normal pattern of thinking of business people. We think in terms of annual costs in budget planning and control, in profit determination, in accounting for operations. Annual costs are, thus, a familiar aspect in business and are easily understood. They are less mistrusted than other less familiar and, therefore, less comfortable bases for comparison.

Comparison of Income with Costs—No Capital Investment. The applications engineer develops a new industrial use for a synthetic fiber which his company produces. The fiber must be slightly altered for this purpose at a small additional cost. No additional capital investment will be required. Market research has been performed to determine the potential demand at various prices as well as the kind and cost of the promotional program which will be required.

The following is a comparison of anticipated annual costs and revenues:

Incremental revenue from new use		$125,000
Incremental expenses:		
Manufacturing	$40,000	
Promotional and sales	35,000	
Administrative and miscellaneous	5,000	
Total		80,000
Net incremental profit		$45,000

Comparison of Annual Costs—No Capital Investment. A rather simple economic evaluation may sometimes be indicated by proposed manufacturing changes. For example, the methods engineer proposes a change in the manufacturing process for a component in a pumping device. The change in process will reduce material wastage but will increase labor time. The following cost analysis is made for the 5,000 components required annually:

Present method:	
Material	$1,500
Direct labor	2,500
Total	$4,000
Proposed method:	
Material	$ 800
Direct labor	2,800
Total	$3,600

It is necessary to consider only those costs which vary with the alternatives being considered. If the cost of insurance remains the same regardless of the alternative chosen, then insurance cost will not affect the relative economy of the alternatives and can be ignored.

Error of Assuming Different Levels of Efficiency. The Doe Manufacturing Company's production-control system is functioning poorly. The president engages an engineer to survey the operations and recommend any steps to improve the services and efficiency. The engineer investigates and analyzes the present operations and requirements. He then submits a report to the president recommending a change to a newly designed system which he has developed. The engineer's cost analysis shows that his proposed system will provide the required production-control service at a total annual cost of $168,000 as compared with the $203,000 annual cost of the present system.

The president is greatly impressed with the engineer's proposal and it is adopted by the company. The engineer supervises the installation of the new system and is then hired to head the production-control department. During the first year of operation under the new system, the total annual cost of production-control activities amounted to $185,000. Although this is greater than the estimate of $168,000, it is still a substantial saving over previous costs and the company management is satisfied.

After five successful years, this engineer leaves Doe Manufacturing and is replaced by a man of considerable production-control experience. After becoming acquainted with the company's operations, the new production-control head submits to the president a plan for improving the system he has inherited from his predecessor. The improved system which he proposes would, according to his estimates, reduce the cost of the production-control services to $150,000.

Upon examining the details of the proposal, the president of the company is surprised to notice that it is almost identical to the system used by the company five years ago. He quite naturally asks why the first system will now be cheaper than the present one, whereas five years ago it was determined to be more expensive.

The new department head is given the detailed cost analysis of five years ago and makes a study of the comparative cost figures used by his predecessor. He discovers that his predecessor had compared the current operating costs of the then existing system with the cost of operations of his proposed system at a very high level of efficiency. The fallacy in his predecessor's cost comparison was twofold:

1. The level of efficiency which his predecessor had assumed would be obtained under the new system was too high. For this reason, only $18,000 of the expected $35,000 annual savings was actually realized.

2. The level of efficiency at which the costs of operations of the then existing system were computed was unconsciously too low. The old system

seemed more expensive than the new only because the old system was operated and managed very inefficiently. If the cost analysis had been based on the operation of the original and the new system at the same level of efficiency of the personnel, then the cost analysis would have disclosed that the then existing system was essentially better than the proposed and adopted one.

What was originally needed in this case was an improvement in management of the department to raise the level of performance of the personnel, not a change of system, as had been proposed by the engineer and adopted by the company five years ago.

Capital Expenditures. Evaluation gets a little more complicated when the problem involves capital expenditures as well as expense items. Thus, the systems analyst for a metal parts manufacturer has developed what he considers an improved material-control-recording procedure. The new procedure requires the investment of $40,000 in office equipment. Time-study analysis shows that as a result of this investment, the cost of clerical labor will be reduced from $40,000 per year to $27,000.

Studies have indicated that a five-year life is a reasonable estimate for this equipment. An annual-cost comparison would, therefore, show:

Present system:
Clerical labor.......... $40,000
Total............... $40,000

Proposed system:
Clerical labor.......... $27,000
Total............... $27,000

Adoption of the proposed system would produce an estimated savings of $13,000 per year, and purchase of the equipment would appear to be indicated. However, there are two elements in this cost analysis which have not been considered. First of all, $40,000 will be spent for equipment with a five-year life and no resale value. This $40,000 cost should be averaged over the five-year period and a depreciation cost of $8,000 per year charged to recover the $40,000 by the end of the five-year period.

Also $40,000 of company cash is being tied up in this equipment. If this money is not invested in this new equipment, it can be invested either in something else which will earn a return or, if there are loans which are repayable, this indebtedness can be reduced and the interest cost saved. An annual interest cost should, therefore, be added to the proposed system.

Many factors enter into a determination of what interest rate should be used and these will be discussed in some detail in a later chapter. In this case, the company has determined that a 10 per cent return is the proper one to use.

Interest Calculation. If we were to add to the costs under the proposed system an interest charge of 10 per cent of $40,000 per year, the cost comparison would now show:

Present system:
Clerical labor... $40,000
    Total.. $40,000

Proposed system:
Clerical labor... $27,000
Depreciation of new equipment, $(\frac{40,000}{5})$...................... 8,000
Interest on investment in new equipment, $(40,000)(0.10)$........... 4,000
    Total.. $39,000

This analysis, if correct, would indicate an expected saving of only $1,000 per year. However, we computed annual interest on the $40,000 original investment despite the fact that the investment was being reduced each year by the depreciation-recovery charge of $8,000 per year. Actually, $4,000 is the valid interest charge for the first year only; $3,200 (10 per cent of the $32,000 undepreciated book value of the equipment during the second year) is the correct charge for the second year; $2,400 (10 per cent of the $24,000 undepreciated book value of the equipment during the third year); $1,600 for the fourth year; and $800 for the fifth year. The average annual interest is thus the average of this decreasing arithmetic progression, the first term of which is $4,000 and the last of which is $800. The average interest over the five-year period is then $(4,000 + 800)/2 = \$2,400$. Expressed in general terms, if P represents the original cost, i the interest rate per period (in this case per year since it is compounded annually), and n the number of periods (in this case years), then $\frac{1}{2}\left(Pi + \frac{Pi}{n}\right)$, or $Pi\left(\frac{n+1}{2n}\right)$ is the average interest cost per year.

The annual costs of the proposed system should therefore read:

Clerical labor...................... $27,000.00
Depreciation, $\frac{40,000}{5}$................ 8,000.00
Interest, $40,000(0.10)(\frac{6}{10})$........... 2,400.00
    Total........................ $37,400.00

This analysis now shows a distinct saving for the proposed system.

Erroneous Use of Book Values. The foreman in a furniture factory proposes the substitution of an automatic shaper costing $9,000 for the two hand shapers presently used. The one automatic shaper will be able to handle the volume of work presently performed by the two hand machines and will reduce the direct labor cost from $5,000 to $2,000 annually. However, the shapers were purchased 6 years ago at a cost of $4,000 each and were being depreciated $400 each per year on the basis of straight-line depreciation for an estimated life of 10 years. The book values of each of the hand shapers were thus $1,600 each. It is a company policy that all new installations must pay for themselves in 4 years with interest at 10 per cent.

The foreman made the following comparison of annual costs, assuming no salvage value for any of the machines at the end of their estimated lives:

Hand shapers:
Depreciation, $\frac{8,000}{10}$... $ 800.00
Interest, $(8,000)(0.10)(\frac{11}{20})$...................................... 440.00
Direct labor... 5,000.00
Maintenance, repairs, power, supplies, insurance, etc................. 1,000.00
    Total... $7,240.00

Automatic shaper:
Depreciation, $\frac{9,000}{4}$... $2,250.00
Interest, $(9,000)(0.10)(\frac{5}{8})$....................................... 562.50
Direct labor... 2,000.00
Maintenance, repairs, power, supplies, insurance, etc............... 2,000.00
    Total... $6,812.50

On the basis of this analysis, the foreman notes an annual saving of more than $400 if the automatic shaper is used and recommends its adoption to the company.

In determining the annual costs if the hand shapers are kept, the foreman should have considered only those depreciation and interest costs which would be avoided if the automatic shaper were bought. The company is forgoing the present salvage value of the hand shapers if it continues to use the hand shapers. The forgoing of the present salvage value is the equivalent of investing this sum of money in the hand shapers. These shapers could now be sold for only $250 each or $500 total. In analyzing the annual costs of keeping the hand shapers, the foreman should therefore depreciate this $500 investment. The company policy is that new installations must pay for themselves in 4 years. The hand shapers should, therefore, be depreciated over a period of 4 years or their remaining expected life, whichever is less. In this case, the remaining expected life of the hand shapers is at least 4 years. Accordingly, the annual costs, keeping the hand shapers, are:

Depreciation, $\frac{500}{4}$.................................... $ 125.00
Interest, $(500)(0.10)(\frac{5}{8})$............................. 31.25
Direct labor....................................... 5,000.00
Maintenance, repairs, power, supplies, insurance, etc.... 1,000.00
    Total... $6,156.25

The true annual cost of operations on the basis of continuing use of the hand shapers thus turns out to be more than $600 lower than if the change is made to the laborsaving automatic shaper.

The significant costs in this analysis are the opportunity or alternative costs which represent resources which become unavailable because they are used in the alternative being considered. Thus, the opportunity cost of continuing use of the hand shapers is the $500 which could be obtained if they were not used but sold. (The annual depreciation charge of $800 on the hand shapers is a book cost which represents amortization of the past expenditure and does not represent a current payment of cash or increase of liability.)

Erroneous Capitalization of Book-value Loss. An engineer for a chemical manufacturer has come across some new type of equipment which would apparently lower unit costs considerably. In accordance with his detailed estimates of material, labor, supplies, etc., the engineer computes that operating costs will be reduced from $30,000 to $10,000. This new equipment will cost $125,000 and will replace facilities which were purchased just 2 years ago at a cost of $150,000. The present facilities were being depreciated on the books of the company on a straight-line basis over a 10-year life, giving them a book value of $120,000. Their resale value, if the new facilities were purchased, is only $40,000. Using an 8 per cent rate of return on investment, the engineer made the following comparison of annual costs based on a 10-year life for the new equipment and 8 years of remaining life for the old facilities:

Present equipment:

Depreciation, $\frac{40,000}{8}$	$ 5,000.00
Interest, $(40,000)(0.08)(\frac{9}{16})$	1,800.00
Operating costs	30,000.00
Total	$36,800.00

New equipment:

Depreciation, $\frac{(120,000 - 40,000) + 125,000}{10}$	$20,500.00
Interest, $(205,000)(0.08)(\frac{11}{20})$	9,020.00
Operating costs	10,000.00
Total	$39,520.00

Depreciation of the new equipment was calculated on the basis that the cost of the new equipment equals $125,000 plus the loss involved in selling the present equipment for $40,000 when it has a depreciated book value of $120,000.

This analysis has convinced the engineer that his proposal is uneconomical and he therefore drops the whole matter.

Actually, this is a very good proposal and, if analyzed correctly, a very substantial reduction in annual costs can be shown. The $80,000 book loss involved in selling the old equipment for $40,000 is a cost which is not pertinent to the present problem. This $80,000 represents the difference between the actual reduction in the resale value of the equipment and the amount of this reduction which the accountants have charged and recovered as production expense in previous years. The economic advisability of making this replacement is independent of whether past production costs were overstated or understated, although this factor could affect financial ability to make the replacement. We are here concerned solely with determining the relative advisability of two alternative courses of action by comparison of the annual cost increments which each alternative will cause. Past happenings are only significant as guides to the future costs.

One of the alternatives is to invest $125,000 in new equipment which will be used up in 10 years. If this alternative is chosen, then the manufacturer can sell the present equipment for $40,000. The other alternative is to keep the present equipment, which involves the investment of $40,000 in a depreciating asset in the sense that the manufacturer forgoes the $40,000 which he can get by selling the equipment now but will not be able to get 8 years from now.

The manufacturer is thus essentially investing $40,000 in a depreciating asset if he chooses to continue with his present facilities and $125,000 if he decides to install the improved equipment.

Correct analysis of the annual costs using the new equipment, therefore, reveals the following estimate:

$$
\begin{array}{lr}
\text{Depreciation, } \frac{125,000}{10} \ldots\ldots\ldots\ldots\ldots & \$12,500.00 \\
\text{Interest, } (125,000)(0.08)(\frac{11}{20}) \ldots\ldots\ldots & 5,500.00 \\
\text{Operating costs} \ldots\ldots\ldots\ldots\ldots\ldots & \underline{10,000.00} \\
\text{Total} \ldots\ldots\ldots\ldots\ldots\ldots\ldots\ldots & \$28,000.00
\end{array}
$$

Installation of the new equipment will thus result in a substantial reduction in annual operating costs—saving almost $9,000 per year.

The $80,000 difference between the resale value of the present equipment and its book value represents a sunk cost which cannot be changed by either of the alternatives being considered. It is, therefore, irrelevant to the decision and the economy analysis.

Inaccurate Assumption of Future Requirements. A company is setting up a separate plant to manufacture a newly developed product. A special nut, required in this product, can be made on an engine lathe costing $4,000 or on a turret lathe costing $15,000. The turret lathe will have lower material wastage, decreasing material cost from $0.160 to $0.155 per unit. Operating rate using the turret lathe is 30 pieces per hour; using the engine lathe the rate is 10 pieces per hour. Three engine lathes will thus be required to equal the capacity of one turret lathe. The operator of the engine lathe would make $2 per hour; the turret lathe operator $1.60 per hour. Repairs, power costs, tools, and all indirect expenses for each of the engine lathes add up to an average of $1,800 per year. Setup, repair, power costs, tools, and other indirect expenses for the turret lathe add up to an average of \$9,600 per year. Estimating a life of 10 years for the engine lathe and 6 years for the turret lathe, assuming no salvage values, and using a return of 6 per cent on investment, the following unit-cost comparison is made on the basis of a 2,000-hour work year (50 weeks times 40 hours):

Engine lathe:

Direct labor, $\frac{2.00}{10}$ \$0.200

Direct material 0.160

Repairs, power, tools, other indirect expenses, $\dfrac{(1,800)}{(10)(2,000)} = \dfrac{1,800}{20,000}$ 0.090

Depreciation, $(\frac{4,000}{10})(\frac{1}{20,000})$ 0.020

Interest, $(4,000)(0.06)(\frac{11}{20})(\frac{1}{20,000})$ 0.007

   Total cost per nut \$0.477

Turret lathe:

Direct labor $\frac{1.60}{30}$ \$0.053

Direct material 0.155

Repairs, power, tools, other indirect expenses, $\dfrac{(9,600)}{(30)(2,000)} = \dfrac{9,600}{60,000}$ 0.160

Depreciation, $(\frac{15,000}{6})(\frac{1}{60,000})$ 0.042

Interest, $15,000(0.06)(\frac{7}{12})(\frac{1}{60,000})$ 0.009

   Total cost per nut \$0.419

Since the analysis shows a saving of almost 6 cents per nut using the turret lathe, the methods man included turret lathe in his recommendation for new equipment. He neglected to consider one crucial aspect: How many of these special nuts will be required each year? If 60,000 will be needed, then the turret lathe is the more economical machine and the cost comparison is valid. If, however, the new plant is expected to produce 20,000 units of this new equipment per year and only one of these special nuts is used in each equipment, then a correct analysis of unit costs will disclose that the engine lathe is more economical.

The expected requirement for the nuts in this case was actually only 20,000. Therefore, the unit costs of production using the one engine lathe that will be required are the same as those previously calculated—totaling \$0.477. The unit costs using the turret lathe, however, are much higher than those calculated because of the excess machine capacity which will not be required:

Direct labor, $\frac{1.60}{30}$ \$0.053

Direct material 0.155

Setup, repairs, power, tools, other indirect expenses, etc., $\frac{9,600}{20,000}$ 0.480

Depreciation, $(\frac{15,000}{6})(\frac{1}{20,000})$ 0.125

Interest, $15,000(0.06)(\frac{7}{12})(\frac{1}{20,000})$ 0.026

   Total cost per nut \$0.839

Unless it were anticipated that requirements would increase or that the excess capacity of the turret lathe would be otherwise utilized, the methods man should have recommended the engine lathe rather than the turret lathe.

Economy studies deal with future conditions. Implicit in any economy study is a forecast of future requirements. This forecast must be explicitly made if uneconomic pitfalls are to be avoided. One can make grave errors in economy studies by assuming that the maximum output of all equipment will be required, that all equipment will be utilized to its maximum or to its most economic capacity.

Incorrect Use of Overhead Ratio. A machinist submits a proposal under the employee suggestion plan in operation in a large manufacturing company. He suggests using a fixture which he has designed to reduce the labor required in the assembly of a subunit used in the company's products. To show the worth of his suggestion and to provide the basis for the determination of the amount of the suggestion award, the following analysis of cost savings is submitted:

Item	*Amount*
1. Direct labor required per assembly subunit, present method..	8.725 min
2. Direct labor required per assembly subunit, proposed method.	6.307 min
3. Direct-labor savings per assembly subunit, Item 1 − Item 2..	2.418 min
4. Average direct-labor cost................................	$1.20 per hour
5. Number of subunits manufactured and used per year.......	40,000
6. Total direct-labor savings, $\dfrac{\text{Item 3} \times \text{Item 4} \times \text{item 5}}{60}$......	$1,934.40 per year
7. Departmental overhead rate............................	50% of direct-labor dollars
8. Overhead cost savings, Item 6 × Item 7.................	$ 967.20 per year
9. Total savings, Item 6 + Item 8........................	$2,901.60 per year

(The cost of the fixture was negligible and therefore omitted from the analysis.)

The error in this calculation is in the assumption that a reduction in the direct-labor cost required in the assembly of the subunit would necessarily produce a 50 per cent reduction in the overhead costs because the overhead costs for the department average 50 per cent of direct labor. Actually, there might be no overhead-cost savings as a result of the adoption of this suggestion; or there might be some savings, but less than 50 per cent of the direct-labor savings; or there might perhaps be an overhead savings greater than 50 per cent of the direct-labor savings. There might even be an increase in the overhead costs as a result of the adoption of this suggestion. It is necessary to determine by direct analysis the overhead costs, if any, which will be reduced as a result of the adoption of this suggestion.

In the case of the proposal just mentioned, investigation disclosed that practically no reduction in overhead costs would occur as a result of the adoption of this suggestion. Therefore, the correct analysis would show total prospective savings of $1,934.40 rather than $2,901.60.

Improper Interest Rate. The manager of a plant is considering the replacement of a certain machine with a model of improved design which cuts operating costs to less than one-third. He asks two of his methods engineers to make independent surveys and determine whether the replacement is desirable. When he receives the reports, he notes that Engineer A's analysis indicates that the replacement should be made and Engineer B's analysis indicates that the old machine tool should be retained. The two analyses are reproduced below:

Engineer A
Present machine:

Depreciation, $\frac{1,500}{4}$	$ 375.00
Interest, $(1,500)(0.035)(\frac{5}{8})$	32.81
Operating costs	4,000.00
Total	$4,407.81

New improved machine:

Depreciation, $\frac{20,000}{8}$	$2,500.00
Interest, $(20,000)(0.035)(\frac{9}{16})$	393.75
Operating costs	1,200.00
Total	$4,093.75

On the basis of the analysis shown above, annual costs will be lowered more than $300 if the present machine is replaced. Engineer A, therefore, recommends purchase of the new improved machine.

Engineer B
Present machine:

Depreciation, $\frac{1,600}{4}$	$ 400.00
Interest, $(1,600)(0.15)(\frac{5}{8})$	150.00
Operating costs	4,000.00
Total	$4,550.00

New improved machine:

Depreciation, $\frac{20,000}{8}$	$2,500.00
Interest, $(20,000)(0.15)(\frac{9}{16})$	1,687.50
Operating costs	1,200.00
Total	$5,387.50

On the basis of Engineer B's analysis, the total annual costs would be higher by more than $800 if the new improved design were adopted at the present time. Engineer B, therefore, recommends that the present machine be retained.

Both engineers estimated almost the same costs and salvage values. (Engineer A estimated salvage value of $1,500 for old machine; Engineer B estimated $1,600.) The principal difference is caused by the rate of return which each engineer estimated was required on the money investment.

This rate of return should include two components: the return which conservatively invested money can earn and an additional return to compensate for the risks involved in the investment. The greater the risks and possibilities of loss of money because of business fluctuations and changing economic conditions, because of technological changes, because of the highly competitive nature of the business, because of lack of a sound basis for estimating expenses, etc., the greater this second element should be.

On reviewing the two analyses presented by his engineers, the plant manager decided that Engineer A's rate of return was much too low. A $3\frac{1}{2}$ per cent return barely covers the cost of a conservative well-protected loan and certainly makes no allowance for the risks involved in the investment as well as the alternative profitable investments which could be made with the money.

Exact[1] and Approximate Methods of Calculating Capital Recovery. In Chapter 5 devoted to interest calculations, we noted that if I want to recover $10,000 with interest at 4% by equal annual receipts over a five-year period, the amount I should receive each year, R, is

$$R = P \left[\frac{i(1+i)^n}{(1+i)^n - 1} \right]$$
$$= \$10,000 \left[\begin{matrix} \text{CR} \\ i = 4\% \\ n = 5 \end{matrix} \right]$$
$$= \$10,000(0.22463) = \$2,246.30$$

In the examples which we have presented thus far in this chapter in which recovery of capital was involved, we have not used this exact formula, but have instead approximated its value by computing straight-line depreciation on the depreciating capital investment plus average interest on the unrecovered capital. The reason we have done this is that many people are familiar with the calculation of depreciation on a straight-line basis as is done by the accountant and can understand it readily. The calculation of average interest on the declining unrecovered investment is also easily understood. Fewer people are familiar with the derivation and use of interest formulas and tables. Because people are generally inclined to distrust that which they do not understand, it is often better to use

---

[1] The term "exact" refers here to the exactness of the interest formula, not the exactness of the answer which, of course, may not be exact for several reasons: the costs and revenues which must be used in the calculation are inexact forecasts of future values and some of the conventions implicit in the compound-interest formula which is used may not always be in complete accord with reality (e.g., the assumption that all payments occur at the end of the period).

familiar concepts and calculations, even if they are only approximations, provided they will not materially distort the picture.

Straight-line depreciation is equivalent to capital recovery at zero per cent interest. The capital-recovery factor $\left[\dfrac{i(1+i)^n}{(1+i)^n - 1} \right]$ approaches the value $1/n$ as the interest rate (i) approaches a value of zero. This can be readily checked in the interest tables.

Error in Approximate Calculations. The method of straight-line depreciation plus average interest understates the annual costs of capital recovery and interest because it uses an arithmetic average for payments over a period of time rather than a time-adjusted average. It would, therefore, be expected that the amount of distortion will be greater as the period of time for capital recovery becomes longer and as the interest rate for adjusting the time value of money becomes larger. At zero per cent interest, there is no difference between the methods.

A comparison of the annual capital-recovery (including interest) factors using the exact method of the interest-formula derivation of Chapter 5 and the approximate one of straight-line depreciation plus average interest thus far used in this chapter was made by tabulating the values at various values of i and n, computing the approximation error by subtraction, and dividing by the exact value to obtain percentage error. The results are charted in Figure 9-1.

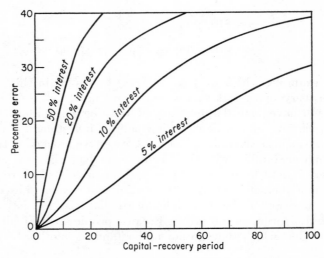

Figure 9-1. Percentage error in using approximate method of calculating capital recovery as a function of the capital-recovery period.

The errors in the approximate method will, therefore, tend to be greatest when

1. There are large differences in the expected lives. (When the expected lives of the alternative investments are almost the same, the percentage error is approximately the same for the alternatives.)

2. The investment costs are high compared with the annual operating costs.

3. There are large differences in the magnitudes of the alternative investments.

4. The interest rates are high and the expected lives are long.

Calculating Capital Recovery by the Exact Method. Let us recalculate the annual costs of the improved material-control-recording procedure on page 120 using the exact method.

Present system:
Clerical labor.. $40,000
   Total... $40,000

Proposed system:
Clerical labor.. $27,000

Capital recovery, $40,000 $\left(\begin{matrix} \text{CR} \\ i = 10\% \\ n = 5 \end{matrix} \right)$ = $40,000(0.26380)............. 10,552

   Total... $37,552

In this case, the $37,552 cost is not significantly different from the $37,400 cost using the approximate method because the capital-recovery period is short. However, we shall see in the next example an economy calculation in which the error introduced by the approximate calculation is crucial.

Salvage Values. In the problems we have considered thus far in this chapter, we have assumed that the capital assets would have no salvage value at the end of their useful lives. In many cases, the salvage value is so small that this assumption is correct for all practical purposes, especially considering the over-all problems and accuracy of estimating future costs and values.

In some cases, however, it is desirable to take into account the expected salvage values at the end of the useful life of the asset. In such cases, capital recovery is calculated only in the depreciating portion of the asset and only interest is charged on the nondepreciating salvage-value portion. If P is the cost of the asset and L its prospective salvage value at the end of n years, then $P - L$ is the depreciating portion of the asset and L is the nondepreciating portion.

The annual capital-recovery-and-interest formula then becomes

Approximate method:

$$\frac{P - L}{n} + (P - L)(i)\left(\frac{n + 1}{2n}\right) + Li$$

Exact method:

$$(P - L)(\mathrm{CR}) + Li$$

Let us consider a sample problem. A small bridge has been weakened by recent floods and consideration is being given to two alternatives. One is to strengthen the existing structure and the other is to replace it with a more modern and stronger one. Strengthening the bridge will cost approximately $50,000, and it is estimated that the bridge should then hold for 10 years before further major repairs would be required. Current salvage value of the bridge is $20,000; if repaired, the bridge would have an expected salvage value of $25,000 at the end of 10 years. A new bridge will cost $200,000 and would have an estimated life of 50 years. Expected salvage value of the new bridge at that time is $40,000. Maintenance on the old bridge is estimated at $18,000 per year and $1,000 per year on the proposed one.

Let us calculate our annual costs with interest at 15 per cent, using the exact procedure first.

Repair old bridge:

Capital recovery, $(P - L) \left(\overset{\mathrm{CR}}{\underset{n = 10}{i = 15\%}} \right) + Li$;

(20,000 + 50,000 − 25,000)(0.19925) + 25,000(0.15) $12,716

Maintenance 18,000

Total $30,716

Replace with new bridge:

Capital recovery, $(P - L) \left(\overset{\mathrm{CR}}{\underset{n = 50}{i = 15\%}} \right) + Li$;

(200,000 − 40,000)(0.15014) + 40,000(0.15) $30,022

Maintenance 1,000

Total $31,022

The capital cost in the alternative of repairing the old bridge consists of the $20,000 opportunity cost which could be obtained if it were scrapped plus the $50,000 to repair it.

Let us now compare this exact solution with the solution using the approximate method.

Repair old bridge:

Depreciation, $\dfrac{P - L}{n} = \dfrac{20,000 + 50,000 - 25,000}{10}$ $4,500

Average interest, $(P - L)(i) \left(\dfrac{n + 1}{2n} \right) + Li$;

(20,000 + 50,000 − 25,000)(0.15)($\frac{11}{20}$) + 25,000(0.15) 7,463

Maintenance 18,000

Total $29,963

Replace with new bridge:

Depreciation, $\dfrac{P - L}{n} = \dfrac{200,000 - 40,000}{50}$ .... $\$3,200$

Average interest, $(P - L)(i)\left(\dfrac{n + 1}{2n}\right) + Li;$

$(200,000 - 40,000)(0.15)(\frac{51}{100}) + 40,000(0.15)$ 18,240

Maintenance 1,000

Total .... $\$22,440$

This is obviously the kind of problem to which the approximate method of computing capital recovery is not suitable for the following reasons: there is a large difference in years of expected life; capital costs and the interest rate are significantly large.

Time-adjusted Averages of Annual Operating Costs. In our calculations thus far, we have used average annual operating costs. We have not mentioned how these averages are calculated if differences may be expected during the life of the investment. It is not unusual to have higher maintenance and operating costs for equipment and buildings as they get older. Taking a simple arithmetic average of these costs may sometimes overstate the value. This is especially true when there is a sharply increasing pattern in later years.

An example will illustrate this. The anticipated maintenance costs on a proposed machine are as follows:

Year	Anticipated maintenance	Year	Anticipated maintenance
1	0	6	$1,000
2	0	7	2,000
3	0	8	2,000
4	0	9	3,000
5	$1,000	10	3,000

Total anticipated maintenance over the 10-year period is $12,000, or an arithmetic average of $1,200 per year.

A time-adjusted average is calculated, using a 10 per cent minimum attractive rate of return.

Year	Anticipated maintenance	SPPW	Present worth of maintenance
5	$ 1,000	0.6209	$ 621
6	1,000	0.5645	565
7	2,000	0.5132	1,026
8	2,000	0.4665	933
9	3,000	0.4241	1,272
10	3,000	0.3855	1,157
	$12,000		$5,574

Each maintenance cost is multiplied by the appropriate present-worth factor to find the equivalent sum as of the beginning of the first year. The present worths of the future maintenance charges are then totaled to obtain $5,574. The uniform annual equivalent of this total is obtained by multiplying by the CR for $i = 10\%$, $n = 10$, 0.16275. We thus obtain $5,574(0.16275), or $907 as the equivalent annual cost compared with the arithmetic average of $1,200.

It would be expected that the equivalent annual cost taking time into account would be considerably less than the simple arithmetic average in this case because the simple arithmetic average does not discount distant future payments, but gives them the same standing as a current one. For this reason, it overstates the average of a series of increasing payments and understates the average of a series of decreasing payments.

The more exact, but more complicated, way of averaging annual operating costs need be used only when cost estimates can be made with precision and when the error introduced by the simple arithmetic averaging procedure affects significantly the accuracy of the economy study.

We previously noted that when capital recovery is calculated using the approximate method of straight-line depreciation plus average interest, the true annual costs are understated. We have just noted here that when an arithmetic average is used for costs which increase as the facility grows older, which is typically the case, the true costs are overstated. These two types of error thus tend to counterbalance each other in many economy studies.

Use of Uniform-gradient Conversion Factor. When costs such as maintenance are expected to increase in an approximately uniform manner throughout the life of an asset, the tables of the uniform-gradient conversion factor in the Appendix may be useful for computing the uniform equivalent annual cost. For example, if annual maintenance costs are expected to start at $1,000 a year during the first year of operation and then increase each year at a uniform rate of about $400 per year during the 15-year expected life of the asset, then, at 10 per cent interest, the uniform equivalent annual costs of maintenance will be

$$\$1,000 + \$400 \begin{pmatrix} \text{UGC} \\ i = 10\% \\ n = 15 \end{pmatrix} = \$1,000 + \$400(5.28) = \$3,112$$

Meaning of Equal Total Annual Costs. In interpreting the significance of differences in total-annual-cost comparisons of projects involving capital investments, we must be careful to understand the following meaning of the comparison. When the annual costs of performing a service are equal, we are earning that rate of return on the extra investment which we used in computing the annual interest cost. Thus, if we are considering the choice of investing $20,000 in a manually controlled punch press or $45,000 in a tape-controlled punch press, analysis discloses the following:

Manually controlled press:
Capital recovery, 6 years, 15% interest, 20,000(0.26424)........... $ 5,285
All affected operating costs.................................... 14,000
   Total.. $19,285

Tape-controlled press:
Capital recovery, 5 years, 15% interest, 45,000(0.29832)........... $13,424
All affected operating costs.................................... 5,860
   Total.. $19,284

This means that the savings in operating costs of using the tape-controlled machine just counterbalance the extra cost at 15 per cent interest of the extra investment of $25,000 in the tape-controlled machine. Thus, if we consider a 15 per cent return on investments as adequate, and no other considerations are involved, we should invest in the tape-controlled machine.

Multiple Interest Rates. When a person puts money in what he considers an investment with high risk, he expects a higher return than when he invests in a project in which he is very certain that he will receive the expected future returns. This means, then, that he may decide that he requires a 20 per cent return on the money he risks in alternative A and only a 10 per cent return if he adopts alternative B because the risk of loss is so much greater in alternative A.

Income Taxes. There is no simple, completely satisfactory way of taking income taxes into account explicitly in annual-cost comparisons. Our cost comparisons have, therefore, been made on a before-income-tax basis. Savings in operating costs which are translated into profits and gains or losses on disposal of fixed assets will, of course, be subject to income tax. The average amount of income tax can be calculated and the costs of the appropriate alternatives adjusted. In general, however, such a calculation will be complicated. (In rate-of-return determinations in Chapter 11, explicit account is taken of the effect of income taxes.)

The simple procedure in annual-cost comparisons is the one followed in this chapter of taking income taxes into account implicitly by setting the interest rate at a before-income-tax value. Thus, if an 8 per cent return is the minimum desired after income taxes and the company is paying 52 per cent of its income to the tax collector, the before-income-tax rate of return used in our annual-cost comparisons will be adjusted as follows to provide an 8 per cent return after income taxes:

$$(1.00 - 0.52)(\text{before-income-tax rate of return}) = 8.0\%$$

$$\text{Before-income-tax rate of return} = \frac{0.08}{1.00 - 0.52} = 16.7\%$$

PROBLEMS

1. The operator of an ice skating rink is considering the desirability of adding 5 weekday morning figure skating sessions for housewives to his present 16-session schedule of afternoon and evening sessions every day and morning sessions only on week-ends. He has conducted some research to determine the number of persons who would attend this morning session as well as the effect it will have on attendance at the other regular sessions. He estimates that the net increase in attendance will be 80 persons each weekday morning session who will pay $1.25 admission, for a total income of $100 per session. To run these extra five sessions, no additional investment in equipment or facilities is required. He estimates that all operating, administrative, and promotional costs for the 21 sessions would total $1,680 per week, or $80 per session. At the present time all costs for 16 sessions total $1,120 per week, or $70 per session. Should the weekday morning sessions be added?

2. You are the chief engineer of a company. One of your engineers has developed an improved design for a machine to perform the work presently performed by a Perna machine purchased 6 years ago. He presents the following analysis of relative economy of his newly designed machine to demonstrate that it should be installed in place of the Perna machine:

Perna machine:
First cost, $50,000
Depreciation charge per year, 10-year life, $5,000 per year
Age, 6 years
Book value, ($50,000 − $30,000), or $20,000
Resale value today, $5,000
Loss if sold today, $20,000 − $5,000, or $15,000
Annual costs:

Capital recovery, $20,000 $\left(\overset{CR}{\underset{n\,=\,2}{i\,=\,10\%}} \right)$ = $20,000(0.57619) $11,524

Direct labor. 20,000
Overhead at 100% of direct labor. 20,000

Total. $51,524

Improved design:
First cost, $60,000
Capital-recovery period, 10 years
No salvage value
10% return desired on investment
Annual costs:

Capital recovery, ($60,000 + $15,000*) $\left(\overset{CR}{\underset{n\,=\,10}{i\,=\,10\%}} \right)$ = $75,000(0.16275). $12,206

Interest on loan, $60,000 at 5% interest. 3,000
Depreciation, $\frac{60,000}{10}$ 6,000
Direct labor. 7,500
Overhead at 100% of direct labor. 7,500

Total. $36,206

* Book-value loss on sale of old machine.

Evaluate your engineer's economy analysis. What errors, if any, are made in this analysis? Separately justify each correction you make.

3. Ten years ago, $10,000 was paid to build a wooden storage shack. Today it is estimated to have another five years of useful life, after which its salvage value is expected to be negligible. Because of rising prices, an identical new shack would cost $12,000 today. A new steel shack, lasting 60 years, would cost $23,000. The sum of $3,000 has been offered for the lumber of the old shack. Using a minimum attractive rate of return of 10 per cent, an engineer has submitted the following analysis:

Keep old wooden shack:

Straight-line depreciation, $\frac{10,000}{15}$ . . . . $ 667

Average interest, $(10,000)\,(0.10)\left(\frac{16}{30}\right)$ 533

Average annual maintenance cost. 750

Total annual cost. $1,950

Build new wooden shack:

Straight-line depreciation, $\dfrac{12,000 - 3,000}{15}$ . . . . $ 600

Average interest, $(12,000 - 3,000)\,(0.10)\left(\frac{16}{30}\right)$ 480

Average annual maintenance cost. 650

Total annual cost. $1,730

Build new steel shack:

Straight-line depreciation, $\dfrac{23,000 - 3,000}{60}$ . . . . $ 333

Average interest, $(20,000)\,(0.10)\left(\frac{61}{120}\right)$ 1,030

Average annual maintenance cost. 350

Total annual cost. $1,713

Accepting the engineer's estimates (i.e., first cost, life, salvage values, maintenance costs, interest rate), do you agree with his comparisons? If you disagree, specifically state why, and give your corrected solution.

4. It has been suggested that periodic changes in production methods and operating procedures are desirable to increase personnel efficiency. These changes are recommended even if, as in the example cited in the text as an error in assuming different levels of efficiency, the proposed change lowers costs only because of an increase in personnel efficiency which should have been obtainable under the old system. The argument is that it is easier to persuade people to improve their work habits when a clean sweep is being made. Comment on this proposition.

5. A company is about to purchase a piece of chemical processing equipment. It has used two types of equipment for this process in the past. Type A costs $15,000, has a prospective life of 4 years, and no salvage value. Type B costs $25,000, has a prospective life of 6 years, and a $3,000 salvage value. Based upon past experience with these two types of equipment, the following operating and maintenance costs are anticipated:

Year of life	Type A	Type B
1	$2,000	$1,000
2	3,000	1,500
3	5,000	2,500
4	8,000	4,000
5	......	5,000
6	......	6,000

Using interest at 8 per cent and calculating capital recovery by the exact method, compare the desirability of the two types of equipment using annual costs.

6. Two pumping systems (one using gasoline and one electric power) are being considered for a requirement at a remote location. This service requirement is expected to last indefinitely. The gasoline pump will cost $3,500, has a life of 6 years, salvage value of $500, and annual operating and repair costs totaling $2,000 during the first year. The annual operating and maintenance costs are expected to be $300 higher in each succeeding year, reaching $3,500 for the sixth year. The electric pumping system will cost $12,000, has a life of 15 years, salvage value of $1,000, and annual operating and maintenance costs totaling $1,000 in the first year and increasing by $150 each year, reaching $3,100 for the 15th year. Using interest at 10% and capital-recovery calculations by the exact method, compare the equivalent annual costs of the two pumping systems.

7. You are considering whether to purchase a facility costing $50,000 or one costing $80,000 to perform a required service. Both facilities will give you the same quality and duration of service and both will provide the required capacity. Using the required interest rate of 8 per cent, you calculate annual costs using exact methods and find that they are equal. Which facility should you choose? Explain your reasoning.

8. A refinery can provide for water storage with a steel tank on a steel tower adjacent to the plant or a concrete standpipe on a hill some distance away. The elevated tank is estimated to cost $82,000, while the standpipe and extra length of service line is estimated to cost $60,000. The standpipe installation will require an additional capital expenditure of $6,000 for pumps and controls. Operating and maintenance costs for the pumps and standpipe are estimated at $500 per year. The maintenance cost of the elevated tank is estimated to be $150 per year. Using an interest rate of 5 per cent, a life of 30 years, and assuming no salvage value, compute the equivalent annual cost for each plan, using the exact method.

9. An engineering firm is considering the purchase of dictation recording equipment. The equipment consists of five recorders and one transcriber, each of which costs $400, carries an estimated maintenance charge of 5 per cent per year, has a life expectancy of 10 years, and has no salvage value. The recorders will be used by five engineers, each of whom dictates an average of 500 letters per year. The average letter requires 5 minutes to dictate, either to a stenographer or to the recorder, and 10 minutes to transcribe and type, either from

notes or from the transcriber. Assume the total cost for time at $6 per hour for an engineer and $3 per hour for stenographic work, the cost of recording media at 1 cent per letter, and interest at 12 per cent. Would it be advisable for the firm to purchase the equipment? Show all calculations.

10. In the planning of a state police radio system, it is desired to maintain a specified minimum signal strength at all points in the state. Two plans for accomplishing this are proposed for comparison. Plan I involves the establishment of six transmitting stations of low power. The investment at each of these in buildings, ground improvements, piping, and tower, all assumed to have a life of 25 years, is estimated as $35,000. The investment in transmitting equipment for each station—assumed, because of the probability of obsolescence, to have a life of 8 years—is estimated at $25,000. The monthly disbursements for operation of each station are estimated as $1,050. Plan II involves the establishment of only two transmitting stations of much higher power. The investment in buildings, etc., at each of these stations is estimated as $45,000, and the useful life of these facilities is estimated at 25 years. The investment in transmitting equipment at each station is estimated as $220,-000, and the life of this equipment is estimated as 8 years. The monthly operating cost is established as $1,400 per station. Using 6 per cent interest, compare the annual costs of these plans using (a) straight-line depreciation plus average interest, (b) exact capital recovery.

11. It is desired to determine whether to use no insulation or to use insulation 1 inch thick or 2 inches thick on a steam pipe. The heat loss from this pipe without insulation would cost $1.50 per year per foot of pipe. A 1-inch insulation will eliminate 89 per cent of the loss and will cost $0.40 per foot. A 2-inch insulation will eliminate 92 per cent of the loss and will cost $0.85 per foot. Using an interest rate of 10 per cent, compare the annual costs per 1,000 feet with no insulation and with the two thicknesses of insulation, using a life of 10 years for the insulation with no salvage value. Use (a) straight-line depreciation and average interest, (b) exact-capital-recovery calculation.

12. To undertake production of a new product, an inventor purchased a simple machine that required much hand labor. The machine cost $4,400 and was estimated to have a useful life of 5 years, at the end of which there would be no salvage value. Annual operating and maintenance costs, exclusive of depreciation and interest, were $2,600. At the end of the first year he was urged to purchase a semiautomatic machine for $6,200, which could match production of the first machine and which would have an annual operating and maintenance cost, exclusive of depreciation and interest, of $800. Trade-in value of the first machine on the new machine would be $1,600. The new machine is estimated to have a life of 4 years and no salvage value. Using an interest rate of 8 per cent, calculate the difference in equivalent annual cost for the two machines, using the exact method and state whether the one-year-old machine should be replaced.

13. Two possible routes for a power line are under consideration. Route A is around a lake, 15 miles in length. The first cost will be $6,000 per mile, the yearly maintenance will be $2,000 per mile, and there will be a salvage value at the end of 15 years of $3,000 per mile. Route B is a submarine cable across the lake, 5 miles long. The first cost will be $31,000 per mile, the annual upkeep $400 per mile, and the salvage value at the end of 15 years will be $6,000 per mile. The yearly power loss will be $550 per mile for both routes.

Interest rate is 6 per cent, annual taxes are 3 per cent of the first cost. Compare the two routes on the basis of annual costs, using (a) straight-line depreciation plus average interest, (b) capital recovery by the exact method.

14. A flood has demonstrated that the drainage structure of a certain area is not adequate. In planning the improvement, three possible courses are considered: (1) Leave an existing undamaged 24-inch corrugated steel culvert in place and install another of the same size alongside. (Assume the existing culvert has a remaining life of 20 years.) (2) Remove the above-mentioned 24-inch culvert and replace it with a single 36-inch culvert. (3) Remove the above-mentioned culvert and replace it with a reinforced concrete culvert of adequate cross section. The present 24-inch pipe has a salvage value of $300. Estimates of the new installation have been made as shown below:

	24-inch	36-inch	Concrete
Cost of pipes, delivered....	$750.00	$1,500.00	
Installation cost..........	375.00	525.00	$2,100.00
Estimated life............	20 yr	20 yr	40 yr

Interest is charged at 5 per cent annually. Assume replacement costs of the 24- and 36-inch steel culverts 20 years hence to be the same as today's costs. Determine the relative economy of the three possible courses of action. (a) Compare the annual costs of the three alternatives using straight-line depreciation and average interest. (b) Compare the annual costs of the three alternatives calculating capital recovery by the exact method. (c) Evaluate the significance of the differences in the two comparisons, (a) and (b).

Note: Problems 8 through 14 have been adapted from professional engineers' examinations.

10 Present-worth and Premium-worth Comparisons

To compare proposed alternative investments by the present-worth method, we compute the discounted present worths of future revenues and costs.

Comparing the Present Worth of Future Costs. When comparing two alternative methods of performing a required service, the present worths of the costs using each of the methods for a given number of years are computed. These furnish a measure of how much money the firm would theoretically have to set aside now to provide for the future services under each of the respective methods. The monies which are theoretically set aside are assumed to earn interest at the rate which was used in discounting the future expenditures.

We have two possible methods of performing a metal-forming operation required in the manufacture of a new product. One will require the purchase of machine A for $6,000 and the expenditure of $5,000 per year in operating costs. The machine has an estimated life of 15 years, with a salvage value of $1,000. The other method will require the purchase of machine B for $10,000. Machine B has an estimated life of 10 years and no salvage value. Operating costs for machine B are estimated at $3,000 per year.

In making present-worth comparisons, we must provide for the same number of years of future service in all the alternatives. The shortest period we can use is the least common multiple of the lives of the assets. In this case, it is expected that the services of the machines will be required for at least 30 years, which is the least common multiple of the asset lives.

Determination of the proper interest rate to use in cost comparisons is discussed in another chapter of this book. In no case should the interest rate used for discounting the prospective future expenditures under each alternative be lower than the minimum rate of return (before income taxes) at which the company will invest its funds in projects of comparable risk. In our present illustration, let us use a 6 per cent rate of return.

Machine A:

Cost of original machine.................................... $ 6,000

Present worth of cost of replacement machine at end of year 15,

$$(\$6,000 - \$1,000)* \left(\begin{array}{c} \text{SPPW} \\ i = 6\% \\ n = 15 \end{array} \right) = \$5,000(0.4173) = \quad 2,087$$

Present worth of operating costs for 30 years,

$$\$5,000 \left(\begin{array}{c} \text{USPW} \\ i = 6\% \\ n = 30 \end{array} \right) = \$5,000(13.765) = \quad 68,825$$

$$\overline{\$76,912}$$

Less, Present worth of salvage value at end of year 30,

$$\$1,000 \left(\begin{array}{c} \text{SPPW} \\ i = 6\% \\ n = 30 \end{array} \right) = \$1,000(0.1741) = \quad -174$$

Total.. $\overline{\$76,738}$

Machine B:

Cost of original machine.................................... $10,000

Present worth of cost of replacement machine at end of year 10,

$$\$10,000 \left(\begin{array}{c} \text{SPPW} \\ i = 6\% \\ n = 10 \end{array} \right) = \$10,000(0.5584) = \quad 5,584$$

Present worth of cost of replacement machine at end of year 20,

$$\$10,000 \left(\begin{array}{c} \text{SPPW} \\ i = 6\% \\ n = 20 \end{array} \right) = \$10,000(0.3118) = \quad 3,118$$

Present worth of operating costs for 30 years,

$$\$3,000 \left(\begin{array}{c} \text{USPW} \\ i = 6\% \\ n = 30 \end{array} \right) = \$3,000(13.765) = \quad 41,295$$

Total.. $\overline{\$59,997}$

If the expected requirement for the services of the machines were only 10 years, the comparison would be restricted to the present worth of the costs of 10 years' service. It is anticipated that Machine A would have a salvage value of $1,500 at the end of 10 years. The present-worth cost comparison would then be as follows:

Machine A:

Cost of original machine.................................... $ 6,000

Present worth of operating cost for 10 years,

$$\$5,000 \left(\begin{array}{c} \text{USPW} \\ i = 6\% \\ n = 10 \end{array} \right) = \$5,000(7.360) = \quad 36,800$$

Less, Present worth of salvage value at end of 10 years,

$$\$1,500 \left(\begin{array}{c} \text{SPPW} \\ i = 6\% \\ n = 10 \end{array} \right) = \$1,500(0.5884) = \quad -883$$

Total.. $\overline{\$41,917}$

---

* The expenditure for the new machine is $6,000 minus the $1,000 salvage value on the old machine.

Machine B:

Cost of original machine.. $10,000

Present worth of operating costs for 10 years,

$$\$3,000 \left(\begin{array}{c} \text{USPW} \\ i = 6\% \\ n = 10 \end{array} \right) = \$3,000(7.360) = \quad 22,080$$

Total... $32,080

Capitalized-cost Comparisons. When it is anticipated that a service will be required indefinitely into the future, the calculation of the present worth of the cost of perpetual service (capitalized cost) may be appropriate. This type of situation may be applicable in utility and governmental investments where anticipated service requirements are frequently long and the assets are frequently long-lived.

We can make a capitalized-cost comparison using the previous problem as follows:

Machine A:

Cost of original machine... $ 6,000

Present worth of infinite number of renewals of machine,

$$\$5,000 \left(\begin{array}{c} \text{SFP} \\ i = 6\% \\ n = 15 \end{array} \right) \left(\frac{1}{i} \right) = \$5,000(0.04296)\left(\frac{1}{0.06}\right) = \quad 3,580$$

Given S
Find R

Present worth of perpetual operating costs, $\quad \$5,000 \left(\frac{1}{0.06}\right) = \quad 83,333$

Total... $92,913

Machine B:

Cost of original machine... $10,000

Present worth of infinite series of renewals of machine,

$$\$10,000 \left(\begin{array}{c} \text{SFP} \\ i = 6\% \\ n = 10 \end{array} \right) \left(\frac{1}{i} \right) = \$10,000(0.07587)\left(\frac{1}{0.06}\right) = \quad 12,645$$

Present worth of perpetual operating costs, $\quad \$3,000 \left(\frac{1}{0.06}\right) = \quad 50,000$

Total... $72,645

The use of present-worth and capitalized-cost computations for purposes of comparing alternative investment proposals is usually not as effective as some of the other methods discussed in this book. Managers and engineers are more accustomed to think in terms of annual costs and rates of return than in terms of present worth of future costs. It is usually more difficult to understand the significance of present-worth comparisons than annual-cost or rate-of-return determinations. Present-worth and capitalized-cost comparisons should, therefore, be used only in specialized situations in which they are particularly advantageous.

Premium-worth Determination. We can compare the prospective annual revenues and costs of a project, including capital recovery and interest charges as costs, at the minimum acceptable rate. Then, the excess of revenues over costs will represent an extra profit above the minimum return required to justify the investment. This can be considered extra profits. The present worth of these extra profits can be used as a measure of the desirability of the proposed venture.

We are considering investing $200,000 in a project which will return the following estimated earnings (revenues minus cost, not including the interest or return of capital) in the future and have no salvage value at the end of six years.

Year	Income less cash expenses
1	$40,000
2	60,000
3	80,000
4	80,000
5	80,000
6	55,000

We can evaluate this investment opportunity by computing a uniform capital-recovery charge for the six years at the minimum acceptable return of 15 per cent and subtracting this charge from the earnings each year. The capital-recovery cost is

$$\$200,000 \left(\begin{array}{c} \text{CR} \\ i = 15\% \\ n = 6 \end{array} \right) = \$200,000(0.26424) = \$52,848$$

We then compute the present worth of these future extra total profits (over and above our minimum return) using the minimum return of 15 per cent as the discount rate, as shown in Table 10-1.

Table 10-1. **Calculation of Present Worth of Future Extra Profits**

Year	Income less cash expenses	Capital-recovery cost	Extra total profits	SPPW	Present worth of extra profits
1	$40,000	$52,848	$ −12,848	0.8696	$ −11,173
2	60,000	52,848	7,152	0.7561	5,408
3	80,000	52,848	27,152	0.6575	17,852
4	80,000	52,848	27,152	0.5718	15,526
5	80,000	52,848	27,152	0.4972	13,500
6	55,000	52,848	2,152	0.4323	930
Total	....	....	....	......	$ 42,043

This present worth of the extra profits (premium worth) can be used as a profitability measure. It tells us how much added investment we would require to obtain the same total future returns if our investment earned only the minimum return. It can thus be considered a bonus investment.

We could also have computed this premium worth of the extra profits by computing the present worth of the income less cash expenses and then subtracting the investment from this present worth. This is shown in Table 10-2.

Table 10-2. Calculation of Present Worth of Future Extra Profits

Year	Income less cash expenses	SPPW	Present worth of income less cash expenses
1	$40,000	0.8696	$ 34,784
2	60,000	0.7561	45,366
3	80,000	0.6575	52,600
4	80,000	0.5718	45,744
5	80,000	0.4972	39,776
6	55,000	0.4323	23,776
			$242,046
Investment..	....	......	−200,000
Total.......	....	......	$ 42,046

Premium-worth Percentage. When comparing the present worths of the extra profits of various proposals, we find it difficult to evaluate these bonus worths because they are produced by investments of varying sizes. We can compute a relative profitability measure by dividing the bonus investment by the actual investment. This gives us a bonus-investment percentage which may be useful for comparative evaluation purposes.

For the investment we are currently considering, the calculation is as follows:

$$\text{Premium-worth percentage} = \frac{\text{bonus investment}}{\text{actual investment}}$$
$$= \frac{\$42,046}{\$200,000} = 21\%$$

Valuation of Future Income by Discounting. If two people each promise to pay me $6,000 five years from now, how much is each of these promises worth to me today?

If the financial resources and the integrity of each of these persons are similar, then I would assess that the risks of not being paid are almost equal. To value each of these promises, I would first have to decide what return I required to invest my money in proposals in which the risk of future nonpayment is comparable to these risks. In this decision I would consider the return I can obtain by other investment of my money at this time. Let us assume that I decide that I would be satisfied with a 6 per cent return on this type of low-risk investment. Then I would value each of these promises at their present worth, using 6 per cent interest,

$$\$6,000 \left(\begin{matrix} \text{SPPW} \\ i = 6\% \\ n = 5 \end{matrix} \right) = \$6,000(0.7473) = \$4,484$$

Assume, however, that the financial resources of one of these persons are decidedly less than the other. I, therefore, adjudge the risk of failure to make payment five years from now to be distinctly higher in one case than in the other. I may require a prospective 10 per cent return for investments with the higher level of risk. Then, the present worth of this more risky promise would be

$$\$6,000 \left(\begin{matrix} \text{SPPW} \\ i = 10\% \\ n = 5 \end{matrix} \right) = \$6,000(0.6209) = \$3,725$$

I place a lower present value on this more risky promise.

Thus, the more risk that a future revenue will not materialize, the higher should be the interest rate used when discounting the expected future revenue to value its present worth.

Valuation of Bonds. Valuation of bonds is a case of valuation of future income. Corporation bonds are promises to pay the principal of the bonds at a given date in the future and to pay interest until then at a given rate. The interest is usually paid semiannually. Thus, a $1,000 5 per cent bond issued on July 1, 1960, and due on July 1, 1975, will pay $25 interest every six months for 15 years and $1,000 at the end of the period.

If you are considering the purchase of this bond immediately after the July 1, 1962, interest payment, how much should you be willing to pay for it if you decided that your investment should yield a 6 per cent return (compounded semiannually)?

To answer this question, you discount the returns of the remaining 13 years before the redemption of the bonds at 6 per cent interest compounded semiannually.

Present worth of 26 remaining interest payments,

$$\$25 \left(\begin{matrix} \text{USPW} \\ i = 3\% \\ n = 26 \end{matrix} \right) = \$25(17.877) = \qquad\qquad \$447$$

Present worth of $1,000 principal repayment,

$$\$1,000 \left(\begin{matrix} \text{SPPW} \\ i = 3\% \\ n = 26 \end{matrix} \right) = \$1,000(0.4637) = \qquad\qquad \underline{464}$$

Bond value = $911

PROBLEMS

1. A tool manufacturing company is considering the purchase of a new lathe. A semiautomatic lathe will cost $10,000 and can be operated for $6,000 per year. A fully automatic lathe will cost $16,000 and can be operated for $4,000 per year. The semiautomatic machine has an estimated life of 12 years, with a $1,000 salvage value, and the fully automatic machine has an estimated life of 8 years with no salvage value. Average annual taxes are estimated as 2 per cent of first cost. Average annual insurance costs are estimated to be 1 per cent of the cost of the machine, plus 3 per cent of the operating cost of the fully automatic lathe, and 5 per cent of the operating cost of the semiautomatic lathe. Compare the cost of the two lathes, using the present-worth method with interest at 8 per cent.

2. A town wishes to build a new town hall and a public works garage on the same site. The town board asks you to evaluate two plans for construction. Plan A calls for the construction of the town hall now and the construction of a separate garage at the end of 8 years. Each structure will cost $250,000. Plan B involves the construction of one facility now, at the cost of $350,000 to serve both purposes. Both plans will meet anticipated requirements and will provide the same capacity and services after the 8th year. The buildings will be usable for about 50 years from the present in both cases. Maintenance costs are estimated for plan A at $6,000 per year for the first 8 years and $20,000 per year thereafter. For plan B, maintenance costs are estimated at $30,000 per year throughout the period. Compute the present worth of each plan, using interest at 4 per cent, and state which is more economical.

3. A municipality is considering whether to build a wooden or a steel bridge over a stream which passes through the town. The wooden trestle costing $30,000 would have an estimated life of 20 years. A steel bridge, costing $100,000 would have an estimated life of 75 years. Annual maintenance costs will average $2,000 for the wooden trestle and $1,000 on the steel bridge. What is the capitalized cost of perpetual service for each alternative using 5 per cent interest?

4. Mr. Warren is considering the purchase of a 10 per cent interest in a venture for $250,000. The venture is expected to produce the following returns to the investors and Mr. Warren would receive 10 per cent of the amounts shown:

End of year	Amount
1	$ 500,000
2	1,500,000
3	2,500,000
4	1,250,000

The venture will be liquidated after the fourth year with no additional return to the investor. Considering the risks of the venture, alternative uses to which he can put his investment funds, and the amounts of money he has available for investment, he has decided that he should receive a minimum return of at least 20 per cent.

    a. What is the premium worth of this potential investment?

    b. What is the premium-worth percentage?

5. How much should you be willing to pay for a $1,000 bond yielding 5 per cent interest, paid semiannually, if the bond becomes due in 15 years and you desire an 8 per cent return on your investment?

6. A section of roadway pavement costs $400 a year to maintain. What expenditure for a new pavement is justified if no maintenance will be required for the first 5 years, $100 per year for the next 10 years, and $400 a year thereafter? Assume money to cost 5 per cent.

7. The owner of a quarry signs a contract to sell his stone on the following basis: The purchaser is to remove the stone from certain portions of the pit according to a fixed schedule of volume, price, and time. The contract is to run 17 years, as follows: 7 years excavating a total of 20,000 yards per year at 10 cents per yard; the remaining 10 years excavating a total of 50,000 yards per year at 15 cents per yard. On the basis of equal year-end payments during each period by the purchaser, what is the present worth of the pit to the owner on the basis of 5% interest?

8. A company is licensed to manufacture a patented article on which the patent has 7 years to run. The company makes 7,500 pieces per year and pays the inventor $100 per year, plus 5 cents per piece. The inventor offers to sell the patent for $3,000. If a return of 6 per cent is desired on the investment, will it pay the company to buy the patent?

Note: Problems 6 through 8 are adapted from professional engineers' examinations.

11 Determination of Rate of Return

In the annual cost and present-worth methods for comparing alternative investment proposals, an acceptable rate of return must be specified before a comparison can be made. In the rate-of-return approach, which will be discussed in this chapter, we calculate this prospective rate of return and then decide whether it is high enough to justify the investment.

Capital Investment with No Depreciation on Investment. The possibility of investing some of your funds in the purchase and operation of a parking lot has come to your attention. This would require $50,000 for the land and $5,000 for working capital (cash, accounts receivable, etc.) a total investment of $55,000. Operating and other expenses are estimated at $12,500 and income at $20,000 per year.

We can analyze this possible investment as follows:

$$\begin{array}{ll} \text{Income} & \$20,000 \\ \text{Expenses} & \underline{12,500} \\ \text{Net income} & \$\ 7,500 \end{array}$$

$$\text{Rate of return on investment} = \frac{\$7,500}{\$55,000} = 13.6\%$$

Thus, the apparent rate of return on this investment is 13.6 per cent. This return is before income taxes.

Actual Rate of Return on Investment. The actual rate of return which you will receive from this investment of $55,000 will be definitely determined only after you have operated the parking lot for as many years as you own it and then sell it for whatever sum it will bring. Until this has been done, all we can do is conjecture. In our analysis, we have conjectured a net income of $7,500 per year and either perpetual ownership and operation or a sale of the land at the same price as was paid for it.

Let us move several years ahead and assume that the parking lot was operated for four years with the following financial results and the land was then sold for $60,000.

Year	Income	Expenses	Net income
1	$19,000	$12,000	$7,000
2	20,000	12,500	7,500
3	21,000	11,500	9,500
4	20,000	12,000	8,000

What return did you actually earn on your investment of $55,000 in the parking lot?

To answer this question we need one additional piece of information. How much money, if any, did you withdraw or receive from the business each year?

Year	Withdrawals from business
1	$5,500
2	7,500
3	8,500
4	8,000

Thus, in return for your investment of $55,000, you received $5,500 the first year (leaving $1,500 of that year's net income in the business to increase the working capital to $6,500), $7,500 the second year, $8,500 the third year, and $75,500 the fourth year [$60,000 from the sale of the land, $8,000 in withdrawals from the business, and the $7,500 of working capital when the parking lot business was disposed of on sale of the land (original $5,000 plus $1,500 from the first year plus $1,000 from the third year].

We want to determine the interest rate which will give these returns for an investment of $55,000. Let us start by assuming as a first guess that this interest rate is 15 per cent. If 15 per cent is the correct interest rate, if I invested $55,000 at 15 per cent I should be able to withdraw the sums stated above in the indicated years. In other words, at 15 per cent interest, $55,000 would be equivalent to those future sums, and the present worths of those future sums at 15 per cent interest would be equal to $55,000. Let us see if the present worths at 15 per cent interest are actually equal to $55,000. (For simplicity, we are assuming that all payments were made at the end of the year. The error introduced by this assumption is small.)

Year	Receipts	SPPW	Present worth of receipt
1	$ 5,500	0.8696	$ 4,783
2	7,500	0.7561	5,671
3	8,500	0.6575	5,589
4	75,500	0.5718	43,171
Total	. . . .	. . . . . .	$59,214

This calculation shows that if we had invested $59,214 at 15 per cent interest we could have withdrawn the stated sums. Since we invested only $55,000, we obviously received a return greater than 15 per cent on our investment.

Let us next try 20 per cent.

Year	Receipts	SPPW	Present worth of receipt
1	$ 5,500	0.8333	$ 4,583
2	7,500	0.6944	5,208
3	8,500	0.5787	4,919
4	75,500	0.4823	36,414
Total	. . . .	. . . . . .	$51,124

These calculations show that if we had invested $51,124 at 20% interest we could have withdrawn the stated sums. Since we invested more than $51,124, we received a lower return.

The return is thus greater than 15 per cent and less than 20 per cent. We can obtain a close approximation by linear interpolation.

Let x = the actual rate of return on the investment.

$$\frac{59,214 - 55,000}{59,214 - 51,124} = \frac{15 - x}{15 - 20}$$

$$\frac{4,214}{8,090} = \frac{15 - x}{-5}$$

$$x = 17.6\%$$

Here we have, of course, calculated rates of return before income taxes.

Apparent Annual Rate of Return on Invested Business Capital. The question of how much a business is earning on its invested capital is different from the question we just answered. This can be determined each year or more frequently by dividing the profits of the business by its invested capital at the time. In the case of the parking lot, the capital invested in the business each year changed with the earnings and withdrawals. The calculation of annual rates of return is illustrated in Table 11-1. We have calculated the apparent annual rates of return before income taxes.

Table 11-1. Calculation of Apparent Annual Rates of Return on Parking-lot Investment

Year	Net income	Withdrawals from business	Retained earnings	Investment in business at end of year	Apparent annual rate of return*
0	. . . . . .	. . . . . .	. . . . . .	$55,000	
1	$7,000	$5,500	$1,500	56,500	12.7%
2	7,500	7,500	. . . . . .	56,500	13.3
3	9,500	8,500	1,000	57,500	16.8
4	8,000	8,000	. . . . . .	57,500	13.9

* Net income as a percentage of investment at beginning of year (end of previous year).

Apparent Rates of Return on a Depreciating-asset Investment.
Mr. Daniels invested $10,000 in a machine which has an estimated average
life of five years. He then rented the machine to a manufacturing company. The company paid all expenses in connection with the use and
operation of the machine. The rental during the first two years was set
at $3,000 per year and was negotiated at the beginning of each succeeding
year as follows: $2,800 during the third year, $2,800 the fourth year,
$2,500 the fifth year, $1,500 the sixth year, $500 the seventh year. The
machine is now too old for use by the company (repair costs are getting
out of line). Mr. Daniels, after some indecision, sells it during the
eighth year for $500.

Mr. Daniels' apparent rates of return on this investment are shown in
Table 11-2. Straight-line depreciation of the cost of the machine is used
with a five-year life. Mr. Daniels is in the 40 per cent income tax bracket.

**Table 11-2. Calculation of Apparent Rates of Return
on a Depreciating-asset Investment**

Year	Income	Depreciation expenses*	Profit	Profit after 40% income tax	Book value or unrecovered investment (at beginning of year)	Apparent rate of return
1	$3,000	$2,000	$1,000	$600	$10,000	6%
2	3,000	2,000	1,000	600	8,000	$7\frac{1}{2}$
3	2,800	2,000	800	480	6,000	8
4	2,800	2,000	800	480	4,000	12
5	2,500	2,000	500	300	2,000	15
6	1,500	0	1,500	900	0	Infinite
7	500	0	500	300	0	Infinite
8	500	0	500	400†	0	Infinite

* Mr. Daniels has no cash expenses in connection with the machine because they
are all borne by the company.

† The $500 from the sale of the machine which has been fully depreciated is taxed
as if it were a capital gain at half the normal rates.

The total cash returns each year are calculated in Table 11-3. We can
now compute the actual rate of return on the $10,000 investment by trial-
and-error determination of the interest rate which will equate the cash
returns shown in Table 11-3 with a present sum of $10,000. By linear
interpolation between 10 and 12 per cent, this rate of return is found to be
approximately 11.26 per cent.

The two examples of apparent rates of return presented here indicate
that apparent rates of return do not have any rational relationship to
prospective rates of return or to the rates of return which are actually
received on an investment. They illustrate the kind of incongruous results

we can obtain with apparent rates of return when we are using depreciating assets.

Table 11-3. Calculation of Actual Rate of Return on a Depreciating-asset Investment

Year	Income	Depreciation expenses	Profit	Profit after 40% income tax	Total cash return	SPPW 10%	Present worth of cash returns, 10% interest	SPPW 12%	Present worth of cash returns, 12% interest
1	$3,000	$2,000	$1,000	$600	$2,600	0.9091	$ 2,364	0.8929	$2,322
2	3,000	2,000	1,000	600	2,600	0.8264	2,149	0.7972	2,073
3	2,800	2,000	800	480	2,480	0.7513	1,863	0.7118	1.765
4	2,800	2,000	800	480	2,480	0.6830	1,694	0.6355	1.576
5	2,500	2,000	500	300	2,300	0.6209	1,428	0.5674	1,305
6	1,500	0	1,500	900	900	0.5645	508	0.5066	456
7	500	0	500	300	300	0.5132	154	0.4523	136
8	500	0	500	400	400	0.4665	187	0.4039	162
							$10,347		$9,795

Linear interpolation for rate of return:

$$\frac{10{,}347 - 10{,}000}{10{,}347 - 9{,}795} = \frac{10 - x}{10 - 12}$$

$$x = 11.26\%$$

Investment in Laborsaving Facility. The Ara Manufacturing Company is considering the purchase of a newly developed machine which will substitute for a hand-polishing operation. It will cost $18,000 and, based on forecasted volume of operations, will produce an estimated net saving of $6,000 per year in labor and supplies. The estimated expected life of the machine is six years. What is the prospective rate of return on the $18,000 investment?

By investing $18,000 now, we expect to receive (in savings) $6,000 a year for six years. What interest rate will equate these sums?

$$\$18{,}000 = \$6{,}000 \left(\begin{array}{c} \text{USPW} \\ i = ? \\ n = 6 \end{array} \right)$$

$$\left(\begin{array}{c} \text{USPW} \\ i = ? \\ n = 6 \end{array} \right) = \frac{\$18{,}000}{\$6{,}000} = 3.00$$

We can now refer to the uniform-series present-worth interest chart of the Appendix and estimate the interest rate by visual interpolation as 24 per cent. We can get a slightly more accurate approximation by linear interpolation from the tables, but, considering the possible errors and uncertainties of estimating and forecasting, it is not worth the effort.

In this case, we would interpolate to find the interest rate from the values in the 25 and 20 per cent tables. The interpolated value is 24.3 per cent. An exact solution, using the formula, is definitely not worth the effort.

Return on a Bond Investment. I am offered a 5 per cent $1,000 bond due 14 years from now for $900. What is my expected return on this investment? (Interest is paid semiannually, which is a common procedure on corporate bonds. This bond, therefore, will pay $25 interest every six months, with the return of the $1,000 principal at the end of the 14 years.)

If I were to pay $1,000 for the bond, my rate of return would obviously be 5 per cent compounded semiannually. However, since I am paying less, my return is greater.

If I were to receive a 6 per cent return, I would pay only the present worth of the future interest and principal payments at 6 per cent interest.

$$\$25 \left(\begin{array}{c} \text{USPW} \\ i = 3\% \\ n = 28 \end{array} \right) + \$1,000 \left(\begin{array}{c} \text{SPPW} \\ i = 3\% \\ n = 28 \end{array} \right)$$

$$\$25(18.764) + \$1,000(0.4371) = \$906.20$$

If I were to receive an 8 per cent return, I would pay the present worth of the future interest and principal payments at 8 per cent interest.

$$\$25 \left(\begin{array}{c} \text{USPW} \\ i = 4\% \\ n = 28 \end{array} \right) + \$1,000 \left(\begin{array}{c} \text{SPPW} \\ i = 4\% \\ n = 28 \end{array} \right)$$

$$\$25(16.663) + \$1,000(0.3335) = \$750.08$$

The interest rate which I will earn if I hold the bond to maturity is the rate which will make the $25 semiannual interest payments and the $1,000 principal payment equal to a present payment of $900. The rate of 6 per cent does not discount the future payments enough and is, therefore, too low; and 8 per cent discounts the future payments too much and is, therefore, too high. Interpolating to find the approximate rate which will equate the present worth of these future receipts to $900, we arrive at 6.08 per cent. An exact answer to this type of problem can be obtained from bond-yield tables. Also, this solution is for rate of return before income taxes.

Expected Return on Speculative Land Investment. I purchase a parcel of land for $20,000 with the expectation that it will more than double in value in five years, at which time I plan on selling it for approximately $50,000. After paying sales commissions and legal and other expenses totaling $6\frac{2}{3}$ per cent, I should net $46,667. Real estate taxes on the parcel are $720 a year; I anticipate no other expenses or income. What is my expected after-tax return on the $20,000 investment?

My investment consists of $20,000 now plus $720 at the end of each year for five years. The $720 real estate tax is an allowable deduction from taxable income on my income tax return. Since I am in the 50 per cent tax bracket, this $720 expense is reduced by $360. The present worth of my total investment is, therefore,

$$\$20{,}000 + (\$720 - \$360) \begin{pmatrix} \text{USPW} \\ i = ? \\ n = 5 \end{pmatrix} = \$20{,}000 + \$360 \begin{pmatrix} \text{USPW} \\ i = ? \\ n = 5 \end{pmatrix}$$

As previously noted, I expect to receive $46,667 in five years for this parcel. The capital-gains tax will reduce the net cash receipt by 25 per cent of the capital gain (see Chapter 8). The capital gain is

$$\$46{,}667 - \$20{,}000 = \$26{,}667$$

The capital-gains tax equals 25 per cent of $26,667, or $6,667. The net amount I will receive after capital-gains tax is thus $40,000. What interest rate will make my total investment equivalent to $40,000 five years hence?

$$\left[\$20{,}000 + \$360 \begin{pmatrix} \text{USPW} \\ i = ? \\ n = 5 \end{pmatrix} \right] \left[\begin{matrix} \text{SPCA} \\ i = ? \\ n = 5 \end{matrix} \right] = \$40{,}000$$

We can now solve this equation or we can put it in more convenient form for trial-and-error approximate solution by linear interpolation.

$$\$20{,}000 + \$360 \begin{pmatrix} \text{USPW} \\ i = ? \\ n = 5 \end{pmatrix} = \$40{,}000 \begin{pmatrix} \dfrac{1}{\text{SPCA}} \\ i = ? \\ n = 5 \end{pmatrix}$$

$$\$20{,}000 + \$360 \begin{pmatrix} \text{USPW} \\ i = ? \\ n = 5 \end{pmatrix} = \$40{,}000 \begin{pmatrix} \text{SPPW} \\ i = ? \\ n = 5 \end{pmatrix}$$

In this last form, we have the present worth of the investment equated to the present worth of the expected revenues. In other words, that interest rate which will make the present worth of $40,000 five years from now equal to the present worth of the investments is the expected rate of return.

As a first guess, we may look at the SPCA column of the interest tables and see what interest rate will double our money in five years. We know, of course, that our expected rate of return is less than this because of the real estate taxes we must pay each year. In the 15 per cent interest table, SPCA at five years is 2.011. Therefore, let us try 15 per cent. Solving,

$$\$40{,}000 \begin{pmatrix} \text{SPPW} \\ i = 15\% \\ n = 5 \end{pmatrix} - \$20{,}000 - \$360 \begin{pmatrix} \text{USPW} \\ i = 15\% \\ n = 5 \end{pmatrix} \overset{?}{=} 0$$

$$\$40{,}000(0.4972) - \$20{,}000 - \$360(3.352) \overset{?}{=} 0$$

$$-\$1{,}318.72 \neq 0$$

This calculation shows that the present worth of the $40,000 future return has been discounted at too high an interest rate when $i = 15\%$ is used.

Let us now try 12 per cent.

$$\$40,000 \begin{pmatrix} \text{SPPW} \\ i = 12\% \\ n = 5 \end{pmatrix} - \$20,000 - \$360 \begin{pmatrix} \text{USPW} \\ i = 12\% \\ n = 5 \end{pmatrix} \overset{?}{=} 0$$

$$\$40,000(0.5674) - \$20,000 - \$360(3.605) \overset{?}{=} 0$$
$$+\$1,398.20 \neq 0$$

This calculation shows that the present worth of the $40,000 future return has been discounted at too low an interest rate when $i = 12\%$ is used. The interest rate which will solve this equation and give us the rate of return is between 12 and 15 per cent. Since we have no tables in between these two values, we use linear interpolation to obtain our solution of 13.5 per cent. We can also use a graphic interpolation for successively narrowing the estimate and interpolating for the approximate solution, as shown in Figure 11-1.

Return on Extra Investment—Cost-saving Facility. We are considering the relative economy of two machines which are designed to perform exactly the same required service. One machine requires a larger investment than the other, but requires lower operating costs. We can consider this as a problem of determining whether or not the extra investment in the more expensive machine is worthwhile. Our decision criterion can then be the adequacy of the rate of return earned on the extra investment.

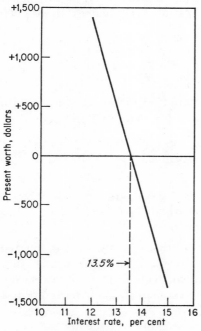

Figure 11-1. Estimation of interest rate by graphic linear interpolation.

On page 133 we made an annual-cost comparison between a manually controlled punch press costing $20,000 and a tape-controlled one costing $45,000. Using 15 per cent interest we found that the annual costs were the same for the tape-controlled as for the manually controlled press. This meant that the costs of the extra investment of $25,000 (interest and return of capital) were provided for at 15 per cent interest by the operating savings of $8,140.

Thus, to compute the return on the extra investment in a cost-saving facility, we find that interest rate which will equate the costs of the two alternatives. The answer will be the same whether we equate the annual costs or the present worth of the future costs.

Because his current plating capacity is inadequate, a manufacturer is considering whether to purchase a modern automatic plating machine which will cost \$100,000 including installation or buy a secondhand one, which is not as efficient but will adequately produce the desired quality of plating, for \$40,000 installed. He estimates an economic life of 8 years for the new automatic machine (with a \$15,000 salvage value at that time) and a life of 6 years for the secondhand one (with no salvage value at the end). Operating costs are forecasted at \$90,000 per year for the new machine and \$120,000 for the secondhand machine. What is the prospective rate of return on the extra \$60,000 investment for the modern new machine?

We want to find that interest rate which will make the annual costs under both alternatives equal to each other.

$$(\$100,000 - \$15,000) \left(\begin{array}{c} \text{CR} \\ i = ? \\ n = 8 \end{array} \right) + \$15,000(i) + \$90,000$$

$$= \$40,000 \left(\begin{array}{c} \text{CR} \\ i = ? \\ n = 6 \end{array} \right) + \$120,000$$

$$\$85,000 \left(\begin{array}{c} \text{CR} \\ i = ? \\ n = 8 \end{array} \right) + \$15,000(i) = \$40,000 \left(\begin{array}{c} \text{CR} \\ i = ? \\ n = 6 \end{array} \right) + \$30,000$$

Let us try an interest rate of 50 per cent.

$$\$85,000(0.52030) + \$15,000(0.50) \stackrel{?}{=} \$40,000(0.54812) + \$30,000$$
$$\$51,726 < \$51,925$$

The rate of return on the extra \$60,000 investment in the new machine is thus slightly more than 50 per cent.

In another case, this manufacturer was considering whether to buy one of two types of metal-bending equipment. Quality of product was the same for both. Type A cost \$6,000, with estimated operating costs of \$8,000 per year. Type B cost \$12,000, with estimated operating costs of \$6,500 per year. Economic lives of 10 years were estimated for both types. What is the prospective rate of return on the extra \$6,000 investment in type B?

Since there are no significant prospective salvage values and the economic lives of both alternatives are equal, the problem reduces to determining the rate of return on an investment of $6,000 which saves $1,500 a year for 10 years.

$$\$6,000 \left(\begin{matrix} \text{CR} \\ i = ? \\ n = 10 \end{matrix} \right) = \$1,500$$

$$\left(\begin{matrix} \text{CR} \\ i = ? \\ n = 10 \end{matrix} \right) = \tfrac{\$1,500}{\$6,000} = 0.2500$$

Using the capital-recovery chart of the Appendix of this book, we observe that the rate of return on the extra investment is approximately 21 per cent.

Approximations of True Rate of Return on Investment. There is no simple method of approximating the true rate of return on investments without using compound-interest formulas, tables, or charts. The available methods will not even give results which are consistently biased in one way or another. Depending upon the circumstances of the investment, all the simple approximate methods will usually give values which are higher or lower than true rates of return, with the error running as much as 50 per cent or more of the true rate.

The simplest and most common method of approximating a rate of return on investment without using compound-interest formulas is to ignore the timing of receipts and disbursements. The forecasted total of the disbursements, including the original investment, is subtracted from the total of the forecasted revenues. This excess of revenues over disbursements is then converted to an annual figure by dividing by the number of years involved in the operation. The rate of return is calculated by dividing by the original investment.

Let us consider the determination of the rates of return on a proposed chemical processing facility in a large city. Several sizes and designs of the chemical-processing facility are being considered for this one site. The forecasted construction and other initial investment costs, as well as annual revenues and disbursements for five alternate designs are shown in Table 11-4. In this case, we determined an average annual gross rental from which was subtracted average expenses to obtain expected net profit. We included an annual depreciation charge on a straight-line basis, with a 15-year life, in the expenses, but charged no depreciation on the land. Prospective net profit was divided in each case by the total investment to get the return on the investment.

We could have computed these returns in a slightly different, but equivalent, manner. First, the total expected revenue over the 15-year period would be computed including the $100,000 for which the land could presumably be sold at the end of the 50-year period. Then the total expenditures over the same period, including the investment cost, would

Table 11-4. Calculation of Rates of Return by Approximate Method for Five Alternate Designs of a Chemical Processing Facility

	Design A	Design B	Design C	Design D	Design E
Investment:					
Land......................	$100,000	$100,000	$100,000	$100,000	$100,000
Chemical processing facility......	235,000	400,000	625,000	785,000	840,000
Total......................	$335,000	$500,000	$725,000	$885,000	$940,000
Annual gross receipts..............	$146,000	$330,000	$435,000	$467,000	$507,000
Annual expenses:					
Depreciation*.................	15,667	26,667	41,667	52,333	56,000
All other costs.................	60,542	131,458	170,416	189,729	206,208
Total......................	$ 76,209	$158,125	$212,083	$242,062	$262,208
Net profit.....................	$ 69,791	$171,875	$222,917	$224,938	$244,792
Taxes at 52%.................	36,291	89,375	115,917	116,968	127,292
Net profit after taxes.............	$ 33,500	$ 82,500	$107,000	$107,970	$117,500
Return on investment.............	10.0%	16.5%	14.8%	12.2%	12.5%

* Depreciation on a straight-line basis with a 15-year life on the facility. No depreciation on the land.

be computed. Subtracting the total expenditures[1] from the total revenues gives a total excess of revenues. Divide this excess by the 15 years to obtain the annual net profit, which is divided by the total investment to calculate the rate of return. For example, in the case of design A:

1. Total receipts: $15 \times \$146,000 = \$2,190,000$
   Sale value of land $= \quad 100,000$

   $\quad\quad\quad\quad\quad\quad\quad\quad\quad\quad \$2,290,000$
2. Total expenditures: $15 \times \$60,542 = \$ \quad 908,130$
   Total taxes: $15 \times \$36,291 = \$ \quad 544,365$
   Total investment $= \quad 335,000$

   $\quad\quad\quad\quad\quad\quad\quad\quad\quad\quad \$1,787,495$
3. Excess of receipts over expenditures $= \$ \quad 502,505$
4. Average excess of receipts per year $= \$ \quad 33,500$
5. Approximate rate of return $\frac{\$33,500}{\$335,000} = \quad 10.0\%$

The results of this arithmetic are the same as what was done in Table 11-4.

If it is assumed that the estimated receipts and disbursements are uniformly distributed over the 15-year life, then this approximate method gives an understatement of the true rate of return. In Table 11-5, the true rates of return using compound interest are calculated. The annual

[1] This does not include the depreciation charges, which are expenses but not cash expenditures.

disbursements do not include the noncash expense of depreciation, which is part of the capital recovery.

Table 11-5. Calculation of True Rates of Return on Investment (Using Compound Interest)

	Design A	Design B	Design C	Design D	Design E
Total investment................	$335,000	$500,000	$725,000	$885,000	$940,000
Annual receipts..................	146,000	330,000	435,000	467,000	507,000
Annual disbursements* including income taxes....................	96,833	220,833	286,333	306,697	333,500
Annual net return after taxes.......	49,167	109,167	148,667	160,303	173,500
Land value at end of 50 years......	100,000	100,000	100,000	100,000	100,000
Return on investment†...........	13.0%	20.9%	19.3%	16.7%	17.1%

* Does not include the noncash item of depreciation.

$$\dagger\ 0 = (\text{annual net return}) \begin{pmatrix} \text{USPW} \\ i = ? \\ n = 15 \end{pmatrix} + \$100,000 \begin{pmatrix} \text{SPPW} \\ i = ? \\ n = 15 \end{pmatrix} - \text{total investment.}$$

The rates of return calculated by the approximate and the compound-interest methods are compared in Table 11-6. It will be seen that the approximate method understated the return in all designs, in some cases as much as 27 per cent.

Table 11-6. Comparison of Rates of Return Calculated by Approximate and Compound-interest Methods

Method	Design				
	A	B	C	D	E
Approximate.....................	10.0	16.5	14.8	12.2	12.5
Compound-interest...............	13.0	20.9	19.3	16.7	17.1
Difference......................	3.0	4.4	4.5	4.5	4.6
Per cent understatement..........	23%	21%	23%	27%	27%

When there is no salvage value (or an insignificant one) at the end of the life of the investment, the approximate method for calculating rate of return which was just illustrated in the previous section will frequently understate the return. The reason is that we ignore the fact that the amount of money invested decreases over the life of the project as cash returns are received. We can try to correct this by dividing the average annual return by an average investment (one-half the depreciating investment plus the salvage value). However, this will tend to overstate, to varying degrees, the rate of return on this type of investment.

The approximate method does not always understate the rate of return. When a large portion or all of the revenues, including salvage returns, is obtained at or toward the end of the investment period, it will tend to overstate the prospective return. The problem of the expected return on the speculative land investment which was previously discussed (page 152) can be used to illustrate this overstatement by the approximate calculation. We obtained a return of 13.5 per cent by the compound-interest calculations. Now let us make an approximate computation:

```
Total receipts.............................................. $40,000
Total disbursements ($20,000 + $1,800 net real estate taxes)........  21,800
Total excess of receipts....................................  18,200
Average return ($18,200/5)..................................   3,640
Approximate rate of return ($3,640/$20,000)................   18.2%
```

This 18.2 per cent rate calculated by the approximate method overstates the return by 4.7 per cent, which is an overstatement of 35 per cent of the true rate.

Rate of Return on Extra-investment–Alternative-revenue Projects. In the previous section, we illustrated the rate of return computation for five alternative designs and sizes of a chemical processing facility on a proposed site. However, we did not use the results to decide which alternative was the most economic.

Management has decided that it would like to invest as much of its funds as possible in facilities such as these provided it can earn at least 15 per cent on such investments. In Table 11-5, all the designs except design A show returns in excess of 15 per cent. We may, therefore, reason that design E is the most desirable because it invests the most funds with a prospective return greater than 15 per cent.

But we have not yet really analyzed the alternatives which are open to us. Design A is obviously not eligible because the return on the investment is below 15 per cent. However, designs B, C, D, and E are all eligible. Let us compare designs B and C first. The question of choosing which of these two is preferable can be stated as follows: Is the extra investment of $225,000 worthwhile? Obviously it is only worthwhile if it will bring a return of 15 per cent or more. Our preference between designs B and C is thus based on the rate of return on this extra investment.

In Table 11-7 we have calculated rates of return on the extra investment of each design over its next cheaper alternative. We see that design C gives us a 15.5 per cent return on the extra investment of $225,000 and is, therefore, a desirable alternative. However, design E, which requires the largest investment, will give us a 22.9 per cent return on the last increment of extra investment, which is well above the 15 per cent requirement. Design E could, therefore, be considered the most desirable one.

However, this last conclusion is fallacious. It is true that the extra investment of $55,000 in design E over design D will earn a 22.9 per cent

Table 11-7. Returns on Extra Investments (Using Compound Interest)

	Design A	Design B	Design C	Design D	Design E
Total investment...............	$335,000	$500,000	$725,000	$885,000	$940,000
Return on total investment.........	13.2%	20.9%	19.4%	16.7%	17.1%
Extra investment*.................	....	$165,000	$225,000	$160,000	$ 55,000
Extra net return.................	....	$ 60,000	$ 39,500	$ 11,636	$ 13,197
Return on extra investment........	....	36.0%	15.5%	1.1%	22.9%

* All this extra investment is in the chemical-processing facility, so that no salvage value for land is involved.

return. Therefore, design E is more desirable than design D. But is design D desirable? The answer to this question is no! The extra $160,000 investment in design D as compared with design C will earn only a 1.1 per cent return. The fallacy of our concluding that design E was most desirable on the basis of the return-on-extra-investment analysis is caused by comparing the higher investment alternative with a lower investment alternative (design D) which is not as desirable as some still lower investment alternative (design C). The significant comparison in this case is the rate of return on the extra investment in design E as compared with the most desirable lower investment alternative, design C. (Design C is more desirable than design B because of its 15.5 per cent return on the extra investment.) Comparing design E with design C in Table 11-8, we note that the return on the extra investment of $215,000 in design E is only 7.8 per cent, well below the 15 per cent requirement.

Our analysis indicates that design C is thus the most desirable alternative.

Nonuniform Investment, Receipt, and Expenditure Patterns. In all our examples for calculating prospective rates of return on proposed projects thus far, the forecasted investments were concentrated at one point in time, the present, and the forecasted receipts were assumed to be uniform.

Table 11-8. Return on Extra Investment in Design E
Compared with Design C

	Design C	Design E
Total investment..................	$725,000	$940,000
Return on total investment..........	19.4%	17.1%
Extra investment..................	$225,000	$215,000
Extra net return..................	....	$ 24,833
Return on extra investment.........	....	7.8%

Thus, the previous calculations are based on the assumption of uniform gross rentals and expenses throughout the life of the structure. In actuality, rental income will sometimes be higher in the earlier years and maintenance and repair expenditures higher in the later years. The use of a simple arithmetic average of the net receipts, ignoring the timing of the high and low years, can sometimes give misleading results.

These calculations also assume that the investment in land and building will be made at one point in time. In actuality, there may be a spread of several years between the purchase of land, the beginning of construction, and the actual occupancy of the building.

Sometimes these discrepancies cause significant decision-making errors.

Importance of Timing. The extent to which the timing of receipts can influence the rate of return received on an investment can be illustrated by a simple example. Assume we invest $1,000 in each of three projects A, B, and C. We receive a total of $1,500 after taxes over a five-year period on each project, but the timing varies as shown below.

End of year	Project		
	A	B	C
1	$100	$300	$500
2	200	300	400
3	300	300	300
4	400	300	200
5	500	300	100

The rates of return, calculated using compound interest are A, 12.0 per cent; B, 15.3 per cent; and C, 20.3 per cent. This is logical because we receive more of our money in the earlier years in project C and it can be reinvested to earn more returns during the time our investments and returns of project A are still tied up.

Individual-annual-return Method. To obtain a more accurate estimate of the prospective rates of return for the five alternative designs of the chemical processing facility previously discussed, each year's cash intake and outgo should be considered separately.

We have already developed the theoretical framework for handling the situations where these nonuniform factors are significant. The calculations of the actual rate of return on the parking lot investment earlier in this chapter involved nonuniform receipts and expenditures. A generalization of this procedure will provide the framework for all possible variations of investment, receipt, and expenditure patterns.

We can establish our framework by considering that a business enterprise involves investments and withdrawals of cash to and from its various ventures continuously. As monies are returned to the business from earnings or depreciation charges, they are continuously invested in other activities in the business. (Some are distributed to owners at various intervals.)

A typical capital investment in a new product may involve expenditures for market and product research, development, design, testing and tooling over several years. Large investments in working capital become necessary as the product is brought to market. Further machine and tooling expenditures become necessary as the sales volume increases. Some capital replacements are required during the life of the product.

Receipts may be low and operating expenses high in the initial period of product introduction. Sales may then build up over a period of time and then taper off because of competition and new technology. Operating expenses may be reduced as starting-up expenses decrease and additional experience is gained with the new process.

In other cases, the pattern may be reversed. High initial sales of a new item may decrease as the novelty wears off or as the market for the line becomes more limited to replacements rather than new consumers. Some production costs may tend to increase over the years as equipment becomes older and requires more maintenance and repairs.

Evaluating the return on our changing investment in a project involves the following steps:

1. Determine the investments which will be required. This would include a yearly time schedule showing the amount and dates when dollars will be required for capital items such as:
   a. Research, development, design, and testing
   b. Land
   c. Site preparations
   d. Building construction
   e. Equipment, tooling, and service facilities
   f. Moving and relocation expenses
   g. Losses and other one-time expenses which will result from project
   h. Working capital for
      (1) Accounts receivable
      (2) Raw material, in-process, and finished-goods inventories
      (3) Other requirements
   It is especially important that requirements for funds in future years for working as well as plant capital for replacement and expansion purposes be included.
2. Prepare a schedule of forecasted sales volume and net income for each year.
3. Prepare a schedule of estimated total expenses, excluding the noncash expenses of depreciation and depletion, for each year.
4. Summarize investment requirements in a format such as Table 11-9.

In this example, if the proposed project is adopted, the site for a new factory is to be purchased in 1961 for $200,000. The factory will be erected in 1962 at a cost of $900,000. In addition, $600,000 will be spent on equipment during 1962. Another $500,000 will go for equipment during 1963 and $40,000 for relocation costs. Operations will commence in the same year and $100,000 of working capital will be required. Expanding operations will require $250,000 additional working capital in 1964, $150,000 more in 1965, $70,000 in 1966, $50,000 in 1967, and $50,000 additional in 1968. In 1967, a $175,000 additional expenditure will be required to expand the capacity of a finishing process.

5. Compute prospective depreciation and depletion allowances for each group of depreciable capital assets, showing the amounts which will be charged each year during the prospective lives of all of these assets. Summarize these to obtain a schedule of depreciation and depletion charges for each year, as shown in Table 11-10.

In Table 11-10, the assets are depreciated by the estimated life allowed for tax purposes. Depreciation for one-half year is charged during the first year on all depreciating assets.

6. Prepare a summary of prospective cash returns from the proposal, such as Table 11-11.

Table 11-9. Summary of Investment Requirements

Year	Nondepreciating Items		Depreciating Items		Total
	Fixed assets	Working capital	Capitalized	Expensed	
1961	$200,000	....	....	....	$ 200,000
1962	....	....	$1,500,000	....	1,500,000
1963	....	$100,000	500,000	$40,000	640,000
1964	....	250,000	....	....	250,000
1965	....	150,000	....	....	150,000
1966	....	70,000	....	....	70,000
1967	....	50,000	175,000	....	225,000
1968	....	50,000	....	....	50,000

Income, column A, is reduced by all expenses except depreciation and depletion charges, column B, and then by depreciation and depletion charges, column C, to obtain net profit, column D. Net profit after deduction of a 52 per cent corporate income tax is computed by taking 48 per cent of the net profit, column D, to obtain net profit after taxes, column E. The total cash return, column E, consists of the net profit after taxes, column D, plus the depreciation and depletion charge, column C, which represents the income-tax-free return of cash invested in depreciating assets.

Table 11-10. Schedule of Depreciation Charges,
Straight-line Depreciation

Year	Factory building, 35 years, $900,000	Equipment					Total $2,175,000
		20 Years		15 Years			
		$200,000	$150,000	$400,000	$350,000	$175,000	
1962	$12,857	$ 5,000	......	$13,333	....	....	$ 31,190
1963	25,714	10,000	$3,750	26,667	$11,667	....	77,798
1964	25,714	10,000	7,500	26,667	23,333	....	93,214
1965	25,714	10,000	7,500	26,667	23,333	....	93,214
1966	25,714	10,000	7,500	26,667	23,333	....	93,214
1967	25,714	10,000	7,500	26,667	23,333	$ 5,833	99,047
1968	25,714	10,000	7,500	26,667	23,333	11,667	104,881
1969	25,714	10,000	7,500	26,667	23,333	11,667	104,881
1970	25,714	10,000	7,500	26,667	23,333	11,667	104,881
1971	25,714	10,000	7,500	26,667	23,333	11,667	104,881
1972	25,714	10,000	7,500	26,667	23,333	11,667	104,881
1973	25,714	10,000	7,500	26,666	23,333	11,667	104,880
1974	25,714	10,000	7,500	26,666	23,334	11,667	104,881
1975	25,714	10,000	7,500	26,666	23,334	11,667	104,881
1976	25,714	10,000	7,500	26,666	23,334	11,667	104,881
1977	25,714	10,000	7,500	13,333	23,334	11,667	91,548
1978	25,714	10,000	7,500	....	11,667	11,666	66,547
1979	25,714	10,000	7,500	....	....	11,666	54,880
1980	25,714	10,000	7,500	....	....	11,666	54,880
1981	25,714	10,000	7,500	....	....	11,666	54,880
1982	25,714	5,000	7,500	....	....	5,833	44,047
1983	25,714	....	3,750	....	....	....	29,464
1984	25,714	....	......	....	....	....	25,714
1985	25,714	....	......	....	....	....	25,714
1986	25,714	....	......	....	....	....	25,714
1987	25,715	....	......	....	....	....	25,715
1988	25,715	....	......	....	....	....	25,715
1989	25,715	....	......	....	....	....	25,715
1990	25,715	....	......	....	....	....	25,715
1991	25,715	....	......	....	....	....	25,715
1992	25,715	....	......	....	....	....	25,715
1993	25,715	....	......	....	....	....	25,715
1994	25,715	....	......	....	....	....	25,715
1995	25,715	....	......	....	....	....	25,715
1996	25,715	....	......	....	....	....	25,715
1997	12,857	....	......	....	....	....	12,857

Table 11-11. Summary of Cash Returns

Year	(A) Income	(B) Expenses (excluding depreciation)	(C) Depreciation and depletion	(D) Net profit (A) − (B) − (C)	(E) Net profit after taxes (0.48)(D)	(F) Total cash return (C) + (E)
1961						
1962	....	....	$ 31,190	$− 31,190	$− 14,971	$16,219
1963	$ 600,000	$1,050,000	77,798	− 527,798	−253,343	−175,545
1964	1,500,000	1,500,000	93,214	− 93,214	− 44,743	48,471
1965	2,500,000	2,200,000	93,214	206,786	99,257	192,471
1966	3,000,000	2,500,000	93,214	406,786	195,257	288,471
1967	3,500,000	2,700,000	99,047	700,953	336,457	435,504
1968	4,000,000	2,850,000	104,881	1,045,119	501,657	606,538
1969	4,500,000	3,000,000	104,881	1,395,119	669,657	774,538
1970	4,500,000	3,100,000	104,881	1,295,119	621,657	726,538
1971	4,500,000	3,100,000	104,881	1,295,119	621,657	726,538
1972	4,500,000	3,250,000	104,881	1,145,119	549,657	654,538
1973	4,500,000	3,250,000	104,880	1,145,120	549,658	654,538
1974	4,500,000	3,250,000	104,881	1,145,119	549,657	654,538
1975	4,500,000	3,350,000	104,881	1,045,119	501,657	606,538
1976	4,500,000	3,350,000	104,881	1,045,119	501,657	606,538
1977	4,500,000	3,350,000	91,548	1,058,452	508,057	599,605
1978	4,500,000	3,500,000	66,547	933,453	448,057	514,604
1979	4,500,000	3,500,000	54,880	945,120	453,658	508,538
1980	4,500,000	3,500,000	54,880	945,120	453,658	508,538
1981	4,500,000	3,500,000	54,880	945,120	453,658	508,538
1982	4,500,000	3,500,000	44,047	955,953	458,857	502,904
1983	4,500,000	3,500,000	29,464	970,536	465,857	495,321
1984	4,500,000	3,600,000	25,714	874,286	419,657	445,371
1985	4,500,000	3,600,000	25,714	874,286	419,657	445,371
1986	....	....	25,714	− 25,714	− 12,343	13,371
1987	....	....	25,715	− 25,715	− 12,343	13,372
1988	....	....	25,715	− 25,715	− 12,343	13,372
1989	....	....	25,715	− 25,715	− 12,343	13,372
1990	....	....	25,715	− 25,715	− 12,343	13,372
1991	....	....	25,715	− 25,715	− 12,343	13,372
1992	....	....	25,715	− 25,715	− 12,343	13,372
1993	....	....	25,715	− 25,715	− 12,343	13,372
1994	....	....	25,715	− 25,715	− 12,343	13,372
1995	....	....	25,715	− 25,715	− 12,343	13,372
1996	....	....	25,715	− 25,715	− 12,343	13,372
1997	....	....	12,857	− 12,857	− 6,171	6,686

In calculating this cash return to the business, it is assumed that the company is making enough profits in its other operations to obtain the tax benefit of losses and depreciation charges in years in which the proposed project itself is not earning a profit.

When the facility, or parts of it, will outlast the requirements on the project, and will have a significant salvage value at the conclusion, this salvage income is usually handled as follows:

a. If the facility has been fully depreciated and it is anticipated that it will be sold, then the estimated salvage income is taxed at only one-half the normal rate. (It is treated the same as a capital gain.)

b. If the facility has not been fully depreciated and the estimated salvage value is the same as the book value, then the salvage income is not taxed at all because it represents recovery of capital.

c. If the estimated salvage income is less than the book value, the amount by which it is less represents a long-term loss on a depreciable business asset. This is treated as an ordinary loss and is fully deductible from income in the year in which it occurs.

d. If the estimated salvage income is more than the book value, the income above the book value is treated the same as a capital gain.

If the facility has not been fully depreciated but it is anticipated that the facility will be retained for other purposes at the end of the project, then the income tax credits for the remaining depreciation charges in future years will be included in the rate-of-return calculation. This is the case for our proposed project.

7. Determine the interest rate which makes the present worth of the investments equal to the present worth of the net cash receipts. This gives us the interest rate at which the investments would have to be invested to yield the net receipts.

In making this calculation, we could, for theoretical validity, adhere to two refinements which, for most applications, are unnecessary.

a. We could use present-worth interest factors based on a continuous compounding of interest. We are not using this in our example because the difference of such refinement as compared with annual interest is not significant considering the inaccuracies, uncertainties, and risk inherent in the cost and revenue forecasts. In addition, continuous compounding sometimes has an unclear meaning to a businessman who has never paid or received interest compounded continuously.

b. We could distinguish between expenditures and receipts which are made or received on a continuing basis during the year (such as some construction expenditures and operating income and expenses), and other expenditures and receipts (such as the purchase of a plant site or a piece of equipment) which are made at one time. Here again, this refinement is usually not worth the effort considering all of the uncertainties of forecasting exact timing as well as values. We shall, therefore, in our example treat all cash values as if they occurred at the end of the year in which they fall, similar to the practice we have thus far followed in this volume.

Trial-and-error Computation System. It is advantageous to develop a systematic pattern for the trial-and-error computations of the last stages of this procedure. Forms, such as used in Tables 11-12 and 11-13 are advantageous for this purpose.

Table **11-12. Cash-investment-expenditure Present-worth Calculations**

Year	Time from base	0% Net cash disbursements	12%		15%	
			Factor	Present worth	Factor	Present worth
1961	1	$ 200,000	0.8929	$ 178,580	0.8696	$ 173,920
1962	2	1,500,000	0.7972	1,195,800	0.7561	1,134,150
1963	3	640,000	0.7118	455,552	0.6575	420,800
1964	4	250,000	0.6355	158,875	0.5718	142,950
1965	5	150,000	0.5674	85,110	0.4972	74,580
1966	6	70,000	0.5066	35,462	0.4323	30,261
1967	7	225,000	0.4523	101,768	0.3759	84,578
1968	8	50,000	0.4039	20,195	0.3269	16,345
Total	...	$3,085,000	......	$2,231,342	......	$2,077,584

The year in which operations of any kind start is our zero point, the present. This is the year in which the first investments, expenses, or income occur. All values must be discounted to this zero point in our trial-and-error computation. We desire to find that interest rate at which the present worth of the investments will equal the present worth of the cash returns. This interest rate will represent the return on the investments.

The 0 per cent interest column is first filled in for both Tables 11-12 and 11-13. In Table 11-12, this column represents the actual undiscounted net-cash-investment disbursements. In Table 11-13, this column represents the actual undiscounted net-cash returns. After totaling these 0 per cent columns, an approximate interest calculation, as in Table 11-14, can be readily made to guide our first trial-and-error present-worth interest computations. This calculation, which is, of course, subject to large errors, shows an approximate rate of return of 7.4 per cent.

We proceed by making our first trial calculation. If the returns are highest in the early years or fairly uniform, we make our first guess at a higher value than the approximately calculated value. If the returns are highest in the later years, we make our first guess at a lower value than the approximately calculated value. In this case, we guess that the true rate is somewhat greater than the approximate result of 7.4 per cent and will try 12 per cent first in Tables 11-12 and 11-13. We find that, at 12

Table 11-13. Cash-return Present-worth Calculations

Year	Time from base	0% Net cash return	12%		15%	
			Factor	Present worth	Factor	Present worth
1961	1	....	0.8929	....	0.8696	
1962	2	$ 16,219	0.7972	$ 12,930	0.7561	$ 12,263
1963	3	−175,545	0.7118	−124,953	0.6575	−115,421
1964	4	48,471	0.6355	30,803	0.5718	27,716
1965	5	192,471	0.5674	109,208	0.4972	95,697
1966	6	288,471	0.5066	146,139	0.4323	124,706
1967	7	435,504	0.4523	196,978	0.3759	163,706
1968	8	606,538	0.4039	244,981	0.3269	198,277
1969	9	774,538	0.3606	279,298	0.2843	220,201
1970	10	726,538	0.3220	233,945	0.2472	179,600
1971	11	726,538	0.2875	208,880	0.2149	156,133
1972	12	654,538	0.2567	168,020	0.1869	122,333
1973	13	654,538	0.2292	150,020	0.1625	106,362
1974	14	654,538	0.2046	133,918	0.1413	92,486
1975	15	606,538	0.1827	110,814	0.1229	74,544
1976	16	606,538	0.1631	98,926	0.1069	64,839
1977	17	599,605	0.1456	87,302	0.0929	55,703
1978	18	514,604	0.1300	66,899	0.0808	41,580
1979	19	508,538	0.1161	59,041	0.0703	35,750
1980	20	508,538	0.1037	52,735	0.0611	31,072
1981	21	508,538	0.0926	47,091	0.0531	27,003
1982	22	502,904	0.0826	41,540	0.0462	23,234
1983	23	495,321	0.0738	36,555	0.0402	19,912
1984	24	445,371	0.0659	29,350	0.0349	15,543
1985	25	445,371	0.0588	26,188	0.0304	13,539
1986	26	13,371	0.0525	702	0.0264	353
1987	27	13,372	0.0469	627	0.0230	308
1988	28	13,372	0.0419	560	0.0200	267
1989	29	13,372	0.0374	500	0.0174	233
1990	30	13,372	0.0334	447	0.0151	202
1991	31	13,372	0.0305	408	0.0135	181
1992	32	13,372	0.0276	369	0.0120	160
1993	33	13,372	0.0247	330	0.0105	140
1994	34	13,372	0.0218	292	0.0090	120
1995	35	13,372	0.0189	253	0.0075	100
1996	36	13,372	0.0172	230	0.0067	90
1997	37	6,686	0.0155	104	0.0059	39
Total	...	$11,499,000	......	$2,451,430	......	$1,788,971

per cent interest, the present worth of the cash returns is greater than the present worths of the investment expenditures. This means that the investment expenditures are actually earning more than 12 per cent.

Table 11-14. **Determination of Approximate Rate of Return**

1. Total cash returns.............................	$11,499,000
2. Total investment disbursements................	3,085,000
3. Excess of cash returns (1) − (2)................	8,414,000
4. Number of years.............................	37
5. Annual excess of cash returns (3) ÷ (4).........	227,405
6. Approximate rate of return (5) ÷ (2)...........	7.4%

We, therefore, next try 15 per cent and find that the present worth of the cash returns is less than the present worths of the investment expenditures. The investment expenditures are, therefore, earning less than a 15 per cent return.

The true rate of return is between 12 and 15 per cent. We can interpolate algebraically to obtain our answer of 13.3 per cent.

The analysis of Tables 11-12 and 11-13 could have been combined into one table showing cash flows for all years (plus for cash returns and minus for cash disbursements). The interest rate which will make the present worth of the cash flows equal to zero is obviously the same as the interest rate which will make the present worth of the cash returns equal to the present worth of the cash disbursements. (PW of cash returns) = (PW of cash disbursements) is equivalent to (PW of cash returns) − (PW of cash disbursements) = 0.

Multiple-interest-rate Problem. In all the cases in which we have computed a rate of return, the project or proposal initially required more money than it generated and eventually generated enough additional funds in later years to repay this excess early requirement or investment. (The cumulative cash flows in these examples always went from negative to positive.) However, it is possible to have an unusual situation in which this pattern is varied in a manner which will result in an erroneous solution for the rate of return.

In an example from the petroleum industry,[1] the problem is to determine the profitability of acquiring a small oil-producing property. Normally, the free flow of oil from a reservoir (primary recovery) diminishes with the passage of time. In some cases, however, secondary recovery measures, such as injection of water into the reservoir, may result in a substantial increase in the total amount of oil produced. The primary reserves in this case have been nearly exhausted, and an investment of $2.5 million by the buyer will be needed at the appropriate time for a

---

[1] Taken from J. G. McLean, "How to Evaluate New Capital Investments," *Harvard Business Review*, November–December, 1958, pp. 59–69. The suggested method of solution, however, is different in some respects.

water flood to accomplish recovery of the secondary reserves. No immediate payment will be made to the seller, but he will receive $12\frac{1}{2}$ per cent royalty on all oil produced from the property, whether from primary or secondary reserves.

The calculations in Table 11-15 are made under the assumption that the water-flooding investment will be made in the fourth year. The $2,500,000 negative cash flow in year 4 is reduced by income of $700,000 (positive cash flow), giving the net negative cash flow of $1,800,000 shown in the table. During the first three years all the primary reserves will be recovered, and income in the fourth to the tenth years will be attributable solely to the water-flood project. As shown by the table, the discounted-cash-flow analysis gives two solutions to this problem. At both 28 per cent and 49 per cent, the net present worth of the cash flow is zero; i.e., the present worth of the cash income is equal to the present worth of the $2.5 million investment.

Table **11-15. Multiple-interest-rate Solution**
(Figures in thousands of dollars)

Year	Cash flow	Present worth of cash flow at						
		10%	20%	28%	30%	40%	49%	50%
1	$ 200	$ 182	$ 167	$156	$ 154	$ 143	$134	$ 133
2	100	83	69	61	59	51	45	44
3	50	38	29	24	23	18	15	15
4	−1,800	−1,229	−868	−671	−630	−469	−365	−356
5	600	373	241	175	162	112	82	79
6	500	282	167	114	104	66	46	44
7	400	205	112	71	64	38	24	23
8	300	140	70	41	37	20	12	12
9	200	85	39	21	19	10	5	5
10	100	39	16	8	7	3	2	2
Total	$ +650	$ +198	$+42	0	$ −2	$ −8	0	$ +1

The positive cash flows of $200,000 in year 1, $100,000 in year 2, and $50,000 in year 3, when compounded at 28 per cent interest to year 4, will counterbalance some of the negative cash flow (investment) of $2,400,000. At 49 per cent interest, the counterbalancing effect of the compounding of the first 3 years' cash flows will be even greater. However, the present worths of the future positive cash flows (years 5 through 10) will be greater at 28 per cent interest than at 49 per cent interest. This accounts for the fact that there are two interest rates which make the present worth of the cash flows equal to zero.

If the positive cash flow funds of years 1, 2, and 3 can be invested to earn 28 per cent, then 28 per cent may be considered the correct solution.

If, however, these positive cash flow funds in the early years can be invested to yield only 10 per cent, we should calculate our rate of return on this investment by first calculating the value which the positive cash flows of the first three years will total at the time of the investment, year 4, using 10 per cent interest. Then we would subtract this compound amount from the $2,400,000 to determine the net investment which is being made in anticipation of the cash flows from the secondary reserves in years 4 through 10.

Multiple-interest-rate solutions may occur when the cumulative net cash flow switches from positive to negative at some stage in the life of the project, usually as a result of additional capital outlays required at that time. There may be as many interest-rate solutions as there are cumulative cash-flow switches from positive to negative during the life of the project.

Use of Continuous Compounding and More Accurate Timing. In some situations, the refinement of continuous compounding and more accurate timing of receipts and expenditures may appear desirable. The procedures illustrated here can be readily adapted for this purpose.

A table of uniform-continuous-payment present-worth factors is given in Chapter 5 (Table 5-3). In those years in which it is desirable to evaluate separately expenditures or receipts made on a continuing basis during the year from those made at particular times during the year, extra lines can be inserted in the interest calculation and the appropriate compound interest factors used to discount the separate values. For most practical purposes, interest factors for fractional parts of the year can be approximated quite closely by linear interpolation between the full-year values.

Advantages of Rate-of-return Approach. The amount of detailed estimation and calculation involved in the rate-of-return approach should vary with the size and complication of the proposal being evaluated. With simple proposals, many short cuts can be taken. When large commitments of funds are involved, greater expenditure of time and effort is desirable to achieve more accurate results. In any case, evaluation of alternative investments by a rate-of-return computation possesses a number of important advantages over the annual-cost and present-worth methods.

The annual-cost and present-worth comparisons require that a minimum acceptable rate of return be determined beforehand. The value of this specified rate of return will determine which individual proposals and alternatives will appear most desirable. The rate-of-return approach possesses the advantage of not requiring the prior specifications of a rate of return.

When proposals are evaluated by annual-cost or present-worth calculations, it is very difficult to rank the relative profitability and desirability of proposals which require investments of different sums of money for various periods of time. The rate-of-return approach simplifies this ranking problem. Of course, the ranking problem is still a very difficult task, fraught with possibilities of judgmental error because of intangible factors. Some limitations and dangers of misinterpretation of rate-of-return calculations are presented in the discussion of capital planning and budgeting in Chapter 16.

The rate-of-return concept can be directly related to the profit goals and planning of a company. The establishment of profit goals, the establishment of capital-planning policies, and the determination of investment decisions can thus be more readily coordinated using rate-of-return economic evaluations.

The rate-of-return-on-investment concept is useful in the management and control of decentralized operations in a company. The use of rate of return as an economic evaluation technique can thus fit in with the operating management philosophy in many companies. (It is important to recognize, of course, that the accounting for rates of returns earned on past investments usually follows different techniques from those used in the economic evaluation of returns for prospective future investments. However, the differences can be reconciled whenever it is desirable.)

The rate-of-return type of analysis is conducive to effective follow-up after an investment has been made to ascertain whether actual results were better, equal to, or poorer than originally estimated. When annual-cost and present-worth comparisons are used, the meaningful comparison of anticipated with actual results becomes especially complicated if the investment costs did not turn out exactly as estimated. In such cases, it is difficult to interpret properly the differences in actual and anticipated annual costs or present worths.

PROBLEMS

Unless otherwise stated, income taxes on ordinary corporate income are at the 52 per cent rate.

1. A farming corporation is considering the purchase of a tract of farm land for $2,000,000. The depreciable assets on the land are negligible. With the investment of an additional $300,000 for working capital, the corporation estimates that it can earn $1,500,000 of income per year, with $800,000 of expenses. Determine the prospective after-tax rate of return on this investment.

2. The actual receipts and expenditures from the corporation's investment in problem 1 and the amount of working capital actually used in farming the tract of land are as follows:

Year	Receipts	Expenses	Actual working capital used
1	$1,400,000	$1,300,000	$400,000
2	1,350,000	1,000,000	400,000
3	1,600,000	900,000	350,000
4	1,700,000	850,000	350,000
5	1,650,000	900,000	300,000

What apparent rates of return after taxes are earned each of the five years?

3. At the end of the fifth year, the corporation of problems 1 and 2 is offered $2,000,000 for the tract of land. For many reasons, including a pressing need for cash, it sells the tract. What actual after-tax rate of return on the monies invested in the land and its operation did the corporation receive?

4. The Dyer Service Corporation was organized in 1956 to rent computer time to organizations who thereby avoided the expenses of purchase or rental of a computer which would be used only a relatively small proportion of the time. The corporation has purchased a computer and auxiliary equipment for $2,000,000 and has an additional $200,000 invested as working capital. Following are the actual rental receipts and cash expenditures of the corporation, which started business on January 2, 1957.

Year	Rental receipts	Cash expenditures	Dividend payments
1957	$ 900,000	$325,000	$ 16,500
1958	1,150,000	350,000	147,500
1959	1,200,000	350,000	219,500
1960	1,000,000	375,000	234,500

Sum-of-digits depreciation of the computer and auxiliary equipment is used with an estimated economic life of five years and an estimated salvage value of $500,000. At the end of 1960 the computer and the auxiliary equipment were sold for $700,000, the corporation dissolved, and the proceeds from the sale of the equipment plus the $200,000 original working capital plus the earnings and depreciation recoveries which were retained as additional working capital were distributed to the stockholder-organizers. Corporate income taxes from 1957 to 1960 were at the 1960 rates shown in the text.

(a) What was the apparent after-tax rate of return on the total investment in the corporation each year?

(b) What was the actual after-tax rate of return on the owners' investment in the business?

5. The methods engineer of the B and G Corporation proposes that the company purchase a group of tape-controlled automatic presses for $600,000. These presses will have an estimated economic life of eight years with an estimated $50,000 salvage value at that time. The new presses will save an estimated $150,000 per year of labor and will have negligible effects on other costs. If these new presses are purchased, they will replace currently used equipment which has a salvage value of $50,000 today. It is estimated that the salvage value will decrease to zero in five years. What is the prospective before-tax rate of return on the investment in the new presses?

6. You can purchase a 6 per cent $1,000 bond, interest paid semiannually, for $800. The bond is due in seven years. You are in a 34 per cent income tax bracket. What after-tax rate of return will you earn if you make this purchase?

7. Mr. Kay has been offered a tract of forest land for $60,000 as a speculative investment. He anticipates that it will be worth $250,000 in 15 years as the result of economic development which he expects will occur in the region. Taxes, insurance, and all other expenses will average about $1,500 per year. What is Mr Kay's prospective after-tax rate of return on his investment if he is in a 43% income tax bracket?

8. The Morrow Company is considering whether to build a wood or steel ware·house to handle its increased requirement for finished-goods storage space- A wood structure, with an expected life of 25 years, will cost $150,000, and a steel structure, with an expected life of 50 years, will cost $225,000. Expected average annual maintenance costs are $4,000 for the wood structure and $2,500 for the steel building. What is the prospective before-tax rate of return on the extra investment in the steel structure?

9. A manufacturer is considering the introduction of a new product. He makes the following forecasts of income and expenditures:

Year after go-ahead decision	Income	Expenditures	
		Expense	Investment
1	0	$ 100,000	
2	0	40,000	$410,000
3	$ 200,000	120,000	30,000
4	300,000	150,000	
5	450,000	180,000	
6	700,000	190,000	10,000
7	500,000	185,000	
8	330,000	150,000	
Total	$2,480,000	$1,115,000	$450,000

The $100,000 expenditure in year 1 is for research and engineering. These costs will be "expensed" and will reduce the corporation's net income before taxes, which currently is in excess of $1,000,000 per year. The $450,000 in year 2 is divided as follows: $40,000 for engineering and tooling which is "expensed"; $30,000 for working capital; and $380,000 for facilities having an estimated salvage value of $100,000 at the end of 7 years. These facilities are depreciated on a straight-line basis. The $150,000 in year 3 is divided as follows: $30,000 for additional working capital and $120,000 for labor, material, promotional and other expenses. The expenditures shown in years 4 through 8 are for labor, material, promotional and other expenses, except for the addition to working capital of $10,000 in year 6. All the income shown is from sale of the new product except in year 8 in which $100,000 of the $330,000 is from the sale of the facilities which originally cost $380,000 and $70,000 is the return of working capital. Compute the rate of return after income tax.

10. The total market for the new product of problem 9 is fixed by population characteristics which the company cannot change. However, by investing $80,000 in a promotional campaign during years 2, 3, 4, and 5, it will be possible to increase sales in the early years at the expense of later years. Income and expenditures would be changed as follows:

Year after go-ahead decision	Income	Expenditures	
		Expense	Investment
1	0	$ 100,000	
2	0	60,000	$410,000
3	$ 350,000	160,000	30,000
4	700,000	220,000	10,000
5	700,000	220,000	
6	250,000	160,000	
7	200,000	150,000	
8	280,000	125,000	
Total	$2,480,000	$1,195,000	$450,000

All income, except the $170,000 for year 8 which is explained in problem 9, is from sale of the new product. All expenditures are also the same as explained in problem 9 with the following three exceptions. $20,000 is included in the expenditures of years 2, 3, 4, and 5 for promotion (a total of $80,000); the investment of $10,000 in added working capital is in year 4 instead of year 6 expenditures; and the costs of production (labor, material, etc.) are moved to earlier years to coincide with the earlier income from sales. Compute the after-tax rate of return when this investment of $80,000 in a promotional campaign is made.

12 Determinations of Equal Cost and Payout

Equal-cost calculations and payout-period calculations may be useful tools in investment analysis when certain types of uncertainty are present. In addition, payout-period determinations may be useful in some cases in which a firm is short of capital funds.

Equal-cost Calculations and Factor Sensitivity. Economic decisions require forecasts, with risks and uncertainties, of the future values of technical and economic factors. When a large change in the value of a factor will not change the choice of alternative, the decision is not sensitive to variations in the value of this factor and it is not necessary to spend much time and energy in estimating the expected future value of the insensitive factor. Equal-cost calculations may then be a simple means of arriving at a decision.

In equal-cost calculations, we equate the annual costs of alternative courses of action, keeping the uncertain factor as an unknown in the equation. We then solve for the value of the uncertain factor which will make the alternatives equally desirable. If the range of expected values of the uncertain factor is definitely larger or smaller than the equal-cost value, the factor is insensitive and we are able to choose the lower cost alternative with a high degree of confidence without carefully estimating values for the insensitive factor. Examples illustrating the application of this technique to several different types of uncertainty situations are presented in this chapter.

Uncertain Sales Forecast. A company requires a punch press to manufacture a new product. It is considering a semiautomatic and a fully automatic model. The semiautomatic model will cost $8,000, will have an expected life of 15 years with no salvage value, and will have maintenance and operating costs of $2,000 a year plus production costs of $0.20 per unit. The automatic model will cost $20,000, will have an expected life of 10 years with no salvage value, and will have maintenance and operating costs of $3,000 a year, plus production costs of $0.08 per unit. A 15 per cent return before income taxes is required on this type of investment. The company is very uncertain as to the annual sales of the new product

An equal-cost analysis may be helpful in this case. At what output volume will the annual costs be the same regardless of whether the semiautomatic or the fully automatic model is purchased?

Let Q represent the quantity manufactured and sold.

Annual costs using semiautomatic press:

$$\$8,000 \left(\begin{array}{c} \text{CR} \\ i = 15\% \\ n = 15 \end{array} \right) + \$2,000 + \$0.20Q$$

Annual costs using automatic press:

$$\$20,000 \left(\begin{array}{c} \text{CR} \\ i = 15\% \\ n = 10 \end{array} \right) + \$3,000 + \$0.08Q$$

Equating the annual costs:

$$\$8,000(0.17102) + \$2,000 + \$0.20\,Q = \$20,000(0.19925)$$
$$+ \$3,000 + \$0.08Q$$
$$Q = \$30,140$$

Annual costs will be the same using the semi- or the fully automatic machine if the output is 30,140 units. If output is above 30,140 units, the fully automatic press is more economical. If output is less than 30,140 units, the semiautomatic press is more economic. The company's best estimate of future annual sales volume is between 50,000 and 100,000 units per year. Therefore, despite the uncertainty and wide range of the sales estimate, the more economical alternative is the fully automatic press.

Uncertainty of Future Costs. A new process has been developed to reduce the costs of manufacturing a chemical compound. Laboratory and pilot-plant studies have been made of yields and costs using various grades of available raw material. However, there is still a great deal of uncertainty as to what the yields and consequent material and labor costs will be.

A plant to manufacture the chemical compound will cost $600,000 and should last at least five, probably ten, years if it should prove economic to operate. Requirements for the compound total 250,000 lb a year. A 25 per cent return before taxes will be required to justify this type of investment. It currently costs the company $2.80 per pound for material and labor to produce the compound. There would be no salvage return if the present facilities are replaced.

Let C represent all operating costs (material and labor) to make a pound of the compound using the new process. Then, using an economic life of 5 years to be on the conservative side, even though the facility will probably have a 10-year life,

$$\$600,000 \left(\begin{array}{c} \text{CR} \\ i = 25\% \\ n = 5 \end{array} \right) + 250,000C = 250,000(\$2.80)$$

$$C = \$1.91$$

Even though the company is very uncertain of the prospective yields and resultant operating costs, it is very certain that the costs will not be as high as \$1.91 per pound. Therefore, despite the uncertainty about operating costs and life of the facility, it appears to be a desirable investment.

Uncertainty As to Expected Economic Life. It is very difficult to estimate the prospective economic life of an asset. The number of years it will remain economic to continue to use an asset depends upon many factors which are very difficult to forecast: future markets, costs, technological progress, etc. Thus, when we are considering the replacement of an asset, an equal-cost analysis may be helpful to simplify the problem of deciding on an appropriate economic life.

It has been proposed that tape-controlled automatic stamping equipment be purchased to replace the current facility. The new equipment will cost \$110,000. Operating costs using the new equipment will total \$8,000 per year compared with \$36,000 per year using current equipment. A 20 per cent return before taxes is required for this type of investment. Salvage value from sale of the present equipment will be negligible after deducting dismantling costs.

Letting Y represent the expected life of the new tape-controlled equipment, we have

$$\$110,000 \left(\begin{array}{c} \text{CR} \\ i = 20\% \\ n = Y \end{array} \right) + \$8,000 = \$36,000$$

$$\left(\begin{array}{c} \text{CR} \\ i = 20\% \\ n = Y \end{array} \right) = 0.25454$$

Using the capital-recovery chart of the Appendix, we find that n is between 8 and 9 years. Unless we can expect the new equipment to have an economic life of 9 years or longer, we should not adopt the proposal.

Uncertainty As to Required Rate of Return. When we compare two alternative projects requiring capital investments of different sizes, we can determine the interest rate which will result in equal annual costs for both alternatives. We demonstrated, in Chapter 11, that this interest rate was the prospective rate of return on the extra investment in the alternative having the larger investment. Our decision in such investment problems is simplified if this rate of return on the extra investment is considerably above or below the general range of values which management considers as acceptable returns.

Usefulness of Equal-cost Analysis. The equal-cost type of analysis is most useful in economy analyses when

1. Uncertainty is concentrated in only one of the aspects which must be forecast.

2. The equal-cost value of the uncertain variable is found to be considerably higher or lower than the expected range of values of the uncertain variable.

When more than one factor is uncertain, we can make several equal-cost calculations with different assumed values for each uncertain factor to examine the range of variation of the equal-cost points.   However, this procedure can sometimes become cumbersome.

Payout Period. The speed with which invested funds are returned to the business may be a criterion of some importance in capital-investment decision-making under two circumstances:

1. When the funds available for capital investment are limited compared with the opportunities which exist for profitable investment and it is expected that future investment opportunities will be more profitable than current ones

2. When a high degree of uncertainty exists as to how long the profitability of a proposed venture will continue into the future

When one or more of the above conditions is present, the use of payout period as *one* of the investment criteria may be justified.

The payout period (sometimes also called payback period) is the number of years which elapse between the time an investment is made and the time the earnings or savings from the investment equal the investment with no interest. It measures the speed with which invested funds are returned to the business.

Calculation of the Payout Period. An equipment proposal requires the investment of $8,000 and will result in savings of $2,000 per year after income taxes. The payout period is

$$\frac{\$8,000}{\$2,000} = 4 \text{ years}$$

It is important that the effect of income and other taxes be taken into account when computing the payout period. The earnings or savings figure used in the calculation should be the cash earnings or net savings (cash flow) after taxes on the accrued earnings.

In the equipment proposal just discussed, the net prospective savings in operating cost will total $3,200. The equipment will be depreciated on a straight-line basis with an 8-year life. The depreciation charge is, therefore, $1,000 per year. The taxable earnings resulting from the equipment savings will be $3,200 minus $1,000, or $2,200. With a 54 per cent corporate income tax rate, the company will pay 54 per cent of $2,200 or approximately $1,200 in income taxes. The $3,200 of savings will, therefore, be reduced by $1,200, leaving a net figure of $2,000 annual savings after taxes.

Availability of Funds for Future Investments. A company which is short of capital funds may find the payout period a useful tool in combination with the methods which take rate of return into account.

Investment in projects A and B is being considered.

	Project A	Project B
Investment....................	$100,000	$100,000
Prospective rate of return.......	14%	17%
Payout period.................	4 years	8 years

Project B gives a 17 per cent rate of return as compared with 14 per cent on project A. However, the payout period is only 4 years for project A and is 8 years for project B. Project B has a higher prospective rate of return than project A because it is anticipated that it will earn more money in the years after its payout period has expired than will project A. The payout-period criterion ignores all earnings beyond the payout period.

The company anticipates increasingly more profitable investment opportunities in the near future for which it will have difficulty arranging financing. It is anticipated that these investments will earn returns in excess of 20 to 25 per cent. Accordingly, it may be more profitable to invest in project A so that the company will have the funds available for the new profit opportunities later on.

Uncertain Future Profitability. A company is considering two investment possibilities.

	Facility M	Facility N
Investment..........	$60,000	$60,000
Rate of return.......	25%	30%
Payout period.......	3 years	8 years

It is worried about the possibility of new technological developments which may make the facilities obsolete. There is no way of knowing when or how rapidly such developments may occur. However, the longer the time before the investment is recovered, the greater is the risk that the facility will be obsolete before its cost has been entirely recovered. The company may, therefore, choose facility M in preference to facility N.

Use and Misuse of Payout Period. Because it is relatively simple to calculate and because managers instinctively like to recover their investment as rapidly as possible, the payout calculation, in this or modified forms, is frequently used to evaluate investment proposals. When used in conjunction with other measures, as just illustrated, payout period is useful in promoting wise investment decision-making. When used as the sole or principal criterion for investment decisions, payout period is dangerous because it may result in the choosing of less profitable investments which yield high initial returns for short periods as compared with more profitable investments which will provide profits for longer periods of time. (The payout-period calculation also ignores the timing of the returns which occur prior to the payout date.)

PROBLEMS

1. The equipment engineer in a company proposes to mechanize an assembly operation by designing and building a new piece of equipment which will eliminate 90 per cent of the labor cost of $120,000 per year. The machine will have an estimated economic life of 10 years, but the cost of design and construction cannot be closely estimated. Determine the maximum cost of designing and constructing the equipment which will be permissible if the investment in the equipment is to yield a 20 per cent prospective return.

2. A manufacturer is undecided whether or not to purchase a facility which will enable him to reduce his distribution expenses by $200,000 a year on a new product because he is uncertain how long demand for the product will continue into the future. The facility will cost $600,000 and is highly specialized. It will therefore have an insignificant salvage value whenever abandoned. What is the minimum life for the facility which will assure a 30 per cent return on the investment?

3. Two 150-hp motors are being considered for installation at a sewage treatment plant. The first costs $1,500 and has an efficiency of 83 per cent. The second costs $1,200 and has an efficiency of 80 per cent. If all the charges such as insurance, maintenance, etc., amount to a total of 15 per cent of the original cost and power costs are at 1.8 cents per kwhr, how many hours of full load of operation per year are necessary to justify purchase of the more expensive motor, if both motors have a life of 25 years and an interest rate of 6 per cent is used?

4. A new water line must be constructed from an existing pumping station to a reservoir 2,000 ft distant. An estimate of costs for three pipe sizes has been made as follows:

Pipe size, inches	Cost per hour for pumping	Estimated construction cost
8	$2.00	$19,000
10	1.50	37,000
12	0.75	62,000

The pipe has a life of 16 years at the end of which there will be no salvage value. Interest is at 15 per cent per annum.

(a) How many hours of pumping per year would be required to make the 8-inch and 10-inch pipes equally economical?

(b) How many hours of pumping per year would be required to make the 10-inch and 12-inch pipes equally economical?

(c) For what ranges of required pumping hours per year is each size of pipe most economical?

5. A manufacturer offers an inventor the choice of two contracts for the exclusive right to manufacture and market the inventor's patented article. Plan A calls for an immediate single lump-sum payment of $30,000. Plan B calls for an annual payment of $1,000 plus a royalty of 50 cents for each unit sold. The remaining life of the patent is 10 years. Using interest compounded annually at 10 per cent, what must be the uniform annual sale of the article to make plan B as attractive to the inventor as plan A? (Disregard income tax considerations.)

6. A telephone switchboard containing 150-pair cable can be made up with either enameled wire or tinned wire. There will be 550 soldered connections. The cost of soldering a connection on the enameled wire will be 1.85 cents; on the tinned wire, 1.25 cents. A 150-pair cable made up with enameled wire costs 65 cents per linear foot; made up with tinned wire, 83 cents per linear foot. (a) Calculate the length of cable run in feet so that the cost of each installation will be the same. (b) For most economical operation, what rule should be applied in deciding whether to use enameled wire or tinned wire?

7. A fruit canner is considering the purchase of an automatic packaging machine which will save $30,000 a year of labor. The machine will cost $60,000, has an estimated economic life of 10 years, and will be depreciated on a straight-line basis. The company's net profit is usually between $500,000 and $1,000,000 per year and it pays only Federal income taxes at the 52 per cent rate on annual profits over $25,000. (a) What is the prospective rate of return after income taxes on this investment? (b) What is the payout period? (c) Under what circumstances might the payout-period calculation be important in deciding whether to purchase the packaging machine?

8. Define the circumstances under which the payout period and the capital-recovery period of a prospective investment would be equal.

Note: Problems 3 through 6 are adapted from professional engineers' examinations.

PART FOUR

Capital Management

13 Capital Investment and Theory of Planning

Some idea of the magnitude of the sums of money invested each year in profit-making and non-profit-making capital projects may be gleaned from the following statistics for 1959:

$37 billion were spent on nonfarm producers' plant and equipment.

$5 billion were spent on farm equipment and on construction and $3 billion on other private construction including religious, educational, social and recreational, and hospital and institutional.

$4 billion additional were invested in inventories.

Expenditures for research and development totaled approximately $12 billion.

Additional billions were invested in working capital by industry.

Many additional billions were spent for capital purposes by Federal, state, and local governments.

What Are Capital Investments? From a capital-planning and -budgeting viewpoint, a capital expenditure is one in which the company's funds are committed for projects which will return the invested funds and profits during future periods.

Capital expenditures, from this planning point of view, need not coincide with the accounting or tax conventions. The criterion for planning purposes is the length of time that the enterprise's resources are committed. From the accounting or tax point of view, capital assets are usually tangible fixed assets which are relatively permanent. In addition, they are not readily convertible to cash or its equivalent (negotiable investments or credit) on short notice; or they will not normally be converted into cash or its equivalent in the normal course of operation of the business, except in so far as a depreciation charge is added to the cost of goods sold and subtracted from the asset value as a depreciation reserve.

Capital expenditures from the accounting viewpoint will, thus, usually cover the procurement, erection, and replacement of such items as buildings, machinery and equipment, automotive vehicles, furniture, etc.

185

Items such as cash, inventories, and accounts receivable are classified as current assets for accounting and tax purposes because they normally turn over into cash one or more times within the accounting year, and management can make adjustments in the sizes of these assets during the year. The cost of machinery, however, must usually be recovered over a period of years and the level of investment is, therefore, not as controllable on short notice.

From a capital-planning point of view, however, this distinction is not valid. If the amount of required cash, inventories, and accounts receivable will be increased by $1,500,000 with the introduction of a new product, then the capital investment required for this new product should include the $1,500,000 cost as a nondepreciating investment. Obviously, $1,500,000 of the enterprise's funds will be tied up in these current assets just as surely as the $600,000 for the nondepreciating land assets on which the new plant is to be built.

Thus, from a planning viewpoint, capital expenditures may include expenditures for items which the accountant and the tax authorities would consider noncapital assets.

Moreover, using this planning concept, capital expenditures may be spent for items which do not even appear as assets on a company financial statement. Thus, expenditures for research and long-term advertising are usually treated as expenses by the company accountants and the tax authorities. (There are usually tax advantages to the company to consider them as expenses.) From the economic planning point of view, however, these expenditures may represent capital investments as important or more important to the long-range future welfare of the enterprise than investments in fixed assets.

Demand Schedule for Capital. A simple theory of capital planning starts with the assumption that we gather together all the capital-investment opportunities in the company. With varying degrees of risk and uncertainty, we can determine for each proposed investment of funds a prospective rate of return. We can then prepare a schedule, such as is shown in Table 13-1, which shows the demand for investment funds arranged in order of decreasing rate of return. With this schedule, the demand for capital in the company is cumulated in Table 13-2 and

Table 13-1. **Schedule of Capital Expenditures**
Year Beginning July 1, 1962

Expected rate of return	Dollars of proposed investment (in thousands)
50% and over	$ 300
40–49.9%	800
30–39.9	2,400
20–29.9	6,200
10–19.9	15,300
5– 9.9	86,700

Table 13-2. **Schedule of Cumulative Demand for Capital**
Year Beginning July 1, 1962

Expected rate of return	Cumulative demand (in thousands)
50% or more	$ 300
40% or more	1,100
30% or more	3,500
20% or more	9,700
10% or more	25,000
5% or more	111,700

plotted in the form of a demand schedule in Figure 13-1.

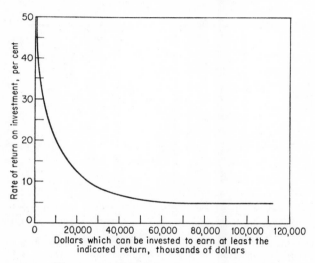

Figure 13-1. Schedule of capital demand.

This demand for capital includes investment proposals for projects to be started during the 1962–1963 fiscal year beginning July 1, 1962. This schedule is a simplification of the actual situation because it does not consider future projects. To provide funds for future projects, it may be desirable to forgo capital investments this year and accumulate cash, government bonds, or other liquid investments; or it may be desirable to invest in capital projects which are short-lived and will return the invested funds rapidly even if the rate of return is relatively low. (When this alternative is being considered, the expected loss in return on investment which is occasioned by the maintenance of this liquid position should be charged to the future project.)

Capital Rationing with No External Supply. If management policy is that all of the monies which will be used for capital expenditures will come from internal sources, that there will be no additional financing from outside the company, then the total supply of funds is fixed. It is the amount which is internally generated by retained earnings and depreciation charges.

We can then have three possible capital-rationing situations, depending upon the following factors: the supply of funds; the minimum rate of return which is specified to justify investment of company money; the demand schedule for capital funds. Figures 13-2 to 13-4 show the three possible situations, in all of which the specified minimum rate of return is 25 per cent and the available capital funds total $2,000,000.

Figure 13-2 shows more funds than projects which will yield the specified minimum return of 25 per cent. The capital-investment pro-

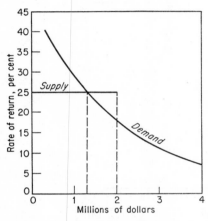

Figure 13-2. Schedules of capital demand and supply—internal supply greater than required for profitable investment (policy of no external financing).

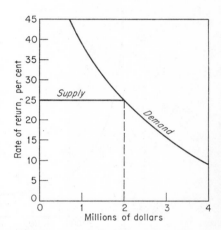

Figure 13-3. Schedules of capital demand and supply—internal supply equal to profitable investment requirements (policy of no external financing).

posals yielding 25 per cent or more total $1,300,000 whereas the funds available for capital investment total $2,000,000.

Figure 13-3 illustrates the infrequent situation in which the funds are just adequate to cover the capital-project demands. Capital-investment proposals yielding 25 per cent or more total $2,000,000 and funds available for capital improvements also total $2,000,000.

In Figure 13-4, the project demand is greater than the available funds and some capital-investment projects will either be postponed or rejected. Capital-investment proposals yielding 25 per cent or more total $2,500,000. Of these investments, $2,000,000 show prospective rates of return of 33 per cent or more. We would postpone or reject the projects totaling $500,000 which yield returns less than 33 per cent but more than 25 per cent unless we decided to obtain further funds by external financing.

Capital Rationing with External Supply. In effect, we have raised the minimum acceptable return in the example of Figure 13-4 from 25 to 33 per cent because the opportunities for profitable investment of funds are so much greater than the supply of funds. At some point we may decide that it is worthwhile to obtain funds from outside sources rather than forego profitable investment opportunities.

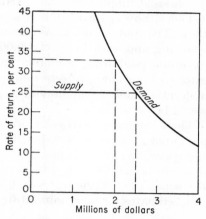

The cost of these outside funds cannot be readily measured. If the funds are raised by sale of stock, the rate of earnings of the present stock may be a first approximation of the incremental cost, but this earnings rate may be misleading because of intangible factors and accounting and tax considerations. If borrowed funds are obtained, the incremental cost is considerably above the interest

Figure 13-4. Schedules of capital demand and supply—internal supply less than required for profitable investment (policy of no external financing).

rate because the additional debt increases the risks and costs of the equity capital.

In any case, management will require a high prospective return on the projects before deciding to obtain external capital. This return will be

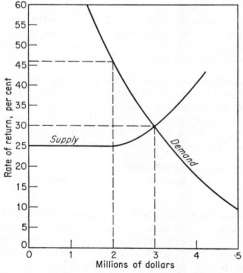

Figure 13-5. Schedules of capital demand and supply—internal and external sources of capital.

higher than if all projects are financed from internal sources. The curve for the supply of capital will, therefore, slope upward at the point where the internal supplies are exhausted.

This situation with external supply of capital is illustrated in Figure 13-5. The project-demand schedule has increased. Without internal financing and with only $2,000,000 of funds available for investment, we would establish a minimum prospective return of 46 per cent. With external financing, projects totaling $3,000,000 of investment would be undertaken and the minimum prospective return on any of these projects would be 30 per cent.

These simple theoretical models for capital-investment planning are presented as a framework for the discussion of capital planning in the enterprise. In our discussion of actual planning procedures, this presentation will be modified to take into account the complicating characteristics which exist in the real world, as well as our inability to obtain accurate estimates for uncertain future events.

PROBLEMS

1. Why is the payment of $2,000,000 for direct labor and $8,000,000 for direct materials this year any less of a capital investment than the payment of $500,000 for equipment?

2. Justify the following statement: Direct labor and direct material are not capital investments, but an investment in inventory (which consists of direct labor, direct material, and indirect expenses) required to manufacture and sell a product is a capital investment.

3. A company which has been using a rate-of-return criterion in budgeting its capital expenditures has made a number of capital investments in which the assets were obsolete before their cost had been fully recovered, with some impairment of the company's cash position. It has therefore been proposed that payout period rather than rate of return be used as the criterion for future capital decisions. Discuss the possible desirability of this change.

4. Can you develop a demand schedule for capital funds using payout period as the criterion? If yes, illustrate such a schedule using assumed data. If no, give the reasons.

5. Referring to the situation shown in Figure 13-2, in which the specified minimum return of 25 per cent results in more funds available than projects, would it be desirable to lower the specified minimum rate of return to increase the number of available projects with high enough prospective rates of return? On what bases would you decide whether to lower it and how much? If you decided not to lower it, would you leave the funds idle or what would you do with them?

14 The Enterprise's Assets and Sources of Funds

The balance sheet of an enterprise lists the assets of the enterprise and discloses where the funds were obtained to acquire the assets. It constitutes a summary statement of the condition of the enterprise as of a given date.

Since it is not practical to add lathes, government bonds, notes receivable, buildings, land, etc., and come up with a meaningful result, the common denominator used in this summary statement is dollars.

To promote ease of understanding the balance sheet statement and to facilitate analysis, the assets and liabilities of the enterprise are classified into convenient groupings. These classifications have been relatively standardized by accounting practice over a period of time. When the balance sheet has been prepared in accordance with accepted practice, fairly definite meanings can be applied to the classifications.

Assets. The assets of an enterprise consist of its property of all categories, what it owns and what is owed to it. The assets can be conveniently divided into four principal categories:

1. Current assets: assets which can be converted to cash or its equivalent (negotiable instruments or credits) on short notice or which will be converted into cash or its equivalent in the normal course of operation of the business. These current assets, with the exception of temporary investments in negotiable securities, are converted through successive current asset stages until they become cash or its equivalent. Six of the major types of current assets are listed here:
   a. Cash (on hand or in bank)
   b. Negotiable government securities and marketable securities on short-term investment
   c. Notes receivable (from sale of the company's product)
   d. Accounts receivable (from sale of the company's product, less reserve for bad debts)
   e. Inventories—finished goods, work in process, and raw materials (obsolete material should not be carried on the books)
   f. Advances on inventory purchases

2. Fixed assets: assets which are relatively permanent and are not converted to cash or its equivalent in the normal course of operation of the business (except in so far as a depreciation charge is added to the cost of goods sold and subtracted from the asset value as a depreciation reserve). The major types of fixed assets are the following:

   a. Land
   b. Buildings and any leasehold improvements
   c. Factory machinery, equipment, and tools
   d. Office equipment, furniture, and fixtures
   e. Automobiles, trucks, and other vehicles

3. Intangible assets: assets which are not available for paying the debts of a company and which are frequently converted to expenses over a number of years. Some of these intangible items are listed here:

   a. Good will
   b. Copyrights
   c. Organization expenses
   d. Development expenses
   e. Franchises
   f. Mailing lists
   g. Patents
   h. Trade names and trademarks
   i. Designs and processes

Some of these intangible assets, such as copyrights, patents, etc., have a limited life. Their asset value should therefore be amortized over this limited life by charging periodically a portion of the value in the operating statements of the company. Even assets with unlimited lives, such as organization expenses and perpetual franchises, are usually amortized over a limited period of time.

4. Miscellaneous assets: assets which do not fit into any of the previous three categories. The more usual types of miscellaneous assets are:

   a. Prepaid expenses, such as unexpired insurance or prepaid rent
   b. Deferred charges, representing expenses for materials and services the benefits of which will extend into the future
   c. Investments which are not temporary or are not negotiable and readily marketable (These cannot be considered current assets because there may be some question as to the amount of money they will bring if they have to be sold on short notice.)
   d. Special funds earmarked for specific purposes and, therefore, not available for general purposes

Liabilities. The liabilities of an enterprise disclose where the funds were obtained to acquire the assets.[1] They can be conveniently divided

---

[1] The term "equities" is sometimes used instead of liabilities to denote the claims of creditors and owners in the assets of the business. When this is done, the term "liabilities" is used to include only the claims of creditors (debt equity).

into three principal categories:

1. Current liabilities: obligations to short-term creditors, generally due and payable within one year. Current liabilities include the following categories:
   a. Notes payable
   b. Accounts payable
   c. Accrued expenses (wages, salaries, interest, rent, taxes, etc., owed but not yet necessarily due for payment)
   d. Advance payments and deposits from customers
   e. Unpaid declared dividends
   f. Funded debt (or portion thereof) maturing within a year
2. Other liabilities: consisting of all noncurrent obligations to nonowners. The principal categories are:
   a. Long-term liabilities, such as bonds, mortgages, long-term notes, etc. (items which are due and payable more than one year in the future)
   b. Reserves for general contingencies—if a reserve is for a specific contingency which probably will occur during the next year, it should be set up as a current liability
   c. Unearned income—received for materials and/or services which have not yet been completely rendered
3. Net worth: consisting of the liability of the enterprise to its owners. It represents the owner's equity in the business and is the amount which is available to the owners after all other debts of every kind have been paid. It indicates the direct and indirect contributions of the owners toward the procurement of the assets of the enterprise. The principal categories are:
   a. Preferred stock
   b. Class A, B, C, D, etc., stock
   c. Common stock
   d. Unearned or capital surplus (derived from sale of stock at a price in excess of par or book value, write-up of fixed assets, donations, etc.)
   e. Earned surplus or undistributed profits

Determination of Balance Sheet Values. Current assets, such as cash and advances on inventory purchases, are taken at actual value. Securities and new-material inventories should usually be valued at purchase price or market price, whichever is less. Receivables are taken at face value less a deduction for bad debts determined by careful analysis. Work-in-process and finished-goods inventory values contain material, labor, overhead, and depreciation costs, some of which are necessarily estimated costs.

Fixed assets, such as land, are usually valued at cost or market value, whichever is less.   Buildings, equipment, vehicles, etc., should generally be valued at cost, plus improvements, less accumulated depreciation. Because of wide inflationary and deflationary fluctuations in the actual economic value of such assets, balance sheet values may bear little relationship to the actual value of a fixed asset.

Since intangible assets cannot be physically valued, the methods for determining the values shown on the balance sheet are numerous. They may be estimates, or guesses, or they may be related to expenditures or surveys by various types of formulas.

Miscellaneous assets should never be valued in excess of market value.

With the exception of reserves for contingencies, liability values are generally definite fixed amounts. Contingency reserves are, of course, estimates which must be made after careful appraisal of all the facts in the situation.

Contingent liabilities that are sometimes omitted from the balance sheet statement, or carried in a footnote, must nevertheless be considered in any financial analyses. The ratio analyses considered later may be biased considerably if such liabilities are not considered. Thus, if notes receivable have been discounted at the bank with recourse (this means that the bank has purchased the note for cash or credit but will have a claim against the company if the signer of the note fails to pay the amount owed), then, for analytic purposes the amounts of discounted notes should be added to the current assets side and the current liabilities side of the balance sheet.

Balance Sheet of a Representative Enterprise. A balance sheet of a representative enterprise is shown in Table 14-1.

Current Assets. The item of $800,000 cash represents money on deposit in the bank and bills and coin in the till. United States government securities of $200,000 represent assets which can be readily converted into cash. The company has $60,000 of notes receivable owed to it by customers who gave notes instead of cash payment. Accounts receivable of $200,000 represents the net amount owed and expected to be paid to the company by customers who purchased on credit. The actual face value of these accounts receivable is $210,000, but $10,000 was set up as a reserve for bad debts which the company expects because some customers will probably fail to pay their bills.

The company has $310,000 of finished-goods inventories representing the products which are ready for sale; it has $140,000 worth of partially finished goods which are in various stages of manufacture; and it has $200,000 of raw materials which are available for use in manufacturing its products. In addition it paid for, but has not yet received, $15,000 worth of items used in the enterprise. The total current assets—items that are readily convertible into cash or that will be converted to cash in a relatively short time in the normal operation of the business—thus total $1,925,000.

Table 14-1. The Schabe Corporation
Balance Sheet as of September 30, 1960

Assets			*Liabilities*		
Current Assets:			Current Liabilities:		
Cash		$ 800,000	Notes Payable		$ 150,000
U.S. Government Securities		200,000	Accounts Payable		200,000
Notes Receivable		60,000	Accrued Expenses		60,000
Accounts Receivable		200,000	Customer Advances		25,000
Inventories:			Maturing Debt		10,000
Finished Goods	$310,000		Total Current Liabilities		$ 445,000
Work in Process	140,000		Other Liabilities:		
Raw Material	200,000	650,000	First Mortgage Bonds, 8%, 1980	$1,000,000	
Purchase Advances		15,000	Long-term Notes, 4 to 7%	290,000	
Total Current Assets		$1,925,000	Reserve for Contingencies	200,000	
Fixed Assets:			Unearned Income	25,000	
Land		$ 200,000	Total Other Liabilities		$1,515,000
Buildings	$1,100,000		Net Worth:		
Less: Reserve for De-			4½% Preferred Stock (authorized		
preciation	185,000	915,000	5,000 shares, issued 4,000 shares		
Machinery and Equip-			of $100 par value)		$ 400,000
ment	$ 900,000		Common Stock (authorized and		
Less: Reserve for De-			issued 400,000 shares of no par		
preciation	280,000	620,000	value)		1,000,000
Total Fixed Assets		$1,735,000	Unearned Surplus		200,000
Intangible Assets:			Earned Surplus		350,001
Patents		$ 60,000	Total Net Worth		$1,950,001
Good will		1			
Total Intangible Assets		$ 60,001			
Miscellaneous Assets:					
Prepayments		$ 20,000			
Deferred Charges		100,000			
Permanent Investments		70,000			
Total Miscellaneous Assets		$ 190,000			
Total		$3,910,001	Total		$3,910,001

Fixed Assets. The company owns land costing $200,000 and worth a bit more at present market prices. Its buildings, costing $1,100,000, have a book value of $915,000 because of accumulated depreciation totaling $185,000. Its machinery and equipment, originally costing $900,000, now have a book value of $620,000, since the amount depreciated is $280,000. The fixed assets of the company—items which last a relatively long time— thus total $1,735,000.

Intangible Assets. The intangible assets of the company total $60,001. Actually they may be worth considerably more or less, but it is difficult to measure them accurately. The value of the patents is carried at $60,000. Good will, which can have a substantial value, is in this case carried at a nominal $1.

Miscellaneous Assets. The company rents a small warehouse and pays its rent in advance each year. Since the manufacturer has not yet received the benefits from the use of this warehouse for which it has paid, but possesses the right to receive the benefits in the future, this is an asset coming to the enterprise in the future. This prepayment is valued at $20,000.

Last year the company retained the services of a marketing specialist and spent $200,000 in preparing for and introducing a new product. Because the benefits from this expenditure will accrue to the manufacturer over a period of years, he has decided to defer a portion of these charges to the future years in which the benefits will be obtained. On our current balance sheet, the amount of this deferment is $100,000.

The firm has investments in the securities of other firms. These investments cost $70,000 at the times of purchase. They now have a market value somewhat in excess of this figure.

Current Liabilities. The manufacturer owes $150,000 to bearers of short-term promissory notes which it has given to some of its suppliers in payment for raw materials. In addition, the company owes $200,000 on unpaid bills for material, supplies, electricity, insurance, etc. Besides these debts, however, the company owes its employees wages for work performed since the last payroll date; it owes contributions to the pension fund; it has taxes for the past year which can be estimated, even though they have not been billed; all of these accrued expenses total $60,000.

Customers have sent in $25,000 in advance of shipment of the merchandise by the company. The company is, therefore, obligated to these customers to the extent of $25,000. In addition, $10,000 of the long-term notes of the company will come due for payment during the next fiscal year.

Other Liabilities. Besides the current liabilities mentioned above, the company owes funds to people on a long-term basis. Thus, the company has a liability of $1,000,000 to the owners of its outstanding first-mortgage bonds. These bonds constitute a promise to pay the face value of the bonds totaling $1,000,000 in 1980 and to pay 8 per cent interest each year until then. Security for the loan is provided by a mortgage on some of the company property. The firm also owes $290,000 in long-term notes which bear from 4 to 7 per cent interest and mature over a period of years.

The company guarantees certain assemblies in its products for 25 years. As a precaution against the contingency that a number of these assemblies may not perform properly, a $200,000 reserve is set up to cover expenses in backing up the guarantee. If this contingent liability were not set up on the statement and the company incurred these expenses in connection with the guarantee, the surplus would have been overstated and the financial position would have appeared better than it really was.

The manufacturer has service contracts with some local concerns and has received $25,000 on these contracts for service to be rendered during the coming year. This represents unearned income.

Net Worth. The stockholders of the company have an equity in its assets totaling $1,950,001. The preferred stockholders own 4,000 shares having a par value of $400,000. The common stockholders have an equity totaling $1,550,001 in the company's assets. This equity is carried on the balance sheet under three classifications: 400,000 shares of no par value common stock carried on the books at $2.50 per share; $200,000 of unearned surplus; $350,001 of earned surplus.

Ratio Analysis. Ratio comparisons of items appearing on the balance sheet and operating statement of a company are sometimes useful in understanding the significance of the dollar values in each asset classification and the amounts of money obtained from the various sources to acquire the assets. Every time you compare one item on a balance sheet with another, you are making a ratio comparison.

It is frequently considered desirable to use tangible net worth values rather than total net worth in computing financial ratios. Tangible net worth is lower than net worth by the amount of intangible assets. Items of an intangible nature are not as commonly carried on balance sheets as they were years ago. When they are, the value carried on the books frequently bears little relationship to the real values.

For our illustrative example of the Schabe Corporation, whose balance sheet is shown in Table 14-1 and whose profit and loss statement is shown in Table 3-1, we can compute the following types of ratios.

Relating sources of funds (ownership versus borrowed) and types of assets

1. Percentage of tangible assets purchased with ownership funds

$$\frac{\text{Tangible net worth}}{\text{Total tangible assets}} = \frac{\$1,890,000}{\$3,850,000}(100) = 49\%$$

2. Debt as a percentage of ownership funds

$$\frac{\text{Total liabilities}}{\text{Tangible net worth}} = \frac{\$1,960,000}{\$1,890,000}(100) = 104\%$$

3. Current debt as a percentage of ownership funds

$$\frac{\text{Total current liabilities}}{\text{Tangible net worth}} = \frac{\$445,000}{\$1,890,000}(100) = 24\%$$

4. Percentage of ownership funds invested in fixed assets

$$\frac{\text{Total fixed assets}}{\text{Tangible net worth}} = \frac{\$1,735,000}{\$1,890,000}(100) = 92\%$$

5. Funded debt (long-term liabilities) as a percentage of net working capital. (Net working capital is equal to the excess of current assets over current liabilities.)

$$\frac{\text{Long-term liabilities}}{\text{Net working capital}} = \frac{\$1,290,000}{\$1,480,000}(100) = 87\%$$

The ratio of net worth to total assets shows the proportion of the business assets which is owned by the stockholders or owners. The ratio of liabilities to net worth measures the relative proportion of the business assets owned by creditors and stockholders (the ratio of owed to owned). The ratio of liabilities to net worth is equal to the reciprocal of the ratio of net worth to total assets minus one.

Obligations to creditors must be paid when they become due: bond-holder interest payments and repayment of principal and accounts and notes receivable payments cannot be postponed at management's discretion. Stockholders, however, receive dividends only at the discretion of the management. These dividends are, thus, not fixed obligations of the company. Therefore, the higher the proportion of the funds which comes from creditors, the higher the fixed obligations and risks to the company if business is poor and losses occur. On the other hand, it is good business to borrow money at say 5 per cent interest if the business can earn a 25 per cent return using the money. However, it is necessary to be sure that too large a proportion of the company's funds are not acquired through debt obligations or the company will not be able to withstand adverse economic conditions.

Current debt to net worth is the ratio of short-term obligations to stockholder investment. It is a measure of the short-term risks and stability of the company.

The ratio of fixed assets to net worth discloses what proportion of the stockholder's money is tied up in fixed assets. The stockholders should usually own all of the plant and equipment and in addition have some of their ownership capital left for other purposes.

When the ratio of funded debt to net working capital is equal to or greater than one, the entire working capital of the company is coming from long-term creditors.

Measuring liquidity—the ability to meet current debts

1. Current assets as a percentage of current liabilities—the current ratio

$$\frac{\text{Total current assets}}{\text{Total current liabilities}} = \frac{\$1,925,000}{\$445,000} (100) = 433\%$$

2. Quick assets (current assets less inventories) as a percentage of current liabilities—the acid test

$$\frac{\text{Total quick assets}}{\text{Total current liabilities}} = \frac{\$1,275,000}{\$445,000} (100) = 287\%$$

3. Cash as a percentage of current liabilities—the cash position

$$\frac{\text{Total cash}}{\text{Total current liabilities}} = \frac{\$800,000}{\$445,000} (100) = 180\%$$

4. Current debt as a percentage of inventory

$$\frac{\text{Total current liabilities}}{\text{Total inventory}} = \frac{\$445,000}{\$650,000} (100) = 68\%$$

The current ratio is the most commonly used measure of the ability of a company to pay its current debts promptly. Current assets are used to pay current debts as the assets are converted to cash in the normal course of business. However, a company with a high percentage of its current assets in inventory is usually in a far poorer position to meet its current obligations than another with the same current ratio, but with a smaller percentage of its current assets in inventory.

The acid-test ratio therefore uses quick assets as a percentage of current liabilities. It excludes inventories, including only cash, temporary investments quickly convertible to cash, and accounts and notes receivable.

The cash-position liquidity ratio uses only cash as a percentage of current liabilities to measure ability to meet current debts.

Current debt as a percentage of inventory is useful as a means of converting the current ratio to the acid-test ratio. The acid-test ratio equals the current ratio minus the reciprocal of the current-debt-to-inventory ratio.

Measuring operating effectiveness

1. Receivables as a percentage of sales

$$\frac{\text{Accounts and notes receivable}}{\text{Net sales}} = \frac{\$260,000}{\$4,850,000} (100) = 5.4\%$$

When information is available on net credit sales,

$$\frac{\text{Accounts and notes receivable}}{\text{Net credit sales}} = \frac{\$260,000}{\$4,400,000*} (100) = 5.9\%$$

2. Collection period

$$\frac{\text{Accounts and notes receivable}}{\text{Net credit sales}} (365) = \frac{\$260,000}{\$4,400,000*} (365) = 22 \text{ days}$$

3. Ratio of sales to inventory

$$\frac{\text{Net sales}}{\text{Total inventory}} = \frac{\$4,850,000}{\$650,000} = 7.5$$

4. Inventory-turnover rate

$$\frac{\text{Cost of goods sold}}{\text{Average inventory}} = \frac{\$2,900,000}{\$765,000\dagger} = 3.8$$

5. Inventory as a percentage of net working capital

$$\frac{\text{Total inventory}}{\text{Net working capital}} = \frac{\$650,000}{\$1,480,000} (100) = 44\%$$

* $450,000 of the $4,850,000 net sales shown in the profit and loss statement were for cash.
† From internal company records.

6. Sales as a percentage of total assets

$$\frac{\text{Net sales}}{\text{Total tangible assets*}} = \frac{\$4,850,000}{\$3,850,000} (100) = 126\%$$

7. Sales as a percentage of fixed assets

$$\frac{\text{Net sales}}{\text{Total fixed assets*}} = \frac{\$4,850,000}{\$1,735,000} (100) = 280\%$$

8. Sales as a percentage of net worth

$$\frac{\text{Net sales}}{\text{Tangible net worth*}} = \frac{\$4,850,000}{\$1,890,000} (100) = 257\%$$

9. Sales as a percentage of total permanent capital investment

$$\frac{\text{Net sales}}{\text{Tangible net worth* + long-term liabilities*}}$$
$$= \frac{\$4,850,000(100)}{\$1,890,000 + \$1,290,000} = 153\%$$

The ratio of receivables to sales (preferably credit sales only) is a measure of the effectiveness of the credit and collection performance. If this ratio is multiplied by the 365 days in the year, we obtain the number of average day's sales which are uncollected. This collection period should be related to the credit terms which the company extends to its customers.

Sales as a ratio to inventory gives an approximate indication of the rate at which inventory moves through the business. It gives an indication when the size of the inventory is too large or the merchandising of the company's products is too slow. When the figures are available for its computation, inventory-turnover rate gives a more accurate representation of inventory movement.[1]

As a business expands, its inventory-turnover rate may remain constant, but the total investment in inventory relative to net working capital may increase. If this ratio increases too much, the business may become vulnerable to bankruptcy if the value of the inventory were to drop suddenly. Net working capital may then be seriously reduced.

Sales as a percentage of fixed assets can also be considered a turnover ratio. Other things being equal, the higher the ratio of sales to fixed assets, the greater the flexibility to operate at relatively low sales volumes and still make a profit.

---

* The end-of-year value is used here, although it would be more logical to use an average if it were available. A simple average of the beginning- and end-of-year figures would be suitable in some cases.

[1] When there is a highly seasonal pattern in the industry, the collection period and receivables as a percentage of sales calculations may not be indicative of average conditions throughout the year when calculated using receivable values as of one date rather than more representative average values.

The ratio of sales to net worth is a measure of how rapidly the owner-ship money is being turned over. The ratio of sales to net worth and long-term liabilities shows how sales compare with the total relatively perma-nent investment of funds by both owners and creditors.

Measuring profitability

1. Profit as a percentage of sales

$$\frac{\text{Net profit after taxes}}{\text{Net sales}} = \frac{\$316,320}{\$4,850,000} \, (100) = 6.5\%$$

2. Profit as a percentage of net worth

$$\frac{\text{Net profit after taxes}}{\text{Tangible net worth*}} = \frac{\$316,320}{\$1,890,000} \, (100) = 17\%$$

3. Profit as a percentage of net working capital

$$\frac{\text{Net profit after taxes}}{\text{Net working capital*}} = \frac{\$316,320}{\$1,480,000} \, (100) = 21\%$$

4. Profit as a percentage of total assets

$$\frac{\text{Net profit after taxes}}{\text{Total tangible assets*}} = \frac{\$316,320}{\$3,850,000} \, (100) = 8.2\%$$

5. Pretax profit as a percentage of permanent capital investment

$$\frac{\text{Net profit before taxes + interest on long-term obligations}}{\text{Tangible net worth* + long-term liabilities*}}$$
$$= \frac{\$316,320 + \$94,000}{\$1,890,000 + \$1,290,000} \, (100) = 13\%$$

Profit as a percentage of sales measures the profit margin per dollar of sales.

Profit as a percentage of net worth measures the return on the owner-ship investment and is thus usually closer to a measure of how well the enterprise is achieving its objectives. This ratio can be calculated by multiplying profit as a percentage of sales by the previously computed turnover ratio of sales as a percentage of net worth.

Profit as a percentage of total assets measures the return on the total investment in assets from all sources, including ownership and long- and short-term liabilities. It is equal to the profit margin per dollar of sales times the turnover ratio of sales to total assets.

Pretax profit as a percentage of permanent capital investment measures the return on the total investment of owners and long-term creditors. It is done on a pretax basis here to give the same treatment to profits (which

---

* The end-of-year value is used here, although it would be more logical to use an average if it were available. A simple average of the beginning- and end-of-year figures would be suitable in some cases.

are subject to income tax) and to interest expenses (which are not subject to income tax).

It is important to remember that ratios give a static picture of a dynamic situation and that they may therefore be misleading. The ratios change continually and may change drastically during a year of normal operations if the business follows a sharp seasonal pattern. Thus, a ratio at any given time may not be typical of the enterprise's inherent condition.

For example, a firm with current assets equal to $400,000 and current liabilities equal to $100,000 before the start of its busy season purchases $500,000 worth of merchandise on open account. This increases its current assets to $900,000 and its current liabilities to $600,000. Its current asset to current liability ratio then goes down from 4.00 to 1.50.

Many additional ratios, which will not be mentioned here, can be constructed to shed light on balance sheet and profit and loss relationships in specific situations. However, an individual ratio comparison, no matter how impressive it may look, will not by itself be very meaningful. A high or low ratio value can never be considered always good or bad. We must establish some bases for comparison to give the ratio any real meaning. These ratios acquire meaning:

1. When the ratio values for other similar firms are available for comparison. Firms in different industries have markedly different production and marketing characteristics which will affect their ratios. Differences in size will also have a great influence on these values in many instances. Differences in accounting practice and classification between companies may detract from the validity of some comparisons. Changes in the value of the dollar can also distort ratio comparisons between firms: for example, one firm may have acquired its assets when prices were low and another when prices were higher.

2. When changes in the ratio values over a period of time are examined. This provides us with historical standards to compare our ratios with our own past and the past of other similar firms. Of course, changes in the value of the dollar may distort some historical comparisons.

3. When the different ratios which reveal complementary aspects of the business are used in conjunction with each other. For example, a lowering of the inventory-turnover ratio may be accompanied by a rise in the profit ratio because the company can now charge more when it provides faster customer service.

4. When one relates the changes in values over time with changes in the goals and operating policies and procedures of the company. For example, a company may have a plan for long-run growth in profits which envisages a development period in which operations will not be as profitable as in the immediate past.

Table 14-2. 1959 Ratios with Interquartile Range, Manufacturers

Line of business (and number of concerns reporting)	Interquartile range	Current assets to current debt	Net profits on net sales	Net profits on tangible net worth	Net profits on net working capital	Net sales to tangible net worth	Net sales to net working capital	Collection period	Net sales to inventory	Fixed assets to tangible net worth	Current debt to tangible net worth	Total debt to tangible net worth	Inventory to net working capital	Current debt to inventory	Funded debts to net working capital
		Times	Per cent	Per cent	Per cent	Times	Times	Days	Times	Per cent	Per cent	Per cent	Per cent	Per cent	Per cent
Furniture (139)	Upper Quartile	4.59	5.23	17.45	28.24	4.20	7.57	32	8.2	17.3	18.1	38.7	49.8	49.7	8.8
	Median	2.82	3.12	8.94	15.34	3.05	5.34	41	6.3	33.3	33.8	66.6	79.3	67.9	22.7
	Lower Quartile	1.97	1.15	3.48	5.30	2.46	3.88	51	4.3	53.2	66.7	107.8	116.4	103.0	47.2
Hardware and tools (98)	Upper Quartile	5.00	5.66	14.57	23.06	3.49	6.33	34	6.6	23.8	18.1	30.2	52.9	42.7	11.1
	Median	3.35	3.71	7.84	12.90	2.53	4.05	40	4.7	33.6	28.2	44.6	77.4	55.4	26.8
	Lower Quartile	2.57	1.80	4.87	9.09	1.77	3.01	45	3.3	51.4	42.7	69.4	98.9	81.8	38.9
Hosiery (74)	Upper Quartile	5.67	4.52	8.59	16.94	3.43	6.71	25	10.1	29.8	11.9	28.8	50.9	37.1	10.5
	Median	3.12	2.83	5.93	11.25	2.09	4.09	38	5.4	42.5	23.0	53.4	76.5	56.9	52.3
	Lower Quartile	2.00	0.61	1.63	4.65	1.47	2.81	46	4.2	62.0	42.1	115.3	117.8	103.6	82.5
Lumber (74)	Upper Quartile	5.88	8.80	11.52	27.23	3.16	6.15	28	8.2	24.0	11.2	35.9	41.6	40.5	25.1
	Median	3.04	4.00	8.87	15.85	1.72	3.14	36	5.2	44.7	20.6	59.7	75.8	70.0	62.8
	Lower Quartile	1.91	2.20	5.14	7.56	0.92	1.98	45	3.8	61.0	38.3	90.0	102.3	103.2	171.4
Machine shops (143)	Upper Quartile	5.16	4.42	9.84	22.55	2.95	8.03	34	16.6	33.1	13.9	32.0	37.6	47.6	22.9
	Median	2.76	2.07	3.82	8.83	1.84	4.71	43	7.1	51.8	31.4	60.4	66.2	89.0	42.1
	Lower Quartile	1.75	0.23	0.37	0.73	1.40	2.53	55	4.1	70.2	50.6	88.7	95.0	206.8	71.1
Machinery, industrial (439)	Upper Quartile	4.65	5.79	11.74	17.95	3.08	4.55	39	6.4	21.7	18.5	35.1	51.9	45.0	12.7
	Median	3.34	3.43	7.49	11.39	2.06	3.11	52	4.3	32.3	29.5	54.9	71.4	68.8	26.2
	Lower Quartile	2.31	1.31	3.26	4.37	1.61	2.39	65	3.2	44.0	49.0	81.9	93.0	102.6	39.4
Meats and provisions, packers (69)	Upper Quartile	3.28	2.54	13.21	39.74	9.65	34.15	9	38.7	42.2	20.8	44.5	46.6	71.9	34.9
	Median	2.34	1.18	8.10	22.24	6.76	17.52	12	28.2	60.4	34.2	73.7	68.0	126.9	60.5
	Lower Quartile	1.70	0.75	5.14	12.67	5.52	11.53	15	18.4	76.3	59.1	108.7	105.4	194.1	121.0

SOURCE: Roy A. Foulke, *How Does Your Business Compare with Others in Your Line?*, Dun & Bradstreet, Inc., New York, 1961, pp. 4–5.

Table 14-3. Median Ratios for 1955 to 1959, Manufacturers

Number of concerns	Current assets to current debt	Net profits on net sales	Net profits on tangible net worth	Net profits on net wkg. cap.	Net sales to tangible net worth	Net sales to net wkg. capital	Collection period	Net sales to inventory	Fixed assets to tangible net worth	Current debt to tangible net worth	Total debt to tangible net worth	Inventory to net working capital	Current debt to inventory	Funded debts to net wkg. capital
	Times	Per cent	Per cent	Per cent	Times	Times	Days	Times	Per cent	Per cent	Per cent	Per cent	Per cent	Per cent
Furniture:														
1955...144	3.12	2.88	10.38	15.32	3.25	5.29	43	8.1	32.5	30.6	57.7	67.5	75.2	28.0
1956...146	2.94	3.30	10.54	14.12	3.08	4.78	42	6.4	33.0	33.0	68.8	69.4	78.3	24.6
1957...146	3.17	2.22	7.70	12.90	2.97	4.90	41	5.9	31.5	29.8	59.7	68.7	72.2	23.0
1958...141	3.24	1.79	5.63	8.90	2.78	4.27	48	6.2	29.8	28.8	54.8	68.2	67.4	26.9
1959...139	2.82	3.12	8.94	15.34	3.05	5.34	41	6.3	33.8	33.6	66.8	79.3	67.9	22.7
Five-year average	3.06	2.66	8.64	13.32	3.03	4.92	43	6.6	32.1	31.2	61.6	70.6	72.2	25.0
Hardware and Tools:														
1955...95	3.44	5.88	12.12	18.68	2.06	2.95	37	4.2	33.6	29.2	46.9	79.6	59.8	19.8
1956...96	3.25	4.95	10.40	16.35	2.30	3.52	38	4.7	35.5	29.1	46.0	80.7	59.0	28.2
1957...102	3.57	3.69	10.25	15.44	2.30	3.36	34	4.8	36.8	24.9	43.5	75.7	50.4	24.8
1958...100	4.07	3.23	6.98	11.00	2.03	3.42	42	4.6	37.0	23.5	52.0	67.6	58.6	34.8
1959...98	3.35	3.71	7.84	12.90	2.53	4.05	40	4.7	33.6	28.2	44.6	77.4	55.4	26.8
Five-year average	3.54	4.29	9.52	14.87	2.24	3.46	38	4.6	35.3	27.0	46.6	76.2	56.6	26.9
Hosiery:														
1955...73	3.32	1.68	3.97	11.16	2.21	4.85	34	5.8	49.6	23.3	49.7	79.4	56.5	41.0
1956...77	4.13	1.41	3.07	6.04	2.31	4.95	30	5.3	44.8	15.9	53.9	68.6	48.3	35.6
1957...75	3.47	1.67	3.89	7.32	2.58	4.49	31	5.8	42.1	19.6	52.2	72.3	55.9	27.5
1958...71	3.52	1.11	3.95	7.78	2.20	4.08	41	5.2	41.8	20.4	92.4	68.3	58.8	45.6
1959...74	3.12	2.83	5.93	11.25	2.09	4.09	38	5.4	42.5	23.0	53.4	76.5	56.9	52.3
Five-year average	3.51	1.74	4.16	8.71	2.28	4.49	35	5.5	44.2	20.4	60.3	73.0	55.3	40.4
Lumber:														
1955...67	3.54	6.53	11.53	24.81	1.68	4.32	29	5.8	39.0	19.4	39.1	69.1	62.8	44.9
1956...73	3.31	4.80	7.17	14.00	1.61	4.02	26	4.6	33.0	16.2	48.5	74.7	54.5	44.1

204

1957...72	3.63	3.54	5.32	9.56	1.66	3.72	32	5.5	31.1	17.3	49.5	77.8	55.5	38.8
1958...74	3.51	3.30	7.67	13.71	2.29	3.67	38	5.9	37.0	18.9	56.4	75.3	55.8	51.4
1959...74	3.04	4.00	8.87	15.85	1.72	3.14	36	5.2	44.7	20.6	59.7	75.8	70.0	62.8
Five-year average	3.41	4.43	8.11	15.59	1.79	3.77	32	5.4	37.0	18.5	50.6	74.5	59.7	48.4
Machine Shops:														
1955...146	2.90	3.25	7.05	13.91	2.07	3.82	38	5.8	42.8	28.7	65.4	70.6	88.1	30.0
1956...162	2.60	4.94	12.77	21.72	2.43	4.24	37	5.4	44.5	35.5	64.1	76.8	84.4	34.6
1957...151	2.88	3.99	10.90	17.97	2.28	4.50	33	8.5	45.2	28.2	49.8	69.2	91.9	31.8
1958...145	3.93	2.38	3.91	6.11	1.56	3.28	40	4.9	44.8	17.8	33.8	60.2	67.3	34.4
1959...143	2.76	2.07	3.82	8.83	1.84	4.71	43	7.1	51.8	31.4	60.4	66.2	89.0	42.1
Five-year average	3.01	3.33	7.69	13.71	2.04	4.11	38	6.3	45.8	28.3	54.7	68.6	84.1	34.6
Machinery, Industrial:														
1955...360	2.80	3.38	8.66	14.05	2.51	3.72	48	4.6	34.4	37.1	65.5	76.1	77.2	24.6
1956...389	2.78	4.06	11.17	16.78	2.62	3.89	46	4.4	35.1	36.9	68.5	79.5	72.1	22.8
1957...364	3.09	3.76	10.16	15.14	2.50	3.69	44	4.6	32.6	31.2	60.3	74.6	69.7	25.6
1958...358	3.68	2.98	6.16	9.59	2.04	3.07	47	4.6	32.4	25.5	49.3	63.7	66.8	23.0
1959...439	3.34	3.43	7.49	11.39	2.06	3.11	52	4.3	32.3	29.5	54.9	71.4	68.8	26.2
Five-year average	3.14	3.52	8.73	13.39	2.35	3.50	47	4.5	33.4	32.0	59.7	73.1	70.9	24.4
Meats and Provisions, Packers:														
1955...71	2.13	1.04	7.80	18.10	8.05	16.61	12	25.6	57.7	34.0	70.9	73.0	112.3	45.7
1956...72	2.23	0.85	8.31	19.92	7.29	15.20	13	23.6	63.1	35.2	65.7	76.4	106.4	43.5
1957...72	2.42	0.78	6.04	15.66	7.36	16.88	11	24.7	58.4	31.7	66.7	64.4	98.1	50.2
1958...68	1.99	0.58	5.57	12.99	9.68	20.32	10	26.0	62.9	41.0	71.7	87.0	104.8	52.2
1959...69	2.34	1.18	8.10	22.24	6.76	17.52	12	28.2	60.4	34.2	73.7	68.0	126.9	60.5
Five-year average	2.22	0.89	7.16	17.78	7.83	17.31	12	25.6	60.5	35.2	69.7	73.8	109.7	50.4

SOURCE: Roy A. Foulke, *How Does Your Business Compare with Others in Your Line?*, Dun & Bradstreet, Inc., New York, 1961, p. 11.

Information for comparisons with other individual firms may be obtained from their annual reports as prepared for stockholders or for the Securities and Exchange Commission, where available. The latter are usually preferable because of the prescribed uniformity and more detailed information.

Data for industry-wide comparisons are frequently available from many trade associations and other industry groups. The groups will sometimes carefully define the accounting terminology and concepts used in the reporting to assist in obtaining comparable data from all firms.

Other sources of ratio data are organizations such as Dun & Bradstreet, Inc., and Robert Morris Associates who prepare ratio information by industry. Table 14-2 shows a portion of the tables issued by Dun & Bradstreet, Inc., showing the interquartile range[1] for 14 ratios in 72 lines of business activity. This table thus reveals something about the variation of ratio values among firms in the industry. Table 14-3 shows a portion of other tables issued by Dun & Bradstreet, Inc., showing the 14 median ratios for the same 72 lines of activity for 1955–1959 to provide a historical basis for comparisons.

PROBLEMS

Problems 1 through 9 refer to the Trane Company whose balance sheet is shown in Table 14-4.

1. Why are inventories considered current assets?

2. Why are patents considered intangible assets?

3. Investments are listed as $300,000 in current assets and $650,000 in miscellaneous assets. Can this be logical? Explain.

4. Should any adjustments be made in the balance sheet based on each of the following facts? If yes, indicate what adjustments should be made. If no, give reason. (a) The inventory value of $1,200,000 is the cost to Trane. The market value is $1,400,000. (b) The Trane Company has not made any allowance in the above statement for uncollectible accounts receivable.

---

[1] Explanation of interquartile ranges: The median ratio of current assets to current debt of manufacturers of furniture is 2.82. To obtain this figure the ratios of current assets to current debt for each of the 139 concerns were arranged in a graduated series with the largest ratio at the top and the smallest at the bottom. The median ratio of 2.82 was the ratio halfway between the top and the bottom. The ratio of 4.59 representing the upper quartile was one-quarter of the way down the series from the top (or halfway between the top and the median). The ratio of 1.97 representing the lower quartile was one-quarter of the way up from the bottom (or halfway between the median and the bottom).

4% of those outstanding are estimated to be uncollectible on the basis of past experience. (c) There was a cost of $1,500,000 for the research leading to the discoveries resulting in the patents which are valued at $400,000 on the balance sheet. (d) The investments, which are valued, respectively, at $300,000 and $650,000 based on their costs to the company, have current market values of $450,000 and $750,000, respectively.

Table 14-4. Trane Company
Consolidated Balance Sheet, December 31, 1960
Assets

Current Assets:

Cash	$1,800,000	
Accounts Receivable	1,000,000	
Inventories	1,200,000	
Investments	300,000	
Total Current Assets		$ 4,300,000
Property, Plant, and Equipment	$7,500,000	
Less Reserve for Depreciation	3,000,000	
Net Property		4,500,000
Investments	$ 650,000	
Prepayments	200,000	
Patents	400,000	
Total Miscellaneous Assets		1,250,000
Total		$10,050,000

Liabilities

Current Liabilities:

Accounts Payable	$ 750,000	
Accrued Taxes	850,000	
Accrued Wages and Interest	400,000	
Total Current Liabilities		$ 2,000,000
5% Debenture Bonds, due 1980		3,000,000
6% Preferred Stock—authorized and issued 10,000 shares of $100 par value	$1,000,000	
Common Stock—authorized and issued 400,000 shares	1,000,000	
Surplus:		
Capital	1,630,000	
Earned	1,420,000	
Total Net Worth		5,050,000
Total		$10,050,000

5. The $3,000,000 accumulated depreciation shown in the balance sheet is the result of the straight-line depreciation charges which the company has been using exclusively over the years. An analyst has calculated that the accumulated depreciation on the $7,500,000 of currently used assets would total $4,000,000 instead of $3,000,000 if sum-of-digits depreciation had been used. Assume that the company would have paid the same dividends and done everything the same regardless of the method of computing depreciation and that the effective income tax rate was 55 per cent throughout the period, which items on the balance sheet would be different if the sum-of-digits method had been used? Calculate what these values would have been.

6. (*a*) Compute the ratios for the Trane Company which will assist you in evaluating the sources of funds and the types of assets in which they are invested.

(*b*) Explain the meaning or lack of meaning of each ratio or percentage.

(*c*) What additional information, if any, would you like to have to assist your evaluation?

7. Trane's president has lunch with a banker friend who inquires about Trane's current ratio. When the president informs the banker that it is less than 3 to 1 (300 per cent), the banker suggests that the company's cash position is not liquid enough. (*a*) Do you agree with the banker? Explain. (*b*) Suggest the easiest and fastest ways to raise the current ratio over 300 per cent. (*c*) Do your suggestions actually improve the liquidity of the company? (*d*) Compute the remaining liquidity ratios for the Trane Company and explain the significance of each. (*e*) What additional information, if any, would be helpful?

8. Trane Company's net sales were $8,600,000 and gross profit totaled $3,700,000 in 1960. There were no cash sales. Inventories averaged $1,600,000, based on cost. (*a*) Compute operating-effectiveness ratios. (*b*) Explain the significance or lack of significance of each. (*c*) What additional information, if any, would give added significance to these ratios?

9. The Trane Company's net profits, after taxes, in 1960 were $220,000. (*a*) Compute ratios to measure profitability. (*b*) Interpret the results. (*c*) What additional information, if any, would be helpful?

10. Obtain the balance sheet and operating statement of a publicly owned company, either in the library or by writing directly to the company. Compute the ratios to assist in evaluating the sources of funds and types of assets in which they are invested, the liquidity, the operating effectiveness, and the profitability of the company. Prepare a brief interpretation regarding the significance of the various ratio values and, when possible, over-all evaluation of the company with respect to the previously mentioned items.

15 Sources of Future Capital Funds

Funds for future capital expenditures by the business are derived from both internal and external sources.

Internal Sources. The internal sources are chiefly depreciation-charge recoveries and retained earnings. The sale of fixed assets and the reduction of working-capital requirements through operational changes are other internal sources which are usually of secondary importance.

External Sources. External sources of capital funds are principally the sale of capital stocks, bonds, and mortgages to the public, insurance companies, and financial institutions.

Although short-term loans from banks or other institutions are not usually considered sources of funds for capital investment, they may, in some cases, release long-term funds for capital investment or they may be a temporary expedient either to postpone long-term financing to a more propitious time or until internal sources provide the required funds.

Instead of borrowing money to finance the purchase or construction of a facility, there are sometimes advantages in selling the facility to an institutional or individual investor and then leasing the facility for a long period of years. Some possible advantages include greater liquidity and tax savings. An economy study must be made to determine the desirability of such a sale-lease-back procedure.

Depreciation Charges. Depreciation and depletion charges are a source of funds for replacement and for new investments. The various purposes and methods of making depreciation and depletion charges have been discussed in some detail in Chapter 6. Because of income taxes, different depreciation methods result in differences in the availability of funds for replacement or for new capital expenditures.

We previously discussed the inadequacy of historical depreciation charges to furnish sufficient funds for replacement of assets in an inflationary economy. In so far as these depreciation charges are insufficient to cover replacement costs of equipment and facilities, they may cause an inflation of the earned surplus figures on the balance sheet.

Retained Earnings. Earnings which have been retained in the business instead of distributed to the owners, who are the stockholders in the case of a corporation, are another internal source of funds. Obviously, the amounts which are available from this source depend, first of all, upon the amount of the earnings; and, second, on what proportion of these earnings are distributed to the stockholders and what proportion are retained in the business.

The policy of firms with respect to retention of earnings for internal investment varies considerably. A number of the theories which have been propounded on this subject are discussed below.

Retaining a Fixed Percentage of Earnings. Some firms operate under a policy of retaining a certain percentage of earnings for growth and to meet future contingencies.

Maintaining a Fixed Dividend. Another group maintains that a company should establish an announced dividend policy of a fixed quarterly dividend which it expects to meet out of earnings under most conditions and then maintain these regular dividend payments whenever possible. With some variations, this is a rather popular policy. It accounts for much of the stability of dividends as compared with relatively wide fluctuations in earnings of many companies.

This policy has much to commend it. Large blocs of stockholders attach great importance to a consistent dividend policy. This will tend to improve the financial rating of the company's securities, increase its price-earnings ratio which decreases its cost of equity capital, as well as improve marketability and decrease the cost of debt financing.

Of course, retained earnings will tend to fluctuate considerably under this theory because it is the residue remaining after the constant dividends have been subtracted from the earnings. During poor times, very little, if anything, will be retained whereas under boom conditions, the amount of retained earnings will be extremely high, as in the recent postwar period. This may have some logic because there are generally more investment opportunities in the business with attractive-appearing prospective returns during boom times than during depression times.

Retention of Earnings Based on Internal-investment Earnings Rate. This dividend policy is based on the following reasoning: a company should retain all the earnings which it can invest in its business as long as the rate of return on the investments exceeds the maximum rate that it pays for equity or debt capital. This will frequently mean retaining a high percentage of earnings.

Studies covering a long period of time indicate that the stocks of firms which retain a large share of their earnings do not have as high a price relative to the total earnings of the company as do those of companies which have more liberal dividend policies. This indicates that retaining a large portion of earnings may depress the price of a company's common stock and thus raise the company's cost of equity capital. This would increase the rate of return required to justify capital expenditures in the business and might, therefore, decrease the demand for capital funds from projects which cannot produce the required higher rate of return.

However, it is not always true that retaining a high percentage of earnings will necessarily depress the price of a company's stock. In recent years, there have been many notable exceptions to this general rule, especially in rapidly expanding companies in growth industries. Moreover, even when the factor of depressed prices does operate, it may not be significant, especially if the firm is not planning on seeking outside funds.

Stockholder Attitudes. Another factor in dividend policy is management's desire to avoid stockholder discontent. Dividends must, therefore, be kept sufficiently high to avoid antagonizing large blocs of stockholders who may be upset by reduced income or by having the stock price depressed by a low dividend policy. (On the other hand, a very successful growth company, large or small, can frequently maintain a low dividend policy without stockholder discontent as long as it keeps increasing dividends on a progressive basis.)

Stockholder attitudes toward retention of earnings are likely to depend upon the personal-income-tax bracket of the stockholder. The high-income-bracket investor is usually more interested in capital-gains prospects than in dividend income in order to reduce his income tax liability.

Small companies, especially when they are new, usually have more to gain by retaining a larger percentage of their earnings than large companies because they cannot raise new equity or debt funds from external sources as readily as larger, well-established companies. In addition, many smaller company's stockholders frequently purchase the stock in the hope of capital gains rather than regular dividend income and will, therefore, tend to be more favorable toward a reduced dividend policy.

When a company retains little of its earnings, it may indicate a lack of investment opportunity in the business and little planning for future growth.

Many policies for retention of earnings contain elements from several of these theories. The policies of a company will sometimes vary as conditions in the business, industry, and economy change. In general, there is an optimum balance to be achieved between retaining so large a proportion of earnings as to depress stock prices and thus raise the costs of equity capital and promote stockholder distrust and retaining so small a proportion that funds for growth and for contingencies are not available in large enough quantities.

Unincorporated Ownership Funds. Small businesses may be operated under individual ownership—the simplest way to operate. The individual provides the ownership capital and is responsible personally for all indebtedness of the business. This type of ownership has several limitations: ownership (equity) capital is limited to the resources of the individual; the owner has unlimited liability for all debts; the enterprise dissolves and all debts become payable when the individual owner dies; and it is therefore difficult for the individual owner to obtain long-term loans.

Formation of a partnership can increase the ownership capital available to a business by including the resources of all the partners, although it is still a limited amount. When any partner dies, the partnership ends and each general partner is liable for all the debts of the partnership. Thus, the partnership has many of the disadvantages of individual ownership as well as some additional limitations on its usefulness.

Corporate Ownership Funds—Capital Stock. Most businesses are conducted under a corporate form of ownership and control. A corporation is an artificial entity created under a contract or charter with a state (articles of incorporation) and endowed by this charter with certain rights and privileges: perpetual life; limited liability of the owners (stock-holders); the right to engage in the activities specified in the charter. To change these articles, the corporation must apply for a revision of its charter or for a new charter.

Ownership funds are raised by the sale of stock to individuals and to other companies and institutions. The types of stock which a corporation may issue and sell are stated in the articles of incorporation (corporation charter).

Common stock is usually a voting stock which participates in the profits of the corporation. Preferred stock is usually nonvoting, but is given a preference in dividends: no dividends may be paid on the common until the preferred has received a fixed dividend. If there is also a provision that any missed dividends on preferred stock must be made up in the future before common dividends are paid, the stock is called cumulative preferred.

However, there may be some nonvoting classes of common stocks and voting preferred stocks. Some preferred stocks may participate in profits above the minimum rate of preference to dividends. For example, there may be a provision that after the common stockholders have received dividends at the same rate as the preferred, remaining dividends will be distributed equally among shares of all classes of stock. Some preferred stock may be convertible into common stock or bonds during specified periods of time and at specified conversion rates. The corporation may have redemption rights during certain periods of time at specified prices. The rights of different classes of stockholders to the assets of the company on liquidation are also specified in the charter of the corporation. There is wide latitude in how the articles of incorporation may spell out the rights and privileges of the different types of stock of the corporation.

Stock may have a par value; it may have no par value, but have stated value; or it may have neither par nor stated values. Neither par value nor stated value represents the price paid for the stock or the current value of the stock. No par value stock is usually taxed the same as $100 par value stock. A low par value results in a reduction in these taxes, especially the transfer tax.

Mortgages and Bonds. A mortgage is a pledge or conditional conveyance of property as security for the repayment of a loan. The mortgage on the property is canceled when the loan is repaid. Unless the mortgagee defaults in his payment obligations, he retains title to the property. A holder of a first mortgage has first claims to an asset in case of default. When junior (such as second or third) mortgages are issued, the holders of these mortgages receive monies from the sale of the property on a defaulted mortgage only if funds are available after the first mortgage holders are paid in full. Junior mortgages are, therefore, subject to greater risk.

A mortgage bond is a long-term loan secured by a mortgage on certain properties of the corporation. If the corporation defaults in its payments on the loan, the bondholders can obtain possession of the mortgaged property through court action and sell it to obtain funds to repay the loan and unpaid interest.

A collateral bond is similar to a mortgage bond, but the security is some form of commercial security other than a property mortgage. The security may be the stocks or bonds of a subsidiary corporation.

Debentures are bonds which are not secured by any specified assets of the corporation. They are promises to pay principal and interest.

The trust agreements under which bonds are issued may sometimes contain clauses which restrict freedom of activity in the corporation in order to provide additional security to the bondholder. For example, it may provide that no dividends may be declared unless profits exceed specified amounts. It may restrict the amount of additional long-term indebtedness the corporation may incur. Such restrictions are more prevalent in debentures than in mortgage bonds.

Leverage of Debt Financing. A simple example will illustrate how debt financing increases the profit-making leverage of the business and, at the same time, increases the risks to the equity capital.

Company A has $1,000,000 of assets, of which $200,000 are provided by debt and $800,000 by stockholder investment (original investment plus retained earnings). Let us assume that a 20 per cent loss in the assets of the company occurs, which reduces the asset value to $800,000. The company still has the $200,000 of debt, but the stockholders' equity in the business is reduced by 25 per cent, from $800,000 to $600,000.

Company B also has $1,000,000 of assets, of which $800,000 are provided by debt and $200,000 by stockholder investment. Assuming the same 20 per cent loss in the assets, the stockholders' investment in the business will be completely wiped out when the assets are worth only $800,000.

However, Company B has a tremendous profit-making leverage compared with Company A. Assume that profits are $200,000 in a given year before interest on debt is paid. Company A pays 6 per cent interest on the $200,000 debt, or $12,000, leaving $188,000 for the return on the $800,000 of common stock. This is a 23.5 per cent return to the stockholders.

Company B pays 8 per cent on its $800,000 debt, or $64,000, leaving $136,000 for the return on its $200,000 of common stock. This is a 68 per cent return to the stockholders. (The interest rate which Company B pays on its debt is higher than Company A pays. The risks of the lenders are generally greater in the high-leverage company and the creditors therefore demanded a higher interest rate on the Company B loans.)

Optimum Plan for External Financing. Consideration of the technical intricacies of the external financing of a company's long-term capital needs is beyond the scope of this volume. The most desirable methods and timing of financing with different types of stocks and bonds sold to individuals, insurance and other companies and institutions depend upon many factors. The goal is to provide the required funds in such a way that the total cost of the monies from all sources will be as low as possible in the long run and, at the same time, to keep the debt-ownership ratio low enough that the company's financial stability will not be threatened during periods of adverse business conditions.

The choice of debt capital (bonds) or equity capital (stocks) for financing capital investments involves numerous considerations. Debt capital gives greater profit leverage (profit possibilities), but higher risks (loss possibilities in a downturn). The interest costs of bonds are income tax deductible as compared with the taxability of stock dividends. On the other hand, equity capital financing may jeopardize present ownership control, but it keeps capitalization conservative.

The choice between common or preferred stock and the privileges attached to the stock must take many factors into consideration. The question of voting privileges and control of the company may be important. Relative marketability and the price the company can obtain for different types of shares are factors. Some institutional investors are not permitted by law or by their charter to buy common stocks, but can buy preferred stock.

The choice of public financing (public sale to individuals, companies, and institutions) or private sale of securities to investors or to institutions is also complicated. Public financing provides an open market for the company's securities, which can have substantial advantages in the future if private placement of the firm's securities becomes undesirable. (Eventual listing of the company's securities on a stock exchange may also be desirable if the company contemplates future financing. The securities may have to become seasoned first in the over-the-counter market.) Public financing also may avoid some restrictive agreements which private buyers may insist upon to safeguard their investment, but which may handicap management. Wide distribution of stock ownership may provide less jeopardy to current management control of the company than a private placement to one or a few persons or institutions. On the other hand, private sale eliminates the bother, the expense, and the public-information disclosures required by the Securities and Exchange Commission registration. The time required to make the sale can be reduced, and the costs of administering a public issue saved. All or a portion of the investment bankers' commissions are also saved.

Correlating Cash Position with Capital Requirements. The company long-range planning should include a continuing review of its prospective cash position several years into the future. The cash position forecast must project the following items into the future, preferably on a monthly basis for the first few years: forecasting sales and subtracting budgeted or estimated cost of goods sold, selling, administrative, and other expenses give a forecast of net income; to this are added estimated depreciation charges and subtracted estimated capital-investment expenditures, increases in working-capital requirements, increases in other investments of the company, income tax payments, and common and preferred stock dividends to obtain the forecasted cash position.

When this review indicates that additional cash will be needed by the company, decisions concerning the amount, nature, and timing of external financing must be made or certain projected investments must be eliminated or curtailed.

PROBLEMS

1. What are the two principal internal sources of funds for future capital needs? What are some other sources of internal funds for capital expenditure?

2. A company can finance its expansion from external sources through increasing its debt or seeking additional equity capital. Discuss the pros and cons of these alternative approaches.

3. If a corporation needs funds for expansion, is it logical for it to distribute some of its earnings as dividends when it is also borrowing money to pay for expansion? Discuss the factors which should determine its policy.

4. What factors may influence the decision of a company to sell preferred as opposed to common stock when raising equity capital?

5. Why are the individual ownership and partnership forms of business frequently more suitable for small enterprise than the corporation form? Why

is the corporation form frequently more suitable for large enterprise? Discuss the pros and cons in each case.

6. Why may a corporation make its preferred stock or bond issue convertible into common stock?

7. Explain how the question of control of the company will affect the choice of the following financing methods: (a) bonds versus stock, (b) common versus preferred stock, (c) private versus public sale of stock.

8. Discuss how you would determine whether you would prefer an investment yielding a 10 per cent return with high leverage as opposed to one yielding a 5 per cent return with low leverage? Assume all other factors except leverage are the same in both situations.

9. How do income taxes and inflation affect the tendency of some companies to avoid debt?

10. When a company retains earnings for internal investment instead of distributing them to stockholders, it is determining how the stockholders' earnings will be used or invested instead of giving the stockholders the privilege of deciding whether to consume the earnings or where the earnings should be invested. Explain your answers to the following: (a) Is retention of earnings therefore undemocratic? (b) Does retention of earnings foster the allocation of resources to the most economic investments as well as having the stockholders make investments in a free market? (c) How do income taxes affect these questions?

16 Capital Planning and Budgeting

The subject of capital planning, budgeting, and management is crucial to the operation of an enterprise. Broadly conceived, it represents the basic top-management function in the enterprise: the investment of funds in those activities where they will be most productive in promoting the profitability and long-range growth of the enterprise.

The management problem of determining the amount and manner of investment of funds for capital purposes is generally the primary management function about which all the other activities of the enterprise must be aligned. The capital budget mirrors the plan of future activities for the enterprise. Because it involves long-range commitments of funds, it is usually one of the first steps in establishing new directions and policies for the company.

Capital-planning Procedures. Because capital planning is so crucial to the success of the business, it is important for management to establish procedures and devote top-management time to accomplish the following:

1. Long- and short-range planning for the growth and development of the company, including economic and market forecasts
2. Development of capital-investment proposals
3. Review and evaluation of these proposals
4. Development of long-range and short-range capital-investment budgets
5. Projection of the supply of money for capital investment, its sources, its costs, and their interaction with the capital structure of the company

Planning Periods. The basic instrument for investment planning in the enterprise is the capital budget. The budgeting process must, therefore, start with the development of the master plan for the long-range development of the company.

The plans for the future of the business should be as long-range as possible. Naturally, the farther into the future these extend, the more tentative and subject to change these plans will be. How far into the future should this planning be carried? This depends on a number of factors.

Most companies cannot visualize and forecast with great accuracy their future requirements. But some industries, such as electric power generation for a residential area, can make long-range-demand forecasts with much greater precision than others, such as titanium production for use in military equipment. The reason is the different character of the use and users of the product. Obviously, the greater the accuracy with which the long-range future can be forecasted, the greater the value of longer-range planning.

Large projects frequently take a considerable time from approval to the actual operation. This, in itself, will sometimes force longer-range planning.

In some cases, the optimum plant size is large and cost savings are great if the optimum-size rather than a smaller-size unit is built or purchased. This type of situation calls for long-range forecasting of future demand growth and consideration of the economies of building or purchasing in anticipation of the demand.

The cash planning requirements of the business will frequently dictate longer-range planning, even if on a tentative basis. Financial planning is required to assure that the funds will be available for the future growth of the business. It is, therefore, necessary to make a comparison of future cash requirements for capital as well as operating purposes, with a forecast of the cash which will be generated from all sources. Advance planning for obtaining any necessary outside funds with the most appropriate timing will then be possible.

Budget Periods. Despite this desirability for long-range planning, it nevertheless remains true that for most businesses it is hard to predict far ahead with precision. Changes in the size and character of industry demand, changes in competitors' plans and shares of market, new technical advances and new research developments leading to new products can change the plans. The long-range capital budget is to a great extent a reflection of these plans. Long-range capital budgeting must, therefore, be flexible, with provisions for continual review and change as new developments unfold.

The approved capital budget should be restricted to a one- or two-year period, with plans for succeeding years kept up to date by periodic review and revision. Even within the one-year budget period, flexibility should usually be maintained by management-review procedures which may result in changes in items already on the approved capital budget for the year.

Even when the market and technological factors in the business are so changeable that plans are no more than guesses which must be continually revised, it is valuable to plan and budget as far ahead as possible. The budgeting process encourages the search for and discovery of new investment opportunities. By pinpointing the discrepancy between expected and actual occurrences, the budgeting process will also sharpen management's planning and forecasting abilities.

Projecting capital budgeting far into the future, even on a very tentative basis, has the additional advantage of providing a better perspective for establishing proper minimum rate-of-return requirements. Wide fluctuations in rate-of-return requirements from year to year will cause incorrect capital decision-making. Long-range budgeting will tend to bring stability to this activity.

Developing Capital Proposals. Proposals for capital investment develop at all levels of management and in all departments as a corollary to the regular activities of the personnel. A dearth of proposals is an indication of poor initiative and unimaginative management. It indicates that management is not making the effort and creating the conditions where the search for investment opportunities will be fruitful. A healthy condition for a company is to have many more proposals for the investment of funds at high rates of return than can be handled by available funds.

The research division will discover new products and processes which create investment opportunities. The design engineering division will create improved designs in product and packaging which require capital investment. The manufacturing division will propose the introduction of more efficient facilities which have been developed by the equipment industries. The industrial engineering division will discover cost-reduction proposals which will give substantial returns on required capital investment. The marketing and sales divisions will propose investment programs involving deeper penetration into existing markets or entry into new markets. The controllers division will propose the installation of automatic data-processing equipment.

The company's environment should encourage the origination of investment proposals at all levels of the organization: operating, supervisory, and staff personnel; research and design engineers, section and department heads, as well as top management.

Preparation of Proposals. The technical, marketing and other facets of each capital-investment proposal must be completely described in a format which is most suitable to each individual case. However, the financial implications of all capital-expenditure proposals should be prepared and summarized in a standardized manner so that they may be evaluated on a uniform base. Figures 16-1 and 16-2 illustrate some of the forms used by the Armstrong Cork Company for this purpose.

The development of capital-investment proposals is interdisciplinary in scope. For effective performance, it requires the close collaboration of the engineering, managerial, and economic talents in the company. There is no hard and fast formula which can give the right answer to the many problems of determining the proper future demands and costs to be used in presenting and evaluating alternative proposals for capital investment.

Job No. _____   _____"M" REQUEST   Date __1/1/61__

Supersedes "D"
Order No. _____ Plant ____Floor____ Bldg. ____135____   Proj.
                                                                  No. __555700__

Est. Cost $ __110,000__   Obsolescence ____10,000____   Est. Comp.
                                                                  Date __7/1/61__

Reason for Request _____Cost Reduction_____

Data in this Block to be Approved by Operations Controller _____ Date _____

Summary of Estimated Economics

Efficient Productive Period ___5+___ Yrs.   Average Added Profit after Tax $_25,000_ /Yr.*

Recovery Period ___3.3___ Yrs.

Return on Average Total   *NOTE: Before Charge for Expense and Obsolescence
Added Capital Employed ___36.8___ %*   of $_10,000_ after Tax in First Year

Title:

        Replace Flim Mixers with Flam High Speed Mixers.

Plant Mgr.	Date	Asst. Dir. of Research	Date
Chief Architect	Date	Dir. of Research	Date
Asst. Dir. of Engr.	Date	V.P. Mfg.	Date
Dir. of Engr.	Date	Controller	Date
Prod. Mgr.	Date		Date
Dept. Mgr.	Date		Date
Oper. Gen. Mgr.	Date	Noted: Pres. Office	Date
Account		Exec. Comm.	Date Granted

Figure 16-1. Armstrong Cork Company—capital-investment summary and approval form.

Review and Authorization Procedure. The proper procedure for review of capital proposals will depend on the organizational structure of the company. The capital-budget proposals should generally go up the channels of authority, with review and approvals required at each step along the way. After being checked carefully, the proposals are consolidated into a coordinated budget request by each division manager before being forwarded to the capital-budgeting officer. Further checking, evaluating, consolidating, and ranking are performed by the budget

TITLE	Replace Flim Mixers with Flam High Speed Mixers on Commodity "A" line	Date 1/1/61

Project No. 555700

PLANT Floor P. & L. STATEMENT COMMODITY "A"

(1) Total Funds Requested $ 110,000
 (a) Capital $ 100,000   (c) Capital plus Expense
 (b) Expense 10,000   after Tax $ 105,000

(2) Obsolescence Requested $ 10,000
(3) Estimated Efficient Productive Period { 5 or More Yrs. [X] _____ Yrs.

Use lines numbered (4) through (21) to support any estimated cost reduction indicated in any request regardless of category if line numbered (1) is $2,000 or more.

	AVG. YEAR DURING E.E.P.P. [ ] 5 YRS. [X]	
	A. PRESENT FACILITIES	B. PROPOSED FACILITIES
(4) Material	$ 500,000	$ 480,000
(5) Labor	100,000	80,000
(6) Scrap	50,000	40,000
(7) Salaries	—	
(8) Employee Benefits (20% × (#5 +#7))	15,000	12,000
(9) Power	5,000	8,000
(10) Repairs and Maintenance	20,000	10,000
(11) Depreciation	2,000	10,000
(12)	8,000	10,000
(13)		
(14) Total Costs Affected (#4 Thru #13)	700,000	650,000 *
(15) Average Added Profit before Tax (#14A - #14B)	———	50,000 *
(16) Average Added Profit after Tax (50% of #15B)	———	25,000 *
(17) Add: Dep'n. Difference (#11B - #11A)	———	8,000
(18) Average Annual Amount Recovered (#16 + #17)	———	33,000
(19) Recovery Period (#1 (c) ÷ #18)	———	3.1 Yrs.

The Operations Controller will use lines numbered (22) through (39) in accordance with the procedure outlined in Section 13.2 of the Accounting Manual.

	FORECAST FOR CURRENT YEAR	AVG. YEAR DURING E. E. P. P. [ ] 5 YRS. [X]	
		A. PRESENT FACILITIES	B. PROPOSED FACILITIES
	(000)	(000)	(000)
(20) Sales Units — Pieces	800	1,000	1,000
(21) Net Sales	$ 800	$1,000	$1,000
(22) Plant Direct Cost		670	620 *
(23) Plant Period Cost		100	100 *
(24) Selling Expense		80	80
(25) Administrative Expense		50	50
(26) Profit before Tax		100	150 *
(27) Profit after Tax 50%		50	75 *
(28) Average Added Profit after Tax (#27B - #27A)		———	25 *
(29) Add: Dep'n. Cost in #23B Less Dep'n. Cost in #23A		———	—
(30) Average Annual Amount Recovered (#28 + #29)		———	—
(31) Recovery Period (#1 (c) ÷ #30)		———	— Yrs.
(32) Cash		$71	$69
(33) Receivables		90	90
(34) Inventories		150	150
(35) Property, Plant, and Equipment		400	470
(36) Miscellaneous		—	—
(37) Average Total Capital Employed		711	779
(38) Return on Average Total Capital Employed (#27 ÷ #37)		7.0%	9.6 % *
(39) Return on Average Total Added Capital Employed (#28 ÷ (#37B -#37A))		———	36.8% *

Note: Before Charge for Expense and Obsolescence of $ 10,000 After Tax in First Year.

Comments:
 Steady growth of acceptance of this product, especially in prefab housing. The Flam Mixers will be modified for our "X" Process which will be difficult to duplicate.

Donald L. Smith
INDUSTRIAL ENGINEER
Robert V. Jones
ACCOUNTANT
Richard M. Black
OPERATIONS CONTROLLER

} Lines numbered (1) (c) and (4) through (19).
} Lines numbered (3) and (20) through (39).

Figure 16-2. Armstrong Cork Company—estimates of period for recovery of cost and return on capital employed.

officer, the president, and an executive or budget or other committee or committees of officers. The final review and approval is usually made by the company's board of directors.

In evaluating a major investment proposal, the judgments of many department heads in the company may be required. The director of research and the chief engineer will evaluate the technical feasibilities and problems. The marketing and sales heads will evaluate the marketing difficulties and the sales forecasts. The controller will check the cost estimates and the rate-of-return calculations. The treasurer will be concerned with its effect on cash requirements, the director of personnel with any special labor requirements, the production manager with any manufacturing problems, and so on.

The board of directors will ordinarily not be concerned with the approval of each item on the capital budget, but will primarily concern itself with its over-all plan: the total size; what areas are being emphasized; how it fits in with the long-range plans for the company; the estimated profitability of the projects; the sources of funds.

Even after a project has been included in an approved capital budget, the project cannot be started without further authorization by management. Practice varies widely in industry in how far down the managerial line authority is delegated to make capital expenditures of varying amounts of money. Some indication of industry practice is given in Table 16-1.

Lump-sum Appropriation for Small Expenditures. The various divisions of a company will have requirements for small capital expenditures each year which it would be cumbersome to attempt to budget individually, even if they could all be predicted far enough in advance of their required dates. It is, therefore, logical to provide moderate lump-sum appropriations for capital expenditures below a small fixed dollar value for each division in the company. These small capital expenditures should usually require the approval of designated personnel in each division.

Timing. Timing is a key element in capital-budgeting procedure. In general, capital budget decision-making is not deciding whether to adopt or reject a proposal, but whether to adopt the proposal at any given time. If the proposal is adopted, a timing decision is made: it will be started next week, next month, or next year and proceed according to a specified schedule. If the proposal is not adopted and is still feasible in the future, a not-adopt decision is frequently a postponement of the decision to the future.

Follow-up on Capital Expenditures. Procedures for following up on authorized capital projects should be concerned with ensuring that planned objectives are achieved as well as pointing up errors so that future planning can be more accurate and effective. Is the time schedule for com-

Table 16-1. Some Examples of Capital Expenditures Limitations

Companies	Type of authority					
	Board of directors (1)	President (2)	Exec. vice pres. (3)	Divisional or departmental vice pres. (4)	Division managers (several plants) (5)	Plant managers (6)
Large Chemical Company (1)	Over $1,000	Up to $1,000	Up to $1,000	Up to $1,000	Up to $1,000	Up to $500
Large Chemical Company (2)	Over $10,000	Up to $10,000	....		Up to $1,000	Up to $500
Large Food Company (1)	Over $25,000		....	$5,000		
Large Food Company (2)	Over $250,000	$10,000–$250,000	....	$4,000–$10,000	$500–$4,000	Up to $5,000
Large Oil Company	Over $300,000	$100,000–$300,000	$25,000–$100,000	$5,000–$25,000	Up to $5,000	To $1,000
Large Materials Company	Over $50,000	$25,000 –$50,000	$10,000–$25,000	$5,000–$10,000	$1,000–$5,000	
Large Light and Power Company	....	Over $10,000	....	$1,000–$10,000	Up to $1,000	
Medium-sized Heavy Capital Goods Company	Over $10,000	Up to $10,000	....	Up to $10,000		
Medium-sized Textile Company	Over $50,000	$5,000–$50,000	....	Up to $5,000		
Management Guide of the Standard Oil Company of California. (This is hypothetical and does not refer to the actual expenditure limitations of the company.)	Over $5,000	$1,000–$5,000	....	Up to $1,000	Up to $1,000	Up to $1,000

SOURCE: E. Dale, *Planning and Developing the Company Organization Structure*, Research Report 20, American Management Association, New York, 1952.

pletion and operation being met? How do the actual investment costs of the projects compare with estimated costs? How do actual revenues, operating costs, savings, and return on investments compare with forecast?

Monthly summary or other periodic statements of investment expenditures, giving detailed information on expenditures and progress on each approved capital project over a given minimum size, should furnish data to control the capital expenditures. These reports should be designed to provide the controls related to the first two of the above questions.

To provide effective follow-up on the profitability of the expenditures, a review should be made after each project is completed and operating to compare the estimated revenues, operating costs, savings, investment, return on investment, and other expected benefits with the actual results being obtained. For large expenditures, this review should be repeated periodically.

The purpose of these follow-ups is not just to pinpoint responsibility for errors but also to discover the types of discrepancies and biases which occur and their causes. In this way, these errors can be avoided whenever possible in the future. In addition, if this type of control-reporting information is available and properly used, management will be better able to appraise the risks and uncertainties of various types of estimating errors.

Rate-of-return Criterion. In the previous chapters of this book devoted to methods of comparing alternatives, we discussed and illustrated various techniques for determining the desirability of proposed investments. Each of these techniques assumed decision criteria. Some of these criteria were compatible with each other in that they would always indicate the same course of action for any given set of circumstances. Others could indicate conflicting courses of action.

Rate of return has many advantages as a criterion for evaluating the desirability of investments. The concept of rate of return as a measure of profitability is simple to understand and is directly related to the profit goals of the enterprise. Because profitability is stated as a percentage, it facilitates comparisons of alternatives involving different total sums. This criterion enables management to select for approval those investments showing the highest rates of return.

Use of rate of return as the capital-budgeting criterion is also conceptually comfortable because it fits in with a simple theoretical exposition of the supply and demand for capital in the enterprise, such as previously presented. This is useful even though practical considerations will not permit actual capital planning in exact accordance with this model.

The procedures for calculating rates of return on investment and rate of return on extra investments were discussed in some detail in a previous chapter.

Minimum Rate of Return. What is the minimum rate of return that a proposal should earn to justify investment of the business's funds?

Except where other intangible benefits are involved, this rate of return should certainly be above the cost of capital to the firm. If the rate of return on a proposed investment is not above the cost of the funds, the firm would be better off not investing its funds.

The acceptable rate of return for new investments should be above the cost of capital to the firm by an amount which will cover investments which must be made even though they will not earn an adequate return. Examples of this would include investments for facilities to promote employee morale or safety.

As a practical matter, the acceptable rate of return should rarely approach the cost of capital. An effective management should usually be capable of developing investment opportunities at more attractive rates of return which exceed the available finances of the company and which exceed the available time for management to cope with the potential new projects.

Cost of Capital. The problem of determining the firm's cost of capital is complicated by several factors: the company's funds usually come from various sources, such as preferred and common stockholders, bondholders, retained earnings, etc. The cost of money raised by issuing bonds or stock fluctuates markedly from time to time, and for capital-planning purposes we are interested in the relatively long-term pattern of future costs.

We must, therefore, estimate the relative proportions of future funds which will come from these various sources, the future costs of funds from each of these sources, and then compute a weighted average of these estimates.

The true cost of borrowed money to a corporation is not generally equal to the coupon rate on its bonds. Thus, when a corporation issues $20,000,000 of 5 per cent 15-year bonds, it may sell them to investment bankers for $18,800,000, or $940 per $1,000 bond. (The investment bankers, in turn, will sell them to investors at $960 for a $1,000 bond.) In addition, the corporation must pay for engraving the bonds as well as legal and accounting expenses in connection with the bond issue and the related registration statements which must be filed with the Securities and Exchange Commission, amounting to $250,000 in this case. Each year, the corporation must pay the cost of making interest payments and must pay fees to the registrar(s) and trustee(s) of the bond issue, $40,000 a year in this case. Thus, the corporation has received $18,550,000 ($18,800,000 minus $250,000) for which it must pay $520,000 [$\frac{1}{2}$ ($1,000,-000 + $40,000)] every six months for 30 periods plus $20,000,000 at the end of the 15 years. To the borrowing corporation, the effective interest cost for these conditions is about 5.94 per cent compounded semiannually.

To the lending investors, the effective interest rate is determined by a return of $25 every six months for 15 years plus $1,000 at the end of 15 years on a $960 investment. This equals about 5.44 per cent compounded semiannually.

The cost of capital is usually greater than the cost of borrowed money. When a company sells bonds at 5 per cent interest to raise capital, it changes the capital structure of the company and increases the risks of the equity (stockholder) capital. Should business conditions become unfavorable, the equity capital must sustain any losses before debt capital is impaired.

When the ratio of debt to equity gets high, the cost of equity capital rises. The high leverage makes the equity in the business more risky and investors expect a higher return on their equity investments to compensate for the higher risks. Other things being equal, the rate of interest which must be paid for the borrowed funds will increase as the proportion of debt to equity capital in the company increases. For this reason alone, it is not logical to consider the cost of borrowed money as the cost of capital. The cost is usually considerably greater. Projects should earn substantially more than the cost of borrowed capital to justify investment of capital funds.

Opportunity Cost of Capital. The cost appropriate for establishing a minimum acceptable return is essentially the opportunity cost of the money. This opportunity cost is the best return which can be obtained, with comparable risks, by investing the firm's available funds either internally or externally. The opportunity cost only approaches the cost of capital when there is a paucity of profitable investment opportunities.

The opportunity-cost concept requires that all present and future investment possibilities be considered simultaneously before a minimum acceptable return is adopted. Obviously, this can be done only in an approximate way.

Screening and Categorization Procedures. Prospective rate of return is the most universally advantageous device for initially measuring the desirability of capital-budget proposals. However, other methods must be used in conjunction with rate of return in determining which projects should be approved.

A desired minimum rate of return for capital investments should be established by top management taking into consideration the costs of capital as well as the over-all demand for capital in the company.

In applying this rate-of-return measure of desirability, we should categorize our proposals into several groups according to the risk and uncertainty of realizing their indicated profitabilities. We would set higher minimum rate-of-return requirements for those categories which involve the greater risk and uncertainty. (In the following discussion, the term "risk" is used to include both risk and uncertainty.)

For certain types of investment proposals, a rate-of-return evaluation approach will not be possible. Replacement of toilet facilities and building a recreation center would be examples of these. These will have to be judged on more qualitative bases, including how they fit in with long-range policies and plans.

A separate category in the capital budget must be maintained for investments in which the monetary return is of minor importance compared with the intangible benefits for which it is too difficult to estimate specific dollar advantages. The evaluation of these proposals requires even more careful judgment and analysis than those in the various risk categories which have tangible evaluations. Some of the methods discussed in Chapter 27 for evaluating intangible factors should prove useful in considering these proposals.

Payout-period calculations may assume some importance in the capital-budget screening process when capital funds are limited; when there is the expectation that available funds in the future will not be large enough to finance future projects of great profitability; or when the risks of obsolescence loom important.

For investment proposals involving relatively small sums of money, it will not be economic to make as detailed forecast and cost estimates as on major proposals. Simplified evaluation procedures should, therefore, be used on minor proposals.

Developing Risk Categories. To evaluate the risk of capital-investment proposals, we must answer such questions as the following:

How accurate are the revenue and cost forecasts?
What is the purpose of the investment?
What types of industries are involved?
What functional areas in the industry are involved?
How much managerial talent will be needed to implement the proposal and how much is available?
How salvageable is the investment if the project is to be liquidated later?
How great are the risks of obsolescence or supersession?

Accuracy of Revenue and Cost Forecasts. Many factors affect the accuracy of the revenue and cost forecasts used to evaluate capital proposals. The risk that actual values will vary from forecasted values depends upon many questions which are difficult to evaluate.

What is the size of the market for the product or service?
Will the company be able to achieve the market share it anticipates?
What new technological developments may affect the market for the product?
What will be the economic life of the new facility? How long will it be required?

How will material costs change in the future?

What kind of efficiency will be maintained in the operation?

What level of material waste or product yield will be achieved?

Purpose of Investment. The risks involved in the various types of investments differ depending upon the purposes of the investment. Replacement investments will usually involve fewer risks of estimating and forecasting errors than expansion investments because personnel are more familiar with the operation, costs, and market with which they are currently dealing. Likewise, diversification investments will frequently involve still further risks because they may include aspects which are new to the company personnel and management.

When a capital expenditure is proposed for a project which is not directed in accordance with the master plan for the growth of the company, the risks of it not producing expected profits are usually increased.

Type of Industry. The marketing or production characteristics of one industry are more risky than others. For example, the demand for telephone service is more stable and less subject to unforecastable fluctuation than the demand for movie entertainment. The production of staple items which have been in existence many years usually involves fewer technical quality and cost problems than the production of newly developed products, such as new synthetic fibers, solid rocket fuels, or nuclear power plants.

Functional Area in Industry. Investments in the research, production, and marketing areas of a specific company will typically involve different levels of risk. When these functions are performed by separate nonintegrated companies in an industry, it is typical to expect the highest return on investments in the highest-risk activity, research; next highest, in production; and lowest, in the lowest-risk activity, marketing.

It would also be expected that the highest-risk companies will tend to have the highest proportion of equity capital, which normally involves higher capital costs than debt capital.

This same type of reasoning can be extended to other functional areas, such as advertising, purchasing, transportation, etc.

Managerial Talent. When a company's managerial talent is fully occupied in attempting to obtain better results from its current complement of facilities and resources—either because too little top-management talent is available or because the present complement has not yet developed to its full potential—the risks of not obtaining expected profits from proposed capital expenditures are expanded considerably. Depending upon the circumstances, it may be desirable temporarily to pass up potentially profitable investments which will require large amounts of managerial attention until the additional managerial talent and time are available.

Shortages of managerial talent will have two effects in capital planning. One effect may be the forgoing of profitable investments, which should result in a raising of the minimum rate of return considered attractive enough to justify investment. Proposals with lower rates of return which may otherwise be adopted must be postponed until new managerial talent is acquired or developed.

A second effect which this shortage may have is that projects which will require more managerial time and talent, or more of certain types of managerial or other scarce talent, will be classified as having a greater risk. A higher rate of return will be required before such projects will be adopted.

Salvageability and Liquidity of Investment. The salvageability and liquidity characteristics of the assets in which the monies are being invested may be important in determining the size of the loss if the investment is liquidated. A working-capital investment is usually more easily recovered than specialized facilities. Depending on its location, terrain, etc., land may or may not be readily marketable if no longer desired. Securities of a corporation listed on a major stock exchange are more liquid than those of a closely held unlisted one.

Risk of Obsolescence and Supersession. Because technological change and progress are so rapid in our present economy, the risk of obsolescence and supersession of facilities, processes, and products is generally great, although difficult to evaluate in magnitude. Other things being equal, the longer the time span, the greater the risks.

One approach to this problem is to determine the payout period—how long it will take to recover the investment cost with no return. If this period is very short, other things being equal, the risk of not recovering the original investment will be reduced. In other words, the risks of obsolescence are greater with the passage of longer periods of time, and the accuracy of scientific and engineering evaluations of prospective new technological developments decreases as the length of time into the future increases.

Furthermore, if the payout period is compared with the estimated economic life of the new facility, a further means of evaluating this risk is presented. A short payout period relative to estimated economic life gives a greater margin of safety.

It is difficult to evaluate with any precision the magnitude of the risks and uncertainties of the investment caused by these factors. Nevertheless, estimates of the magnitude of these risks can be made. Proposals can then be categorized into several groupings depending on the estimated magnitude of these risks.

Working Capital. As illustrated in some examples in previous chapters, adoption of a capital-investment proposal will result in many cases in requirements for additional working capital. This working capital is a part of the nondepreciating investment in the same manner as a fixed asset, such as land, and should not be overlooked or ignored in the economic evaluation.

This additional working capital is caused by the incremental amounts of current assets (cash, inventories, accounts receivable, notes receivable, etc.) which will be required in the business if the proposed project is adopted. Any related current liabilities (such as incremental accounts payable and notes payable) should be subtracted from the added current assets to obtain a net additional working capital. Any interest costs on these liabilities, such as those associated with notes payable, should be added to the cost of the project.

Use of Existing Facilities. When estimating the investment cost of a new project for calculating the prospective rate of return, not only should the cost of new facilities and additional working capital be estimated, but the value of existing facilities which the new project will use should also be considered as an opportunity or alternative cost. This is necessary because these facilities could otherwise be used for other income-producing purposes. Thus, the proportionate share of existing facilities may include a share of the current investment in power plants and other non-manufacturing facilities.

Future Investment Opportunities. When comparing projects with different expected lives, the rate-of-return approach carries the implication that the monies earned in the shorter-lived investment can be reinvested at a comparable rate of return in the future.

Rate of return as a capital-investment criterion thus loses some of its validity if we cannot assume that future investment opportunities in the business will be roughly comparable to the current ones. This becomes apparent in the case in which we compare the relative worth of two investment opportunities of differing expected durations, if the short-lived proposal has a higher return than the long-lived one, but the long-lived return is still above the minimum acceptable return for its category of risk.

However, it is usually true that future investment opportunities will be as good or better than the present ones if the management is alert and aggressive. Assurance as to the validity of this assumption of future investment opportunities is obtained by long-range capital budgeting coupled with aggressive management initiative in developing new investment opportunities.

To some extent, the rate-of-return procedure has a bias toward short-lived, high-return projects. Considering the increasing rate of technological obsolescence in industry as a whole and the difficulty of forecasting far into the future with great accuracy, this kind of bias may be both reasonable and desirable. It tends to keep management in a position to take advantage of newly developing investment opportunities without the possible drag of obsolescent facilities which have not paid for themselves.

Of course, if there are valid reasons for expecting that investment opportunities in the future will not offer as high a return, then a modified procedure should be used. Although the basic criterion for the capital-budget decision-making program outlined in this chapter is the rate of return, classified into risk categories, modifications in the ranking by rate of return may sometimes be in order. For example, a project with an estimated life of 30 years earning a 35 per cent return may be preferred to a project earning 38 per cent with an economic life of only 5 years provided that the minimum acceptable return is less than 35 per cent and that the firm does not expect to be able to find many opportunities for future investment of funds in projects yielding returns in the neighborhood of 35 per cent or better.

Mutually Exclusive (Alternative) Projects. The capital-budgeting procedure described in this chapter is based on the proposition that the demand for capital funds will be from projects which are not mutually exclusive (adoption of one does not preclude adoption of others, except for the availability of funds).

When projects are mutually exclusive, choice of the alternative to be considered in the budgeting should depend upon the return on the extra investment in the alternative projects requiring the larger investments. This will avoid the possibility of choosing an investment, for example, of $100 yielding a 200 per cent return in preference to a $10,000 investment yielding an 80 per cent return.

Comparing Large and Small Investments. It may be argued that, even if projects are not mutually exclusive, the rate-of-return criterion may result in the choice of a smaller investment proposal yielding a higher return over a larger investment proposal yielding a satisfactory, but lower, return. The smaller-investment-and-higher-return proposal will be more desirable only if the remaining funds can be invested at a high enough return in other capital proposals. This argument would apply, for instance, if $500,000 can be invested at a 25 per cent return and $200,000 at a 40 per cent return; the total sum available for capital investment is $600,000; and there are no other investment opportunities yielding an adequate return.

It is unusual that other investments of the required profitability level are not available or will not be available in the near future to an alert management. In the rare case where there is a scarcity of high-profitability investments available to management, it may be desirable to examine the proposals to ensure that some larger proposals with smaller but adequate returns are not rejected when opportunities do not exist for better utilization of the larger sums of money. Of course, if the proposals are mutually exclusive (alternative), then the previous comment on interdependent projects applies.

The Error of Piecemeal Analysis. When components of a facility fail to operate properly or to give the required quality of product or service, we are faced with the choice of replacing the malfunctioning parts or losing the revenues of the entire facility. If we then relate the cost of the replacement to the revenues which would be foregone if we did not replace, we will generally obtain an unusually high rate of return on the investment in the new component.

When another component fails the next year, we are again faced with the alternative of replacing this second component or losing the revenues of the entire facility. Again, an unusually high rate of return is indicated on the added investment.

Each time a part of the facility fails, we find a prospective high rate of return on the relatively small investment to rescue the total revenues of the facility. But each time we are rescuing the same revenues.

Our error in these analyses is in taking an incomplete short-term view of the future. Our view is incomplete because each time we have been ignoring the replacements which will be required in future years.

What is required is a long-range view of all costs and revenues for the entire facility. Using forecasts of prospective replacements of all components, of future operating costs, of quality of output, of obsolescence, etc., as well as of future revenues, the economy of keeping the entire facility in continued operation in future years should be analyzed. Perhaps the entire facility has outlived its economic life and funds should be channeled into entirely new facilities or ventures.

When considering the performance of one aspect of a production process, we should examine the economic future of the whole process to be certain that improvements and replacement of components in the process are justified. We do not want to end up with a production facility which has excellent equipment for each separate operation, but is obsolete as a whole because of new requirements or newly developed technology.

This kind of situation arises when we consider replacing pumps and other components in chemical processing plants; when we consider replacing components on an airliner; and when we consider whether we should build a new power plant or repair the old. It can occur whenever we consider a capital expenditure to replace old equipment for the purpose of maintaining production, improving efficiency and quality, or expanding capacity.

Relative and Absolute Returns. Rate-of-return calculations for cost-saving proposals can sometimes be misleading because the rate of return which is calculated on a cost-saving investment is usually a relative rather than an absolute return.

This distinction is important. The prospective rate of return on a cost-saving investment is dependent upon the efficiency of the currently used facility. If a very inefficient facility is currently used, an investment in a facility which is less inefficient may show a very high return despite the fact that the new facility is very inefficient and costly compared to other available facilities. In fact, the more inefficient the current facility, the higher will be the rate of return which the economy analysis will show. As a result, production costs may still be so high after the high-return investment has been made that competitive prices still cannot be met without operating at a loss.

An example will illustrate this phenomenon. A proposed new facility will cost $100,000, have an estimated life of six years, no salvage value, and save $30,000 per year in operating costs compared with the current facility, which has no resale value. The prospective rate of return on this investment is approximately 20 per cent. If we were using a still more inefficient process than we are, one having operating costs of $10,000 more per year, our savings would be $40,000 per year and our prospective rate of return for this same new facility would be more than 32 per cent.

Moreover, our production costs may still be too high with this new facility if a still more efficient one is available and used by our competitors. We will be realizing these high-percentage returns compared with our previous costs, but will still be losing money. If we now make an economy analysis of replacing our new facility with the more efficient one we overlooked, we will show a high enough prospective return on the new investment to justify junking the facility we just procured. (We must consider the unrecoverable portion of the previous investment as a sunk loss.) However, we may not have the money to purchase the still more efficient facility.

The only practical answer to the problem which is posed by the relativity of the rate-of-return calculation for this type of investment is to recognize that the calculated returns are relative and to make thorough investigations to be sure that the most efficient alternatives are considered in the economy study.

Payout Period as a Criterion. The payout period (time required to recover the capital investment out of the earnings or savings) which was discussed in Chapter 12 may be a valuable yardstick to aid in appraising capital expenditures under certain conditions. When funds are or will be limited, the question of how fast the monies will come back may assume great importance.

When the business cycle is at a low point and prospective returns on available projects are correspondingly low, cash payout period gathers more importance because a short payout period will return the money to the business for reinvestment in more profitable projects when the business cycle has improved.

The payout-period calculation completely ignores all earnings beyond the payout years and thus penalizes projects which have long-life potentials in favor of those which offer high earnings or savings for a relatively short period of time. Whereas it is true that the future should be discounted because of uncertainties as well as the time value of money, completely ignoring long-term potential is not the logical answer. For example, project X involves an investment of $10,000 with net after-tax cash flow totaling $2,000 a year for 20 years whereas project Y involves an investment of the same amount of money with net after-tax cash flow totaling $2,500 a year for 5 years. Payout period for project X is $10,000/$2,000, or 5 years and for project Y is $10,000/$2,500, or 4 years. Project Y may have the shorter payout period, but it appears very likely that project X is the more profitable because its profits will continue for a much longer period of time.

Premium Worth and Premium-worth Percentage as a Criterion. The premium worth of a proposal is the present value discounted at the minimum acceptable rate which investments are expected to earn. The calculation of this premium worth and the premium-worth percentage are both discussed in Chapter 10. Either one can be used as a capital-rationing criterion: all proposals with a positive premium worth or premium-worth percentage would be accepted; when proposals are mutually exclusive (alternative), those with the highest premium worth or premium-worth percentage would be accepted. This criterion has some advantages over the rate-of-return criterion, but also some serious disadvantages.

The premium worth takes account of all earnings throughout the expected life of the asset and is simpler to calculate than the rate of return because the trial-and-error solutions are eliminated. When comparing alternatives with different expected lives, an explicit assumption is made in the evaluation regarding the future rates which a company's funds can earn. This compares with the implicit assumption made in the rate-of-return approach that monies can be reinvested at the same rates as those which will be earned by the projects under consideration.

However, the problem of determining the minimum acceptable rate of return which projects are expected to earn remains for both the premium-worth and premium-worth-percentage criteria. The rate-of-return method of capital rationing provides a rationale for determining a minimum acceptable rate of return whereas in the premium-worth methods the rate of return must be first established in advance by some other method which would probably be comparable to a rate-of-return rationale. (It may be necessary to determine separate minimum acceptable rates of return for different categories of investment proposals.) The premium-worth criterion also assumes that additional funds can always be obtained from outside sources for all investments which appear desirable.

When the premium worth is used as the capital-budgeting criterion, an investment yielding a $200,000 premium worth will appear more desirable than one yielding only $150,000 premium worth even though the one yielding $150,000 requires the investment of only $50,000 whereas the one yielding $200,000 premium worth requires the investment of $1,000,-000. The use of the premium-worth percentage avoids this difficulty, but adds some difficulties of its own. It is impossible in many cases to distinguish between investment and expense expenditures to determine the number of dollars by which the premium worth is to be divided to obtain the percentage. (For example, are research, development, and advertising expenses a part of the investment?) Also, when the timing of the investments are not all concentrated at the initiation of the project (some of them occurring later in the life of the project), the premium-worth percentage can be misleading as an indication of relative desirability.

Depreciation Charge as a Criterion. At times, some companies have followed a practice of allocating to each division of the enterprise the amount of its own depreciation and depletion charges. This practice is based on the theory that the funds were generated by depreciation charges for assets in each division; each division, therefore, should be allowed these funds for new or replacement investments designed to strengthen its profit-making potential.

This practice has a number of important drawbacks. It assumes that the capital funds resulting from depreciation charges in the various divisions of the company should be used in each division to replace existing assets roughly in the order in which they are depreciated. It promotes a *status quo* business strategy. It may result in some of the enterprise's funds being used for investments in one division which are less beneficial to the enterprise and earn lower returns than alternative investments in other divisions which are forgone because of lack of funds allocated to these other divisions.

Model Building. Where the investment decision is important enough, it may be desirable and economic to build a mathematical, physical, or analog model of the expected behavior. We can then simulate the alternative possibilities of what may occur in the future and evaluate the economic consequences. We can also take account of risks and uncertainties in some of these simulations. Plant investments, warehousing proposals, plant location problems are amenable to this approach when the projects are important enough to justify the study costs.

Various aspects of model building, simulation, Monte Carlo analysis, etc., are discussed in Part Six of this volume.

Investments in Research, Advertising, etc. The same types of procedures which have been used in analyzing the advisability of investments in tangible assets and production and engineering programs can be used for examining the economy of investments in research programs, advertising campaigns, and other expenditures which are usually treated as expenses by the accountants and tax authorities. Of course, it is frequently not possible to make a detailed analysis with much precision in the forecasts.

However, even a broad-term analysis can be very revealing in some situations. For example, a proposed research program may have a potential estimated by its enthusiastic sponsors of returning $4 for every $1 invested in the research. To the uninitiated, this may seem like a very valuable investment, yielding a potential 400 per cent return. However, if a simple economy analysis is made, taking into account that money has earning power if used elsewhere, it may reveal a relatively low prospective rate of return on the investment considering the risks and uncertainties.

Consider the research program previously mentioned. It calls for the expenditure of the following sums of money.

Year	Budgeted research expenditures
1	$50,000
2	25,000
3	10,000
4	10,000
5	5,000

Its enthusiastic sponsors estimate the following net returns from this program.

Year	Forecasted net cash return (income less cash expenditures)
6	
7	
8	$10,000
9	20,000
10	30,000
11	50,000
12	75,000
13	75,000
14	75,000
15	65,000

The prospective rate of return on this research investment which will return $4 for each $1 is only 14.3 per cent even if the figures of the enthusiastic proponents are accepted.

Even this kind of analysis is possible only in certain situations in which quantitative estimates can be made. Much research and advertising defy this type of analysis except in even more approximate terms. The evaluation is thus largely intangible, and some of the methods of evaluation discussed in the chapters of Part Six may be useful.

PROBLEMS

1. Why is it difficult to apply directly the supply-and-demand approach of Chapter 13 in capital budgeting?

2. The capital-budgeting procedures developed in the text use rate of return as the primary criterion for ranking proposals. It has been proposed that the premium worth or premium-worth percentages be used as the primary criterion. (a) What arguments can you marshal to support the use of the premium-worth or premium-worth-percentage criterion? (b) What would be the principal drawbacks to using the premium-worth or premium-worth-percentage criterion?

3. Prepare a set of procedural instructions (in outline format) for the operation of a capital-budgeting system in a medium-sized manufacturing company, specifying all the policies and steps necessary for a successful system.

4. Write a detailed procedure specifying how the follow-up on approved capital projects should be conducted, including whatever forms and reports you consider appropriate.

5. Company A retains all its earnings. Company B distributes 50 per cent of its earnings as dividends. Company B must then borrow money to finance some of its capital expenditures whereas Company A does not need to borrow. Does this mean that Company B has a higher cost of capital than Company A? Explain your answer.

6. A shortage of managerial talent to implement capital-investment proposals has been cited as one factor which will increase the risk and uncertainty of the proposals. Cannot this shortage be easily overcome by the employment of additional managers from outside the company? Explain your answer.

7. How is the piecemeal-analysis error related to the problem of suboptimization discussed in Chapter 2?

8. Savings on cost-saving investments are dependent upon the efficiency of the current operation. An analysis may therefore make a proposal appear very desirable even though it is quite undesirable when compared with better alternatives. Does this make cost-saving investments less desirable than income-producing ones? Explain.

9. Would the allocation of investment funds to each division of a company on the basis of depreciation charges be a reasonable procedure under any circumstances? Explain.

17 The Economy of Replacement and Retirement (Economic Life)

The quantity of future services which a facility will produce is very important in determining the relative economy of the potential investment in the facility. Quite obviously, the greater this quantity, the higher the prospective return from the investment.

This quantity of future services is dependent upon the rate of production and the length of time the facility will be used. This length of time depends upon the rate at which the utility of the machine depreciates. The faster this occurs, the sooner it becomes economical to replace or retire the asset. Physical deterioration of equipment may cause excessive maintenance, reduced efficiency, poor quality. New production or service requirements may render facilities inadequate. Improved facilities may be developed for better performance. Equipment may be rendered obsolete by technological advances.

Economic Life. If we could forecast with precision the future values of these factors, we could calculate the average cost of retaining a facility in operation for any given life. The longer we keep a facility in operation before replacing it, the lower will be the average annual capital-recovery cost and the higher will be the operating costs, the loss of revenue from poorer quality of product, loss of potential savings from improved equipment, etc. Thus, as illustrated in Figure 17-1, we have two opposing tendencies as we keep the facility longer: the decreasing average capital-recovery costs and the increasing operating and other costs of using older equipment. These combine to produce a curve which is concave upward with a minimum value at one point. This point corresponds to the number of years the facility should be kept in service before retirement to achieve the lowest average annual cost or the maximum return. It is the theoretical economic life of the facility.

Simplified Model of Reality. Some insights into the interaction of factors which determine the economic lives of facilities may be gained by the consideration of simplified models of reality. Studies of economic life under restrictive assumptions are useful only if the assumptions are clearly understood. Otherwise, misinterpretations and misapplications may result.

As machines get older, the general pattern is as follows:

1. Increasing maintenance and repairs
2. Decreasing operating rate with consequent increasing costs
3. Decreasing receipts for product or service and increased costs because of declining quality
4. Decreasing operating costs of improved machines as compared with deteriorating facilities
5. Decreasing receipts for product or service because of relative quality declines as compared with higher quality of product of improved machines (This is a comparison of the product or service of improved machines with the deteriorating facility.)
6. Possible obsolescence of product or service on a gradual or more sudden basis

This pattern of deterioration is not uniform nor do each of the factors have the same importance or effect in different cases. The first two items result in a pattern of increasing costs as the machine ages. The third factor, declining quality, results in a decline in income which can be considered a cost or price of keeping the machine rather than replacing it with a new but unimproved version.

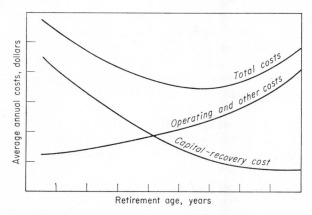

Figure 17-1. Theoretical economic-life curve.

The fourth, the decrease in operating costs which would be possible each time an improved machine is developed if the new one were used, is a relative increase in annual operation costs compared with the improved design.

The fifth factor is the decreasing relative receipts because of relative inferiority of the quality of product as compared with improved machines. In some cases, machine improvements are made at frequent intervals, annually or every couple of years. In many cases, they appear less frequently and represent more dramatic breakthroughs. The sixth factor represents a decrease in the demand for the product or service produced by the facility because of obsolescence. Most obsolescence takes place over a period of time although it may not always be recognized in its early stages. However, there are examples of rather sudden obsolescence.

Our present discussion aims to gain an insight into how these factors affect the economic life of an asset without implying that explicit economic-life calculations can or should usually be made for each facility. Rather, a knowledge of how these factors affect economic life will enable better judgment to be used in assessing the importance of expected variations in these factors.

In actual practice, it is not practical to make explicit estimates of the behavior of each of these factors in each year of the life of a machine whose procurement is being considered. Each of these factors should nevertheless be considered in appraising the desirability of procuring a facility and in estimating the expected economic life of the asset.

A machine does not have an inherent economic life. Many of the factors, such as technological progress, which affect economic life are exterior to the machine and its performance and will occur in the future. In addition, the values for the various forecasted costs are averages. Some of the machines will have higher costs than the average and some lower.

An aspect of machine retirement which is ignored in this economic-life model is the downgrading of equipment to other less demanding services or to stand-by service in the enterprise. In this model, such downgrading is considered the same as a retirement. Retirement of the asset does not necessarily mean that the asset is dismantled and sold or scrapped.

Calculation of Economic Life. Let us start with the assumption that we desire a 10 per cent rate of return on our investments in facilities. We want to determine the economic life of machine Q whose first cost is $5,000.

Inherent Costs. In Table 17-1 are summarized the inherent costs of machine Q. Cost of operation, cost of decreasing capacity, and cost of declining quality are forecasted for each of nine years and then totaled to obtain an estimate of the alternative costs of the inherent deterioration of the machine.

The cost of operation, as shown in this table, includes maintenance and repair costs which generally increase as the machine gets older. In some years, especially when the machine is relatively new, there may be no change from year to year. There may be decreases in some years for two reasons: maintenance may be deferred for one or more years after it should normally be performed; in some years, large sporadic maintenance and repair costs may occur because of accidents or because some of the maintenance is performed in a cycle covering several years.

The effective capacity of a machine will usually decrease when it gets old because it requires more down time for repairs, has more frequent breakdowns, and sometimes cannot be run at rated capacity. This reduced operating rate results in smaller production per unit time. This means that the machine must be run more hours to achieve the same output or that more machines must be operated. The lost output, therefore, represents an increased cost. One pattern for this cost is shown in Table 17-1.

Table 17-1. **Inherent Costs of Machine Q**

Year	Cost of operation	Cost of decreasing capacity	Cost of declining quality	Total inherent costs
1	$5,950	0	0	$ 5,950
2	5,950	0	0	5,950
3	6,000	0	0	6,000
4	6,100	0	$ 25	6,125
5	6,200	$ 150	100	6,450
6	6,400	400	225	7,025
7	6,700	800	500	8,000
8	7,200	1,000	1,025	9,225
9	8,000	1,000	1,700	10,700

The quality of the product or service produced by an asset will frequently be reduced as the ability of the machine to hold tolerances or perform with perfection decreases with age. The selling price for the lower-quality product or service declines. The net reduction in receipts has the same effect as a comparable increase in costs. This declining capability of the equipment will also result in a larger production of reject product, which must be reworked or scrapped. The cost of declining quality thus includes the labor cost of rework, scrapped material, extra inspection and sorting, etc., as well as the reduced revenues from the lower prices which can be charged for poorer-quality product.

Costs Relative to Improved Models and Obsolescence. Each year improvements are made in the design of equipment. New processes are discovered and technological breakthroughs are successfully accomplished. This improved equipment will frequently produce at lower costs than the unimproved equipment and/or will produce a higher-quality product.

The operating cost inferiority of an existing machine must take account not only of the operating savings which a new design would produce but also any difference in the price of the improved machine and the currently used model. There is thus a decline in quality on the old machine relative to the quality on the new improved machines. This decline in relative quality means a decline in receipts relative to the new machine and can be considered an increased cost. There is also an increased cost of operating the older designed machine relative to the improved new model, and this is an additional relative cost. Both of these cost inferiorities of the old machine over improved new models can be represented as annual costs. They are alternative or opportunity costs.

Another alternative cost is represented by the decreasing net income caused by obsolescence affecting the machine's products or services. The demand for the products produced by the machine may decrease or disappear abruptly or gradually because technology has developed better substitute products.

The costs relative to improved models and obsolescence for machine Q are summarized in Table 17-2.

Table 17-2. Costs of Machine Q Relative to Improved Models and Obsolescence

Year	Operating cost inferiority	Quality inferiority	Obsolescence	Total relative costs
1	0	0	$ 50	$ 50
2	$ 25	$ 25	100	150
3	50	50	150	250
4	100	75	200	375
5	150	100	300	550
6	250	125	400	775
7	350	150	500	1,000
8	500	175	600	1,275
9	700	200	700	1,600

The economic-life calculation is performed in Table 17-3, using the estimated data on inherent and relative costs of Tables 17-1 and 17-2 as well as estimated salvage values of the equipment each year. The total cost of service each year is obtained by adding together the inherent and relative costs, the estimated decrease in salvage value during the year, and the interest on the value at the beginning of the year. The annual equivalent cost of service if retired at the end of the year is determined from the annual total cost of service figures by first multiplying each annual cost of service value by the appropriate single-payment present-worth factor at 10 per cent interest to find its present worth of cost of service during year; then calculating the present worth of cost of service since placed in service by summing the present worths of cost of service during each year up to the year in question; and finally multiplying this present value of the cost of service since placed in service by the capital-recovery factor to obtain annual equivalent cost if retired at end of the year.

Table 17-3. Economic-life Calculation

Year	Inherent costs	Relative costs	Total inherent and relative costs	Est. decrease in salvage value during year	Value at beginning of year	Interest on value at beginning of year, 10%	Total cost of service during year	SPPW 10%	PW of cost of service during year	PW of cost of service since placed in service	CR 10%	Annual equivalent cost if retired at end of year
1	$ 5,950	$ 50	$ 6,000	$2,000	$5,000	$500	$ 8,500	0.9091	$7,727	$ 7,727	1.10000	$8,500
2	5,950	150	6,100	1,000	3,000	300	7,400	0.8264	6,115	13,842	0.57619	7,976
3	6,000	250	6,250	500	2,000	200	6,950	0.7513	5,222	19,064	0.40211	7,666
4	6,125	375	6,500	300	1,500	150	6,950	0.6830	4,747	23,811	0.31547	7,512
5	6,450	550	7,000	200	1,200	120	7,320	0.6209	4,545	28,356	0.26380	7,480
6	7,025	775	7,800	150	1,000	100	8,050	0.5645	4,544	32,900	0.22961	7,554
7	8,000	1,000	9,000	125	850	85	9,210	0.5132	4,727	37,627	0.20541	7,729
8	9,225	1,275	10,500	100	725	72	10,672	0.4665	4,978	42,605	0.18744	7,986
9	10,700	1,600	12,300	75	625	62	12,437	0.4241	5,275	47,880	0.17364	8,314

The minimum value for the annual equivalent cost occurs if the facility is retired at the end of five years. This is also shown in Figure 17-2, on which is plotted the annual equivalent total cost. Annual equivalents of the increasing inherent and relative costs and annual equivalents of the decreasing capital-recovery costs were separately computed, and separate curves for the two components of the annual equivalent total cost are also shown on this chart.

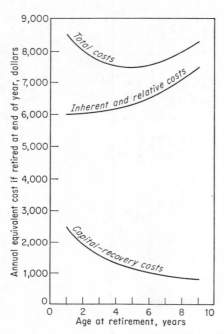

Figure 17-2. Economic-life curve of machine Q.

Specialized Utility of Economic-life Concept. We can see from our previous models that a machine does not have a natural economic life. This life depends upon the inherent deterioration costs which are subject to changes as cost and market conditions change; upon the extent of technological advances which influences the relative decline caused by obsolescence and supersession; upon the rate of return which management desires on its capital investments (which in turn is related to many other factors); and upon the prices of the machines when new and at various ages when used (which are in turn related to many of the above items).

This economic-life model is not realistic in the sense that we can use it to forecast the life of an asset. It is realistic in that it describes how various factors affect the economic life of an asset. We cannot use the model for forecasting purposes because the forecast data it requires cannot be readily obtained with the required degree of accuracy. However, we can use the model to ascertain how changes in various factors will affect the economic lives of facilities.

Economic Life and Price of Facility. How will variations in the price of a facility affect its economic life? In Figure 17-3 are plotted economic-life curves for facilities costing $1,000, $5,000, $10,000, and $25,000. All the inherent and relative costs are the same as in the original example. The percentage decreases in salvage value each year are also the same. A 10 per cent desired rate of return is used.

We can see that, as the price of the facility increases, with all other factors held constant, the economic life of the asset increases. The $1,000 facility has an economic life of 3 years; the $5,000 facility, 5 years; the $10,000 facility, 6 years; and the $25,000 facility has an economic life of 8 years.

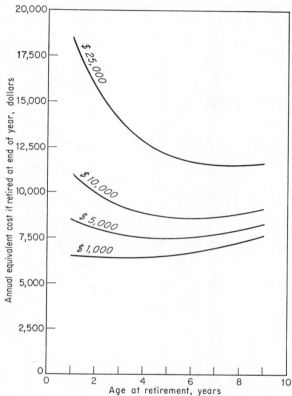

Figure 17-3. Economic-life curves for facilities costing $1,000 to $25,000.

Economic Life and Rate of Return. The rate of return which a company desires on a facility depends upon many factors, including the prevailing interest rates and the alternatives available.

Some industries require higher prospective rates of return on investments than others. The availability of investment funds changes and these changes affect interest rates and required rates of return. How do variations in the size of this required return affect the rapidity with which equipment is replaced by more modern facilities? How would changes in the required rate of return affect our economic-life calculation for the $5,000 and $10,000 facilities in the previous example?

We can calculate economic-life curves for the two facilities using different interest rates. These changes in economic life are summarized in

Figures 17-4 and 17-5. As the interest rate increases, the annual equivalent costs increase and the economic life of the asset increases. Thus, in the $5,000 facility of Figure 17-4, the minimum point on the 0 per cent curve

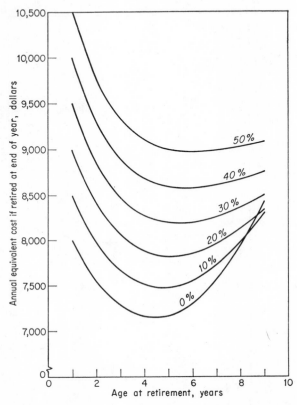

Figure 17-4. Economic-life curves at interest rates from 0 to 50 per cent, $5,000 facility.

shows a 4-year economic life; the 10 through 30 per cent curves show a 5-year economic life; and the 40 and 50 per cent curves show a 6-year economic life. For the $10,000 facility of Figure 17-5, the minimum point on the 0 per cent curve shows a 5-year economic life; the 10 and 20 per cent curves show a 6-year economic life; the 30 and 40 per cent curves show a 7-year economic life; and the 50 per cent curve shows a 8-year economic life.

We can see that raising the rate of return increases the economic life of the asset. The higher the required rate of return, the less frequently we will replace our assets. How greatly the size of the interest rate will affect economic life depends upon the relative importance of capital costs, which are affected by the interest rate, and changes in the inherent and relative costs.

In the $5,000 facility, the increases in inherent and relative costs as the facility grows older are large compared with the capital costs, which decrease as the facility is kept longer. For this reason, increases in the interest rate have smaller effects in increasing the economic life than in other cases in which the facility costs are relatively larger. Thus, in the $10,000 facility example, the interest rate increases have a greater effect in prolonging economic life than in the case of the $5,000 facility.

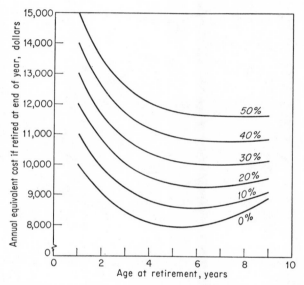

Figure 17-5. Economic-life curves at interest rates from 0 to 50 per cent, $10,000 facility.

Economic Life and Wage Rates. Wage rates vary between regions, industries, occupations, etc. How do these variations affect the economy of machine replacement?

Labor costs constitute the largest percentage of inherent and relative costs. Two examples of the effect of increasing the inherent and relative costs 0, 10, 20, 40, and 100 per cent are shown in the economic-life curves of Figures 17-6 and 17-7.

In Figure 17-6 are plotted the economic-life curves of a $5,000 machine which already has a relatively short economic life. The economic life of the $5,000 facility remains at 5 years for the 0, 10, and 20 per cent increase in inherent and relative costs; it decreases to 4 years for the 40 and 100 per cent increases. In Figure 17-7 are plotted the economic-life curves of a $10,000 facility which has a somewhat longer economic life.

The economic life of the $10,000 facility remains at 6 years for the 0, 10, and 20 per cent increase in inherent and relative costs; it decreases to 5 years for the 40 and 100 per cent increases. We see that in both cases the increasing inherent and relative costs tend to shorten the economic life of the machine, making earlier replacement economic.

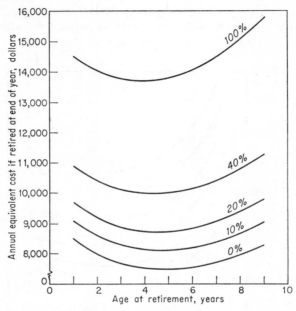

Figure 17-6. Economic-life curves with increasing inherent and relative costs, $5,000 facility.

It would thus appear that increasing wage rates will decrease the economic life of assets and cause them to be replaced sooner, other things being held constant. However, increases in wage rates in the industry making the asset will also increase the replacement price of the facility. We noted in a previous section that as the price of the facility increases, the economic life of the asset increases. Whether the over-all effect of increasing wage rates will cause increases or decreases in economic life will depend upon the relative size of the changes in the asset-manufacturing industry and the asset-using industry.

Economic Life and Rate of Technological Progress. The rate of development of new technology will affect the size of relative costs of obsolescence as well as the operating and quality cost inferiorities. Increasing rates of progress will thus increase the inherent and relative costs compared with the investment costs. As shown in Figures 17-6 and 17-7, these increases will tend to shorten the economic life of the asset.

The faster the rate of technological progress, the shorter will be the economic life, other things being equal.

It is important to remember that the various effects on economic life which use of this model has disclosed are based upon simplified illustrations. They represent tendencies which will have different values in each actual situation. In any given situation, all of the interactions which are present must be considered. Will the capital cost of the replacement of the facility rise when wage rates are increased? Will higher wage rates, by making replacement more economic, encourage a faster rate of technological progress? When facility costs are increased, will salvage values increase proportionately?

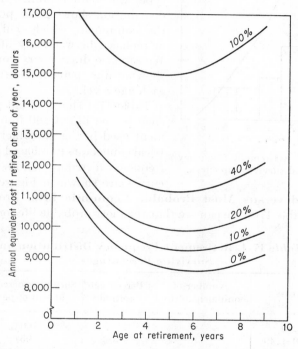

Figure 17-7. Economic-life curves with increasing inherent and relative costs, $10,000 facility.

Dispersion of Economic Lives. The preceding discussions of economic-life models assumed that there was one value for the maintenance and repairs on each type of machine each year of its life. Actually, there is a dispersion of values for each year—some equipment will have values close to the average for the year whereas others will have much higher or lower figures. Dispersions of values will also occur with all the other costs involved in the economic-life model. As a result, some machines will be replaced before the average economic life for the type of machine has been reached. Others will be replaced later than this expected average number of years. *Replacement decisions must be based not on economic-life studies, but on economic comparisons of the advantages and disadvantages of continuing with current facilities and replacing them with the best available alternatives.* Age of the facility is pertinent only in so far as it affects such items as expected costs, quality of service, and revenues.

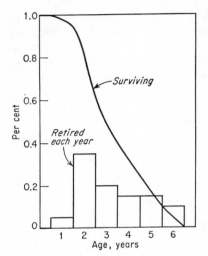

Figure 17-8. Retirement frequency histogram and survivorship curve.

For any group of equipment of one type, we could establish a frequency distribution showing the percentage of the equipment which will be retired or replaced between any life intervals. We can also draw a survivorship curve, showing the percentage surviving to each age level.

Table 17-4 shows recent past experience in the life of 160 items of equipment used in the manufacture of electrical connectors purchased in 1950. The frequency distribution and survivorship curves are shown in Figure 17-8.

Expected versus Most Probable Economic Life. From the statistics in Table 17-4, we can see that the most probable life for this equip-

Table 17-4. **Retirement Frequency Distribution and Surviving Percentages**

Years	Number of equipment retired	Percentage retired	Surviving percentage at end of period
0–0.49	0	. . . .	100%
0.50–1.49	8	5%	95
1.50–2.49	56	35	60
2.50–3.49	32	20	40
3.50–4.49	24	15	25
4.50–5.49	24	15	10
5.50–6.49	16	10	0
	160	100%	

ment is 2 years. Thirty-five per cent of the equipment is retired with a life between 1.5 and 2.5 years. No other age has as large a percentage retiring as the modal age of 2 years. However, this most likely or probable life is considerably less than the average or expected life, which is more than $3\frac{1}{4}$ years, shown by expected value of 3.30 in calculations of Table 17-5. (Expected and most probable values are discussed in Chapter 21.)

Table 17-5. Expected- (Average) Life Calculation

Years	Percentage retired	Value
1	0.05	0.05
2	0.35	0.70
3	0.20	0.60
4	0.15	0.60
5	0.15	0.75
6	0.10	0.60
	1.00	3.30, Expected value

Determination of Actual Service Lives. In the preceding example, we assumed that the prospective economic service life of an asset could be estimated from the distribution of service lives that the same or similar assets had in the immediate past. This is based on the assumption that management retains an asset in service only until it is no longer economic to do so: that it recognizes when it is most economic to replace each asset and acts on this knowledge. For some of the same reasons that we cannot forecast expected economic life with precision, management cannot be certain exactly when a machine should be replaced for more economic operation. Moreover, as noted in a preceding section, the cost curves for varying lives tend to be very flat at the bottom, little difference in average costs being caused by deviating a few years one way or the other from the economic life.

Knowledge of the actual lives and retirement characteristics of recently retired assets can be very useful in determining retirement and expected-life characteristics of current or prospective new capital assets. There are two principal approaches to determining actual service lives: (1) the original-group approach, (2) the annual-rate approach.

The Original-group Approach. The original-group approach is based on the records of the retirements each year of all units of one type of asset which were placed in service in one year. These calculations were previously illustrated in Table 17-4. This approach possesses two principal disadvantages:

1. The retirement experience is limited to one period's purchases. The size of the sample is therefore restricted to a relatively small number in many cases.

2. Most of the group must have been retired before the method can be applied. It, therefore, does not give as current a picture of the lives of the

asset as the annual-rate approach. This is of special importance for long-lived assets.

Figure 17-8 shows the survivorship curve for a group of assets which was obtained by the original-group approach. When all of the original group of assets have not been retired before the analysis date, we may extrapolate to zero survivors to obtain an approximation of the completed curve.

The Annual-rate Approach. The annual-rate approach is based upon an analysis of the rate of retirement of the assets in each age group which were in service during one or more given recent years. This calculation is illustrated in Table 17-6 and refers to retirement experience during the four-year period 1957 to 1960.

Table 17-6. **Number in Service at Beginning of Each Age Group and Number Retired During Age Group Period**

Age	Year placed in service										1957-1960 Experience	
	1951	1952	1953	1954	1955	1956	1957	1958	1959	1960	Number in service at beginning of age group	Number retired during age group
0- 0.49	35(0)	31(0)	38(0)	33(0)	26(0)	28(0)	22(0)	39(0)	47(0)	39(0)	147	0
0.50- 1.49	35(1)	31(1)	38(0)	33(3)	26(2)	28(1)	22(0)	39(3)	47(0)	39	136	4
1.50- 2.49	34(3)	30(2)	38(3)	30(1)	24(1)	27(1)	22(2)	36(2)	47		109	6
2.50- 3.49	31(2)	28(3)	35(6)	29(5)	23(4)	26(4)	20(3)	34			98	16
3.50- 4.49	29(8)	25(8)	29(9)	24(10)	19(7)	22(8)	17				94	34
4.50- 5.49	21(11)	17(8)	20(10)	14(6)	12(7)	14					63	31
5.50- 6.49	10(4)	9(4)	10(3)	8(2)	5						37	13
6.50- 7.49	6(0)	5(1)	7 (2)	6								
7.50- 8.49	6(1)	4(1)	5									
8.50- 9.49	5(0)	3										
9.50-10.49	5											

The units in service in each age group during the period are calculated by adding together the number of units of the asset which were in service in each age group in 1957, 1958, 1959 and 1960. For example, purchases were as follows:

1957	22
1958	39
1959	47
1960	39
Total	147

Therefore, 147 new machines were in service during this period. For simplicity, machines placed in service during a year are considered to have been acquired at the middle of the year and are, therefore, in age group 0–0.49.

None of the machines purchased in 1957 to 1960 were retired in this first year. During 1957 to 1960, the following number of machines in age group 0.50–1.49 were in service: the 108 purchased in 1957 to 1959 plus the 28 purchased in 1956.

In Table 17-6, the history of all the machines purchased from 1951 to 1960 is shown. The number of units in service at the beginning of each age group, which correspond to the beginning of successive years, is shown. Alongside, in parentheses, are shown the retirements during the age group. The units corresponding to 1957 to 1960 experience on the various original groups purchased from 1951 to 1960 are bracketed in between heavy lines. These are summed up in the last two columns on the right.

In Table 17-7, the percentage retirements in each age group are calculated by dividing the number retired by the number in service at the beginning of each age group. The percentage retired during the period is obtained by multiplying the percentage of age group retired by the preceding percentage of survivors at the end of the age group. This percentage retired during the period is then subtracted to obtain this age group's percentage of survivors at the end of the age group.

Table 17-7. Retirement Data for 1957, 1958, 1959, 1960

Age group	Number in service at beginning of age group	Number retired during age group	Percentage of age group retired	Percentage retired during period	Percentage of survivors at end of age group
0–0.49	147	0	0.00	0.00	100.00
0.50–1.49	136	4	2.94	2.94	97.06
1.50–2.49	109	6	5.50	5.34	91.72
2.50–3.49	98	16	16.33	14.98	76.74
3.50–4.49	94	34	36.17	27.76	48.98
4.50–5.49	63	31	49.21	24.10	24.88
5.50–6.49	37	13	35.14	8.74	16.14

For example, in 1.50 to 2.49 age group, the 6 retirements are divided by the 109 in service at beginning of age group, which gives us 5.50 per cent as the percentage of the age group retired. This 5.50 per cent is multiplied by 97.06 per cent, the preceding percentage of survivors at end of age group, to obtain 5.34 per cent for the percentage retired. This 5.34 per cent is then subtracted from the preceding percentage of survivors at end of age group, 97.06 per cent, to obtain this age group's percentage of survivors, which is, therefore, 91.72 per cent.

The frequency distribution for percentage retired and the survivorship curve for this equipment are shown in Figure 17-9.

This same method could be applied to 1 year's or 10 years' experience. Using the most recent 1-year period will give most current results, but will be based on a smaller sample of experience and may have unusual factors present in that year. The 10-year period has the disadvantage of being based on older experience, but may be desirable if the larger sample of experience is necessary.

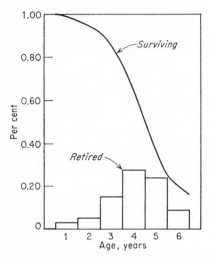

Figure 17-9. Retirement frequency histogram and survivorship curve.

Completing Survivorship Curves. Incomplete survivorship curves are extrapolated to zero to permit the calculation of the average or expected life. Of course, where the distribution of lives is approximately normal, the median life (age at which 50 per cent of the units are retired) will be close to the average.

Extrapolation may be done in a number of ways. Some of these are as follows:

1. By visual means to obtain a smooth curve.

2. By statistical fitting of a curve, such as a least-squares line (see Chapter 31).

3. By selection of a suitable type of survivorship curve which has been previously developed. The Iowa Engineering Experiment Station has developed a comprehensive set of survivorship curves which may be very useful in this connection.[1]

The use of the Iowa-type curves is illustrated in Figure 17-10. Each type of survivorship curve is drawn on a transparent sheet of paper with curves for a range of average service lives as shown in the two examples. The Iowa curves on the transparent sheet are then matched to the original incomplete survivorship curve to obtain the best fit. In the example of Figure 17-10, we see that the L_3 type curves in the top panel provide a reasonably good fit for survivorship curve A, but not for survivorship curve B. The R_2 type curves of the bottom panel provide a reasonably good fit for survivorship curve B.

Limitations of Usefulness. Data on past retirement history are very useful but have limitations when estimating economic lives.

[1] These are described in A. Marston, R. Winfrey, and J. C. Hempstead, *Engineering Valuation and Depreciation,* McGraw-Hill Book Company, Inc., New York, 1953.

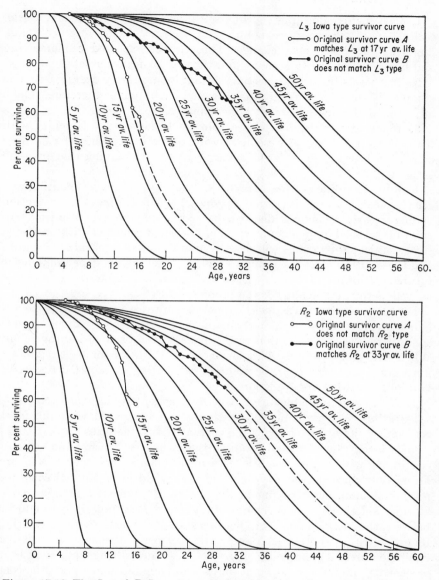

Figure 17-10. The L_3 and R_2 Iowa-type survivorship curves drawn to specific average service lives. SOURCE: A. Marston, R. Winfrey, and J. C. Hempstead, *Engineering Valuation and Depreciation*, McGraw-Hill Book Company, Inc., New York, 1953.

255

1. Past history does not repeat itself in exactly the same way. Costs, technological progress, economic and market conditions, company financing problems, etc., change. These affect expected economic life and must be taken into account in estimates for future assets.

2. The assets themselves change, so that we are rarely dealing with one completely homogenous group of assets. We must, therefore, make adjustments for the effects of these changes.

3. When we are dealing with a completely new type of facility with little or no past history, we can only use statistical studies of past lives of related types of facilities as a starting point in making economic-life estimates.

Remaining Economic Life of a Facility. When calculating the relative economy of an investment proposal which involves the production of incremental revenue which can be estimated, the rate-of-return calculation is based upon a comparison of projected revenues with projected costs. Projected revenues will depend upon forecasted market conditions and these future market conditions will, to some extent, depend upon the future costs of production of this company and of competitive companies as well as future demand for the product or service.

For many capital-investment proposals, however, incremental revenue is not involved because the anticipated benefits are cost reductions or a combination of cost reduction with expansion and product improvement. When evaluating proposed replacement of facilities for cost-reduction purposes, grave errors can be made in calculating anticipated returns if two important factors are ignored:

1. If the best available alternative replacement is not evaluated

2. If this best available alternative is not compared with the most economical life expectancy for the currently used facilities

This latter consideration requires that when estimating the costs of continuing with current facilities in a replacement study, we use a future life of only one additional year if this will yield lower annual costs for retaining the present equipment than will a life of more than one year.

In considering the replacement of an asset, the comparison should be between the cost and quality of performance of the new equipment during its expected life and the cost and quality of performance of the existing equipment over its remaining expected life. If the existing equipment is at or past the minimum-cost point on its economic-life curve, then the cost of service for one more year is the suitable cost of the existing facility.

MAPI Replacement Formula and Business Investment Charts. Much attention has been centered in recent years (but with limited application in industry[1]) on formula and chart methods for evaluating

---

[1] This is based upon personal observation of the author in his consulting practice as well as discussion with Dr. Arthur Lesser, Jr., who is currently (1961) making a survey of capital-management practices in industry.

replacement and investment decisions which were developed under the direction of George Terborgh[1] by the Machinery and Allied Products Institute (MAPI). The formula is based on a theoretical background which presents its own new vocabulary in order to obtain conceptual precision.

The Replacement Formula. There are a number of assumptions in this formula:

1. Future challengers will repeat the adverse minimum of the present one.

2. The present challengers will accumulate operating inferiority at a constant rate.

A challenger is the best unit, or group of units, available at a given time for the replacement of the defender, which is an asset now in service whose replacement is being considered. Operating inferiority is the amount by which the defender is operationally inferior to the challenger, taking both physical deterioration and obsolescence into account. The adverse average is the sum of the time-adjusted averages of operating inferiority and capital cost for a specific period. The adverse minimum is the value of the adverse average at its lowest point. Thus, it is assumed in the MAPI formula that the sum of the alternative costs of physical deterioration and obsolescence increases by a constant amount each year. This annual rate at which the inferiority gap widens is called the inferiority gradient. It is determined by experience with the presently used machine.

The MAPI system is to compare the adverse minimum of the challenger with that of the defender, assuming just one more year's service for the defender. To calculate these adverse minimums, formulas are recommended which provide for the following approximations: in lieu of the uniform annual equivalent of operating inferiority, the simple average is computed; in lieu of the uniform annual equivalent of capital cost, average depreciation plus interest on the average of the purchase price and salvage value.

Two formulas using these assumptions are presented:

Life average of operating inferiority and capital costs

$$= \frac{g(n-1)}{2} + \frac{c-s}{n} + \frac{i(c+s)}{2}$$

where g is the annual inferiority gradient, c the acquisition cost, s the terminal salvage value, n the number of years in the period of service, and i the rate of interest (in decimals).

However, the above formula is presented as a secondary device to be

[1] G. Terborgh, *Dynamic Equipment Policy*, McGraw-Hill Book Company, Inc., New York, 1949.

used only when the anticipated salvage values are large enough to alter the replacement decision indicated by the following no-salvage-value formula:

$$\text{Adverse minimum} = \sqrt{2cg} + \frac{ic - g}{2}$$

The first formula, with salvage values, was originally considered defective because the service life must be stipulated. It was, therefore, not called a true adverse minimum. In later publication,[1] however, the challenger's adverse minimum is always computed from the estimated service life.

The Business Investment Charts. In a recent MAPI publication[2] Terborgh presented a modification of his replacement-formula system. This new system, based on the use of charts, was designed to cover all types of capital-budgeting decisions, including replacements.

It uses as the basis for comparing investments a next-year rate of return called the MAPI urgency rating, rather than dollar-cost figures. The urgency rating is after income taxes at an assumed rate of 50 per cent (with adjustment factors for other rates) using either sum-of-the-digits or straight-line depreciation. It is computed by discounting expected future dollars beyond one year at an average interest rate of 8.25 per cent, assuming that 75 per cent of the capital comes from equity with a 10 per cent return and 25 per cent from debt at 3 per cent return. (The older replacement formula was based on a dollar-cost comparison before income taxes.)

The new approach provides separate charts for the accumulation of deterioration and obsolescence over the life of the investment at an increasing rate, at a decreasing rate, as well as at a constant rate. (The older replacement formula provided only for a constant rate.)

The MAPI formula and charts possess some disadvantages. Many of these are inherent in any procedure which is based on severely restricted conditions.

1. When a formula is used, people tend to lose sight of its limitations and restrictions and eventually tend to apply it by rote.

2. The assumptions are not applicable to all cases and it is difficult to insure that it will not be applied when the assumptions will cause significantly distorted results.

3. When it is apparent that assumptions are not valid, it is cumbersome to modify the formula to handle the problem.

---

[1] *MAPI Replacement Manual*, Machinery and Allied Products Institute, Washington, 1950.

[2] G. Terborgh, *Business Investment Policy*, Machinery and Allied Products Institute and Council for Technological Advancement, Washington, 1958.

4. Some assumptions are unrealistic in a large percentage of the cases even if the unrealistic aspects do not always affect the answer.

5. Because of the necessary complications of its derivation, it is extremely difficult for many people to understand fully all the implications of the assumptions and approximations in the formula without diligent study and continued use. This can lead to incorrect conclusions even though theoretically the errors may be avoidable.

There are no theoretical advantages which make the MAPI formula and charts superior to the less formalized, more generally applicable methods which require explicit statement of the assumptions and which are presented in this book. The practical advantage which the formula and charts possess—providing a mechanical procedure for computing the relative economy of alternatives—has an important drawback inherent in this very advantage: people tend to forget the assumptions when they use a mechanical procedure.

Despite the disadvantages of his method, Terborgh has made a significant contribution to an understanding of the essentials of replacement analysis. His books provide perceptive presentations of the theory of replacement and investment and are recommended for study by serious students of the subject.

PROBLEMS

1. Listed below are pairs of items. In each case, indicate the factors which would produce a longer or shorter life for one as compared with the other. Explain which tendency would be of predominant importance in each case. (a) A slide rule or a desk calculator, (b) a desk calculator or an electronic computer, (c) a bench lathe or an automatic screw machine, (d) a manually operated punch press or a tape-controlled automatic press, (e) a meat packing facility or an antibiotic manufacturing facility.

2. Would you expect that each of the following items would have a longer or a shorter economic life in an industrially underdeveloped country than in the United States? Explain which factors would tend to produce a longer or shorter life and which tendency would be of predominant importance in each case. (a) A computer used to calculate and issue payroll checks, (b) a punch press to produce replacement parts for automobiles, (c) a chemical-processing plant to produce agricultural fertilizer, (d) a manual water pump for use in industrial plants.

3. The retirement history for special high-compression valves used by the Bover Company is tabulated as follows:

Number Remaining in Service Each Year
(Number retired in parentheses)

Age (years)	Year of purchase					
	1955	1956	1957	1958	1959	1960
0–0.49	277(17)	391(27)	263(15)	246(11)	289(19)	310(18)
0.50–1.49	260(62)	364(86)	248(61)	235(62)	270(49)	292
1.50–2.49	198(97)	278(135)	187(88)	173(83)	221	
2.50–3.49	101(52)	143(76)	99(49)	90		
3.50–4.49	49(24)	67(34)	50			
4.50–5.49	25 (9)	33				
5.50–6.49	16					

(a) Calculate and plot a frequency distribution for percentage retired and a survivorship curve for these special high-compression valves using 1960 experience only.

(b) Do the same as in (a), but use the experience of 1959 as well as 1960.

(c) Do the same as in (a), but use the experience of 1958, 1959, and 1960.

4. The replacement of a boring machine is being considered by the Reardorn Furniture Co. The new improved machine will cost $30,000 installed, will have an estimated economic life of 12 years, and $2,000 salvage. It is estimated that annual operating and maintenance costs will average $16,000 per year. The present machine has a book value of $6,000 and a salvage value of $4,000. Its estimated costs for the next 3 years are shown below.

Year	Salvage value at end of year	Book value at end of year	Operating and maintenance costs during year
1	$3,000	$4,500	$20,000
2	2,500	3,000	25,000
3	2,000	1,500	30,000

Using interest at 15 per cent, make an annual-cost comparison, using exact capital recovery, to determine whether it is economical to make the replacement.

5. (a) Examine the statements in the text regarding some of the assumptions in the MAPI replacement formula. In many cases, the actual circumstances will be close to these assumptions. In others in which there are significant differences between actuality and these assumptions, the decision may or may not be sensitive to these differences. For each assumption describe a situation in which the MAPI formula would be unrealistic, with possible misleading results.

(b) Repeat (a) for the MAPI business investment chart statements of assumptions in the text.

PART FIVE

Determinations of Minimum Cost
and Maximum Profit

18 Minimum-cost Functional Relationships

Economic decisions frequently involve the choice of size or amount of a facility or a production factor. An appropriate way of handling these problems is to determine the minimum-cost point of the total cost function.

The total cost function in these problems may be composed of three categories of cost elements: elements which increase as the size of the facility or other design variable increases; elements which decrease as the size of the facility or other design variable increases; and elements which do not change as the size of the facility or other design variable increases or decreases.

The illustrations which will be presented in this chapter demonstrate the methods of developing formula or tabular total-cost models for making minimum-cost-point decisions. These methods do not take explicit account of risk or uncertainty. Risk and uncertainty are considered in the next section of this volume.

Algebraic Determinations: Directly and Inversely Proportional Costs. If some costs vary in direct proportion and other costs in inverse proportion to the size of a facility or other design variable, we can generalize an algebraic expression of total costs as follows:

$$C = AX + \frac{B}{X} + K$$

where C = total cost
X = size of facility or other design variable
A, B, and K = constants which are positive or equal to zero

To find the minimum point for the total cost, we differentiate to find the first derivative of C, set it equal to zero, and solve for X.

$$\frac{dC}{dX} = A - \frac{B}{X^2} = 0$$

$$X = \sqrt{\frac{B}{A}}^*$$

* Although mathematically X can also equal $-\sqrt{B/A}$, X is a positive quantity by definition.

263

We check to ensure that this is a minimum rather than a maximum value by computing the second derivative, $\dfrac{d^2C}{dX^2} = \dfrac{2B}{X^3}$, and noting that it has a positive value when $X = \sqrt{B/A}$.

At the value $X = \sqrt{B/A}$, the minimum-cost point, the directly proportional costs, AX, are exactly equal to the inversely proportional costs, B/X. This can be seen by substituting the value $\sqrt{B/A}$ in the expressions for the directly proportional and the inversely proportional costs.

Directly proportional costs at minimum-cost point:

$$AX = A\sqrt{\frac{B}{A}} = \sqrt{AB}$$

Inversely proportional costs at minimum cost point:

$$\frac{B}{X} = \frac{B}{\sqrt{\dfrac{B}{A}}} = \sqrt{AB}$$

The graph of this total-annual-cost curve is shown in Figure 18-1.

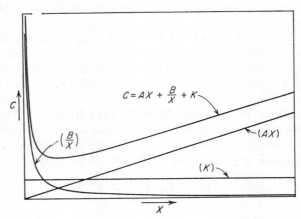

Figure 18-1. Total-annual-cost curve: $C = AX + \dfrac{B}{X} + K$.

The total-annual-cost curve, C, is composed of three elements: a constant element, K, represented by a horizontal line; a uniformly increasing element, AX; and a uniformly decreasing element, B/X. The minimum point in the total-cost curve is at the intersection of these latter two curves, the constant element, K, having no effect on the X value of the location of the intersection.

It is important to remember that this relationship of the minimum-cost point being at the point of intersection of the directly varying and inversely varying costs (the point at which these costs are equal to each other) is true only where the variations are directly and inversely proportional.

Kelvin's law is a classical example of the algebraic determination of a minimum-cost point where the costs are directly and inversely proportional. In connection with specification of the size of wire to conduct electric current, Lord Kelvin showed some years ago that the most economical wire size was one in which the investment costs, which vary directly with the size of the wire, equal the energy loss, which varies inversely with the size of the wire.

We will let

S = size of wire, measured by cross-section area
R = electrical resistance of wire, measured in ohms
I = amount of current conducted, measured in amperes
C_1, C_2, C_3 = constants, as explained below

The investment cost is composed of capital-recovery costs and taxes. With a given interest rate and capital-recovery period, capital-recovery costs are dependent only on the cost of the wire, which in this case is assumed to be proportional to its cross-section area. Taxes, insurance, etc., are a fixed percentage of the cost of the wire.

Thus,

Cost of wire = $C_1 S$
Capital-recovery cost = $C_1 S(\text{CR})$
Taxes, insurance, etc. = $C_2 S$
Total investment costs = $C_1 S(\text{CR}) + C_2 S = S[C_1(\text{CR}) + C_2]$

The energy loss, in watts, is $I^2 R$. The electrical resistance, R, is inversely proportional to the cross-section area of the wire, S. We can, therefore, write $R = C_3/S$. The energy loss then becomes $(I^2 C_3)/S$. I, the amount of current to be conducted, is constant in any given application.

We follow Kelvin's law to solve the problem by setting the investment cost equal to the energy loss:

$$S[C_1(\text{CR}) + C_2] = \frac{I^2 C_3}{S}$$

$$S = \sqrt{\frac{I^2 C_3}{C_1(\text{CR}) + C_2}}$$

We can use differential calculus to check Kelvin's law. Let T represent the total investment cost plus energy loss.

$$T = S[C_1(\text{CR}) + C_2] + \frac{I^2 C_3}{S}$$

To find the minimum-cost point, we calculate the first derivative and set it equal to zero.

$$\frac{dT}{dS} = C_1(CR) + C_2 - \frac{I^2C_3}{S^2} = 0$$

$$S = \sqrt{\frac{I^2C_3}{C_1(CR) + C_2}}$$

This is a minimum point since $\dfrac{d^2T}{dS^2} = \dfrac{2I^2C_3}{S^3}$ is positive when

$$S = \sqrt{\frac{I^2C_3}{C_1(CR) + C_2}}$$

Of course, Kelvin's law is true only if both sets of costs are actually directly and inversely proportional to changes in the size of the wire. For the investment costs to be directly proportional to the wire size, the price of wire per pound per foot must be the same regardless of the wire size (diameter); the cost of suspending the wire must be the same regardless of the size; and the expected lives of the wires must be the same regardless of the size. Similar restrictions apply to the proportionality of the cost of energy loss. Thus, Kelvin's law considers only energy loss due to resistance of the conductor and does not consider leakage and corona losses, which are important in high-voltage transmission.

Tabular Determination: Nonproportional Costs. In most practical minimum-cost problems, costs are not exactly proportional to the size or other design variable. In addition, it is frequently less tedious and more appropriate to solve a minimum-cost problem by tabular rather than by algebraic analysis.

In designing a bridge to cover a 1,500-ft crossing, the length of the space between each pier determines the number of piers which will be required. The longer the span length between the piers, the fewer the number of required piers, but the greater the amount of steel in the superstructure required to support the longer span. Maintenance costs are approximately the same regardless of the pier–span-length relationship. The relevant cost estimates for various numbers of piers and span lengths are shown in Table 18-1.

Examination of the table of cost estimates shows that the design with six piers gives the lowest total cost.

Economic Order Quantities and Inventory Levels. The determination of economic order quantities and inventory levels is a minimum-cost functional relationship problem. The functional relationship may be relatively simple or very complex, depending upon the procurement and manufacturing circumstances and the sales requirements.

Uniform Known Usage and Negligible Procurement Lead Time. If we assume that sales or usage of an item is uniform at a rate U pieces

Table 18-1. Estimated Costs of Building 1,500-ft Bridge
(Excluding Costs of Deck)

No. of piers	Span length (ft)	Cost of piers	Cost of steelwork	Total cost
4	500.0	$1,600,000	$4,040,000	$5,640,000
5	375.0	2,000,000	3,200,000	5,200,000
6	300.0	2,360,000	2,600,000	4,960,000
7	250.0	2,700,000	2,280,000	4,980,000
8	214.3	3,020,000	1,975,000	4,995,000
9	187.5	3,340,000	1,780,000	5,120,000

per year, and that the time to procure or produce the item is negligible, we could place an order for Q pieces of the item when its stock reaches zero, or we could place the order so that delivery is made when the stock reaches zero. The variations in inventory level under these conditions can be graphically presented as shown in Figure 18-2. No cushion or safety

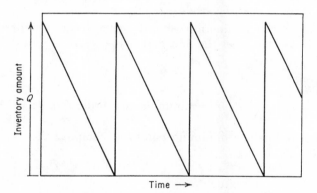

Figure 18-2. Pattern of variations in inventory level with uniform known usage and negligible procurement lead time.

stocks are shown in this presentation. They are unnecessary if we have a known demand. As illustrated, an order for inventory replacement would be placed at a uniform time interval for an economic amount, Q. This amount will be ordered U/Q times a year.

In this illustration, the unit-procurement or production cost of the item is a constant. If the item is purchased, the unit cost of the item will not vary with the quantity within the range of values we are considering. If it is manufactured, the unit material and direct-labor cost will not vary within the range of values we are considering.

Let us designate C_1 as the cost of placing a purchase order. If the item is manufactured rather than purchased, C_1 will represent the ordering and setup costs. The annual cost per year of placing orders or of making setups for the item is then C_1 times the number of times it is ordered per year, or $C_1(U/Q)$.

Let us designate C_2 as the cost of holding one unit of the item in inventory for a year. This includes the interest cost on the investment as well as accounting, obsolescence, deterioration, warehouse rental, handling, and storage costs. The annual cost of holding the item in inventory is then equal to C_2 times the average inventory level. The average inventory level is one-half the order quantity, or $Q/2$. The annual holding cost is, therefore, $C_2(Q/2)$.

The cost of manufacture or purchase is independent of the order quantity in this example. It is equal to the annual requirement, U, times the unit production cost or purchase price, which we will designate as C_3. This annual cost is therefore C_3U.

The total cost, C_T, consists of the cost of setup or placing the order plus the holding cost plus the cost of manufacture or purchase.

$$C_T = \frac{C_1U}{Q} + \frac{C_2Q}{2} + C_3U$$

To calculate the minimum-cost order quantity, we differentiate C_T with respect to Q and set the first derivative equal to zero.

$$\frac{dC_T}{dQ} = \frac{-C_1U}{Q^2} + \frac{C_2}{2} = 0$$

$$Q = \sqrt{\frac{2C_1U}{C_2}} = \text{minimum-cost order quantity}$$

To test that this is a minimum point, we compute the second derivative: $\dfrac{d^2C_T}{dQ^2} = \dfrac{2C_1U}{Q^3}$. This is positive when $Q = \sqrt{\dfrac{2C_1U}{C_2}}$, indicating that we have a minimum point.

Thus, $Q = \sqrt{\dfrac{2C_1U}{C_2}}$ should be ordered U/Q times a year for a minimum total annual cost. The total annual cost, C_T, when the economic quantity is ordered is

$$C_T = \frac{C_1U}{\sqrt{\dfrac{2C_1U}{C_2}}} + \frac{C_2}{2}\sqrt{\frac{2C_1U}{C_2}} + UC_3$$

$$C_T = \sqrt{2C_1C_2U} + UC_3$$

The term UC_3 represents the production or purchase cost of one year's requirements and the term $\sqrt{2C_1C_2U}$ represents the annual inventory and setup or order costs.

The average amount in inventory under this economic order policy is $Q/2$ or $\sqrt{C_1U/2C_2}$. This would indicate that, other things being equal and with no safety stocks, the size of the average inventory should vary as the square root of sales, $\sqrt{U}$.

Letting $C_1 = \$15$, $C_2 = \$0.06$, $C_3 = \$0.40$, and $U = 20,000$ per year, we can plot a graph of costs as a function of order quantity, Q, as shown in Figure 18-3. We are interested in operating at the minimum-cost point

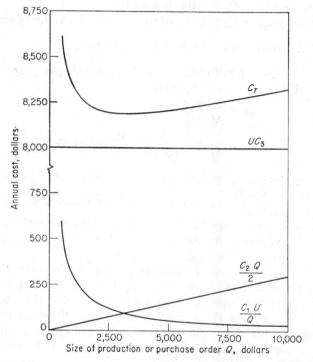

Figure 18-3. Variation of costs with size of production or purchase order when $C_1 = \$15$, $C_2 = \$0.06$, $C_3 = \$0.40$, and $U = 20,000$.

of C_T, which in this case occurs as $Q = \sqrt{2(15)(20,000)/0.06} = 3,162$. Our total-cost equation is

$$C_T = \frac{15(20,000)}{Q} + \frac{0.06Q}{2} + 0.40(20,000)$$

$$= \frac{15(20,000)}{3,162} + \frac{0.06(3,162)}{2} + 0.40(20,000)$$

$$= \$8,190$$

National Manufacturers, Inc., produces several switches exclusively for export under a contract which provides for shipment of specified quantities each week. On one type of these switches, National is supposed to supply 208,000 switches per year at a uniform rate of 4,000 per week.

Manufacturing capacity is 50,000 per day. Setup costs for the manufacture of the switch are $100 and holding costs have been estimated at 20 per cent of the average inventory value.

We can use the economic-lot-size formula we just developed because we have a uniform known usage and a negligible procurement lead time.

$$\text{Setup costs} = C_1 = \$100 \text{ per setup}$$
$$\text{Holding costs} = C_2 = 20\% \text{ of unit inventory value of switch}$$

Since the inventory value of this switch is $0.075,

$$C_2 = 0.20(0.075) = \$0.015 \text{ per unit per year}$$
$$\text{Usage} = U = 208,000 \text{ per year}$$
$$Q = \sqrt{\frac{2C_1 U}{C_2}}$$
$$= \sqrt{\frac{2(100)(208,000)}{0.015}} = 52,650$$

We should thus make these switches in batches of 52,000 every three months $\left(\dfrac{U}{Q} = \dfrac{208,000}{52,650} = \text{approximately four times a year}\right)$ for lowest costs. If the contract were to be quadrupled to 832,000 per year, we should make batches of $52,000 \sqrt{4} = 104,000$ every month and a half, (eight times a year) for lowest cost performance.

Size of Interest Charge in Holding Cost. An important element of holding cost is usually the interest cost on the capital tied up in the inventory. The size of the interest rate used in calculating this charge is significant in determining the economic order quantities. We may revise this formula to highlight the importance of using the proper interest rate and to assist in judging how variations in this interest rate will affect the economic order quantity.

The cost of holding may be divided into two parts: C_2' will represent all holding costs other than the interest cost on capital tied up in the inventory; the interest cost will be equal to the value of the average inventory, $QC_3/2$, times the interest rate, i, or $QC_3 i/2$.

The total annual cost would then be

$$C_T = \frac{C_1 U}{Q} + \frac{C_2' Q}{2} + \frac{QC_3 i}{2} + UC_3$$

Determining the minimum-cost point,

$$\frac{dC_T}{dQ} = \frac{-C_1 U}{Q^2} + \frac{C_2'}{2} + \frac{C_3 i}{2} = 0$$
$$Q = \sqrt{\frac{2C_1 U}{C_2' + iC_3}} = \text{minimum-cost order quantity}$$

The second derivative is positive at this value of Q, verifying that we have a minimum-cost point on the total-cost curve.

An example will illustrate the potential importance of the interest rate in determining economic order quantities. National Manufacturers purchases a component which it then markets under its own brand name.

$$\text{Purchasing costs} = C_1 = \$15 \text{ per order}$$
$$\text{Holding costs} = C_2 = C_2' + iC_3$$
$$C_2' = \$0.005 \text{ per unit}$$
$$C_3 = \$0.14 \text{ per unit}$$
$$i = 6\% \text{ or } 12\%$$
$$\text{Usage} = U = 100,000 \text{ per year}$$
$$Q = \sqrt{\frac{2C_1U}{C_2' + iC_3}}$$

For $i = 6\%$,

$$Q = \sqrt{\frac{2(15)(100,000)}{0.005 + (0.06)(0.14)}} = 14,950$$

For $i = 12\%$,

$$Q = \sqrt{\frac{2(15)(100,000)}{0.005 + (0.12)(0.14)}} = 11,750$$

Economic-order Tables. The factors which determine the most economic size of order are

1. The cost of making a setup or placing an order, C_1
2. The unit cost of holding inventory, C_2
3. Usage, U

To avoid the necessity of computing separately economic lot sizes for a large number of items, tables can be constructed which present the economic order or lot sizes for various values of these factors. Table 18-2 is an example of such a table. This table is calculated with U, the annual forecasted usage, expressed in dollars; C_1, the order or setup cost, expressed in dollars per purchase order or per setup; C_2, the inventory holding cost, expressed in dollars per unit per year; and Q, the economic order amount, expressed in dollars, and equal to $\sqrt{C_1/C_2}\sqrt{2U}$.

To illustrate use of the table: It is estimated that a bracket requires the expenditure of \$40 for ordering and production setup and costs \$0.50 a year to hold a unit in inventory. C_1/C_2 therefore equals 80. Annual usage runs about \$10,000 a year. The $C_1/C_2 = 75$ column is closest to the 80 value. We read off the order amount of \$1,225 at \$10,000 annual usage.

If we were to calculate this from the formula, we would get:

$$Q = \sqrt{\frac{2C_1U}{C_2}} = \sqrt{\frac{2(40)(10,000)}{0.50}} = \$1,265$$

Considering the risks and uncertainties of the cost estimates, the difference is insignificant.

One way of using an economic order table such as Table 18-2 is to

Table 18-2. **Economic Order Quantities**

Annual usage (U)	Order amount in dollars (Q)				
	$C_1/C_2 = 25$	$C_1/C_2 = 50$	$C_1/C_2 = 75$	$C_1/C_2 = 100$	$C_1/C_2 = 150$
$\quad$ 1,000	$ 224	$ 316	$ 387	$ 447	$ 548
1,500	274	387	474	548	671
2,000	316	447	548	632	775
3,000	387	548	671	775	949
4,000	447	632	775	894	1,095
5,000	500	707	866	1,000	1,225
7,500	612	866	1,061	1,225	1,500
10,000	707	1,000	1,225	1,414	1,732
20,000	1,000	1,414	1,732	2,000	2,449
30,000	1,225	1,732	2,121	2,449	3,000
40,000	1,414	2,000	2,449	2,828	3,464
50,000	1,581	2,236	2,739	3,162	3,873
75,000	1,936	2,739	3,354	3,873	4,743
100,000	2,236	3,162	3,873	4,472	5,477
200,000	3,162	4,472	5,477	6,325	7,746
300,000	3,873	5,477	6,708	7,746	9,487
400,000	4,472	6,325	7,746	8,944	10,954
500,000	5,000	7,071	8,660	10,000	12,247
750,000	6,124	8,660	10,607	12,247	15,000
1,000,000	7,071	10,000	12,247	14,142	17,321

analyze the setup and procurement costs (C_1) and the holding costs (C_2) of all materials and parts. The items would then be categorized based upon the approximate C_1/C_2 values which were calculated. Knowing the C_1/C_2 category and estimating annual usage, we can refer to an economic-order table to establish the economic order amount. The range of C_1/C_2 values covered in the order-size tables will vary from company to company depending upon the actual range of C_1/C_2 values.

Delivery Time. Let us make our assumptions a little more realistic. In many manufacturing situations, a significant amount of time elapses between the time the manufacturing department starts delivering an order and the entire order is delivered. The variations in inventory level under this type of situation are shown in Figure 18-4.

If we let P equal the rate of production per day, then Q/P is the number of days it takes to complete the production order for quantity Q. During this period, the inventory is accumulating at a rate which is less than P per day by the amount of daily usage, $U/260$. The inventory is thus increasing $[P - (U/260)]$ units per day and will reach its maximum at the end of Q/P days with a value of $\left(P - \dfrac{U}{260}\right)\left(\dfrac{Q}{P}\right).$

The average inventory will be one-half this maximum value, or

$$\frac{Q}{2P}\left(P - \frac{U}{260}\right) = \frac{Q}{2}\left(1 - \frac{U}{260P}\right)$$

Following the reasoning in our previous analysis,

$$C_T = \frac{C_1 U}{Q} + \frac{C_2 Q}{2}\left(1 - \frac{U}{260P}\right) + UC_3$$

$$\frac{dC_T}{dQ} = \frac{-C_1 U}{Q^2} + \frac{C_2}{2}\left(1 - \frac{U}{260P}\right) = 0$$

$$Q = \sqrt{\frac{2C_1 U}{C_2[1 - (U/260P)]}} = \text{minimum-cost order quantity}$$

Since $\dfrac{d^2 C_T}{dQ^2}$ is positive at this order quantity, this is a minimum-cost point.

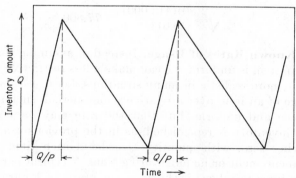

Figure 18-4. Pattern of variations in inventory level with uniform known usage and significant delivery time.

National Manufacturers' capacity for producing another one of the switches which it exports exclusively under contract is limited to 3,000 per day. The contract calls for 416,000 switches per year. Setup costs for this switch are $80 and holding costs have been estimated at 22 per cent of the average inventory value.

Because of capacity restrictions the ratio of the usage rate and production rate on this switch $[416,000/260(3,000) = 0.533]$ is of significant size. Procurement lead time will, therefore, make some difference in the calculation of the minimum-cost order quantity. We will, therefore, use our new formula.

Setup costs $= C_1 = \$80$ per setup

Holding costs $= C_2 = 22\%$ of unit inventory value of switch

The inventory value of this switch is \$0.050. Therefore,

$$C_2 = 0.22(0.050) = \$0.011 \text{ per unit}$$
$$\text{Usage} = U = 416{,}000 \text{ per year}$$
$$\text{Production} = P = 3{,}000 \text{ per day}$$

$$Q = \sqrt{\frac{2C_1 U}{C_2[1 - (U/260P)]}}$$

$$= \sqrt{\frac{2(80)(416{,}000)}{0.011\left[1 - \dfrac{416{,}000}{260(3{,}000)}\right]}} = 114{,}000$$

The minimum-cost production-lot size is thus 114,000 units.

If we had ignored the procurement lead time and used the formula assuming negligible lead time, we would have computed

$$Q = \sqrt{\frac{2C_1 U}{C_2}}$$

$$= \sqrt{\frac{2(80)(416{,}000)}{0.011}} = 77{,}800$$

Varying Known Rates of Usage. Instead of assuming that the sales or usage of an item is uniform, we can make a less restrictive assumption which will be more realistic in many situations. Let us assume only that sales or usage of an item over a relatively long period, such as a year or two, is known and uniform, but that the rate may vary during this period. The inventory is replenished, as in the previous examples, each time it reaches zero, with quantity Q ordered each time. There is a negligible procurement or manufacturing time. A typical pattern for the variations in inventory level is shown in the graph of Figure 18-5.

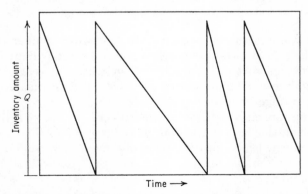

Figure 18-5. Pattern of variations in inventory level with varying known rates of usage and negligible procurement time.

If we use a year as the period for which we know the demand, then U/Q represents the number of production or purchase orders which we will issue during the year. The annual cost of these orders is C_1U/Q as in the previous example.

Our average inventory is $Q/2$, so that our holding cost is still $C_2(Q/2)$. Our total cost C_T is thus

$$C_T = \frac{C_1U}{Q} + \frac{C_2Q}{2} + UC_3$$

This is exactly the same as in the previous examples for uniform usage. Minimum-cost points and economical-lot sizes are therefore the same as in the case of uniform usage.

When there is a significant procurement or manufacturing time, the variations in inventory level frequently follow a pattern approximately as shown in Figure 18-6. The annual cost of orders is still C_1U/Q.

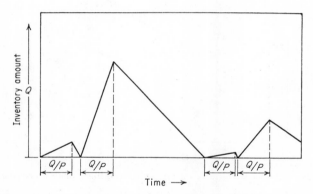

Figure 18-6. Pattern of variations in inventory level with varying known rates of usage and significant delivery time.

Our average inventory, however, is now $(Q/2)[1 - (U/260P)]$, the same as in the case for uniform usage. The economical order quantities and minimum-cost points are also the same as for uniform usage.

Quantity Purchase Discounts. In many cases, raw materials and parts can be purchased at quantity discounts. Ordering larger quantities to obtain lower freight rates has the same effect as a quantity discount since the purchase price of the raw material or part, C_3, includes the freight cost. How do we take quantity discounts into account in minimum-cost calculation?

Let us consider a simple example in which there is one price break. When the quantity ordered is greater than a given amount, k_1, the price is reduced from C_3 to C_3'. The total annual costs, C_T, when the order quantity is less than k_1, are

$$C_T = \frac{C_1 U}{Q} + \frac{C_2 Q}{2} + U C_3$$

When the order quantity is greater than k_1, total annual costs become

$$C_T' = \frac{C_1 U}{Q} + \frac{C_2' Q}{2} + U C_3'$$

C_2' is less than C_2 because the amount of capital per unit tied up in inventory is reduced when the purchase cost of the inventory is less.

Curves for C_T and C_T' are shown in Figure 18-7. The C_T' curve does not extend below $Q = k_1$ because the quantity discount price of C_3' does

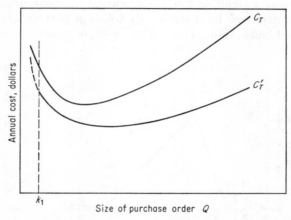

Figure 18-7. Annual-cost variations with quantity purchase price discount, situation I.

not apply to quantities below k_1. If the lower price did apply to order quantities below k_1, the annual costs would follow the dashed line shown on the chart.

We previously saw that the total annual costs, when the economic order quantity is used, are

$$C_T = \sqrt{2 C_1 C_2 U} + U C_3$$

When the economic order quantity equals or exceeds k_1, the quantity discount takes effect and C_T' applies:

$$C_T' = \sqrt{2 C_1 C_2' U} + U C_3'$$

C_2' and C_3' are less than C_2 and C_3, respectively. Therefore, C_T' using its economic order quantity will always be less than C_T using its economic order quantity. This is also apparent in Figure 18-7.

However, there is always the possibility that the economic order quantity computed for C_T' will turn out to be less than k_1. This is true in Figures 18-8 and 18-9. When this occurs, we cannot use the C_T' order

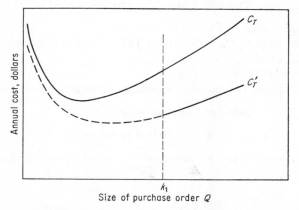

Figure 18-8. Annual-cost variations with quantity purchase price discount, situation II.

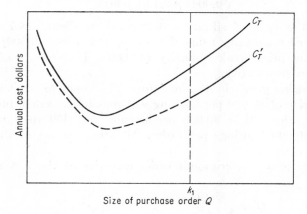

Figure 18-9. Annual-cost variations with quantity purchase price discount, situation III.

quantity because we cannot obtain the C_T' price discount below k_1. The C_T' curve does not exist below k_1. We must choose between ordering k_1 at price C_3' or using the C_T economic order quantity.

If C_T' at k_1 is less than C_T at its economic order quantity, we will order k_1 at the discount price C_3'. In Figure 18-8 C_T' at k_1 is less than C_T at its economic order quantity (minimum-total-cost point). We shall, therefore, order k_1.

If C_T' at k_1 is more than C_T at its economic order quantity, we will order the C_T economic order quantity. In Figure 18-9, C_T' at k_1 is more than C_T at its economic order quantity. We shall, therefore, order the C_T economic order quantity and forgo the discount.

For example, National Manufacturers buys 600,000 of one type of housing per year. The following data are assembled on these housings:

Purchasing cost = C_1 = \$15 per order
Holding costs = C_2 = \$0.004 + 12% of value per housing
Price of housing,
  C_3 = \$0.040 per housing
  C_3' = \$0.036 per housing on orders of 40,000 housings or more

Therefore, k_1 = 40,000 housings per order

$$\text{Usage} = U = 600,000 \text{ housings per year}$$

We first compute the economic order quantity using the discounted price

$$Q = \sqrt{\frac{2C_1 U}{C_2'}}$$
$$= \sqrt{\frac{2(15)(600,000)}{0.004 + 0.12(0.036)}} = 46,500$$

This is the type of situation illustrated in Figure 18-7 where the economic order quantity using the discounted price (46,500) is greater than k_1, the price-break quantity (40,000). Therefore, 46,500 is our economic order quantity.

The following year, the vendor informs National Manufacturers that the base price of \$0.040 per housing will remain the same, but that the discounted price will be \$0.038 per housing and that the quantity will start at 100,000 housings per order. All other factors in the problem remain the same.

We compute a new economic order quantity at the new discounted price.

$$Q = \sqrt{\frac{2C_1 U}{C_2'}}$$
$$= \sqrt{\frac{2(15)(600,000)}{0.004 + 0.12(0.038)}} = 45,900$$

Since 45,900 is less than the quantity discount point, k_1 = 100,000, we must compute the total annual cost, C_T', at the lowest order quantity at which the quantity discount will apply, 100,000.

$$C_T' = \frac{C_1 U}{Q} + \frac{C_2' Q}{2} + UC_3'$$
$$= \frac{15(600,000)}{100,000} + \frac{[0.004 + 0.12(0.038)][100,000]}{2} + 600,000(0.038)$$
$$= \$23,318$$

We want to compare this $23,318 annual cost with the minimum annual cost ordering less than 100,000 housings per order at a price of $0.040 per housing. The annual cost at the economic order point will be

$$C_T = \sqrt{2C_1C_2U} + UC_3$$
$$= \sqrt{2(15)[0.004 + 0.12(0.040)](600,000)} + 600,000(0.040)$$
$$= \$24,398$$

The $24,398 is greater than the $23,318 previously obtained using lots of 100,000 with a quantity price discount. We thus see that it would be more economic to order in lots of 100,000 and obtain the quantity discount. This is the type of situation illustrated in Figure 18-8.

Let us see how our answer might be changed if the quantity price discount in this problem came at 500,000 housings per order rather than 100,000.

We must calculate a new C_T' at the lowest order quantity at which the discounted price will apply, now 500,000 housings per order.

$$C_T' = \frac{C_1U}{Q} + \frac{C_2'Q}{2} + UC_3'$$
$$= \frac{15(600,000)}{500,000} + \frac{[0.004 + 0.12(0.038)](500,000)}{2} + 600,000(0.038)$$
$$= \$24,958$$

Since $24,958 is larger than the annual cost using the economic order quantity with no price discount, $24,398, we should, therefore, order in lots of

$$Q = \sqrt{\frac{2C_1U}{C_2}}$$
$$= \sqrt{\frac{2(15)(600,000)}{0.004 + 0.12(0.040)}} = 45,200$$

Our procedure can be summarized as follows:

1. Using the formula $Q = \sqrt{\frac{2C_1U}{C_2'}}$, we compute the economic order quantity using a purchase price of C_3'. If this quantity is equal to or greater than k_1, then this is the optimum order quantity.

2. If this economic quantity is less than k_1, we compute the economic order quantity using the C_3 undiscounted purchase price. We then compare the annual costs using the undiscounted order quantity with the annual costs using k_1 as the order quantity. The one with the lower annual costs is the optimum order quantity.

A similar procedure can be applied when there are two price breaks at which quantity discounts are applied.

1. We compute the economic order quantity at the lowest price C_3'' (highest discount). If this quantity is equal to or greater than the re-

quired volume for the second discount, k_2, then this is the optimum order quantity.

2. If this economic quantity is less than k_2, then we compute the economic order quantity at the middle price C_3'. This new economic order quantity must be less than k_2. If it is equal to or more than k_1, then compare the annual costs using this new economic order quantity with the annual costs using k_2 as the order quantity with the lowest price, C_3''. The one with the lower total is the optimum order quantity.

3. If this economic order quantity at the middle price, C_3', is less than k_1, then we compute the economic order quantity at the undiscounted price. We then compare the annual costs using this last economic order quantity with the undiscounted price; the annual costs using k_1 as the order quantity with the middle price, C_3'; and the annual costs using k_2 as the order quantity with the lowest price, C_3''. The one with the lowest total costs is the optimum order quantity.

This same general procedure can be readily extended to cover the situation in which any number of price breaks occur.

Another method of taking quantity discounts into account in minimum-ordering-cost problems is to use the total-annual-cost tables which are presented in the next section.

Total-annual-cost Tables. In establishing decision rules for production and purchase ordering, it is sometimes valuable to develop tables showing total annual costs for various order sizes and annual usages. Table 18-3 is an example. These tables can simplify minimum-cost ordering decisions of all kinds, especially when quantity discounts are involved.

The total annual cost, C_T, was previously given as

$$C_T = \frac{C_1 U}{Q} + \frac{C_2 Q}{2} + U C_3$$

Using this formula, we can construct total-annual-cost tables for any given set of values of the ordering or setup cost, C_1, and holding cost, C_2. In Table 18-3, $C_1 = \$15$ per order and $C_2 = 20\%$ of the unit-inventory value per year. Thus, for an annual usage of $500 and a $100 order quantity, we have:

$$C_T = 15(\tfrac{500}{100}) + 0.20(\tfrac{100}{2}) + 500 = \$585$$

This is the value shown in the upper-left-hand corner of the table in the column labeled "Size of order equals $100" and row labeled "Annual usage equals $500."

The difference between the annual usage and the total annual costs shown in the table is the annual cost of ordering and holding. For any estimated annual usage, the economic order quantity is found by observing the size of order which results in the lowest total annual costs. Thus,

Table 18-3. Total Annual Cost
Ordering or setup cost = $15 per order
Holding cost = 20% of average inventory value per year

Annual usage	Size of order													
	$100	$200	$400	$700	$1,000	$1,500	$2,000	$3,000	$4,000	$5,000	$7,000	$10,000	$15,000	$20,000
$ 500	$ 585	$ 558	$ 559	$ 581	$ 608	$ 655	$ 704	$ 803	$ 902	$ 1,002	$ 1,201	$ 1,501	$ 2,000	$ 2,500
1,000	1,160	1,095	1,078	1,091	1,115	1,160	1,208	1,305	1,404	1,503	1,702	2,002	2,501	3,001
2,000	2,310	2,170	2,115	2,113	2,130	2,170	2,215	2,310	2,408	2,506	2,704	3,003	3,502	4,002
4,000	4,610	4,320	4,190	4,156	4,160	4,190	4,230	4,320	4,415	4,512	4,709	5,006	5,504	6,003
7,000	8,060	7,545	7,303	7,220	7,205	7,220	7,253	7,335	7,426	7,521	7,715	8,011	8,507	9,005
10,000	11,510	10,770	10,415	10,284	10,250	10,250	10,275	10,350	10,438	10,530	10,721	11,015	11,510	12,008
20,000	23,010	21,520	20,790	20,499	20,310	20,350	20,350	20,400	20,475	20,560	20,743	21,030	21,520	22,015
30,000	34,510	32,270	31,165	30,713	30,550	30,450	30,425	30,450	30,513	30,590	30,764	31,045	31,530	32,023
50,000	57,510	53,770	51,915	51,141	50,850	50,650	50,575	50,550	50,588	50,650	50,807	51,075	51,550	52,038
75,000	86,260	80,645	77,853	76,677	76,225	75,900	75,763	75,675	75,681	75,725	75,861	76,113	76,575	77,056

with a $4,000 annual usage, orders of $700 result in total annual costs of $4,156. This is less than for any other size order.

Price discounts are handled in a relatively simple manner using this table. In the previous example of an item with a $4,000 annual usage, we are permitted to take 2 per cent discount on orders of $1,000 to $1,999, 5 per cent on orders of $2,000 to $4,999, and 10 per cent on orders of $5,000 or more. Will it be economic to issue orders for more than the $700 previously determined economic order quantity, ignoring the price discounts?

If we place orders for $1,000 worth, total annual cost will be $4,160 (Table 18-3 value in Size of order column labeled $1,000 and Annual usage row labeled $4,000) less the 2 per cent price discount of $80 (2 per cent of the $4,000 annual usage), or $4,080. This is less than the $4,156 total annual cost using orders of $700 each.

If we place orders for $2,000 each time and qualify for the 5 per cent discount, total annual cost will be $4,230 less the 5 per cent price discount of $200 (5 per cent of $4,000), or $4,030. This is less than the $4,080 using orders of $1,000 each.

If we place orders for $5,000 each time and qualify for the 10 per cent discount, total annual cost will be $4,512 less $400 (10 per cent of $4,000), or $4,112. This is greater than the cost using orders of $1,000 or $2,000, but less than for orders of $700 each.

Effects of Risk and Uncertainty on Inventory Planning. Our previous discussions of economic order quantities assumed that we know in advance the usage of each item without risk of being wrong and that we can get immediate delivery of orders or know in advance with certainty how long it will take to get delivery. In a large percentage of cases in industry these assumptions are not true.

In the chapters of Part Six, we shall discuss several analytic techniques applying to various types of inventory economy problems under uncertainty. We shall review here briefly some of the practical adaptations of minimum-cost analysis which are desirable to take account of risk and uncertainty. (There are, of course, other types of uncertainty in the minimum-cost calculations, such as the accuracy of estimates of present and future costs, which we are not considering here.)

Practical inventory-planning procedures must be designed to take uncertainty into account. We cannot allow inventories to fall to zero before they are replenished. We must, therefore, plan on having a safety or cushion stock to provide a safety margin when uncertainties cause inventories to be depleted faster than we expect.

Figure 18-10 shows how inventory balances are expected to vary on the average with safety stocks when sales are expected to be uniform. Ordering of the economic quantity occurs at an order point which is above the safety-stock level by the amount of usage expected during the lead time (the time elapse between the placing of the order and the delivery of the stock).

The size of the safety stock is dependent upon the amount of risk we are willing to take of running out of stock. Assuming the lead time is fixed, this risk is dependent on the probability of having usage or sales requirements for the item during the lead time which are greater than the order-point level. The larger the safety stock, the steeper will be the maximum-usage rate covered by the safety stock, as shown in Figure 18-10, and the smaller will be the risk of running out of stock.

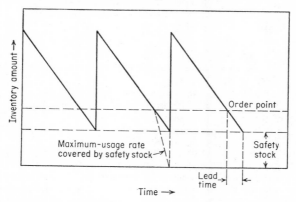

Figure 18-10. Pattern of variations in inventory levels when safety stock is carried

The risk of run-out is not independent of the order or lot size. The safety-stock level determines the risk of run-out each time the inventory amount approaches the minimum stock. However, the larger the order or lot size, the less frequently will the inventory amount approach minimum stock and, therefore, be exposed to this risk. Thus, if there is a 10 per cent risk of running out each time the stock level approaches the minimum stock and the order quantity is three months' supply, the 10 per cent risk will occur every 13 weeks. The risk per week is, thus, 10 per cent divided by 13, or 0.77 per cent. If the average opportunity cost of a stock-out is $15, the annual cost of stock-outs is $15(52)(0.0077) = $6.01. If the same safety stock is kept, but the order quantity is increased to 6 months' supply, the 10 per cent risk will occur every 26 weeks. The risk per week is then 10 per cent divided by 26, or 0.38 per cent. The average inconvenience and cost of running out of stock is reduced by 50 per cent.

The handling of this interaction in establishing economic order quantities is discussed in Chapter 21.

The purpose of the presentations in this chapter has been to demonstrate the development of formula and tabular models suitable for solving minimum-cost problems. This presentation was not aimed at providing ready-made formulas suitable for indiscriminate use in all kinds of situations. Each of the formulas which were developed is based upon specified assumptions. Consequently, the formulas should not be used when the assumptions do not apply.

PROBLEMS

1. A new water line must be constructed from an existing pumping station to a tank 1,500 feet away. An analysis of costs for these sizes of pipe has been made as follows.

Pipe size	Cost per hour for pumping	Estimated construction cost
8	$1.60	$15,000
10	1.20	30,000
12	0.60	50,000

The annual cost is to be computed on the basis of straight-line depreciation and average interest, using a life of 15 years with no salvage value and an interest rate of 6 per cent per year. Determine the most economical pipe size for pumping 4,000 hours per year.

2. A certain chemical compound is purchased for use as a raw material in a manufacturing plant. The clerical and accounting costs involved in making a purchase are $21 per purchase order regardless of the size of the lot purchased. Throughout the year 3,000 gallons of this compound are consumed at a fairly uniform rate. It is purchased and stored in 50-gallon drums. Its purchase price per gallon, including freight, is $3.30. Annual storage costs are estimated as 50 cents per drum of maximum inventory. Annual carrying charges are estimated as 12 per cent on average inventory. To assure continuous operations, at least 200 gallons should be maintained on hand at all times as an emergency stock. What is the most economical size of lot to purchase? (State your answer in terms of drums.)

3. The Prene Company uses 50,000 of a certain type bracket per year. It can produce the bracket with negligible procurement lead time and no difficulty at a cost of $0.60 per piece, so no minimum stock is maintained. Ordinary and setup costs are $80 per order. Storage costs are $0.04 per year per bracket in average inventory. All other holding or carrying costs total 15 per cent of the average inventory value (at cost). What is the economic order quantity for these brackets?

4. The Prene Company manufactures hundreds of parts for which it would like a simple table to determine the order quantity for items such as those of problem 3. The annual usage of these items varies from $1,000 to $50,000. Ordering and setup costs for the various items are from $30 to $100 per order. The cost of holding one of these items in inventory varies from $0.10 to $0.50 per year. Prepare a table which the Prene Company can use to determine economic order quantities.

5. The Prene Company manufactures a gear component which has a significant delivery time. The company can produce this component at a rate of 600 per week. It uses 10,000 units a year. Cost of production is $0.40 a unit. Ordering and setup costs are $150 per order. Storage costs are $0.03 per year per unit in average inventory. All other holding costs total 15 per cent of the average inventory value. What is the economic order quantity for this gear component?

6. The Prene Company purchases 5,000 timers per year. Order costs, including the obtaining of quotes, etc., total $50. Storage costs are $0.06 per unit in average inventory. All other holding costs total 15 per cent of the average inventory value. The price is $6.25 for orders of less than 1,000 units and $6.00 for orders of 1,000 units or more. What is the economic order quantity?

7. The vendor in problem 6 has informed Prene that the price will be $6.25 for orders of less than 2,000 units and $6 for orders of 2,000 units or more. Does this change the economic order quantity? If yes, what is the new economic order quantity?

8. The vendor in problem 7 now informs Prene that in the future it will require orders of 5,000 units or more before it will grant the $0.25 discount from $6.25 to $6. Does this change the economic order quantity? If yes, what is the new economic order quantity?

9. Your company has been using Table 18-3 in the manner described in the text to determine economic order quantities where price discounts are involved. Your assistant tells you that there is an error in that procedure. If we assume that the annual requirements for an item are constant regardless of price reductions through quantity discounts, the annual usage in dollars will decrease each time the unit price is decreased by a quantity discount. Yet in our procedure we contine to speak of our dollar usage as if it remained constant and of placing orders of specified dollar amounts which will result in different unit quantities depending upon the price. Evaluate the validity of your assistant's argument.

Note: Problems 1 and 2 are adapted from professional engineers' examinations.

19 Programming for Minimum Cost or Maximum Profit

Many economy problems involve the optimum allocation of limited resources to achieve a minimum-cost or maximum-profit objective. We shall, therefore, concern ourselves in this chapter with methods of programming for minimum cost or maximum profit.

Let us use a simplified example to illustrate this type of programming problem.

We produce two types of clamps: type A and type B. We can sell up to 180,000 type A clamps per week and up to 100,000 type B clamps per week and no more. We make a profit of $0.03 per type A clamp and $0.05 per type B clamp. How many type A and type B clamps should we produce with our current limited production capacity to maximize profits?

If we could produce 180,000 type A and 100,000 type B clamps in a 40-hour work week, we would maximize profits by so doing. However, the cutting department can cut only 7,000 type A clamps per hour and only 3,000 type B clamps per hour. The assembly department can assemble type A clamps at the rate of 5,000 per hour and type B clamps at the rate of 4,000 per hour.

Letting A represent the number of type A clamps made per week and B the number of type B clamps made per week, we can write the following inequalities to represent the production restrictions under which we must operate.

Cutting department,

$$\frac{A}{7,000} + \frac{B}{3,000} \leq 40$$

or
$$3A + 7B \leq 840,000$$

Assembly department,

$$\frac{A}{5,000} + \frac{B}{4,000} \leq 40$$

or
$$4A + 5B \leq 800,000$$

The sales restrictions under which we must operate if we are to avoid inventory variations are

$$A \leqq 180,000$$
$$B \leqq 100,000$$

Figure 19-1 graphically illustrates the limitations imposed by these restrictions on our freedom to vary production of type A and type B clamps. We plot limiting equations to represent our production restrictions: $3A + 7B = 840,000$ and $4A + 5B = 800,000$. We must operate at or below each of these lines. We plot limiting equations to represent our sales restrictions: $A = 180,000$ and $B = 100,000$. We must also operate at or below these values. The shaded area represents the possible combinations of type A and B clamp production which will satisfy the restrictions.

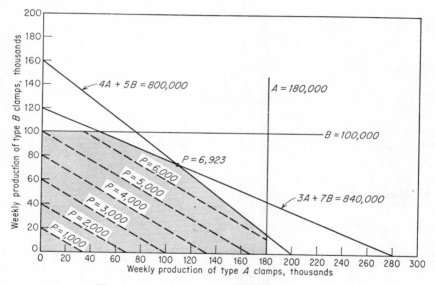

Figure 19-1. Programming for maximum profit.

Our weekly profit equals $0.03A + 0.05B$. This value will vary depending upon which permissible combination of types A and B production is chosen. However, there are various combinations of A and B which will yield equal profit. The line $0.03A + 0.05B = \$6,000$ is one such line. We plot this line on the chart containing our previous restrictions. We can operate on any point on this line within the shaded area and obtain a $6,000 per week profit. Similarly, we plot the other equal-profit lines shown in the chart.

Since we desire to maximize our profit, we will operate on the maximum-equal-profit line or point which satisfies the sales and production restrictions. This optimum program, as shown in Figure 19-1, is at $A = 107,692$

clamps per week and $B = 73,846$ clamps per week. The profit, P, equals $6,923 at this point.

Trial-and-error Programming Method. You manufacture five parts in one division of your company. You can make these parts on any one of three types of machines, A, B, or C, with the time required dependent on which type machine is used, as specified in Table 19-1. The avail-

Table 19-1. Time to Manufacture (hours per piece)

Machine type	Parts				
	010	020	030	040	050
A	6	2	3	1	7
B	4	3	7	2	7
C	5	6	9	6	5

able machine-hours (practical capacity) are shown in Table 19-2. The

Table 19-2. Available Machine Time

Type	
A	600 hr per week
B	350 hr per week
C	1,500 hr per week
Total	2,450 hr per week

number of each part required next week is shown in Table 19-3.

Table 19-3. Number of Parts Required Next Week

010	100
020	200
030	150
040	100
050	50
Total	600

There are no significant differences in the cost per machine-hour on each type of machine. Quality of product and material usage are also the same. Manufacturing time in hours can, therefore, be used instead of cost as the variable to be minimized in this problem of making the most economic allocation of parts to machines.

If available capacities permit, you would certainly assign each part to the machine which requires the least time to manufacture that part. Even if available capacities do not permit, following this rule provides a first step in developing the most economic answer. This is done in Table 19-4.

Table 19-4. Assignments (in hours) Assuming Available Capacity

Machine type	Parts						Available machine-hours
	010	020	030	040	050	Total	
A	. . .	400	450	100	. . .	950	600
B	400	. . .	. . .	. . .	. . .	400	350
C	. . .	. . .	. . .	. . .	250	250	1,500

We see from this table that machines A and B will be overloaded under this schedule. To relieve this situation, we start juggling assignments by trial and error, applying the principle of opportunity or alternative costs. Machine A is overloaded by 350 hours. We have two choices. We could move 350 hours of 020 parts from machine A to B at a cost of 175 additional hours (in Table 19-1, machine A manufactures 020 parts in 2 hours and machine B manufactures them in 3 hours). Or, we could move 350 hours of 030 parts to machine B at a cost of 467 additional hours (in Table 19-1, machine A manufactures 030 parts in 3 hours and machine B manufactures them in 7 hours). Naturally, the first choice is preferable. Our first adjusted assignment, as shown in Table 19-5, has corrected the overloading of machine A. However, these changes to machine B, which was already overloaded, aggravates its overloaded condition further.

Table 19-5. First Adjusted Assignments (in hours)

Machine type	Parts						Available machine-hours
	010	020	030	040	050	Total	
A	. . .	50	450	100	. . .	600	600
B	400	525	. . .	. . .	. . .	925	350
C	. . .	. . .	. . .	. . .	250	250	1,500

To correct the machine B overloading, we could consider moving all 525 hours of the 020 production to machine C instead of B, but this would involve additional costs of 525 hours whereas we could shift 400 hours of 010 production to machine C from machine B at an additional cost of only 100 hours. The latter is definitely more advantageous.

Since machine B has only 350 hours available capacity, we have no alternative but to shift 175 hours of 020 production to machine C at an additional cost of 175 hours. Our final adjusted assignments are shown in Table 19-6.

In this example our final adjusted assignments result in shifting 400 hours of 010 from B to C at an additional cost of 100 hours; 233 hours of 020 from A to B at an additional cost of 117 hours; and 117 hours of 020 from A to C at an additional cost of 233 hours. Further consideration of other possible shifts does not disclose any better alternatives, although other assignments at the same total cost in hours are possible. For example, instead of shifting 117 hours of 020 from A to C, 117 of 030 could be shifted from A to C at the same additional cost of 233 hours.

Table 19-6. Final Adjusted Assignments (in hours)

Machine type	Parts						Available machine-hours
	010	020	030	040	050	Total	
A	...	50	450	100	...	600	600
B	...	350	...	...	...	350	350
C	500	350	...	...	250	1,100	1,500

We see from this last observation, that the additional costs per hour shifted are the same when the ratio of hours (cost) using C compared to A are the same. The ratio of hours on C and on A for 020 is 6 to 2, or 3.0. The ratio of hours on C and on A for 030 is 9 to 3, or 3.0.

For this reason, the ratio of hours (cost) on each machine to the best machine (lowest cost) can provide a convenient guide to more economic assignments. In the example we just worked out, we could have proceeded by first computing these ratios, as in Table 19-7.

Table 19-7. Ratio of Cost on Each Machine to Lowest-cost Machine for Each Part

Machine type	Part				
	010	020	030	040	050
A	6 / 1.50	2 / 1.00	3 / 1.00	1 / 1.00	7 / 1.40
B	4 / 1.00	3 / 1.50	7 / 2.33	2 / 2.00	7 / 1.40
C	5 / 1.25	6 / 3.00	9 / 3.00	6 / 6.00	5 / 1.00

We would make our first assignments just as we did previously to the machines with the least hours, ratio of 1.00. Then based on available hours on each machine, we could shift production from the overloaded machines going up in ratios from 1.00 as little as possible. The answers we previously decided upon for this problem follow this criterion.

This example was based on no setup time requirements. The procedure would be similar if setup times were involved, except that the total hours would include setup time.

We chose a rather simple example to illustrate this trial-and-error method of programming to determine economic machine assignments. However, the same procedure would apply to the considerably more complicated examples which involve more machines, more products, and more accurate cost data. The increased complexity in these cases will, however, make us less certain that we have reached an optimal or near-optimal solution.

We shall examine more involved and time-consuming techniques which provide greater assurance that the optimum assignments were made. Trial-and-error approach, if properly used by a person with good judgment, will usually give an optimal or near-optimal solution, and is frequently the only one we can afford to use because of the cost and time required for some of the more involved approaches.

However, we are not certain that we have reached an optimum solution when we use this trial-and-error method. The desirability of the solution will depend to some extent on the ability and judgment of the scheduler. When the problem is more complicated than the simplified version illustrated here, it becomes increasingly difficult to be certain of the optimality of the solution. Therefore, where major expenses or profits are involved, it may be worthwhile to employ more time-consuming mathematical programming techniques, such as the simplex method.

The simplex method will (1) test whether or not the trial-and-error procedure has actually resulted in an optimum solution (minimum cost or maximum profit), (2) provide a systematic approach to reach this optimum solution when the test reveals it has not been reached.

Simplex Technique for Linear Programming. When the simultaneous variations of several variables must be considered in minimizing costs or maximizing profits or other objectives, the simplex technique of linear programming may provide an effective method of solving an economy problem.

The simplex technique requires that the cost or profit or other quantity which is to be minimized or maximized be represented or expressed algebraically as a linear equation. The restrictions which limit the amount and manner of attainment of the objective to be minimized or maximized must also be stated in a linear algebraic form of equation or inequality.

Let us illustrate the simplex technique by an example.

A manufacturer makes three products, A, B, and C, using common facilities. There are two processes in its manufacture which we shall call

V and W. Manufacturing times (in hours) for each unit are as follows:

Product	Process V	Process W
A	9	11
B	5	18
C	20	6

There are 400 hours per week of machine time available in process V and 750 hours per week available in process W. The profits per unit returned by the products are as follows: A — \$32, B — \$20, C — \$60. Assuming all of products A, B, and C which can be produced can be sold, how much of each product should be produced for maximum profit?

Let us now state the goal and restrictions on its accomplishment algebraically. Our goal is to maximize weekly profits P.

$$P = 32Q_A + 20Q_B + 60Q_C$$

where Q_A = units per week manufactured of A
Q_B = units per week manufactured of B
Q_C = units per week manufactured of C
Our restrictions are

$$9Q_A + 5Q_B + 20Q_C \leq 400$$
$$11Q_A + 18Q_B + 6Q_C \leq 750$$

which means that the total work assigned to process V must be less than or equal to 400 hours and for process W must be less than or equal to 750 hours.

If there were limits to the amounts of A, B, or C which could be sold, these would be handled as additional restrictions in the permitted values of the variables.

To eliminate the inequalities in these restrictions, we add another variable, called a "slack variable" to each inequality.

$$9Q_A + 5Q_B + 20Q_C + S_1 = 400$$
$$11Q_A + 18Q_B + 6Q_C + S_2 = 750$$

The "slack variable" equals zero when the entire capacity of the process is used. Otherwise, it equals the value of the unused capacity in the process.

Using these equations we can now follow the simplex procedure. The procedure provides for successive approximations according to fixed rules, which can be followed by a clerk or a computer. The rules of this simplex algorithm ensure that we shall conclude with an optimum solution, assuming that our objective and restriction equations are valid.

Table 19-8 provides the starting point for successive, systematic trial-and-error solutions. This table has restriction equations in rows 3 and 4.

Thus, considering the heavy line as an equals sign and ignoring the first two columns, the third line reads: $400 = 1S_1 + 9Q_A + 5Q_B + 20Q_C$. The coefficients in the goal or objective equation are entered in the first row of the table. The fifth or criterion row in the first tableau has the same values as the coefficients of the objective equation, with signs reversed. We establish our first feasible solution by setting values for the two slack variables equal to the constants in the restriction equations, meaning no production and no profit. We start with this feasible solution because it is easy to specify. In Table 19-8, this feasible solution is indicated by the insertion in the variable columns of S_1 and S_2 alongside the constant values of 400 and 750, respectively.

Table **19-8. Initial Simplex Tableau**

Objective			0	0	32	20	60
	Variable	Constant	S_1	S_2	Q_A	Q_B	Q_C
0	S_1	400	1	0	9	5	20
0	S_2	750	0	1	11	18	6
Criterion		0	0	0	-32	-20	-60

We now desire to substitute feasible amounts of production of A, B, and C into the solution so that we shall increase the value of the criterion function (profit). We therefore establish successive tableaux in which we insert into our solution the variables which will add to the total profit more than will be withdrawn by the elimination of variables which are currently in the solution. The variable chosen for addition in each case is given by the column with the most negative criterion value. In Table 19-8, this is Q_C, which has a criterion value of -60 in this first tableau. Each additional unit of C will add \$60 to the profits of the objective equation. We therefore insert Q_C into the solution in the second tableau. We must always remove a variable whenever we insert a new one into the solution. Each removed variable should take out less profit than is added by the variable which is newly inserted in the solution. The coefficients in the successive tableaux are manipulated according to specified rules which ensure that each successive tableau results in a feasible solution with an increased total profit. (The total profit is shown by the criterion value in the constant column. You will note that this is zero for the first feasible solution shown in Table 19-8.)

We continue the procedure of introducing the variable with the most negative criterion value into successive tableaux until there is no further possibility of increasing the value of the criterion measure. This value occurs in the tableau in which there are no negative values in the criterion row and represents the maximum value of the objective equation which will also satisfy the restriction equations.

The simplex method of calculating the coefficients for the successive tableau for solving our problem is presented in the appendix to this chapter. The final tableau is shown there in Table 19-12. You will note that there are no negative values in the criterion row of the fourth tableau. The criterion value in the constant column of $1,471 indicates the profit if a weekly production rate of 33.28 units of A and 21.94 units of B is used.

Restrictions with Equalities. We sometimes have problems in which the restrictions will not allow underutilization of capacity or overfulfillment of quality or other specifications. In these cases, we do not require "slack" variables to convert inequalities to equalities since the restrictions will be stated as equalities. This, however, causes difficulty in applying the simplex solution technique.

We therefore introduce "artificial" variables, A_1, A_2, A_3, etc., into each equality just as we previously introduced the "slack" variables in our previous example. We treat these "artificial" variables exactly the same as the slack variables except that we take one step to ensure that they will eventually be driven down to zero in the simplex solution. We do this by inserting the "artificial" variable in the objective or goal equation and making its coefficient in this equation so high that it will be too costly to use any of the variables in the final solution.

For example, in the previous case of the manufacture of products A, B, and C by processes V and W, let us assume that we want to assure that all of the capacity of process W is used regardless of the effect it has on profits. Our restrictions would then become

$$9Q_A + 5Q_B + 20Q_C \leqq 400$$
$$11Q_A + 18Q_B + 6Q_C = 750$$

which means that the total work assigned to process V must be less than or equal to 400 hours, but for process W must equal exactly 750 hours.

We next add a "slack" variable to the first equation and an "artificial" variable to the second equation:

$$9Q_A + 5Q_B + 20Q_C + S_1 = 400$$
$$11Q_A + 18Q_B + 6Q_C + A_1 = 750$$

Our goal or objective equation now becomes

$$P = 32Q_A + 20Q_B + 60Q_C - MA_1$$

where M is a large unspecified amount. In solving the simplex tableau M is always considered larger than any other amount to which it is compared. This assures that A_1 will be driven out by the simplex solution since any amount of A_1 will reduce the attainment of the goal more than the substitution of any other variable. As long as A_1 is in the solution, the

criterion row will contain a negative value and the computational procedure requires the construction of further tableaux which will eliminate
any "artificial" variables.

Minus Slack Variable. Sometimes a restriction may be in the following
form:

$$2X_1 + 3X_2 \geqq 17$$

To convert this to an equality, we must introduce a minus "slack"
variable, $-S_1$.

$$2X_1 + 3X_2 - S_1 = 17$$

In this case, the coefficient of S_1 is -1 rather than the usual $+1$.
We must, therefore, introduce an artificial variable A_1 with a $+1$ coefficient to provide the standard pattern for our simplex solution,
$2X_1 + 3X_2 - S_1 + A_1 = 17$. At the same time, we ensure that the A_1
will not enter into the final solution by associating a cost of M with it in
the goal or objective equation, M being larger than any other number or
numbers.

Alternate Optimal Solutions. In some cases, alternate solutions to a
linear programming problem are possible which will result in several
solutions which are optimal, each yielding the same total return. The
determination of these alternate solutions by simplex calculations is
discussed in the appendix at the end of this chapter.

Clerical Labor and High-speed Computers. From this example and
its solution as illustrated in the appendix to this chapter, it is apparent
that once the problem has been set up, the simplex procedure follows a set
pattern and can be performed by a clerk or on a high-speed computer.
Linear-programming problems are very adaptable for solution on high-
speed computers. When the problem is complicated, and most practical
ones are, a computer is a necessity.

It is also apparent that the amount of labor involved in a formal simplex
solution can be very great. For this reason, approximate trial-and-error
solutions will frequently be preferable when the economy of making the
economy analysis is considered.

Minimization of Costs or Other Variables. Sometimes the objective
is to minimize costs or other variables. The procedure that is used is
exactly the same as the one illustrated, except that the objective or goal
function is written differently. If we maximize the negative of the objective function, then we are in effect minimizing the objective function.

To solve a minimizing problem, we multiply each term in the objective
or goal function by -1. We then use the simplex technique to maximize
this negative function.

This procedure is illustrated in the next example of a distribution-cost
problem.

Minimizing Transportation or Distribution Costs. A manufacturer of a household appliance has three factories, one in the East, one in the Southeast, and one in the Southwest. The appliance is distributed by six distributors scattered around the country, each of whom maintains a central warehouse from which all shipments to wholesalers in his territory are made.

The cost of producing the appliance in each factory is somewhat different because of differences in age and technology of the facilities as well as some wage-rate differences. To determine the cost of the appliance delivered to each of the distributor's warehouses, it is necessary to add the transportation cost from each factory to each warehouse to the cost of producing at each factory. Table 19-9 shows the costs of producing and delivering one appliance to each warehouse from each factory. Table 19-10 shows the capacities of each factory in units per day and Table 19-11 specifies the market requirements in units per day.

Table 19-9. Unit Cost of Producing and Delivering to the Warehouse

Factory	Warehouse				
	W_1	W_2	W_3	W_4	W_5
F_1	$16	$14	$17	$21	$18
F_2	18	15	16	13	12
F_3	17	19	18	11	13

Table 19-10. Factory Capacities per Day
$F_1 = 550$ units
$F_2 = 800$ units
$F_3 = 300$ units

Table 19-11. Market Requirements per Day
$W_1 = 250$ units
$W_2 = 500$ units
$W_3 = 125$ units
$W_4 = 400$ units
$W_5 = 75$ units

We start by defining the unknowns:

Factory	Warehouse				
	W_1	W_2	W_3	W_4	W_5
F_1	Q_{11}	Q_{12}	Q_{13}	Q_{14}	Q_{15}
F_2	Q_{21}	Q_{22}	Q_{23}	Q_{24}	Q_{25}
F_3	Q_{31}	Q_{32}	Q_{33}	Q_{34}	Q_{35}

Thus, Q_{11} represents the average amount shipped per day from factory F_1 to warehouse 1, Q_{21} the amount shipped from factory F_2 to warehouse 1, and so on.

The restriction equations are established by factory capacities and market requirements:

$$Q_{11} + Q_{12} + Q_{13} + Q_{14} + Q_{15} \leqq 550$$
$$Q_{21} + Q_{22} + Q_{23} + Q_{24} + Q_{25} \leqq 800$$
$$Q_{31} + Q_{32} + Q_{33} + Q_{34} + Q_{35} \leqq 300$$

$$Q_{11} + Q_{21} + Q_{31} = 250$$
$$Q_{12} + Q_{22} + Q_{32} = 500$$
$$Q_{13} + Q_{23} + Q_{33} = 125$$
$$Q_{14} + Q_{24} + Q_{34} = 400$$
$$Q_{15} + Q_{25} + Q_{35} = 75$$

Adding the "slack" variables to the factory-capacity restrictions and the "artificial" variables to the warehouse-requirement restrictions,

$$Q_{11} + Q_{12} + Q_{13} + Q_{14} + Q_{15} + S_1 = 550$$
$$Q_{21} + Q_{22} + Q_{23} + Q_{24} + Q_{25} + S_2 = 800$$
$$Q_{31} + Q_{32} + Q_{33} + Q_{34} + Q_{35} + S_3 = 300$$
$$Q_{11} + Q_{21} + Q_{31} + A_1 = 250$$
$$Q_{12} + Q_{22} + Q_{32} + A_2 = 500$$
$$Q_{13} + Q_{23} + Q_{33} + A_3 = 125$$
$$Q_{14} + Q_{24} + Q_{34} + A_4 = 400$$
$$Q_{15} + Q_{25} + Q_{35} + A_5 = 75$$

We desire to minimize total cost of producing and delivering to the warehouse. The goal or objective equation which we desire to minimize is

$$\begin{aligned} C = \ & 16Q_{11} + 14Q_{12} + 17Q_{13} + 21Q_{14} + 18Q_{15} + 18Q_{21} + \\ & 15Q_{22} + 16Q_{23} + 13Q_{24} + 12Q_{25} + 17Q_{31} + 19Q_{32} + \\ & 18Q_{33} + 11Q_{34} + 13Q_{35} + MA_1 + MA_2 + MA_3 + MA_4 + MA_5 \end{aligned}$$

To convert this to a form which we can handle as a maximization problem in standard procedure, we multiply each term by -1.

$$\begin{aligned} -C = \ & -16Q_{11} - 14Q_{12} - 17Q_{13} - 21Q_{14} - 18Q_{15} - 18Q_{21} - 15Q_{22} - \\ & 16Q_{23} - 13Q_{24} - 12Q_{25} - 17Q_{31} - 19Q_{32} - 18Q_{33} - \\ & 11Q_{34} - 13Q_{35} - MA_1 - MA_2 - MA_3 - MA_4 - MA_5 \end{aligned}$$

We can now set up the tableau and solve this problem in the standard simplex manner.

This type of problem, in which all of the modifying coefficients in the restrictive equations are 1, is known as a transportation or distribution problem. A programming procedure, easier to apply than the simplex method, has been developed for this special type of problem. This procedure, known as the transportation technique, was independently developed by both F. L. Hitchcock[1] and T. C. Koopmans.[2] Application of the transportation technique is explained in publications by both G. B. Dantzig[3] and A. Charnes and W. W. Cooper.[4]

Mathematical Theory of Linear Programming. The introduction to linear programming presented in this chapter has been kept as free of mathematical symbolism as well as mathematical theory as possible. The mathematical theory of linear programming is expounded in a number of publications.[5] Much of the pioneering work in this field was done by T. C. Koopmans and others at the Cowles Commission.[6] The simplex technique for solving linear-programming problems was developed by G. B. Dantzig.[7]

Applications of Linear Programming in Economic Decision-making. Many types of economy problems can be effectively solved by the techniques of mathematical programming. Although nonlinear-programming techniques have been developed for the solution, within an arbitrary degree of approximation, of certain nonlinear functions,[8] these are more complicated than the linear-programming techniques discussed in this chapter. Thus, one of the prime requirements when linear programming is used is that all the relationships be linear. This means that changes in the various factors result in proportional changes in other factors. In addition, methods have been developed for solving dynamic programming problems, in which a series of consecutive decisions must be made. Even though each decision is individually optimal, the over-all series of decisions will not be optimal unless dynamic programming techniques are used to integrate the series of decisions.[9]

[1] F. L. Hitchcock, "The Distribution of a Product from Several Sources to Numerous Localities," *Journal of Mathematical Physics*, vol. 20, pp. 224–230, 1941.

[2] T. C. Koopmans, "Optimum Utilization of the Transportation System," *Proceedings of the International Statistical Conferences*, Cowels Commission Paper, New Series, no. 34, Washington, 1947.

[3] G. B. Dantzig, "Application of the Simplex Method to a Transportation Problem," Chapter 23 of T. C. Koopmans (ed.), *Activity Analysis of Production and Allocation*, Cowles Commission Monograph 13, John Wiley & Sons, Inc., New York, 1951.

[4] A. Charnes and W. W. Cooper, "The Stepping Stone Method of Explaining Linear Programming Calculations in Transportation Problems," *Management Science*, October, 1954, pp. 49–69; and W. W. Cooper, and A. Charnes, *Transportation Scheduling by Linear Programming*, Proceedings of the Conference on Operations Research in Marketing, Case Institute of Technology, Cleveland, 1953.

[5] See in particular the Lectures on the Mathematical Theory of Linear Programming by A. Charnes in Part II of A. Charnes, W. W. Cooper, and A. Henderson, *An Introduction to Linear Programming*, John Wiley & Sons, Inc., New York, 1953.

[6] Koopmans (ed.), *op. cit.*

[7] G. B. Dantzig, "Maximization of a Linear Function of Variables Subject to Linear Inequalities," Chapter 21 in Koopmans (ed.), *op. cit.*

[8] See, for example, A. Charnes and C. E. Lemke, "Minimization of Nonlinear Separable Convex Functionals," *Naval Research Logistics Quarterly*, 1954, pp. 301–312.

[9] See R. Bellman, *Dynamic Programming*, Princeton University Press, Princeton, N.J., 1957.

What are some of the areas of economic analysis in which linear-programming techniques can be fruitfully applied?

Establishing the basis for salary compensation

Allocating orders onto machines or into machine centers

Planning production to meet a seasonal sales pattern

Determining optimum locations for warehouses to reduce total costs

Planning new facilities investments and selecting new equipment

Planning most profitable product mixes for existing facilities and markets

Evaluation of proposed alternative new business ventures

Determination of production rates and inventory to meet seasonal requirements at lowest costs

APPENDIX A. SIMPLEX CALCULATIONS FOR SOLVING LINEAR-PROGRAMMING PROBLEM

We shall use for our example the problem (previously presented in the text) of determining how much of products A, B, and C should be produced for maximum profit.
Objective or goal equation,

$$P = 32Q_A + 20Q_B + 60Q_C$$

Restriction equations,

$$9Q_A + 5Q_B + 20Q_C + S_1 = 400$$
$$11Q_A + 18Q_B + 6Q_C + S_2 = 750$$

where Q_A = units per week manufactured of A

Q_B = units per week manufactured of B

Q_C = units per week manufactured of C

In the first tableau of Table 19-12, we have entered the constants and coefficients of the two restriction equations in rows 3 and 4. Thus, considering the heavy line as an equal sign, we have $400 = 1S_1 + 9Q_A + 5Q_B + 20Q_C$. We have followed the usual convention of placing our slack-variable columns ahead of the interdependent variables.

We have entered the coefficients of the goal or objective equation in row 1 of the first tableau $(0S_1 + 0S_2 + 32Q_A + 20Q_B + 60Q_C)$. In column 1 we enter the coefficients in the objective equation of the variables in column 2. In the first tableau the variable column contains the slack variables of the restriction equations, which have zero coefficients in the objective equation, since they do not appear therein.

The criterion row is computed by

1. Multiplying the numbers in each column by the value in the objective column in the row

2. Adding together these products for all the numbers in the column

3. Subtracting the objective coefficient of the column from the sum in (2)

For example, for column Q_A:

1. 9×0 (value in objective column for this row) $= 0$, $11 \times 0 = 0$

2. $0 + 0 = 0$

3. $0 - 32 = -32$

This completes the first tableau. The feasible solution in this tableau, which is not an optimum one, is given by setting the variables in the variable column equal to the constants in the constant column:

$$S_1 = 400$$
$$S_2 = 750$$

If this solution is followed, we have the following by substituting in the restriction equations:

$$9Q_A + 5Q_B + 20Q_C + 400 = 400$$

or

$$9Q_A + 5Q_B + 20Q_C = 400 - 400 = 0$$

And

$$11Q_A + 18Q_B + 6Q_C + 750 = 750$$

or

$$11Q_A + 18Q_B + 6Q_C = 0$$

Therefore, this feasible solution with which we start involves zero output for all processes and zero profit.

Table 19-12. Simplex Tableaux

	Objective			0	0	32	20	60	
		Vari-able	Con-stant	S_1	S_2	Q_A	Q_B	Q_C	
First									
Tableau	0	S_1	400	1	0	9	5	(20)	→
	0	S_2	750	0	1	11	18	6	
	Criterion		0	0	0	−32	−20	−60	
								↓	
Second	60	Q_C	20	0.05	0	0.45	0.25	1	←
Tableau	0	S_2	630	−0.3	1	8.3	(16.5)	0	→
	Criterion		1,200	3	0	−5	−5	0	
							↓		
Third	60	Q_C	10.46	0.055	−0.015	(0.324)	0	1	→
Tableau	20	Q_B	38.18	−0.018	0.061	0.503	1	0	←
	Criterion		1391	2.909	0.303	−2.485	0	0	
						↓			
Fourth	32	Q_A	32.28	0.170	−0.046	1	0	3.086	←
Tableau	20	Q_B	21.94	−0.103	0.084	0	1	−1.552	
	Criterion		1,471	3.331	0.188	0	0	7.670	

The rules for testing whether an optimal solution has been reached are as follows:
1. If all the values in the criterion row are zero or positive, then we have obtained a maximum value for P.
2. If any values in the criterion row are negative, then
   a. If some values in a column having a negative criterion value are positive, further calculations and tableaux are required.
   b. If all values in the columns having negative criterion values are equal to zero or negative, the maximum value for P which is infinitely large has been obtained.

Our first tableau falls under rule 2a above and further calculation is, therefore, required.

We proceed as follows to create the second tableau. We choose the most negative criterion in the first tableau, and the column variable corresponding to this criterion is introduced into our solution as a row variable. To determine the row it replaces, divide each positive value in the column into the corresponding value in the constant column. The lowest ratio indicates the variable to be replaced.

In this case, we choose Q_C as the variable to be inserted and indicate by an arrow going down. We compute $400 \div 20 = 20$ and $750 \div 6 = 125$. Since 20 is the smallest ratio, we circle this number and refer to it as the circled number in the future. S_1 goes out of the variable row and this is indicated by an outward arrow.

In the second tableau, we insert Q_C in place of S_1 and place an arrow-in on that row. We divide each value in the arrow-out row of the first tableau by the circled number.

In our problem, the circled number is 20 and the Q_C row on the second tableau is obtained by dividing each value of the S_1 row of the first tableau by 20. The objective value of 60 applies to the Q_C row in the same manner as it applies to the Q_C column and is so inserted.

To derive the remaining values (other than objective values) for the second tableau, we proceed as follows for each value:

1. Find number in arrow-out row of the column (previous tableau).
2. Find number in arrow-out column of the row (previous tableau) on which you are working.
3. Multiply these two numbers and divide by the circled number (previous tableau).
4. Subtract this result (step 3) from the value in the previous tableau on which you are working.

To illustrate for number 750 in the first tableau:

1. 400 — number in arrow-out row
2. 6 — number in arrow-out column
3. $\dfrac{(400)(6)}{20} = 120$
4. $750 - 120 = 630$

To illustrate for 6, in the arrow-out column:

1. 20
2. 6
3. $\dfrac{(20)(6)}{20} = 6$
4. $6 - 6 = 0$

The remaining derived values for the second tableau, including the criterion row, are computed by following these 4 steps and are shown in Table 19-12.

Our second tableau solution, $Q_C = 20$ and $S_2 = 630$ provides a feasible solution which will provide a profit of \$1,200 ($60Q_C$), as shown in the constant column of the criterion row. This profit can be realized by producing 20 of product C per week. This will result in 630 hours per week of process W in unused capacity.

All the values in the criterion row are not zero or positive. Therefore, based on our rules for testing, we have not yet reached an optimal solution. We, therefore, proceed to our third tableau in the same manner as previously.

We should choose the most negative criterion value in the second tableau, but we have a tie in this case. It makes no difference which we choose although one choice may involve more tableaux and therefore take a longer time to obtain the answer.

The third and fourth tableaux are completed in Table 19-12. The fourth tableau gives us an optimal solution showing a profit in the criterion row of 1,471. The solution is 32.28 units of A per week, 21.94 of B per week, and no production of C. These figures are operating rates and the fractional parts are completed in the succeeding periods. We can check the optimal-profit calculation by the formula

$$P = 32Q_A + 20Q_B + 60Q_C$$
$$= 32(32.28) + 20(21.94) + 60(0) = 1471.7$$

Since none of the "slack" variables appear in the solution, the entire capacity of 400 hours in process V and 750 hours in process W are used in the production of A and B and there is no unused capacity in the optimal solution. This can be checked by multiplying out the loads on processes V and W from 32.28 units of A and 21.94 units of B per week.

The criterion values under the slack variables in the final tableau indicate the added profits which could be derived by increasing the capacity of the related process by one unit, in this case, hours. Thus additional profits of \$3.33 could be expected if process A's capacity were increased by one hour and only \$0.19 additional profits if process B's capacity were increased by one hour.

Analysis of the computation method reveals that

1. All derived values in the arrow-out column except the circled one become zeros in the next tableau.

2. If there is a zero in an arrow-out row, the column in which it appears will not change in the next tableau. Correspondingly, if there is a zero in an arrow-out column, the row in which it appears will not change in the next tableau.

3. When a column of a variable meets a row of the same variable, a 1 will result at the intersection point and all other values in the column will equal zero.

Degeneracy. When our rule for testing whether an optimal solution has been reached indicates that a better solution would be developed by introducing a new variable which has a negative criterion value, we must determine which row variable will be replaced. To determine the row variable which will be replaced, we divide each positive value in the column (of the new variable) into the corresponding value in the constant column. The row with the lowest ratio indicates the variable to be replaced.

If two or more rows have the same lowest ratio, a condition known as "degeneracy" results and we are confronted with the question of how to proceed. We can arbitrarily choose one of the lowest rows and proceed with our replacement of the variable and we will obtain the right answer. However, a better rule is to divide the positive value of the new variable column in the tied rows into the row values in successive columns going from left to right. The ratios are compared at each column. At the first column at which the tie is broken, the row variable which has the smallest ratio is replaced.

Other Solutions Which Are Also Optimal. Sometimes there may be several solutions to a linear-programming problem which will yield the same optimum return. These solutions will all result in the same total profit. Whenever there is a zero in the criterion row in the column of a variable which is not in the variable column in the final tableau, we have alternate optimal solutions.

We may understand this relationship a little better if we refer to the tableaux of Table 19-12. We can observe that the change in profit from one tableau to the next, as shown in the criterion row of the constant column, is always equal to the product of the number (with sign reversed) in the criterion row of the variable being inserted into the next tableau times the ratio of the constant column value to the circled value in the arrow-out row. Thus, the increase in profit from the second tableau to the third tableau is $1,391 - 1,200$ or 191. The number (with sign reversed) in the criterion row of the variable being inserted into the third tableau is 5. The ratio of the constant column value to the circled value in the arrow-out row is $630/16.5 = 38.2$. Then, 5 times $38.2 = 191$.

Since this relationship is always true, if we have a zero value in the criterion row in the column of a variable which is not in the variable column, we can designate the column as the column-out and construct a new tableau. This new tableau will have the same criterion value in the constant column as the previous one. The solution with the new variable will then be an alternate solution.

PROBLEMS

1. The Rowland Corp. manufactures two qualities of wire staplers. It makes a profit of $1.00 on each high-quality stapler, stapler H, and $0.60 on each poorer-quality stapler, stapler P. The company can sell up to 2,000 H and 4,000 P per week. Both staplers are made with the same facilities. If only P staplers were made, the stamping section could handle 6,000, the assembly section 5,000, and the paint section 8,000 each week. H staplers take 25 per cent more stamping time, 50 per cent more assembly time, and 150 per cent

more printing time than P staplers. Determine the number of H and P staplers which should be made for maximum profit. Solve this problem graphically by plotting limiting equations to represent the area restrictions imposed by production and sales limitations and superimposing the profit lines. The profit line which is farthest from the origin within the permissible area gives the maximum profit.

2. Referring to problem 1, formulate the restriction equations and the goal or objective equation in a form which will allow solution of the problem by the simplex method.

3. Use the simplex method to solve the formulation of problem 2.

4. Refer to the assignment problem in the text which was solved by trial-and-error programming to determine the best machine assignments. Formulate the restriction equations and the goal or objective equation in a form which will allow solution of the problem by the simplex method.

5. Use the simplex method to solve the formulation of problem 4.

6. A coffee company sells under four different brand names. The types and proportions of coffee beans included in each are shown below:

Brand name	Bean type		
	A	B	C
Bromley............	Minimum of 5%	....	Maximum of 80%
Mokar.............	....	....	Maximum of 60%
Gokar.............	....	Minimum of 50%	Maximum of 10%
Johnson...........	Minimum of 70%		

Costs are as follows: A—$0.40 per pound; B—$0.35 per pound; and C—$0.20 per pound. All other costs are constant regardless of brand or proportions of bean type used. The following quantities of each bean type are available: A—2,000 lb per day; B—15,000 lb per day; C—4,000 lb per day. Prices which the company can obtain for each brand are as follows: Bromley—$0.50; Mokar—$0.55; Gokar—$0.60; Johnson—$0.70. Formulate the restriction equations and the objective equation which will permit a simplex solution to the problem which will maximize profits.

PART SIX

Risk, Uncertainty, and Intangibles

20 Risk, Uncertainty, and Intangibles

Engineering and business decision-making involves the choosing of one course of action from all available alternatives. Evaluation of the relative worth of each of these alternatives requires estimates of present conditions about which we frequently have incomplete knowledge as well as forecasts of future events. Forecasts of future events involve risks and uncertainties, especially when economic consequences are involved. In many cases, income or costs are associated with events which may or may not occur.

Although future events are uncertain, we must nevertheless forecast, guess, or estimate what will occur if we are to make a rational decision. When we buy a lathe, we must forecast our requirements for the products which will be made on the lathe in the future. When the engineer or businessman is confronted with making a decision, with choosing one alternative course of action or design, an important factor in that decision is the relative expected future income and/or costs associated with the alternatives.

Definition of Risk and Uncertainty. The words "risk" and "uncertainty" refer to the possibility that the desirability or profitability of a project will turn out to be different than it is forecasted at the time of evaluation. In most cases, however, management is not likely to be as disturbed if the results turn out to be more favorable than anticipated as they would if the results turn out to be less favorable.

For most purposes there is no need to distinguish between the meanings of the words "risk" and "uncertainty" and they can be used interchangeably. When we want to consider how to deal explicitly with risk and uncertainty, however, there is an advantage to more careful definition. We shall define risk as the dispersion of the probability distribution of the event whose value is being predicted.[1] Uncertainty will be measured by the degree of lack of confidence that the estimated probability distribution is correct.

---

[1] In statistical decision theory, the term "risk" is sometimes used with altogether different meanings, such as the expected loss. In statistical sampling theory, it is used with still other meanings. In common usage, the term "risk" is also used to mean probability, e.g., the risk of failure. It is sometimes used in this latter sense in this volume.

For example, it is estimated that the distribution of the economic lives of a certain type of machine is as shown in Table 20-1. We can calculate the mean of this estimated distribution. It is 7 years. We can use 7 years as the expected economic life of a new machine of a similar type which we plan to build. Assuming our estimated distribution is correct, there is still a risk of 54 in 100 that the life of our new machine will be less than 7 years. (Our distribution shows 1 per cent having an economic life of 3.0 to 3.9 years, 6 per cent with a life of 4.0 to 4.9 years, etc.)

Table 20-1. **Distribution of Machine Life**

Life (years)	Per cent of machines with indicated life
2.0– 2.9	0
3.0– 3.9	1
4.0– 4.9	6
5.0– 5.9	18
6.0– 6.9	29
7.0– 7.9	21
8.0– 8.9	14
9.0– 9.9	7
10.0–10.9	2
11.0–11.9	1
12.0–12.9	1
	100

In addition to this risk, we are uncertain as to how close this distribution of the estimated economic lives of a similar machine will be to the actual distribution of economic lives of the new machine we plan to build.

Risk is the variation from the average (expected) value which occurs in random, chance patterns. The larger this variation, the larger the risk. The individual factors causing these random variations are numerous and are not important enough to be recognized separately by any of their effects. They interact with each other statistically and produce a distribution of values for the variable. Risk thus covers those variations caused by many random influences we cannot attempt to forecast. Responsibility for the differences between the average (expected) value and the actual ones which occur because of risk cannot be assigned to any error in forecasting any variable.

Uncertainty is caused by errors in forecasting one or more factors which are significant in determining the future values of the variable or by the complete absence of a forecast. Differences between expected value and actual ones caused by uncertainty can be assigned to individual factors which have been incorrectly forecast or which have not been forecast.

The assignable factors which cause uncertainty in economic decision-making are affected by many circumstances. How stable are the objectives, policies, and strategies of the enterprise which determine the stability of the criteria being used to evaluate the alternatives? How changeable are the markets and demands for our products and/or services? How will this affect our product and market strategies? How certain are we of the plans of our competitors and their reactions to our plans? Will consumer reactions perhaps change our market characteristics? Will producer reactions to our plans change our costs? How will future advances in technology, which cannot be predicted, affect the desirability of the alternatives? How may innovations affect revenues and costs? What will be the actual operating conditions under each alternative plan? What significant unlikely events may occur and how will they alter quality of production, amount of spoilage, cost of materials and operations?

Expected Value of an Alternative. The expected value of an alternative is the average value which the alternative will have in the long run. If there is a 0.15 probability that I will receive $100,000 if I follow alternative A, then alternative A has an expected value of

$$0.15(\$100,000) = \$15,000$$

The expected value is equal to the value the alternative may have times the probability that it will occur, assuming that nothing will occur otherwise.

If I follow alternative B, there is a 0.15 probability that I will receive $100,000, a 0.10 probability that I will receive $50,000, and a 0.50 probability that I will receive $18,000. Then alternative B has an expected value equal to the sum of the expected values of each of the possible events:

$$
\begin{aligned}
0.15(\$100,000) &= \$15,000 \\
0.10(50,000) &= 5,000 \\
0.50(18,000) &= 9,000 \\
\text{Total expected value} &= \$29,000
\end{aligned}
$$

Costs are negative values. Expected costs have analogous meanings to expected values and are computed in exactly the same way as expected values. If I adopt alternative X, there is a 0.70 probability that I will incur $20,000 of expenses, a 0.25 probability that I will incur $50,000 of expenses, and a 0.05 probability that I will incur a $150,000 expense. The expected cost of alternative X is as follows:

$$
\begin{aligned}
0.70(\$20,000) &= \$14,000 \\
0.25(50,000) &= 12,500 \\
0.05(150,000) &= 7,500 \\
\text{Total expected expense} &= \$34,000
\end{aligned}
$$

A manufacturer is considering submitting a bid on a government contract. If his bid is accepted, he considers that there is a 0.40 probability he will make a profit of $10,000, a 0.50 probability that he will make only $5,000, and a 0.10 probability of losing $50,000. What is the expected value of this contract, if accepted, based on his profit and probability estimates?

$$
\begin{array}{rcl}
0.40(\quad \$10,000) & = & \$4,000 \\
0.50(\quad\ 5,000) & = & 2,500 \\
0.10(-\ 50,000) & = & -5,000 \\
\hline
\text{Total expected value} & = & \$1,500
\end{array}
$$

Contingency Evaluations. If there is uncertainty about the action that a competitor may take, or about the technical performance of a new process, or about the possibility of a new technological breakthrough, or about the labor rates which will prevail in the future, or about some other contingency which has a possibility of occurring and would influence the desirability of the investment, it may be valuable to calculate the profitability or desirability of the alternative course of action assuming one or more of these events occurred. The possible effects if these events occur would be indicated in these analyses. The seriousness of the risks and uncertainties caused by these possible occurrences could then be better evaluated.

Of course, it would not be practical and economical to make too many "contingency" calculations for possible events which were not very likely to occur. Too many such calculations would only confuse and hinder rather than aid intelligent evaluations of the significant facets of the decision-making problem.

Estimating Expected Values and Costs of Contingencies. We may go one step further in evaluating the possible effects of contingencies that could significantly affect results. We can make an estimate of the probability of occurrence of the favorable or unfavorable events. The previously calculated favorable and unfavorable effects of the events can then be converted into expected values and costs by multiplying the adverse effect of the event by the probability of its occurrence. We can then calculate an expected profit or benefit and use our usual tangible criterion for reaching a decision.

Even though these probabilities and expected values must frequently be judgmental, they will be helpful in arriving at a logical decision. Sometimes the magnitude of the differences in revenues and/or costs will be so great that, even allowing for the possibility of large estimating errors, one alternative is clearly superior to another. In these cases, little or no difference will be indicated in the choice of desirable alternatives by a moderate error in the assigned probabilities.

The use of approximate, rough estimates of probabilities is almost always better than ignoring the problem. In the absence of a formal analysis of the probabilities and formal computation of the expected values of the alternatives, the businessman or engineer will make an intuitive decision as to which alternative to choose. In this case, he may not make the choice which is most logical, even assuming his own intuitive judgment of the probabilities is correct.

Probability Distributions for Risk. It may sometimes be helpful to evaluate risks by developing a distribution showing the relative frequency of the possible values. The amount of labor which it is worthwhile to spend on these efforts will depend upon the relative importance of the risks in determining the advisability of adopting the proposal as well as how much uncertainty there will be with regard to the applicability of the developed distributions.

These frequency distributions can be developed in a number of ways, with varying degrees of accuracy and uncertainty.

1. When frequency distributions of the same or similar situations are available from actual past data, they can be used or modified to apply to the current situation as good judgment dictates. This is illustrated in the distribution of the economic life of a new piece of equipment which was previously presented.

2. In some cases, analytic methods can be used to develop a frequency distribution. For example, the technical conditions may indicate that a Poisson distribution is correct and the appropriate distribution may be developed (see Chapter 22).

3. Where these first two methods are not possible, the "Monte Carlo" technique (see Chapter 25) could be used. This technique should be used only in connection with decisions in which the risks are a highly significant factor and where it is worth the effort and cost.

Estimating Range of Values. Another approach in evaluating risks and uncertainties is to estimate a range of possible values for the revenues or desired benefits, and the investment and operating costs, rather than attempt to construct an entire frequency distribution.

In addition to estimating expected values of investment income and expense, an optimistic value (very small probability of being better) is estimated as well as a pessimistic value (very small probability of being worse). If the project appears desirable even when the pessimistic values are used, it should be adopted. If the project appears undesirable even when the optimistic values are used, it should be rejected. Where the optimistic value and the expected values make the project appear desirable, but the pessimistic do not, further study of the factors causing the risks and uncertainties should be made.

Validity of Expected Value or Cost As a Criterion. A proposal may have a high expected profit when evaluated using probability estimates of the possible contingencies. Yet, it may nevertheless not be as desirable to some businesses or individuals as another proposal with a lower expected profit.

For example, I am offered the opportunity to wager $50,000 on a throw of one true die. If the die shows 2, I will receive $1,000,000. If it shows any other number, I lose my $50,000. Using expected profit as my criterion, I should accept this offer. Since the die will show 2 once in six throws on the average, the expected value of the offer is $\frac{1}{6}$ of $1,000,000 minus $\frac{5}{6}$ of $50,000 equals $166,667 minus $41,667, or $125,000. Nevertheless, if $50,000 represents my entire net worth, I would be loathe to take advantage of this offer despite its large expected profit. However, if the wager and the reward were both reduced to 5 per cent of their original sums, say, $2,500 and $50,000, respectively, I would accept the offer. The loss of $50,000 represents more than 20 times the loss of $2,500 to me because $50,000 is my entire net worth. To a person with a net worth of 1 or 2 million dollars, the loss of $50,000 might represent just about 20 times the loss of $2,500.[1]

The principle this example illustrates is that expected or average value or cost calculations are valid only when the absolute size of the maximum loss is small enough relative to the net worth of the person or business and ability to withstand the loss without serious ill effect. As the size of the maximum loss becomes relatively large compared with the net worth of the enterprise, there is a reduction in the value of the proposal to the enterprise. Of course, the magnitude of this reduction varies with individual attitudes, as well as with the financial condition of the business.

How large does the maximum possible loss have to be before expected cost is not a valid criterion for economic decisions? We can establish three areas of magnitude of maximum loss.

A possible loss area is one in which it is logical to use expected value and cost as the criterion for making an economic decision. The worst possible loss which will fall in this area will depend upon the ability of the firm to withstand one or more such losses for the sake of the long-run expected gains. In one company, this may be $1,000 whereas in another, much larger company it may be $1,000,000. Determination of the upper limit of this area is a difficult top-management decision.

Another possible loss area is one in which the worst possible loss is so great that it is never logical for the company to take a risk no matter how small the probability of the occurrence nor how large the expected profits. It would normally be foolish for a company to risk the loss of so large a sum of money that the company would be bankrupt or would be unable to operate effectively. It is for this reason that most companies carry

---

[1] We can make the generalization that the utility value of additional units of money decreases as the absolute amount of money increases. An increase of annual profit from $100,000 to $150,000 clearly has more utility value than an increase from $10,000,000 to $10,050,000. Also, the relative utility values of each of these $50,000 annual-profit increases are subjective, varying from person to person. Some decision theorists disagree with this generalization. They argue that a person would never gamble when the expected dollar values were equal because the possible loss of money has greater (negative) utility than the gain of that same amount if this generalization were true. This argument, however, ignores the utility which a person receives from the gambling experience.

fire insurance. The probability of a $10,000,000 factory burning down in any year may be only one in 2,000. The expected (average) annual loss is, therefore, only $5,000. The insurance premium may be $8,000 per year. The company is willing to pay the extra $3,000 per year because the $10,000,000 loss would be acutely embarrassing if it occurred in any one year. However, if the company had a hundred factories scattered throughout the country, so that there was no risk of them all burning down at the same time, the loss of one factory would not bankrupt it. Although fire losses in some years could exceed the premium of $800,000 which would be saved by not insuring, the expected (average) cost would be less by an average of $300,000 per year. The company is able to withstand the financial drain during the years when there are more than average fire losses.[1]

In between the area in which expected costs are completely applicable and in which they are not applicable at all is an area in which they have limited applicability. The possible loss is not so great that the alternative is completely ruled out. Neither is it so small that we can apply expected value without judgmental evaluation of all the potential consequences and intangible aspects of the alternatives.

In another case, I am given the opportunity of making a sure profit of $5 or a possible profit of $30. I estimate the probability of making the $30 as one in four, or 0.25. The expected profit in the latter case is 0.25($30), or $7.50, and I will, therefore, choose the $30 possible profit.

I am also given the opportunity to make a sure profit of $500,000 or a possible profit of $3,000,000. I estimate the probability of making the $3,000,000 as one in four, or 0.25. The expected profit in the latter case is 0.25($3,000,000), or $750,000, and yet I will choose $500,000.

The reasons for this latter behavior are analogous to the reasons for not being guided by expected costs when there is a possibility of large loss. The worth of the extra possible $2,500,000 is not great enough to counteract the possible loss of an otherwise certain $500,000. Just as a company is not willing to risk the possibility of unusually large possible losses regardless of possible big expected profits, it also may not be willing to forego a large relatively secure profit for larger expected profits which have greater risks of not occurring.

For any company, there are three areas of possible gain, analogous to the possible loss areas, but frequently with different dollar value limits:

1. An area in which expected value calculations are completely valid as a decision criterion

2. An area in which expected value considerations are not the decision-making criterion

---

[1] The factor of repeatability also enters into the usefulness of expected value as a criterion. When an event recurs frequently, expected (long-run) value calculations have more meaning than when the event occurs only once.

3. The area in between the first two areas in which judgmental evaluation of all the potential consequences and intangible circumstances surrounding the alternatives is necessary

Company Differences in the Importance of Risk and Uncertainty. Based on our previous discussion, we can see that the same risks would have a different importance to two business firms. Two firms (Ajax and Mohawk) are offered similar contracts to supply a standard component used by an automobile manufacturer. Because of the uncertainties in the manufacturing process and future costs, each firm realizes that there are risks of loss. Let us assume, for the sake of illustration, that each firm has the same cost functions and calculates its risks of profit and loss in the same manner. It figures that, 9 chances out of 10, it will clear a net profit of $150,000 on this contract. However, because of the uncertainties just mentioned, each realizes that there is a small chance, say 1 in 10, that it may lose as much as $100,000. We may then calculate that each has an expected (average) profit of $125,000, as shown below.

Possible profit or (loss)	Probability of occurrence	Expected profit or (loss)
$150,000	0.9	$135,000
(100,000)	0.1	(10,000)
		$125,000

Another way of calculating this expected (average) profit is to consider that if it were possible to make this same investment 10 times with these probabilities of profit and loss, on the average we would expect to make a profit of $150,000 9 times and we would expect to lose $100,000 once. Our average (expected) profit for the 10 times is 9($150,000) less the $100,000 loss, divided by 10. This equals $125,000.

Even though there is the same expected profit of $125,000 for both manufacturers, it may not be equally desirable to them. Remember that there is one chance in ten that a $100,000 loss will occur. Ajax may be in a much stronger financial position than Mohawk. A $100,000 loss would be undesirable for both and would mean reduced profits for both. However, for Mohawk it would mean a serious financial crisis. For Ajax the loss would not be catastrophic. For this reason, the small risk of loss of $100,000, even though it has been taken into account in the calculation of the expected profit, is an important intangible factor mitigating against the contract for Mohawk. It does not mitigate against the contract for Ajax because Ajax can afford to take the risk.

Risk and Uncertainty as Intangible Factors. A company is considering the investment of $1,000,000 in one of two projects, L and M. Project L uses a conventional process and has expected (average) annual profits of $250,000 per year in accordance with the following probability estimates.

Annual profit	Percentage probability
$200,000–$219,999	10 %
220,000– 239,999	20
240,000– 259,999	40
260,000– 279,999	20
280,000– 299,999	10

Project M uses a newly developed process and has expected annual profits of $250,000 in accordance with the following probability estimates.

Annual profit	Percentage probability
$150,000–$189,999	10 %
190,000– 229,999	20
230,000– 269,999	40
270,000– 309,999	20
310,000– 349,999	10

Although the expected profits are the same, the dispersion of the distribution of the estimated profits (risk) is much greater for M than for L. This lower risk for project L is an intangible factor in its favor.

We may generalize by saying that if alternative A and alternative B have the same expected returns, but A has a lower risk (dispersion of returns), then A is preferable to B. If alternative C and alternative D have the same risks, but C has a higher expected return than D, then C is preferable to D. If neither the expected returns nor the risks of the alternatives being considered are equal or nearly so, then an intangible analysis of the importance of the lower risk is necessary.

Not only is the risk lower for project L, but there is less uncertainty as to the probability distribution of potential profits because it uses a conventional process whereas project L uses a newly developed process. There is much more historical evidence to estimate the probability distribution for L than for M, with whose process we have had very limited experience. There is, therefore, less uncertainty about the validity of L's distribution than M's. The lower uncertainty regarding the validity of its distribution is also an intangible factor in L's favor.

Complete Uncertainty as to Contingencies. All the factors in an economic decision may be capable of tangible evaluation in dollars: all of the values and costs of each alternative can be estimated in dollars for each possible future contingency. Yet, if the circumstances are such that no estimate, not even a vague approximation, of the probabilities of occurrence of the contingencies is possible, expected profit cannot be used to assist in the decision-making process. We are confronted with the problem of decision-making involving contingencies with complete uncertainty.

How should we decide whether or not to double our plant capacity? The contending local political parties have opposing views on legislation which will affect the desirability of the plant expansion. If political party A wins the next local election, we shall show a loss of $150,000 if we double our capacity, and shall show a profit of $150,000 if we do not. If political party B wins the next local election, we shall show a profit of $500,000 if we double the capacity, and $50,000 if we do not. The local political situation is such that there is no basis for placing any probabilities on the outcome of the election.

Let us examine some of the possible ways of handling problems with complete uncertainty as to contingencies and see how they would apply to our problem.

We can present the expected profits under each contingency in the form of a simple matrix.

Alternative	Contingency	
	A wins election	B wins election
Double plant capacity..........	−$150,000	+$500,000
Not double plant capacity.......	+$150,000	+$ 50,000

Maximin Criterion. We can be pessimistic and conservative and say that we will examine what the smallest profit for each alternative will be under any contingency and then select the alternative which has the highest value of this smallest profit.

Alternative	*Smallest profit under any contingency*
Double capacity.............	−$150,000
Not double capacity.........	+$ 50,000

Not doubling capacity has the highest minimum profit and is, therefore, chosen. This criterion maximizes the minimum profit and is, therefore, called the maximin criterion.

Maximax Criterion. We can be optimistic and speculative and say that we will examine what the largest profit for each alternative will be under any contingency and then select the alternative which has the highest value of the largest profit.

Alternative	*Largest profit under any contingency*
Double capacity.............	+$500,000
Not double capacity.........	+$150,000

Doubling capacity has the highest maximum profit and is, therefore, chosen. This criterion maximizes the maximum profit and is, therefore, called the maximax criterion.

Maxim Criterion. If we are feeling neither completely conservative nor completely speculative, but somewhere in between, we can maximize a criterion measure using any proportions of the maximin and maximax criteria. Thus, if we are feeling 70 per cent conservative and 30 per cent speculative, we would have the following.

Alternative	70% of smallest profit under any contingency	30% of largest profit under any contingency	Criterion value
Double capacity..............	−$105,000	+$150,000	+$45,000
Not double capacity...........	+$ 35,000	+$ 45,000	+$80,000

Not doubling capacity has the higher criterion value and is, therefore, chosen.

However, if we are feeling only 30 per cent conservative and 70 per cent speculative, we would have the following.

Alternative	30% of smallest profit under any contingency	70% of largest profit under any contingency	Criterion value
Double capacity..............	−$45,000	+$350,000	+$305,000
Not double capacity..........	+$15,000	+$105,000	+$120,000

Doubling capacity has the higher criterion value and is, therefore, chosen.

Minimax Criterion. If we are pessimistic and conservative and are dealing with costs rather than profits, we would examine the highest cost for each alternative under any contingency and choose the alternative which had the lowest value of this highest cost. This criterion minimizes the maximum cost and is, therefore, called the minimax criterion.

Minimin Criterion. If we are optimistic and speculative and are dealing with costs rather than profits, we would examine the lowest costs for each alternative under any contingency and choose the alternative which had the lowest value of this lowest cost. This criterion minimizes the minimum cost and is, therefore, called the minimin criterion.

Minim Criterion. If we are feeling neither completely conservative nor completely speculative, but somewhere in between, and are dealing with costs rather than profits, we can minimize a criterion measure using any proportions of the minimax and minimin criteria. We do this in a manner similar to the procedure previously used for maxim criterion where we are dealing with profits.

Minimax Regret Criterion. If we choose one alternative and another one would have given us a higher profit under the contingency which actually occurs, we shall be regretful to the extent that our profits are

318   RISK, UNCERTAINTY, AND INTANGIBLES

smaller than they could have been. We can measure the maximum potential regret by subtracting the estimated profit for each alternative under each contingency from the maximum estimated profit under each contingency under any alternative. We then list the largest maximum potential regret for each alternative. We choose the alternative which has the smallest potential regret in this listing.

Applying this criterion to our problem, we compute the maximum potential regrets and list the largest maximum potential regret for each alternative.

Alternative	Contingency		Largest maximum potential regret
	A wins election	B wins election	
Double capacity.........	$300,000	0	$300,000
Not double capacity.....	0	$450,000	$450,000

Doubling capacity has the smallest value in the listing of the largest maximum potential regrets and is, therefore, chosen.

We have computed our maximum potential regret if a contingency comes true which would have resulted in a higher profit. We have then minimized this maximum regret according to our minimax regret criterion.

Although one or more of the preceding procedures may have an intuitive appeal to some persons, none is really logical as the sole criterion for a decision. For example, using the maximin criterion, I would choose not to double capacity even if the potential profit of doubling capacity if B wins the election were raised to $500,000,000 and, at the same time, the potential loss of $150,000 of doubling capacity if A wins the election were changed to a potential profit of $25,000. This same type of illogical result can be obtained with the other criteria.

The consideration of additional alternatives can change the results using the minimax regret criterion even though the additional alternatives are not themselves desirable. Let us add a third alternative to our previous example, the alternative of changing the production process, leaving the capacity the same as at present. Our expected profits are then as shown below.

Alternative	Contingency	
	A wins election	B wins election
Double capacity...........	−$150,000	+$500,000
Not double capacity........	+$150,000	+$ 50,000
Change process...........	+$400,000	0

We compute the maximum potential regrets and list the largest maximum potential regret for each alternative.

Alternative	Contingency		Largest maximum potential regret
	A wins election	B wins election	
Double capacity.........	$550,000	0	$550,000
Not double capacity.....	$250,000	$450,000	$450,000
Change process..........	0	$500,000	$500,000

Not doubling capacity now has the smallest value on the listing of the largest maximum potential regrets and is therefore chosen. Previously, when we did not consider in our analysis the third alternative of changing the process, the minimax regret criterion indicated the choice of doubling capacity. It is not reasonable to have the decision switch when a new alternative, which does not turn out to be desirable, is added to our consideration.

Many additional decision rules under complete uncertainty have been suggested at various times. However, they all suffer from the same kind of inadequacies which these have and generally lack some of the intuitive appeal one or more of the preceding ones may have for some applications.

Under some circumstances the criteria which we have presented will give logical results. Thus, the maximin or minimax criteria may be logically applied as a supplementary criterion under the circumstances previously described in this chapter when the possible loss to a company is so great that the expected-value or expected-cost criterion is no longer valid.

However, none of these approaches is satisfactory as the sole criterion for a decision. They are not consistent. They can lead to nonsensical conclusions. Yet they represent the only possible type of approach if complete uncertainty is present.

But complete uncertainty is quite rare. More often, the decision-maker is confronted with the problem of making probability estimates which are very highly uncertain. Because they are so uncertain, he finds it unusually difficult to estimate probabilities and, therefore, prefers to consider them completely uncertain. However, the lack of a really logical approach under complete uncertainty makes it desirable to use even highly uncertain estimates of probabilities.

Take the case of the election-result contingencies in our illustration: the reason the election was considered completely uncertain is because the outcome is completely in doubt. However, it is not really completely uncertain. To say the outcome is completely doubtful indicates that, in the estimator's opinion, the estimated probability of either party winning is not far from 0.50.[1] We are, therefore, not very uncertain at all and can make the probability estimates necessary for the expected value calculations required to assist our economic evaluation.

We need not consider alternatives which are insignificant (or dominated) in our evaluation. An alternative is insignificant (or dominated) if another alternative is preferable to it regardless of which contingency may occur in the future. If all alternatives except one are insignificant, then it is not necessary to estimate the probabilities of the contingencies.

For logical decision-making when the alternatives are significant, we must have explicit or implicit estimates, no matter how hazardous, of the probabilities of occurrence of the contingencies. This places a burden on decision-makers to make estimates even though they will be highly incorrect a certain percentage of the time.

There is usually an estimate of the probabilities of contingencies when logical decisions are being made. The estimates may only be implicit, remaining in the subconscious mind of the decision-maker, rather than explicitly stated as required by formalized procedures such as are discussed in this book. But they exist. Our limited discussion of attempts to establish criteria for decision-making on the assumption of complete uncertainty serves to emphasize that we cannot avoid this estimating if we are to have decisions which are truly logical in promoting the objectives of the enterprise.

Choosing the Evaluation Procedures. The best procedure for evaluating alternatives will depend upon the individual circumstances. Where all of the factors can be made tangible, the most scientific and least subjective type of evaluation can usually be made unless there is complete uncertainty as to the relative probabilities of occurrence of the contingencies.

We have previously pointed out that the basic difference between a tangible and intangible factor is the ease and cost of evaluating in dollars the advantages and disadvantages of each factor associated with each alternative. When it is uneconomic to make a quantitative evaluation of risk and uncertainty, they must be treated as intangible factors.

Chapters 21 to 26 are devoted primarily to topics which will assist in making tangible evaluations of risk. Tangible analysis is not always economic or possible, however, for all factors affecting many types of decisions. Analytic methods of evaluating intangibles are therefore discussed in Chapter 27.

---

[1] This is a subjective probability: how confident is the estimator that one party or the other will win.

PROBLEMS

1. You are analyzing the problem of shipping customers' orders. You must estimate the number and size of orders which are received each day. Distinguish between the risks and uncertainties in your estimate.

2. Mr. Arnold is considering the purchase of a business. He estimates that it has the following probabilities of having the indicated profits or losses next year.

Profit or loss	Probability of occurring
$60,000	0.1
40,000	0.3
20,000	0.3
0	0.2
−20,000	0.1
	1.0

Based on Mr. Arnold's estimates, what is the expected profit or loss next year?

3. Give an example of a situation in which estimation of ranges of values would be useful in solving an economy problem.

4. There is 1 chance in 10 that a certain event will occur in any year. If it does occur, a $500,000 expenditure will be required. (*a*) Using expected costs as the decision-making criterion and interest at 10 per cent, how much would it be justified to spend now to eliminate this risk for 50 years? (*b*) How much would it be justified to spend to reduce the risk from 1 in 10 to 1 in 20? (*c*) Under what circumstances would expected costs not be a suitable criterion for making these decisions?

5. I am completely uncertain as to the outcome of exploratory operations which are being conducted by my competitor. I have estimated the following payoff matrix for an investment which I can make now or postpone until the success or failure of my competitor's explorations are determined.

	Explorations successful	Explorations unsuccessful
I make investment now........	+$100,000	−$50,000
I postpone investment.........	−$ 25,000	+$50,000

(*a*) Determine the decision which should be made using each of the following: (1) maximin criterion, (2) maximax criterion, (3) maxim criterion based on a 60 per cent optimistic–40 per cent conservative feeling, (4) minimax regret criterion.

(*b*) Is there any basis for saying that one of these criteria is most valid in this case?

6. The Bordel Corporation is undecided whether or not to install new equipment to reduce costs in a foreign country. Under existing conditions, rental of the new equipment will yield a significant reduction in costs. However, the legislature in the foreign country has been debating the adoption of labor

laws which would make use of the new equipment uneconomic. There is complete uncertainty as to whether the legislature will adopt these labor laws in the near future or ever. Costs under each contingency are shown below.

	New labor law adopted	New labor law not adopted
Install new equipment..........	$70,000	$25,000
Not install..................	40,000	40,000

(a) Determine the decision which should be made using each of the following: (1) minimax criterion, (2) minimin criterion, (3) minim criterion based on a 50 per cent optimistic–50 per cent conservative feeling, (4) minimax regret criterion.

(b) Is there any basis for saying that one of these criteria is most valid in this case?

21 Descriptive Statistics, Probability, and Expected Cost

Quantitative analysis provides the basis for much engineering economic analysis and managerial decision-making. Numbers are the basis for quantitative analysis. It will, therefore, be helpful to consider a few aspects of how we can present, describe, and analyze groups of numbers (descriptive statistics).

The engineering and economic analyst usually has reason to doubt that any particular number or numerical relationship that he may use to describe an economic variable is exactly true. He therefore has reason to doubt the conclusions of his study. Probability calculations provide a means of expressing quantitatively the degree of assurance the analyst may have in his numerical evaluations. It will therefore be helpful to consider in this and succeeding chapters some elements of probability theory and its applications.

Taking a Sample. I would like to know the number of different items included in orders which the Wimpole Company received from its customers in 1960. To accomplish this, I will take a sample of 50 of the orders received by the company during 1960 and count the number of items on each of the orders in the sample. One way of presenting the results of this study would be to list the results of this count, as shown in Table 21-1.

Frequency Distribution. I can arrange this data in the form of a frequency distribution, as shown in Table 21-2, by tabulating the frequency of occurrence of each value.

Frequency Histogram. I can plot this frequency distribution in the form of a frequency histogram, as shown in Figure 21-1. This gives me a graphic picture of the frequency distribution.

Grouped Frequency Distribution. I could group the data into classes and obtain a frequency distribution of the form shown in Table 21-3. When the size of the sample is 50 or more, one sacrifices little in the way of accuracy by doing this. In fact, the underlying shape of the frequency distribution may sometimes be better revealed by a good grouping, as in the present example. The frequency histogram for the grouped data is shown in Figure 21-2.

Table 21-1. Number of Items on Sample of 50 Orders
Received by the Wimpole Company during 1960

Sample number	Number of items	Sample number	Number of items
1	52	26	49
2	55	27	51
3	53	28	51
4	74	29	54
5	51	30	46
6	55	31	51
7	48	32	52
8	52	33	57
9	42	34	51
10	53	35	50
11	65	36	78
12	50	37	52
13	57	38	54
14	36	39	53
15	59	40	48
16	53	41	56
17	47	42	65
18	46	43	44
19	55	44	51
20	51	45	63
21	63	46	50
22	57	47	60
23	53	48	55
24	45	49	59
25	53	50	46

It is convenient to express the frequencies in a frequency distribution so that they will add up to 1.00. In this way, the frequency in each class interval represents the relative proportion of the values falling in that class interval. Using relative frequencies facilitates comparison of frequency distributions composed of varying total numbers in the sample or population. Figure 21-2 shows the relative frequencies as well as the absolute frequencies.

Discrete and Continuous Variables. In our previous example, we were concerned with the number of items appearing on incoming orders. Thus, there were 50 items on some orders, 51 on others, 52 on others, etc. There would never be 51.6 or any fraction of an item on an order. Number of items is, therefore, called a discrete variable to distinguish it from continuous variables which can take additional values in between any two numbers.

Table 21-2. **Frequency Distribution of Number of Items on 50 Orders Received by the Wimpole Company during 1960**

Number of items	Frequency of occurence	Number of items	Frequency of occurence
36	1	53	6
42	1	54	2
44	1	55	4
45	1	56	1
46	3	57	3
47	1	59	2
48	2	60	1
49	1	63	2
50	3	65	2
51	7	74	1
52	4	78	1

When we are concerned with the variations in dollar values of each order, we will be dealing with a continuous variable. No matter how close the value of the two numbers may be, it is theoretically possible to have additional values between them. For example, between \$1,181.74 and \$1,181.75 we can have \$1,181.746. Of course, we cannot measure below a certain value, such as cents or tenths of a cent. This measurement problem creates the effect of discreteness in every distribution. If we have a frequency distribution of weights, theoretically we have a continuous

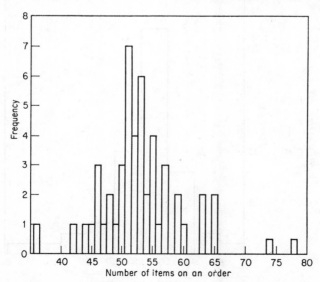

Figure 21-1. Frequency histogram for number of items on 50 orders received by the Wimpole Company during 1960 (ungrouped data).

Table 21-3. Frequency Distribution of Number of Items on 50
Orders Received by the Wimpole Company during 1960

Class interval	Mid-point of class interval	Frequency	Relative frequency
35–39	37	1	0.02
40–44	42	2	0.04
45–49	47	8	0.16
50–54	52	22	0.44
55–59	57	10	0.20
60–64	62	3	0.06
65–69	67	2	0.04
70–74	72	1	0.02
75–79	77	1	0.02
Total		50	1.00

variable. In actual practice, however, a measuring scale may give us
readings only to the nearest pound.

Descriptive Statistics. I ask you: Based on this sample, how many
items appear on each order? How can you answer me? You can show me
the frequency distribution or frequency histogram. But if I desire a
numerical answer, which can be more readily manipulated for analytic
purposes, what value or values would you give me?

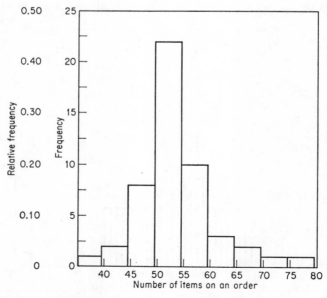

Figure 21-2. Frequency histogram for number of items on 50 orders received by the
Wimpole Company during 1960 (grouped data).

Mode. You could tell me that the most popular value is 51 items on an order. The value 51 occurs with more frequency than any other value and is, therefore, the most likely single value to occur on any order. It is called the mode (most fashionable, à la mode).

Median. You could tell me that $52\frac{1}{2}$ is the middle value. There are an equal number of values above and below this middle value, which is called the median. An order selected at random is just as likely to have more than 52 items as less than 52 items.

Arithmetic Mean. If I add up all the values, which I shall call ΣX (summation of X values), and divide by the number of values, $N = 50$, I shall obtain the arithmetic mean, labeled $\bar{X}$.

$$\bar{X} = \frac{\Sigma X}{N} = \frac{2,671}{50} = 53.42$$

This is the value which most people would call the average or expected value of the sample.

The arithmetic mean is the most commonly used measure of what we call the central tendency of a distribution. The sum of the differences between each value in the distribution and the arithmetic mean is always equal to zero. [$\Sigma(X - \bar{X}) = 0$.] The sum of the squares of the differences between each value in the distribution and the arithmetic mean is less than the sum of the squares of the differences between each value and any other value. [$\Sigma(X - \bar{X})^2$ is a minimum.]

When computing the arithmetic mean from grouped data, we assume that the frequencies are uniformly distributed in each class interval and use the formula

$$\bar{X} = \frac{\Sigma[f(MP)]}{N}$$

where MP = the mid-point of each class interval and f = the frequency in each class interval. Using the grouped data, we compute a value of $\bar{X} = 53.6$, shown in Table 21-4. This compares with the value of 53.42 we obtained previously using the raw data.

Except in special situations, such as when some unusually high or low values distort the meaning of the arithmetic mean for certain purposes, the arithmetic mean is the most useful and usual measure of central tendency. In a perfectly symmetrical, unimodal distribution (such as the normal distribution discussed later), the mean, median, and mode are the same. In a large percentage of cases where they are different, the differences are not significant.

Central Tendency and Dispersion. The mode, median, and arithmetic mean are measures of the central tendency of the distribution. To describe the distribution of values more completely, we should measure the spread of values about the central value. The measures of spread are often referred to as measures of dispersion.

Table 21-4. **Calculation of Arithmetic Mean of Grouped Data for the**
Number of Items on 50 Orders Received by the
Wimpole Company during 1960

Class interval	Mid-point of class interval (MP)	Frequency (f)	f(MP)
35–39	37	1	37
40–44	42	2	84
45–49	47	8	376
50–54	52	22	1,144
55–59	57	10	570
60–64	62	3	186
65–69	67	2	134
70–74	72	1	72
75–79	77	1	77
Total	. . .	50	2,680

$$\bar{X} = \frac{\Sigma[f(MP)]}{N} = \frac{2,680}{50} = 53.6$$

Range of Values. The difference between the highest and lowest value
in the distribution is the range of values. It is the simplest measure of
dispersion, easy to calculate, easy to understand, and very useful in the
solution of many industrial problems. However, it is greatly affected by
unusual occurrences because the size of the range is dependent only on
the two extreme values in the distribution. This limits its usefulness for
some purposes.

Standard Deviation. A very useful and widely used measure of
dispersion is called the standard deviation, represented traditionally by the
Greek letter σ (sigma). The standard deviation, σ, is the square root of the
arithmetic mean of the squares of the deviations of each value from the
arithmetic mean

$$\sigma = \sqrt{\frac{\Sigma(X - \bar{X})^2}{N}}$$

This measure of the dispersion of the values in the distribution is
affected by every value in the sample. Extremely large or small values
have a great relative effect on the value of the standard deviation both
because the deviations are squared and because they are arithmetically
averaged.

For grouped frequency distributions, the formula becomes

$$\sigma = \sqrt{\frac{\Sigma f(MP - \bar{X})^2}{N}}$$

Computation of the standard deviation for the grouped data of the number of items on an order is shown in Table 21-5. We compute a value of $\sigma = 7.1$ for this sample.

Table 21-5. Calculation of Standard Deviation of Grouped Data for the Number of Items on 50 Orders Received by the Wimpole Company during 1960

Class interval	Mid-point of class interval (MP)	Frequency (f)	$(MP - \bar{X})^2$	$f(MP - \bar{X})^2$
35–39	37	1	275.56	275.56
40–44	42	2	134.56	269.12
45–49	47	8	43.56	348.48
50–54	52	22	2.56	56.32
55–59	57	10	11.56	115.60
60–64	62	3	70.56	211.68
65–69	67	2	179.56	359.12
70–74	72	1	338.56	338.56
75–79	77	1	547.56	547.56
Total	. . .	50	1,604.04	2,522.00

$$\sigma = \sqrt{\frac{\Sigma f(MP - \bar{X})^2}{N}} = \sqrt{\frac{2,522}{50}} = 7.1$$

We shall see later that we can predict the percentage of values which will fall within any distance from the mean, measured in standard-deviation units.

Standard Deviation as a Measure of Risk. To evaluate alternative methods for processing the Wimpole Company's customer orders, it is necessary to calculate the expected costs using each alternative. The number of items appearing on each order is a factor in determining these costs. Using an average of 54 items per order, we can calculate expected costs for each alternative. Even if we are completely certain that 54 items per order is the correct average, individual orders will have more or less than 54 items. We therefore run the risk that the costs of processing these orders will vary from the expected values calculated using the average of 54 items per order. As explained in Chapter 20, the size of this risk is measured by the dispersion of the frequency distribution. If the standard deviation were 3 items per order rather than the 7 items per order previously calculated, the probabilities of having individual actual-order-processing costs vary from the calculated average processing costs would be considerably less and the previously mentioned risk would be smaller.

Skewness and Kurtosis. The measures of central tendency indicate the position of the central values of our frequency histogram on the X, or value, axis and the measures of dispersion indicate the amount of spread around the central values. Further description of the distribution is provided by measures of skewness, which indicate the degree of non-symmetry, and measures of kurtosis, which indicate the degree of peakedness.

Skewness is usually measured by computing

$$\frac{\Sigma(X - \bar{X})^3}{N}$$

and dividing this by σ^3 to get a relative measure.

For grouped data, this becomes

$$\frac{\Sigma f(MP - \bar{X})^3}{N} \left(\frac{1}{\sigma^3}\right)$$

A positive value indicates a right-skewed distribution (tail to the right as in Figure 21-3 with mean greater than mode) and a negative value indicates a left-skewed distribution (tail to the left as in Figure 21-4 with

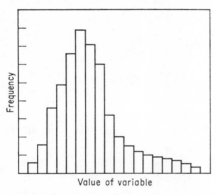

Figure 21-3. Frequency histogram of a right-skewed distribution (positive skewness).

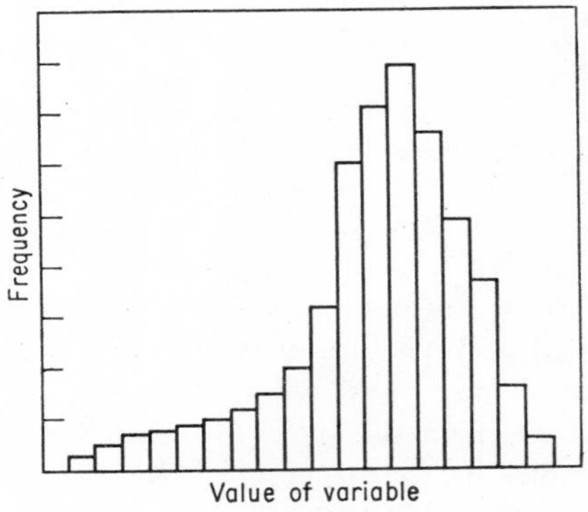

Figure 21-4. Frequency histogram of a left-skewed distribution (negative skewness).

mean less than mode). The normal distribution (discussed later) is symmetrical and, therefore, has zero skewness.

Kurtosis is usually measured by computing

$$\frac{\Sigma(X - \bar{X})^4}{N}$$

and dividing this by σ^4 to get a relative measure. For grouped data this becomes

$$\frac{\Sigma f(MP - \bar{X})^4}{N} \left(\frac{1}{\sigma^4}\right)$$

The normal distribution has a kurtosis value of $+3$. Distributions with values less than $+3$ are flatter than the normal curve, whereas those with values greater than $+3$ are more peaked than the normal curve.

The skewness and kurtosis measures of our distribution of number of items on an order are computed in Table 21-6. Skewness equals 0.891 and kurtosis 4.901.

Calculation Short Cuts. Various short-cut methods for computing measures of central tendency, dispersion, skewness, and kurtosis are presented in books on statistical methods.[1] These short cuts are particularly useful when large amounts of data must be analyzed.

Table 21-6

Class interval	Mid-point of class interval (MP)	Frequency (f)	$(MP - \bar{X})^3$	$f(MP - \bar{X})^3$	$(MP - \bar{X})^4$	$f(MP - \bar{X})^4$
35–39	37	1	−4,574.30	−4,574.30	75,933.31	75,933.31
40–44	42	2	−1,560.90	−3,121.80	18,106.39	36,212.78
45–49	47	8	−287.50	−2,300.00	1,897.47	15,179.76
50–54	52	22	−4.10	−90.20	6.55	144.10
55–59	57	10	39.30	393.00	133.63	1,336.30
60–64	62	3	592.70	1,778.10	4,978.71	14,936.13
65–69	67	2	2,406.10	4,812.20	32,241.79	64,483.58
70–74	72	1	6,229.50	6,229.50	114,622.87	114,622.87
75–79	77	1	12,812.90	12,812.90	299,821.95	299,821.95
Total	...	50	....	15,939.40	....	622,670.78

$$\frac{\Sigma f(MP - \bar{X})^3}{N}\left(\frac{1}{\sigma^3}\right) = \frac{15,939}{50}\left(\frac{1}{357.91}\right) = 0.89$$

$$\frac{\Sigma f(MP - \bar{X})^4}{N}\left(\frac{1}{\sigma^4}\right) = \frac{622,671}{50}\left(\frac{1}{2,541.2}\right) = 4.90$$

Definition of Probability. Probability can be considered relative frequency in the long run. The probability that an event will occur can be defined as follows: the ratio of the number of occurrences of the event to the number of opportunities or trials for the event to occur as the number of opportunities or trials is indefinitely increased.

For example, if I estimate that the probability of receiving an order with more than 70 items on it is 0.15, then I am saying that I believe that if we count each order received by the company as an opportunity or trial; if we count each order with 71 or more items on it as an occurrence; if we divide the number of occurrences by the number of opportunities or trials; and if we make a large enough number of trials to have small sampling errors, then the ratio of the number of occurrences to the number of opportunities or trials will equal 0.15.

For another example, let us consider the distribution of number of

[1] See, for example, F. E. Croxton and D. J. Cowden, *Practical Business Statistics*, Prentice-Hall, Inc., Englewood Cliffs, N.J., 1960.

units of catalogue item 1282 sold per week, shown in Table 21-7. This table shows 50 weeks of sales experience. If I can assume that, as the number of weeks of sales experience is increased indefinitely, the same relative frequency will hold, then I can say that the probability of selling 6 units per week is $\frac{1}{50}$, or 0.02, the probability of selling 7 units per week is $\frac{8}{50}$, or 0.16, and so on.

Table 21-7. **Sales per Week of Item 1282 during 50-Week Period**

Number of units sold per week X	Number of weeks f	fX
6	1	6
7	8	56
8	16	128
9	12	108
10	4	40
11	3	33
12	2	24
13	2	26
14	1	14
15	1	15
Total	50	450

$$\bar{X} = \frac{fX}{N} = \frac{450}{50} = 9$$

Probability Relationships. Let us consider some relationships between the probabilities of occurrence of events.

Addition of Probabilities. If the probability of less than 30 items occurring on an order is 0.10 and, as previously stated, the probability of more than 70 items is 0.15, then the probability of an order having less than 30 or more than 70 items is 0.25. The probability of occurrence of any number of mutually exclusive events is the sum of the probabilities of occurrence of the individual events.

In the example of sales of item 1282, the probability of selling 6, 8, or 10 units per week is 0.02 + 0.32 + 0.08 = 0.42. And the probability of selling less than 8 units or more than 12 units in any one week is (0.02 + 0.16) + (0.04 + 0.02 + 0.02) = 0.26.

If two events are not mutually exclusive, then the probability of occurrence of both events is equal to the sum of the probabilities of occurrence of the two individual events minus the probability that both events will occur together. For example, the probability that an order will total more than $100 is 0.20; the probability that an order will have less than 30 items is, as previously stated, 0.10; and 0.15 of orders totaling more than $100 have less than 30 items. These probabilities can be represented by the two overlapping areas of Figure 21-5. Thus, the larger area, with the left-slanted lines, represents the probability (0.20) that an order will total more than $100. The smaller area, with the right-slanted lines, represents the probability (0.10) that an order will have less than 30 items. The overlap area, with crosshatch lines, represents the probability that an order will have less than 30 items and total more than $100. The overlap area covers 0.15 of the "more than $100" area and 0.30 of the "less than 30 items" area; 0.15 of the "more than $100" area equals 0.15 times 0.20, or 0.03; 0.30 of the "less than 30 items" area equals 0.30 times 0.10, or 0.03. Thus, 0.03 represents the probability that an order will have less than 30 items and total more than $100.

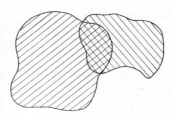

Figure 21-5. Representation of probabilities which are not mutually exclusive.

If we were to say in this case that the probability that an order will have less than 30 items or will total more than $100 is represented by the sum of the larger right-slanted area (0.20) and the smaller left-slanted area (0.10), we would be counting the overlap crosshatch area twice.   We must therefore subtract this overlap area (0.03) from the sum of the two separate areas. Therefore, the probability of occurrence of an order which will have less than 30 items or will total more than $100 equals 0.02 + 0.10 − 0.03, or 0.27.

Multiplication of Probabilities. What is the probability that any two orders chosen at random will both have more than 70 items? In only 15 out of 100 times will the first one chosen have more than 70 items. In only 15 out of 100 of these 15 out of 100 times will the second order also have more than 70 items. The probability of both orders having more than 70 items is thus (0.15) (0.15), or 0.0225. Whenever a compound event consists of separate and independent events, the probability of the compound event occurring is equal to the product of the probabilities of the separate events occurring.

What is the probability that of any two orders chosen at random, one will have more than 70 items and one will have less than 30 items? In only 15 out of 100 times will the first one chosen have more than 70 items. In only 10 out of 100 of these 15 out of 100 times will the second order have less than 30 items. Therefore, the probability that the first order will have more than 70 items and the second order less than 30 items is (0.15) (0.10), or 0.0150. However, the first order chosen could have less than 30 items and the second one more than 70 items. The probability of this occurrence is also (0.10) (0.15), or 0.0150. Therefore, the probability that one order will have more than 70 items and one will have less than 30 items is 2(0.10) (0.15), or 0.0300.

Conditional Probabilities. When the events are not independent, then the probability of the compound event occurring is equal to the product of the probability of one event occurring and the probability of the other ones occurring, assuming the first has occurred. Thus, we have 100 meters in stock of which, based on past experience, we know that 8 are defective. The repairman takes two meters chosen at random with him on each repair job so that he has an extra one with him if one proves defective. He does not test them in advance to determine if they are defective. What is the probability that he will take two defective ones? The probability that the first one chosen is defective is $\frac{8}{100}$. The probability that the second one chosen is defective, assuming the first one chosen was defective, is $\frac{7}{99}$. Therefore, the probability that the repairman will choose both defective ones is $(\frac{8}{100})(\frac{7}{99}) = 0.0057$. ($\frac{7}{99}$ is called a conditional probability.)

If the policy were changed to require him to take three meters, what would be the probability that all three would be defective? The probability that the third one chosen is defective, assuming the first two were defective, is $\frac{6}{98}$. Therefore, the probability that all three will be defective is $(\frac{8}{100})(\frac{7}{99})(\frac{6}{98}) = 0.00035$.

When the repairman takes just two meters with him, what is the probability that one is good and one is defective? We can answer this by observing that there are only three possibilities: they are both good, both defective, or one good and one defective. Therefore, the probabilities of these three possibilities must add up to certainty, or a probability of 1.0.

Labeling,

P_1 = probability that both are good
P_2 = probability that both are defective
P_3 = probability that one is good and one is defective
$P_1 + P_2 + P_3 = 1$
$P_3 = 1 - P_1 - P_2$

We previously calculated $P_2 = 0.0057$. We are now able to calculate $P_1 = (\frac{92}{100})(\frac{91}{99}) = 0.8457$. Therefore, $P_3 = 1 - 0.8457 - 0.0057 = 0.1486$.

We could also answer this question by considering that what we desire is the probability of two mutually exclusive events: one event is choosing a good meter and then a defective one; the second event is choosing a defective one and then a good one. The probability of the first event is $(\frac{92}{100})(\frac{8}{99}) = 0.0743$. The probability of the second event is $(\frac{8}{100})(\frac{92}{99}) = 0.0743$. Therefore, the probability of both of these mutually exclusive events is $0.0743 + 0.0743 = 0.1486$.

Maintenance Application. How many meters should this repairman take with him on each assignment? Let us analyze the case in which the repairman returns to his maintenance headquarters after each assignment, in which he requires a new meter on each assignment, and in which he is the only repairman who uses this stock of meters. When the meter or meters which the repairman has taken on the assignment are all defective, then he must return to his headquarters. This results in a cost in lost time, transportation, inconvenience to customer, etc., of $14. However, when extra meters which are not required are taken on a repair assignment, costs of inventory control, paperwork, handling, possibility of loss, etc., are incurred totaling $0.75 for each extra good meter which must be returned at the end of each assignment.

We need not consider in this problem the cost of taking a good meter which is used on the repair assignment because this will be the same fixed amount regardless of the number of meters taken per trip. We also need not consider the cost of returning extra meters which prove defective because this cost will also occur regardless of the number of meters taken per trip. We are therefore only concerned with the expected costs per trip of returning to headquarters to obtain additional meters and of taking good meters which must be returned.

We would like to minimize the total of the expected cost of returning to headquarters to obtain additional meters and the expected cost of taking extra meters. These costs are summarized in Table 21-8 for 1, 2, and 3 meters taken per assignment. The table shows a minimum total cost of $0.714 per trip when 2 meters are taken.

Table 21-8. **Expected Costs per Assignment as a Function of Number of Meters Taken on Assignment**

Number of meters taken on assignment	Expected cost per assignment of returning to obtain additional meters	Expected cost per assignment of returning extra good meters	Total cost per assignment
1	$1.120	$0.000	$1.120
2	0.080	0.634	0.714
3	0.005	1.320	1.325

If the repairman takes only 1 meter, 8 times in 100 it will prove defective when he installs it. The expected cost of lost time, transportation, etc., is then 0.08($14) = $1.120 per trip. If he takes 2 meters, the probability of both being defective was previously calculated as 0.0057. The expected cost is then 0.0057($14) = $0.080 per trip. If he takes three meters with him, the probability of all three being defective was previously calculated as 0.00035. The expected cost is then

$$0.00035(\$14) = \$0.005 \text{ per trip}$$

If the repairman takes only 1 meter, there is no possibility of returning an extra good meter. If he takes 2 meters, he will return 1 good meter if both meters prove to be good. The probability of both meters being good was previously calculated at 0.8457. The expected cost of returning extra good meters is therefore 0.8457($0.75) = $0.634.

If 3 meters are taken on each trip, the repairman will return 2 good meters if all 3 are good and 1 good meter if only 2 are good. We must add together the expected costs of both of these possibilities. The probability that all 3 will be good is $(\frac{92}{100})(\frac{91}{99})(\frac{90}{98}) = 0.7766$. The expected cost of returning the 2 good meters in this case is then 2(0.7766)($0.75) = $1.165 per trip. The probability that only 2 of the 3 meters are good is the sum of the following terms, each of which represents the probability of choosing 2 good and 1 defective meters in a different sequence:

$$(\tfrac{92}{100})\ (\tfrac{91}{99})\ (\tfrac{8}{98}) = 0.069$$
$$(\tfrac{92}{100})\ (\tfrac{8}{99})\ (\tfrac{91}{98}) = 0.069$$
$$(\tfrac{8}{100})\ (\tfrac{92}{99})\ (\tfrac{91}{98}) = \underline{0.069}$$
$$0.207$$

The expected cost of returning 1 of these 2 good meters is

$$(0.207)\ (\$0.75) = \$0.155 \text{ per trip}$$

The expected cost of returning extra good meters if 3 meters are taken on each trip is then $1.165 + $0.155 = $1.320.

Risk of Running Out of Inventory Stock. If the lead time for the replenishment of inventory stock is fixed, the risk of running out of stock is dependent upon variations in usage or sales requirements for the item. These sales requirements will usually show random variations which can cause stock shortages, depending upon the size of the safety stock. (The requirements will also frequently vary seasonally, which we shall not consider here.)

We would like to determine the risk of running out of stock of catalogue item 1282. The distribution of sales variations for item 1282 over the past 50 weeks was shown in Table 21-7. Sales average 9 units per week. There would be no risk and safety stock would not be necessary if these variations did not occur, because we can obtain delivery of new stock in exactly one week. We could place an order when the stock level declined to 9. This would be exactly one week before our stock level is scheduled to hit zero were it not for variations in the rate of sales.

Because of these variations in rate of sales, if we place an order when stock level declines to 9 units, we shall run out of stock a certain proportion of the time before the replenishment order arrives. From Table 21-9, we see that we shall run out 26 per cent of the ordering cycles, since this is the proportion of the time that sales exceed 9 units per week.

If we keep a safety stock of 1 unit, we shall order when the stock level declines to 10 units. We shall then run out of stock only 18 per cent of the time. If we keep a safety stock of 5 units, we shall order when the stock level declines to 14 units. We shall then run out of stock only 2 per cent of the time. We can eliminate run-outs entirely by keeping a safety stock of 6 units.

Table 21-9. **Calculation of Proportion of Time Weekly Sales of Item 1282 Exceed Given Values**

Number of units sold per week	Number of weeks	Relative frequency	Proportion of time sales exceed value in Col. 1
5	0	0.00	1.00
6	1	0.02	0.98
7	8	0.16	0.82
8	16	0.32	0.50
9	12	0.24	0.26
10	4	0.08	0.18
11	3	0.06	0.12
12	2	0.04	0.08
13	2	0.04	0.04
14	1	0.02	0.02
15	1	0.02	0.00

However, the larger the safety stock, the greater the costs of storage, investment in inventory, etc. These inventory carrying costs can be calculated and the cost of carrying a large enough inventory so as never to run out of stock determined. This cost will typically be very high and management will be reluctant to spend such a large sum. A reasonably low risk of run-out can be obtained with much lower inventory levels. Based upon a comparison of inventory costs at various risks of running out of stock at each reorder, management can decide upon a reasonably economic balance of these two factors.

Economic Lot Size with Risk of Variations in Requirements. The size of the safety stock determines the risk of run-out each time the inventory approaches minimum stock levels at reorder time. The larger the size of the reorder which is periodically placed, the more infrequent will the reorders be. The inventory will therefore be exposed to run-out less frequently. The expected or average costs per year of running out of stock will then be smaller.

Whenever we run out of stock, we experience an opportunity cost because of loss of sales and/or loss of customer good will. Estimating the cost of being out of stock is usually more difficult than estimating holding costs. In fact some people will say it is impossible to make any estimate. What they really mean is that it is impossible to make an estimate as accurate as they normally like to have their estimates. However, for most inventory-control purposes, just having the right average order of magnitude will usually be sufficient to give near-optimum results.

In our illustrative problem, the opportunity cost of running out of stock is estimated to be $6 per unit. When we carry extra items in a safety stock, inventory holding costs increase. These costs are estimated at $15 per item per year.

In Table 21-10 are shown the out-of-stock costs and the holding costs when various sizes of safety stock are carried and various sizes of safety stock are required. (The holding costs in the upper right segment of the table are dollars per year. The out-of-stock costs shown in the lower left segment are dollars per ordering cycle.) The minimum safety stock that we are considering is -3 units, meaning that the order is placed when 6 units are on hand. Since the average consumption during the one-week lead time is 9 units, this represents a planned safety stock carried of -3 units. There would be no point in carrying less than a -3 unit safety stock because the minimum usage during the lead time is 6 units. There will never be any old stock available when the new order is delivered. Obviously, the minimum safety stock which is required is also -3 units.

Table **21-10. Out-of-stock and Holding Costs**

Safety stock required	Safety stock carried									
	-3	-2	-1	0	1	2	3	4	5	6
-3	0	15	30	45	60	75	90	105	120	135
-2	6	0	15	30	45	60	75	90	105	120
-1	12	6	0	15	30	45	60	75	90	105
0	18	12	6	0	15	30	45	60	75	90
1	24	18	12	6	0	15	30	45	60	75
2	30	24	18	12	6	0	15	30	45	60
3	36	30	24	18	12	6	0	15	30	45
4	42	36	30	24	18	12	6	0	15	30
5	48	42	36	30	24	18	12	6	0	15
6	54	48	42	36	30	24	18	12	6	0

When the safety stock required and the safety stock carried are equal, there are no out-of-stock costs and there are no carrying costs. However, when more is required than is carried, we have out-of-stock costs totaling $6 times the number of units short. Thus, when 3 units are required and -2 are carried, the out-of-stock cost is 5 times $6, or $30. When more safety stock is carried than is required, we have holding costs totaling $15 per item per year. Thus, when 1 unit of safety stock is required and 4 units are carried, the holding costs total $45 per year.

In Table 21-11, we compute the total expected or average out-of-stock costs and the total expected or average holding costs for each assumed level of safety stock carried. Carrying a safety stock of 2 units, holding costs are $75 whenever only -3 units are required (only 6 units sold dur-

Table 21-11. Total Expected (Average) Out-of-stock (O) and Holding (H) Costs*

Safety stock carried

Safety stock required	Relative frequency	−3 O	−3 H	−2 O	−2 H	−1 O	−1 H	0 O	0 H	1 O	1 H	2 O	2 H	3 O	3 H	4 O	4 H	5 O	5 H	6 O	6 H
−3	0.02	$			$0.30		$0.60		$0.90		$1.20		$1.50		$1.80		$2.10		$2.40		$2.70
−2	0.16	0.96					2.40		4.80		7.20		9.60		12.00		14.40		16.80		19.20
−1	0.32	3.84		$1.92					4.80		9.60		14.40		19.20		24.00		28.80		33.60
0	0.24	4.32		2.88		$1.44					3.60		7.20		10.80		14.40		18.00		21.60
1	0.08	1.92		1.44		0.96		$0.48					1.20		2.40		3.60		4.80		6.00
2	0.06	1.80		1.44		1.08		0.72		0.36					0.90		1.80		2.70		3.60
3	0.04	1.44		1.20		0.96		0.72		0.48		0.24					0.60		1.20		1.80
4	0.04	1.68		1.44		1.20		0.96		0.72		0.48		0.24					0.60		1.20
5	0.02	0.96		0.84		0.72		0.60		0.48		0.36		0.24		0.12					0.30
6	0.02	1.08		0.96		0.84		0.72		0.60		0.48		0.36		0.24		0.12			
Total	1.00	$18.00		$12.12	$0.30	$7.20	$3.00	$4.20	$10.50	$2.64	$21.60	$1.56	$33.90	$0.84	$47.10	$0.36	$60.90	$0.12	$75.30		$90.00

* Out-of-stock costs are in dollars per ordering cycle and holding costs are in dollars per year.

339

ing the one-week lead time). The relative frequency of selling only 6 units in a week is 0.02. The expected or average holding cost for this contingency is, therefore, only 0.02 of $75, or $1.50. Similarly, the expected holding costs when -2 units of safety stock are required is 0.16 of $60, or $9.60. The average holding cost with a safety stock of 2 is the sum of the expected costs under all the possible requirements which will produce holding costs. They total $33.90 in this case.

The expected out-of-stock costs are computed in the same manner as the holding costs. For the 2-unit safety stock a $6 out-of-stock cost will occur when 3 units of safety stock are required. And 3 units of safety stock will be required when 12 units are sold in a week or 0.04 of the time. The expected or average out-of-stock cost for this contingency is therefore, 0.04 of $6, or $0.24.

The out-of-stock costs shown in the table occur each time reordering takes place. It is like a setup or order cost. However, the carrying cost is an additional annual cost unrelated to the size and frequency of ordering.

In Chapter 18 we established a minimum-cost economic-order quantity assuming uniform known rates of usage. No safety stocks were required under such conditions. When there is a risk of running out of stock, as in the example currently being considered, the expected out-of-stock cost should be added to the ordering and setup costs in determining the economic lot size. We shall have 10 different economic lot sizes depending upon which safety-stock level we choose.

Our previously established economic-lot-size formula was

$$Q = \sqrt{\frac{2C_1 U}{C_2}}$$

where C_1 = setup and order costs
$\quad\quad C_2$ = holding costs per unit per year
$\quad\quad U$ = annual usage
In this example, $C_1 = \$12$, $C_2 = \$15$, and $U = 468$ units.

We now apply this formula, adding our expected out-of stock costs (O_E) to the setup and order costs,

$$Q = \sqrt{\frac{2(C_1 + O_E)U}{C_2}}$$

-3 safety stock: $\quad Q = \sqrt{\dfrac{2(12 + 18)(468)}{15}}$

$$= \sqrt{\frac{2(468)}{15}} \sqrt{12 + 18}$$

$$= \sqrt{62.4} \sqrt{12 + 18} \quad\quad = 43.27$$

-2 safety stock: $\quad Q = \sqrt{62.4} \sqrt{12 + 12.12} = 38.79$

-1 safety stock: $\quad Q = \sqrt{62.4} \sqrt{12 + 7.20} \ = 34.61$

0 safety stock: $Q = \sqrt{62.4}\,\sqrt{12 + 4.20}\ \ = 31.79$
1 safety stock: $Q = \sqrt{62.4}\,\sqrt{12 + 2.64}\ \ = 30.22$
2 safety stock: $Q = \sqrt{62.4}\,\sqrt{12 + 1.56}\ \ = 29.09$
3 safety stock: $Q = \sqrt{62.4}\,\sqrt{12 + 0.84}\ \ = 28.31$
4 safety stock: $Q = \sqrt{62.4}\,\sqrt{12 + 0.36}\ \ = 27.77$
5 safety stock: $Q = \sqrt{62.4}\,\sqrt{12 + 0.12}\ \ = 27.50$
6 safety stock: $Q = \sqrt{62.4}\,\sqrt{12 + 0}\ \ \ \ \ = 27.36$

Which one of these lot sizes will give us the lowest total costs? We apply our total-cost formula of Chapter 18, $C_T = \dfrac{C_1 U}{Q} + \dfrac{C_2 Q}{2} + C_3 U$. We need not consider $C_3 U$ in our comparison of costs using various lot sizes and safety stocks since $C_3 U$ is unaffected by the lot size or safety stock. We add O_E, expected out-of-stock cost to the setup and ordering cost C_1 and we add a term, H_E, for the extra expected holding costs per year because of the safety stock. The equation becomes

$$C_T = \frac{(C_1 + O_E)U}{Q} + \frac{C_2 Q}{2} + H_E$$

Total annual costs (excluding $C_3 U$) for each safety-stock level are

-3 safety-stock level:

$$C_T = \frac{(12 + 18)468}{43.27} + \frac{15(43.27)}{2} + 0 \qquad = \$649.00$$

-2 safety-stock level:

$$C_T = \frac{(12 + 12.12)468}{38.79} + \frac{15(38.79)}{2} + 0.30 = \$582.23$$

-1 safety-stock level:

$$C_T = \frac{(12 + 7.20)468}{34.61} + \frac{15(34.61)}{2} + 3.00 \ \ = \$522.20$$

0 safety-stock level:

$$C_T = \frac{(12 + 4.20)468}{31.79} + \frac{15(31.79)}{2} + 10.50 = \$487.42$$

1 safety-stock level:

$$C_T = \frac{(12 + 2.64)468}{30.22} + \frac{15(30.22)}{2} + 21.60 = \$474.97$$

2 safety-stock level:

$$C_T = \frac{(12 + 1.56)468}{29.09} + \frac{15(29.09)}{2} + 33.90 = \$470.23$$

3 safety-stock level:

$$C_T = \frac{(12 + 0.84)468}{28.31} + \frac{15(28.31)}{2} + 47.10 = \$471.69$$

4 safety-stock level:

$$C_T = \frac{(12 + 0.36)468}{27.77} + \frac{15(27.77)}{2} + 60.90 = \$477.48$$

5 safety-stock level:

$$C_T = \frac{(12 + 0.12)468}{27.50} + \frac{15(27.50)}{2} + 75.30 = \$487.81$$

6 safety-stock level:

$$C_T = \frac{(12 + 0)468}{27.36} + \frac{15(27.36)}{2} + 90.00 \quad = \$500.46$$

From these calculations, we note that the minimum total annual costs occur at a safety-stock level of +2. Our economic order quantity for this safety-stock level is therefore 29 units.

PROBLEMS

Listed below for use in problems 1 through 5 are the number of working hours between receipt of telephone subscription orders for a newspaper and the entry of the new subscriber's name in the master addressing file (75 orders were sampled).

2.4	1.4	2.5	2.2	2.5	1.9	2.3
1.3	2.8	2.9	3.6	2.7	2.4	2.8
3.9	1.7	3.3	1.8	1.9	3.6	0.8
2.1	2.9	0.9	2.1	3.1	2.1	2.3
2.6	1.6	2.9	3.7	2.4	1.2	2.7
1.2	2.6	3.4	1.3	1.5	3.4	1.9
2.3	3.7	2.7	1.4	6.8	2.4	2.5
1.7	2.4	3.5	2.6	2.5	4.2	3.2
2.2	1.1	2.3	3.3	3.1	2.1	1.6
3.1	2.7	0.6	2.7	1.1	1.8	
5.3	4.7	2.9	1.5	2.2	1.6	

1. Set up a grouped frequency distribution for the data on the entry of the 75 telephone subscription orders. (Make the class interval width equal to $\frac{1}{2}$ hr.) Express the frequencies in relative form as well as the absolute values.

2. Plot the frequency distribution of problem 1 in the form of a histogram, labeling the scale for relative frequencies as well as absolute values.

3. (a) What is the modal class interval for working hours between receipt of a telephone order and its entry in the master file? (b) In which class interval is the median value?

4. (a) What is the arithmetic mean of the number of working hours between receipt of a telephone order and its entry in the master file? (b) What is the range of values in this distribution? (c) What is the standard deviation? Calculate from the grouped data.

5. Calculate the measures of skewness and kurtosis for the distribution of problem 4. (a) Does the skewness value indicate lack of symmetry in this distribution? (b) Is this distribution flatter or more peaked than a normal distribution?

6. Which of the following variables are discrete and which continuous? (a) Weight of children at birth, (b) number of children per family, (c) diameter of shafts in a control mechanism, (d) daily sales of a department store, (e) number of defects in samples of 500 parts, (f) per cent defectives in samples of 500 parts.

7. A careful and exhaustive study in your city has disclosed the following information on the morning papers each person primarily reads:

$$
\begin{array}{ll}
\textit{The Daily Chronicle} \dots \dots \dots \dots & 20,000 \\
\textit{The Globe} \dots \dots \dots \dots \dots & 56,000 \\
\text{No morning newspaper} \dots \dots \dots & 4,000
\end{array}
$$

At random, you ask persons living in your city which morning paper each primarily reads. What is your estimate of the probability that the next person you ask will tell you that he primarily reads (a) *The Daily Chronicle*, (b) *The Globe*, (c) *The Daily Chronicle* or *The Globe*, (d) No morning newspaper?

8. Referring to the primary readership study of problem 7, (a) What is the probability that, of the next two persons chosen at random, one will tell you that he reads *The Daily Chronicle* and the other that he reads *The Globe*? (b) What is the probability that the next two persons will tell you that they read *The Daily Chronicle* or *The Globe*? (c) What is the probability that the next five persons will tell you they read *The Daily Chronicle*?

9. You have a meeting with twenty of your neighbors. Four (20 per cent) primarily read *The Daily Chronicle* and sixteen (80 per cent) primarily read *The Globe*.

(a) If you ask two of them at random which newspapers they primarily read, what is the probability that (1) both will say they read *The Globe*? (2) both will say they read *The Daily Chronicle*? (3) one will say he reads *The Globe* and one *The Daily Chronicle*?

(b) If you ask four of them at random which newspapers they primarily read, what is the probability that (1) all four will say they read *The Globe*? (2) all four will say they read *The Daily Chronicle*? (3) one will say he reads *The Globe* and three *The Daily Chronicle*? (4) one will say he reads *The Daily Chronicle* and three *The Globe*?

10. You desire to broaden the scope of the newspaper readership study in problem 7 by considering the entire readership, rather than just primary

readership. The expanded study shows the following information regarding the morning newspapers read by each person:

Only *The Daily Chronicle*.............. 18,000
Only *The Globe*...................... 50,000
The Daily Chronicle and *Globe*.......... 8,000
No morning newspaper.............. 4,000

At random, you ask persons living in your city which morning paper each primarily reads. (*a*) What is your estimate of the probability that the next person you ask will tell you that he reads *The Daily Chronicle? The Globe? The Daily Chronicle* or *The Globe?* no newspaper? (*b*) What percentage of *The Daily Chronicle* readership also reads *The Globe?* (*c*) What percentage of *The Globe* readership also reads *The Daily Chronicle?*

11. Refer to the illustration in the text on the determination of economic lot size taking account of variations in requirements. The method requires an estimate of the opportunity cost of being out of stock. Using an opportunity cost of $6 per unit, we determine that a safety stock of $+2$ and economic order quantity of 29 units give us a minimum total cost, excluding the cost of the item, of $470.23. (*a*) Using an opportunity cost of being out of stock of $12 per unit and keeping all other costs the same, determine the safety stock, economic order quantity, and minimum total cost. (*b*) Compare the results of your calculation with the one in the text using an out-of-stock opportunity cost one-half the size of yours. Does the comparison indicate anything about the sensitivity of the economic order quantity and safety-stock determination to errors in the estimate of the opportunity cost of running out of stock?

12. In order to estimate the opportunity cost of running out of stock, it is possible to work the economic-lot-size calculation in reverse. Using the current stock levels, ordering quantities, setup and holding costs, etc., we can determine the opportunity cost of run-out which would make the current practice economic. This would give us management's implied estimate of the opportunity cost of running out of stock. Management can then decide whether the opportunity cost implicit in its inventory decisions is reasonable. What are the pros and cons of this approach?

22 Probability Distributions

In an economy analysis, there are always elements of risk and some doubt as to the conclusions we reach. It has been previously noted that an understanding of probability theory and its applications will improve our ability to evaluate the risk in economy analyses and thus our ability to make economic decisions. Therefore, we shall briefly review in this chapter the use of the following common probability distributions: binomial, Poisson, exponential, and normal.

Constructing a Binomial Frequency Distribution. If the probability of an event occurring at any trial is constant and independent of previous trial results and is designated as p, then the probability of 0, 1, 2, 3, . . . , n occurrences in n trials is given by the successive terms of the binomial $(q + p)^n$ where $q = 1 - p$. The successive terms of the binomial expansion are as follows:

$$(q + p)^n = q^n + nq^{n-1}p + \frac{n(n - 1)}{(1)(2)} q^{n-2}p^2$$
$$+ \frac{n(n - 1)(n - 2)}{(1)(2)(3)} q^{n-3}p^3 + \cdots$$

For example, if the probability of obtaining more than \$100,000 of new orders in any day is constant at 0.1, then the probability of not having more than \$100,000 of new orders in any one of the next 5 days is given by the first term of the expansion or $(0.9)^5$; the probability of one day with more than \$100,000 new business is $5(0.9)^4 (0.1)$; and so on.

The binomial distribution for the number of days we shall obtain more than \$100,000 of new orders is shown in Table 22-1. The frequency histogram for this distribution is drawn in Figure 22-1.

Size of Shipping Department Vacation Staff. The company management is considering the size of staff to maintain in the shipping department during the 5-day period in which the remainder of the factory will be closed for vacation. The normal shipping department staff can handle orders totaling up to \$100,000 per day without delaying any shipments. (When other departments in the factory are operating during the year, the policy is to transfer people temporarily to the shipping department when orders total more than \$100,000 per day.)

What is the probability that orders will be delayed during the 5-day vacation period if only the normal staff works in the shipping department? Delays will only occur if more than $100,000 of new orders are received in any day during this 5-day period. We have previously calculated in Table 22-1 that the probability of receiving no orders totaling more than $100,000 during the 5-day period is $(0.9)^5 = 0.6$. Therefore, the probability is $1 - 0.6$, or 0.4, that some shipments will be delayed. Using the probabilities of Table 22-1, we can estimate the probabilities of having 1, 2, 3, 4, or 5 days in the 5-day period in which orders will total more than $100,000 and cause delays in some shipments.

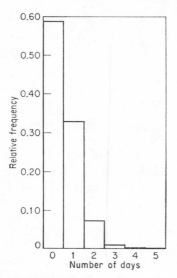

Figure 22-1. Histogram of binomial distribution ($p = 0.1$ and $n = 5$).

Binomial Distribution Values. The arithmetic mean of any binomial distribution is equal to np. For our example,

$$\bar{X} = 5(0.10) = 0.5 \text{ day}$$

in a 5-day period or once in every 10-day period. The standard deviation of any binomial distribution is equal to $\sqrt{np(1 - p)}$, or $\sqrt{npq}$. For our example, $\sigma = \sqrt{5(0.1)(1 - 0.1)} = 0.671.$[1] The computation of $\bar{X} = np$ and $\sigma = \sqrt{np(1 - p)}$ in our example can be checked by calculating these values from the distribution of Table 22-1, using the method for computing standard deviations described in Chapter 21.

To reduce the necessity of making tedious calculations, various tables of probabilities for the binomial distribution have been published.[2] In addition, the binomial distribution may be approximated by the normal distribution under certain circumstances explained later.

A Binomial Illustration. When a machine is producing castings under conditions of statistical control, the probability of any particular casting being defective is a constant which we can designate as p. If we take random samples of 10 castings periodically and test them to determine the defective ones, we can record the number defective in each sample. Let us say that the average percentage defective turns out to be 15 per cent. Then the distribution of the number of defective castings in

---

[1] No distinction in notation is made between sample and population values of $\bar{X}$, σ, p, and c in this chapter. These distinctions are made in Chapter 23, which discusses sampling and confidence limits, and in succeeding chapters.

[2] See, for example, *Tables of the Binomial Probability Distribution*, National Bureau of Standards, Applied Mathematics Series 6, Washington, 1950.

the samples of 10 should follow the binomial distribution, with a mean of $np = (0.15)(10) = 1.5$ and a standard deviation of

$$\sqrt{np(1 - p)} = \sqrt{10(0.15)(0.85)} = 1.129$$

If the distribution of the number of defectives in samples of 10 differs significantly from what would be expected under the binomial distribution, the casting process is not under statistical control. When a process is not under statistical control, assignable causes other than chance factors are causing variations in the value of p and the distribution will not follow the binomial pattern.

Table 22-1. Binomial Probability Distribution
($p = 0.1$ and $n = 5$)

Number of days	Relative frequency (or probability)	
0	$(0.9)^5$	$= 0.59049$
1	$(5)(0.9)^4(0.1)$	$= 0.32805$
2	$\dfrac{(5)(4)}{(1)(2)}(0.9)^3(0.1)^2$	$= 0.07290$
3	$\dfrac{(5)(4)(3)}{(1)(2)(3)}(0.9)^2(0.1)^3$	$= 0.00810$
4	$\dfrac{(5)(4)(3)(2)}{(1)(2)(3)(4)}(0.9)(0.1)^4$	$= 0.00045$
5	$\dfrac{(5)(4)(3)(2)(1)}{(1)(2)(3)(4)(5)}(0.1)^5$	$= 0.00001$
		$\overline{1.00000}$

Poisson Distribution. The expected number of occurrences of an event within a given unit of space or time may be constant and independent of what has previously occurred, but the probability of the event occurring at any particular point in the unit space or time may be extremely (infinitesimally) small and constant and the number of possible points may be extremely (infinitely) large. When these conditions hold, the distribution of the number of occurrences per unit of space or time follows a Poisson distribution. For example, the expected or average number of incoming telephone calls in an hour is 4.5. The probability of a telephone call coming in at any particular instant in a day is infinitesimally small, the number of instants in a day is infinitely large, and the successive calls are independent of each other. Under these conditions, the distribution of the number of telephone calls per day can be expected to follow the Poisson distribution.

For any given value of np (average number of occurrences), the Poisson is the limiting value of the binomial as n (number of trials or points in space or time in which the event may occur) increases indefinitely as np

is held constant. The successive terms of the binomial expansion,

$$(q + p)^n = q^n + nq^{n-1}p + \frac{n(n-1)}{(1)(2)} q^{n-2}p^2 + \cdots$$

become the Poisson series

$$e^{-c} + ce^{-c} + \frac{c^2e^{-c}}{(1)(2)} + \frac{c^3e^{-c}}{(1)(2)(3)} + \cdots$$

where $e = 2.71828$, the base of natural or Naperian logarithms

c = average number of occurrences (np)

The probability of one occurrence is c times the probability of none. Probability of two occurrences is $c/2$ times the probability of one. Probability of three occurrences is $c/3$ times the probability of two, and so on.

Constructing a Poisson Frequency Distribution. The frequency distribution for our telephone-call example is computed in Table 22-2. The histogram of the distribution is plotted in Figure 22-2.[1]

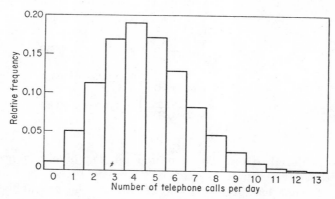

Figure 22-2. Histogram of Poisson distribution ($c = 4.5$).

The arithmetic mean of the Poisson distribution is c and the standard deviation is $\sqrt{c}$. Thus, for our telephone-call illustration

$$\bar{X} = c = 4.5$$
$$\sigma = \sqrt{c} = \sqrt{4.5} = 2.12$$

This can be checked by calculation from the distribution of Table 22-2.

The Poisson chart in the Appendix to this book provides a means for graphically determining probabilities of the Poisson distribution for values of up to $c = 30$. Thus, to determine the probability of receiving 4 telephone calls in one day in the illustrated problem, we would enter the

[1] Although the presentations of Table 22-2 and Figure 22-2 go only to 13 calls per day, they can be carried as far as desired toward infinity.

Table 22-2. **Poisson Probability Distribution**
$(c = 4.5)$

Number of telephone calls in day	Relative frequency (or probability)	Number of telephone calls in day	Relative frequency (or probability)
0	$P_0 = e^{-4.5} = 0.01111$	9	$P_9 = \frac{4.5}{9}P_8 = 0.02317$
1	$P_1 = 4.5P_0 = 0.05000$	10	$P_{10} = \frac{4.5}{10}P_9 = 0.01043$
2	$P_2 = \frac{4.5}{2}P_1 = 0.11250$	11	$P_{11} = \frac{4.5}{11}P_{10} = 0.00427$
3	$P_3 = \frac{4.5}{3}P_2 = 0.16875$	12	$P_{12} = \frac{4.5}{12}P_{11} = 0.00160$
4	$P_4 = \frac{4.5}{4}P_3 = 0.18984$	13	$P_{13} = \frac{4.5}{13}P_{12} = 0.00055$
5	$P_5 = \frac{4.5}{5}P_4 = 0.17086$	.	.
6	$P_6 = \frac{4.5}{6}P_5 = 0.12815$	.	.
7	$P_7 = \frac{4.5}{7}P_6 = 0.08238$	.	.
8	$P_8 = \frac{4.5}{8}P_7 = 0.04634$		

table at the abscissa value of $c = 4.5$, go up vertically to the $d = 4$ curved line, read off on the ordinate scale the value 0.54, which is the probability of receiving 4 telephone calls or less in one day. We would next go up vertically to the $d = 3$ curved line and read off on the ordinate scale the value 0.35, which is the probability of receiving 3 telephone calls or less in one day. The difference between the probability of 4 or less calls, 0.54, and the probability of 3 or less calls, 0.35, is the approximate probability of exactly 4 calls, 0.19. In general, we can determine Poisson probabilities to two significant figures from this table, with some approximation attached to the second figure. For most, but not all, economic applications, this is sufficient accuracy.

Poisson values up to $c = 100$ to six decimal places are given in published tables.[1] In addition, the Poisson distribution may be approximated by the normal distribution under certain circumstances which are discussed later.

Additional Examples of a Poisson Process. When a machine is producing optical lenses of 1-in. diameter under conditions of statistical control, the probability of a defect at any one point on the lens is infinitesimally small, the number of possible points at which a defect could occur is infinitely large, and the probability of a defect occurring on any lens is a constant. The distribution should therefore be Poisson. However, if the machine is not operating under conditions of statistical control, factors other than chance will cause variations in the probability of a defect occurring on a lens. The process then ceases to be Poisson.

The probability of a machine breaking down at any particular point in time is infinitesimally small and the number of possible points in time in which it can break down is infinitely large. Although the probability

[1] See E. C. Molina, *Poisson's Exponential Binomial Limit*, D. Van Nostrand Company, Inc., Princeton, N.J., 1949.

of a breakdown in any week may be constant if the machine usage is constant, we have not fulfilled the requirements for a Poisson process if the machine breakdowns result from wear and tear rather than accidental causes. Breakdowns from wear and tear are not independent of each other. The fact that a machine has just broken down and been repaired makes it less likely to break down from the same cause again right away. We would, therefore, not expect the number of breakdowns to follow the Poisson distribution. (However, we are sometimes surprised to find that distributions follow patterns contrary to what our theoretical reasoning would lead us to expect.)

In Chapter 26 we shall discuss economics of waiting-line (queuing) problems in which the probability of an arrival is always the same regardless of what has happened previously or the length of the waiting line. The arrivals therefore follow a Poisson distribution in this queuing model.

Exponential Distribution. The exponential distribution has its origins in the Poisson process. Thus, if our previous distribution of the number of incoming telephone calls follows a Poisson distribution, then the distribution of the lengths of time between successive telephone calls follows the exponential distribution. Since each Poisson event (telephone call) is independent of all previous and future ones, it does not matter where we start counting intervals.

The probability formula for the exponential distribution is ce^{-cX} where c is the average number of Poisson occurrences per unit space or time, e is the base of the Naperian or natural system of logarithms, with a value of 2.71828, and X is the interval between occurrences. (The probability formula is sometimes written in the form $(1/k)\, e^{-X/k}$, where k is equal to $1/c$, the average time interval between occurrences.) For our telephone example, where $c = 4.5$, this becomes $4.5e^{-4.5X}$.

The mean and standard deviation of the exponential distribution are

$$\bar{X} = \frac{1}{c}$$

$$\sigma = \frac{1}{c}$$

In our telephone example,

$$\bar{X} = \frac{1}{c} = \frac{1}{4.5} = 0.222$$

$$\sigma = \frac{1}{c} = \frac{1}{4.5} = 0.222$$

Exponential Distribution in Industry. Maguire, Pearson, and Wynn[1] studied the time intervals between successive accidents for one

[1] B. A. Maguire, E. S. Pearson, and A. H. A. Wynn, "The Time Interval between Industrial Accidents," *Biometrika*, vol. 39, pp. 168–180, 1952.

shift in one section of a mine. As long as safety conditions remain fairly consistent and the risk of accident therefore constant, we would expect a Poisson process. The distribution obtained in this study is shown in Figure 22-3, which indicates a rather good fit to an exponential distribution.

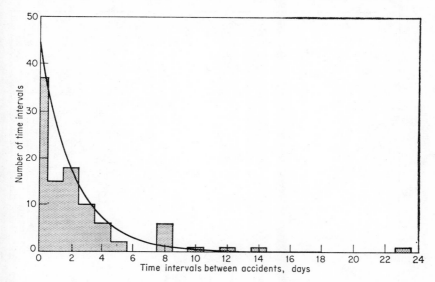

Figure 22-3. Histogram of time intervals between successive accidents in one district of a mine with fitted exponential curve.

In some cases we would not expect an exponential distribution based on the theoretical considerations and yet the exponential distribution gives a good fit to the data. In the examination of numerous cases of the servicing times in waiting-time problems we find exponential distributions when we would not expect them.

Thus, Brigham[1] reports on a study of the time required to serve mechanics at a tool crib in connection with his analysis of the optimum number of clerks to be placed behind service counters. His study shows an approximately exponential distribution of service times. Distribution curves of serving times were made up for two tool cribs to compare the actual frequencies of serving times to the theoretical frequencies which would be expected for an exponential distribution. The actual serving times conformed very closely to the theoretical distribution, as can be seen in Figure 22-4 for one of the tool cribs.

We would not have expected that this would follow a Poisson process. The probability of the service ending at any instant is independent of what has happened in all previous instants. A Poisson assumption would,

[1] G. Brigham, "On a Congestion Problem in an Aircraft Factory," *Operations Research*, vol. 3, no. 4, pp. 412–428, November, 1955.

therefore, imply that a person is as likely to require the same amount of additional service at the tool crib after having been serviced for a time as if he had not been there, that he is not any more likely to leave after having been there a while than if he had just arrived.

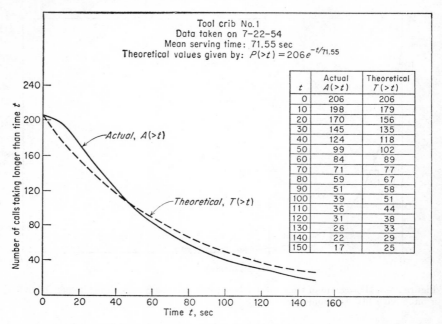

Tool crib No.1
Data taken on 7-22-54
Mean serving time: 71.55 sec
Theoretical values given by: $P(>t) = 206\,e^{-t/71.55}$

t	Actual $A(>t)$	Theoretical $T(>t)$
0	206	206
10	198	179
20	170	156
30	145	135
40	124	118
50	99	102
60	84	89
70	71	77
80	59	67
90	51	58
100	39	51
110	36	44
120	31	38
130	26	33
140	22	29
150	17	25

Figure 22-4. Distribution of serving times, machine shop tool crib.

Thus, the exponential distribution is present in a considerable percentage of cases even when there are weak theoretical grounds for expecting that it will exist. In the queuing model presented in Chapter 26 for the solution of certain types of economic problems involving waiting time, the servicing rates are assumed to follow an exponential distribution.

Normal Distribution. The most commonly used distribution in industrial and commercial decision-making is the normal distribution (also called the Gaussian distribution). The equation of the normal curve is

$$f(X) = \frac{1}{\sigma \sqrt{2\pi}}\, e^{-(X-\bar{X})^2/2\sigma^2}$$

The normal distribution is shown in Figure 22-5. A table of areas under the normal curve is presented in the Appendix to this book.

The table tells us the relative frequency between the mean and any value in a normal distribution. The table values disclose the fractional parts of the total area (1.00000) under the normal curve between the mean and a perpendicular erected at various numbers of standard deviations from the mean $[(X - \bar{X})/\sigma]$. Thus, 0.24857, or 24.857 per cent, of the area lies between the mean and 0.67σ of a normal distribution.

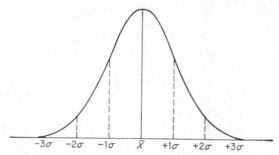

Figure 22-5. Normal distribution.

The normal distribution is symmetrical about the mean. The area between $\bar{X}$ and $\bar{X} + 0.67\sigma$ is exactly the same as the area between $\bar{X}$ and $\bar{X} - 0.67\sigma$. Thus, almost 50 per cent (24.857% + 24.857% = 49.714%) of the values in a normal distribution occur between $\bar{X} \pm \frac{2}{3}\sigma$; 68.268 per cent, or more than two-thirds, of the frequencies fall between $\bar{X} \pm 1\sigma$; and 95.45 per cent of the area is between $\bar{X} \pm 2\sigma$. The 3-sigma limits ($\bar{X} \pm 3\sigma$) include 99.73 per cent of the total frequency.

We can also say that less than 0.3 per cent of the values will be outside $\bar{X} \pm 3\sigma$; less than 5 per cent outside $\bar{X} \pm 2\sigma$; and less than 32 per cent outside $\bar{X} \pm 1\sigma$.

If I determine that the arithmetic mean of the time for performing a certain operation is 2.4 hr, the standard deviation is 0.2 hr, and the distribution is normal, what percentage of the time will the operation take between 2.0 and 2.8 hr? Let $X_L =$ the lower limit = 2.0 hr and $X_U =$ the upper limit = 2.8 hr.

$$\bar{X} = 2.4 \text{ hr}$$
$$\frac{X_L - \bar{X}}{\sigma} = \frac{2.0 - 2.4}{0.2} = -2$$
$$\frac{X_U - \bar{X}}{\sigma} = \frac{2.8 - 2.4}{0.2} = 2$$

The area between $\bar{X}$ and $\bar{X} - 2\sigma$ is 0.47725, using the table of areas under the normal curve. The same area is between $\bar{X}$ and $\bar{X} + 2\sigma$. Adding the two equal areas together, we get 0.9545, or approximately 95.5 per cent.

What percentage of time will it take between 2.0 and 3.0 hr?

$$\frac{X_L - \bar{X}}{\sigma} = \frac{2.0 - 2.4}{0.2} = -2$$
$$\frac{X_U - \bar{X}}{\sigma} = \frac{3.0 - 2.4}{0.2} = 3$$

From the table of normal areas, between $\bar{X}$ and $\bar{X} - 2\sigma$ is 0.47725 of the distribution; between $\bar{X}$ and $\bar{X} + 3\sigma$ is 0.49865. Adding these two relative frequencies together, we get 0.9759, or approximately 97.6 per cent.

What is the probability of it taking more than 3 hr?

$$\frac{X - \bar{X}}{\sigma} = \frac{3 - 2.4}{0.2} = 3$$

We desire to know the relative frequency of values greater than $\bar{X} + 3\sigma$. The area on each side of the mean in a normal distribution is one-half the total area, or 0.50000. The table of normal areas tells us that 0.49865 of the values are between $\bar{X}$ and $\bar{X} + 3\sigma$. If all the values greater than $\bar{X}$ total 0.50000 and those between $\bar{X}$ and $\bar{X} + 3\sigma$ total 0.49865, then those which are greater than $\bar{X} + 3\sigma$ total $0.50000 - 0.49865 = 0.00135$, or 0.14 per cent. The probability of it taking more than 3 hr is less than 14 in 10,000.

The normal distribution is symmetrical and therefore has zero skewness. When a distribution is only slightly skewed, the area under a normal distribution still gives a reasonable approximation to the probability values for most purposes.

The kurtosis (peakedness) of a normal distribution has a value of +3.

Normal Approximations to Other Distributions. The normal distribution gives a reasonable enough approximation to many other distributions. Because of the ease with which normal-curve areas can be used and analytically manipulated and because, in many cases, the answers obtained using the normal distribution do not differ significantly from those obtained using the true distribution, the normal distribution is widely used in decision-making instead of the more precise distributions it approximates. We can thus avoid spending a lot of effort to obtain a great theoretical accuracy which has little practical significance.

The binomial distribution approaches the shape of the normal distribution as the number of trials, n, becomes very large. Also, the closer the value of p is to 0.5, the faster does the binomial approach the normal distribution as the size of n increases. We thus find that the error of using the normal distribution as an approximation to the binomial is small, even with relatively small values of n, if p is reasonably close to 0.5. In general, if np is greater than 5, the normal distribution will give an approximation to the binomial which is good enough for most economic decision-making purposes.

The probability of a part being defective is 0.05. What is the probability that there will be 15 or more defective parts in a lot of 200 parts? We compute

$$\bar{X} = np = 200(0.05) = 10$$
$$\sigma = \sqrt{np(1 - p)} = \sqrt{200(0.05)(0.95)} = 3.08$$

We desire to know the relative frequency of lots which will have more than 14 defective parts.

$$\frac{X - \bar{X}}{\sigma} = \frac{14 - 10}{3.08} = 1.30$$

Using the table of areas under the normal curve, we find that 0.4032 of the area is between $\bar{X}$ and $\bar{X} + 1.30\sigma$. Therefore,

$$0.5000 - 0.4032 = 0.0968$$

of the area is above $\bar{X} + 1.30\sigma$. Therefore, approximately 10 per cent of the time there will be 15 or more defectives in a lot of 200 parts.

The Poisson distribution also approaches the shape of the normal curve as the expected or average number of occurrences, c, becomes very large. Thus, for most economic decision purposes, when the average number of occurrences is greater than 50, the probabilities of the normal distribution may be used as a reasonable approximation of the Poisson.

For example, the number of telephone calls received by the sales department on Mondays averages 81. What is the probability of receiving more than 100 calls on a Monday (assuming that the Poisson process does not change)?

$$\bar{X} = c = 81$$
$$\sigma = \sqrt{c} = \sqrt{81} = 9$$
$$\frac{X - \bar{X}}{\sigma} = \frac{100 - 81}{9} = 2.11$$

Using the table of areas under the normal curve, we find that 0.4826 of the area is between $\bar{X}$ and $\bar{X} + 2.11\sigma$. Therefore,

$$0.5000 - 0.4826 = 0.0174$$

of the area is above $\bar{X} + 2.11\sigma$. The probability of receiving more than 100 calls on a Monday because of chance factors is therefore slightly less than 2 per cent.

Statistical Control. The binomial, Poisson, exponential, normal, and other probability distributions are based upon the process operating under physical conditions of statistical control. A condition of statistical control exists when the expected or average probabilities of occurrence of events remain constant and when variations from these expected values are caused by numerous independent causes of the same order of magnitudes. The numerous causes are frequently called chance causes. When these chance causes tend to cause deviations above and below the mean to equal degrees, the distribution tends to be normal.

In practice, one cannot blindly assume that a distribution will follow a normal or any other pattern based solely upon the physical conditions of the process or operation. It is necessary to compare the shape of the sample distribution with the theoretical one to ascertain if the assumption is a reasonable one.[1]

Distributions of Sums. If we determine that the mean time to pick a a customer's order is 3.6 min with $\sigma = 0.3$ min and the mean time to pack it for shipment is 4.3 min with $\sigma = 0.2$ min, then the mean time to pick and pack an order is $\bar{X}_{\text{pick and pack}} = \bar{X}_{\text{pick}} + \bar{X}_{\text{pack}} = 3.6 + 4.3 = 7.9$ min. If I receive 500 orders, the mean time to pick and pack them is

$$7.9(500) = 3{,}950 \text{ min}$$

How much dispersion can I expect about this mean value? If the time to pick and the time to pack are not affected or related to each other (independent, not correlated), the standard deviation of the time to pick and pack is equal to the square root of the sum of the squares of the individual standard deviations of the time to pick and the time to pack.

$$\sigma_{\text{pick and pack}} = \sqrt{\sigma^2_{\text{pick}} + \sigma^2_{\text{pack}}} = \sqrt{(0.3)^2 + (0.2)^2} = 0.36$$

The standard deviation of 0.36 is less than the arithmetic sum of 0.3 and 0.2. This is reasonable. The operation of chance will cause some of the longer pick times to be coupled with some shorter pack times and some shorter pick times will be coupled with longer pack times. This will result in an averaging out of some of the dispersion in the separate distributions.

Distributions of Differences. If a picker and a packer worked as a team, with no intermingling of functions, how much time, on the average, would the picker be idle if a big enough reservoir of work were always available to keep the packer busy. The mean idle time for the picker would be $\bar{X}_{\text{pack}-\text{pick}} = \bar{X}_{\text{pack}} - \bar{X}_{\text{pick}} = 4.3 - 3.6 = 0.7$ min per order.

What is the standard deviation of this idle time, still assuming independence of the two variables, pick and pack? The standard deviation of the difference ($\sigma_{\text{pack}-\text{pick}}$) is the same as the standard deviation of the sum ($\sigma_{\text{pick}+\text{pack}}$).

$$\sigma_{\text{pack}-\text{pick}} = \sqrt{\sigma^2_{\text{pack}} + \sigma^2_{\text{pick}}}$$

It is reasonable to expect that the standard deviation of the difference will be the same as the standard deviation of the sum and be less than the arithmetic sum of the separate standard deviations. You would expect that the operation of chance will cause some of the longer pack times to be coupled with longer pick times and the shorter pack times with the shorter pick times to average out some of the dispersion in the separate distributions. This should operate in the same proportion of cases that chance factors cause some of the longer pack times to be coupled with shorter pick times and shorter pack times with longer pick times, which causes

---

[1] Statistical procedures for testing an assumption of normality or any other pattern are presented in the probability and statistics references cited in the Bibliography at the end of this book.

the standard deviation of the sum to be less than the arithmetic sum of the separate standard deviations.

Normality of Sums or Differences. When values from normal distributions are added or subtracted from each other, the distributions of the sums or differences are normal. Thus, if the distribution of the time to pick an order and the distribution of the time to pack an order are both normal, the distributions of their sums and differences will both be normal.

Prospective Cost of Rejects. We assemble three sections of a shaft end to end in the manufacture of a control mechanism. The sections are chosen randomly. The tolerance for the length of the shaft is 8.000 $\pm$ 0.020. In the production of the shafts, we are able to obtain the following values for the mean and standard deviations of each section.

Section	Mean length	Standard deviation of length
1	3.500	0.003
2	1.750	0.002
3	2.750	0.006

The distributions of the lengths of each section are normal.

To enable us to estimate the cost of assemblies which will be rejected because they are outside the tolerance, we want to determine the percentage of the assemblies which will be outside the tolerance limits. The mean length of the sum of the three sections is

$$\bar{X}_s = \bar{X}_1 + \bar{X}_2 + \bar{X}_3 = 3.500 + 1.750 + 2.750 = 8.000$$

The standard deviation of the sum of the three section lengths is

$$\sigma_s = \sqrt{\sigma_1{}^2 + \sigma_2{}^2 + \sigma_3{}^2} = \sqrt{(0.003)^2 + (0.002)^2 + (0.006)^2} = 0.007$$

The tolerance limits of 8.000 $\pm$ 0.020 give us an upper value of 8.020 and a lower value of 7.980.

$$8.020 \text{ is equal to } \bar{X}_s + \frac{0.020}{0.007}\sigma_s = \bar{X}_s + 2.86\sigma_s$$

$$7.980 \text{ is equal to } \bar{X}_s - \frac{0.020}{0.007}\sigma_s = \bar{X}_s - 2.86\sigma_s$$

Using the table of areas under the normal curve, we find that

$$0.4979 + 0.4979 = 0.9958$$

or, almost 99.6 per cent of the shaft assemblies will be within tolerance and approximately 0.4 per cent will therefore be outside tolerance.

If the reject cost is high, we may investigate the relative desirability and economy of such alternatives as changing the production process on one or more of the shaft sections to obtain less dispersion in the lengths; increasing the tolerances if this can be done without materially decreasing the usefulness of the product; changing the material or other aspects of the design. The preceding methodology will enable us to estimate costs of rejects under various alternatives.

PROBLEMS

1. You toss three true dice at one time. You would like to know the relative frequencies (probabilities) that you will obtain no 5, one 5, two 5s, and three 5s on a single throw. (a) Why would you expect these frequencies to follow the binomial distribution? (b) Write the successive terms of the binomial distribution which will indicate these probabilities and compute their values. (c) Plot a frequency histogram for this binomial distribution. (d) What is the arithmetic mean of this binomial distribution? (e) What is the standard deviation of the distribution?

2. The probability of a defective part being produced when a certain press in a factory is operating under statistical control has been established as 0.04. Assuming that it will continue to operate under control, (a) why would you expect that the number of defective parts produced should follow the binomial distribution? (b) What is the expected number (arithmetic mean) of defective parts in a sample of 50? (c) What is the standard deviation of the number of defective parts in samples of 50?

3. The average number of surface defects on a certain type and size of earthenware jar produced by the Mordel Company is 6.2 when the process is under control. (a) Why would you expect the distribution of number of surface defects to follow the Poisson distribution? (b) Write the successive terms of the Poisson distribution which will indicate the relative frequencies of obtaining jars with 0 to 13 surface defects and compute their values. (c) Plot a frequency histogram for this Poisson distribution. (d) What is the arithmetic mean of the number of defects on a jar? (e) What is the standard deviation of the number of defects on a jar?

4. A machine, operating under statistical control, is producing a certain type of optical lens of $\frac{3}{4}$-in. diameter with an average of 0.225 flaws per lens. Using the Poisson graph, determine the probability of obtaining a lens with (a) no flaws, (b) 4 or more flaws.

5. The Mordel Company kept a record of the lengths of time between receipt of successive incoming telephone calls in the sales department. It found that the distribution of these times did not conform to the exponential distribution. (a) Why would some people think it should be an exponential distribution? (b) What are some of the possible reasons that it is not an exponential distribution in this case?

6. The average number of working days between significant injuries requiring first aid in the cutting department of a company is 3.4. If this distribution follows an exponential pattern, what is the standard deviation of this distribution?

7. The average weight of a die casting is 4.25 oz; the standard deviation is 0.20 oz; and the distribution of die casting weights follows the normal distribution. (a) What percentage of castings are outside the specifications of 4.00 to 4.75 oz? (b) What percentage of the castings weigh more than 5.05 oz? (c) If we can adjust the die casting machine to change the average weight of casting produced but not the amount of dispersion about the average, what average weight will give us the lowest percentage outside the specifications? What will this lowest percentage be?

8. Answer the following questions, using the normal distribution for an approximate solution wherever it is appropriate. (a) The number of defects per 10,000 sq yd of a certain cloth is 61. What is the probability of having less than 40 defects in a shipment of 10,000 sq yd? (b) The probability that the diameter of a shaft will fall outside specifications is 0.1. What is the probability that there will be 1 shaft with diameter outside specifications in a lot of 10? (c) The number of accidents per month in a certain department of a company averages 0.80. What is the probability of having no accidents in a month? (d) The percentage defectives produced by a machine is 0.004. What is the probability that there will be 2 or more defectives in a shipment of 3,000 pieces?

9. The Marlow Manufacturing Co. is considering the purchase of two new pieces of equipment to replace two currently used machines to manufacture four components which are assembled together end to end. The nominal dimensions of the components are 1.000, 1.500, 2.750, and 4.000 in. The specifications call for a total length of 9.250 in. ± 0.015 in. The currently used machines are capable of manufacturing these components with the following standard deviations, respectively: 0.005, 0.004, 0.010, and 0.008 in. The distributions are approximately normal and the machines can be kept adjusted so that their arithmetic means are always equal to the nominal dimensions of each of the components. The new machines will be capable of manufacturing these components with the following standard deviations respectively: 0.002, 0.003, 0.005, and 0.002 in. Each year 10,000 components are required. The average out-of-pocket factory cost of each component rejected because it is outside specification is $4.65. There is 100 per cent inspection of all components.

    (a) Determine the annual cost of rejected components using the current machines.

    (b) Determine the prospective annual savings in the cost of rejected components using the two new pieces of equipment.

    (c) If the current equipment has no salvage value and all costs will remain the same for the new equipment, except the afore-mentioned saving in cost of rejected components, how much would Marlow be justified in spending on this new equipment if a 10 per cent before-tax return is desired on the investment and if the economic life of the new assets is estimated at 12 years with no salvage value?

10. The critical dimension in a product is the difference between the outside diameter of a shaft and the inside diameter of a sleeve which fits over the shaft. The nominal diameter of the shaft is 1.400 in. and the nominal inside

diameter of the sleeve is 1.406 in. The clearance in each case is equal to the difference between the sleeve inside diameter and the shaft outside diameter. Since the machines which produce these parts can be kept adjusted so that their arithmetic means are always equal to the nominal dimensions of the shafts and the sleeves, the average clearance is 0.006 in. The minimum clearance for assembly is 0.001 in. The currently used equipment is capable of manufacturing shafts and sleeves with standard deviations of 0.002 and 0.004 in. respectively. The distributions are approximately normal. What percentage will be capable of being assembled if shafts and sleeves are assembled randomly?

23   Sampling and Confidence Limits

The problem of sampling is to determine what can be said about a population or universe when we have examined only a limited number of its members. It is frequently impossible and usually uneconomic to try to examine an entire population.

In Chapter 21 we estimated that the average number of items on orders received by the Wimpole Company was 53.6. We determined this by examining a sample of 50 orders. When making an economic evaluation, we may then assume that the mean number of items on all orders of the Wimpole Company is 53.6. In making this assumption, we understand that there is a risk that the actual number of items on any order will be more or less than 53.6 by varying amounts; and that there is uncertainty that 53.6 is the true mean of all orders received by the Wimpole Company. The theory of sampling is concerned with this latter question: how confident are we that 53.6 is the true mean?

To ascertain the average number of items on the orders received by the Wimpole Company, we selected at random 50 orders. We then used this sample of 50 orders as representative of all orders received and to be received by the Wimpole Company. All of the orders is called the population or universe from which we took a sample of 50.

The mean of our sample distribution of number of items on an order was 53.6 and the standard deviation was 7.1. What is our best estimate of the mean and standard deviation of the entire population of values?

Unbiased Estimates of Population Parameters. We shall denote the population mean as $\bar{X}'$ and the population standard deviation as σ' to distinguish them from the sample values of $\bar{X}$ and σ.

$\bar{X}$ is an unbiased[1] estimate of $\bar{X}'$. This means that since our sample mean number of items on an order was 53.6, our unbiased estimate of the mean number on all orders is the same 53.6. However, σ is not an unbiased estimate of σ'.

$$\sigma'_{\text{est}} = \sqrt{\frac{\Sigma(X - \bar{X})^2}{N - 1}} = \sigma\sqrt{\frac{N}{N - 1}}$$

[1] A statistic is an unbiased estimate of a population parameter, such as a mean or a standard deviation, if its average (expected) value is the parameter value. Thus, the average of sample means, $\bar{X}$, is equal to the population mean, $\bar{X}'$. However, the average of sample standard deviations, $\bar{\sigma}$, is not equal to σ'.

Thus the σ of our sample, which equals 7.1, must be multiplied by $\sqrt{\frac{50}{49}}$ to obtain our estimate of the standard deviation we would have obtained if we had examined the entire population. Our σ'_{est} thus equals 7.17.

The factor $\sqrt{N/(N-1)}$ becomes insignificant when N becomes large. When N is small, however, the size of the sample does not allow enough room for variation about the sample mean value to produce an unbiased estimate of the population mean.

If I were to take another random sample of 50 orders and determine the mean, chances are that the mean would not be exactly 53.6. If I were to take a very large number of samples of 50 orders each, I could obtain a distribution of sample means. The mean of the sample means would be equal to the mean of the population ($\bar{X}'$) if I took enough samples. Therefore, when I have several samples, my best estimate of $\bar{X}'$ is $\bar{\bar{X}}$, the mean of the sample means.

Standard Error of the Mean. How much dispersion will there be of the sample means about the population mean? The larger the size of the sample, the less the dispersion we would expect. Each larger random sample will be more representative of the population and the means from these samples should vary less from the population mean than the means from smaller samples. The standard deviation of the sample means is called the standard error of the mean ($\sigma_{\bar{X}}$). It is equal to the standard deviation of the population divided by the square root of the size of the samples.

$$\sigma_{\bar{X}} = \frac{\sigma'}{\sqrt{N}}$$

In our example the standard error of the mean number of items on an order equals $\dfrac{\sigma'_{est}}{\sqrt{N}} = \dfrac{7.17}{\sqrt{50}} = 1.01$, or 1.0.

Even though the distribution of the population of values is not normal, the distribution of mean values tends to be normal. For example, the skewness of the distribution of means equals (skewness of population)/N and the kurtosis equals [(kurtosis of population -3)/N] $+3$. Thus, the larger the sample size, the more nearly normal will be the distribution of $\bar{X}$ values even if the population values are not normal. For example, if a sample of 50 is taken from a population with a skewness value of 8 (highly skewed) and a kurtosis value of 10 (highly peaked), the distribution of means would have skewness and kurtosis values very close to normal: skewness equal to $\frac{8}{50}$, or 0.16, and kurtosis equal to [(10 -3)/50] $+3$, or 3.14.

This property of the distribution of the mean of samples is important in many applications because it enables us to use the normal distribution to evaluate the precision with which we can make cost and other estimates based upon our samples.

Confidence Limits. Our $\bar{X}'_{\text{est}} = 53.6$ for the number of items on an order was computed from a sample of 50 randomly chosen orders. The probability that the true mean of the population of all orders is exactly 53.6 is infinitesimally small. We can express our confidence in the precision of this estimate of 53.6 in terms of confidence or fiducial limits.

If the population mean were as low as 51.6, the probability distribution of sample means would be as shown in Figure 23-1. From this chart we can see that the probability of obtaining a sample mean as high as 53.6 or higher from a population with a mean of 51.6 is given by the area outside the 2σ distance from the mean on one side of the normal curve. The table of areas under the normal curve shows 0.47725 of the area between the mean and 2σ. Therefore, $0.50000 - 0.47725 = 0.02275$, which is outside the 2σ limits on one side of the normal curve. Only 2.28 per cent of the time would we get a sample mean as high as 53.6 or higher from a population with a mean of 51.6. If we were to say, therefore, that our sample mean of 53.6 came from a population with a mean no lower than 51.6, we would be wrong only 2.28 per cent of the time. We are, therefore, 97.72 per cent confident that the sample mean came from a population with a mean of 51.6 or higher.

If the population mean were as high as 55.6, the probability distribution of sample means would be as shown in Figure 23-2. We can see from this

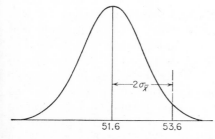

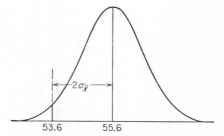

Figure 23-1. Distribution of sample means—assumed population mean of 51.6 items.

Figure 23-2. Distribution of sample means—assumed population mean of 55.6 items.

chart that the probability of obtaining a sample mean as low or lower than 53.6 is also given by the area outside the 2σ distance from the mean on one side of the normal curve and is therefore equal to 0.02275. Only 2.28 per cent of the time would we get a sample mean as low as 53.6 or lower from a population with a mean of 55.6. If we were to say, therefore, that our sample mean of 53.6 came from a population with a mean no higher than 55.6, we would be wrong only 2.28 per cent of the time. We are, therefore, 97.72 per cent confident that the sample mean came from a population with a mean of 55.6 or lower.

And we would, therefore, be wrong only 2.28 per cent plus 2.28 per cent, or 4.56 per cent, of the time if we were to say that our sample mean came from a population with a mean between 51.6 and 55.6. These two figures, 51.6 and 55.6, are our 95.46 per cent confidence or fiducial limits. We are approximately 95 per cent confident that the sample mean of 53.6 came from a population with a mean between 51.6 and 55.6.

Let us generalize the procedure just described for computing confidence limits for a sample mean value. Our confidence limits are obtained by adding and subtracting a certain number of standard errors of the mean to and from the sample mean. The number of $\sigma_{\bar{x}}$s is based on the normal distribution and depends upon what confidence level we desire. Table 23-1 summarizes these values for various commonly used confidence levels.

Table **23-1. Normal Distribution Confidence Limits**

Confidence level	Number of standard deviations or standard errors
90.0%	1.65
95.0	1.96
95.5	2.00
99.0	2.58
99.7	3.00
99.9	3.29

Stability of Population and Statistical Control. It might be well at this point to pause and examine briefly some of the implications and assumptions of what we have done. It was pointed out in Chapter 22 that a condition of statistical control exists when the expected or average probabilities of occurrence of events remain constant or change in accordance with a predetermined pattern and when variations from these expected values are randomly distributed. From a sampling viewpoint, a condition of statistical control exists when it is possible to predict the probability of future values falling within specified limits. This is possible only when the probability of future values falling within specified limits is constant or is changing in accordance with a known pattern.

A sample mean is an unbiased estimate of the population mean only if a condition of statistical control exists. If the population is unstable (does not exhibit the characteristics of statistical control), then confidence limits cannot be assigned to an estimate of the population mean.

In our example, we established as our population the number of items on all orders received by the Wimpole Company. It is possible that orders received on Monday tend to have a different average number of items per order than those received during the remainder of the week. If the ratio of the number of orders received on Monday to the rest of the week is constant, excluding random variations, this need not produce instability. However, if this ratio is not constant, then the population is unstable and we do not have statistical control. What we may do, in this case, is to divide our orders into two populations: orders received on Monday; and orders received during the remainder of the week. We can now compute separate estimates of the population means and variances for Mondays and for the remainder of the week.

Confidence limits are not statistically valid unless the phenomenon is under statistical control, although they may nevertheless be useful. Statistical control can sometimes be obtained by dividing one population into several more homogeneous populations and working separately with each population. This possibility was previously suggested for the number of items on orders of the Wimpole Company. In other cases, the cause of the instability can be eliminated. Thus, if material usage and costs exhibit instability because of variations in the composition of raw material delivered by different suppliers, the suppliers may be required to maintain more uniform composition standards and inspection procedures may be established to enforce these standards.

The use of statistical methods and graphic control charts to test for the stability of a population is discussed briefly in Chapter 24.

Student's t **Distribution.** When we use a small sample to estimate the standard deviation of the population, we find that we cannot use the normal distribution to estimate the area between the mean and any given deviation from the mean. The distribution of the probability of deviations when σ' is estimated from small samples is known as Student's t distribution. This distribution is more spread out than the normal distribution and is different for each sample size used to estimate σ'.

Student's t distribution is presented in the Appendix to this book. The values in the body of the table indicate the number of standard-error unit deviations from the mean of the universe $[(\bar{X} - \bar{X}')/\sigma_{\bar{x}}]$ which will give an area outside these deviations equal to the probabilities shown in the column headings.

The degrees of freedom refer to the sample size from which σ' is estimated. If σ' is estimated from one sample of 18 items, the number of degrees of freedom is 17. (One degree of freedom is lost in calculating $\Sigma(X - \bar{X})^2$: given the mean, $\bar{X}$, and 17 other items, the 18th item value is determined and cannot vary.) If σ' is estimated by weighting two sample standard-deviation values, one of 18 items and the other of 10 items, the degrees of freedom are $(18 - 1) + (10 - 1)$, or 26. If the 28 individual random items in the two samples are combined to calculate the σ'_{est}, then the degrees of freedom are $28 - 1 = 27$.

As the size of sample used to estimate σ' increases, Student's t distribution approaches the normal one. Student's t distribution is exactly the same as the normal distribution when the sample is infinite. For practically all purposes of economic evaluation, the normal distribution can be used in place of Student's t distribution when the sample size exceeds 30.

Confidence Limits Using Student's t Distribution. The basis for establishing confidence limits when using Student's t distribution is exactly the same as when the normal distribution is used. For example, the average weight of a sample of 9 castings produced on a machine under controlled conditions is 34.2 lb and $\sigma'_{est} = 1.5$ lb. With what confidence can I estimate the population mean as 34.2 lb?

If I desire to establish 99 per cent confidence limits, then I want to be able to say that only 1 per cent of the time will I be wrong. Student's t distribution shows that for 8 degrees of freedom and a probability of 0.01, my deviation from the mean is $3.355\sigma_{\bar{x}}$. My 99 per cent confidence limits therefore become $\bar{X}' \pm 3.355\sigma_{\bar{x}} = 34.2 \pm 3.355 (1.5/\sqrt{9}) = 35.9$ to 32.5. The 90 per cent confidence limits would be $34.2 \pm 1.860 (1.5/\sqrt{9}) = 35.1$ to 33.3 and 99.9 per cent confidence limits would be $34.2 \pm 5.041 (1.5/\sqrt{9}) = 36.7$ to 31.7. The higher the degree of confidence we desire, the wider the range of possible population values we must specify. The narrower the permitted range, the lower the confidence level, other things being equal.

Student's t distribution is valid for sampling from a normal population. We noted in our previous discussion of the sampling distribution of the mean that the distribution of sample means from nonnormal populations is more normal than the population. The larger the sample, the greater is this normalizing effect. Thus, even with samples of less than 30, we can usually use Student's t distribution safely with distributions which are moderately nonnormal. This includes the kinds of distributions most frequently occurring in industrial and business decision-making.

Confidence Limits on Distribution of Differences of Sample Means. In considering the advantages of purchasing two alternative pieces of equipment, an engineer measured the number of minutes the operator spent to produce a random sample of 15 components on machine A and the time to produce a random sample of 10 components on machine B. The results are summarized below.

Machine A	Machine B
$N_A = 15$	$N_B = 10$
$\bar{X}_A = 18.4$ min	$\bar{X}_B = 12.8$ min
$\sigma_A = 1.7$ min	$\sigma_B = 1.9$ min

There is a difference of $18.4 - 12.8 = 5.6$ min in the average time to produce a component. How much confidence do we have in this estimated saving of time?

If the two population standard deviations are equal, then our best estimate of the standard deviation of the populations is

$$\sigma'_{est} = \sqrt{\frac{N_A\sigma_A{}^2 + N_B\sigma_B{}^2}{N_A + N_B - 2}} = \sqrt{\frac{(N_A - 1)(\sigma'_{A,est})^2 + (N_B - 1)(\sigma'_{B,est})^2}{N_A + N_B - 2}}$$

Both forms of the above equation are equivalent. Either can be used, depending upon whether σ or σ'_{est} of the individual samples were originally computed. The numerators under the square root in both cases equal $\Sigma(X_A - \bar{X}_A)^2 + \Sigma(X_B - \bar{X}_B)^2$. The denominators equal the number of degrees of freedom, $(N_A - 1) + (N_B - 1) = N_A + N_B - 2$.

For our example,

$$\sigma'_{est} = \sqrt{\frac{15(1.7)^2 + 10(1.9)^2}{15 + 10 - 2}} = 1.86$$

The standard error of the difference between two means is

$$\sigma_{\bar{X}_A - \bar{X}_B} = \sqrt{\sigma_{\bar{X}_A}^2 + \sigma_{\bar{X}_B}^2}$$

This equation is analogous to the standard deviation of a difference previously presented in Chapter 22.

$$\sigma_{\bar{X}_A - \bar{X}_B} = \sqrt{\frac{(\sigma')^2}{N_A} + \frac{(\sigma')^2}{N_B}} = \sigma' \sqrt{\frac{1}{N_A} + \frac{1}{N_B}}$$

For our example,

$$\sigma_{\bar{X}_A - \bar{X}_B} = 1.86 \sqrt{\tfrac{1}{15} + \tfrac{1}{10}} = 0.76$$

If we knew σ' or estimated it from a large enough sample, we could establish the confidence limits using the normal distribution. In this case, we estimated σ' from samples having a total of 23 degrees of freedom, so we use Student's t distribution.

Our 95 per cent confidence limits (0.05 outside the limits) are given by

$$(\bar{X}_A - \bar{X}_B) \pm 2.069\sigma_{\bar{X}_A - \bar{X}_B}$$
$$(18.4 - 12.8) \pm 2.069(0.76) = 5.6 \pm 1.6$$

We are 95 per cent confident that the true difference in the average times is between 7.2 and 4.0 min.

Confidence Limits for a Proportion. To estimate the percentage of orders received for less than \$10 worth of merchandise, we take a random sample of 100 orders. We find 27 are below \$10 in value. The proportion below \$10 in value is thus $\tfrac{27}{100} = 0.27$. How confident are we of this proportion?

We can establish confidence intervals using the normal distribution as an approximation to the binomial because the sample is large and the proportion is not very small. However, we have charts available for determining the 80, 90, 95, and 99 per cent confidence limits for population proportions. These are presented in Figures 23-3 to 23-6. These charts present confidence belts for various sample sizes.

To determine the 80 per cent confidence limits for our sample, we enter the chart of Figure 23-3 at the abscissa value of observed proportion of

0.27 and go up vertically until we come to the first $n = 100$ line. At this point we move horizontally to the ordinate scale and read off the population proportion of 0.215 as our lower confidence limit. To determine our upper confidence limit, we return to our abscissa proportion of 0.27 and continue up vertically until we reach the second $n = 100$ line. We move over horizontally at this point and read off on the ordinate scale the population proportion of 0.33 as our upper confidence limit.

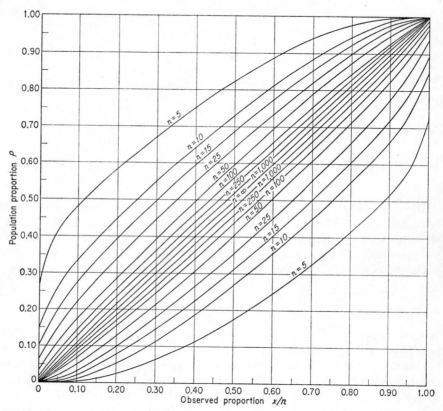

Figure 23-3. Eighty per cent confidence belts for population proportion. SOURCE: Eisenhart, C., M. W. Hastay, and W. A. Wallis, *Selected Techniques of Statistical Analysis*—OSRD, McGraw-Hill Book Company, Inc., 1947.

Following similar procedures, we can determine the 90, 95, or 99 per cent confidence belts, which, of course, are wider as the confidence percentage increases.

For sample sizes other than those shown in the charts, we can interpolate visually to estimate approximate confidence limits which are accurate enough for most economic decision-making purposes.

Confidence Limits on Range of Values. If we take a random small sample, we can not have much confidence that the range of the sample will include a large percentage of the population.   The larger the sample we take, the greater our confidence that the range of the sample includes a given percentage of the population. S. S. Wilks[1] developed a formula which tells us quantitatively how much confidence we can have that the highest and lowest values of a random sample will include a given

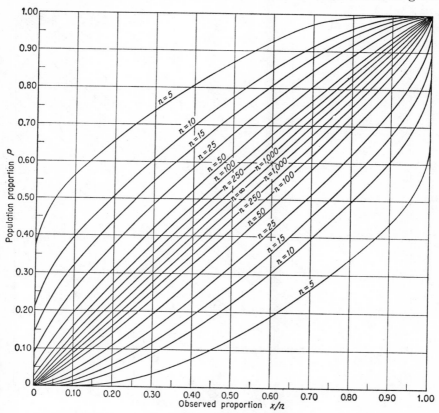

Figure 23-4. Ninety per cent confidence belts for population proportion. SOURCE: Eisenhart, C., M. W. Hastay, and W. A. Wallis, *Selected Techniques of Statistical Analysis*—OSRD, McGraw-Hill Book Company, Inc., 1947.

percentage of the population. If we let ϵ represent the assurance that we desire that 100β per cent of the population is included within the range of a random sample, the size of the sample, N, should satisfy the following relationship:

$$N\beta^{N-1} - (N - 1)\beta^N = 1 - \epsilon$$

[1] S. S. Wilks, *Mathematical Statistics*, Princeton University Press, Princeton, N.J., 1943, p. 94.

Birnbaum and Zuckerman[1] developed a graphic method for determining the sample size, N, based on this formula.

In many economy studies, we want to estimate the worst and best results which may occur under various possible alternative courses of action. The Birnbaum and Zuckerman procedure can sometimes give us an insight into how much confidence we should have that the range of our sample values (best and worst values) is wide enough.

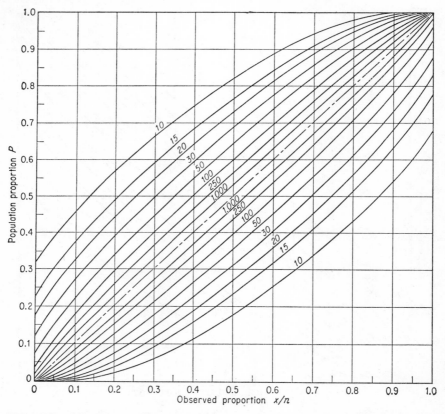

Figure 23-5. Ninety-five per cent confidence belts for population proportion. Source: Eisenhart, C., M. W. Hastay, and W. A. Wallis, *Selected Techniques of Statistical Analysis*—OSRD, McGraw-Hill Book Company, Inc., 1947.

For example, we plan on taking a random sample of the setup costs under present operating conditions for certain types of milling operations in our factory. We want to obtain smallest and largest values to obtain best and worst estimations for our economy analysis. How large a sample

[1] Z. W. Birnbaum and H. S. Zuckerman, "A Graphical Determination of Sample Size for Wilks' Tolerance Limits," *Annals of Mathematical Statistics*, vol. 20, pp. 313–316.

should we take if we desire to be 98 per cent certain of including 95 per cent of the cases under current conditions in the factory (assuming they are under control). The graphic solution to this problem using Wilks' formula is shown in Figure 23-7. ϵ is equal to 0.98 and β equals 0.95. We need a sample of 115 to be 98 per cent certain that the highest and lowest values of our sample will include 95 per cent of all setup costs for this type of milling operation.

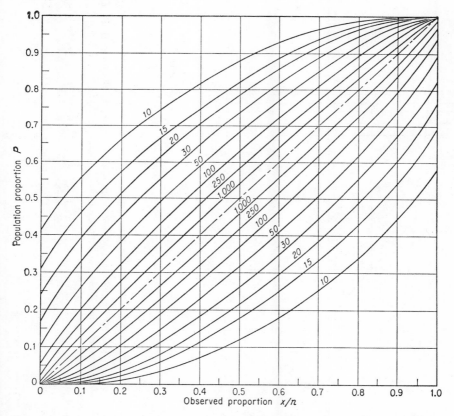

Figure 23-6. Ninety-nine per cent confidence belts for population proportion. SOURCE: Eisenhart, C., M. W. Hastay, and W. A. Wallis, *Selected Techniques of Statistical Analysis*—OSRD, McGraw-Hill Book Company, Inc., 1947.

Sampling from Finite Populations. The theoretical background of the preceding discussions of sampling was based on the assumption that the samples come from an infinite population. As long as the population is large enough so that the size of the sample is small as compared with the size of the finite population, any error from using the preceding relationships will not significantly affect our answer. In most cases we will be sampling under these circumstances.

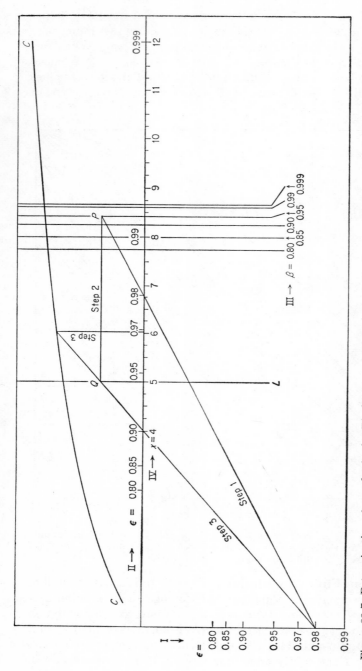

Figure 23-7. Determination of sample size by Birnbaum and Zuckerman chart. Source: Zuckerman, H. S., and Z. W. Birnbaum, "A Graphical Determination of Sample Size for Wilks' Tolerance Limits," *Annals of Mathematical Statistics*, vol. 20, pp 313–316.

To find an approximate solution of the equation $N\beta^{N-1} - (N-1)\beta^N = 1 - \epsilon$

Step 1-connect ϵ on Scale I and ϵ on Scale II with a straight line; this line cuts verticle line marked β on Scale III at point P,

Step 2-locate on line L the point with the ordinate of P; call this point Q,

Step 3-connect ϵ on Scale I with Q; the connecting line cuts curve C at a point which has abscissa x on Scale IV, read off x,

Step 4-compute $N = x\dfrac{\beta}{1-\beta} = 6.05\dfrac{.95}{1-.95} = 115.$

To determine the standard error of the sample mean from a finite population where the sample size is a significant proportion of the population size, we should multiply the σ'_{est} of the population by

$$\frac{1}{\sqrt{N_s}} \sqrt{\frac{N_p - N_s}{N_p - 1}}$$

where N_s = size of sample and N_p = size of population. When N_s is very small compared with N_p, $\sqrt{(N_p - N_s)/(N_p - 1)}$ approaches 1 and the formula is the same as for an infinite population.

Simple Random Sampling. Our previous presentations are predicated upon the taking of simple random samples, which means that the samples are chosen in such a way that each member of the population has an equal opportunity of being included in the sample. Random sampling also implies that every combination of members of the population has an equal opportunity of being included.

When the sampler has an element of choice in choosing the sample, there is always the danger of a bias being introduced unconsciously. To avoid such biases, randomness may be obtained by numbering the members of the population and then using a table of random numbers (see Chapter 25) or drawing numbers at random from a bowl to choose the population members to be included in the sample.

Many other methods of sampling are used. Under some conditions, these will give more precise knowledge of population values at the same cost or lower cost or give the same knowledge at lower cost than simple random sampling. These other sampling procedures include

1. Systematic random sampling
2. Stratified random sampling
3. Cluster sampling
4. Random sequential (variable-size) sampling
5. Judgment (purposive) sampling

Systematic Random Sampling. Systematic random sampling occurs when the members of the population are ordered or listed and every member at a fixed interval from the first one selected is chosen as part of the sample. The first one is selected at random, using a table of random numbers or some other device. In this method, every member has an equal opportunity of being included in the sample by virtue of the random choice of the first member. However, every combination of members does not have an equal opportunity of being included unless the order or listing is itself random.

When the order or listing is not random, then our previous formulations do not apply. The samples may nevertheless sometimes be more representative than a random sample; and they may sometimes give a considerably distorted result.

An example of a more representative systematic sample would be a study of buying habits or intentions of residents of an area. Systematic random sampling would not sample neighboring homes which resemble each other most, whereas simple random sampling would sample neighboring houses in a certain proportion of the cases.

Examples of distorted systematic sampling would be the sampling of the work load in the sales department at 9:30 a.m. and every 24 hours thereafter; or the sampling of the number of customers in one department of a store at intervals of every seven days. These samples would not be representative of other times of the day in the first case or of the other days of the week in the second case.

Stratified Random Sampling. In stratified random sampling the population is divided into subgroups or strata and random samples are taken from each subgroup. Stratified sampling requires a prior knowledge of population characteristics so that the population can be divided into subgroups which are more homogeneous (have less dispersion about the mean of the characteristics in the subgroup being studied). The sample values from each subgroup are combined to obtain an estimate for the entire population.

If we are studying the potential market for a new consumer product and desire to ascertain consumer attitudes to the new product and possible design variations, we would set up separate subgroups based upon criteria which have an effect on consumer buying attitudes toward the type of product we are planning to introduce. Some of these may be age, sex, education, rural-urban location, etc. Thus, one subgroup may be 30 to 40 years of age, female, college graduate, rural. The purpose is to get homogeneous groups which are different from each other. The degree of stratification and the total size of the sample will depend upon the relative costs and results desired.

The size of the sample in each subgroup may be

1. Proportionate to the size of each subgroup in the population.

2. Proportionate to the dispersion of values in each subgroup as well as the subgroup sizes in the population. If there is no dispersion of values in a subgroup with respect to the characteristic being studied, then the sample of one tells everything we want to know. If there is a great deal of dispersion of values in a subgroup, we need a larger sample to obtain the same standard error than we do from a subgroup with less dispersion of values.

If the costs of sampling are higher in some subgroups than in others, this factor may also be used to modify the sample sizes to obtain the greatest over-all accuracy at the allowable cost.

Where the size of the subgroup samples are proportionate to the size of the population in each subgroup, the simple arithmetic mean of the entire sample is computed as the best estimate of the population mean.

Where the relative dispersion in the subgroups, the costs of sampling, or other factors have resulted in nonproportionate subgroups, the mean of the population is estimated by weighting each subgroup sample mean by the proportion of the entire population in the subgroup to compute a weighted average.

The standard error of the sample mean of each subgroup can be computed in the manner previously described in this chapter. The confidence limits for each of these subgroup sample means can then be determined in the manner previously described for random samples.

We can compute the standard error of the stratified sample mean of the entire population from the estimated standard deviations of the subgroup populations. We shall use the following notation:

$\bar{X}_g$ = mean of subgroup sample

$\sigma'_{g,\text{est}}$ = estimated standard deviation of population of subgroup

N_p = number in entire population

N_{gp} = number in population of subgroup

N_{gs} = number in sample of subgroup

I_g = relative importance of subgroup (equals N_{gp}/N_p when population is finite)

$$\sigma'_{g,\text{est}} = \sqrt{\frac{\Sigma(X - \bar{X}_g)^2}{N_{gs} - 1}}$$

When the population is infinite or when the population is finite but the population in each subgroup is very large compared with the sample size in each subgroup,

Standard error of stratified sample mean $= \sigma_{\bar{X}} = \sqrt{\sum \left[\frac{I_g^2 (\sigma'_{g,\text{est}})^2}{N_{gs}} \right]}$

When the population is finite and the population in each stratum is not very large compared with the sample size, we apply a correction to our previous formula and obtain the following formula:

$$\sigma_{\bar{X}} = \sqrt{\sum \left[\frac{I_g^2 (\sigma'_{g,\text{est}})^2}{N_{gs}} \right] - \sum \left[\frac{I_g (\sigma'_{g,\text{est}})^2}{N_p} \right]}$$

Obviously, the better the stratification plan, i. e., the more homogeneous the subgroups which have been arranged, the smaller will be the $\sigma'_{g,\text{est}}$ values and the smaller will be the standard error of the mean of the total sample.

When the sample sizes are large, we can compute the standard error of the mean using this formula and determine our confidence limits using the normal distribution. When each subgroup provides only a few degrees of freedom, Student's t distribution is frequently used (though not strictly applicable, but the more exact methods are too complex to be worth the trouble in most economic analyses).

The standard error of the mean of a stratified random sample can be considerably less than that of an unstratified random sample when there is logical subgrouping. Thus, to estimate the average inventory which retailers carry of a certain item, we could take a random sample of 900 of the 90,000 retailers in the population and obtain $\bar{X} = 778$ and $\sigma'_{est} = 100$. We could divide the retailers into urban and rural subgroups. Taking a random sample of 500 of the 50,000 urban retailers, we obtain $\bar{X}_g = 1,000$ and $\sigma'_{g,est} = 60$. Taking a random sample of 400 of the 40,000 rural retailers, we obtain $\bar{X}_g = 500$ and $\sigma'_{g,est} = 50$. Since $\frac{5}{9}$ of the retailers are urban, $\bar{X}'_{est}$ of the entire population for the stratified sample equals

$$\frac{500(1,000) + 400(500)}{900} = 778.$$

For the random sample,

$$\sigma_{\bar{X}} = \frac{\sigma'_{est}}{\sqrt{N}} = \frac{100}{\sqrt{900}} = 3.3$$

For the stratified sample,

$$\sigma_{\bar{X}} = \sqrt{\sum \left[\frac{I_g{}^2(\sigma'_{g,est})^2}{N_{gs}} \right]} = \sqrt{\frac{(\frac{5}{9})^2(60)^2}{500} + \frac{(\frac{4}{9})^2(50)^2}{400}} = 1.9$$

Cluster Sampling. In cluster sampling, representative subgroups are selected by random sampling. This is done by one of the following methods:

1. Simple random sampling with each subgroup having an equal probability of being chosen

2. Random sampling with each subgroup having an opportunity of being selected proportionate to the number of population members in the subgroup

3. Stratified random sampling of the subgroups

The selected sample of the population would include one of the following:

1. All members in each selected subgroup

2. A simple random sample from each selected subgroup

3. A stratified random sample from each selected subgroup

For example, hourly earnings of factory workers in the United States may be sampled by selecting representative factories (subgroups of workers) by one of the following methods:

1. Simple random sampling of all factories in the United States, with each factory having an equal opportunity of being chosen

2. Random sampling of all factories in the United States, with each factory having an opportunity of being chosen proportional to its number of factory workers

3. Stratified random sampling of the factories, based upon subgroups of factories broken down by geographic area, industry, size, etc.

The selected sample of the population would include one of the following:

1. All the workers in the selected factories
2. A simple random sample of the workers in each selected factory
3. A stratified random sample of the workers in each selected factory

Random Sequential (Variable-size) Sampling. In sequential sampling after each small random sample of one or more members of the population is taken, a decision is made to continue or stop the random sampling. The decision is based upon the estimated population values disclosed by analysis of the samples taken up to that point. The mathematical procedures thus far developed for sequential sampling are chiefly useful in industrial inspection acceptance procedures.

Judgment (Purposive) Sampling. In many types of economic decisions, it is not economic to attempt to sample on a random basis. The time and costs involved are too large. A purposive sample may then be used in which the members of the sample are chosen based upon the judgment of the sample selector. The selector chooses the sample to agree with those aspects of the population which he considers significant for the purpose.

Purposive samples may be stratified and/or clustered and/or sequential. However, since the sample members are not chosen randomly, since each member of the population does not have an equal probability of being included in the sample, we cannot use probability distributions to place confidence limits on the population estimates.

Choice of Sampling Procedure. Choosing a sampling procedure is, in itself, an economic decision. How much is it worth spending for a greater confidence in the economic analysis? How much confidence is placed in the judgment of individuals in a purposive sample as opposed to the more objective determination of confidence possible when the samples are based upon procedures using probability laws?

PROBLEMS

1. You take a random sample of 40 bottles of a liquid product, measure the contents of each, and compute that the mean content ($\bar{X}$) equals 28.4 oz and the standard deviation (σ) equals 0.13 oz. What is your unbiased estimate of the population mean and standard deviation?

2. One of your colleagues proposes to repeat the process of taking samples of 40 bottles of the product of problem 1 many times and each time compute the mean of the number of ounces in the bottles. What is your best estimate of the mean and standard deviation (standard error) of the distribution of means which he will obtain?

3. Determine the 95, 99, and 99.9 per cent confidence limits for an estimate of the population-mean content of the bottles of problem 1 based upon this one random sample.

4. Carefully and explicitly state the meaning of the 99 per cent confidence limits you computed in problem 3.

5. Unaware of your sampling in problem 1, one of your colleagues took a random sample of 10 bottles rather than 40. His sample revealed an $\bar{X}$ of 28.4 oz and a σ of 0.13. (By coincidence, this is the same as the $\bar{X}$ and σ which you obtained in problem 1 with a sample of 40.) What is his unbiased estimate of the population mean and standard deviation?

6. (a) What are the 95, 99, and 99.9 per cent confidence limits for an estimate of the population mean content of the bottles based on your colleague's sample of problem 5? (b) Compare the differences in confidence limits calculated in problem 3 and those just calculated in (a) of this problem.

7. A methods engineer has redesigned the workplace layout for an assembly operation. He observed the times it took an operator to produce a random sample of 8 assemblies using the existing method as well as a random sample of 6 assemblies using his new proposed method. The times are shown below.

Present layout, minutes	Proposed layout, minutes
4.62	3.76
3.97	4.31
4.53	3.92
4.65	3.56
3.78	4.22
4.22	3.16
4.81	
4.40	

(a) What is your best estimate of the savings in assembly time which the new workplace layout will produce?

(b) How much confidence do you have in this estimate? (Express your confidence by computing 99 per cent confidence limits.)

8. To help evaluate some alternative proposed personnel policies, the Romberly Corporation desires to estimate the proportion of its 3,000 factory employees who own their own homes. It takes a random sample of 50 employees and finds that 23, or 46 per cent, of them own their own homes. From this sample, how confident can the Romberly Corporation be of the percentage of its factory employees who own their own homes? (Express this confidence using 95 per cent confidence limits.)

9. An engineer in the Romberly Corporation is investigating the operating economy of an automatic machine loading device which the company uses. One important factor is the amount of time required to connect the device each time a new setup is made on a machine. It is desirable to know the

longest and shortest times generally required for the connection. How large a random sample is needed to be 99 per cent certain that the highest and lowest values in the sample include 96 per cent of the population values of connection times?

10. What types of sampling design would be appropriate to determine each of the following? Explain why. (*a*) Voting intentions in a large city, (*b*) size of brackets being produced by a machine, (*c*) work load in a secretarial pool, (*d*) number of defects in 5,000 castings produced by a foundry, (*e*) buying intentions of housewives in a suburb, (*f*) buying intentions of housewives in a large city, (*g*) buying intentions of housewives in the United States.

24 Model Building and Simulation

In previous sections of this volume, we forecast the annual profits or costs of several alternative ways of performing an operation, manufacturing a product, or operating an entire business. In effect, we were simulating the real situation and arriving at a decision by the cut-and-try examination of the results.

Simulation is used here to mean the use of a model which takes account of those essentials of reality which are significant to the decision-making objective. A decision is reached by running various alternatives through the model and comparing results. The model does not have to look like reality, but it must give the results which reality will give with respect to the problems under study.

The inventory-control formulas in Chapters 18 and 21 are simulations of reality. They are useful only in those industrial situations which they truly simulate. The various rate-of-return computational procedures in Chapter 11 are good simulations only in the various industrial situations in which the realities of the situation match the assumptions in the different models. Some of the simpler models provide good simulations of certain types of business situations. However, they are applicable to a more limited number of situations than the more elaborate rate-of-return models which have fewer limiting assumptions.

Simulation and model building are thus terms used to describe activities in which we all engage a good deal of the time when we are making decisions.

Recent advances in mathematical and statistical methods and the development of high-speed computers have made it possible to use simulation and model building more effectively in many areas of economic decision-making. Models can now be more complex and more realistic and still be within the capacity of the new computing machines. High-speed computers in conjunction with simulation techniques also assist in evaluating risk and uncertainty: Monte Carlo techniques can be used in many situations to assist in evaluating risk; the economic consequences of possible alternative outcomes can be determined to assist in evaluating uncertainty.

Before proceeding to the main body of our discussion of models and simulation, one word of caution is in order. It is not always economic to attempt to develop realistic, refined, or mathematical models. One should relate the costs of model construction to the potential benefits from its use.

Models. Models provide ways of simulating reality. We are all familiar with many varieties of models. The models we most commonly recognize as such are those in which some spatial relations are preserved, in which the model resembles reality in appearance to a great degree: a physical duplication, such as the prototype of a new aircraft design; a smaller-sized version of reality, such as a reduced-size model of a bridge or a globe with elevations and depressions corresponding to the earth's surface; a reduced capacity, and sometimes simplified, operation, such as a pilot plant; a reduced dimension, as well as reduced-size model, such as a photograph (two dimensions instead of three).

Next we come to models in which appearance starts to deviate from reality, but in which all of the properties of the actual situation which are important for the analytic purposes at hand are represented by other analogous properties. For example, a contour map of one section of the earth's surface shows by contour lines the changes in elevation which are pictured on the globe. A road map may have heavy solid lines to indicate highways of four lanes or more, light solid lines to indicate other first-class all-weather hard-surfaced roads, and dashed lines to indicate all other roads. It then shows what a composite aerial photograph would reveal, but the road map does not preserve the real appearance of the roads. A layout diagram of a factory shows diagrammatically spatial relationships but does not preserve the appearances as a real model or photograph would.

Charts and graphs of all kinds are analogous models of reality: length of a bar or distance from an axis used to represent any property we can measure, such as distance, area, size, weight, quantity, differences or percentages, etc. A flow chart showing the flow of materials in a process or of information in a reporting system is another example of an analogous model. Sometimes we can construct devices which will operate in an analogous manner to another machine or a whole factory. (A computer may be programmed to act as such a device.)

Finally, we come to mathematical models which are even further removed from the physical appearance of reality. In these models, symbolism is used to specify succinctly the significant relationship using mathematical notations to describe how the factors under scrutiny behave in reality. The mathematical formulations in the inventory models of Chapter 18 and in the maximization and minimization models of Chapter 19 are examples. The optimum alternative in these cases is determined analytically from the mathematical manipulation of the model.

Experimentation and analysis are facilitated more and more as we move from reality to models preserving the appearance of reality, to the analogous models, to the mathematical ones. Thus, experimentation on the operating characteristics of a chemical process under a wide variety of types of changes in all kinds of conditions can be performed in the real plant only at prohibitive cost. It can be done more economically in a pilot plant.

Manipulation of variables could be done still more economically in a device such as a computer programmed to act in a manner analogous to the plant. A series of mathematical equations would generally be the cheapest to manipulate and solve for various optimum solutions. However, the economy of experimentation and analysis must be balanced against the costs of developing the models which are adequate representations of reality. Considering the costs, difficulties, and hazards, of developing computer or mathematical models, the pilot plant may be the cheapest in total cost for many situations.

Models are at the heart of scientific methodology. The development of theories and laws of nature involves the development of general models of reality. Advancement of the science of engineering and economics involves the development of better models which can be used to predict future behavior. This will enable the selection of nearer optimum solutions to engineering and business problems.

Determining the Optimum Alternative from a Model. From the point of view of making an economic decision, of choosing an alternative course of action, models can be divided into two types:

1. Mathematical ones in which an optimum solution can be deduced analytically by manipulation of the model—the inventory models of Chapter 18 and the programming models of Chapter 19 provide examples of this type of solution. Many models require the use of complex mathematical procedures to solve analytically for the optimum solution.

2. All others, including some mathematical ones, in which various possible alternative values or courses of action must be tried and results compared to obtain a trial-and-error solution—the annual-cost models of Chapter 9 are examples of this type of model.

Computer Simulation of a Business Operation. In the discussion of suboptimization in Chapter 2, it was noted that one of the reasons it was necessary to restrict the scope of the system being designed and evaluated is our inability to handle design and evaluation problems when the scope of the system is too broad. When the number of elements and the number of interactions among the elements become large, we have difficulty in analyzing the possible effect of alternative courses of action. However, large electronic computers enable us to enlarge our horizons considerably in building realistic models to test alternative business proposals.

Many problems in business operations cannot be conveniently isolated from the entire business system or major portions of it. Thus, quality level affects material and labor costs, plant capacity (because of rework of defectives), production control, marketing strategy, pricing, customer service, distribution and transportation costs (because of returns of defectives), etc. When there are many questions involving the quality levels of many products in numerous plants and when these questions include methods of distribution, plant location, plant capacity, product-line strategy, and other interacting factors, simulation on a computer may be economic.

Of course the investments or decisions must be important enough to justify the expense of building a model of the expected behavior of the system to be used on a computer. This model can then be utilized to evaluate alternative courses of action in order to make the best decision. Where risks and uncertainties are significant, the computer can be used to simulate a series of consequences of each alternative course of action, assuming different values for the uncertain variables. This will aid considerably in determining the character and importance of the uncertainties in each alternative course of action.

How large and detailed a model to build will vary with the purposes, potential benefits, and capacities of the computer. Once the model has been built, programmed onto the computer, tested, and refined where necessary, it can be used to evaluate in a rapid fashion the effects of many alternatives. In fact, the construction of the model and the results of computer runs will usually suggest more potentially optimum alternatives for investigation.

Testing Adequacy of Model. The fundamental test of the adequacy of a model is: Does it effectively simulate the real world? does it give the same answers as actually occur? does it accurately predict what will occur?

These questions suggest ways of testing a model. We examine the real world situation. Using all available evidence, we evaluate in a logical and practical way whether the model meets the test of realism in all significant aspects which will affect the business or engineering decision.

The model is a statement of the existence of certain relationships. It is a hypothesis. We can deduce or draw conclusions from this hypothesis. Are these conclusions substantiated by the real world? Do they actually occur?

The ability to forecast accurately is the fundamental test of scientific theories and hypotheses. This also applies to economic models. Newton's law of gravity and Einstein's theory of relativity are accepted or rejected as models of reality only in so far as they can be used to forecast physical phenomena with accuracy. However, the degree of forecasting precision obtainable with economic models is usually much lower than with physical models.

However, the real test of any model is, does it work? Is it useful? The model may provide an imperfect simulation of reality. It may give relatively inaccurate forecasts of what will occur. The solutions and decisions derived from its use may be quite far from optimal. And yet it may provide the most effective means available for making the required decisions. If it will enable better, though far from perfect, decision-making than any other available method which can be economically applied, it has passed the test for the present.

Follow-up to Adapt Model to Changes. Economic decisions are based upon models which simulate the real state of affairs. These real conditions will change over a period of time. The values or size of various factors will change. New factors which were formerly insignificant will become significant. Others which were significant will become insignificant. And the relationships of the factors with each other and to the effectiveness of the system will change.

It is thus necessary to follow up to ensure that models are adapted to changes as required. This poses an economic problem because

1. The values of the factors and their interrelationship are continually changing. However, we are interested only in significant changes in which the potential improvement from changing the model will be greater than the cost of making the change.

2. It is difficult to ascertain promptly when significant changes in pertinent factors or their relationships have occurred. Not only must the values of all the factors in the model be considered, but other factors which were not relevant when the model was developed, and therefore not included in the model, may become significant and have to be included.

It would therefore be uneconomic, in general, to attempt a continual follow-up on each factor which may change and render the model less effective.

In some cases, however, the potential losses from below-optimal performance are great enough to warrant the establishment of procedures calling for relatively continuous follow-up on the factors which currently have a significant effect on the performance of the system or may have significant effects if their values changed. These procedures have three aspects:

1. Discovering when changes in the factors will occur or have occurred

2. Communicating the information about the change to the decision-maker or his analyst

3. Determining whether the change or changes will have a significant enough effect on the utility of the model to justify the cost of changing it

We shall consider in detail some of the problems of discovering when changes have occurred.

Categories of Factor Changes. There are two categories of factors which may change. One category concerns those factors which we control or have definite knowledge of future values. We decide if and when we will change the items or models we sell or the designs or quality of the models. We decide when we will change our service and pricing policies, although competitive market conditions may force us in one direction or the other. Other factors, such as the date for tax payments, the number of days of annual paid vacation for employees, the number of working days in a year, are not decided by us, but we have definite knowledge of their current and, up to a point, future values.

The second category concerns those factors which we must forecast. For example, two of the factors in our inventory models are annual requirements and storage costs. Changes in our annual-requirements forecast or in our storage-costs forecast will change the constants in the inventory equation model. (The storage cost used in the inventory model is sometimes the past storage cost if no change is anticipated in the future, just as the annual requirement would be the past year's figure if no change were anticipated. However, annual requirements are usually more variable than storage costs and it is less usual to find no anticipated changes from year to year.)

Sampling Changes versus Population Changes. For this second type of factor which must be forecasted, we have the problem of distinguishing between sampling variations from the true population value and actual changes in population value. We can test the deviations by assuming no true change in population value has occurred. We then determine the probability that a sampling variation that is as great as or greater than actually occurred would occur just due to chance.

Type I and Type II Errors. Let us say that the probability of obtaining a sampling deviation that is as great or greater turns out to be 0.003. If we consider 0.003 small enough, we will reject our assumption or hypothesis and say that a true change in population value has occurred. We will be wrong only 3 times in 1,000. Rejecting our hypothesis when it is really true, saying that the population value has changed when it really has not, is called a type I error by statisticians. Using the symbol α to represent the magnitude of this probability, $\alpha = 0.003$ in this case.

We have established that we are willing to have no more than a 0.3 per cent probability of a type I error. When the probability of obtaining a sampling deviation turns out to be 0.004, we shall not reject the hypothesis. We are thus saying that the population value has not changed. A certain percentage of the time when we make this statement the population value will have actually changed and we shall be wrong. This kind of error is called a type II error. We shall use the symbol β to represent the magnitude of the probability of type II errors.

The probabilities of a type II error depend upon a number of considerations:

1. We will be more likely to make a type II error if the population value has not shifted very much than if it has shifted a great deal.

2. The smaller the sample size, the larger the risks of a type II error.

3. The smaller the probability we are willing to have of a type I error, rejecting the hypothesis when it is not true, the larger the probability of a type II error.

In Figure 24-1, our hypothesis is that our samples are coming from the unchanged population whose frequency curve for sample means is indicated by the solid line and whose mean is $\bar{X}'_H$. The probability of a type I error is shown by the shaded area under this curve labeled α.

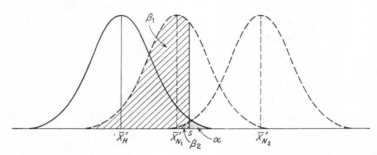

Figure 24-1. Probabilities of type I and type II errors when population mean has shifted from $\bar{X}'_H$ to $\bar{X}'_{N_1}$ and to $\bar{X}'_{N_2}$.

If the population mean shifted from $\bar{X}'_H$ to $\bar{X}'_{N_1}$, we would still obtain most of our sample values to the left of S and would therefore accept our hypothesis and make a type II error. The proportion of time we will do this, β_1, is shown by the crosshatched area under the frequency curve for sample means from the new population.

If the population mean shifted from $\bar{X}'_H$ to $\bar{X}'_{N_2}$, we would obtain very few of our sample values to the left of S. It is therefore very unlikely that a population shift as great as this will go undetected. β_2 is very small.

The dispersion or spread of the distribution of means shown in Figure 24-1 is given by the formula $\sigma_{\bar{X}} = \sigma'/\sqrt{N}$. The larger the sample size, N, the smaller will be the spread which is inversely proportional to the square root of the sample size. The smaller the spread of the distributions, the less they will overlap. β, the area in the new shifted distribution which is to the left of α cutoff on the original distribution, would be smaller if the dispersions are smaller. Figure 24-2 shows the frequency curves for the sampling distribution of means from a larger sample than in Figure 24-1. The dispersions are smaller. The β_1 value for the probability of a type II error if the population mean shifted to $\bar{X}'_{N_1}$ is much smaller and the β_2 value if the mean shifted to $\bar{X}_{N_2}$ is so small that it cannot be shown in the figure. This demonstrates how increasing the sample size reduces the probability of a type II error.

We can also decrease the probability of a type II error if we are willing to increase the probability of a type I error, as shown in Figure 24-3. We shall reject our hypothesis more readily and, as a result, be wrong in this rejection a larger α proportion of the time. Conversely, the β proportion of the time, when we shall not reject our hypothesis even though it is really incorrect, will decrease.

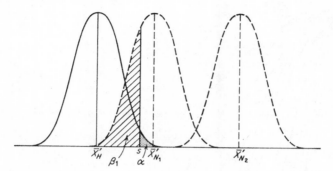

Figure 24-2. Probabilities of type I and type II errors when population mean has shifted from $\bar{X}'_H$ to $\bar{X}'_{N_1}$ and to $\bar{X}'_{N_2}$—larger sample size.

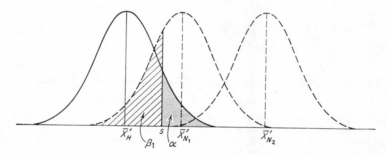

Figure 24-3. Probabilities of type I and type II errors when population mean has shifted from $\bar{X}'_H$ to $\bar{X}'_{N_1}$ and to $\bar{X}'_{N_2}$—larger type I error.

Operating-characteristic Curves. For given values of α and N we can draw curves for each kind of statistical test which will show the probability of accepting our hypothesis. These curves are called operating-characteristic curves. Figures 24-4 and 24-5 show the operating-characteristic curves for the two-sided normal-distribution test and the Student's t distribution test. The probability of a type I error, α, has been set at 0.05 for an error in either direction. A two-sided test means that the probability of 0.05 applies to the probability of obtaining a deviation from the mean value on either the high side or the low side of the distribution.

In Figures 24-4 and 24-5 for the normal and Student's t test, we see that if the true difference between the means is 0, there is a 0.95 probability of accepting the hypothesis that the true difference is 0 (that the sample mean is different from the population value only because of sampling variations). This corresponds to a probability of 0.05 (1.00 − 0.95) of rejecting the hypothesis when it is true, a type I probability of $\alpha = 0.05$. This is true regardless of sample size.

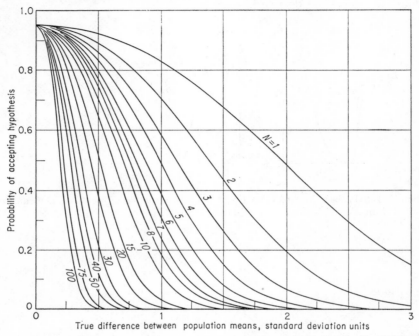

Figure 24-4. Operating characteristics of the two-sided normal test (significance level: $\alpha = 0.05$). SOURCE: C. D., Ferris, F. E. Grubbs, and C. L. Weaver, "Operating Characteristics for the Common Statistical Tests of Significance," *Annals of Mathematical Statistics*, vol. 17, pp. 178-197, June 1946.

The probability of accepting the hypothesis when it is not true is less than 0.95. This probability becomes smaller as the true differences, measured in standard-deviation units, become greater. The curves of Figures 24-4 and 24-5 show that the probability of accepting a false hypothesis decreases more rapidly as the extent of the falsity increases when the sample sizes are larger. Thus, for the normal test of Figure 24-4, the probability of accepting a false hypothesis when the true difference is equal to one-half a standard-deviation unit is more than 0.80 for a sample size of 4, more than 0.60 for a sample size of 10, a little less than 0.40 for a sample size of 20, about 0.20 for a sample size of 30, and close to zero for a sample size of 100.

If we are satisfied with a probability of 0.40 of accepting the hypothesis when it is not true, when the true difference is equal to one-half a standard-deviation unit, we can use a sample size of 20. If, however, we desire a probability of no more than 0.20 of accepting the hypothesis when this true difference exists, then a sample size of 30 is required.

Testing a Null Hypothesis. The assumption or hypothesis which we have been discussing is frequently called a null hypothesis because it is often used when we desire to prove the opposite of the hypothesis. For

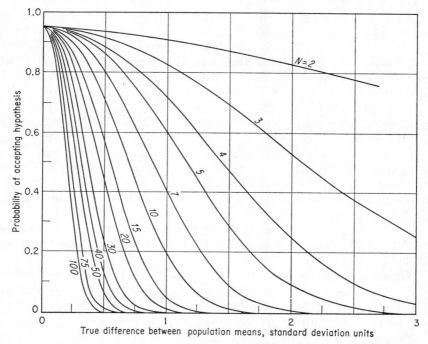

Figure 24-5. Operating characteristics of the two-sided t test (significance level: $\alpha = 0.05$). SOURCE: C. D., Ferris, F. E. Grubbs, and C. L. Weaver, "Operating Characteristics for the Common Statistical Tests of Significance," *Annals of Mathematical Statistics*, vol. 17, pp. 178-197, June 1946.

example, if we want to prove that the inventory-storage cost has decreased significantly, we shall first null-hypothesize that it has not changed. The average storage cost per unit has been $0.68 per month. Our null hypothesis is that the average cost of $0.66 per month for the last 400 units is just due to sampling variations, that the true mean of the population from which the sample came is still $0.68. Then, if we can show that the probability of this null hypothesis being true is so small that it is unlikely, we have proved that storage costs have decreased significantly.

We compute a $\sigma'_{\text{est}} = \$0.08$ per month. Then,

$$\sigma_{\bar{x}} = \frac{0.08}{\sqrt{400}} = \frac{0.08}{20} = 0.004$$

$$\frac{\bar{X} - \bar{X}'}{\sigma_{\bar{x}}} = \frac{0.66 - 0.68}{0.004} = -5$$

Using the table of areas under the normal curve, the area 5σ and further from the mean on one side is 0.0000002867. Our null hypothesis is, therefore, very improbable and a statistically significant improvement in storage costs has occurred.

Control Charts. When we desire to test a null hypothesis on a periodic systematic basis, a control chart may provide a convenient graphic device for accomplishing this purpose. A simple control chart is presented in Figure 24-6 in connection with problem 5 at the conclusion of this chapter.

Economy of Sampling to Discover Changes. In observing and taking samples of values to discover when changes have occurred which may affect our model, cost is of prime importance. The total cost of discovering and making changes in the model must be more than matched by the benefits from the changes. We want to minimize the sum of the following opportunity costs:

1. The costs of the sample observations, the statistical analysis to determine the significance of changes, and the investigation to correct the model properly where necessary—these depend upon the size, frequency, and method of sampling as well as upon the types of testing and analytic procedures used

2. The costs involved because of type I and II errors—changing the model when it should not be changed and not changing the model when it should be changed

The sizes of α and β determine the second group of costs. We can reduce the size of α and β by increasing our sample size N and increasing our first group of costs. We should do this as long as the decrease in error costs will be greater than the increase in sampling and analysis costs.

How about the relative sizes of α and β? We can decrease one by increasing the other. In theory, the relative sizes should be inversely proportional to the cost which will be incurred if the type of error is made. In practice, this is hard to determine.

Relating Model to Reality. Models are necessary to aid in decision-making. However, we must always examine the results critically to be sure that the course of action which appears best in terms of the model will actually be best in reality.

It may not be best in some situations for either or both of two reasons: the model may be lacking in its portrayal of reality in one or more aspects, such as the omission of a significant factor, the inclusion of insignificant factors, or a misrepresentation of the relationships between the factors and the criteria used for making the decision; or the criteria of effectiveness may not be the best ones for achieving the over-all objectives of the enterprise or organizational unit. These problems of relating our solutions to reality, the relevance of both the model and the criteria, are discussed in practical terms in many places in this volume when different types of models and criteria suitable for various economic situations are presented and their use illustrated.

The problem of relating our models to reality is a continuing one because economic, engineering, and operating conditions change. These will frequently render our models obsolete. It is therefore necessary to reexamine periodically the decision models used in the enterprise to be certain that the values and relationships are still valid.

PROBLEMS

1. "Science is a branch of study concerned with observation and classification of facts, especially with the establishment of verifiable general laws, chiefly by induction and hypotheses."[1] Reconcile this definition of science with the statement in the text that advancement of the science of engineering and economics involves the development of better models which can be used to predict future behavior.

2. Discuss the problem of follow-up to keep up to date the model used in Chapter 19 to determine the volumes of products A, B, and C, which should be produced for maximum profit. Include a discussion of the problem of discovering and communicating when significant changes will occur or have occurred.

3. Setup costs for punch press jobs in the Reardom Corporation have averaged $58.42, with $\sigma' = \$6.38$. The distribution appears to be approximately normal.

   (a) A random sample of the setup costs of four current jobs is taken. The average of the setup costs for this sample is $67.99. Calculate the probability of obtaining an average setup cost of $67.99 or higher as a result of sampling variations, assuming that our null hypothesis is true, that the population mean value of $58.42 has not changed. (*Answer:* 0.0014)

   (b) Another random sample of the setup costs of four current jobs is taken and the average of this sample is $48.85. Calculate the probability of obtaining an average setup cost of $48.85 or lower as a result of sampling variations alone, assuming our null hypothesis is still true. (*Answer:* 0.0014)

   (c) Assuming our null hypothesis remains true, what is the probability of obtaining a random sample of four setup costs outside the range $48.85 to $67.99 as a result of sampling variations? (*Answer:* 0.0028)

4. Referring to problem 3, the Reardom Corporation continues to take random samples of four setup costs in an attempt to ensure that the population mean value of $58.42 has not changed. As long as the sample means are between $48.85 and $67.99, it assumes that the null hypothesis has not been disproved.
   (a) What is the probability of a type I error when using this control procedure?
   (b) What is the probability of a type II error when using this control procedure if the true population mean value shifts from $58.42 to $62.00?

5. Referring to problem 3, it is decided to continue to take random samples of four setup costs and to plot the mean of the random samples to give a graphic picture of these cost variations. The ordinate scale is labeled average cost

---

[1] *Webster's New Collegiate Dictionary*, G. & C. Merriam Co., Springfield, Mass., 1959.

and the abscissa scale is labeled sample number, as in Figure 24-6. (This graph, used for testing a null hypothesis, is called a control chart.) At the hypothesized population mean value of $58.42 a horizontal line is drawn. If the null hypothesis were true and there were no sampling variation, all sample means would fall on this line. However, the actual sample means will be scattered about this line. Horizontal dashed lines have also been drawn at $48.85 and $67.99, which represent $\bar{X}' \pm 3\sigma_{\bar{x}}$ and at $52.04 and $64.80, which represent $\bar{X}' \pm 2\sigma_{\bar{x}}$.

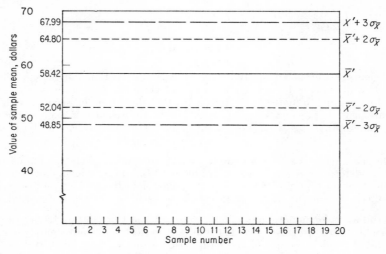

Figure 24-6. Control chart for setup costs.

(a) What is the probability of a type I error (α) if a decision is made that the null hypothesis is disproved only when (1) One point falls outside either $3\sigma_{\bar{x}}$ (dashed) line? (2) One point falls outside either $2\sigma_{\bar{x}}$ (dashed) line? (3) Two successive points fall outside either $2\sigma_{\bar{x}}$ (dashed) line?

(b) What is the probability of a type II error if a decision is made that the null hypothesis is disproved only when one point falls outside either $2\sigma_{\bar{x}}$ (dashed) line and the true population mean has risen to $62.00? Use Figure 24-4 to get an approximate answer.

25 Simulating Risk
(Monte Carlo Technique)

Many economic decisions require the comparison of alternatives involving risks. The Monte Carlo technique is a device for simulating these risks. Risk is the result of the variations in the values of a variable which are caused by the action and interaction of many factors. Each of these factors exerts such an insignificant influence on the variations in the values of the variable that their individual effects cannot be isolated. This pattern of variation in the values of the variable is called chance or random variation.

Random Numbers. In the Monte Carlo technique, this pattern of chance variation is simulated by means of random numbers. Random numbers are numbers which have been generated in such a way that there is an equal probability of any digit appearing each time, regardless of any past appearances. Spinning a perfectly true roulette wheel; drawing numbers out of a box, being careful to ensure that each number has equal opportunity of being drawn each time; or throwing perfectly true dice are possible ways of generating random numbers.

Using a table of random numbers which has been generated with great care to ensure randomness is frequently the simplest way of obtaining these numbers. A table of random numbers is presented in the Appendix of this book. These numbers were generated so that the probability of any integer from 0 to 9 appearing in each space in each column is exactly 0.1.

Generating Random Samples. These random numbers can be used to obtain random samples without actually taking a physical sample.

For example, we would like to obtain a random sample of 25 of the 1,582 male assembly workers in an electronic component manufacturing company. If each worker has a payroll number, we may go to the table of random numbers and starting in any column take the first 25 payroll numbers which appear in the table. If payroll numbers have not been previously assigned, we would number the workers from 0000 to 1582. Then, starting with any column we would note each number between 0000 and 1582 until we have 25 different numbers. The employees with these 25 numbers would be our random sample.

The two examples of simulation illustrated in this chapter are simplified examples to illustrate the methodology. In actual practice, it will usually be necessary to use more complicated Monte Carlo models to make them more realistic and valid and to use larger Monte Carlo samples to make the simulation more reliable. In their present simplified forms, both of the examples presented here are capable of analytic solution.

Monte Carlo Sampling: Empirical Distribution. Let us consider how the Monte Carlo technique can assist us in forecasting costs. We manufacture and sell a perishable food product which must be thrown away if it is not sold the same day it is produced. On any day in which we cannot supply the amounts demanded, the sales are lost to us. We would like to estimate the total cost of leftover waste product and lost sales at various output levels so that we can determine an optimum level at which to operate. To do this we must forecast how often we will run out and what our average leftover product and our average lost sales will be when operating at various output levels.

Based on past experience, the sales to our distributors are expected to vary as shown in the frequency distribution of Table 25-1. The distribution is plotted in Figure 25-1. The expected (average) sales rate is 2,755 units per day.

Table 25-1. Frequency Distribution of Daily Sales

Daily sales	Mid-point	Relative frequency
2,450–2,549	2,500	0.05
2,550–2,649	2,600	0.15
2,650–2,749	2,700	0.25
2,750–2,849	2,800	0.35
2,850–2,949	2,900	0.15
2,950–3,049	3,000	0.05
		1.00

Devoting 9 production units to this product on a one-shift basis, we can expect to obtain the daily production variations shown in the frequency distribution of Table 25-2. This distribution is plotted in Figure 25-2. The expected (average) production rate is 2,755 units per day.

Table 25-2. Frequency Distribution of Production Using 9 Units

Daily production	Mid-point	Relative frequency
2,550–2,649	2,600	0.15
2,650–2,749	2,700	0.30
2,750–2,849	2,800	0.40
2,850–2,949	2,900	0.15
		1.00

We can now simulate what will happen on any number of days we desire to sample. The larger the number of days we sample, the smaller will be the risk that the summary statistics we calculate from our sample values vary significantly from the true values. (Sampling errors are discussed in Chapter 23.) To simplify our illustration of the procedure, we will take a sample of only 15 days. In actual practice, much larger samples may be used.

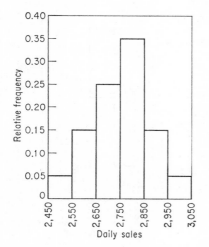 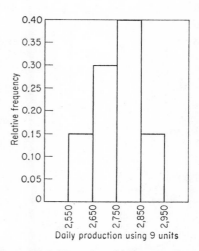

Figure 25-1. Frequency histogram of daily sales.

Figure 25-2. Frequency histogram of production using 9 units.

If we were to take a random sample of the daily sales values on the abscissa (horizontal axis) of Figure 25-2, each sales value should have an equal probability of occurring in the sample. However, we want the probability of a value occurring between 2,550 and 2,649 to be 3 times as great as a value occurring between 2,950 and 3,049 (proportional to the frequencies in the two class intervals).

We therefore plot a cumulative distribution for daily sales in Figure 25-3 and for daily production in Figure 25-4, assuming for simplicity that all production and sales are made at the mid-points of the class intervals.

We would like a random sample of the number sold on each day, with the underlying relative frequencies conforming to our distribution. Thus, we want the probability of selecting a day in which 2,600 units are sold to be 0.15. Therefore, we have constructed our cumulative frequency of sales so that the vertical height at the abscissa value of 2,600 units per day is 0.15 of the total vertical distance on the ordinate scale.

If each frequency has an equal probability of being chosen as the point of entry, then the probability of any particular sales value being chosen will be proportional to the vertical height of its histogram which is proportional to relative frequency. To ensure that the point of entry is randomized with each frequency having an equal probability of being chosen, we choose our point of entry from a table of random numbers. Thus, taking random numbers from the table in the Appendix, we obtain the

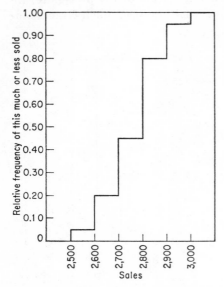

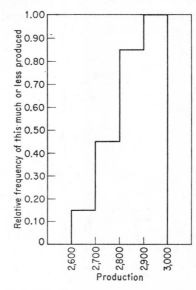

Figure 25-3. Cumulative frequency histogram of sales.

Figure 25-4. Cumulative frequency histogram of production using 9 units.

values for daily sales shown in Table 25-3. Our first random number chosen is 48867. We enter the cumulative distribution of Figure 25-3 on the vertical axis (frequency of this much or less sold), using our first random number of 0.488 and draw a horizontal line across until it meets the cumulative-frequency histogram. We then drop a vertical line to the abscissa and read off our sample value, which is 2,800 for our first random number.

Table **25-3. Simulated Daily Sales**

Random number	Sales	Random number	Sales
488	2,800	881	2,900
322	2,700	834	2,900
274	2,700	913	2,900
557	2,800	327	2,700
931	2,900	077	2,600
986	3,000	552	2,800
682	2,800	890	2,900
179	2,600		

Following the same procedure for production, we obtain the values shown in Table 25-4.

Table 25-4. Simulated Daily Production Using 9 Units

Random number	Production	Random number	Production
339	2,700	218	2,700
697	2,800	367	2,700
031	2,600	990	2,900
052	2,600	383	2,700
506	2,800	667	2,800
865	2,900	641	2,800
948	2,900	517	2,800
308	2,700		

We can now prepare Table 25-5 showing leftover production or lost sales each day using 9 production units. The average daily amount of leftover waste product is 33 and the average daily lost sales is 73. The unit cost of waste product can be estimated and the average daily cost of waste product calculated. Similarly, the profit which is not made because a sale is lost can be estimated (with an additional allowance for loss of customer good will where applicable) and the cost of the average daily lost sales calculated. The average daily combined cost of these losses using 9 production units can then be obtained.

Table 25-5. Leftover Production and Lost Sales Using 9 Production Units

Day	Sales	Production	Leftover production	Lost sales
1	2,800	2,700	. . .	100
2	2,700	2,800	100	
3	2,700	2,600	. . .	100
4	2,800	2,600	. . .	200
5	2,900	2,800	. . .	100
6	3,000	2,900	. . .	100
7	2,800	2,900	100	
8	2,600	2,700	100	
9	2,900	2,700	. . .	200
10	2,900	2,700	. . .	200
11	2,900	2,900		
12	2,700	2,700		
13	2,600	2,800	200	
14	2,800	2,800		
15	2,900	2,800	. . .	100
Total	. . . . .	. . . . .	500	1,100
Daily average	. . . . .	. . . . .	33	73

Using this same procedure, we can calculate the average daily combined cost of leftover production and lost sales when 8 production units are used, when 10 production units are used, and so on. By tabulating these total costs at the various production levels, we can ascertain the optimum number of production units to commit to this production.

Monte Carlo Sampling: Theoretical (Mathematical) Distribution. In the previous example, we established empirical frequency distributions based upon past experience. In some instances, we can estimate the mean and standard deviation of a distribution and have good reason to be confident that the distribution is normal. In other instances, we may have good reason to assume that a binomial, Poisson, or other mathematical distribution is appropriate. Our procedure for Monte Carlo sampling from these distributions is similar to the procedure used in the previous illustration. Let us consider an example using the normal distribution.

We desire to determine how many order pickers (who pack as they pick) we should have in our shipping department. We will refer to the pick and pack operation as picking to keep the notation brief.

An average of 200 orders are received daily. Analysis indicates that the distribution of the number of orders received each day is normal, with a standard deviation of 25.

There is an average of 50 items on each order. The distribution of the average number of items on a day's orders is also disclosed to be normal, with a standard deviation of 10.

The average time for an order picker to pick an item is 0.02 hr. The standard deviation of the daily average time is 0.004 hr. This distribution is also normal.

All orders are shipped in the order of their receipt. We have a commitment to our distributors to ship all orders within two days of their receipt. This commitment is understood to mean that the shipment will be picked up by the common carrier no later than the early morning of the second day following receipt of the order. Overtime with premium pay is authorized whenever necessary to carry out this policy. Whenever required, the order pickers work overtime until all orders received on the previous day have been picked. There is enough labor flexibility in the shipping and other departments to label and have the packed orders ready the following morning for the common carrier.

We know the means and the standard deviations of the number of orders received, the items per order, and the average time to pick an order. We can therefore construct a normal cumulative-frequency distribution for each variable using a table of areas under the normal curve. We wish to simulate random variations in the values of these variables so that we can establish the time requirements for the picking operation for the days in our sample.

We can do this in a manner similar to the procedure used in our previous example. We first plot the cumulative-frequency distributions for each variable. Then, using the table of random numbers, we select random values on the ordinate scale (vertical axis). For each random value, we draw a horizontal line until it meets the cumulative-frequency curve. Then we drop a vertical line to the abscissa (horizontal axis) and read off the value.

This procedure is illustrated in Figure 25-5 for a normal distribution in which the mean equals zero and in which deviations from the mean are expressed in terms of standard deviations.

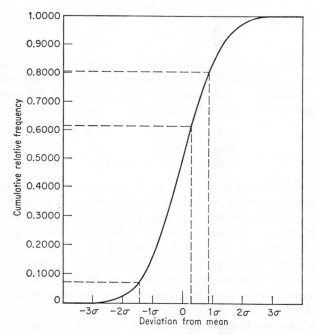

Figure 25-5. Random normal values (deviations from mean).

The probability of a value near the mean occurring in real life is larger than the probability of one occurring farther from the mean: this probability is equal to its relative frequency. The steepness of the cumulative-probability curve is proportional to the relative frequency at each value. The probability of simulated values being chosen when we use random numbers to determine the points on the ordinate scale at which we enter the cumulative-probability curve is proportional to the steepness of the curve and therefore to the relative frequency at each value. Therefore, the probability of a value occurring in the simulation is the same as in real life, provided the graph accurately describes the actual frequencies.

To obtain our random normal values, we use a table of random numbers, such as that in the Appendix, to select randomly cumulative relative frequencies between 0.0000 and 1.0000. Three such random numbers are listed in Table 25-6. For each random number, we draw a horizontal line on the normal cumulative-frequency distribution of Figure 25-5, entering the ordinate at the value of each random number. We read off on the abscissa the random normal value for each random number, in standard deviations from the mean. These are shown in Figure 25-5 and Table 25-6.

Table 25-6. Random Normal Values (Deviations from Mean)

Random numbers	Random normal value (σ deviations from mean)
61357	0.289
80545	0.861
07293	−1.454

We can now apply these random normal values (deviates) to any normal distribution. For example, our first random deviate is 0.289. Our distribution of number of orders received has a mean of 200 and a standard deviation of 25. Therefore, our random values are

$$200 + 0.289(25) = 207.2$$
$$200 + 0.861(25) = 221.5$$
$$200 - 1.454(25) = 163.6$$

The reason for illustrating this procedure on a cumulative normal frequency distribution with $\bar{X} = 0$ and values shown in terms of standard deviations from the zero mean is that this illustrates how we can build up tables of random normal values. A table of random normal numbers (expressed in terms of standard deviations from the mean) can then be used over and over again whenever we desire to take a Monte Carlo sample from a normal distribution. This saves much time and effort. A table of random normal numbers (Gaussian deviates) is presented in the Appendix to this book.

Thus, the first random normal value shown in the table is 1.102σ. This value is expressed as a deviation from the mean of zero in our model. Our distribution of number of orders received has a mean ($\bar{X}$) of 200 and standard deviation (σ) of 25. Therefore, the random value is

$$200 + 1.102(25) = 227.6$$

If this same random normal deviate value is applied to the distribution of the average number of items on a day's orders, the random value is $50 + 1.102(10) = 61.0$. In our problem, it would not be proper to do this, however, because we want each variable to vary independently of the others. We shall therefore take separate sets of random normal numbers independently for each normal variable.

We shall simulate values for each variable for 30 working days in our illustration. In actual practice, we would desire a larger sample in order to reduce sampling error. The simulation procedure is illustrated in Table 25-7.

If exactly 200 orders were received every day with an average of exactly 50 items per order and it took exactly 0.02 hr to pick (and pack) each item, then the daily work load would be exactly 200(50)(0.02), or 200 hr. If the normal number of working hours per worker per day is 7.2 hr, then the number of order pickers required to avoid overtime or accumulation of unpicked orders would be $\frac{1}{7.2}$ (200) = 27.8, or 28 order pickers.

We shall simulate the situation in the shipping department using various numbers of order pickers. (There are presently 28 order pickers in the department.) Let us illustrate the procedures with 25, 26, 27, and 28 pickers.

Column A lists the day. In columns B, D, and G, we list random normal numbers (deviates) from the table of the Appendix. We start at any point in the table for each of these listings, but we use different sections of the table for each of the columns to obtain independent listings.

Column C is calculated by multiplying each random normal deviate by 25, the standard deviation of numbers of orders received daily, to obtain the random deviation in terms of number of orders, and adding 200, the arithmetic average of number of orders received daily. This gives us random values for number of orders received.

The random values for average number of items per order, column E, and for the average time to pick an item, column H, are calculated in the same manner as the random values for number of orders received, column C.

The number of items to be picked, column F, is the product of the random values of the number of orders received, column C, and the random values of the average number of items per order, column E.

The total time to pick the day's orders, column I, is the product of the random value of the average time to pick an order, column H, and the number of items to be picked, column F.

Columns J, K, and L will vary depending upon the number of pickers. The accumulated pick time, column J, consists of the time to pick the current day's orders, column I, plus the pick time remaining after the previous day's regular working period, column K of the previous day, minus the previous day's overtime, column L of the previous day.

The remaining pick time, column K, consists of the accumulated pick time, column J, minus the pick hours expended per day in the shipping department, which is 7.2 times the number of pickers. (The pickers work 7.2 hr per day.) If the accumulated pick time, column J, is less than the pick hours expended per day, the difference is idle time which is lost and cannot be carried forward as a minus remaining pick time.

Table 25-7. Simulation of 30 Working Days

Day	Number of orders received		Average number of items per order		Number of items to be picked	Average time to pick an item		Total time to pick day's orders	25 pickers		
	Random normal deviate	Random value 200 + 25(B)	Random normal deviate	Random value 50 + 10(D)	(E)(C)	Random normal deviate	Random value 0.02 + 0.004(G)	(H)(F)	Accumulated pick time I + prev. (K − L)	Remaining pick time J − 25(7.2)	Overtime K − I when K > 1
A	B	C	D	E	F	G	H	I	J	K	L
1	0.596	214.9	2.291	72.9	15,666	1.130	0.02452	384.1	384.1	204.1	0
2	−1.386	165.4	−1.198	38.0	6,285	1.633	0.02653	166.7	370.8	190.8	24.1
3	0.217	205.4	0.549	55.5	11,400	−1.315	0.01474	168.0	334.7	154.7	0
4	−1.024	174.4	0.165	51.7	9,016	0.817	0.02327	209.8	364.5	184.5	0
5	−0.632	184.2	0.515	55.2	10,168	−0.174	0.01930	196.2	380.7	200.7	4.5
6	−1.628	159.3	−1.731	32.7	5,209	0.163	0.02065	107.6	303.8	123.8	16.2
7	0.010	200.3	0.574	55.7	11,157	0.365	0.02146	239.4	347.0	167.0	0
8	0.170	204.3	1.677	66.8	13,647	1.055	0.02422	330.5	497.5	317.5	0
9	0.688	217.2	−1.102	39.0	8,471	−0.385	0.01846	156.4	473.9	293.9	137.5
10	0.497	212.4	−1.119	38.8	8,241	1.651	0.02660	219.2	375.6	195.6	0
11	−1.166	170.9	1.261	62.6	10,698	−1.835	0.01266	135.4	331.0	151.0	15.6
12	−1.918	152.1	−0.086	49.1	7,468	1.015	0.02406	179.7	315.1	135.1	0
13	1.140	228.5	0.155	51.6	11,791	1.098	0.02439	287.6	422.7	242.7	0
14	−0.390	190.3	−0.054	49.5	9,420	−0.727	0.01709	161.0	403.7	223.7	62.7
15	0.742	218.6	0.048	50.5	11,039	0.349	0.02140	236.2	397.2	217.2	0
16	1.051	226.3	−1.724	32.8	7,423	−1.080	0.01568	116.4	333.6	153.6	37.2
17	1.060	226.5	0.778	57.8	13,092	0.340	0.02136	279.6	396.0	216.0	0
18	−0.332	191.7	0.778	57.8	11,080	−0.002	0.01999	221.5	437.5	257.5	36.0
19	−0.856	178.6	−0.868	41.3	7,376	−1.307	0.01477	108.9	330.4	150.4	41.5
20	1.350	233.8	−0.844	41.6	9,726	−0.346	0.01862	181.1	290.0	110.0	0
21	−0.520	187.0	0.983	59.8	11,183	−1.129	0.01548	173.1	283.1	103.1	0
22	−1.821	154.5	0.111	51.1	7,895	−0.768	0.01693	133.7	236.8	56.8	0
23	−0.450	188.8	0.705	57.1	10,780	−1.521	0.01392	150.1	206.9	26.9	0
24	2.348	258.7	−1.431	35.7	9,236	1.222	0.02489	229.9	256.8	76.8	0
25	−1.261	168.5	−0.227	47.7	8,037	0.375	0.02150	172.8	249.6	69.6	0
26	0.226	205.7	0.008	50.1	10,306	0.605	0.02242	231.1	300.7	120.7	0
27	−1.210	169.8	−0.642	43.6	7,403	1.470	0.02588	191.6	312.3	132.3	0
28	−0.554	186.2	1.086	60.9	11,340	1.864	0.02746	311.4	443.7	263.7	0
29	−0.282	193.0	−0.160	48.4	9,341	−1.223	0.01511	141.1	404.8	224.8	83.7
30	−0.016	199.6	−0.801	42.0	8,383	−0.395	0.01842	154.4	295.5	115.5	0

402

Table 25-7. Simulation of 30 Working Days (Continued)

Day	26 Pickers			27 Pickers			28 Pickers		
	Accumulated pick time I + prev. (K − L)	Remaining pick time J − 26(7.2)	Overtime K − I when K > I	Accumulated pick time I + prev. (K − L)	Remaining pick time J − 27(7.2)	Overtime K − I when K > I	Accumulated pick time I + prev. (K − L)	Remaining pick time J − 28(7.2)	Overtime K − I when K > I
A	J	K	L	J	K	L	J	K	L
1	384.1	196.9	0	384.1	189.7	0	384.1	182.5	0
2	363.6	176.4	9.7	356.4	162.0	0	349.2	147.6	0
3	334.7	147.5	0	330.0	135.6	0	315.6	114.0	0
4	357.3	170.1	0	345.4	151.0	0	323.8	122.2	0
5	366.3	179.1	0	347.2	152.8	0	318.4	116.8	0
6	286.7	99.5	0	260.4	66.0	0	224.4	22.8	0
7	338.9	151.7	0	305.4	111.0	0	262.2	60.6	0
8	482.2	295.0	107.8	441.5	247.1	52.7	391.1	189.5	0
9	451.4	264.2	0	403.5	209.1	0	345.9	144.3	0
10	375.6	188.4	1.2	375.6	181.2	0	363.5	161.9	0
11	323.8	136.6	0	316.6	122.2	0	297.3	95.7	0
12	315.1	127.9	0	301.9	107.5	0	275.4	73.8	0
13	415.5	228.3	41.1	395.1	200.7	0	361.4	159.8	0
14	389.3	202.1	0	361.7	167.3	6.3	320.8	119.2	0
15	397.2	210.0	22.8	397.2	202.8	0	355.4	153.8	0
16	326.4	139.2	0	319.2	124.8	8.4	270.2	68.6	0
17	396.0	208.8	21.6	396.0	201.6	0	348.2	146.6	0
18	430.3	243.1	34.3	423.1	228.7	7.2	368.1	166.5	0
19	330.4	143.2	0	330.4	136.0	27.1	275.4	73.8	0
20	290.0	102.8	0	290.0	95.6	0	254.9	53.3	0
21	275.9	88.7	0	268.7	74.3	0	226.4	24.8	0
22	222.4	35.2	0	208.0	13.6	0	158.5	0	0
23	185.3		0	163.7		0	150.1	0	0
24	229.9	42.7	0	229.9	35.5	0	229.9	28.3	0
25	215.5	28.3	0	208.3	13.9	0	201.1	0	0
26	259.4	72.2	0	245.0	50.6	0	231.1	29.5	0
27	263.8	76.6	0	242.2	47.8	0	221.1	19.5	0
28	388.0	200.8	13.6	359.2	164.8	0	330.9	129.3	0
29	341.9	154.7	0	305.9	111.5	0	270.4	68.8	0
30	295.5	108.3	0	265.9	71.5	0	223.2	21.6	0

Whenever, at the end of any day, the remaining pick time, column K, is greater than the total time to pick that day's orders, column I, it means that some of the previous day's orders have not been picked. On such occasions, the order pickers automatically work overtime until the previous day's orders are picked. In such cases, the amount of overtime, column L, is equal to column K minus column I.

Totaling experience for the 30 days with 25, 26, 27, and 28 pickers, we find the following.

Number of pickers	Total overtime	Average per day	Total per year (260 × daily average)
25	459.0	15.3	3,978
26	252.1	8.4	2,184
27	101.7	3.4	884
28	0	0	0

Regular time costs per picker per hour = \$6
Overtime costs per picker per hour   = \$9

Therefore, the annual costs for regular and overtime are as shown in Table 25-8. (The regular-time hours are computed by multiplying 260 days by 7.2 hr times the number of pickers.)

Table 25-8. Annual Costs for Pickers in the Shipping Department

	25 Pickers		26 Pickers		27 Pickers		28 Pickers	
	Hours	Dollars	Hours	Dollars	Hours	Dollars	Hours	Dollars
Regular time...	46,800	\$280,800	48,672	\$292,032	50,544	\$303,264	52,416	\$314,496
Overtime.......	3,978	35,802	2,184	19,656	884	7,956	0	
Total........	......	\$316,602	......	\$311,688	......	\$311,220	......	\$314,496

Number of Monte Carlo Trials (Sample Size). In our example, we took a Monte Carlo sample of 30 days of activity. In actual practice we may take a larger sample to obtain a more reliable picture of the overtime costs.

The required number of Monte Carlo trials is determined in the same manner as we would decide upon the size of a sample of the actual situation. The sampling-error and confidence determinations of Chapter 23 apply to Monte Carlo sampling just as to real-life sampling. However, with Monte Carlo sampling we can increase the size of the sample at much smaller expense than in real-life sampling. It is therefore economic to run much larger samples and obtain much smaller sampling errors.

Using Other Theoretical Distributions. We illustrated the technique for simulating risk using Monte Carlo methods with normal random numbers. When the theoretical distribution takes any other form—binomial, Poisson, etc.—exactly the same methodology can be employed.

Use of Computers. In actual practice, Monte Carlo simulation will generally be much more complex than the illustrations in this chapter which were oversimplified to promote ease of presentation. In most cases, in which Monte Carlo simulation is applied, high-speed digital computers are required. Large-scale electronic computers are frequently necessary in these cases because of the complexity of the simulations and the large numbers of trials (computer runs) required to reduce sampling error and obtain the desired confidence levels.

Real Life versus Monte Carlo Experimentation. An alternative to these Monte Carlo simulations would be to experiment directly in the company operation. In the first illustration in this chapter of a perishable food product, we would vary the number of production units and consequent output levels. In the second illustration we would experiment directly in the shipping department by varying the number of pickers. These real-life experiments would have the advantage of eliminating the problem of obtaining a good match between the simulation model and actual conditions. However, the disadvantages of the direct experimentation are great.

1. They would be disrupting to company operations.

2. It would be very difficult to have the same operating conditions apply each time.

3. It would be much more costly and take much more time to obtain the same size of sample (and therefore statistical reliability).

4. The Monte Carlo technique allows continued experimentation with many types of alternatives which could not be attempted in real-life experimentation.

We can use these models to evaluate the effects of many types of possible changes in business policies. For example, we can examine the following questions relating to the two cases presented in this chapter: What are the potential financial benefits from policies or investments designed to reduce variations in production output or to reduce the perishability of the product? What effect would a same-day shipping policy have on costs?

Analytic versus Monte Carlo Models. Monte Carlo methods can be used in the solutions of problems for which

1. Methods of solving analytic models have not yet been developed. Many waiting-time (queuing) models are in this category.

2. Solvable analytic models are available, but the mathematical procedures are relatively complex and arduous, so that Monte Carlo techniques provide a simpler method of solution.

3. Solvable analytic models are available, not too complex, but beyond the mathematical ability of available personnel.

Both analytic and Monte Carlo models have some common limitations. In both cases, we must be concerned with the question of the validity of the model. Does the model behave in the same way as the real world? However, with Monte Carlo simulations we can frequently obtain more realistic models than with analytic models.

Monte Carlo solution methods have some disadvantages which are not present in analytic solution methods. In the Monte Carlo method we have the same problem of statistical variations and experimental design that we have in direct experimentation in the real situation. We must take a large enough sample to reduce sampling variation to a sufficiently low level. In some cases, we may also have the problem of ensuring that our simulation continues for a long enough period of time to reach steady-state conditions. Thus, when an analytic model is realistic and can be mathematically manipulated to obtain the optimum solution, it possesses an important advantage over a Monte Carlo model.

PROBLEMS

1. Explain how tables of random numbers can be helpful in obtaining a random sample of (a) the 82 punch presses in a factory, (b) the 1,350 varieties of clamps made by the Harrow Clamp Corporation, (c) the days in the year.

2. The Boonton Manufacturing Co. requires more factory space. One of the alternatives being considered is the purchase of a warehouse 5 miles from the manufacturing plant for the storage of finished-goods stock. This will release for manufacturing purposes the space in the main plant which is presently used for this storage. The plan involves the delivery by company trucks during an 8-hr interval at the end of each workday of all items completed by the factory. To reach a decision on the economic number of trucks to purchase or rent, it is necessary to estimate, assuming various numbers of trucks, the average amount of finished goods which will remain at the plant at the end of the day and the average amount of truck capacity which will be unused. Following is the distribution of daily production figures:

Pounds of product per day	Relative frequency
350,000–374,999	0.03
375,000–399,999	0.09
400,000–424,999	0.18
425,000–449,999	0.24
450,000–474,999	0.30
475,000–499,999	0.10
500,000–524,999	0.05
525,000–549,999	0.01
	1.00

Each truck can carry 4,000 lb per trip. (Weight rather than volume is the limiting factor in all cases.) The number of trips which can be made in the 8 hr after the factory has closed is determined by the loading and unloading time as well as the time to drive the 5 miles separating the manufacturing plant from the new warehouse. The company has records of truck loading and unloading times for these goods as well as travel-time data between plant and warehouse from which it has constructed the following frequency distribution on the number of pounds of product a fully loaded truck can move from plant to warehouse in an 8-hr period.

Pounds of product moved per 8-hr day per truck	Relative frequency
28,000–31,999	0.08
32,000–35,999	0.23
36,000–39,999	0.36
40,000–43,999	0.15
44,000–47,999	0.11
48,000–51,999	0.07
	1.00

How would you determine the average amount of finished goods undelivered at the end of the day and the average amount of unused truck capacity if various numbers of trucks are used? Illustrate by simulating 5 days of activity.

3. The Marrow Company is distributing an appliance which is manufactured for it under contract by another manufacturing company. The contract provides for specification of average daily deliveries at the beginning of each calendar year. This method of delivery should be fairly satisfactory because the sales pattern shows no seasonal pattern and it is possible to forecast sales for the next calendar year with considerable accuracy. It is necessary to carry a cushion or safety stock because there is some daily variation in the deliveries from the manufacturer and in the sales of the Marrow Company. We desire to determine the size of safety stock needed to minimize the total of the costs of stock-out and of holding safety stock. Daily sales are forecast at 200 per day, with a standard deviation of 20, and an approximately normal distribution. Deliveries from the manufacturer will also average 200 per day, with a standard deviation of 10, and an approximately normal distribution. Holding costs are estimated at $100 per appliance per year and the opportunity cost of a stock-out is estimated at $60 per stockout of an appliance. How would you use Monte Carlo methods to determine the economic size of safety stock which the Marrow Company should carry? Illustrate by simulating 5 days of activity with buffer stocks at 0 and 10.

26 Waiting-time (Queuing) Evaluations

Many problems of economic decision-making involve the economics of waiting time (queuing): persons and facilities waiting for work (idle time) and work (items or persons) queuing up and waiting for facilities or persons.

Economic problems involving waiting time and queuing are present in many aspects of enterprise operation when there is random variability in requirements for certain services and/or in the time required to provide the services.

How many order-entry clerks should be employed to obtain the best economic balance between the cost of idle clerical and/or machine time and delay in processing incoming orders?

How many machines should one operator tend to provide the best balance between the cost of machines waiting for the operator when he is overloaded and the operator's waiting (idle) time when his services (setting up, loading, adjusting, and unloading) are not required?

How many wrapping counters should be provided in a department store to obtain the optimum balance between idle wrapping clerks and delays to customers lining up and waiting for wrapping service?

What is the optimum factory layout? How should production be scheduled: to minimize idle machine time or to minimize the production time cycle or operator waiting time?

How many maintenance crews should be employed to obtain the best economic balance between the times when service is delayed and the times the crews will be idle?

These problems involve variable flows and the capacities of facilities to handle these flows. We must strike a balance between costs of waiting and costs of idle time to answer these questions. Economic evaluation of alternatives requires forecasts of waiting times for various flows and capacities.

Types of Systems Changes. The types of alternative courses of action which may require economic evaluation can be classified as follows.

1. Changing the number of servicing stations (e.g., number of maintenance crews)

2. Reorganizing the service stations so that the servicing time is changed (e.g., smaller maintenance crews taking longer per repair or

408

larger crews taking shorter time per repair) and perhaps also changing the number of stations (e.g., increasing or decreasing the number of crews at the same time)

3. Changing queue discipline (e.g., the order in which maintenance repair requests are handled)

4. Changing service policy (e.g., the policy on what kinds of repairs are handled by maintenance crews or the policy on when overtime is authorized for maintenance repairs)

Stable Systems. When the average number of items per hour arriving on a receiving dock is greater than the average hourly capacity of the dock handlers to handle them, incoming materials will obviously continue to accumulate on the receiving dock. The average capacity of the servicing facility must be at least equal to the average flow of arrivals or a waiting line will continue to build up indefinitely. This build-up will continue until the capacity of the servicing facility is increased or the flow of arrivals is reduced. Until one or the other is done, the system is unstable.

In the remainder of this chapter, we shall be concerned with situations in which the system has settled down to stable values. This does not mean that the number on a waiting line becomes stable, but that the probability of a given number being on a waiting line at any time remains constant. We shall not be concerned with the transient state which occurs while the waiting-line probabilities are adjusting from one operating pattern to another. For example, when a repair service opens for business the probability of the first arrivals finding a waiting line is zero. This probability will increase as the business stays open until a steady state is reached: the probability of finding given numbers on the waiting line having stabilized.

Solution of Waiting-time Problems. To solve waiting-time problems, we must know

1. The input pattern—the quantities of paperwork, repair calls, material receipts, etc., which arrive at the servicing facility and the pattern (distribution) of variations of the arrivals

2. Queue discipline—the order in which the arrivals are serviced

3. Output

a. The number of servicing stations (such as wrapping desks, maintenance crews, etc.)

b. The quantities which each servicing station can handle and the patterns (distribution) of variation of service times

4. Service policy—how much service is given under various circumstances

Monte Carlo Methods. Monte Carlo simulation methods are particularly well suited to handle many queuing evaluations. It is frequently impossible or extremely difficult to analyze some queuing problems mathematically to enable the determination of optimal solutions. When solvable mathematical models cannot be conveniently developed, Monte Carlo methods can often be used to simulate the queuing system in a realistic manner. The general approach to be used in these cases was illustrated in Chapter 25.

Mathematical Models. To illustrate the methodology of using analytic queuing models, we shall discuss in this chapter mathematical queuing models which satisfy the following general conditions:

1. Input—the probability of an arrival at any instant is always the same regardless of what has happened previously or the length of the waiting line. Under these conditions, we would expect the arrivals to follow a Poisson distribution.

2. Queue discipline—there is a single line for arrivals, with a rule of first come, first served, and no arrival leaves until it has been serviced.

3. Output—servicing rates follow an exponential distribution. This assumption has proved itself valid in a considerable percentage of cases, even where there have been weak theoretical grounds for expecting that the probability that the servicing will terminate at any instant is independent of what has happened previously. In each case, however, we must review the data and test this assumption in the light of the discussions of Chapter 22.

The following symbols will be used:

A = average number of arrivals per unit time
S = average number of servicings per unit time which each station can perform
N = number of service stations

Single Servicing Station. In a single-station line, the station is busy A/S of the time and is idle $(1 - A/S)$ of the time. A/S is thus a measure of the utilization of the capacity of the service station. For example, if customers in a repair shop arrive at an average rate of 60 per day and they receive service at an average rate of 100 per day, then the facility (station) is busy $\frac{60}{100}$ of the time and is idle $\frac{40}{100}$ of the time.

Proportion of Arrivals Who Must Wait. A customer will have to wait if he arrives when the facility is occupied servicing other customers. The probability that any customer will have to wait is therefore $A/S = \frac{60}{100}$, or 60 per cent of the time because the facility is busy.

Proportion of Time Facility is Idle. As previously noted, the facility is idle $(1 - A/S)$ of the time. In our example, $(1 - \frac{60}{100})$, or 40 per cent of the time.

Average Waiting Time of Arrivals. This equals $A/[S(S - A)]$, or $60/[100(100 - 60)] = 0.015$ day. This average includes the zero waiting times of those who do not wait at all.

Average Length of Waiting Lines. The average length of waiting lines is equal to the average waiting time of arrivals times the arrival rate, or

$A^2/[S(S - A)]$. For our repair-shop example, this equals

$$\frac{3,600}{100(100 - 60)} = 0.90 \text{ customer}$$

or an average of a little less than one customer. This average obviously includes the times zero customers are waiting.

Assuming a service rate of 100 per day, Figure 26-1 shows how these

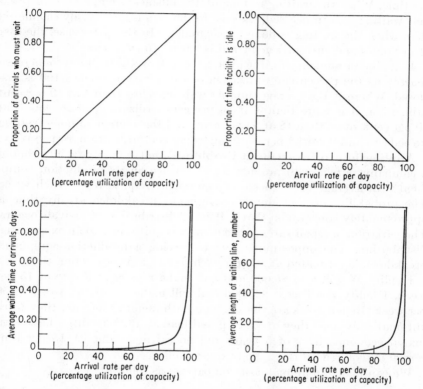

Figure 26-1. Changes in waiting-line values with variation in percentage utilization of capacity in a single service station (service rate = 100 per day).

waiting-line values vary as the arrival rate approaches the service rate. From these charts we can note the following:

1. The number of customers who will have to wait increases proportionately as the arrival rate approaches the service rate (capacity of the station).

2. The cost of idle facilities decreases proportionally as the arrival rate approaches the service rate.

3. However, the average waiting time of arrivals increases sharply as the arrival rate approaches the service rate. Thus, at 60 per cent utiliza-

tion of capacity, the average waiting time is 0.015 day; at 80 per cent utilization it is 0.04 day; at 90 per cent, it is 0.09 day; at 95 per cent, it is 0.19 day, more than twice as long as at 90 per cent utilization; and at 98 per cent and 99 per cent, the average waiting times of arrivals are almost a full half-day and a full day, respectively.

The total waiting time, computed by multiplying the number arriving in any interval by the average waiting time, determines the cost of waiting time. When the waiting is done by the business's employees, or products waiting to be processed, the cost to the firm is more easily calculated than when the waiting is done by customers. In the latter case, the cost of lost sales and customer good will is harder to estimate.

4. A similar tendency for the average length of waiting lines to increase sharply as the percentage utilization of capacity approaches 100 is disclosed. Whereas, the average number waiting is less than 1 at 60 per cent utilization, it is more than 3 at 80 per cent utilization, more than 8 at 90 per cent, more than 18 at 95 per cent, and the average number waiting exceeds 48 and 98 at 98 per cent and 99 per cent utilization, respectively.

Application to Investment Problem. What capacity facility should a company purchase to provide repair service on its production equipment? An average of 12 pieces of equipment require repair each week. The probability of a production-equipment breakdown at any time is approximately constant so that a Poisson distribution of arrivals occurs. The variation in repair rates of the facility is quite close to an exponential distribution. The opportunity cost of having a production-equipment breakdown is estimated at $25 for each day of lost production time.

Facility W will cost $5,000 and will make repairs at a rate of 15 per week. Facility Z will cost $20,000 and will make repairs at a rate of 50 per week. Repair costs are the same on both facilities because they work automatically once they are set up and loaded. Both facilities have estimated economic lives of 5 years and no salvage value. A 15 per cent return is required on this type of investment.

We can make an annual-cost comparison as follows:

Facility W:

Capital-recovery cost,

$$\$5,000 \left(i = 15\% \atop n = 5 \right) = \$5,000(0.29832) = \$1,492$$

Cost of lost production-equipment time,
   Time waiting to be repaired,

$$\text{Average per arrival} = \frac{A}{S(S - A)} = \frac{12}{15(15 - 12)} = 0.27 \text{ week}$$

$$\text{Total per year} = (12)(52)(0.27) = 168.5 \text{ weeks}$$

Time being repaired,
  Average per repair = $\frac{1}{15}$ = 0.07 week
  Total per year = $(12)(52)(0.07)$ = 43.7 weeks
  Total waiting and repair time per year = $168.5 + 43.7 = 212.2$ weeks
  Total cost per year = $(5)(\$25)(212.2)$ = \$26,525
Total annual cost = $\$1,492 + \$26,525 = \$28,017$

Facility Z:

Capital-recovery cost,

$$\$20,000 \left(\begin{array}{c} \text{CR} \\ i = 15\% \\ n = 5 \end{array} \right) = \$20,000(0.29832) = \$5,966$$

Cost of lost production-equipment time,
  Time waiting to be repaired,

$$\text{Average per arrival} = \frac{A}{S(S - A)} = \frac{12}{50(50 - 12)} = 0.006 \text{ week}$$

  Total per year = $(12)(52)(0.006)$ = 3.7 weeks
  Time being repaired,
    Average per repair = $\frac{1}{50}$ = 0.02 week
    Total per year = $(12)(52)(0.02)$ = 12.5 weeks
  Total waiting and repair time per year = $3.7 + 12.5 = 16.2$ weeks
  Total cost per year = $(5)(\$25)(16.2)$ = \$2,025
Total annual cost = $\$5,966 + 2,025 = \$7,991$

Multiple Servicing Stations. The owner of our repair shop has purchased a competing business which has an arrival rate of 120 per day. He plans on routing all the business of the newly acquired firm to his own shop. Thus, his repair-shop arrival rate is being increased to 180 per day. To handle this arrival rate, he established two additional repair facilities, so that he now has three servicing stations ($N = 3$). He has one line for all customers, each of whom is serviced by the first available station (facility) in the order of first come, first served.

The numerical answers to many questions regarding multiple-station waiting-line problems can be evaluated most readily if we know the probability that all stations are idle at any instant (that nobody is being serviced or is waiting at any instant). We will denote this probability that the system or shop is empty of customers by p_0.

$$p_0 = \cfrac{1}{\left[\sum_{n=0}^{N-1} \frac{1}{n!} \left(\frac{A}{S} \right)^n \right] + \frac{1}{N!} \left(\frac{A}{S} \right)^N \left(\frac{NS}{NS - A} \right)}$$

In our example, $A = 180$ per day, $S = 100$ per station per day, and $N = 3$. Therefore,

$$p_0 = \cfrac{1}{\left[\displaystyle\sum_{n=0}^{2} \frac{1}{n!}\left(\frac{180}{100}\right)^n\right] + \frac{1}{3!}\left(\frac{180}{100}\right)^3\left(\frac{3(100)}{3(100)-180}\right)}$$

$$\left[\sum_{n=0}^{2} \frac{1}{n!}\left(\frac{180}{100}\right)^n\right] = 1 + 1.8 + \frac{1}{2}(1.8)^2 = 4.42$$

$$\frac{1}{3!}\left(\frac{180}{100}\right)^3\left[\frac{3(100)}{3(100)-180}\right] = \frac{1}{6}(1.8)^3\left(\frac{300}{120}\right) = 2.43$$

$$p_0 = \frac{1}{4.42 + 2.43} = 0.146$$

Proportion of Arrivals Who Must Wait. In this case, when a customer arrives, he will obtain immediate service if none, one, or two of the stations are not being used at the time. He will have to wait if N or more other arrivals are still there, either being serviced or waiting in line. The probability that an arrival will occur when N or more other arrivals are still there, either being serviced or waiting on line, is

$$\frac{S(A/S)^N}{(N-1)!(NS-A)}\, p_0$$

For our repair shop, the probability that a customer will arrive when 3 or more other customers are in the repair shop is

$$\frac{100\left(\frac{180}{100}\right)^3}{(3-1)![3(100)-180]}\,(0.146) = 0.35$$

This is the proportion of arrivals who must wait.

Proportion of Time Facilities Are Idle. How would we determine the average proportion of time the repair-shop stations will be idle?

Since the number of arrivals per day, 180, is less than the total capacity of all three stations per day, 300, and since in the long run all arrivals are serviced even if they are delayed, the long-run average proportion of time the three stations will be working is $\frac{180}{300}$, or 0.60. Therefore, the average proportion of idle time will be 1.00 minus 0.60, or 0.40.

We know from previous calculation that the probability of all three stations being empty or idle at any instant is 0.146. We also would like to know the probability of two being idle at any instant, which is the same as the probability of one being busy (p_1); as well as the probability of one being idle at any instant, which is the same as the probability of two being busy (p_2).

The probability that a arrivals or customers are in the system, either being serviced or are waiting to be serviced, at any time is

$$p_a = \frac{1}{a!}\left(\frac{A}{S}\right)^a p_0$$

when a, the number of arrivals or customers in the system, is not greater than N, the number of servicing stations ($a \leq N$). This formula becomes $p_a = \frac{1}{N!N^{a-N}}\left(\frac{A}{S}\right)^a p_0$ when the number of customers in the system is greater than the number of servicing stations ($a > N$). This second formula is equivalent to the first when $a = N$.

The probability of two stations being idle is

$$p_1 = \frac{1}{1!}\left(\frac{180}{100}\right)(0.146) = 0.263$$

The probability of one station being idle is

$$p_2 = \frac{1}{2!}\left(\frac{180}{100}\right)^2 (0.146) = 0.237$$

At any instant, the total number of expected idle repair stations would be equal to $3p_0 + 2p_1 + 1p_2$ or $3(0.146) + 2(0.263) + (0.237) = 1.201$.

The average proportion of time any station is idle would be this total, 1.201, divided by 3, the number of repair stations, or 0.40. This checks with our previous calculation at the beginning of this section of average proportion of time idle.

A general formula for the average idle time per station is

$$\frac{Np_0 + (N-1)p_1 + (N-2)p_2 + \cdots + p_{N-1}}{N}$$

Average Waiting Time of Arrivals. The formula for the average waiting time of arrivals is

$$\frac{S(A/S)^N}{(N-1)!(NS-A)^2}p_0$$

For our repair shop, the average waiting time of all customers is

$$\frac{100(\frac{180}{100})^3}{(3-1)![3(100)-180]^2}(0.146) = 0.003 \text{ day}$$

Average Length of Waiting Line. The average length of the single waiting line equals the average waiting time of arrivals times the arrival rate, or

$$\frac{AS(A/S)^N}{(N-1)!(NS-A)^2}p_0$$

For our 3-station repair shop:

$$\frac{(180)(100)(\frac{180}{100})^3}{(3-1)![3(100)-180]^2}(0.146) = 0.53$$

The ratio of arrivals to total capacity in the multistation service facility is 180 to 3(100), or 60 per cent, just as it was in the single-station repair shop. However, note the comparisons in Table 26-1. With the same degree of capacity utilization, only 35 per cent of the arrivals must wait in the 3-station facility compared with 60 per cent in the single-station facility; the facility is completely idle only 0.15 of the time with 3 service stations compared with 0.40 for the single station; the average waiting time is 0.003 day with the 3-station facility compared to 0.015 day; and the average length of the waiting line is reduced to 0.53 customer from 0.90 customer in the single-station facility.

Table **26-1. Comparison of Single- and Three-station Service Facility (Ratio of Arrivals to Total Capacity = 0.60)**

	Single-station repair shop	Three-station repair shop
Proportion of arrivals who must wait...........	0.60	0.35
Proportion of time facility is completely idle.....	0.40	0.15*
Average waiting time of arrivals................	0.015 day	0.003 day
Average length of waiting line.................	0.90 customer	0.53 customer

* Proportion of time all three stations are idle. As explained in the text, the average proportion of time the individual stations are idle is obviously 0.40, one minus the ratio of the arrival rate to the total capacity of all three stations.

Assuming a service rate of 100 per day per station, Figure 26-2 shows how the waiting-line values vary with the number of separate stations serviced by a single waiting line as well as the degree of utilization of capacity. We see that the proportion of arrivals who must wait decreases markedly for the same percentage utilization of capacity as the number of stations increases. Thus at 60 per cent utilization of capacity, the proportion of arrivals who must wait decreases from 0.60 with a single service station, to 0.45 with 2 stations, to 0.36 with 3 stations, to 0.24 with 5 stations. As the percentage utilization of capacity increases toward 100 per cent, the proportion of arrivals who must wait increases more rapidly as the number of service stations are increased. Therefore, at the higher percentage utilizations, the differences between the proportion who must wait with the various number of service stations become smaller and disappear entirely at 100 per cent utilization. Thus, at 90 per cent utilization, 0.90 must wait with a single service station, 0.86 with 2 stations, 0.82 with 3 stations, and 0.77 with 5 stations.

The proportion of time the facilities are completely idle decreases as the percentage utilization increases. It decreases at a much more rapid rate as the number of stations is increased. (The average proportion of time the stations are idle is, of course, equal to one minus the proportionate utilization of the capacity and is the same whether there are one or a dozen stations.)

The average waiting time of arrivals increases sharply as the arrival rate approaches the total capacity of the facility, regardless of the number of stations. However, the increase is suppressed as the number of stations

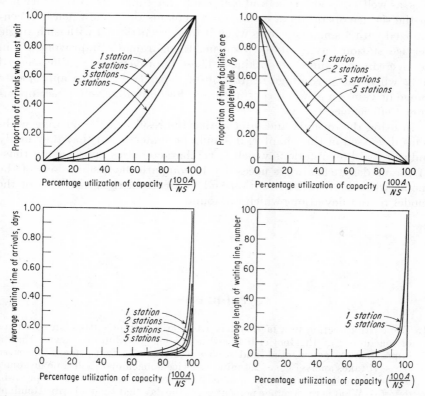

Figure 26-2. Changes in waiting-line values with variations in percentage utilization of capacity and number of service stations (service rate = 100 per station per day).

is increased. Thus, at 60 per cent utilization of capacity, the average waiting time is 0.015 day with 1 service station, 0.006 day with 2 stations, 0.003 day with 3 stations, and 0.001 day with 5 stations. At 80 per cent utilization, the average waiting time is still only 0.006 day with 5 stations whereas it has risen to 0.040 day for a single station. At 99 per cent utilization, the average waiting time is only 0.195 day with 5 stations, 0.327 day with 3 stations, 0.493 day with 2 stations, and 0.990 day with a single station facility.

The average length of waiting line increases sharply as the utilization approaches capacity. As shown in the chart, this rate of increase of waiting-line length is not reduced significantly by increasing the number of stations from 1 to 5.

These charts show how waiting lines and capacity requirements may be affected by centralization in an organization of certain service operations, such as record-keeping, report preparation, and stenographic services, as well as various sales and manufacturing functions. If the efficiency of the service operation of each station remains the same when it is centralized with a single queue as when it was decentralized with each single service station having its own queue, then dramatic improvements in service can sometimes be obtained. These improvements can be secured only when the percentage utilization of capacity is in the appropriate range of values and when centralization does not adversely affect operational efficiencies.

In using the formula and interpreting the results of the queuing problems discussed in this chapter, it should be remembered that they apply only to real-life situations which have characteristics approaching those of the model. It is always necessary to compare the assumptions of the model with the real-life situation and to ascertain the sensitivity of the model to any deviations which are found.

PROBLEMS

1. The cutting section in a factory has a tool crib with one attendant. Arrivals of machinists at the tool crib follow a Poisson distribution, service time is approximately exponential, and service is given on a first-come, first-served basis. It takes an average of 2.4 min to service a machinist each time he comes to the tool crib. The average number of arrivals of machinists is 80 per 8-hr day. (a) What is the average percentage of the day that the tool crib attendant will be idle (not servicing machinists)? (b) What is the probability that a machinist must wait? (c) What is the average length of time that he must wait?

2. The size of the cutting section of problem 1 has expanded and the average number of arrivals is now doubled, 160 per 8-hr day (all other conditions as described). (a) By what percentage has the average proportion of the day that the tool crib attendant will be idle (not servicing machinists) decreased? (b) By what percentage has the probability that a machinist must wait increased? (c) By what percentage has the average length of time that a machinist must wait increased?

3. A second attendant is assigned to the tool crib of problems 1 and 2 after the number of arrivals has doubled to 160 per 8-hr day. The machinists wait on one line and are serviced by the first available attendant in the order of first-come, first-served. (a) How does the average proportion of the day that the

tool crib attendants are idle compare with the situation in problem 2? in problem 1? (b) By what percentage has the probability that a machinist must wait been decreased compared with the situation in problem 2? compared with the situation in problem 1? (c) By what percentage has the average length of time that a machinist must wait been reduced compared with the situation in problem 2? compared with the situation in problem 1?

4. The number of arrivals of machinists requiring tool crib service has now increased to 400 per day. All other conditions are the same as in problem 1. If tool crib attendants cost \$140 each and machinists \$500 each for a 40-hr week (including indirect costs), how many tool crib attendants should be provided for minimum total cost? Set up the equation for the cost which must be minimized, but do not solve for numerical answer.

5. A drug store has two salesclerks and one cashier-wrapper. The salesclerk serves a customer (excluding the wrapping and payment) in an average of 1.2 min. The cashier-wrapper wraps and takes payment in 0.4 min. Fifty customers are served per hour from 2 to 4 P.M. daily. Customer arrivals are approximately Poisson and service times exponential. What would be the effects on average waiting times and average lengths of waiting lines if the cashier-wrapper and the salesclerk jobs were combined, (a) If the average total time to serve, wrap, and take payment becomes $1.2 + 0.4 = 1.6$ min? (b) If the average total time to serve, wrap, and take payment becomes 2.0 min?

6. It is difficult to estimate the opportunity costs of machine breakdown with great accuracy. In the example in the text of the application of waiting-time theory to the evaluation of a proposal to invest in a repair facility, an opportunity cost of \$25 for each day of lost production was used. How much in error can this cost estimate be without affecting the decision in this example?

7. A queuing model rarely approximates reality very exactly. Predictions from a queuing model will therefore deviate from what will happen in real life. Does this make use of queuing models valueless? Explain.

27   Evaluating Intangibles

The subjects discussed thus far in this volume have been directed largely to the problems of making tangible analyses and evaluations of engineering and business alternatives. Properly prepared tangible evaluations will usually be more accurate, objective, and reliable than intangible evaluations. However, it is frequently not possible to evaluate tangibly all the factors which are pertinent to an economic decision. We will therefore discuss in this chapter some of the possible ways of evaluating intangible objectives.

Ignoring Intangibles. Because they are difficult to evaluate, there is sometimes a tendency to ignore intangible criteria. This is poor practice which ultimately proves uneconomic. Even if nonsubjective, quantitative evaluation is impossible, these criteria should be considered. The effects of these intangible factors may sometimes be more important than the tangible ones. Therefore, the logical choice of a course of action cannot be made without evaluation of these intangibles. (If pertinent intangibles are not considered explicitly, the final decision will be based upon unevaluated, implicit values for these intangibles.)

Making Intangibles Tangible by Valuation. It has been suggested previously that intangibles can always be made tangible if one puts enough time and effort into the determination of dollar or other quantitative values and if one is willing to accept a large enough risk and uncertainty as to the accuracy of the estimates. Where to draw the line in quantitative evaluation is a problem of economics and judgment.

The saving of human life would most frequently be considered an intangible objective of great importance. Should we attempt to place a price on a human life and convert this into a tangible objective? There are many ways of doing this, each of which will give us different answers, none of which may be truly valid in any particular case. Suggested means of obtaining values must of necessity be arbitrary and subjective.

One suggestion is that " . . . it appears reasonable to equate the economic (not emotional) value of a human life at that amount of money which can be afforded to prevent its accidental loss in our society. This amount of money varies in a variety of circumstances but can be assessed as normally being less than $100,000 and more than $10,000. To be conservative, we may postulate an allowable expenditure of $50,000 per life saved . . . ."[1] How much society can afford to spend to prevent accidental loss of life depends upon many subjective assumptions. Another method could average the current level of court awards in compensation suits involving accidental death. Another could average the values assigned by independent analysts in the recent past. Another could consider how much companies or governmental units are willing to spend to reduce the risks of loss of life and compute the implied value placed on human life. These are all arbitrary, some involve circular reasoning, and the meanings of the values are not very easy to understand.

Equal-cost Approach to Evaluation of Intangibles. In some cases, where only one of the significant objectives is intangible, an equal-cost approach can be used in evaluating the intangibles and alternatives at the same time. (Methods of making equal-cost calculations were discussed in Chapter 12.) For example, two alternative safety proposals in a chemical plant are being considered. Alternative A will cost $20,000 a year per machine unit and alternative B will cost $35,000 a year per machine unit. The expected reduction in hazards of death from explosion is evaluated as follows.

	Present	Alternative A	Alternative B
Estimated probability of an explosion in any year..........	1 in 100,000, or 0.00001	1 in 500,000, or 0.000002	1 in 1,000,000, or 0.000001
Estimated size of death toll in an explosion if one occurs........	25	10	10
Estimated expected number of lives lost per year (probability of an explosion times death toll in an explosion).............	0.00025	0.00002	0.00001

If alternative A is adopted, we are spending $20,000 per year to save 0.00023 life per year (the difference between the expected number of lives lost per year under present safety conditions and those of alternative A, 0.00025 minus 0.00002). If alternative A is adopted, this places a value of $87,000,000 on a life ($20,000 divided by 0.00023). The total costs of alternative A are no greater than present costs if we place this value on a life.

If alternative B is adopted, we are spending an extra $15,000 (the difference between the $35,000 a year cost of alternative B and the $20,000 a year cost of alternative A) to save 0.00001 life (the difference between the expected number of lives lost per year under alternative A and alternative B, 0.00002 minus 0.00001). This places a value of $1,500,000,000

---

[1] A. L. Stanly, "Evaluating Intangibles for Executive Decision," *Mechanical Engineering*, September, 1955, p. 781.

on a life ($15,000 divided by 0.00001). Total costs of alternatives A and B are equal with a life valued at this figure.

In this example, it was assumed there were no other intangible factors and that the probabilities of an explosion and the size of the death toll in an explosion could be estimated with precision and little risk of error.

This type of equal-cost calculation can provide a basis for decision-making. Instead of deciding on a dollar value for an intangible factor, we calculate an equal-cost value. The decision-makers can then decide merely whether they estimate the dollar value above or below this equal-cost value.

Utility Functions and Values. We noted in Chapter 20 that

1. The value of additional dollars of potential or actual income varies between individuals and between companies.

2. The value of additional dollars of potential or actual income decreases as the total income increases, following the well-known economic law of diminishing returns. We thus have a diminishing marginal value of money. If we denote the value of money as its utility, each individual or company has a utility curve, such as Figure 27-1, which exhibits this diminishing marginal utility.[1] The utility curves of different individuals or companies are difficult to approximate. They indicate relative values of decreases or increases of income to these individuals or companies, but do not indicate anything about relative values of money between individuals or companies. We cannot say that money has more or less utility to one or another individual or company by examining estimated utility functions.

Figure 27-1. Utility curve showing income with a diminishing marginal utility.

3. The expected value or expected utility of additional dollars of potential or actual income is lower as the risk (dispersion) is increased when the dollar values are large compared to the wealth of the individual or company. A certain $100,000 additional income is preferred to a $200,000 income with a 50 per cent risk of no income when a person's other income totals $10,000. However, a person may have no preference between these alternatives if he has $4,000,000 of other income.

[1] An argument has been made for utility curves which have a diminishing marginal utility, as shown in Figure 27-1, for the low-income dollar values; then an increasing marginal-utility portion for middle-income dollar values; and, finally, a diminishing marginal-utility portion for the high-income dollar values. See M. Friedman and L. F. Savage, "The Utility Analysis of Choices Involving Risk," *Journal of Political Economy,* vol. 56, pp. 279–304, 1948.

Differences in utility values occur because of differences in the decision-making environment, the alternatives being considered, and the decision-makers' preferences. Utility values are the results of factors which produce decision-making preferences. Utility values do not produce the preferences. Thus, a utility function is valid only for a particular type of decision situation and cannot be used in another decision situation or with different alternatives. A utility function should not be considered to represent the value of money. It represents a subjective measure of managerial attitudes in a given situation toward risks and incremental revenue or cost.

Quantifying Intangibles (Not in Common Denominator). Even though the anticipated performance with reference to the intangible objective cannot be valued in dollars (or whatever other common denominator is used), in many cases it can be quantified in other units to assist in the evaluation.

It may not be possible to place dollar values on the different accuracies or lack of accuracies of several alternative record-keeping systems. Nevertheless, forecasts of the number of errors of various kinds which may be expected under each alternative would be very helpful in evaluating this intangible.

It may not be possible to place dollar values readily on the different delivery-time cycles required under several alternative proposed inventory and shipping facilities and procedures. However, quantitative knowledge of the average number of days for delivery of a customer's order and the expected variations from the average under each alternative will be valuable in evaluating performance against this intangible criterion.

Basic Procedure for Quantifying Judgment Values. When intangible factors predominate, a basic approach[1] to evaluating alternative proposals is to determine a measure of expected utility by

1. Establishing the criteria for decision-making by determining the relative importance of each of the various objectives of the proposals. Each criterion then has an importance rating.

2. Evaluating how effectively each alternative meets each of these criteria. Each alternative then has an effectiveness (or utility) with respect to each criterion.

3. Obtaining a rated value for each alternative by computing a weighted average of the effectiveness ratings. The effectiveness ratings will be weighted by the relative-importance ratings of (1) above.

A form for making these judgments and calculations and comparing the results is shown in Table 27-1. Each significant objective or criterion is ranked in order of estimated importance, from the most important to the least important. They are then listed in column 1. We assign an impor-

[1] Adapted from N. N. Barish, *Systems Analysis for Effective Administration*, Funk & Wagnalls Company, New York, 1951.

Table 27-1. Evaluation Work Sheet

Objective or criterion	Importance rating	Adjusted importance rating	Alternative proposals									
			Alternative 1		Alternative 2		Alternative 3		Alternative 4		Alternative 5	
			Effectiveness rating	Rated value	Effectiveness rating	Rated value	Effectiveness rating	Rated value	Effectiveness rating	Rated value	Effectiveness rating	Rated value
(1)	(2)	(3)	(4)	(5)	(4)	(5)	(4)	(5)	(4)	(5)	(4)	(5)
1												
2												
3												
4												
5												
Total		100	xxxxxx		xxxxxx		xxxxxx		xxxxxx		xxxxxx	

tance rating of 100 to the most important objective and then assign decreasing values to the other objectives based on our estimates of their relative importances to each other. We place these ratings in column 2. These relative-importance ratings are adjusted so that they total 100 and are placed in column 3. (This is done by adding up the unadjusted ratings, dividing each unadjusted rating by the sum of the unadjusted ratings, and then multiplying the quotient by 100.) Each alternative's effectiveness ratings are listed in the respective columns 4. The rated value components of columns 5 are obtained by multiplying each of the columns 4 effectiveness ratings by the importance ratings of column 3. The total rated values for each alternative are obtained by summing the columns 5 of each alternative and dividing by 100.

Logic and Assumptions of Procedure. The logic of this procedure is based upon having the objectives stated in such a manner that they are

1. Distinct, one not implying any of the others

2. Independent, the achievement of one not influencing or affecting the achievement of any of the others

3. Not contradictory, the achievement of any combination of objectives not being impossible

4. Additive, the achievement of each objective adding to the total desirability regardless of the achievement of other objectives

We can illustrate these conditions by example.

1. If one objective is to decrease maintenance costs and another is to decrease factory costs, the two objectives are not distinct because maintenance costs are a part of factory costs and a decrease in maintenance costs automatically implies a decrease in factory costs if other things remain the same.

2. If one objective is to improve over-all customer service and another is to provide a larger safety stock of finished-goods inventory so that fewer stock-outs develop, the objectives are not independent. The objective of a larger safety stock is not necessarily a part of the objective of improving over-all customer service, but it will certainly have an effect on one facet of customer service.

3. If one objective is to lower the average investment in inventory and another is to increase production lot sizes, the two objectives are contradictory because the increase of production lot sizes is impossible without an increase in average investment in inventory, other things being equal.

4. If I rate high quality as 40 per cent important in an objective and low cost as 30 per cent, then an alternative which will give me both high quality and low price is worth 70 per cent, the simple addition of the importance ratings of the two objectives. Or is it worth 85 per cent in combination? We would like our objectives to be stated so that they are, as much as possible, simply additive. This is, however, very difficult to

achieve. Sometimes, a clearer understanding and specification of objectives can be helpful. Thus, the true objective may actually be high quality within a specified range of costs.

It is frequently difficult to specify objectives so that they satisfy all of the above conditions completely. However, the closer that this can be accomplished, the more accurate will be our evaluation.

Improving the Reliability of Importance Ratings. The first step in the previously described basic procedure for quantifying judgmental evaluation of alternatives when the objectives are intangible was establishing criteria. This was accomplished by determining importance ratings for each objective. How can we improve the reliability and accuracy of our determination of these importance ratings?

We can do so by following a systematic procedure for checking our judgments for consistency of the relative evaluations, by reevaluating our determinations where they are not consistent, and by systematically continuing to recheck and reevaluate until complete internal consistency of value judgments is obtained.

Our checking and reevaluation procedure[1] works essentially as follows:

1. The objectives to which we had previously assigned importance ratings are listed in order of descending importance (as in column 2 of Table 27-1).

2. Compare the first and most important objective with all the remaining ones put together. Do you consider it more important, equally important, or less important than all the others further down on the list put together?

3. If you consider the first objective more important than all the others put together, see if its importance rating is greater than the sum of the importance ratings of all the other objectives. If it is not, change the importance rating of the first objective so that it is greater than the sum of the others.

4. If you consider the first objective of equal importance to all the others put together, see if its importance rating is equal to the sum of the importance ratings of all the other objectives. If it is not, change the importance rating of the first objective so that it is equal to the sum of the others.

5. If you consider the first objective less important than all the others put together, see if its importance rating is less than the sum of the importance ratings of all the other objectives. If it is not, change the importance rating of the first objective so that it is less than the sum of the others.

---

[1] Quite a number of different procedures can be used to make consistency comparisons of the relative importance of objectives in a systematic manner. The procedure presented here is one of several used in the author's industrial consulting practice. It is adapted from a procedure suggested in C. W. Churchman, R. L. Ackoff, and E. L. Arnoff, *Introduction to Operations Research*, John Wiley & Sons, Inc., New York, 1957.

6. If the first objective was considered more important or equally important to all the others put together, apply the same procedure to the second most important objective on the list. Do you consider it more important, equally important, or less important than all the others farther down on the list put together? Then proceed as in (3), (4), or (5) above, applying the proper paragraph to the second objective instead of the first.

7. If the first objective was considered less important than all the others put together, compare the first objective with all the remaining ones put together except the lowest one. Do you consider it more important, equally important, or less important than all the others farther down on the list except the lowest one put together? Then proceed as in (3), (4), or (5) above. If (3) or (4) are applicable, proceed to (6) after applying (3) or (4). If (5) is applicable, proceed as in this paragraph (7) again, comparing the first objective with all the remaining ones put together except the lowest two. As long as (5) is applicable, the procedures of this paragraph (7) are repeated, until after the first objective is compared with the second and third objectives put together. Then, even if (5) is still applicable proceed to (6).

8. Continue the above procedures until the third from the lowest objective has been compared with the two lowest objectives on the list.

In making the necessary adjustments in importance ratings at each step of the procedure, always try not to change the relative values of the importance ratings of the objectives within the "put-together" groups.

All comparisons should be reviewed at the end of the procedure to ensure that later adjustments have not upset relationships which were established earlier. When necessary, portions of the procedure are repeated.

The adjusted importance ratings which add up to 100 are computed by totaling the last revised ratings, dividing each rating by the total, and multiplying by 100.

Criteria Development Sheet. A form is provided in Table 27-2 for applying this procedure. We will illustrate its use with a hypothetical incoming-material-inspection-system proposal.

Space is provided on the form for listing no more than 6 objectives or criteria. When there are more than 6, the procedure becomes cumbersome. A suitable modification of this procedure for 7 or more objectives is presented later.

We list the four objectives for our incoming-material inspection system in the first column in order of decreasing importance: high reliability, low cost, short time requirements, and high flexibility in meeting changing needs. In actual practice, we would define these objectives very carefully to have them meet our previously described assumptions regarding independence, additivity, etc., as closely as possible. It is also usually important to specify the maximum range of permissible variation of achievement of these objectives. For example, we would not consider adopting an alternative which would result in a reliability level below a specified point.

Table 27-2. **Criteria Development Sheet**

Objective or criteria	Initial importance ratings	Importance rating revisions										Adjusted importance ratings
		1	2	3	4	5	6	7	8	9	10	
1. High reliability.................	100	125	125	150								48
2. Low cost......................	60	60	85	85								28
3. Short time requirements.........	50	50	50	50								16
4. High flexibility in meeting changing needs......................	25	25	25	25								8
5.												
6.												

We enter our initial evaluations of the relative importance of these objectives, placing an importance rating of 100 on the first objective and decreasing values on the others going down the list: 100, 60, 50, and 25.

We compare the high-reliability objective with the low-cost, short-time requirements, and high-flexibility objectives put together. Do we consider the former more important, equally important, or less important than the latter? We decide that is is less important.

We now compare the importance ratings we previously gave the individual objectives. Is 100, the rating given the high-reliability objective, less than $60 + 50 + 25$, the sum of the ratings given the low-cost, short-time requirements, and high-flexibility objectives, respectively? Yes, 100 is less than 135. Therefore, no revision of the initial importance ratings is necessary.

Because the high-reliability objective is less important than the low-cost, short-time requirements, and high-flexibility objectives put together, we next compare the high-reliability objective with only the low-cost and short-time-requirements objectives taken together. Do we consider the high-reliability objective more important, equally important, or less important than the two latter objectives? We decide that the high-reliability objective is more important.

We compare the importance ratings given the individual objectives. Is 100, the rating given the high-reliability objective, greater than $60 + 50$, the sum of the ratings given the low-cost and short-time-requirements objectives respectively? No, 100 is less than 110. We therefore revise 100 to make it greater than 110 by an amount which indicates how much more important the high-reliability objective is than the other two combined. We decide that a rating of 125 for high reliability will express our opinon of this relationship. We now have the importance ratings as shown in the first Importance Ratings Revisions column.

We next compare the low-cost objective with the short-time requirements and high-flexibility objectives. Do we consider the former more important, equally important, or less important than the latter? We decide that it is more important. We compare the importance ratings. Is 60 greater than 50 + 25? No, 60 is less than 75. We therefore revise our importance rating for the low-cost objective to 85. We now have the importance ratings as shown in the second revision column.

We conclude the internal-consistency check for this illustration by reviewing all our previous comparisons to be certain that later adjustments have not upset relationships which were established earlier. Is 125 less than 85 + 50 + 25 = 160? Yes. Is 125 more than 85 + 50 = 135? No. We therefore decide to raise the importance rating of the high-reliability objective to 150, as shown in the third revision column.

We start our review again. Is 150 less than 85 + 50 + 25 = 160? Yes. Is 150 more than 85 + 50 = 135? Yes. Is 85 more than 50 + 25 = 75? Yes. Our importance ratings are now internally consistent with our judgment values.

We total the last revised ratings (150 + 85 + 50 + 25 = 310). We divide each rating by 310 and multiply by 100 to obtain the adjusted importance ratings shown in the last column on the right.

Seven or More Objectives. When there are seven or more objectives, the previously described procedure becomes burdensome. A modification of the procedure is therefore described here.

1. List the objectives in order of descending importance.

2. Select any one objective at random.

3. Randomly assign each of the remaining objectives into groups of approximately equal size, with no more than five to a group.

4. Add the selected objective (2) to each group and assign the importance rating 100 to it.

5. Keeping the importance rating of the selected objective (2) at 100, rank the objectives in each group in order of descending importance and assign importance ratings to them.

6. For each group of six or less objectives, follow the procedure for improving the reliability of importance ratings previously described. However, do not change the importance rating of 100 assigned to the selected objective (2) and do not adjust the ratings to total 100.

7. Make a combined listing of all the objectives in order of decreasing importance rating. Compare this listing with the initial one made in paragraph 1. Note any differences in ranking. If you still think the initial listing is correct, repeat the steps of the previous procedure to adjust the affected groups and reconcile the evaluations.

Then adjust the importance ratings to add up to 100 by the usual procedure.

Improving the Reliability of Effectiveness Ratings. The second step in the basic procedure for quantifying judgmental evaluations of alternatives when the objectives are intangible is to estimate how effectively each alternative meets each of the previously established criteria. How can we improve the reliability and accuracy or our determination of these effectiveness (utility) ratings? We can do so by carefully establishing benchmarks which will provide a logical and uniform basis for setting effectiveness ratings for each criterion.

The alternatives being considered, of course, influence the determination of the benchmarks. In addition, each criterion presents a separate problem for establishing benchmarks. Some intangibles lend themselves readily to quantitative evaluation. In other cases, it is more difficult to establish logical benchmarks which can be used with a high degree of reliability. We shall present examples of the establishment of benchmarks for three types of criteria:

1. Tangible criteria, such as profits or costs
2. Intangible quantitative criteria, such as time-cycle requirements
3. Intangible qualitative criteria, such as high flexibility in meeting changing needs

For a tangible criterion, the effectiveness rating is usually directly or inversely proportional to the estimated number of dollars: directly proportional if the criterion is income, revenue, or profits; inversely proportional if it is costs. If the criterion is income, revenue, or profits, we can establish our benchmarks using the chart of Figure 27-2. L represents the lowest forecasted income, revenue, or profit of any alternative being considered and M represents the highest. If the criterion is cost, we can

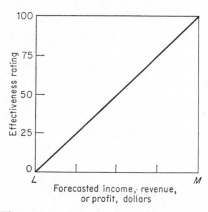

Figure 27-2. Effectiveness rating benchmark chart for income, revenue, or profit criteria.

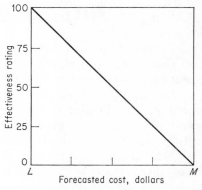

Figure 27-3. Effectiveness rating benchmark chart for cost criterion.

use the chart of Figure 27-3, in which L represents the lowest forecasted cost of any alternative being considered and M represents the highest.

We noted earlier in this chapter and in Chapter 20 that individuals and companies do not always place the same value on dollars and that as the size of potential profits or losses increases, the utility of additional units of dollars tends to decrease. In these cases, the utility function for determining effectiveness ratings for tangible criteria should not be a straight line. A curve of the type shown in Figure 27-4 is therefore sometimes appropriate.

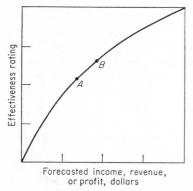

Figure 27-4. Effectiveness rating benchmark chart (nonlinear utility).

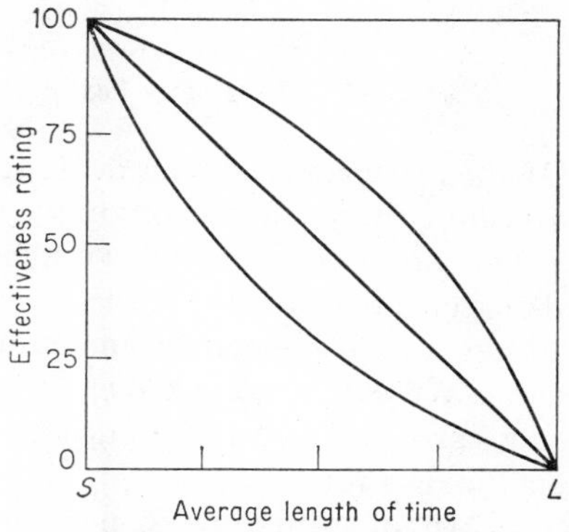

Figure 27-5. Effectiveness rating benchmark chart for intangible criterion.

However, a nonlinear utility curve is required only when the range of alternative potential tangible benefits is very large. This range must be a substantial proportion of the current net worth of the enterprise. In the more common case, the potential expected dollar-value gains cover a range which is only a portion of the range shown in Figure 27-4. Thus, if the potential gains are from A to B in Figure 27-4, this portion of the utility function is essentially a straight line and the linear-utility function of Figure 27-2 is satisfactory for determining effectiveness ratings.

We can also establish graphic benchmark charts for intangible criteria whose values can be measured quantitatively, but not in dollar units. An example of such an intangible criterion is the shortness of the average length of time between receipt of incoming material at the inspection department and dispatch of the material to the stockroom after inspection. One of the lines in the chart of Figure 27-5 may be used as a benchmark for this criterion or a somewhat different shape may be more appropriate in some cases. S represents the shortest time and L represents the longest time of any alternative being considered. The correct shape of curve to use as the benchmark will depend upon how the value to the enterprise of shorter time cycles changes with variations in the size of the time cycle.

Let us next consider how we can establish benchmarks for effectiveness ratings of intangible qualitative criteria, such as high flexibility in meeting changing needs. We can establish rough-and-ready benchmarks using descriptive adjectives to describe the flexibility of the systems alternative and then use a benchmark table, such as the following, to find the effectiveness rating.

Benchmark	Effectiveness rating
Extremely inflexible............	0
Moderately inflexible...........	25
Average flexibility..............	50
Moderately flexible.............	75
Unusually flexible..............	100

If the alternatives being evaluated are consequential enough and if the criterion is important enough, we can do a more reliable job of establishing benchmarks. What do we mean by the flexibility of the system? In this case, we mean how time-consuming is it to adjust to new products and new quality specifications and how costly is it to make these adjustments. We can now, in effect, divide this criterion into two criteria and, using previously presented techniques, establish effectiveness-rating benchmarks for

1. Cost of adjusting to new products and new quality specifications
2. Time required to adjust to new products and new quality specifications

In using the two benchmarks to obtain one effectiveness rating, we must establish a relative importance for time and cost in the flexibility criterion.

If the significance of the alternative and the flexibility criterion is great enough, it may be preferable to consider the time to adjust to new products and new quality specifications and the cost to adjust as separate criteria. Their relative importance ratings will then be determined in the manner previously described in this chapter.

Interaction of Effectiveness Benchmarks on Importance Ratings. There can be a great deal of helpful interaction between the establishment of importance ratings for the objectives and the establishment of benchmarks for effectiveness rating.

Consideration of the problem of establishing effectiveness-rating benchmarks may help clarify the definition of the criterion. It may indicate that the criterion should be subdivided into several more easily measured criteria, as in the example previously discussed.

The range of variation of the effectiveness values will influence the establishment of importance ratings of the objectives. For example, if the estimated costs of all the alternatives have a very small variation of values, the influence of cost as a criterion for choosing the optimum alternative will be much smaller than if the estimated costs had a very wide variation of values, assuming the same importance rating for cost. This is true for time requirements, reliability performance, and all other objectives.

Therefore, it is frequently useful when significant decisions are being made to establish initial effectiveness benchmarks before the importance ratings for the objectives are definitely established.

Individual and Group Evaluation. The procedures for determining importance and effectiveness ratings imply that one person makes the evaluations. In actual practice, it is frequently desirable to have many individuals participate in the evaluations.

When the final economic decision requires the agreement of a number of persons and the issues are rather involved, these evaluation procedures may be valuable in clarifying the thinking of each person on the relative merits and demerits of various proposals. By promoting the organization of thoughts on the essential elements as well as the clarity of communication of these thoughts, these procedures will aid in disclosing the basic items of agreement and disagreement. This will help create understanding of the issues and eventual agreement on a decision.

The participation of persons with different backgrounds and points of view in the evaluation is valuable not only to obtain agreement and mutual understanding but also to reduce bias and improve the accuracy of the evaluation. Comparison of ratings and discussion of the reasons for differences will frequently disclose unconscious biases in the evaluation. When a number of persons with varied backgrounds participate in the evaluation, these biases will tend to disappear or be minimized when the individual ratings are averaged or the group decisions are reached.

There are numerous plans whereby the various decision-making individuals participate in the evaluation. These plans generally involve either individual ratings made independently or group ratings made cooperatively by the decision-makers or a combination of the two. Each has advantages and is appropriate under certain circumstances. A few of these possibilities are described here.

When the individual-rating procedure is used, each decision-maker makes his own evaluations independently. The final ratings which are assigned are the arithmetic mean of the ratings of the individuals.

When the evaluations are made by a group, the bases for the evaluations and differences of opinion are discussed and clarified. Final ratings are assigned by majority vote or, where feasible, the consensus of the group, what the Quakers call "the sense of the meeting."

When the individual-rating procedure is used, group discussion is frequently valuable in clarifying the reasons for differences. This may result in some changes in the ratings of the individuals before an average is computed. Sometimes, the group discussion of the individual ratings may be directed toward arriving at a consensus or at a final decision by majority vote instead of by averaging.

We have discussed in some detail methods of determining importance ratings to establish criteria, effectiveness ratings to estimate how well each alternative will meet the criteria, and a weighted average effectiveness to choose the optimum alternative. These procedures provide for more reliable and accurate evaluation of alternatives because they provide for

1. The objectives to be thought out carefully and defined
2. The relative importance of objectives to be determined
3. Estimates to be made of how well the various alternatives will achieve these objectives, which forces a consideration of methods of measuring and estimating this potential achievement
4. Internal consistency of judgments to be established

The procedures provide a mechanism for comparison of individual differences in the evaluations. These differences can be analyzed and discussed, and possible errors in reasoning disclosed. The judgments of different individuals and groups with different points of view can thus be focused on the various aspects of the evaluation and their viewpoints reflected in the results.

These procedures do not eliminate the need for good judgment. They provide a rationale for systematically channeling this judgment to obtain decisions to improve consistency and highlight contradictions. Their validity, of course, is dependent upon a reasonable conformance between the assumptions implicit in the procedural model and reality.

PROBLEMS

1. Discuss the validity of the possible methods of placing a price on a human life which were presented in the text.

2. How could one place a dollar value on the improved morale which a company recreation center would create?

3. James Root is offered an opportunity in which he estimates that there is a 75 per cent probability of making a profit of $100,000 and a 25 per cent probability of losing $25,000. There are no intangibles in this case except the risks which are as stated above and are known with complete certainty. (a) What is the expected profit to Root if he accepts the offer? (b) Root refuses this opportunity on the basis that it has a negative expected utility to him. Can this be logical? Explain your answer.

4. Instead of refusing the opportunity presented him in problem 3, Root forms a

syndicate with nine other acquaintances. The 10 partners decide to accept the offer, agreeing to share all costs, profits, and losses equally. (a) What is Root's expected profit under this arrangement? (b) Is it logical for Root to have refused the opportunity in problem 3 but to participate in this new syndicated arrangement in which he has a much reduced expected profit? Explain your answer.

5. Diversification of investments by securities investors is based on the idea of reducing risk by not putting all one's eggs in one basket. It thus means that you will not invest all your funds in the venture (or ventures) which has the maximum expected return, but will put a portion of your assets in lower-return investments. Can this be justified on the basis of (a) Maximizing expected profit? Explain. (b) Maximizing expected utility? Explain.

6. Various proposals have been submitted for developing a new state park to increase the recreational opportunities in your state. These proposals call for different sites, facilities, capacities, costs, etc. Outline a procedure for evaluating these alternative proposals. What criteria might be suitable for use in this evaluation?

PART SEVEN

Elements of Economic Measurement,
Analysis, and Forecasting

28 Economics of the Firm

In our discussions of engineering and economic decision-making thus far, we have not explicitly considered economic relationships between the firm's production and its markets and how these relationships affect economic decisions in the enterprise. In this chapter we shall briefly review the economics of the firm to assist in understanding these economic relationships and to provide a background for some of our later discussions of economic forecasting.

Demand Schedule and Curve. The demand schedule for any commodity is a schedule showing the quantities of the commodity which will be purchased at various prices. However, the demand for most products and services is affected by many factors other than price, such as quality of product or service, advertising and promotion, income levels, geographic locations, etc. These other factors are held constant in our demand schedule.

A simple example of a demand schedule is shown in Table 28-1. Thus, 3 units per day of product M will be demanded by buyers if the price is $400; 4 units per day if the price is $380; 5 units per day at $361; and so on. The schedule is plotted to produce the demand curve of Figure 28-1.

Total Revenue. If the companies making product M set the price at

Table 28-1. Demand Schedule for Product M

Number of units per day	Price (dollars per unit)	Number of units per day	Price (dollars per unit)
3	400	10	271
4	380	11	254
5	361	12	238
6	342	13	222
7	324	14	206
8	306	15	191
9	288	16	177

$400 per unit, its total revenue per day will be equal to the 3 units per day which will be sold times $400, or $1,200. If they set the price at $380, its total revenue per day will be 4 times $380, or $1,520. We could also

439

state it another way: If the companies manufacture and offer for sale 4 units per day, they will be able to charge no more than $380 per unit or they will not sell all of them. Their total revenue will therefore be $1,520 per day.

The total revenue for any output volume from 3 to 16 units per day is shown in Table 28-2. A total-revenue curve is plotted in Figure 28-2.

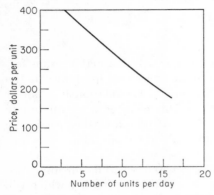

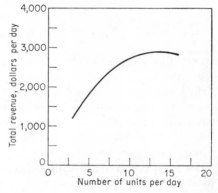

Figure 28-1. Demand curve for product M.

Figure 28-2. Total-revenue curve for product M.

These total-revenue calculations are predicated on the assumption that, at any given time, all of the products are sold at one price. We see that the total revenue of producers of product M will increase as we expand output and sales to 13 units per day. When the output is expanded beyond this figure, total revenue will decrease.

Table **28-2. Total and Marginal Revenue Schedules for Product M**

Number of units per day Q	Price (dollars per unit) P	Total revenue $R = PQ$	Marginal revenue M_R
3	$400	$1,200	
4	380	1,520	$320
5	361	1,805	285
6	342	2,052	247
7	324	2,268	216
8	306	2,448	180
9	288	2,592	144
10	271	2,710	118
11	254	2,794	84
12	238	2,856	62
13	222	2,886	30
14	206	2,884	−2
15	191	2,865	−19
16	177	2,832	−33

If we let Q equal the number of units per day, P equal the price in dollars per unit, and R equal total revenue, then

$$R = PQ$$

Incremental and Marginal Revenue. How much additional revenue will be obtained if the volume of product M is increased from 3 to 10 units per day? From Table 28-2 we can see that the increase in revenue will be $1,510 ($2,710 minus $1,200). This is the incremental revenue resulting from the change in volume.

How much will the revenue increase if the output is increased from 3 to 4 per day? From Table 28-2 we can see that this incremental revenue will be $320 ($1,520 minus $1,200). This incremental revenue resulting from an increased volume of 1 unit is also called the marginal revenue of the last unit. The marginal revenue (M_R) is equal to the additional revenue which would not have been obtained if the last unit had not been sold. It represents the net revenue contribution of the last unit. Thus the marginal revenue of the 7th unit is equal to the total revenue from 7 units per week ($2,268) minus the total revenue from 6 units per week ($2,052), or $216.

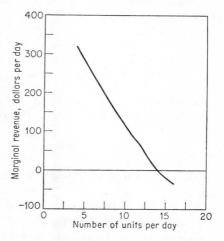

Figure 28-3. Marginal-revenue curve for product M.

The marginal revenues are shown in Table 28-2 for values of Q from 3 to 16 units per day. The marginal-revenue curve is plotted in Figure 28-3.

We can see that the marginal revenue is zero when the total revenue is at its maximum.[1] The marginal revenue represents the revenue contribution by expanding output by the last unit. As long as the marginal revenue is positive, total revenue will increase by expanding sales volume. When marginal revenue becomes negative, total revenue is lower because the last unit was offered for sale. The total revenue is therefore at its maximum at the point where the marginal revenue goes from positive to negative values. The marginal revenue is equal or close to zero at this point. In our example, this point is at 13 units per day.

The slope at any point of the total revenue curve of Figure 28-2 is given by the change in total revenue, ΔR, divided by the change in quan-

[1] With discrete numbers, the marginal revenue is close to, but not exactly, zero at the point of maximum total revenue.

tity, ΔQ. The slope is therefore equal to the marginal revenue. The slope is positive at the lower quantities; decreases as the number of units, Q, increase; reaches zero value (horizontal slope) when the total revenue, R, is at its maximum; and then is negative after the maximum-revenue volume is exceeded.

Mathematical Relationships. We can use continuous-distribution values to approximate the discrete data and can express the previous relationships as follows:

Demand curve,

$$P = f(Q)$$

Total revenue,

$$R = PQ = Qf(Q)$$

Marginal revenue (equal to the slope of the revenue curve and thus equal to the first derivative of the revenue function),

$$M_R = \frac{dR}{dQ} = Qf'(Q) + f(Q)$$

The total-revenue function reaches its maximum at the point where the first derivative, dR/dQ, is equal to zero.[1]

Elasticity of Demand. When the percentage change in the volume of a product which will be purchased when a change in the price occurs is relatively large, the product is said to have a high elasticity of demand or price elasticity. A product is considered to have an inelastic demand when a decrease in price will produce a relatively small increase in the quantity purchased.

The elasticity of demand, E, equals the percentage increase in purchases divided by the percentage decrease in price.

$$E = \frac{\Delta Q/Q}{\Delta P/P} = \frac{P}{Q}\frac{\Delta Q}{\Delta P}$$

or

$$E = \frac{dQ/Q}{dP/P} = \frac{P}{Q}\frac{dQ}{dP}$$

$E = \dfrac{P}{Q}\dfrac{\Delta Q}{\Delta P}$ defines arc elasticity, the elasticity over a range of the demand curve. The range is determined by the size of ΔQ. $E = \dfrac{P}{Q}\dfrac{dQ}{dP}$ defines point elasticity, the elasticity at one point on the demand curve. $E = -1$ is the dividing line between relatively elastic and relatively inelastic price behavior. If a 10 per cent decrease in price will produce a 10 per cent increase in volume purchased, the product has unit elasticity. If a 10 per

[1] For discrete data, setting $dR/dQ = 0$ will yield a value, Q^*, which may not be a whole number. The optimum value, $\hat{Q}$ or $\hat{Q} + 1$, will then be the whole number on either side of Q^*. $(\hat{Q} < Q^* < \hat{Q} + 1.)$

cent decrease in price will produce a 20 per cent increase in volume purchased, the product is relatively elastic. If a 10 per cent decrease in price will produce a 5 per cent increase in volume purchased, the product is relatively inelastic.

In Figure 28-4 we see two demand curves. Quantity purchased per week is more responsive to changes in price in the more elastic demand curve than in the less elastic one. In both cases, the demand functions tend to be more elastic at the high-price sections of the curve than in the lower-price sections. This is apparent from the formula $E = \dfrac{P}{Q}\dfrac{\Delta Q}{\Delta P}$.

The ratio $\dfrac{\Delta Q}{\Delta P}$, which measures the change in quantity per unit change in price, is

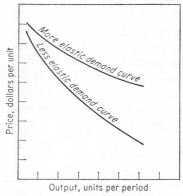

Figure 28-4. Elasticity of demand curves.

multiplied by the ratio of the absolute value of price to quantity, P/Q. The ratio P/Q is highest in the high-price sections of the curve in which P is high and Q is small. As the price of a product decreases, the price elasticity tends to be reduced.

We have previously written

$$\text{Price} = P = f(Q)$$
$$\text{Total revenue} = R = PQ$$

Therefore,

$$\text{Marginal revenue} = M_R = \frac{dR}{dQ} = P + Q\frac{dP}{dQ} = P\left(1 + \frac{Q}{P}\frac{dP}{dQ}\right)$$

Since the elasticity of demand, E, equals $\dfrac{P}{Q}\dfrac{dQ}{dP}$, $\dfrac{1}{E}$ equals $\dfrac{Q}{P}\dfrac{dP}{dQ}$ and we can now write

$$\text{Marginal revenue} = \frac{dR}{dQ} = P\left(1 + \frac{1}{E}\right)$$

Marginal revenue is equal to zero when total revenue is at its maximum. Therefore, at this point of maximum revenue,

$$\frac{dR}{dQ} = P\left(1 + \frac{1}{E}\right) = 0$$

Since P is not equal to 0,

$$1 + \frac{1}{E} = 0$$
$$E = -1$$

Thus, at the point of maximum total revenue the price elasticity is always equal to minus unity, the dividing line between elastic and inelastic demand.

If all the supply of a product is furnished by one company, the price will never move into the inelastic range unless the company decides to operate at a point beyond the maximum-total-revenue point. When many companies produce a product, competition will frequently cause the total production to go beyond this point into the inelastic range.

Short-run Cost Function of a Business. Although there is a wide variation in the shape of short-run cost functions for business enterprises, economic treatises have generally portrayed total-cost functions which are reverse S-shaped, such as shown in Figure 28-5, and average- and marginal-cost functions which are distinctly U-shaped, such as shown in Figure 28-6.

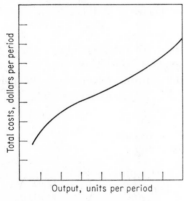

Figure 28-5. Total cost function.

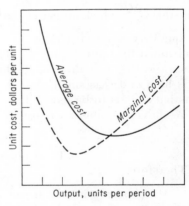

Figure 28-6. Average- and marginal-cost functions.

The average-cost curve decreases initially as the output volume increases primarily because the fixed costs per unit output decrease as their fixed amount is spread over a larger output volume. In addition, variable costs per unit of output will sometimes tend to decrease initially as output increases because more efficient processes, simplified material handling, etc., can be used. For these same reasons, the marginal-cost curve decreases with increases in output. The marginal fixed cost is obviously decreasing at all outputs and the marginal variable cost is decreasing initially as output volume increases.

As output volume is extended beyond a certain point, variable costs per unit of output will tend to increase because of overcrowding, employee attitudes, overtime wage premiums, etc. Also with larger outputs, the effect of spreading fixed costs over additional outputs causes a smaller relative decline in unit cost. We thus reach a point where the increase in the additional amount of variable cost for an additional unit of output equals the decrease in the additional amount of fixed cost for an additional unit of output. This is the output at which the minimum marginal cost occurs.

The average cost per unit continues to decrease at outputs beyond the minimum-marginal-cost point because the increasing marginal costs are still below the average costs at these outputs and continue to pull down the average costs. The minimum-average-cost point (optimum costs for the existing facility) is reached at the point at which the marginal-cost curve crosses the average-cost curve. Beyond this point, marginal costs are above the average costs and pull the average costs up.

The business facilities are designed to operate at optimum efficiency at this minimum-average-cost point. Beyond this point, we obtain higher than optimum average costs. As we shall discuss later, it may nevertheless be more profitable to operate above this optimum efficiency volume even though higher average costs result.

Monopoly and Competition. Pure monopoly is very rare. Under pure monopoly, only one firm supplies a product. However, the monopoly of this firm is very rarely complete. To be complete, the monopolist's product must be indispensable, have no substitutes, and no potential competition or possibility of control by the government. These conditions are practically never completely true, but are sometimes approximated. A new patented product may provide a temporary monopoly. A public utility may have a monopoly which is subject to government regulation. Of course, these monopolies are usually subject to the competition of possible substitutes.

Pure competition, on the other hand, is present when many firms supply a standard product to numerous purchasers. No one of the suppliers or purchasers is large enough to affect the market price significantly by his actions. The quantities produced or purchased by any one firm do not affect the market price. The markets for most agricultural products, such as wheat, corn, tobacco, etc., come close to satisfying the requirements of pure competition.

In most cases neither pure competition nor pure monopoly prevails but some form of imperfect competition, which may take the form of monopolistic competition or oligopoly or both.

Monopolistic competition is imperfect competition because the products of the various producers are differentiated even though they serve a common purpose. Each producer attempts to differentiate his product in the consumer's mind through differences in quality, service, design, style, packaging, brand name, advertising, and promotion. Even if there are no real differences in the products of different producers, the consumer may prefer one brand to another and thus create product differentiation.

Because of this differentiation, one producer may charge more for his differentiated product than another and not lose all his customers to his lower-priced competitor. There will be some buyers who prefer his product enough to pay more rather than purchase his competitor's substitute. However, there is a limit to the amount he can exceed the price of his competitors before his customers will start purchasing his competitors' substitutes. The greater the product differentiation, the greater the pricing freedom of the producer and the more monopolistic his behavior can be. Monopolistic competition is very common in the markets for manufactured consumer goods.

Oligopoly is a form of imperfect competition because the number of the suppliers is small enough so that changes in the output of any one of them will affect the market price. Each firm must consider the effect of changes in his production output upon the market price. He must also consider the possible reaction of his competitors to changes in his prices. Oligopoly is a common market condition, as witness the price, promotion, and advertising wars among rival producers. (Under pure competition, producers ignore each other because the actions of competitors do not affect revenues.)

The term "differential oligopoly" is sometimes applied to the not uncommon situation in which both product differentiation and oligopoly are present.

Let us now examine how firms operate under each of these models of competitive and monopolistic behavior. We realize that none of the models exactly fits reality in any case. They are nevertheless useful in understanding price and output decisions under a wide variety of circumstances.

Pure Monopoly. In discussing elasticity of demand, we noted that if all the supply of a product is furnished by one company, the price will never move into the inelastic lower price range because this range occurs past the point of maximum total revenue. What price and output rate should a monopolist choose to maximize profit? The point of maximum profit occurs at an output volume below the maximum-total-revenue point.

Letting T represent total profit and C represent total cost,

$$T = R - C$$

Since we desire to maximize profit, we differentiate it with respect to output volume, Q, and set the first derivative equal to zero,

$$\frac{dT}{dQ} = \frac{dR}{dQ} - \frac{dC}{dQ} = 0$$
$$\frac{dR}{dQ} = \frac{dC}{dQ}$$

The point of maximum profit is where marginal revenue equals marginal cost. This is illustrated in Figure 28-7 which shows a demand function

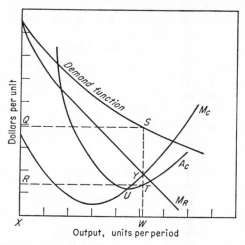

Figure 28-7. Revenue and cost relationships under pure monopoly.

and its derived marginal-revenue (M_R) curve. The demand function shows the price (average receipt) which can be obtained with any given output rate. The marginal-revenue curve shows the additional receipts for each additional unit of output. We have also drawn the average-cost (A_c) and marginal-cost (M_c) curves. Included in these costs are "normal or equilibrium" profits. These are the costs of the equity capital and are the minimum profits needed to obtain or retain equity capital in the industry.

As long as the marginal cost is below the average cost, the average-cost curve will continue to decrease. When the cost of an additional unit of output is less than the average of all previous units, it lowers the average cost of the previous units when the unit is added. At the point of intersection (U) of the marginal- and average-cost curves, the cost of an additional unit is the same as the average of all previous units. Beyond this intersection point (U), the marginal-cost curve is above the average-cost curve, each additional unit of output raising the average of all previous units. The intersection point (U) is thus the minimum point on the average-cost curve. The most efficient operating volume is at this minimum-average-cost point (U).

However, this most efficient operating volume is not usually the most profitable operating volume. The most profitable operating volume depends upon the market demand. As long as the cost of an additional unit of output is less than the revenue from the additional unit, it is worthwhile increasing the output rate. This means that we should increase output as long as marginal costs are less than marginal revenues. Before the point of intersection (Y) of the marginal-revenue and marginal-cost curves, marginal costs are less than marginal revenues. Beyond this intersection point (Y), marginal revenues are less than marginal costs and it would be unprofitable to increase output. At this most profitable output rate, average costs are given by the ordinate value of point T, which is higher than the most efficient cost value of point U.

The total revenue at this most profitable output rate is given by multiplying the price (or average revenue per unit), as shown by the line SW reaching to the demand function, and the number of units, as shown by the line XW. The rectangle $QXWS$ therefore denotes total revenue. The total cost at this output rate is similarly shown by the rectangle $RXWT$. The total profit is therefore shown by $QXWS$ minus $RXWT$, or $QRTS$.

If the demand for the product should decrease, the demand function would move lower and the marginal-revenue line would move down and might then intersect the marginal-cost line before the minimum-average-cost point. For most profitable results, the company will operate in this case below the most efficient output rate.

Pure Competition. When pure competition is present, none of the suppliers or purchasers are large enough to affect the market price by the volume of their output. Each producer can sell all of his production at the market price. The demand function is therefore a straight horizontal line at the level of the market price. The total-revenue line is a straight line which never decreases. The marginal-revenue line coincides with the demand-and-price line because each additional unit of output will yield additional revenue equal to the market price.

Three situations showing the output-rate adjustment of individual producers under pure competition are shown in Figures 28-8 to 28-10. The marginal- (M_c) and average- (A_c) cost lines are similar to those in Figure 28-7 for a monopolist. These costs include a "normal" return on equity capital. The demand function for this producer's output is the same as the marginal-revenue (M_R) line (a straight horizontal line at the level of the market price) because all output can be sold at the market price.

Figure 28-8 shows the condition of a company in which the minimum-average-cost point is below the market price. Output will be expanded until the marginal revenue from an additional unit (the price) is equal to the marginal cost of producing an additional unit. This occurs at Y, which is beyond the output for minimum-average cost. Beyond this point, we receive less additional revenue than we incur additional cost. Profits per unit are lower at output Y than would occur at minimum-average-cost output U, but total profits are higher. Profits (over and above "normal" return) are given by the area $QRTY$, which represents the product of the output volume times the difference between price and average cost.

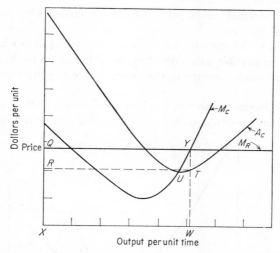

Figure 28-8. Revenue and cost relationships under pure competition (minimum average cost less than price).

Figure 28-9 shows the condition of a company in which the minimum-average-cost point is above the market price, which is the same for all the companies in the industry. The area $QRTY$ represents the loss (reduction of "normal" profit) of the company.

Figure 28-10 shows the condition of a company in which the minimum-average-cost point coincides with the market price. Profits are exactly

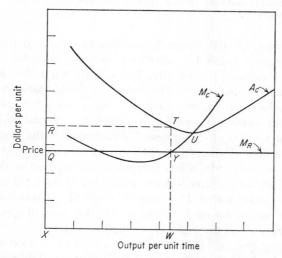

Figure 28-9. Revenue and cost relationships under pure competition (minimum average cost greater than price).

equal to the "normal" amount included in costs. The area $QRTY$ is therefore equal to zero.

Each producer will vary his rate of output with changes in the market price. When the market price declines, he will reduce his rate of output. He will produce each time up to the point where the price line crosses his marginal-cost line.

As the price increases, he will increase production to the amount shown on the right-hand portion of his marginal-cost curve for that price. As

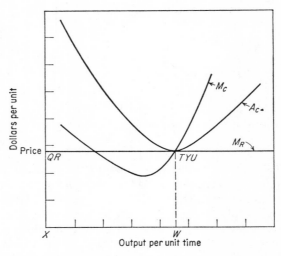

Figure 28-10. Revenue and cost relationships under pure competition (minimum average cost equal to price).

the price declines, he will reduce his output in a corresponding manner. If the price declines below his minimum-marginal cost, he will be better off stopping production completely. Thus, if we knew the marginal-cost function of each producer in the industry, we could forecast the amount he would produce at various prices. Adding up all these individual amounts, we can construct a schedule of the total amount which would be supplied to the market at each price. This schedule is the supply schedule for the commodity. Using this schedule, we can construct the supply curve of Figure 28-11, which is a horizontal summation of the marginal-cost curves of all the producers in the industry. At each price level on the vertical price axis, we add up the horizontal output values of the marginal-cost curves for each producer. We use only the portion of the marginal-cost curve to the right of its minimum point.

Under the purely competitive market in which these producers operate, the market price is always the same for all of them. The market price is determined by the demand function for the product, such as was previously shown in Figure 28-1, and the total rate of supply of the commodity by all the very numerous producers. No one producer can supply a large enough quantity to affect the supply curve significantly. Eliminating any erratic day-to-day market variations which may occur, the price of the commodity at any time is at the point of intersection of the supply curve with the demand curve, which shows the average rate at which the commodity will be purchased at each price level. This is shown in Figure 28-12, where the intersection at point L determines the price and total-

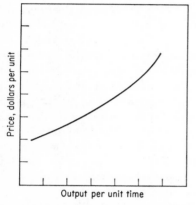

Figure 28-11. Supply curve for a product.

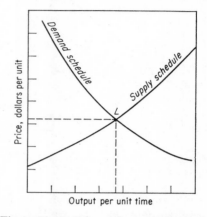

Figure 28-12. Price and output determination as a function of supply and demand schedules.

output rate. The price, L, is a short-term price which will change under the following circumstances:

1. If the demand schedule for the product were to change, modifying the demand curve

2. If the cost schedules of the individual producers were to change modifying the total-supply curve for the product

3. If the number of individual producers were to change, modifying the total-supply curve for the product

If demand for the product is very strong compared with the total capacity in the industry, the short-period price will be high enough so that a proportion of companies will be producing at output rates larger than their optimum-cost output rate, as shown in Figure 28-8. These companies will be induced by this to expand their facilities to enable them to operate closer to their minimum-average-cost point. The presence of profits in excess of "normal" in these companies will also attract the entrance of new producers into the industry. Both of these factors will cause the industry capacity to expand. The supply curve will move to the right. If the demand schedule remains unchanged, the price will gradually decline, as shown in Figure 28-13. S_1, S_2, S_3 represent successive supply curves as industry capacity expands.

The stable-equilibrium position occurs when the price equals the minimum average cost of production (including "normal" profits), as shown in Figure 28-10. This is never completely attained for all firms in an industry. There is a tendency toward this position which may never be reached because many different economic forces may affect the operation of the firm and the market before the equilibrium position is reached.

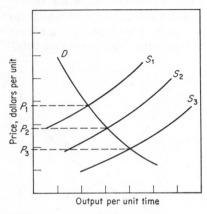

Figure 28-13. Effect of facility expansions on price and output.

Investigations into the technology of production of a product are continually undertaken in most companies which are competitive. These investigations disclose improvements in equipment, methods, materials, etc., which will lower costs or increase quality. At any one time, there is an optimum technology with a plant of optimum size, equipment, methods, organization, etc.

When demand is high relative to supply, the new facilities which are installed will reflect this optimum technology and their marginal-cost curves will have the minimum average costs of this optimum technology. Because of competition, prices will tend to move toward the minimum average costs of the producers using this optimum technology. If demand is weak relative to supply, the facilities which are retired will be the less efficient ones and the marginal-cost curves of the remaining companies will be the more efficient one which will tend to be the ones closest to the optimum-technology curve. There is thus a tendency for the cost curves of the firms to approach the optimum-technology curve as the least efficient technologies are replaced or retired.

If demand for the product is very weak compared with the total capacity in the industry, the short-period price will be low enough so that a proportion of companies will be producing at output rates lower than their optimum-cost output rate, as shown in Figure 28-9. These companies will be discouraged from investing new money to replace or repair existing facilities. As equipment is worn out, it will be retired and capacity reduced. If the price goes low enough, some companies will leave the industry or go out of business. These factors will cause industry capacity to decrease. The supply curve will move to the left. If the demand schedule remains unchanged, the price will gradually rise, as shown in Figure 28-14. S_1, S_2, S_3 represent successive supply curves as industry capacity contracts.

What happens when the demand for the product suddenly increases? Figure 28-15 illustrates this situation. The demand-schedule curve increases from D_1 to D_2. The immediate reaction of the price is to move from L, the price for the current output rate on D_1, to M or close to M, the price for the current output rate on D_2. With the price raised close to M, each individual producer will be expected to increase his output because the price will be greater than his marginal costs which are summarized in the supply curve. Increasing the supply rate will then cause the prices to fall along D_2 until N, is reached, where the supply curve intersects the new demand curve D_2. At this point, all producers are operating at a point in which their marginal costs equal the price. Producers will not expand their output rates with their current facilities beyond N because to do so will result in marginal costs higher than the price. However, the high "excess" profits provided by the increased demand and higher prices will cause new facilities to be constructed to increase capacity. This will move the supply schedule to the right and the price will further decline along D_2. Capacity increases will tend to continue until the price has declined to the minimum average costs of the optimum technology. (The costs contain the "normal" return required to attract capital into the industry.)

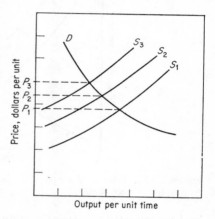

Figure 28-14. Effect of facility contractions on price and output.

The minimum average costs of the optimum technology may be the same when the size of the industry is larger. Or these optimum technology costs may be larger or smaller than they were before the expansion of the industry. Whether they are larger, smaller, or the same depends upon the nature of the industry and the net effect of the tendencies of various cost factors to rise or fall as the industry becomes larger or smaller.

As an industry becomes larger, it will create an increased demand for the items it uses or consumes in the production process: land, machinery, labor, raw materials, parts, and components. To attract these items from other economic uses, higher prices will have to be bid for them or items of poorer quality and productivity utilized. Thus, expansion of a mining industry may require the use of poorer quality ores; expansion of a manufacturing industry may require the paying of a premium price to obtain raw materials which are in short supply.

On the other hand, when an industry expands in size, various types of economies become available to all manufacturers. The larger the industry, the greater the possibilities of specialization within it, which will reduce the operating costs of all companies in the industry. Thus, a well-developed agricultural industry has specialized manufacturers of machinery. They can supply machinery at a lower cost than the farmer can manufacture the machinery himself when the market is too small to justify specialized machinery manufacturers. In the early days of the automobile it was more expensive for each automobile manufacturer to make his own parts in small quantities than it was to purchase these parts from special-

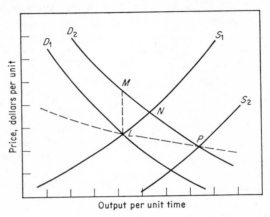

Figure 28-15. Effects of increase in demand in an industry which has decreasing minimum average costs.

ized manufacturers after the industry had grown large enough to justify such specialized production.

There are thus tendencies to both higher and lower average costs in most industries as the size of the industry increases. These tendencies may just about offset each other in some industries, resulting in roughly constant minimum average costs for the optimum technology regardless of the size of the industry. In other cases, the tendencies toward higher costs will outweigh those toward lower costs, producing an increasing trend of minimum average costs of the optimum technology as the size of the industry grows. In still other cases, the tendencies toward lower costs will outweigh those toward higher costs, producing a decreasing trend of minimum average costs.

We can thus draw a dotted line in Figure 28-15 indicating the trend of minimum average costs of the optimum technology as the size of the industry increases. In this case, the trend line is one of decreasing costs. The capacity of the industry in our example will continue to be expanded and the supply curves will continue to move to the right until curve S_2 crosses the intersection of D_2 and the trend line of minimum average costs for the optimum technology at P. The long-term price will tend toward this point which is below the price before the demand schedule increased from D_1 to D_2. We thus see that, when an industry has a trend line of decreasing minimum average costs for the optimum technology, an increase in demand will produce a short-term rise in price; but the long-term price trend resulting from this increase in demand will be a lowering of the price.

Figure 28-16 shows the situation for an industry which has a trend line of increasing minimum average costs. In this case, both the short-term

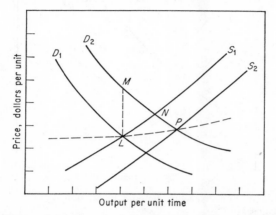

Figure 28-16. Effects of increase in demand in an industry which has increasing minimum average costs.

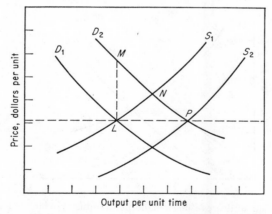

Figure 28-17. Effects of increase in demand in an industry which has constant mini mum average costs.

equilibrium price at N and the long-term equilibrium price at P toward which prices will tend are higher than the prices at L before the demand schedule had increased from D_1 to D_2.

Figure 28-17 shows the situation for an industry which has a trend line of constant minimum average costs. In this case, point N toward which prices will tend in the short term is higher than the initial price L; but point P toward which prices will tend in the long run is the same as at L, the equilibrium price prior to the increase in demand.

Adjustments of price and capacity to decreases in demand in a competitive industry are analogous to those for increases. In Figures 28-18 to

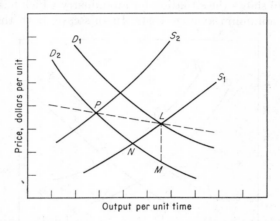

Figure 28-18. Effects of decrease in demand in an industry which has decreasing minimum average costs.

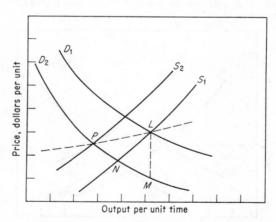

Figure 28-19. Effects of decrease in demand in an industry which has increasing minimum average costs.

28-20, D_2 represents the lower demand schedule and N and P represent the short-term and long-term points toward which prices will tend.

We live in an age of unusually rapid technological progress. New methods are constantly being developed which change and lower the costs of production.[1] How do these changes affect the output rate and price under competitive conditions?

The long-term tendency produced by technological improvements in production processes is shown in Figure 28-21. The minimum average

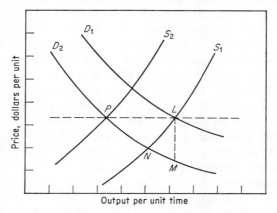

Figure 28-20. Effects of decrease in demand in an industry which has constant minimum average costs.

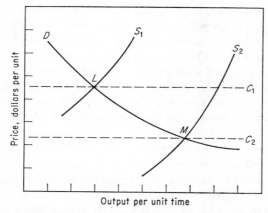

Figure 28-21. Effects of technological advances on price and output.

costs for the optimum technology have shifted from C_1 to C_2. As more and more firms in the industry adopt the methods of the improved technology, the supply curve will move from S_1 toward S_2 and the price will tend to move gradually from L to M.

Short term and long term are relative terms referring to the time it

[1] Other results of technology changes in creating new or improved products cause changes in the demand for existing products. The effect of changes in demand schedule on price and output rate were previously discussed.

takes for the industry to make adjustments in its output. The periods of time involved will vary from industry to industry. The period involved in short-term adjustments depends upon how fast the rate of output using the existing facilities can be changed. The period involved in long-term adjustments during times of increasing demand depends upon how rapidly new equipment can be procured or constructed to increase the capacity of the plant; and during times of decreasing demand it depends upon the economic life and size of the investment in capital facilities and whether or not the facilities can be converted to other uses.

The price and output adjustments discussed in this section occur over varying periods of time. There are day-to-day market-price adjustments caused by day-to-day variations in demand which cannot be met by immediate changes in output rate. There are short-term changes in output rate within the framework of current capacity. There are long-term variations in supply schedules which will change output rate and price. There are technological changes which induce changes in costs and supply schedules as well as demand schedules. These changes occur concurrently and interact on each other. Rarely does a tendency have time to work its way into an equilibrium position before additional changes cause variations to tend in other directions.

Monopolistic Competition. When the products of the various producers in an industry are differentiated even though they serve a common purpose, we have monopolistic competition instead of pure competition. A producer may charge more for his product than another and still not lose all his customers. The individual producer has a separate demand function for his product which is distinct from those of his competitors. His demand curve will have some slope rather than be a horizontal line. The amount of slope will depend upon how much product differentiation he has managed to create by such things as brand advertising or quality differences.

The determination by the producer of the output rate for maximum profit under monopolistic competition is thus similar to the situation for the pure monopolist except that the demand functions are generally much flatter and more elastic. The monopolistic competitor has some of the freedom of the monopolist to adjust his output and prices to maximize his profits. However, unless his product differentiation is very great, his demand curve is nearly horizontal, as in pure competition. This limits the amount of price advantage he can obtain by limiting his output rate.

Figures 28-22 to 28-24 show the economic relationships for the three situations in which a monopolistically competitive firm may find itself. These situations are analogous to those of Figures 28-8 to 28-10 in the purely competitive case.

In Figure 28-22 the company is making a profit of $QRTY$ above the "normal" profit. If the product of the company possesses advantages which cannot be duplicated or otherwise met by competitors, the competitive tendency for the situation to approach the equilibrium of Figure 28-24 will be reduced or eliminated. The area will then represent a monopolistic profit rather than the disequilibrium profit which tends to disappear under the effects of competition.

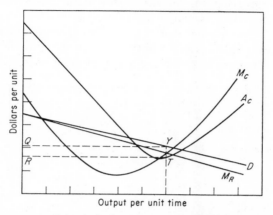

Figure 28-22. Revenue and cost relationships under monopolistic competition (average cost less than price).

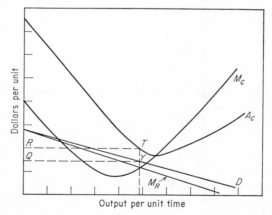

Figure 28-23. Revenue and cost relationships under monopolistic competition (average cost greater than price).

One basic difference we may note between monopolistic competition and pure competition is that there is a tendency for the output rate to be slightly less and the price slightly higher under monopolistic than under pure competition. Thus, in Figure 28-24, the equilibrium position when producers are making only the "normal" profits included in costs, the output rate will be at the point of tangency of the demand curve with the average-cost curve. This occurs to the left of the minimum-average-cost point. The short-term equilibrium toward which prices and output rate will tend is thus at a higher price and lower output rate than under pure competition. The greater the amount of product differentiation, the greater will be the slope of the demand function and the greater this tendency toward operating to the left of the minimum-average-cost point even when monopolistic profit is not present.

Oligopoly. When the number of producers or suppliers of a product is small enough that changes in the output of any one of them will affect the market price, oligopoly is present. Each firm must consider the effects of

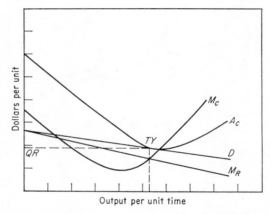

Figure 28-24. Revenue and cost relationships under monopolistic competition (average cost equal to price).

its own actions on the market situation as well as the reaction of its competitors to these actions.

We shall illustrate the oligopoly situation with an example in which there are only two firms in the industry. This is called duopoly. To start off, we have a monopolist who develops a new chemical and patents the process for manufacturing it. It costs him $1.50 per pound to produce. He produces 100,000 lb per year and sells it for $10 per pound for a profit of $850,000 per year. At this output rate marginal revenues equal marginal costs and he is maximizing his profits.

At this time another company develops another process for making the product. It also costs approximately $1.50 per pound to manufacture. If the new duopolist decides to price his output at the current market price of $10 per pound and if he can obtain half of the business, each duopolist will make a profit of $425,000 per year.

If either company decides to cut the price to $9 per pound to attempt to get a larger share of the market for itself, theoretically all the customers will go to the lower-price company because the product is the same. The price-cutting company might then expect a profit of $750,000 per year selling 100,000 lb. However, the other duopolist will not sit idle and allow all of its business to be taken away by its competitor. He will also cut his price. Such a price war could conceivably continue until the price was $1.50 or even lower if each would try to force the other out of business.

To avoid the possibility of creating an unprofitable price war, the duopolists might reach an agreement on sharing the market. The situation would then be as if there were one monopoly producer. Or, without any formal agreement, both duopolists may recognize the hazards of price cutting. They will therefore adopt a live-and-let-live attitude and avoid price-cutting competition. The price will then be near the monopoly price.

The same type of reasoning will apply when there are more than two oligopolists. Frequently, when a live-and-let-live attitude prevails, one of the firms in the industry, usually the largest or one of the larger ones, will emerge as the price leader. The other firms in the industry will customarily follow the prices established by the leader and adjust their output rate to maximize profits at that price. The price established by the leader is usually high enough to allow those already in the industry an adequate profit, but below the monopoly price to avoid attracting new firms into the industry.

Thus, under oligopoly, if each company considers the influence on the market price of his own policies, the price will tend toward the pure-monopoly one. This is more likely when the number of companies is small. If each company ignores the possible reactions of his competitors to his policies, they will act competitively against each other and the price will tend toward the pure-competition one even if there are only two companies. However, this case is more likely when the number of companies is large. The oligopoly output rate and price is thus usually somewhere between the pure-competition and pure-monopoly price.

When relatively few oligopolists dominate a market, it is valuable for the oligopolists to study and understand each other's cost relationships as well as the policies and criteria which their oligopolistic competitors use in establishing output rate and price policies. This will frequently make possible more logical analysis to establish output rate and pricing decisions to maximize profits.

Let us consider the simplified example of two oligopolists each of whom assumes that his competitor will continue to produce at his current output rate regardless of what changes he makes in his own output rate. Each producer has a good idea of the other's total cost function and he knows the other's current production or output rate.

Duopolist A has a cost function

$$C_A = F_A(Q)$$

Duopolist B has a cost function

$$C_B = F_B(Q)$$

As noted previously,

$$\text{Price} = P = f(Q)$$

Total revenue for each duopolist,

$$R_A = Q_A P = Q_A f(Q)$$
$$R_B = Q_B P = Q_B f(Q)$$

Profit for each duopolist,

$$\text{Profit}_A = Q_A f(Q) - C_A$$
$$\text{Profit}_B = Q_B f(Q) - C_B$$

To maximize profit for duopolist A,

$$\frac{d[Q_A f(Q)]}{dQ_A} = \frac{dC_A}{dQ_A}$$

$$f(Q) + Q_A \frac{d[f(Q)]}{dQ} \frac{d(Q_A + Q_B)}{dQ_A} = \frac{dC_A}{dQ_A}$$

$$\frac{d[f(Q)]}{dQ} = \frac{dP}{dQ}$$

$$\frac{d(Q_A + Q_B)}{dQ_A} = \frac{dQ_A}{dQ_A} + \frac{dQ_B}{dQ_A}$$

$$\frac{dQ_A}{dQ_A} = 1$$

$$\frac{dQ_B}{dQ_A} = 0$$

The last relationship is true because duopolist B will continue to produce at his current output rate regardless of what duopolist A does.

We can therefore write

$$f(Q) + Q_A \frac{dP}{dQ} = \frac{dC_A}{dQ_A}$$

By applying similar analysis to duopolist B we can write

$$f(Q) + Q_B \frac{dP}{dQ} = \frac{dC_B}{dQ_B}$$

Having reasonably good estimates of the demand schedule, $f(Q)$, we can compute the first derivative of this function, $\frac{dP}{dQ}$. $\frac{dC_A}{dQ_A}$ and $\frac{dC_B}{dQ_B}$ are the respective marginal-cost curves which we can also estimate. We have two unknowns, Q_A and Q_B, and can therefore usually solve for them with two equations.

When the two duopolists have approximately the same cost functions, $C_A = C_B$ and $\dfrac{dC_A}{dQ_A} = \dfrac{dC_B}{dQ_B}$. Then

$$f(Q) + Q_A \frac{dP}{dQ} = f(Q) + Q_B \frac{dP}{dQ}$$
$$Q_A = Q_B = \tfrac{1}{2}Q$$

The duopolists will share the total output equally.

If variable costs are insignificant, so that total cost is relatively constant regardless of output rate and marginal costs are close to zero, such as in a motion picture theater, the equally shared output is determined by

$$f(Q) + \tfrac{1}{2}Q \frac{dP}{dQ} = 0$$

Multiplying by 2,

$$2f(Q) + Q \frac{dP}{dQ} = f(Q) + \left(f(Q) + Q \frac{dP}{dQ} \right) = 0$$
$$P + \left(P + Q \frac{dP}{dQ} \right) = P + \frac{d(PQ)}{dQ} = 0$$
$$\frac{d(PQ)}{dQ} = -P$$

P is the price and $\dfrac{d(PQ)}{dQ} = \dfrac{dR}{dQ}$ is the marginal receipts. At the output rate for maximum profit, the marginal receipts are equal to $-P$. Under pure monopoly, marginal receipts would be zero at the output rate for maximum profit because marginal costs are insignificant when total costs are relatively constant. This is illustrated in Figure 28-25. The

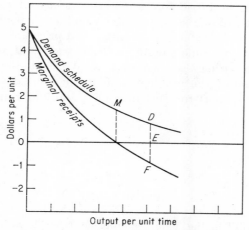

Figure 28-25. Revenue-output relationships under duopoly.

pure-monopoly output rate and price is at M, which is at the output rate where the marginal-receipts line crosses the zero line. The duopoly output rate and price is at D, which is at the output rate where price equals negative marginal receipts ($DE = EF$).

Overcapacity in Highly Fluctuating Industries. Industries with highly fluctuating demand functions tend to suffer from overcapacity a good portion of the time. When the demand is high, companies will frequently assume that it will remain high and they expand capacity. During periods of low demand, the industry will suffer either from a low, unprofitable price structure if it is a competitive industry or from idle capacity if it is a monopolistic industry. This problem is particularly critical in industries with high fixed investments, which make it difficult to leave the industry without unusually severe financial loss on the disposal of capital assets.

In our discussion of prices and costs in this chapter, we have been considering real prices and costs, unaffected by monetary inflation or deflation of their values. Thus, if the price of a product rises from \$2.40 to \$2.55 per unit at the same time that an index number measuring the level of prices rises from 108 to 122, the real price of the product will have decreased because the product price rise of 6 per cent is less than the decline of 13 per cent in the value of the dollar. The use of index numbers for adjusting prices to a fixed dollar value is discussed in Chapter 29.

The presentation in this chapter has been designed to give a general background for some of the practical decision-making techniques presented elsewhere in this book as well as provide the theory for specific types of analyses discussed later. The purpose is to contribute to a general understanding of the operation of a company in the business economy.

In later chapters in this section we shall discuss the nature and measurement of some of the broad forces in the economy which influence the economic position of the company. Such factors as population trends, national income and product distribution, and price-level changes affect the demand and cost functions of each company and are therefore of direct concern in business decision-making. We shall also give particular attention to some of the problems and methods used for determining demand functions, short-run cost functions, and long-run cost functions.

PROBLEMS

The term "profit" in the following problems refers to economic profit, the amount above the normal profit required to keep ownership capital in the business. The terms "prices" and "costs" refer to real prices and real costs in constant dollars.

1. Refer to Table 28-1 in the text, which presents the demand schedule for product M. Because of a technological change in one of the industries using product M, the price at which various numbers of units will be purchased per day has decreased 10 per cent. (*a*) Compute new demand, total-revenue, and marginal-revenue values. (*b*) Draw on a graph the new and old demand curves. (*c*) Has this change in the demand for product M increased or decreased its elasticity of demand?

2. Indicate which of the following industries are increasing-, decreasing-, or constant-cost industries in your estimation and give reasons: (*a*) wheat farming, (*b*) drugs, (*c*) trucking, (*d*) cattle ranching, (*e*) electronic appliances.

3. A large, permanent decrease has occurred in the demand for an agricultural product which is sold under conditions of pure competition and is not under government control or regulation. Describe the effects which this will have on prices, outputs, and acreages under cultivation, in the short and the long run, assuming no other changes in conditions occur.

4. A large, permanent increase in the demand for an electrical appliance sold under conditions of monopolistic competition has occurred. Describe the effects which this will have on prices and outputs in the short and the long run, assuming no other changes in conditions occur.

5. What limits, if any, are there on the price which a pure monopolist will charge if there is no government regulation?

6. Are the prices of products produced and sold under oligopoly always higher than they would be if they were produced under pure competition? Explain.

7. Discuss the validity of using each of the following bases for measuring the degree of competition versus monopoly in an industry: (*a*) the size of profits in the industry, (*b*) the amplitude and frequency of fluctuation of the prices of the industry's products, (*c*) the elasticity of the demand function for the industry's products, (*d*) the amount of concentration of production, sales, employees, or assets in a specified small number of the largest firms.

8. An appliance manufacturer has the following short-run total-cost function: $C = 0.5x^2 + 50x + 800$, where C is total cost per week and x is output in units per week. The company has a monopoly protected by patents. Its demand function is: $p = 250 - 2x$, where p is the price in dollars per unit. (*a*) What weekly output rate will produce maximum profit? (*b*) What will be the monopoly price? (*c*) What will be the profit?

9. The government imposes a tax of $10 per set on the output of the manufacturer under the conditions of problem 8. (*a*) How much of this tax will the manufacturer pass on to his customers in the form of higher prices? (*b*) How much will the company's output and profits be changed?

10. Refer to problem 9. The government would like to determine the size of tax which will produce the maximum tax return. By using a tax rate of t dollars per unit, we can determine the monopolist's output in terms of t. We can then determine the total tax return as a function of t. (*a*) What is the tax rate for maximum tax return to the government? (*b*) How much would this tax rate increase the price?

11. A company which operates under conditions approximating pure competition has a short-run cost function: $C = x^3 - 8x^2 + 15x + 800$, where C is total cost per hour and x is output rate in units per hour. Determine the output rate and profit if the market price is $50.

12. The company of problem 11 decides to attempt to differentiate its product from that of the other producers in the industry. It therefore employs packaging and advertising firms to create a preference for its product in the minds of consumers. This has caused the cost function to change to $C = x^3 - 8x^2 + 18x + 850$. The packaging and advertising programs have created a condition of monopolistic competition in which the company's demand function is $p = 100 - 1.5x$. Determine the output rate, price, and profit under this new situation.

29 Measures of Economic Activity

Forecasting general business conditions is usually an essential prelude to forecasting conditions in the industry and in the firm. Numerous varieties of measures of economic activity, which are published by various organizations, aid in this forecasting process. We shall therefore discuss in this chapter measures of economic activity and relationships which are designed to describe various aspects of the economy and assist in the economic forecasting which is a critical aspect of most business decisions.

Three types of economic measures are described.

1. Total-activity measures, which are designed to measure directly activity in the entire economic system. We shall describe three such systems—national-income accounting, flow-of-funds accounting, and input-output accounting.

2. Index numbers, which are used to measure a wide variety of conditions: prices, employment, production, health, sales potential, inventory level, and quality performance. The index number is a technique for measuring changes in a large or small number of varying items and expressing the net effect of these many variations in a number which can be used for comparative purposes.

3. Economic indicators, which measure one or several aspects of economic activity to provide indicators of what is occurring in the entire economic system or a major portion of it.

This classification of economic measures is not rigidly exclusive. Thus, elements of total-activity measures, such as national-income statistics, are useful as economic indicators. Various index numbers are also useful as economic indicators.

National-income Accounting. The national income and product accounts, published quarterly and annually by the U.S. Department of Commerce, provide quantitative descriptive measures of the way the entire economy is functioning.[1] They reveal important fluctuations and

---

[1] The sources for most of the national-income information in this chapter are *National Income*, U.S. Department of Commerce, 1954; *U.S. Income and Output*, U.S. Department of Commerce, 1958; *Survey of Current Business*, July 1960. These sources should be consulted for more detailed discussion of the economic concepts and statistical techniques of national-income accounting. The development of national-income accounting was pioneered by Simon Kuznets under the auspices of the National

long-term changes in the volume, composition, and use of the country's output, in the industrial structure through which it is produced, and in the distribution of the resultant income. There are three principal facets to the national income-product picture:

1. Gross national product, which is the market value of the output of goods and services

2. Gross national income, which is earnings resulting from the production of goods and services

3. Gross national expenditure, which is the expenditures for the goods and services of the gross national product, including investment expenditures

Each of these facets is a different way of looking at the same economic activity. Gross national expenditures are required to produce gross national product which results in gross national income. They are, therefore, equal to each other. The term "gross national product" is most commonly used to represent this aggregate of the nation's economic activity.

Gross national product or expenditure is the market value of the output of goods and services produced by the nation's economy, before deduction of depreciation charges and other allowances for business and institutional consumption of durable capital goods. Other business products used up by business in the accounting period are excluded. The nation's economy refers to the labor and property supplied by residents of the nation. Gross national product comprises the purchases of goods and services by consumers and government, gross private domestic investment (including the change in business inventories), and net foreign investment.

Net national product or expenditure is the market value of the net output of goods and services produced by the nation's economy. It comprises the purchases of goods and services by consumers and government, net private domestic investment (including the change in business inventories), and net foreign investment. Net national product is equal to gross national product less capital consumption allowances.

National income is the aggregate earnings of labor and property which arise from the current production of goods and services by the nation's economy. Thus, it measures the total factor costs of the goods and services produced by the economy. Earnings are inclusive of taxes and consist of the compensation of employees, the profits of corporate and unincorporated enterprises, net interest, and the rental income flowing to persons. National income essentially equals net national product minus indirect business tax and nontax liability (with adjustments for business

Bureau of Economic Research. The results of his work were published by the National Bureau of Economic Research: *National Income and Capital Formation, 1919–1935* in 1937, *Commodity Flow and Capital Formation* in 1938, and several others in later years.

transfer payments and current surplus of government enterprises less subsidies).

Personal income is the current income received by persons from all sources, inclusive of transfers from government and business but exclusive of transfers among persons. Not only individuals (including owners of unincorporated enterprises), but nonprofit institutions, private trust funds, and private pension, health, and welfare funds are classified as persons. Personal income is measured on a before-tax basis, as the sum of wage and salary disbursements, other labor income, proprietors' and rental income, interest and dividends, and transfer payments, minus personal contributions for social insurance. Personal income essentially equals national income plus net government interest and government and business transfer payments, minus corporate-profits tax liability, corporate retained earnings, and contributions for social insurance (with adjustments for inventory valuation changes and the excess of wage accruals over disbursements).

Disposable income is the income remaining to persons after deduction of personal tax and nontax payments to general government. Disposable personal income, thus, equals personal income less personal tax and nontax payments.

A simplified presentation of the relationship between personal income, national income, and gross national product in 1959 is shown in Figure 29-1. The data for this presentation are shown in the national income and product accounts of Table 29-1. These accounts represent a system for classifying national income and product transactions. They are constructed on the accounting principle that every economic transaction has both a debit and a credit entry in a sector account. Thus, personal saving is a debit to the personal income and outlay account (item 6) and a credit to the gross savings and investment account (item 10). All entries in the accounts of Table 29-1 are cross-referenced to show the counterentry.

The principal descriptive terms used in national income and product accounting are defined in Appendix A of this chapter to assist in understanding the concepts in the summary data of Table 29-1 and to facilitate the use of the statistical data in the detailed accounts published in the *Survey of Current Business* and its supplements.

Supplementing the summary account statements of Table 29-1, but not shown here, are numerous tables of detailed statistics with such information as gross national product by major type of product in current and constant dollars; national income by industry; national income and product by legal form of organization; distribution of consumer units and their family personal income, by income brackets; government expenditures by type of functions; sources and uses of gross saving; new construction activity by type; net change in business inventories; balance of payments on capital account; compensation of employees by industry;

Table 29-1

I. National Income and Product Account, 1959*
(In billions of dollars)

Item		
1	Compensation of employees	277.8
2	Wages and salaries	258.2
3	Disbursements (II-7)	258.2
4	Excess of accruals over disbursements (V-11)	.0
5	Supplements	19.6
6	Employer contributions for social insurance (III-18)	9.5
7	Other labor income (II-11)	10.1
8	Proprietor's income (II-12)	46.5
9	Rental income of persons (II-15)	12.4
10	Corporate profits and inventory valuation adjustment	46.6
11	Profits before tax	47.0
12	Tax liability (III-15)	23.2
13	Profits after tax	23.8
14	Dividends (II-16)	13.4
15	Undistributed (V-12)	10.5
16	Inventory valuation adjustment (V-13)	-.5
17	Net interest (II-18)	16.4
18	NATIONAL INCOME	399.6
19	Business transfer payments (II-21)	1.8
20	Indirect business tax and nontax liability (III-16)	42.6
21	Current surplus of government enterprises less subsidies (III-10)	-.6
22	Capital consumption allowances (V-14)	40.5
23	Statistical discrepancy (V-16)	-1.8
	GROSS NATIONAL PRODUCT	482.1

Item		
24	Personal consumption expenditures (II-2)	313.8
25	Gross private domestic investment (V-1)	72.0
26	Net exports of goods and services	-1.0
27	Exports (IV-1)	22.9
28	Imports (IV-2)	23.8
29	Government purchases of goods and services (III-1)	97.1
	GROSS NATIONAL PRODUCT	482.1

II. Personal Income and Outlay Account, 1959

Item		
1	Personal tax and nontax payments (III-12)	46.0
2	Personal consumption expenditures (I-24)	313.8
3	Durable goods	43.4
4	Nondurable goods	147.6
5	Services	122.8
6	Personal saving (V-10)	23.4
	PERSONAL OUTLAY AND SAVING	383.3

Item		
7	Wage and salary disbursements (I-3)	258.2
8	Manufacturing	84.7
9	Other private	128.2
10	Government	45.3
11	Other labor income (I-7)	10.1
12	Proprietors' income (I-8)	46.5
13	Business and professional	34.7
14	Farm	11.8
15	Rental income of persons (I-9)	12.4
16	Dividends (I-14)	13.4
17	Personal interest income	23.5
18	Net interest (I-17)	16.4
19	Net interest paid by government (III-9)	7.1
20	Transfer payments	27.0
21	Business (I-19)	1.8
22	Government (III-7)	25.2
23	Less: Personal contributions for social insurance (III-19)	7.8
	PERSONAL INCOME	383.3

III. Government Receipts and Expenditures Account, 1959

Item			Item		
1	Purchases of goods and services (I-29)	97.1	12	Personal tax and nontax receipts (II-1)	46.0
2	Federal	53.3	13	Federal	39.8
3	National defense (less sales)	45.5	14	State and local	6.2
4	Other	7.8	15	Corporate profits tax accruals (I-12)	23.2
5	State and local	43.9	16	Indirect business tax and nontax accruals (I-20)	42.6
6	Transfer payments	26.8	17	Contributions for social insurance	17.3
7	To persons (II-22)	25.2	18	Employer (I-6)	9.5
8	Foreign (IV-3)	1.5	19	Personal (II-23)	7.8
9	Net interest paid (II-19)	7.1			
10	Subsidies less current surplus of government enterprises (I-21)	−.6			
11	Surplus or deficit (−) on income and product account (V-15)	−2.5			
	GOVERNMENT EXPENDITURES AND SURPLUS	129.1		GOVERNMENT RECEIPTS	129.1

IV. Foreign Transactions Account, 1959

Item			Item		
1	Exports of goods and services (I-27)	22.9	2	Imports of goods and services (I-28)	23.8
			3	Transfer payments from U.S. Government (III-8)	1.5
			4	Net foreign investment (V-9)	−2.5
	RECEIPTS FROM ABROAD	22.9		PAYMENTS TO ABROAD	22.9

V. Gross Savings and Investment Account, 1959

Item			Item		
1	Gross private domestic investment (I-25)	72.0	10	Personal saving (II-6)	23.4
2	New construction	40.3	11	Excess of wage accruals over disbursements (I-4)	0
3	Residential nonfarm	22.3	12	Undistributed corporate profits (I-15)	10.5
4	Other	18.0	13	Corporate inventory valuation adjustment (I-16)	−.5
5	Producers' durable equipment	25.8	14	Capital consumption allowances (I-22)	40.5
6	Change in business inventories	5.9	15	Government surplus or deficit (−) on income and product account (III-11)	−2.5
7	Nonfarm	5.4	16	Statistical discrepancy (I-23)	−1.8
8	Farm	.5			
9	Net foreign investment (IV-4)	−2.5			
	GROSS INVESTMENT	69.5		GROSS SAVING AND STATISTICAL DISCREPANCY	69.5

* Numbers in parentheses indicate accounts and items of counterentry in the accounts.
SOURCE: *Survey of Current Business*, July, 1960, p. 12.

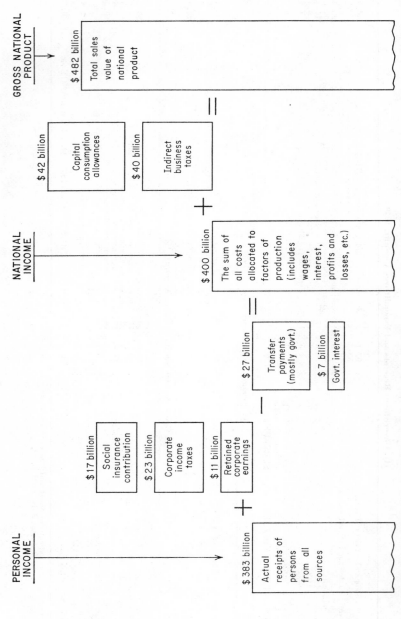

Figure 29-1. Simplified representation of relationship between personal income, national income, and national product (1959 data). Data from *Survey of Current Business*, July, 1960.

GROSS NATIONAL PRODUCT

$ 482 billion

Total sales value of national product

$ 42 billion

Capital consumption allowances

$ 40 billion

Indirect business taxes

NATIONAL INCOME

$ 400 billion

The sum of all costs allocated to factors of production (includes wages, interest, profits and losses, etc.)

$ 27 billion

Transfer payments (mostly govt.)

$ 7 billion

Govt. interest

$ 17 billion

Social insurance contribution

$ 23 billion

Corporate income taxes

$ 11 billion

Retained corporate earnings

PERSONAL INCOME

$ 383 billion

Actual receipts of persons from all sources

corporate profits (before and after tax), net dividend payments, undistributed profits, and depreciation charges, by industry; income and gross product originating in farming.

Flow-of-funds Accounting. The flow-of-funds system[1] of accounts, published quarterly and annually by the Federal Reserve Board, is designed to provide a statistical framework to facilitate the analysis of problems involving relationships among financial and nonfinancial developments in the economy and to permit the tieing together of economic-sector and financial-market analyses into integrated analyses for the economy as a whole.

Table 29-2 shows a summary of flow-of-funds accounts for 1959. It presents a detailed sector-by-transaction matrix of the saving, tangible capital, and financial flows for the entire economy. In this table, the economy has been divided into eleven sectors: (1) consumers and non-profit organizations; three nonfinancial business sectors: (2) farm business, (3) nonfarm, noncorporate business, and (4) corporate business; two government sectors: (5) Federal government, and (6) state and local government; four financial sectors: (7) commercial banks and monetary authorities, including the Federal Reserve System, (8) savings institutions (mutual savings banks, savings and loan associations, and credit unions), (9) insurance companies and private pension plans, and (10) finance not elsewhere classified (security brokers and dealers, open-end investment companies, sales finance companies, etc.); and (11) a sector for the rest of the world (that is, for foreign transactions with the United States). Subsector statements are also prepared for the major components of the financial sectors.

In flow-of-funds accounting, each recorded transaction is reflected in at least four entries in the accounts of participating sectors. For example, a transaction consisting of a purchase of goods for cash is entered as a purchase of goods by the buyer, a sale of goods by the seller, a reduction in cash for the buyer, and an increase in cash for the seller. (Some transactions, such as purchases involving part cash and part credit payment, involve more than four entries.) Such a transaction has two nonfinancial entries—the purchase and the sale—and two financial entries—the reduction and the increase in cash. Some transactions are entirely financial in character, for example, purchases of securities for cash or repayments of

---

[1] The most detailed explanation of the flow-of-funds system is presented in *Flow of Funds in the United States, 1939–53*, Board of Governors, Federal Reserve System, 1955. An additional source for much of the information in this section is "A Quarterly Presentation of Flow of Funds, Savings, and Investment," *Federal Reserve Bulletin*, August, 1959, pp. 828–1062. Discussion of the economic concepts and statistical techniques underlying the system are available in these sources. In particular, detailed descriptions of the sector and transaction categories of Tables 29-2 to 29-23 are given in the latter reference. The pioneering work in this area was performed by Morris A. Copeland. The results of his work were published in his book, *A Study of Moneyflows in the United States*, National Bureau of Economic Research, New York, 1952.

Table 29-2. Summary of Flow-of-funds Accounts for 1959
(In billions of dollars)

Transaction category	Consumer and nonprofit sector U	S	Farm U	S	Noncorporate U	S	Corporate U	S	Federal U	S	State and local U	S	Commercial banking U	S	Savings institutions U	S	Insurance U	S	Finance n.e.c. U	S	Rest-of-world sector U	S	All sectors U	S	Discrepancy U	Natl. saving and investment
A Gross saving		74.0		4.1		8.2		34.8		-4.5		-4.4		1.5		.9		1.2		-.5		2.5		117.8	2.3	115.2 A
B Capital Consumption		43.4		4.1		8.2		23.3																79.0		79.0 B
C Net saving (A − B)		30.6		*				11.4		-4.5		-4.4		1.5		.9		1.2		-.5		2.5		38.7		36.1 C
D Gross investment (E + J)	76.2		4.1		8.2		30.7		-4.5		-3.9		2.4		.7		1.6		-.1		1.8		117.1		-1.6	113.7 D
E Private capital expenditures (net of sales)	65.6		5.4		11.4		32.3						.4				.4						115.4			115.4 E
F Consumer durable goods	43.4																						43.4			43.4 F
G Nonfarm resident. constr.	18.5				1.9		1.9																22.3			22.3 G
H Plant and equipment	3.7		4.9		8.9		25.5						.4				.4						43.8			43.8 H
I Change in inventories			.5		.6		4.8																5.9			5.9 I
J Net financial invest. (K − L)	10.6		-1.3		-3.2		-1.6		-4.5		-3.9		2.0		.7		1.2		-.1		1.8		1.6		-1.6	-1.8 J
K Net acquis. of finan. assets	31.3		-.4		*		13.4		6.3		3.1		4.6		10.0		9.9		4.6		5.8		88.7			4.0 K
L Net increase in liab.		20.7		.9		3.2		15.0		10.8		6.9		2.6		9.4		8.8		4.7		4.0		87.1		5.8 L
M Gold and Treas. currency	.9		-.4		-.3		.2		*	*			-1.0						.1		1.1	*	.1	*	-.1	-1.1 M
N Dem. dep. and currency									.7	*	.5		1.1		-.2		.1		.1		.1	1.1	1.7	1.1	-.6	-.1 N
O Fixed-value redeem. claims	9.6				-.4		-.4			-2.0		-.4		1.2		8.4					-1.0		7.6	7.6		1.0 O
P Time deposits	4.1				-.4		-.4			-.2		-.4		1.2		1.2					-1.0		2.2	2.2		1.0 P

		Values (left → right)
Q	Savings shares	7.3 ... 7.2 7.2 ...
R	U.S. savings bonds	−1.8 ... −1.8 −1.8 ...
S	Saving through life insur.	3.7 ... 3.6 ... 3.7 3.7 ...
T	Saving through pen. funds	7.9 ... 1.8 ... .9 ... 5.2 ... 7.9 7.9 ...
U	Credit and equity mkt. instr.	15.3 20.6 ... 2.0 ... .4 ... 4.8 ... 5.5 11.6 ... 3.8 ... 10.7 ... 2.9 ... 5.1 ... 5.6 ... .1 10.6 ... .9 ... 9.8 ... 4.5 ... 4.7 ... 3.1 ... .8 ... 61.5 61.4 ... −.1 ... −2.3
V	Federal obligations	9.4 ... 4.4 ... 11.3 ... 1.0 ... −7.1 ... .6 ... .2 ... .1 ... 2.8 ... 11.3 11.3 ... −2.8
W	State and local obligations	2.5 ... 1.8 ... .5 ... .4 ... 1.4 ... * ... 4.9 4.9 ...
X	Corp. and foreign bonds	.1 ... 3.3 ... 1.2 ... −.1 ... 3.5 ... .2 ... 1.0 ... .1 ... .5 ... 4.7 4.7 4
Y	Corporate stock	1.1 ... 2.3 ... −.2 ... 1.9 ... 1.0 1.8 ... .2 ... 4.4 4.4 ... −.2
Z	1- to 4-family mortgages	.5 13.2 ... .1 ... .1 1.6 ... .1 ... .1 ... 8.2 ... 1.3 ... .4 ... 13.3 13.3 ...
a	Other mortgages	1.8 .1 ... 1.1 ... 1.4 ... 3.2 ... .6 ... .1 ... 1.1 ... 1.2 ... .2 ... 5.8 5.8 ...
b	Consumer credit	6.3 ... .4 ... .8 ... .1 ... 2.4 ... .8 ... * ... 6.3 6.3 ...
c	Security credit	−.2 * ... 1.9 ... * ... .1 ... *
d	Bank loans n.e.c.	.4 ... .7 ... 2.7 ... 2.5 ... .2 ... 7.9 ... .1 ... .1 ... 1.3 ... .2 ... 7.9 7.9 ... *
e	Other loans	.5 ... .2 ... .6 ... .3 ... .4 ... 1.6 ... −.6 ... −.6 ... .2 ... .8 ... .5 ... 1.0 ... .5 ... −.1 ... 2.8 2.7 ... −.1
f	Trade credit	.1 ... 3.4 ... 6.8 3.3 ... .1 ... .1 ... 6.9 6.9 ...
g	Proprietors' net invest. in noncorporate business	−6.1 ...
h	Misc. financial trans.	−1.1 ... * ... −5.0 ... 1.3 ... .1 ... 1.8 1.0 ... .2 −.1 ... .1 ... 2.4 3.2 ... −6.1 −6.1 ... 5.4 4.6 ... −.8 .8
i	Sector discrepancies (A − D)	−2.2 ... 4.1 ... −.6 ... −.9 ... .2 ... −.4 ... −.4 ... .8 ... .7 .7 ... 1.5

* Less than $50 millions.

NOTE.—U = uses of funds; S = sources of funds. Financial uses of funds represent net acquisitions of assets; financial sources of funds, net changes in liabilities.

Details may not add to totals because of rounding.

debt in cash; in these cases, all entries reflect changes in financial claims. It has been found convenient in describing the accounts to refer to the nonfinancial entries of the transactions recorded as nonfinancial transactions and to call the financial entries financial transactions.

The flow-of-funds accounts include all transactions which (1) involve at least two separate economic units and (2) are effected through transfers of credit and money. This perspective results in the exclusion, as far as possible, of transactions internal to the accounts of a single economic unit, such as a corporation or a family, and of barter and imputed transactions. Internal transactions are such bookkeeping transfers as allocations of funds to various reserve accounts and interplant transfers among the establishments of a single enterprise. Such internal transactions are not recorded in the flow-of-funds system because they do not involve two separate economic units and are not effected through the transfer of money or credit. Some of these internal entries, however, have economic significance. For example, charges to depreciation reserves directly affect tax liabilities and also have a bearing on investment, dividend, and other business policies of the economic unit. Similarly, charges to reserves for bad debts by financial institutions may exert an influence on credit availability.

The transactions of the various sectors are classified in a standard way throughout all sector accounts. Each payment by one economic unit is also a receipt of another, and each debt of one unit is also a financial asset of another; with both sides of each transaction or claim classified similarly, the transactions of one sector can be related to those of other sectors, and transaction accounts can be set up showing the amounts various sectors put into, and receive from, various broad markets. In the financial area, standardization of transaction classification provides a consistent structure of all financial flows.

Financial flows for each sector are recorded on a net-transaction basis for each financial-transaction category; that is, for each sector for each financial-transaction category the asset entry represents funds used to acquire assets of that type in the accounting period less funds realized from the disposition of assets of that type in the accounting period; and the liability entry represents funds raised by borrowing less funds used in repayment in the accounting period. In two respects, however, entries for financial flows are on a gross basis. (1) Liabilities (assets) of one transaction category are not netted against assets (liabilities) of another. For example, consumer borrowing to purchase securities is not netted against consumer purchase of the securities; both are shown in the consumer account. (2) For any sector, asset and liability entries within a single transaction category are not netted; both are shown (except for internal holdings in consolidated sector accounts). For example, consumer mortgage assets are not netted against consumer mortgage liabilities.

Futher explanations of the manner in which transactions are recorded in flow-of-funds accounting is given in Appendix B of this chapter.

The flow-of-funds system of accounts contributes a controlled statistical approach and an internally consistent body of data that highlight the complex of transactions in the economy. The constraints provided by a system in which every flow is consistently recorded both as receipt and payment and in which explicitly recorded sources and uses of funds balance for each sector enforce a consistency of analysis in picturing interrelationships in the economy.

The flow-of-funds accounts focus attention on the interplay between financial and nonfinancial factors in the economy and arrange both flows in a single internally consistent structure. Emphasis is placed on the behavior of groups of economic units. All transactions—current and capital, financial and nonfinancial—of each group of economic units are recorded in a sector account of sources and uses of funds, which covers current income of all types, current expenditures, capital expenditures, borrowing, and lending and other acquisitions of financial assets. However, the flow-of-funds statement does not reflect the total transactions in the economy because, as previously explained, only the net results of transactions in the various categories are indicated.

Input-Output Accounting. Input-output accounting is essentially a system of double-entry bookkeeping which shows, for each sector of the economy during a given period, purchases from and sales to each of the other sectors. It may be considered an extension of national income and and product accounting. It is extended in the sense that it includes sales of intermediate products as well as end-product deliveries to ultimate users.

Table 29-3 shows in summary form the distribution of the value of all output in the United States for 1947 both by industry of origin and industry of destination.[1] Each row in the table lists for a designated industry the dollar amount of its output consumed in 1947 by each of the other 49 industries. Looking at the end of row 1, we see that the total gross output of agriculture and fisheries was $44,263 million in 1947. This is considered to be the value at producer's prices of all the output defined to be included in this industry. The first entry in this row indicates that the industry itself consumed $10,856 million worth of the total produced, mostly as feed and seed. This entry illustrates the fact that each industry group is

---

[1] The data and information on the 1947 interindustry study in this chapter have been adapted from W. D. Evans and M. Hoffenberg, *The Interindustry Relations Study for 1947*, U.S. Bureau of Labor Statistics, 1951. Input-output accounting had its origins in the pioneering work of Wassily Leontief. See the following publications by Leontief: "Quantitative Input-Output Relations in the Economic System of the United States," *Review of Economics and Statistics*, vol. 18, no. 3, pp. 105–125, August, 1936; *The Structure of the American Economy, 1919–1939*, Oxford University Press, New York, 1951; (with others) *Studies in the Structure of the American Economy*, Oxford University Press, New York, 1953.

composed of a large number of separate enterprises, any one of which may sell to or purchase from another.

Continuing along the row, food and kindred products (column 2) purchased $15,048 million worth, mostly for conversion to processed foods. Tobacco manufactures (column 3) purchased $783 million worth, practically all raw tobacco, and so on. Some $250 million went to undistributed (column 43, which is not shown in table) because the destination could not be specifically identified. Farther along the row, we see (column 46) that additions to inventory (no matter where held) took $1,008 million, that exports (column 47) amounted to $1,276 million, and that households consumed $9,785 million worth of agricultural and fishery products. This latter figure does not include consumer expenditures for food produced by the food and kindred products industry (No. 2) nor payments for meals prepared by the eating and drinking places industry (No. 44). The above description for row 1 can be similarly extended to all the other rows.

Since the first entry in each row represents the shipments of that sector to agriculture and fisheries, it follows that the first column is a summary of the purchases in 1947 by this sector. The first entry in the column is, of course, the afore-mentioned intraindustry transfer. Agriculture and fisheries also purchased $2,378 million from food and kindred products (row 2), mostly prepared feed; $830 million from chemicals (row 10), mainly fertilizer and insecticides; and so on for the other industries. One will note large purchases from transportation and trade (rows 31-34). These are transportation costs and trade margins on material items purchased by this industry for production purposes. The rental amount (row 37) of $2,393 million represents gross rent paid for rented land and service buildings. Inventory depletion (row 46), amounting to $2,660 million, accounts for shipments of agricultural products in excess of current production in the period. The household entry (row 50) of $19,166 million includes wage and salary payments, profits, interest payments, and depreciation charges. (Since the output of the agriculture and fisheries sector refers to productive activities, the outlays appearing in the first column are those expenditure items incurred in the process of production. Farmers and fishermen as consumers are not included in the sector; they appear as part of the household segment.) Similarly, the outlays of the other sectors in 1947 may be traced in other columns.

In general, then, the distribution of the products or services of any one industry to each of the others may be traced by reading the entries along its row, and its purchases from other industries by reading down its column. It is this property which first led Leontief to refer to them as "input-output" tables.

The sectors have been divided into two groups. The first 45 may be considered as processing sectors, and for each of these the gross output and gross outlay totals are identical. This is equivalent to saying that in an accounting sense current outlays, with allowance for profits and inventory change, are equal to current receipts. The remaining 5 sectors may be considered as representing end-product demand (the column) or factor payments (the rows). For these sectors individually the gross receipt and outlay totals are not the same, but for the 5 sectors collectively there is a balance. This is roughly equivalent to saying that, in a gross national product sense, factor payments for productive activities equal the sum of consumer expenditures, net investment (including change in stocks and net foreign balance), and government expenditures. With minor adjustments for statistical and conceptual differences, the gross national product may be derived from these figures—on the product side from the columns and on the factor-payment side from the rows.

The ratios shown in Table 29-4 were calculated directly from the data of Table 29-3. This table may be interpreted as showing in simple form the unit-cost structure for each sector in 1947 in terms of its direct purchases from other processing sectors. In the first column, for example, each dollar's worth of current output from agriculture and fisheries required internal transfers (for such items as feed and seed) of 26.1 cents, and purchases from the food processing sector (typically for prepared feeds) of 5.7 cents. Farther down the same column are recorded purchases per dollar of current output of 2.0 cents for chemicals, 1.1 cents for coal and petroleum products, 0.3 cents for rubber products, and so on. The other columns provide similar information for other sectors.

Table 29-5 is also based on figures from Table 29-3, but is computed more directly from Table 29-4. It is of special interest since it shows the combined direct and indirect requirements placed on all sectors by the delivery outside the processing system of $1 of output from each sector. For example, the amount of nonferrous metals required in 1947 to support the delivery of motor vehicles outside the processing system was substantially more than the direct purchases indicated in Table 29-3. In addition, the motor vehicle sector (No. 26) purchased electrical machinery, and this sector (No. 25) was also a substantial purchaser of nonferrous metals. Other more remote ways in which nonferrous metals output was related to motor vehicle production may be found. The table summarizes all these supply connections, direct and indirect, among the sectors, expressing them in terms of requirements per dollar of finished-goods delivery from each sector. Thus the entry in row 26, column 16, indicates that about 7.9 cents of nonferrous metals gross output was directly and indirectly required by the motor vehicle sector in 1947 per dollar of deliveries outside the processing system. The processing system is here defined to include only the activities of the sectors shown in the table. The term "deliveries outside the processing system" refers to sales to sectors excluded from this table (households, investors, foreign buyers, government,

Table 29-3. Interindustry Flow of Goods and Services by Industry of Origin and Destination, 1947
(In millions of dollars)

Producing industry	1 Agriculture & fisheries	2 Food & kindred products	3 Tobacco manufactures	4 Textile mill products	5 Apparel	6 Lumber & wood products	7 Furniture & Fixtures	8 Paper & allied products	9 Printing & publishing	10 Chemicals	11 Products of petroleum & coal	12 Rubber products	13 Leather & leather products	14 Stone, clay & glass products	15 Iron & steel	16 Nonferrous metals	17 Plumbing & heating
1. Agriculture & fisheries	10,856	15,048	783	2,079	19	192	....	9	....	1,211	*	....	....	49	*	....	11
2. Food & kindred products	2,378	4,910	15	60	9	*	*	30	*	685	*	....	444	2	3	*	
3. Tobacco manufactures	....	....	828	....	....	....	....	....	....	1							
4. Textile mill products	64	2	....	1,303	3,882	3	285	43	25	13	2	444	88	33	....	....	*
5. Apparel	44	204	....	....	1,963	....	5	20	....	30	....	....	2	3	....	....	*
6. Lumber & wood products	148	81	18	18	2	1,094	385	267	1	45	6	....	17	17	36	28	*
7. Furniture & fixtures	....	....	....	....	12	....	7	5	....								*
8. Paper & allied products	2	453	65	78	25	5	15	2,597	1,081	331	112	20	54	179	*	*	
9. Printing & publishing	....	39	....	2	....	....	....	....	767	16							
10. Chemicals	830	1,451	25	800	142	26	63	183	97	2,655	213	604	126	116	99	85	
11. Products of petroleum & coal	457	58	*	30	5	74	.1	63	3	325	4,829	12	2	50	846	49	
12. Rubber products	122	9	....	13	18	9	6	9	3	1	1	41	50	8	*	*	
13. Leather & leather products	....	....	....	2	53	4	7	....	4	....	....	....	1,037	....			*
14. Stone, clay & glass products	65	253	1	1	*	14	34	28	....	258	46	7	5	430	180	33	
15. Iron & steel	6	2	....	....	1	10	97	....	....	5	6	14	1	23	3,982	33	1
16. Nonferrous metals	....	....	....	....	....	2	16	....	14	189	1	*	*	13	324	2,599	
17. Plumbing & heating supplies															15		
18. Fabricated structural metal products						5									7		
19. Other fabricated metal products	83	543	15	*	6	35	132	17	1	130	78	12	16	4	24	4	
20. Agric'l, mining & const. machinery	59												5	15	7		
21. Metalworking machinery														8	7		
22. Other machinery (except electric)	....	13	....	35	21	14	11	14	35	1	5	....	2	27	4		
23. Motors & generators																	
24. Radios																*	
25. Other electrical machinery										1				7	8	46	
26. Motor vehicles	111	3	....		1	....		1	*		*		1	*	*	
27. Other transportation equipment	10	....			2	6	32	1	*	*		*	2	1			
28. Professional & scientific equipment						2	6	32	13				1	*			
29. Miscellaneous manufacturing	4	11	....	4	256	1	16	15	....	29	....	*	22	9	5	*	
30. Coal, gas & electric power	61	193	4	105	36	24	18	123	29	188	556	37	15	204	242	104	
31. Railroad transportation	440	548	21	94	60	143	54	224	68	287	270	36	36	145	423	100	
32. Ocean transportation	73	126	3	13	11	9	*	16	*	44	94	*	1	14	30	52	*
33. Other transportation	553	367	16	79	25	138	40	117	25	95	470	7	21	70	140	19	
34. Trade	1,360	418	38	228	369	60	60	176	31	173	19	55	57	52	216	140	
35. Communications	2	41	1	9	19	10	6	8	39	23	15	6	5	10	16	6	
36. Finance & insurance	238	145	1	20	24	77	18	18	23	18	125	7	7	46	44	14	
37. Rental	2,393	91	2	25	96	19	17	26	61	34	....	10	19	18	36	21	
38. Business services	8	533	98	71	97	19	57	22	58	424	42	21	49	11	25	5	
39. Personal & repair services	368	119	*	3	3	42	4	4	20	11	13	1	1	31	3	3	
40. Medical, educ. & nonprofit org's																	
41. Amusements																	
42. Scrap & miscellaneous industries	....	....	....	....	24	....	....	250	....	110	....	7	....	13	650	456	
43. Undistributed	....	2,059	132	438	1,310	880	329	201	610	1,740	788	329	323	570	287	101	2
44. Eating & drinking places									2								
45. New construction & maintenance	199	117	1	39	16	12	7	42	15	36	26	12	19	34	81	20	
46. Inventory change (depletions)	2,660	402	1	120	185	*	14	87	26	140	8	3	33	2	3	102	
47. Foreign countries (imports from)	690	2,001	104	208	279	183	6	621	8	594	258	2	35	143	43	573	*
48. Government	813	1,134	104	639	376	338	112	497	335	762	780	114	136	323	573	245	
49. Gross private capital formation	Depreciation and other capital consumption allowances are included in household row																
50. Households	19,166	6,262	387	3,286	4,013	2,564	1,063	2,161	3,034	3,431	4,907	1,024	1,140	2,255	3,945	1,519	6
Total gross outlays	44,263	37,636	2,663	9,838	13,321	6,002	2,892	7,899	6,447	14,050	13,670	2,825	3,810	4,844	12,338	6,387	1,7

*Less than $500,000.

Note: Each row shows distribution of output of producing industry named at left. Each column shows input distribution for purchasing industry named at top.
SOURCE: Data are from Division of Interindustry Economics. U.S. Bureau of Labor Statistics, October, 1951.

480

Table 29-3. Interindustry Flow of Goods and Services by Industry of Origin and Destination, 1947 (Continued)
(In millions of dollars)

Columns 18–26, 44, 45 are **Purchasing industry**; columns 46–50 are **Final demand**.

No.	Producing industry	18 Fabricated structural metal products	19 Other fabricated metal products	20 Agric'l, mining & const. machinery	21 Metalworking machinery	22 Other machinery (except electric)	23 Motors & generators	24 Radios	25 Other electrical machinery	26 Motor vehicles	44 Eating & drinking places	45 New construction & maintenance	46 Inventory change (additions)	47 Foreign countries (exports to)	48 Government	49 Gross private capital formation	50 Households	Total gross output
1	Agriculture & fisheries										865	92	1,008	1,276	569	21	9,785	44,263
2	Food & kindred products		*			*			*		3,469	2	608	1,528	728		22,141	37,636
3	Tobacco manufactures												77	217	3		1,485	2,663
4	Textile mill products		8	2	1	18	2	9	36	147		47	61	919	101	21	1,469	9,838
5	Apparel		1	*		2		*	*	100	21	1	214	301	193	1	9,987	13,321
6	Lumber & wood products	5	34	15	4	67	3	10	41	46	5	2,330	174	170	14	36	67	6,002
7	Furniture & fixtures					5		102	1	26		198	78	35	52	569	1,459	2,892
8	Paper & allied products	5	79	2	2	39	4	17	48	33	57	170	44	154	59		344	7,899
9	Printing & publishing		11	2	1	5		1	5			30	*	72	156	89	1,491	6,447
10	Chemicals	18	88	17	5	62	10	9	178	111	42	635	305	812	186		1,964	14,050
11	Products of petroleum & coal	3	12	9	4	24	1	2	18	31	15	617	56	680	177	*	2,437	13,670
12	Rubber products	2	5	75	2	53	2	2	31	496	4	56	94	168	21	8	709	2,825
13	Leather & leather products		*	1	3	11	7	*	1	13		1	108	84	30	17	2,065	3,810
14	Stone, clay & glass products	6	52	7	10	57	23	7	92	192	59	1,741	99	205	17	15	341	4,844
15	Iron & steel	553	1,374	532	143	930	118	13	196	1,102		876	57	605	13			12,338
16	Nonferrous metals	63	272	24	23	366	40	26	654	176	2	315	98	167	5		19	6,387
17	Plumbing & heating supplies	41	7			35	1		32	8		878	64	42	7	60	397	1,745
18	Fabricated structural metal products	42	18	33	1	67	*		9	10		1,564	15	67	4	145	13	2,316
19	Other fabricated metal products	90	213	93	67	326	28	63	211	956	24	652	127	280	38	74	537	6,445
20	Agric'l, mining & const. machinery	23		115	20	96			3			116	105	566	82	1,640	66	3,292
21	Metalworking machinery	9	53	51	57	90	7	6	19	223			17	205	11	734	31	1,833
22	Other machinery (except electric)	43	41	307	68	565	50	2	82	402		338	288	990	84	3,450	1,080	10,312
23	Motors & generators	7		32	29	317	17	5	52			3	33	85	11	128		1,095
24	Radios		13			4	8	243	95	19			56	113	83	296	639	1,692
25	Other electrical machinery	9	125	22	16	158	57	165	350	599		716	161	244	76	1,331	673	5,723
26	Motor vehicles		32	24	7	*			12	4,401	1	36	401	1,020	151	2,982	3,128	14,265
27	Other transportation equipment					*				12		1	18	324	1,245	1,203	171	4,001
28	Professional & scientific equipment	3	3	1	2	36	2	3	9	70		22	32	184	79	260	630	2,119
29	Miscellaneous manufacturing	1	18	*	1	45	20	30	61	22	21	32	43	187	85	511	1,934	4,756
30	Coal, gas & electric power	15	52	23	14	68	8	6	39	62	219	30	27	355	195		133	9,205
31	Railroad transportation	37	77	44	12	100	11	13	50	228	253	706	74	590	332	266	2,061	9,952
32	Ocean transportation	*	*	*	*	*	1				1			1,340	126		102	2,292
33	Other transportation	5	17	10	3	29	3	8	19	67	97	572	38	314	186	103	3,860	9,855
34	Trade	54	110	51	22	183	18	34	83	56	1,061	2,506	149	987	45	2,336	27,107	41,657
35	Communications	6	13	6	4	23	3	4	13	16	11	44		38	148		1,269	3,173
36	Finance & insurance	14	19	11	7	32	7	9	23	22	72	400		135	32		6,993	12,814
37	Rental	10	20	6	6	32	2	9	19	21	386	84			223	804	20,289	28,855
38	Business services	4	25	12	11	64	3	25	32	76	55	134		3	38		179	5,097
39	Personal & repair services																	
40	Medical, educ. & nonprofit org's		3	2	1	5	*	*	1	3		228	819		83	271	7,333	14,301
41	Amusements														5,078		7,856	13,385
42	Scrap & miscellaneous industries	4	3	9	6	38	1	*	3			1	128				2,403	2,944
43	Undistributed	172	1,000	356	250	1,463	45	204	822	490	536			30	1			24,711
44	Eating & drinking places																12,075	13,270
45	New construction & maintenance	.5	24	16	6	28	2	7	16	44	73	7			5,464	15,709	154	28,704
46	Inventory change (depletions)	*	3	*	4		*	2	7					22				4,887
47	Foreign countries (imports from)	1	6	35	1	1	1	2	15					1,313			1,325	9,275
48	Government	113	277	167	86	514	64	62	274	656	1,410	470	73	831	3,458	216		220,474
49	Gross private capital formation	→ Depreciation and other capital consumption allowances are included in household row																
50	Households	943	2,335	1,178	930	4,339	534	595	2,092	3,303	4,254	11,492		847	30,058	218	2,116	220,474
	Total gross outlays	2,316	6,445	3,292	1,833	10,312	1,095	1,692	5,723	14,265	13,270	28,704	4,802	17,320	51,060	33,514	191,625	769,248

* Less than $500,000.

Note: Each row shows distribution of output of producing industry named at left. Each column shows input distribution for purchasing industry named at top.

SOURCE: Data are from Division of Interindustry Economics, U.S. Bureau of Labor Statistics, October, 1951.

481

Table 29-4. Direct Purchases per Dollar of Output, 1947

Purchasing industry

Producing industry	1 Agriculture & fisheries	2 Food & kindred products	3 Tobacco manufactures	4 Textile mill products	5 Apparel	6 Lumber & wood products	7 Furniture & fixtures	8 Paper & allied products	9 Printing & publishing	10 Chemicals	11 Products of petroleum & coal	12 Rubber products	13 Leather & leather products	14 Stone, clay & glass products
1. Agriculture & fisheries	.260935	.404140	.294104	.213932	.001496	.032107	......	.001198	......	.087035	......	......	.012851	.000046
2. Food & kindred products	.057168	.131870	.005524	.006206	.000663	.000057	.000125	.003804	.000053	.049224	.000021	......	.117515	.000408
3. Tobacco manufactures	......	......	.310990	......	......	......	......	......	......	.000049	......	......	......	......
4. Textile mill products	.001543	.000046	......	.134117	.295538	.000439	.099330	.005513	.003899	.000965	.000118	.157283	.023296	.006774
5. Apparel	.001067	.005478	......	......	.149402	......	.001738	.002536	......	.002129	......	......	.000392	.000041
6. Lumber & wood products	.003568	.002174	.006881	.001819	.000177	.182243	.133882	.034158	.000094	.003232	.000431	......	.004477	.003518
7. Furniture & fixtures	......	......	......	.001295	......	......	.002433	.000725	......	......	......	......	......	......
8. Paper & allied products	.000038	.012165	.024549	.008046	.001902	.000758	.005253	.332409	.168256	.023798	.008205	.007041	.014306	.037024
9. Printing & publishing	......	.001052	......	.000247	......	......	......	......	.119509	.011132	......	......	......	......
10. Chemicals	.019942	.038979	.009310	.082302	.010810	.004359	.021779	.023454	.015073	.190897	.015605	.214162	.033459	.023855
11. Products of petroleum & coal	.010984	.001557	.000087	.003102	.000339	.012315	.000347	.008089	.000458	.023325	.353491	.004421	.000636	.010286
12. Rubber products	.002934	.000238	......	.001371	.001406	.001449	.002175	.001148	.000480	.000102	.000043	.014385	.013323	.017749
13. Leather & leather products	......	......	......	.000177	.004003	.000611	.002351	......	.000620	......	......	......	.274762	......
14. Stone, clay & glass products	.001555	.006784	.000196	.000059	.000027	.002398	.011905	.003641	......	.018544	.003386	.002467	.000239	.088765
15. Iron & steel	.000146	.000076	......	......	.000071	.001642	.033689	......	.002149	.013614	.000361	.000479	.004822	.000122
16. Nonferrous metals	......	......	......	......	......	.000402	.005536	......	......	......	.000051	.000031	......	.002646
17. Plumbing & heating supplies	......	......	......	......	......	......	.001722	......	......	......	......	......	......	......
18. Fabricated structural metal products	......	......	......	......	......	......	......	......	......	.009333	.005668	.004089	.004311	.000890
19. Other fabricated metal products	.002003	.014592	.005584	.000041	.000480	.005584	.045717	.002231	.000191	......	......	......	......	.001026
20. Agric'l, mining & const. machinery	.001414	......	......	......	......	......	......	......	......	......	......	......	......	......
21. Metalworking machinery	......	......	......	......	......	......	......	......	......	......	......	......	......	......
22. Other machinery (except electric)	......	.000352	......	.003655	.001621	.002325	.003703	.001727	.005496	.000114	.000394	......	......	.000436
23. Motors & generators	......	......	......	......	......	......	......	......	......	......	......	......	......	......
24. Radios	......	......	......	......	......	......	......	......	......	......	......	......	......	.001379
25. Other electrical machinery	......	......	......	......	......	......	......	......	......	.000036	......	......	......	.001516
26. Motor vehicles	.002672	.000067	......	......	......	.000156	......	......	......	......	.000019	......	......	.000095
27. Other transportation equipment	.000240	......	......	......	......	......	......	.000008	......	.000039	.000004	.000028	......	.000207
28. Professional & scientific equipment	......	......	......	......	......	......	.000616	.000768	.004995	......	.000935	.000035	.005973	.001838
29. Miscellaneous manufacturing	.000093	.000302	......	.000380	.019451	.000174	.005614	.001907	......	.002079	......	......	.003996	.042185
30. Coal, gas & electric power	.001475	.005178	.001661	.010805	.002719	.004035	.006038	.015667	.004575	.013513	.040675	.013315	.009532	.030017
31. Railroad transportation	.001573	.014717	.007736	.009633	.004561	.023862	.018910	.028653	.001510	.020651	.019789	.012875	.000150	.002880
32. Ocean transportation	.013299	.009870	.005877	.008067	.001931	.022927	.013749	.014969	.003953	.006862	.034358	.002364	.005480	.014435
33. Other transportation	.032681	.111217	.014443	.023470	.028096	.009900	.020770	.022472	.004823	.012445	.001392	.019369	.014972	.010839
34. Trade	.000037	.001092	.000543	.000892	.001471	.001576	.002066	.001084	.006065	.001666	.001065	.002182	.001282	.002036
35. Communications	.005710	.003900	.000551	.002038	.001839	.012769	.006369	.002339	.003500	.001304	.009152	.002556	.001803	.009475
36. Finance & insurance	......	.002435	.000641	.002607	.007307	.003171	.005837	.003379	.009595	.002501	......	.003419	.005135	.003807
37. Rental	.057526	......	......	......	......	......	......	.002812	.009050	.030467	.003104	.007442	.012901	.002208
38. Business services	.000199	.014309	.036674	.007286	.007344	.003268	.019645	......	......	......	.000950	.000256	.000198	......
39. Personal & repair services	.008846	.003196	.000170	.000318	.000193	.007015	.001236	.000513	.003102	.000775	......	......	......	......
40. Medical, educ. & nonprofit org's	......	......	......	......	......	......	......	......	......	......	......	......	......	......
41. Amusements	......	......	......	......	......	......	......	.031975	......	.007807	......	......	.002459	.002593
42. Scrap & miscellaneous industries	......	......	......	.002418	......	......	......	......	......	......	......	......	......	......
43. Undistributed	......	.055286	.049643	.045045	.099746	.146519	.114328	.025736	.094981	.125094	.057669	.116642	.085508	.117676
44. Eating & drinking places	......	......	......	......	......	......	......	......	.000311	......	......	......	......	......
45. New construction & maintenance	.004783	.003153	.000523	.004016	.001188	.002008	.002419	.005333	.002278	.002611	.001907	.004162	.004886	.006940

Note: Each entry shows direct purchases from industry named at left by industry named at top per dollar of output by latter.

source: Data are from Division of Interindustry Economics, U.S. Bureau of Labor Statistics, November, 1951.

Table 29-4. Direct Purchases per Dollar of Output, 1947 (Continued)

Producing industry	15 Iron & steel	16 Nonferrous metals	17 Plumbing & heating supplies	18 Fabricated structural metal products	19 Other fabricated metal products	20 Agric'l, mining & const. machinery	21 Metalworking machinery	22 Other machinery (except electric)	23 Motors & generators	24 Radios	25 Other electrical machinery	26 Motor vehicles	44 Eating & drinking places	45 New construction & maintenance
1. Agriculture & fisheries		.001717											.065190	.003209
2. Food & kindred products	.000252	.000044			.000022			.000010				.000019	.261397	.000052
3. Tobacco manufactures														
4. Textile mill products			.000062	.000004	.001312	.000496	.000392	.001728	.002145	.005352	.006291	.010346		.001643
5. Apparel			.000071		.000186	.000039		.000162		.000015	.000042	.007001	.001606	.000038
6. Lumber & wood products	.022924	.004538	.012933	.002205	.005236	.004551	.002180	.006476	.003173	.006154	.007168	.003263	.000361	.081185
7. Furniture & fixtures			.000112						.000506	.000436	.000118	.001805		.006886
8. Paper & allied products	.000038	.000008	.004691	.002194	.012251	.000658	.001300	.003772	.003760	.000741	.008356	.002311	.004261	.005929
9. Printing & publishing			.000578		.001647	.000597	.000223	.000500		.000490	.000908		.002221	
10. Chemicals	.008005	.013528	.012260	.007595	.013588	.005093	.002715	.005994	.008911	.005241	.031193	.007774	.003196	.022141
11. Products of petroleum & coal	.068571	.007861	.004090	.001473	.001856	.002557	.002298	.002331	.001193	.001272	.003189	.002171	.001093	.021498
12. Rubber products	.000003	.000021	.000987	.000780	.000781	.022622	.000934	.003146	.001573	.000932	.005459	.034779	.000323	.001952
13. Leather & leather products			.000032	.000003	.000098	.001015	.005824	.000637	.000271	.000001	.000099	.000943		.000017
14. Stone, clay & glass products	.014600	.005260	.004966	.002608	.000281	.002251	.005721	.005500	.020479	.004140	.016145	.013493	.004441	.060646
15. Iron & steel	.322796	.005336	.098731	.238712	.213267	.161508	.078202	.090225	.107698	.037797	.034184	.077329		.030532
16. Nonferrous metals	.026282	.413611	.053701	.027247	.042245	.007315	.012442	.035547	.036539	.015031	.114395	.012332	.000156	.010983
17. Plumbing & heating supplies	.001216		.022322	.017674	.001132			.003371	.000457		.005626	.000524		.030588
18. Fabricated structural metal products	.000562		.011062	.017858	.002831	.010142	.000818	.000528	.000165		.001547	.000678		.054469
19. Other fabricated metal products	.001909	.000632	.041433	.038896	.033105	.028352	.036275	.031639	.025063	.037303	.036815	.067060	.001838	.022707
20. Agric'l, mining & const. machinery	.001245	.001218			.000997		.034863	.010916	.009332		.000188			.004048
21. Metalworking machinery	.000617	.000981	.003200	.004039	.008123	.015401	.031080	.008697	.006726	.003501	.003382	.015646		
22. Other machinery (except electric)	.002146	.000597	.063161	.018488	.006381	.093214	.036997	.054843	.045326	.000930	.014331	.028209		.011765
23. Motors & generators			.019886	.002826	.000139	.009803	.015701	.030802	.015517	.002802	.009137			.000112
24. Radios		.000037	.000401		.002018			.000319	.007462	.143701	.016541	.001301		
25. Other electrical machinery	.000641	.007287	.030154	.003986	.019323	.006786	.008642	.015332	.052118	.097526	.061135	.040234		.024946
26. Motor vehicles	.000001	.000008			.005036	.007212	.003994	.000034			.002164	.308642	.000105	.001257
27. Other transportation equipment	.000198	.000081						.000009			.000020		.000835	.000028
28. Professional & scientific equipment	.000020		.019465	.001171	.000400	.000200	.001050	.003500	.001727	.001997	.001570	.004922		.000766
29. Miscellaneous manufacturing	.000381	.000029	.000811	.000466	.002850	.000288	.004378	.018399	.017803	.010709	.005505	.001613		.001108
30. Coal, gas & electric power	.019598	.016483	.007255	.006501	.008113	.006862	.007801	.006651	.007664	.003794	.006836	.004368	.016524	.001108
31. Railroad transportation	.034254	.015850	.010667	.015817	.011940	.013370	.006663	.009704	.007676					.001055
32. Ocean transportation	.002430	.008363	.000011	.000014	.000011	.000010	.000011	.000028	.000004	.000003	.000010	.000059		
33. Other transportation	.011345	.002958	.003302	.002330	.002593	.002936	.001831	.002765	.003052	.004854	.003358	.004741	.007326	.019921
34. Trade	.017499	.022258	.020785	.023213	.017142	.015448	.012057	.017779	.016588	.019866	.014559	.003937	.079948	.087295
35. Communications	.001326	.000880	.001984	.002592	.002053	.001860	.002304	.002209	.002849	.002640	.002253	.001088	.000834	.001545
36. Finance & insurance	.003580	.002187	.003495	.006053	.003061	.003490	.003836	.003127	.006266	.005164	.003941	.001513	.005433	.013940
37. Rental	.002909	.003299	.002472	.004261	.003073	.001753	.003347	.003116	.001830	.005505	.003321	.001449	.029100	.002911
38. Business services	.002027	.000721	.009018	.004290	.003908	.003525	.005785	.006177	.003196	.014549	.005560	.005385	.004154	.004693
39. Personal & repair services	.000277	.000479	.000718	.001749	.000473	.000590	.000484	.000496	.000239	.000242	.000251	.000190	.017153	.028518
40. Medical, educ. & nonprofit org's														
41. Amusements														
42. Scarp & miscellaneous industries	.052722	.072621	.004533	.001752	.000513	.002807	.003019	.003665	.000461	.000233	.000469			.000034
43. Undistributed	.023296	.016166	.121079	.074349	.155194	.108236	.136390	.141873	.041399	.120847	.143698	.034362	.040349	
44. Eating & drinking places														
45. New construction & maintenance	.006585	.003191	.002811	.002268	.003777	.004911	.003208	.002745	.001697	.003956	.002731	.003074	.005506	.000247

Note: Each entry shows direct purchases from industry named at left by industry named at top per dollar of output by latter.

SOURCE: Data are from Division of Interindustry Economics, U.S. Bureau of Labor Statistics, November, 1951.

Purchasing industry	Producing industry													
	1	2	3	4	5	6	7	8	9	10	11	12	13	14
	Agriculture & fisheries	Food & kindred products	Tobacco manufactures	Textile mill products	Apparel	Lumber & wood products	Furniture & fixtures	Paper & allied products	Printing & publishing	Chemicals	Products of petroleum & coal	Rubber products	Leather & leather products	Stone, clay & glass products
1. Agriculture & fisheries	1.41445	.09706	.00010	.00612	.00295	.00889	.00060	.00955	.00597	.04648	.03699	.00591	.00067	.0054
2. Food & kindred products	.67525	1.20488	.00034	.01022	.01002	.01229	.00121	.04052	.02000	.08977	.03274	.00592	.00210	.0155
3. Tobacco manufactures	.62025	.05661	1.45172	.00787	.00261	.02255	.00127	.07578	.03709	.05067	.02689	.00560	.00221	.0068
4. Textile mill products	.37946	.04421	.00032	1.16140	.00215	.00998	.00250	.03258	.01529	.14143	.02924	.00579	.00210	.0068
5. Apparel	.14820	.02393	.00054	.41081	1.17788	.00962	.00224	.03063	?01881	.08166	.02197	.00787	.00988	.0072
6. Lumber & wood products	.01708	.01228	.00061	.01028	.00217	1.23069	.00202	.02161	.01451	.03072	.04268	.00802	.00480	.0096
7. Furniture & fixtures	.06395	.01486	.00061	.12572	.00430	.17350	1.00448	.03564	.02522	.06584	.03174	.00855	.00705	.0220
8. Paper & allied products	.02759	.01523	.00059	.01691	.00613	.06819	.00195	1.52213	.02288	.05975	.03754	.00509	.00236	.0100
9. Printing & publishing	.01922	.00958	.00049	.01428	.00250	.01806	.00162	.30502	1.15324	.04689	.01891	.00509	.00378	.0062
10. Chemicals	.20918	.09197	.00079	.01339	.00627	.01667	.00203	.07617	.03785	1.27195	.07006	.00679	.00399	.0332
11. Products of petroleum & coal	.01358	.00707	.00035	.00591	.00135	.00674	.00117	.03252	.01077	.04423	1.56855	.00407	.00214	.0102
12. Rubber products	.11527	.03211	.00064	.19426	.00309	.00700	.00213	.04667	.02319	.31339	.03860	1.02067	.00369	.0153
13. Leather & leather products	.16890	.20874	.00054	.05007	.00421	.01757	.00179	.05752	.02367	.10036	.02405	.02432	1.38213	.0111
14. Stone, clay & glass products	.02098	.00994	.00052	.01718	.00281	.01406	.00164	.07946	.01340	.05434	.03946	.00684	.00306	1.1030
15. Iron & steel	.01235	.00701	.00083	.00614	.00193	.01219	.00086	.03331	.03129	.03433	.17714	.00348	.00278	.0288
16. Nonferrous metals	.01817	.00767	.00109	.00671	.00236	.01685	.00080	.04045	.04141	.04591	.04073	.00344	.00326	.0149
17. Plumbing & heating supplies	.01969	.00971	.00074	.01102	.00245	.02754	.00214	.03785	.02529	.04692	.04688	.00745	.00421	.0183
18. Fabricated structural metal products	.01337	.00703	.00058	.00716	.00174	.01165	.00133	.02667	.01969	.03354	.05958	.00531	.00292	.0152
19. Other fabricated metal products	.02079	.01051	.00081	.01260	.00284	.01846	.00226	.04878	.02468	.04951	.05987	.00748	.00452	.0229
20. Agric'l, mining & const. machinery	.01846	.00903	.00068	.01433	.00227	.01594	.00184	.02737	.02067	.04049	.05268	.03012	.00531	.0152
21. Metalworking machinery	.01597	.00900	.00065	.01013	.00212	.01189	.00187	.02592	.01866	.02914	.03535	.00720	.01200	.0162
22. Other machinery (except electric)	.01878	.00932	.00073	.01341	.00251	.01879	.00257	.03337	.02195	.03821	.04050	.01184	.00507	.0177
23. Motors & generators	.01308	.00621	.00043	.00952	.00138	.01193	.00167	.02577	.01471	.03367	.03572	.00563	.00272	.0322
24. Radios	.02522	.01055	.00071	.02756	.00259	.03220	.07309	.04751	.02662	.04475	.02726	.00850	.00454	.0174
25. Other electrical machinery	.02752	.01236	.00079	.02012	.00270	.02166	.00351	.04484	.02427	.07553	.03694	.01255	.00452	.0302
26. Motor vehicles	.02753	.00998	.00053	.03929	.01374	.01598	.00428	.03195	.01972	.05795	.07633	.05619	.00506	.0330
27. Other transportation equipment	.01637	.00772	.00057	.01358	.00511	.02046	.00734	.02977	.01587	.03214	.03873	.00851	.00430	.0110
28. Professional & scientific equipment	.03480	.01537	.00058	.03874	.00308	.01440	.00220	.08670	.02913	.06525	.02334	.00808	.00914	.0230
29. Miscellaneous manufacturing industries	.04000	.02093	.00088	.03445	.00316	.03017	.00275	.05570	.02521	.08407	.02848	.01638	.00847	.0247
30. Coal, gal & electric power	.00708	.00351	.00020	.00414	.00070	.01191	.00066	.00878	.00521	.01790	.10012	.00220	.00123	.0051
31. Railroad transportation	.00932	.01176	.00009	.00148	.00042	.00200	.00028	.00627	.00838	.01016	.05573	.00121	.00049	.003
32. Ocean transportation	.01365	.00869	.00039	.01047	.00147	.00853	.00167	.01445	.01201	.01913	.07633	.00400	.00244	.005
33. Other transportation	.00961	.00719	.00017	.00619	.00120	.00269	.00066	.01017	.01067	.01472	.08019	.01603	.00114	.002
34. Trade	.00868	.00589	.00032	.00574	.00158	.00583	.00106	.03764	.03262	.01462	.01885	.00443	.00188	.004
35. Communications	.00667	.00538	.00016	.00270	.00092	.00248	.00065	.01319	.03005	.00801	.00606	.00161	.00091	.001
36. Finance & insurance agents	.00564	.00296	.00028	.00418	.00088	.00396	.00450	.01644	.03591	.00926	.00888	.00282	.00153	.002
37. Rentals	.00354	.00183	.00012	.00220	.00042	.00873	.00316	.00569	.00481	.00632	.05664	.00123	.00072	.001
38. Business services	.01928	.01018	.00066	.01341	.00252	.00405	.00213	.15162	.52394	.03905	.01933	.00657	.00445	.007
39. Personal & repair services	.01601	.00775	.00042	.01333	.00414	.00736	.00183	.02531	.01728	.03946	.02507	.01341	.00616	.009
40. Medical & educ. organizations	.03876	.03254	.00029	.00613	.00278	.00484	.00133	.01923	.02311	.03401	.01916	.00348	.00255	.004
41. Amusements	.00991	.00535	.00043	.00664	.00143	.00621	.00151	.02014	.03407	.01675	.01525	.00392	.00263	.004
42. Scrap & misc. industries	.03763	.02227	.00746	.03082	.01346	.03544	.00187	.25351	.28465	.07231	.05139	.01256	.01805	.015
43. Nondistributed	.06850	.03663	.00311	.04508	.01008	.03585	.00990	.08861	.05349	.10188	.05940	.02777	.01915	.028
44. Eating & drinking places	.27438	.32435	.00028	.00690	.00544	.00743	.00106	.02753	.01653	.03865	.02294	.00438	.00180	.011

Note: Each entry shows, per dollar of deliveries to final demand by industry named at left, the total dollar production directly and indirectly required from industry named at top. This is the transposed inverse of an identity matrix less the matrix shown in Table 29-4.

SOURCE: Data are from the U.S. Bureau of Labor Statistics, Division of Interindustry Economics, November, 1951.

Table 29-5. Direct and Indirect Requirements Per Dollar of Final Demand (Continued)

Producing industry

Purchasing industry	15 Iron & steel	16 Nonferrous metals	17 Plumbing & heating supplies	18 Fabricated structural metal products	19 Other fabricated metal products	20 Agric'l, mining & const. machinery	21 Metalworking machinery	22 Other machinery (except electric)	23 Motors & generators	24 Radios	25 Other electrical machinery	26 Motor vehicles	44 Eating & drinking places
Agriculture & fisheries	.00843	.00465	.00021	.00046	.00810	.00267	.00071	.00379	.00058	.00025	.00199	.00964	.00133
Food & kindred products	.02160	.01258	.00068	.00146	.02858	.00267	.00194	.01109	.00179	.00068	.00521	.01111	.00472
Tobacco manufactures	.01882	.01124	.00071	.00151	.01961	.00263	.00194	.01126	.00187	.00069	.00524	.01073	.00504
Textile mill products	.01467	.01135	.00060	.00126	.01010	.00207	.00158	.01357	.00168	.00055	.00425	.00832	.00410
Apparel	.02215	.01656	.00104	.00222	.01432	.00276	.00271	.01950	.00285	.00096	.00716	.01136	.00769
Lumber & wood products	.03011	.01755	.00123	.00262	.02219	.00309	.00324	.02182	.00333	.00114	.00841	.01415	.00909
Furniture & fixtures	.09148	.03324	.00135	.00442	.06327	.00309	.00350	.02313	.00327	.00120	.00919	.01308	.00843
Paper & allied products	.02241	.01167	.00079	.00146	.01317	.00183	.00172	.01317	.00191	.00060	.00509	.00965	.00357
Printing & publishing	.02026	.01724	.00092	.00191	.01214	.00225	.00235	.02072	.00259	.00083	.00630	.00975	.00663
Chemicals	.03262	.04715	.00130	.00271	.02915	.00348	.00339	.01984	.00337	.00119	.00925	.01462	.00900
Products of petroleum & coal	.01937	.01101	.00070	.00151	.01782	.00193	.00189	.01158	.00190	.00066	.00514	.00844	.00512
Rubber products	.03400	.02297	.00119	.00251	.02162	.00307	.00308	.01877	.00313	.00108	.00813	.01270	.00854
Leather & leather products	.02507	.01702	.00105	.00223	.02281	.00277	.00276	.01634	.00276	.00098	.00729	.01167	.00767
Stone, clay & glass products	.02973	.01957	.00100	.00210	.01343	.00375	.00258	.01592	.00266	.00093	.00847	.01142	.00710
Iron & steel	1.50757	.07982	.00286	.00260	.01451	.00421	.00302	.01573	.00235	.00072	.00768	.01209	.00347
Nonferrous metals	.04869	1.72290	.00281	.00192	.01360	.00459	.00387	.01449	.00259	.00106	.01994	.01455	.00301
Plumbing & heating supplies	.21406	.13746	1.02509	.01496	.06536	.00432	.00827	.09059	.02679	.00272	.04633	.01409	.00854
Fabricated structural metal products	.40547	.08526	.00201	1.02089	.05537	.01365	.00767	.03745	.00668	.00109	.01360	.01085	.00572
Other fabricated metal products	.36337	.11394	.00324	.00617	1.15386	.00412	.01275	.02963	.00443	.00413	.03244	.02242	.00938
Agric'l, mining & const. machinery	.30959	.05462	.00222	.01415	.05124	1.04070	.02123	.12279	.01718	.00152	.01977	.02369	.00789
Metalworking machinery	.17067	.05330	.00167	.00395	.05614	.01519	1.03636	.06116	.02116	.00157	.02066	.01860	.00827
Other machinery (except electric)	.19489	.09920	.00548	.01014	.05345	.01389	.01379	1.08180	.03719	.00208	.01408		.00891
Motors & generators	.20050	.10055	.00198	.00225	.04031	.00267	.00097	.06124	1.11991	.01074	.06481	.00817	.00447
Radios	.07028	.08043	.00218	.00335	.07011	.00347	.00809	.02475	.00825	1.17159	.13263	.01461	.00971
Other electrical machinery	.10607	.23827	.00780	.00491	.06035	.00396	.00820	.03877	.01437	.02213	1.08039	.01820	.00949
Motor vehicles	.23514	.07809	.00267	.00379	.11825	.00365	.00724	.06070	.00499	.00465	.07550	1.45745	.00602
Other transportation equipment	.19321	.06058	.00337	.01123	.03444	.00732	.00723	.07363	.01887	.00626	.02566	.01101	.00707
Professional & scientific equipment	.05225	.07351	.00131	.00325	.05242	.00297	.00157	.03190	.00929	.00870	.00387	.01162	.00769
Miscellaneous manufacturing industries	.04896	.09061	.00174	.00361	.02971	.00422	.00454	.02677	.00456	.00166	.01633	.01725	.01248
Coal, gas & electric power	.01816	.00774	.00044	.00087	.00619	.00464	.00101	.00717	.00120	.00040	.00509	.00565	.00277
Railroad transportation	.03120	.01319	.00025	.00120	.00575	.00102	.00138	.00809	.00132	.00025	.00506	.00242	.00101
Ocean transportation	.02217	.01189	.00085	.00196	.01276	.00205	.00217	.01404	.00263	.00090	.00586	.00843	.00576
Other transportation	.01325	.00598	.00032	.00072	.00646	.00087	.00115	.00689	.00138	.00044	.00419	.02577	.00274
Trade	.01304	.00767	.00056	.00113	.00841	.00150	.00144	.00901	.00145	.00067	.00442	.01046	.00366
Communications	.00755	.00759	.00038	.00061	.00447	.00072	.00079	.00470	.00091	.00109	.01894	.00376	.00195
Finance & insurance agents	.01062	.00628	.00048	.00098	.00575	.00119	.00119	.00879	.00127	.00044	.00325		.00318
Rentals	.00642	.00342	.00023	.00049	.00333	.00095	.00060	.00372	.00063	.00022	.00189	.00285	.00161
Business services	.02659	.02100	.00127	.00262	.01604	.00309	.00324	.02229	.00342	.00136	.01107	.01457	.00916
Personal & repair services	.03724	.01934	.00102	.00200	.02156	.00655	.00426	.02794	.00302	.00311	.01638	.11946	.00597
Medical & educ. organizations	.01247	.00917	.00058	.00123	.00867	.00152	.00157	.00929	.00161	.00059	.00433	.00703	.01567
Amusements	.01666	.01184	.00081	.00170	.00971	.00207	.00207	.01253	.00214	.00076	.00569	.00924	.00591
Scrap & misc. industries	.20188	.06946	.00686	.00926	.05800	.01173	.00943	.06239	.01198	.00337	.03335	.08626	.00577
Nondistributed	.11519	.07589	.00613	.01312	.07072	.01474	.01583	.09403	.01635	.00556	.03994	.06038	.04711
Eating & drinking places	.01511	.00926	.00056	.00119	.01465	.00191	.00155	.00911	.00149	.00058	.00431	.00978	1.00396

Note: Each entry shows, per dollar of deliveries to final demand by industry named at left, the total dollar production directly and indirectly required from industry named at top. This is the transposed inverse of an identity matrix less the matrix shown in Table 29-4.

SOURCE: Data are from the U.S. Bureau of Labor Statistics, Division of Interindustry Economics, November, 1951.

new and maintenance construction), typically of goods to be used as purchased rather than in carrying out further processing activities.

Further explanation of the methods of construction and the meaning of the input-output accounting statements of Tables 29-3 to 29-5 is presented in Appendix C of this chapter.

Input-output accounting is a valuable means of establishing the interdependences among the various industries in the economy in quantitative terms. It is a means of defining the structure of the economy and measuring the interrelationships between the various industries. Input-output analysis is also useful in assuring that economic forecasts regarding activity in various industries are consistent with the forecasted and possible levels of activity in other sectors of the economy. High- or low-output levels for automobiles require various output levels in other industries, such as steel. Input-output accounting is thus valuable as the basis for translating a general over-all forecast into detailed, consistent forecasts of various segments of the economy.

Input-output analysis has a number of difficulties. First of all, it is based on a static model. When the technology and price structures of the industries change, the ratios or coefficients in the matrix must also be changed if the results are to be valid. Thus, the results of the 1947 study can be used only for approximate analysis years later, even when attempts are made to adjust relationships for the changes which have occurred.

Second, the analysis is most meaningful when the industry breakdown is relatively detailed. However, a 100-industry table has 10,000 entries; a 200-industry table has 40,000 entries; and a 500-industry table has 250,000 entries. As the size of the matrix increases, it becomes more complex, costly, time-consuming, and subject to error at a very rapid rate. Although new large-scale electronic computers will assist in solving some of these data-handling problems, the task of compiling input-output charts is formidable. Thus, the National Income Division of the U.S. Department of Commerce is at present (1961) preparing a small (about 50 sectors) input-output table for the United States referring to the year 1958. Nevertheless, it will be several years before the results will be available.

Third, the assumption that the inputs in each industry vary proportionately with output is contrary to logic and economic thinking. We noted in a previous chapter that some costs are fixed and do not vary with changes in output as compared with variable costs which do vary proportionately with output. When relative price changes occur, input substitutions may occur to change the pattern of variation of input costs with output volume. In addition, the mix of products in the industries will frequently change when the output volume changes and can thus destroy the constant proportional relationship. However, these reasons for expecting nonproportional variation of inputs with output volume need not be of great significance if the error introduced by the assumption of proportionality is sufficiently small. In many cases, the error is so small that it will cause no difficulties. In other cases, the results should be treated as approximations which need to be adjusted by additional study.

The input-output accounting system which has been described here briefly is based on one simple model. Some of this model's limitations have been discussed. More complicated, and, hopefully, more realistic input-output models have also been developed.[1] Some of these use a linear-programming approach, attempting to maximize economic behavior using resource-allocation procedures on a national-economy scale similar to those presented in Chapter 19 for allocating resources within the enterprise.

Price and Cost Indexes. In several places in this volume we refer to the necessity for adjusting prices or costs to take account of changes in the value of the dollar. This must be done prior to using these prices or costs for analysis, prediction, and planning purposes. The suggested procedures involve dividing the unadjusted dollar value by an appropriate price-level index which measures or approximates the purchasing power of the dollar. In this manner, dollars are obtained which have as nearly as possible the same value throughout the period of the study.

Simple Aggregate Index. The simplest way of constructing a price index would be to add up the prices of each item included in the index during each period and divide each of the sums by the sum of the prices in the base period. Thus, if we were constructing an index based upon three items, A, B, and C, and were using 1956 as the base year, we would have the calculations shown in Table 29-6.

Table 29-6. Calculation of Simple Aggregate Index Numbers

| Year | Price | | | | Index number |
	A	B	C	Total	
1956	$2.15 per bushel	$0.98 per pound	$8.52 per gross	$11.65	100.0
1957	2.06	0.94	8.65	11.65	100.0
1958	1.98	1.02	8.72	11.72	100.6
1959	2.02	1.07	8.77	11.86	101.8

If we let p_0 equal the price of an item in the base year and p_n the price in the given year for which we are computing an index number, the simple aggregate index number equals

$$\frac{\Sigma p_n}{\Sigma p_0}$$

[1] An excellent review of the theory of input-output models and presentation of the results of much of the recent research in this area is presented in H. B. Chenery and P. G. Clark, *Interindustry Economics*, John Wiley & Sons, Inc., New York, 1959.

This type of price index number suffers from a serious defect: the relative influence of the items included in the index is not related to their relative importance. This influence is determined by the units in which the prices are quoted. Thus, if the price of item C were quoted per unit rather than per gross, changes in the price of item C would have less than 0.7 per cent of the influence it presently has in determining changes in the index-number values for each year.

Simple Average-of-relatives Index. We can eliminate the influence of the units in which the prices are quoted by first computing a relative price for each item and then averaging these relative values.

Thus, using the prices in our previous example, we compute price relatives for each item, total the price relatives, and divide by three to obtain an average price relative or index number. This is shown in Table 29-7.

Table **29-7. Calculation of Simple Average-of-relatives Index Numbers**

| Year | Price relative (p_n/p_0) | | | | Index number |
	A	B	C	Total	
1956	100.0	100.0	100.0	300.0	100.0
1957	95.8	95.9	101.5	293.2	97.7
1958	92.1	104.1	102.3	298.5	99.5
1959	94.0	109.2	102.9	306.1	102.0

The formula for this method is

$$\frac{\Sigma(p_n/p_0)}{N}$$

This method causes percentage price variations in each commodity in the price index to have an equal weight in determining the index number.

In both the simple aggregate index and the simple average-of-relatives index, the weightings are arbitrary and not related to the importance of the various items included in the index. In the aggregate index, the weighting depends upon the unit in which the price is quoted. In the index of relatives, each item arbitrarily receives the same weighting. We can counteract this by consciously weighting the items in both the aggregate and relatives indexes.

Weighted Aggregate Index. The most usual method of weighting the items in the aggregate index is to use the quantities produced, sold, consumed, or shipped during the base year. In this way, the units in which the prices are quoted have no effect. Thus, for our example, the quantities of each item sold in the base year, 1956, are

$$\text{A—82,620,000 bushels}$$
$$\text{B—26,700,000 pounds}$$
$$\text{C—2,450,000 gross}$$

We now multiply each price by these quantities, as shown in Table 29-8. We divide the sum of the weighted prices in each year, by the sum of the weighted prices in the base year to obtain our index number.

Table 29-8. **Calculation of Weighted Aggregate Index Numbers with Base-year (1956) Weights**

| Year | A | | B | | C | | Total weighted price | Index number |
	Price	82,620,000 bushels times price	Price	26,700,000 pounds times price	Price	2,450,000 gross times price		
1956	$2.15	$177,633,000	$0.98	$26,166,000	$8.52	$20,874,000	$224,673,000	100.0
1957	2.06	170,197,200	0.94	25,098,000	8.65	21,192,500	216,487,700	96.4
1958	1.98	163,587,600	1.02	27,234,000	8.72	21,364,000	212,185,600	94.4
1959	2.02	166,892,400	1.07	28,569,000	8.77	21,486,500	216,947,900	96.6

Using q_0 to represent the base-period quantities for each item, the formula for this weighted aggregate index is

$$\frac{\Sigma p_n q_0}{\Sigma p_0 q_0}$$

The major defect of this procedure is that the relative importance of the items in the index number will usually change over the years. As the period from the base year increases, the quantity weights become less representative of the current relative importance of the items. The usual answer to this problem is to change the base period whenever the old base-period weights become obsolete.

Another, usually less satisfactory, method of taking account of the changing relative importance of the items included in the index is to weight the items by the quantities in the given year. Each year's weight would therefore be different. Thus, in our example, the quantities of each item sold in 1957, 1958, and 1959, were as follows.

	A	B	C
1957	84,280,000	26,100,000	2,010,000
1958	84,750,000	22,260,000	2,640,000
1959	85,970,000	20,130,000	1,890,000

The construction of the index numbers using these weights is shown in Table 29-9. In the years following the base year, two calculations are

Table 29-9. Calculation of Weighted Aggregate Index Numbers with Given-year Weights

Year		A Price	A Quantity (q_n)	A Price times quantity	B Price	B Quantity (q_n)	B Price times quantity	C Price	C Quantity (q_n)	C Price times quantity	Total weighted prices	Index number
1956		$2.15	82,620,000	$177,633,000	$0.98	26,700,000	$26,166,000	$8.52	2,450,000	$20,874,000	$224,673,000	100.0
1957	Base year	2.15	84,280,000	181,202,000	0.98	26,100,000	25,578,000	8.52	2,010,000	17,125,200	223,905,200	96.3
	Given year	2.06	84,280,000	173,616,800	0.94	26,100,000	24,534,000	8.65	2,010,000	17,386,500	215,537,300	
1958	Base year	2.15	84,750,000	182,212,500	0.98	22,260,000	21,814,800	8.52	2,640,000	22,492,800	226,520,100	94.3
	Given year	1.98	84,750,000	167,805,000	1.02	22,260,000	22,705,200	8.72	2,640,000	23,020,800	213,531,000	
1959	Base year	2.15	85,970,000	184,835,500	0.98	20,130,000	19,727,400	8.52	1,890,000	16,102,800	220,665,700	96.0
	Given year	2.02	85,970,000	173,659,400	1.07	20,130,000	21,539,100	8.77	1,890,000	16,575,300	211,773,800	

made for each year: one using the base-year price times the given-year quantity and the other using the given-year price times the given-year quantity. The latter is then divided by the former to obtain the index number.

Using q_n to represent the given-period quantity for each item, the formula for this weighted aggregate index number is

$$\frac{\Sigma p_n q_n}{\Sigma p_0 q_n}$$

This last approach suffers from the fact that the index numbers can be compared only to the base-period value. Direct comparisons between other years are not valid because the prices have been weighted differently in each year. Therefore, differences in the index-number value from one year to another can be caused by changes in the weights as well as changes in the prices.

Weighted Average-of-relatives Index. We can also construct a weighted average-of-relatives index, by weighting the price relatives by the base period or given period values produced, shipped, sold, or consumed. We use value rather than quantity because the price relatives are pure numbers and using quantity weights expressed in various physical units would represent arbitrary meaningless weighting dependent upon the units of measure chosen.

The construction of a weighted average-of-relatives price index using base-period value weights is illustrated in Table 29-10, developed from

Table 29-10. Calculation of Weighted Average-of-relatives
Index with Base-year (1956) Weights

Year	A			B		
	p_n/p_0	$p_0 q_0$	$(p_n/p_0)(p_0 q_0)$	p_n/p_0	$p_0 q_0$	$(p_n/p_0)(p_0 q_0)$
1956	100.0	$177,633,000	$177,633,000	100.0	$26,166,000	$26,166,000
1957	95.8	177,633,000	170,172,414	95.9	26,166,000	25,093,194
1958	92.1	177,633,000	163,599,993	104.1	26,166,000	27,238,806
1959	94.0	177,633,000	166,975,020	109.2	26,166,000	28,573,272

Year	C			Total		Index number
	p_n/p_0	$p_0 q_0$	$(p_n/p_0)(p_0 q_0)$	$p_0 q_0$	$(p_n/p_0)(p_0 q_0)$	
1956	100.0	$20,874,000	$20,874,000	$224,673,000	$224,673,000	100.0
1957	101.5	20,874,000	21,187,110	224,673,000	216,452,718	96.3
1958	102.3	20,874,000	21,354,102	224,673,000	212,192,901	94.4
1959	102.9	20,874,000	21,479,346	224,673,000	217,027,638	96.0

the data of our previous example. The formula is

$$\frac{\sum \left[\frac{p_n}{p_0} (p_0 q_0) \right]}{\Sigma p_0 q_0}$$

The problem of adjusting the weight values for changing importance of the various items included in the index is similar to the problem in the weighted aggregate index. In fact, the value of weighted average-of-relatives index using base-period weights is always the same as the weighted aggregate index. The formula for the weighted average-of-relatives index is mathematically equivalent to the weighted aggregate index, when base-year weights are used,

$$\frac{\sum \left[\frac{p_n}{p_0} (p_0 q_0) \right]}{\Sigma p_0 q_0} = \frac{\Sigma p_n q_0}{\Sigma p_0 q_0}$$

The weighted average-of-relatives index does not give the same results as the weighted aggregate index when given-year weights are used.

The construction of a weighted average-of-relatives index using given-period weights follows the formula,

$$\frac{\sum \left[\frac{p_n}{p_0} (p_n q_n) \right]}{\Sigma p_n q_n}$$

We, of course, do not have direct comparability between prices in each year because the prices have been weighted differently each year. Some of the year-to-year changes are caused by weight rather than price changes. The index number therefore measures changes only from the base-period values.

The weighting of relatives in constructing a price index is frequently more convenient than weighting prices directly. This is true when we are interested in the movements of the prices of individual items and individual subgroups of items which are included in the index as well as the entire index value. Comparative analysis of changes in these prices is facilitated when price relatives are used.

Shifting Index Base Year. If we wish to shift the base year of an index-number series, we simply divide each index number by the index-number value of the new base year and multiply by 100.

We have an index-number series for prices in industry A using a 1954 base and another series for prices in industry B using a 1956 base, as shown in Table 29-11. We desire to convert the industry A series to a 1956 base to make it easier to compare the price variations of the two indexes. We therefore divide each index-number value of the industry A series by 127, the industry A index number for 1956, and multiply by 100.

Thus, for 1951, 86 divided by 127 equals 0.68 and multiplied by 100 gives 68; for 1956, 127 divided by 127 equals 1.00 and multiplied by 100 equals 100; and for 1960, 169 divided by 127 equals 1.33 and multiplied by 100 equals 133. The industry A price index numbers are now more readily comparable with the industry B series. We see that, compared with 1956, industry A prices have risen less, rather than more, than industry B prices.

Table 29-11. Shifting Base Year of an Index-number Series

	Index of industry A prices 1954 = 100	Index of industry B prices 1956 = 100	Index of industry A prices 1956 = 100
1951	86	65	68
1952	94	72	74
1953	101	86	80
1954	100	88	79
1955	118	97	93
1956	127	100	100
1957	134	113	106
1958	149	126	117
1959	161	138	127
1960	169	146	133

Splicing Indexes. Sometimes we want to compare price or quantity changes over a period of time which is longer than the period covered by one index series. We may then splice two index-number series together provided that the two series measure approximately the same phenomena and that there is at least one period of overlap. The procedure is illustrated in Table 29-12, where we adjust the values of an old index so that its value in the overlap year, 1956, is equal to the value of the new series.

Table 29-12. Splicing Two Index-number Series

	Old index	New index	Spliced index I	Spliced index II
1951	156.2	.....	116.1	156.2
1952	158.5	.....	117.8	158.5
1953	160.1	.....	119.0	160.1
1954	161.3	.....	119.9	161.3
1955	162.9	.....	121.1	162.9
1956	164.7	122.4	122.4	164.7
1957	.....	126.8	126.8	170.6
1958	.....	129.3	129.3	174.0
1959	.....	134.7	134.7	181.3
1960	.....	138.6	138.6	186.5

To obtain spliced index I, we multiply each value of the old index by 122.4/164.7 so that the values of the old index join the values of the new index with the new value of 122.4 in 1956. In this case, we have converted the old index values to join with the more recent values of the new index.

To obtain spliced index II, we multiply each value of the new index by 164.7/122.4 so that values of the new index are adjusted to join with the old index value of 164.7 in 1956. This is the less usual case in which the new index values are converted to join the old index values.

Dollar-value Adjustments (Deflation of Data). During periods of inflation, rising prices cause a decline in the value of the dollar. During deflationary periods, declining prices cause an increase in the value of the dollar. Various indexes have been constructed to measure the level of prices. The index or component of an index which is most appropriate to use as a measure of price level varies with the problem being studied or the decision being made. The two most common indexes used in this connection, either as a whole or one or more components, are the consumer price index and wholesale price index.

If prices rise more rapidly than income rises, "real" income has declined. We must adjust or deflate dollar values so that they measure "real" value. We do this by dividing each dollar value by an appropriate price index which measures the price level in each period.

In Table 29-13 we show the average weekly earnings of maintenance employees in a company from 1953 through 1959. We show alongside these earnings figures the average value of consumer price index for each of these years. We compute our deflated average weekly earnings by dividing the average weekly earnings by the consumer price index for each year and multiplying by 100. Thus, for 1953, ($71.34 ÷ 114.4)100 equals $62.36.

Table **29-13. Deflating Average Weekly Earnings of Maintenance Employees with Consumer Price Index**

Year	Average weekly earnings of maintenance employees	Average consumer price index 1947–1949 = 100	Deflated average weekly earnings 1947–1949 dollars
1953	$71.34	114.4	$62.36
1954	71.82	114.8	62.56
1955	73.02	114.5	63.77
1956	77.51	116.2	66.70
1957	77.82	120.2	64.74
1958	77.84	123.5	63.03
1959	78.66	124.6	63.13

We can now see that although the uncorrected earnings figures indicate rising earnings for the maintenance workers, their "real" earnings (in terms of the goods and services which they can purchase with their earnings) declined from \$66.70 in 1956 to \$63.13 in 1959.

This same type of procedure would apply to many other situations: we would deflate commodity sales figures using a wholesale price index or retail sales figures using a retail price index to obtain "real" dollar total sales figures.

Importance of Base-year Selection. The management and the employees in a company were interested in determining whether the salaries of its office staff had increased in proportion to the changes in the cost of living index; or whether the salaries had increased more or less than this index.

The company had been maintaining annual summary records of the salaries paid its office workers. Since 1944, it had computed an index relating the salary level each year with the salary level in 1944. To compare changes since 1948 in the cost of living with changes in the office-staff-salary index, Table 29-14 was constructed. It showed that the office-salary index stood at 128.9 compared with a consumer price index value of 124.6. This meant that the salary index was high relative to the consumer price index.

Table 29-14. Comparison of Consumer Price Index Series and Office-staff-salary Index Series

	Consumer price index 1947–1949 = 100	Office-staff-salary index 1944 = 100
1948	102.8	110.0
1949	101.8	111.1
1950	102.8	111.8
1951	111.0	112.7
1952	113.5	113.6
1953	114.4	113.8
1954	114.8	117.4
1955	114.5	117.5
1956	116.2	119.2
1957	120.2	124.9
1958	123.5	127.6
1959	124.6	128.9

However, someone pointed out that the base years for the two indexes were different. It was not fair to compare the salary index using a 1944 base year with the consumer price index using a 1947–1949 base year. To compare properly the values of the two indexes, their base years should be shifted to a common period. A new table was prepared, Table 29-15, in which the base year for both indexes was shifted to 1948. This table shows that office salaries have not kept up with the cost of living. The

1959 index value for the office salaries is only 117.2 as compared with a consumer price index value of 121.2.

Table 29-15. Comparison of Consumer Price Index Series and Office-staff-salary Index Series

	Consumer price index 1948 = 100	Office-staff-salary index 1948 = 100
1948	100.0	100.0
1949	99.0	101.0
1950	100.0	101.6
1951	108.0	102.5
1952	110.4	103.3
1953	111.3	103.5
1954	111.7	106.7
1955	111.4	106.8
1956	113.0	108.4
1957	116.9	113.5
1958	120.1	116.0
1959	121.2	117.2

However, an analyst in the comptroller's division thought that 1948 was too distant a year to use as the base period for the indexes. He considered that a more recent year, 1953, would be more suitable. He, therefore, constructed Table 29-16, showing the values of the two indexes with 1953 as the base year. Now, the office salary index compares very favorably with the cost of living index for recent years. In fact, in 1959, the office salary index stands at 113.3 and the consumer price index at 108.9.

This example illustrates the importance of the correct choice of base year for an index number. It also points up a prime reason that many people distrust index numbers.

Table 29-16. Comparison of Consumer Price Index Series and Office-staff-salary Index Series

	Consumer price index 1953 = 100	Office-staff-salary index 1953 = 100
1953	100.0	100.0
1954	100.3	103.2
1955	100.1	103.3
1956	101.6	104.7
1957	105.1	109.8
1958	108.0	112.1
1959	108.9	113.3

Importance of Correct Weighting.   Let us assume that there are only two commodities in a price index and the commodities are of equal importance. Table 29-17 shows the prices of each in 1958 and 1959 and the weighted average-of-relatives index numbers using first 1958 and then 1959 as the base years.

Table 29-17. **Calculation of Simple Average of Price Relatives Index Numbers with 1958 and with 1959 as Base Year**

	Price		Price relatives 1958 = 100		Price relatives 1959 = 100	
	1958	1959	1958	1959	1958	1959
A	1.00	2.00	100	200	50	100
B	0.50	0.25	100	50	200	100
Total	....	....	200	250	250	200
Average	....	....	100	125	125	100

Comparing 1959 with 1958, A has doubled in price (200 per cent) and B has dropped to 50 per cent of its former price. Prices have therefore increased an average of 125 per cent. Comparing 1958 with 1959, A was 50 per cent of its 1959 price in 1958 and B was 200 per cent of its 1959 price in 1958. Therefore, prices in 1958 are 125 per cent of 1959 prices. Thus, when 1958 is used as the base year, the price index (average of the relatives) shows 1959 prices (125) higher than 1958 (100). When 1959 is used as the base year, the price index shows 1959 prices (100) lower than 1958 (125).

To ascertain the reason for this discrepancy, let us recalculate our weighted average of relatives, showing explicitly the equal weights which have been implicitly assigned the price relatives of items A and B. This is done in Table 29-18. When 1958 is the base year, $p_0 = p_8$, p_8 being the price in 1958. The weighting factor $p_0 q_0$ is then $p_8 q_8$. If p_{A8} and p_{B8} are the prices of A and B respectively in 1958 and q_{A8} and q_{B8} are the quantities of A and B respectively in 1958, then the assumption of equal importance for the price relatives of A and B means that $p_{A8} q_{A8} = p_{B8} q_{B8}$. Therefore, $\dfrac{q_{A8}}{q_{B8}} = \dfrac{p_{B8}}{p_{A8}} = \dfrac{0.50}{1.00} = \dfrac{1}{2}$. This means that twice as much B as A is sold in 1958. When 1959 is the base year, the assumption of equal importance means that $p_{A9} q_{A9} = p_{B9} q_{B9}$. Therefore, $\dfrac{q_{A9}}{q_{B9}} = \dfrac{p_{B9}}{p_{A9}} = \dfrac{0.25}{2.00} = \dfrac{1}{8}$. This means that eight times as much B as A is sold in 1959 if our assumption of equal importance is correct when we use our new base year of 1959.

Thus, prices have increased from 1958 to 1959 if we weight the prices by the implied quantities sold in 1958. However, they have decreased from 1958 to 1959 if we weight the prices by the implied quantities sold in 1959.

This example illustrates the significant effects which differences in weighting may produce. It also reveals the importance of considering explicitly the effects of alternative weightings on the resulting index number. The 1958 base may be more suitable for some purposes and the 1959 base may be more suitable for others.

Table 29-18. **Calculation of Simple Average of Price Relatives Index Numbers with 1958 and with 1959 as Base Year—Explicitly Showing Weights Which Have Been Implicitly Assigned**

	Price		1958 = 100					
			1958			1959		
	1958	1959	$\frac{p_n}{p_0} = \frac{p_8}{p_8}$	Weight $p_0q_0 = p_8q_8$	$\frac{p_8}{p_8}(p_8q_8)100$	$\frac{p_n}{p_0} = \frac{p_9}{p_8}$	Weight $p_0q_0 = p_8q_8$	$\frac{p_9}{p_8}(p_8q_8)100$
A	1.00	2.00	1.00	1	100	2.00	1	200
B	0.50	0.25	1.00	1	100	0.50	1	50
Total (Σ)				2	200		2	250
$\sum \left[\dfrac{p_n}{p_0}(p_0q_0)\right] \Big/ \Sigma p_0q_0$					100			125

	Price		1959 = 100					
			1958			1959		
	1958	1959	$\frac{p_n}{p_0} = \frac{p_8}{p_9}$	Weight $p_0q_0 = p_9q_9$	$\frac{p_8}{p_9}(p_9q_9)100$	$\frac{p_n}{p_0} = \frac{p_9}{p_9}$	Weight $p_0q_0 = p_9q_9$	$\frac{p_9}{p_9}(p_9q_9)100$
A	1.00	2.00	0.50	1	50	1.00	1	100
B	0.50	0.25	2.00	1	200	1.00	1	100
Total (Σ)				2	250		2	200
$\sum \left[\dfrac{p_n}{p_0}(p_0q_0)\right] \Big/ \Sigma p_0q_0$					125			100

"Figures don't lie, but liars figure." This statement is applicable to all types of statistical presentations, but especially to index numbers. Correctly used, index numbers can help reveal important relationships. Incorrectly used, they can mislead.

Activity Indexes. Indexes of business activity are constructed and published by various organizations to give approximate measurement to economic trends. These indexes measure changes in production, shipments, sales, or consumption. These changes are measured in physical quantity or in value units.

Quantity Index Numbers. Quantity index numbers are useful for such purposes as measuring changes in the industrial production, department store sales volume, or consumption of goods and services in the entire United States or any portion of the country. If we assume that the price of an item measures its economic importance, quantity index numbers can be constructed in a manner similar to those for price except that price and quantity are interchanged.

The weights used for aggregate quantity index numbers are prices. For average-of-relatives quantity index numbers, value (price times quantity) weights are used.

Thus, the weighted aggregate quantity index number with base-year weights is

$$\frac{\Sigma q_n p_0}{\Sigma q_0 p_0}$$

With given-year weights, the weighted aggregate quantity index number is

$$\frac{\Sigma q_n p_n}{\Sigma q_0 p_n}$$

The weighted average-of-relatives quantity index number with base-year weights is

$$\frac{\Sigma[(q_n/q_0)(p_0 q_0)]}{\Sigma p_0 q_0}$$

This is equal to the weighted aggregate quantity index number with base-year weights since $\dfrac{\Sigma[(q_n/q_0)(p_0 q_0)]}{\Sigma p_0 q_0} = \dfrac{\Sigma q_n p_0}{\Sigma q_0 p_0}$. With given-year weights, the weighted average-of-relatives quantity index number is

$$\frac{\Sigma[(q_n/q_0)(p_n q_n)]}{\Sigma p_n q_n}$$

Useful index numbers are constructed by many government and private organizations to measure changes in various facets and sectors of the nation's economy. We shall consider in this book three of these: the wholesale price index, the consumer price index, and the FRB (Federal Reserve Board) index of industrial production.

Wholesale Price Index. The wholesale price index, published by the Bureau of Labor Statistics, is based on approximately 4,000 separate price quotations for some 2,000 commodities. Official monthly indexes are available separately for major groups of commodities as well as for the total index since 1890. A finer classification by subgroups of commodities is available since 1913. In 1952, a third level of classification—product class—was introduced; this has been extended back to 1947. The index is a measure of price movements at other than the retail level. It is used as a measure of the purchasing power of the dollar (excluding retail, where the consumer price index is used). Specific segments of the index (sometimes coupled with statistics on wages or earnings in specific industries) are also used to adjust for changes in the prices of specific categories of materials. As a measure of general and specific price trends, it is widely used in budget making and review, both in industry and government; in planning the cost of plant-expansion programs; in appraising inventories; in establishing replacement costs, etc. The index is also used in LIFO accounting by some organizations.

A brief discussion of the methods used in the construction of the wholesale price index as well as of its limitations and reliability is presented in Appendix D of this chapter.

Consumer Price Index. The consumer price index, also prepared by the Bureau of Labor Statistics, is a statistical measure of changes in prices of the goods and services bought by families of city wage earners and clerical workers. Since price change is one of the most important factors affecting the cost of living over short periods of time, this index provides an approximation of changes in the cost of living of urban wage-earner and clerical-worker families. Widespread acceptance of this use is shown by the inclusion in labor-management agreements of automatic wage-adjustment clauses based on the consumer price index.

Appendix E of this chapter contains a brief discussion of the methods used in the construction of the consumer price index as well as of its limitations and reliability.

FRB Index of Industrial Production. The Federal Reserve Board index of industrial production and its component indexes and series are important tools for improving our understanding and ability to forecast general economic and business conditions. These quantity indexes are also extremely useful for developing industry and company forecasts of changes in demand and sales. The industry and market components are particularly suited to assist in making comparisons and correlations which will enable a better understanding and forecasting of trends in various sectors of the economy.

A brief description of the FRB index of industrial production and its component series and the methods used in its construction is presented in Appendix F of this chapter.

Economic Indicators. Economic indicators are statistical series of data which reveal what is happening in various parts of the economy and serve as indicators or barometers of what is happening in the entire economy or in a significant segment of the economy. The aim is to be able to use these indicators to forecast the turning points in business cycles as well as to assess the magnitude of rising or declining economic activity. (Time series analysis to evaluate cycles is discussed in Chapter 30.)

The number of economic indicators which are prepared and the number of sources which publish these indicators are very numerous. To attempt to mention, discuss, and explain all of them would require a whole volume devoted to this topic alone.

The National Bureau of Economic Research has been studying business cycles since its organization in 1920. It has examined many hundreds of economic measures to assess their usefulness as indicators of what will occur, is occurring, or has occurred in the economic system. Of the numerous statistical series which were examined and tested, 21 were selected as being the most useful indicators for forecasting and measuring cyclical changes in business activity.[1]

The list of 21 indicators is given in Table 29-19. In general, series in the leading group have usually reached cyclical highs or lows several months before the business-cycle peak or trough; those in the roughly coincident group at the time of the cycle peak or trough or within a few months on either side; and those in the lagging group a few months after the cycle peak or trough. Statistics on the leads and lags of each indicator with respect to business-cycle peaks or troughs are given in Table 29-20. An analysis of the behavior of these indicators during the period (1948–1958) after that used in selecting them is given in the Fortieth Annual Report of the National Bureau of Economic Research, May, 1960, Part III, Section 3.

Adjustment of indicators for the repetitive movement within each year undergone by most economic data because of the "season," differences in length of the month, occurrence of holidays, etc., is a prerequisite to their effective use in analyzing business cycles. Comparisons with the same month a year ago are often misleading, especially in the neighborhood of business upturns or downturns. It is highly desirable, therefore, to eliminate seasonal movements by dividing each month's figure by an index representing the usual level of activity in that month relative to the average level of activity for the year. Seasonal indexes are discussed in Chapter 30.

Diffusion Indexes. Numerous experiments with methods of summarizing the movements of a collection of business indicators have been carried out. One of the simplest is to count the number that are rising at any given time and take this as a percentage of the total number. (If some are "unchanged," they can be counted as one-half and added to the number rising.) The resulting percentage is called a diffusion index since it shows how widely diffused an expansionary movement is among the indicators. During business-cycle expansions, diffusion indexes generally are above 50 per cent and during contractions they are generally below it. But diffusion indexes based on leading indicators usually shift their posi-

[1] The information on the work of the National Bureau of Economic Research on economic indicators is summarized from *The National Bureau's Research on Indicators of Cyclical Revivals and Recessions*, National Bureau of Economic Research, New York, August, 1960.

Table 29-19. Sources of Current Data for 21 Indicators

Indicator	Unit	Data for December 1958 Orig.	Data for December 1958 Seas. adj.	Survey of Current Business Monthly	Survey of Current Business Weekly supp.	Federal Reserve Bulletin Monthly	Economic Indicators Monthly	Press release or other primary source[a]
Leading Group								
1. Business failures, liab., indus. and comm.	Mil. $	57.07	54.88	U	U	n.a.	n.a.	Dun and Bradstreet, Inc., Business Economics Department, *Business Trend News, Monthly Failures*
2. Common stock price index, industrials, Dow-Jones	$ per share	566.43	*	U*	U*	n.a.	n.a.	*Barron's National Business and Financial Weekly* (second issue of month)
3. New orders, durable-goods mfg. industries, value	Mil. $	13,796	13,673	S	S	n.a.	n.a.	OBE, *Business News Reports, Manufacturers' Sales, Orders, and Inventories*
4. Residential building contracts, fl. sp.	Mil. sq. ft.	89.07	124.50	n.a.	n.a.	n.a.	n.a.	F. W. Dodge Corporation, *Construction Contracts, United States Summary* (U)
5. Comm. and indus. building contracts, fl. sp.	Mil. sq. ft.	23.82	29.06	n.a.	n.a.	n.a.	n.a.	See 4
6. Average workweek, mfg.	Hrs. per wk.	40.2	29.8	U	U	U	U	BLS, *Monthly Report on the Labor Force, Employment, Unemployment, Hours and Earnings*
7. New business incorporations	Number	16,512	15,577	U	U	n.a.	n.a.	Dun and Bradstreet, Inc., Business Economics Department, *Business Trend News, Monthly New Incorporations*
8. Index of spot market prices, basic commodities	1947–49 = 100	86.0	*	n.a.	n.a.	n.a.	n.a.	BLS, *Daily Indexes and Spot Market Prices*, quotation of the 15th or nearest date of the month (U*)

Roughly Coincident Group

	Unit						Source[a]
9. Employment in nonagricultural establishments	Thous. persons	51,935	50,844	S	S	S	See 6
10. Unemployment	Thous. persons	4,108	4,166	U	U	U	See 6; seasonal adjustment factors given in source
11. Bank debits outside New York City	Bil. $	146.3	133.0	U	U	U	FRB, *Bank Debits* (No. G. 6)
12. Freight carloadings	Thous. cars per wk.	531	597	U[b]	n.a.	U	Association of American Railroads, Car Service Division, *Revenue Freight Loaded and Received from Connections*
13. Industrial production index (incl. utilities)	1947–49 = 100	149	151	S	S	S	FRB, *Business Indexes* (No. 12. 3.)
14. Wholesale price index, excl. farm prod. and foods	1947–49 = 100	127.2	126.8	U	U	U	BLS, *Wholesale Price Index* (weekly release)
15. Corporate profits after taxes (Q)	Bil. $ at ann. rates	n.a.	22.7[c]	S	S	S	OBE, *Business News Reports, National Income and Corporate Profits*[d]
16. Gross national product, current dollars (Q)	Bil. $ at ann. rates	482.0[e]	457.1[c]	S	S	S	OBE, *Business News Reports, National Income and Product*[d]

Lagging Group

	Unit						Source[a]
17. Personal income	Bil. $ at ann. rates	n.a.	366.9	S	S	S	OBE, *Business News Reports, Personal Income*
18. Sales by retail stores	Mil. $	21,174	17,603	S	S	S	Census, *Advance Retail Sales Report*
19. Consumer installment debt (end of month)	Mil. $	34.080	33,576	U	U	U	FRB, *Consumer Credit, Short- and Intermediate-Term* (No. G. 19)
20. Manufacturers' inventories, book value (end of month)	Mil. $	49,468	49,179	S	n.a.	S	See 3
21. Bank interest rates on business loans (last month of quarter)	Per cent	4.50	*	U*	U*	n.a.	*Federal Reserve Bulletin*

Note: The *Survey of Current Business* is published by the U.S. Department of Commerce, Office of Business Economics; the *Federal Reserve Bulletin* by the Board of Governors of the Federal Reserve System; and *Economic Indicators* by the Joint Economic Committee (prepared by the Council of Economic Advisers).

* No seasonal adjustment required.

n.a. = Not available.

[a] The sources cited are those in which the current figures are first released, sometimes in rounded or preliminary form. Note, however, that these sources do not ordinarily provide revised figures for earlier dates, which the monthly periodicals listed at the left do.

[b] Monthly figures in *Survey of Current Business* are totals for weeks ending within the month. Monthly figures in *Economic Indicators* (and used by NBER) are weekly averages, with weeks ending on the first, second, or third day of the month included in preceding month.

[c] [e] Figure covers the last quarter of 1958.

[d] Advance figures are published in *Economic Indicators*.

Source: *The National Bureau's Research on Indicators of Cyclical Revivals and Recessions*, National Bureau of Economic Research, New York, August, 1960, p. 9.

Table 29-20. Leads and Lags of 21 Indicators at Business-cycle Peaks and Troughs, through 1958

Indicator and period covered	Number of coincidences				Median lead (−) or lag (+) (months)[b]	Longest	
	Leads	Exact	Rough[a]	Lags		Lead	Lag (months)
LEADING GROUP							
1. Bus. failures, liab., indus. and comm., 1875–1959, inverted[c]	14	1	3	2	−7	−28	+3
	16	1	2	1	−7	−13	+7
2. Industrial common stock price index, Dow-Jones, 1897–1959	10	1	7	2	−3	−30	+3
	11	1	4	1	−7	−18	+1
3. New orders, durable goods mfg. industries, value, 1920–59	7	0	0	0	−6	−35	−4
	7	1	6	0	−2	−8	0
4. Residential building contracts, value, 1915–18; floor space, 1919–59	7	0	1	1	−16	−31	+8
	7	1	3	0	−5	−9	0
5. Comm. and indust. building contracts, floor space, 1919–59	6	0	2	1	−9	−32	+2
	5	1	6	2	−1.5	−5	+3
6. Average workweek, mfg., 1920–59	6	0	2	1	−7	−20	+2
	5	2	2	1	−4	−8	+5
7. No. of new incorporations, 1860–1959	14	1	8	4	−2	−28	+15
	17	1	4	3	−6	−18	+21
8. Wholesale price index, basic commodities, BLS, 1935–59: Bradstreet's, 1892–1933	10	0	7	3	−2	−29	+8
	10	2	6	2	−1	−11.5	+14
ROUGHLY COINCIDENT GROUP							
9. Employment in nonagr. establishments, 1929–59; factory employment, 1889–1928	5	4	10	7	0	−20	+10
	6	9	12	1	0	−10	+2
10. Total unemployment, 1929–59, inverted[c]	3	0	2	2	−4	−10	+2
	0	2	4	4	+1.5	0	+14
11. Bank debits outside NYC, 1919–59; clearings, 1875–1918	4	2	11	10	+1.5	−7	+10
	15	1	11	1	−3	−10	+1
12. Freight carloadings, 1918–59	7	2	5	1	−3	−31	+1
	2	5	8	3	0	−8	+7
13. Industrial production (incl. utilities), FRB, 1919–59; business activity, Babson, 1889–1918	6	4	10	7	0	−15	+10
	10	6	10	1	−1	−12	+4
14. Wholesale price index, excl. farm products and foods, 1913–59	3	0	4	3	0	−15	+6
	0	1	6	6	+1	0	+7
15. Corporate profits after taxes (Q), 1920–59	6	2	4	0	−4	−20	0
	6	1	6	2	−2	−9	+1
16. Gross national product, in current dollars (Q), 1921–59	1	2	6	3	+0.5	−2	+3
	5	0	5	2	−1	−5	+4
LAGGING GROUP							
17. Personal income (Q), 1921–28; (M) 1929–59	2	1	5	5	+1	−5	+9
	7	2	7	0	−2	−12	0
18. Sales by retail stores, 1935–1959; department store sales, 1919–34	0	2	3	4	+2.5	0	+9
	3	1	5	2	−0.5	−7	+3
19. Consumer instalment debt (end of month), 1929–59	0	0	1	4	+5.5	+2.5	+7.5
	1	0	2	3	+3.5	−1.5	+5.5
20. Manufacturers' inventories (end of month), 1926–59	2	0	2	5	+1.5	−9.5	+7.5
	1	0	2	6	+3.5	−7.5	+12.5
21. Bank interest rates on business loans, FRB (last month of Q), 1939–59; customers' loans, Riefler, 1919–39	1	1	2	6	+5	−20	+13
	0	0	3	9	+5	+2	+39

Note: Entries are based on comparisons of the cyclical peaks and troughs in each indicator with business cycle peaks and troughs. Comparisons with business cycle peaks are shown in the first line, trough comparisons on the second. The timing record for each indicator includes entries derived from related historical series where they are available for earlier cycles.

a Includes leads of 1–3 months, exact coincidences, and lags of 1–3 months.

b Middle figure in the array of timing observations from longest lead to longest lag. Where the number of timing observations is even, the median is the average of the two middle observations.

c Troughs in the data are compared with business cycle peaks, peaks with business-cycle troughs.

SOURCE: *The National Bureau's Research on Indicators of Cyclical Revivals and Recessions.* National Bureau of Economic Research. New York, August, 1960, p. 10.

tion prior to those based on coincident indicators, and the latter move prior to those based on lagging indicators. Although the movement and meaning of each individual indicator should not be lost sight of, the diffusion index provides a convenient background against which to compare and analyze the changes in particular indicators.

Table 29-21. Diffusion Indexes and Directions of Change of 21 Economic Indicators, 1958, Rise(+), No Change(0), Fall(−)

Indicator	Span in months[a]	Jan.	Feb.	Mar.	Apr.	May	June	July	Aug.	Sept.	Oct.	Nov.	Dec.
Leading group													
1. Business failures, liabilities	6	−	+	−	−	−	+	+	−	+	−	+	+
2. Industrial stock prices	4	+	+	+	+	+	+	+	+	+	+	+	+
3. New orders, durable goods mfrs.	6	−	−	+	+	+	+	+	+	+	+	+	+
4. Constr. contracts, residential, fl. sp.	6	−	+	+	+	+	+	+	+	+	−	−	−
5. Constr. contracts, comm. & indus., fl. sp	6	−	−	−	−	+	+	+	+	−	+	−	−
6. Aver. workweek, mfg	4	−	−	+	+	+	+	+	+	+	+	+	+
7. New incorporations, no	6	−	+	+	+	+	+	+	+	+	+	+	+
8. Prices, basic	3	+	+	+	−	−	+	+	+	+	+	0	−
Roughly coincident group													
9. Employment, nonagr., BLS	2	−	−	−	−	+	+	+	+	+	+	+	+
10. Unemployment	5	−	−	−	−	−	−	+	+	+	+	+	+
11. Bank debits outside N.Y.C.	6	−	−	−	+	+	+	+	+	+	+	+	+
12. Carloadings	5	−	−	−	+	−	+	+	+	+	+	+	+
13. Production, FRB	2	−	−	−	0	+	+	+	+	+	+	+	+
14. Prices, wholesale, exc. farm & food	2	−	−	−	−	−	+	+	+	+	+	+	+
15. Corp. profits after taxes (Q)	3	−	−	−	+	+	+	+	+	+	+	+	+
16. GNP (Q)	3	−	−	−	+	+	+	+	+	+	+	+	+
Lagging group													
17. Personal income	2	−	+	+	+	+	+	+	+	+	+	+	+
18. Retail sales	4	−	−	−	+	+	+	0	+	+	+	+	+
19. Consumer instalment debt	1	+	−	−	−	−	−	−	+	+	+	+	+
20. Manufacturers' inventories	1	−	−	−	−	−	−	−	−	−	+	−	−
21. Bank rates on business loans (Q)	3	−	−	−	−	−	−	−	−	+	+	+	+
Diffusion indexes (% rising)													
Leading group		25.0	62.5	75.0	62.5	75.0	100.0	100.0	87.5	87.5	75.0	68.8	62.5
Roughly coincident group		0	0	0	56.2	62.5	87.5	100.0	100.0	100.0	100.0	100.0	100.0
Lagging group		20.0	20.0	20.0	40.0	40.0	40.0	30.0	60.0	60.0	100.0	80.0	80.0
21 indicators		14.3	28.6	33.3	54.8	61.9	81.0	83.3	85.7	85.7	90.5	83.3	81.0

[a] When the span is six months, the change from January to July is entered in April, February to August in May, etc. For five-month spans the change from January to June is entered in April, etc. Entries are made up to the month prior to the last available month of data by using successively shorter intervals. E.g., when the span is six months and the last available figure is July, a preliminary entry for May is obtained by comparing February with July, and an entry for June by comparing March with July.

Source: *The National Bureau's Research on Indicators of Cyclical Revivals and Recessions*, National Bureau of Economic Research, New York, August, 1960, p. 14.

505

Table 29-21 shows the construction of diffusion indexes for 1958. The direction of change in each indicator is measured over a span of one to six months, longer spans being used for more erratic series in order to reduce the influence of erratic movements and expose the cyclical swing in the data.

APPENDIX A. DEFINITIONS OF PRINCIPAL TERMS IN NATIONAL INCOME AND PRODUCT ACCOUNTING

The items comprising gross national product in the right-hand section of the national income and product account, 1959, of Table 29-1 will be defined first. *Personal consumption expenditures* consists of the market value of purchases of goods and services by individuals and nonprofit institutions and the value of food, clothing, housing, and financial services received by them as income in kind. It includes the rental value of owner-occupied houses but does not include purchases of dwellings, which are classified as capital goods. *Gross private domestic investment* consists of acquisitions of newly produced capital goods by private business and nonprofit institutions and of the value of the change in the volume of inventories held by business. It covers all private new dwellings, including those acquired by owner-occupants. *Net foreign investment* is the net change in international assets and liabilities, including the monetary gold stock, arising out of the current international flows of goods and services, factor incomes, and cash gifts and contributions. Thus it measures the excess of (1) domestic output sold abroad over purchases of foreign output, (2) production abroad credited to United States-owned resources over production at home credited to foreign-owned resources, and (3) cash gifts and contributions received from abroad over cash gifts and contributions to foreigners. The net transfer of cash gifts and contributions offsets corresponding entries in personal consumption expenditures and government purchases of goods and services. *Government purchases of goods and services* measures purchases of goods and services by government bodies, exclusive of acquisitions of land and used depreciable assets and of current outlays of government enterprises. It consists of general government expenditures for compensation of employees, purchases from business (net of sales by government of consumption goods and materials), net government purchases from abroad and international contributions, and the gross investment of government enterprises. Therefore, government purchases of goods and services excludes transfer payments, government interest, and subsidies, as well as loans and other financial transfers outside the scope of income and product transactions.

The items comprising national income in the left-hand section of the National Income and Product Account, 1959, are next defined. *Compensation of employees* is the income accruing to persons in an employee status as remuneration for their work. From the employer's standpoint, it is the direct cost of employing labor. It is the sum of wages and salaries and supplements to wages and salaries. *Wages and salaries* consists of the monetary remuneration of employees commonly regarded as wages and salaries, inclusive of executives' compensation, commissions, tips, and bonuses, and of payments in kind which represent income to the recipients. *Supplements to wages and salaries* is the monetary compensation of employees not commonly regarded as wages and salaries. It consists of employer contributions for social insurance; employer contributions to private pension, health, and welfare funds; compensation for injuries; directors' fees; pay of the military reserve; and a few other minor items of labor income. *Income of unincorporated enterprises* measures the monetary earnings and income in kind of sole proprietorships, partnerships, and producers' cooperatives from their current business operations—other than the supplementary income of individuals involved from renting property. As with corporate profits, capital gains and losses are excluded and no deduction is made for depletion. *Inventory valuation adjustment* measures the excess of the value of the change in the volume of nonfarm business inventories, valued at average prices during the period, over the change in the book value of nonfarm inventories. This adjustment is required because corporate profits and income of unincorporated enterprises are taken inclusive of inventory profit or loss, as is customary in business accounting, whereas only the value of the real change in inventories is counted as current output in the national product. No valuation adjustment is required for farm inventories because farm income is measured exclusive of inventory profits.

Rental income of persons consists of the monetary earnings of persons from the rental of real property, except those of persons primarily engaged in the real estate business; the imputed net rental returns to owner-occupants of nonfarm dwellings; and the royalties received by persons from patents, copyrights, and rights to natural resources. *Corporate profits before tax* is the earnings of corporations organized for profit which accrue to residents of the nation, measured before Federal and state profit taxes, without deduction of depletion charges and exclusive of capital gains and losses. Profits accruing to residents are measured by eliminating intercorporate dividends from profits of domestic corporations and by adding the net receipts of dividends and branch profits from abroad. In other major respects, the definition of profits is in accordance with Federal income tax regulations. *Corporate profits tax liability* comprises Federal and state taxes levied on corporate earnings. Disbursements of tax refunds are deducted from tax liability in the year in which the tax liability was incurred. *Net interest* measures total interest (monetary and imputed, private and government) accruing to United States persons and governments minus total interest paid by United States governments. Government interest (Federal, state, and local) is deducted because it is not considered income arising in current production. It is necessary not only to exclude the portion of it paid directly to persons and governments but also to deduct the portion of it paid to business, because the latter is reflected in the incomes paid out or retained by the business system. The imputed interest component of net interest is measured in general as the excess of property income received by financial intermediaries from funds entrusted to them by persons over property income actually returned in monetary form by these intermediaries to persons. A portion of imputed interest is numerically equal to the value of financial services received by persons without explicit payment; the remainder represents property income withheld by life insurance companies and mutual financial intermediaries on the account of persons.

Definitions of the items reconciling national income to gross national product in the left-hand section of the National Income and Product Account, 1959, are next presented. *Business transfer payments* consists of monetary income receipts of individuals from business for which no services are rendered currently, of corporate gifts to nonprofit institutions, and of individuals' bad debts to business. *Indirect business tax and nontax liability* consists of tax liabilities incurred by businesses, except corporate income taxes, and other general government revenues from business. It includes all sales taxes. It includes payments for such specific services as are provided within the framework of general government activity. It excludes, however, purchases from government enterprises. Government receipts from the sale of surplus property are not included in this item. Tax liabilities are net of refunds. *Current surplus of government enterprises less subsidies* is shown as a single item because of the difficulties involved in segregating subsidies paid through Federal government enterprises from other expenditures of these enterprises. Current surplus of government enterprises represents the excess of sales receipts over current operating costs of government enterprises. In the calculation of the current surplus, no deduction is made for charges to depreciation or other reserves and interest is not counted in either receipts or costs. Subsidies are the monetary grants provided by government to private business.

Capital consumption allowances consists of depreciation charges, capital outlays charged to current expense, and accidental damage to fixed capital. Depreciation charges represents the charges made by private business against receipts for the current consumption of durable capital goods and comparable allowances for nonprofit institutions. It includes depreciation charges against owner-occupied houses. Depreciation reported by business is not adjusted for changes in the replacement value of capital goods, except for farm enterprises. Capital outlays charged to current expense represents new construction and purchases of new durable capital goods included in gross private domestic investment that are charged as current expense by business rather than entered on capital account. Accidental damage to fixed capital measures the value of the physical losses by fire, natural events, and other accidents to fixed capital of private business, not covered by depreciation charges.

Statistical discrepancy is the excess of the value of the estimated gross national product computed by the final-products method over its independently estimated value computed by adding the necessary conceptual adjustments to national income in the manner just described.

We next consider the items comprising personal income in the right-hand section of the personal income and outlay account, 1959, of Table 29-1. *Wage and salary disbursements* is equal to wages and salaries, except that retroactive wages are counted when paid rather than when earned. *Other labor income* is the same as supplements to wages and salaries exclusive of employer contributions for social insurance in national income. *Proprietors' and rental income* is the sum of income of unincorporated enterprises and inventory valuation adjustment and rental income of persons as given in the components of national income. *Dividends* measures cash dividend disbursements by corporations organized for profit to stockholders who are United States persons. *Personal interest income* measures total interest (monetary and imputed, private and government) accruing to United States persons. The imputed interest component of personal interest income is the same as in national income. *Transfer payments* consists of monetary income receipts of individuals from government and business (other than government interest) for which no services are rendered currently, of government payments and corporate gifts to nonprofit institutions, and of individuals' bad debts to business. *Personal contributions for social insurance* consists of payments by both employees and self-employed. Contributions of the self-employed, which relate to old-age and survivors insurance, were first made in 1952.

Personal outlay and saving is, of course, equal to personal income. The items comprising personal outlay and saving in the left-hand section of the personal income and outlay account, 1959, are defined next. *Personal tax and nontax payments* consists of the taxes levied against individuals, their income, and their property that are not deductible as expenses of business operations, and of other general government revenues from individuals in their personal capacity. It includes payments for such specific services as are provided within the framework of general government activity. It excludes, however, purchases from government enterprises. Tax refunds are deducted from payments as of the time of refund. *Personal consumption expenditures* is the same as in gross national product. *Personal saving* is the excess of personal income over personal consumption expenditures and personal tax and nontax payments. It consists of the current saving of individuals (including owners of unincorporated businesses), nonprofit institutions, and private pension, health, welfare, and trust funds. Personal saving may be in such forms as changes in cash and deposits, security holdings, indebtedness, and reserves of life insurance companies and mutual savings institutions, the net investment of unincorporated enterprises, and the acquisition of real property net of depreciation.

Government Receipts and Expenditures Account, 1959, summarizes receipts and expenditures of the government sector of the economy. Foreign Transactions Account, 1959, summarizes receipts from and payments to foreign countries. Gross Savings and Investment Account, 1959, summarizes investment expenditures and the sources of savings funds for these expenditures. It will be noted from the left-hand section of this account that domestic investment expenditures are considered to include only new construction, producers' durable equipment (items having a useful life of one year or more), and changes in business inventories. Moreover, new construction includes residential units as well as business facility expenditures. This definition of investment expenditures thus does not encompass some of the noncapitalized types of investment expenditures, such as in certain types of research which we have discussed in the earlier sections of this volume, and it does include nonbusiness residential investments by consumers.

APPENDIX B. FURTHER EXPLANATION OF FLOW-OF-FUNDS ACCOUNTING STATEMENTS

In order to keep the flow-of-funds accounting statement of Table 29-2 to manageable proportions, current account receipts and outlays for each sector are summarized into a single entry for saving. However, more of the current account detail is shown in the separate account statements for each sector. Thus, the statement for the consumer and nonprofit organization sector for 1959, Table 29-22, shows more of the detail than the summary of Table 29-2. The $30.6 billion of net saving shown for this sector in the summary table is derived in Table 29-22. (Income receipts include payrolls, dividends, and income withdrawls from unincorporated business. Life insurance premiums paid are net dividends received. Insurance and retirement credits include credits received in connection with insurance, pension, and retirement policies.)

For each sector and for the economy as a whole, gross saving measured from the current transactions account (row A of Table 29-2) is conceptually equal to gross investment measured from the capital transactions account (row D). In practice, however, the two measures are not necessarily equal because of statistical discrepancies. The difference between gross saving and gross investment is shown for each sector as a sector discrepancy transaction (row i). The conceptual equality of saving and investment in these accounts is an alternative statement of the conceptual equality of sources and uses of funds. The gross saving entry (row A) in the rest-of-world sector represents the rest of the world's surplus in current transactions with the United States.

Gross investment (row D) in each sector includes net investment in the financial assets of other sectors (row J) as well as private capital expenditures within the sector (row E). The financial investment flows from one domestic sector to another, row J—net financial investment, should cancel each other out in the national total for the economy as a whole (all sectors column). The discrepancy column sector entry for row J (and for row D, which has the row J values as one of its components) is therefore a correcting entry which brings the flows among the domestic sectors into balance. In the all sectors column, net financial investment (row J) is thus properly equal to zero when the discrepancy entry is taken into account and gross investment (row D) is equal to private capital expenditure (row E) when the row D discrepancy entry is taken into account. Therefore, gross saving (row A) should equal private capital expenditures (row E) in the all sectors column. The difference between gross saving (row A) and private capital expenditures (row E) is a discrepancy which is recorded for convenience on line A of the discrepancy column.

The national saving and investment column gives totals for the domestic sectors of the economy. The financial entries in this column are net uses of funds plus the corrections for items in the discrepancy column. Net financial investment (row J) is equal, but opposite in sign, to the net financial investment (row J) in the rest of the world sector column.

Because it is impossible to measure actual current income withdrawals by proprietors, this item is considered equal to the net income of unincorporated businesses, both farm and nonfarm. Unincorporated business retained income, or net saving, is therefore considered to be zero. Row g, proprietors' net investment in noncorporate business, therefore, includes not only the net flow of new equity funds but also the net earnings retained in the business.

The nonfarm residential construction entry (row G) represents, in the consumer sector, 1- to 4-family dwellings completed and purchases of additions and alterations to them. In the noncorporate and corporate business sectors, the entries in this row (G) represent all other private residential construction, including work in process on 1- to 4-family dwellings.

Table 29-22. Consumer and Nonprofit Organization Sector Statement of Sources and Uses of Funds, 1959
(In billions of dollars)

A	Current receipts	361.5	W	Fixed-value redeem. claims	9.6
B	Income receipts	331.8	X	Time deposits	4.1
C	Transfer receipts	29.7	Y	Savings shares	7.3
D	Income taxes and other deductions	50.1	Z	U.S. savings bonds	−1.8
E	Taxes less tax refunds	42.1	a	Saving through life insurance	3.7
F	Pension and OASI deductions	8.0	b	Saving through pension funds	7.9
G	Cur. receipts after deduct. (A − D)	311.4			
H	Cur. expend. for goods and serv	246.4	c	Cr. and equity mkt. instr.	15.3
I	Net life insurance premiums	2.6	d	Federal obligations	9.4
J	Current surplus (G − H − I)	62.4	e	State and local obligations	2.5
K	Insurance and retirement credits	11.6	f	Corporate and foreign bonds	.1
L	Capital consumption	43.4	g	Corporate stock	1.1
M	Net saving (J + K − L)	30.6	h	Mortgages	2.3
N	Gross saving (L + M)	74.0	i	Net invest. in noncorp. bus	−6.1
O	Gross investment (P + T)	76.2	j	*Net increase in liabilities*	20.7
P	*Capital expend. (net of sales)*	65.6	k	Consumer	20.1
Q	Residential construction	18.5	l	1-4 family mortgages	13.2
R	Consumer durable goods	43.4	m	Consumer credit	6.3
S	Plant and equip. (nonprofit)	3.7	n	Security credit	*
T	*Net financial investment* (U − j)	10.6	o	Other loans	.5
U	*Net acquis. of finan. assets*	31.3	p	Nonprofit organizations	.6
V	Demand deposits and currency	.9	q	Discrepancy (N − O)	−2.2

* Less than $50 million.

The financial liabilities of row L and the succeeding detailed rows include equity as well as debt claims.

Sector and transaction discrepancies, which are indicated in the discrepancy column and in row (i) are caused by many factors: inconsistencies in timing, valuation, coverage, and classification as well as errors in data. When one of the entries in a sector or transaction account is estimated as a residual (obtained by subtracting the other entries from the total in the account), the discrepancies are automatically transferred to this entry and no discrepancy will be shown in the table.

There are a number of differences between national-income and flow-of-funds accounting in concept and measurement of similar economic series. Although detailed discussion of these is beyond the scope of this section, we shall present one illustration. Consumer net saving in the flow-of-funds accounts differs from net personal saving in the national-income accounts in several respects. It is larger by the amount of three items not reflected in the national-income personal-saving figure: (1) purchases of consumer durable goods, net of depreciation on such goods; (2) saving through government life insurance; (3) saving through government employee retirement funds and through the railroad retirement fund. It is less than the national-income series by the amount of the internal saving of life insurance companies and of mutual financial institutions, which is reflected in the national-income series.

APPENDIX C. FURTHER EXPLANATION OF INPUT-OUTPUT ACCOUNTING[1]

All entries in Table 29-3 are in producer's (rather than purchaser's) values. For example, the $44.3 billion output of agriculture and fisheries is the value before addition of any marketing charges on farm or fishery products. The entries for trade and transportation (rows 31 to 34) in the first column represent charges for these services on the products purchased by agriculture and fisheries. The marketing margins on farm and fishery products are charged to the sectors which purchased them.

The output totals include the value of products and services "sold" by an industry to itself, even though there may have been no monetary transaction involved; e.g., the output totals will include all corn grown by farmers even though some corn was fed to hogs raised on the same farm. In general, those transactions which clearly represent a production stage are represented in the industry totals. Others, such as the intermediate fresh meat which eventually becomes cured meat, or the crude vegetable oil which is refined in the same plant, are generally excluded.

The total gross output of any industry, as defined in this table, is the value of all output of the industry, plus "transfers." These "transfers" include the value of the products primary to the industry but produced in other industries, imports of competitive products, and inventory depletions of products primary to but held outside the industry.

The output of the transportation industries (Nos. 31 to 33) and trade (No. 34) is, in general, the value added to commodities in the process of distribution to users. The disposition of the output of these industries appears in the table as the transportation and trade charges attached to the commodities that each industry purchases. Of course, the output of transportation is not limited to the above services, for it also includes carrying of passengers, mails, and other services. A further marketing charge appears in the form of government excise taxes (part cf the amounts in row 48).

The new construction and maintenance industry (No. 45) needs special mention because the allocations of output along the row are for maintenance construction alone, except to industries 48 and 49. The allocation to government (No. 48) is for public construction, both new and maintenance, and the allocation to gross private capital formation (No. 49) is the total of all new private construction. The other allocations to gross private capital formation are mainly the value of producer durables. The largest other allocation is from the rental industry (No. 37), referring to charges involved in real property transactions.

The treatment of foreign countries (No. 47) is somewhat special in that imports classed as "competitive" are transferred to the related domestic industry and distributed from the latter, whereas imports classed as "noncompetitive" are assigned directly to the industry using the item. The foreign trade row includes all listed imports (at

[1] Adapted from W. Evans, and M. Hoffenberg, *The Interindustry Relations Study for 1947*, U.S. Bureau of Labor Statistics, Washington, 1951.

foreign port value) and a number of invisible items, such as costs to the United States of foreign ocean transportation, travel abroad, offshore purchases by the Federal government, gifts, and other unilateral payments. The foreign trade column includes all listed exports and such invisibles as foreign purchase of United States ocean transportation, air transportation, motion picture royalties, insurance payments by foreigners, income on investments abroad, etc.

The government row (No. 48) shows essentially estimates of the amounts of taxes, postage, and other miscellaneous payments to the government by the various sectors. Activities of the government which closely parallel those of a private sector, such as government printing activities, the production of synthetic rubber, public school activities, government-owned hospitals, etc., have been excluded from government and included in the appropriate industry group. The government column shows outlays to other sectors for services, wages and salaries, supplies, and equipment.

The household sector (row 50) was defined to include all wages and salaries, interest payments, depreciation charges, payments for entrepreneurial services, contributions, and various other minor income payments. It is in large measure composed of payments made to individuals by other sectors. The household column shows individual or consumer outlays for the varied goods and services offered by other sectors. For consistency in treatment, the rental figure (row 37) in the household column includes, in addition to rental payments by consumers, other costs of household operation (such as fuels for heating) and imputed rentals for homeowners.

The ratios of Table 29-4 were computed in two stages, as follows:

1. The gross output figure for each sector shown in Table 29-3 was adjusted to refer to output during the year by subtracting inventory depletion during the year (from row 46). Thus, gross output for agriculture and fisheries (sector 1) amounting to $44,263 million was reduced by $2,660 million (row 46, column 1) to give an adjusted gross output figure of $41,603 million for this sector.

2. The column entries for each sector in Table 29-3 were then divided by the adjusted gross output level for the sector to produce the ratios shown in the present table. For example, total internal transactions within the agriculture and fisheries sector of $10,856 million (row 1, column 1 of Table 29-3) divided by $41,603 million yields 0.261, the entry at row 1 and column 1 of the present table. The sales of $2,378 million (row 2, column 1 of Table 29-3) of the food and kindred products sector to agriculture and fisheries divided by $41,603 million gives 0.057, the entry at row 2 and column 1 of the present table. The other ratios may be similarly derived. The ratios have been computed only for those sectors (1 to 45) considered to have processing functions.

The meaning of Table 29-5 may be illuminated by reference to Table 29-4, which shows that in 1947 the production of $1 of gross output by the agriculture and fisheries sector was accompanied by $0.2609 of intrasector transactions (row 1, column 1). To allow for this consumption within the sector of seed, feed, and other items, then, delivery outside the processing system of $1 of output (to household consumers, foreign buyers, or other final demand sectors) required at least $1.2609 gross output by the sector. Farther down in column 1, it is shown that $0.0572 per dollar of farm and fishery production was purchased from the food and kindred products sector (No. 2), $0.0190 from the chemicals sector (No. 10), and so on. One may conclude that in 1947 the delivery of $1 of farm and fishery output outside the processing system required gross production of at least $1.2609 from the agriculture and fishery sector, $0.0721 from the food and kindred products sector (0.0572 times 1.2609), $0.0251 from the chemicals sector (0.0199 times 1.2609), and so on.

To extend the chain of inference, we may turn to column 2 of Table 29-4, which shows the unit cost structure of the food and kindred products sector. Per dollar of output in this sector, there were $0.1319 of intrasector transactions, and purchases of $0.4041 from agriculture and fisheries, $0.0390 from chemicals, and so on. One may now make the critical assumption that these purchases were made by establishments in the food and kindred products sector in order to carry out their function of supplying their markets and that a pro rata share of the purchases may properly be attributed to the demand for food and kindred products by each of the other sectors. On this basis, the above $0.0721 of food and kindred products output generated by $1 of end-product deliveries by farms and fisheries entailed in turn additional gross output of $0.0291 in the agriculture and fisheries sector (0.0721 times 0.4041), $0.0095 in the food and kindred products sector (0.0721 times 0.1319), $0.0028 in the chemicals sector (0.0721 times 0.0390), and so on.

Totaling the figures, we now conclude that delivery outside the processing system of $1 of agricultural and fishery products required on the average, in 1947, gross output of at least $1.2900 from sector 1, $0.0816 from sector 2, $0.0279 from sector 10, and so on. Proceeding step by step in this way, and including all the sectors in the calculations, one could slowly build up a table of the total requirements on all sectors entailed by deliveries outside the processing system from any one sector. (In actual practice, this laborious procedure can be shortened.)

Each row in Table 29-5 shows the gross output in 1947 required directly and indirectly from each sector to support the delivery outside the processing system of $1 by the sector named at the beginning of the row. For example, in row 1, delivery of $1 of farm and fishery products required a total gross output of $1.4144 from the agricultural and fisheries sector (No. 1), 9.71 cents from the food and kindred products sector (No. 2), 4.65 cents from the chemicals sector (No. 10), and varying amounts from all others. To give another example, the entry in row 26, column 15, shows that 23.51 cents of gross iron and steel output was required directly and indirectly per dollar of end-product deliveries by the motor vehicle sector (which includes parts, accessories, etc.).

As the table stands, all entries are related to deliveries outside the processing system rather than to total production. To illustrate, the external delivery of $1 by the motor vehicles sector required $1.457 gross production by that sector (row and column 26). One may conclude then, that 23.51/1.457 cents of gross iron and steel output, or 16.14 cents, was required directly and indirectly per dollar of motor vehicle sector production. The other entries in the table may be adjusted similarly to refer to production rather than external end-product deliveries by dividing all entries in each row by the entry at the intersection with the corresponding column (e.g., divide row 1 by the entry in row 1, column 1, etc.).

Note also that all figures refer to gross output (including intrasector transactions) rather than net output (referring only to transactions with other sectors). The figures may be adjusted to exclude intrasector transfers by multiplying each column by 1 minus the entry at the intersection of the corresponding row and column in Table 29-4. Thus, each entry in the first column would be multiplied by 1 minus 0.2609, or 0.7391. The adjusted entry for row 1 and column 1 would be 1.4144 times 0.7391, or 1.0454. This might be interpreted as showing that external delivery of $1 of farm and fishery products would require $1.0454 output from the sector net of all intrasector transfers. Since the latter are excluded, the excess of 4.54 cents over $1 represents the "feedback" effects on itself of agriculture and fisheries purchases from other sectors. (If adjustments to a net output concept and to a production level rather than external deliveries basis are both to be applied, the former must be carried through first and the latter based on its results.)

Each column in Table 29-5 shows the gross output from a single sector required directly and indirectly per dollar of deliveries outside the processing system by each of the sectors. The entries in the first column, for example, reflect the dependence of agricultural production on demand for processed foods, tobacco products, textiles, apparel, chemicals, and leather products. The entries in column 5 show that most apparel moves directly to the ultimate consumer rather than through other processing channels. Other columns may be interpreted similarly. If a set of specified end-product deliveries is applied to the entries in any given column, the result will show the total gross output from the sector required to support the stipulated deliveries from the processing system. In effect, this will represent the "set-aside" against the sector's gross output implied by the stipulated deliveries—the amount preempted by this expression of purpose, and hence not available for other uses.

The new construction and maintenance sector (No. 45), shown as a processing sector in Tables 29-3 and 29-4 was excluded from computation of Table 29-5. Its inclusion would have frozen within the computations the 1947 product composition of this variegated sector. It was omitted to gain added flexibility in the treatment of construction for some analytical purposes.

APPENDIX D. BLS WHOLESALE PRICE INDEX[1]

"Wholesale" as used in the title of the wholesale price index refers to sales in large lots, not to the prices paid or received by wholesalers, distributors, or jobbers. The price data used in constructing this index are those which apply at primary market levels—that is, the first important commercial transaction for each commodity. Most of the quotations are the selling prices of representative manufacturers or producers, or prices quoted on organized exchanges or markets.

Index Groups. The classification system of the wholesale price index is essentially based on products or commodities rather than on industry, source, or end use. The basic index is divided into 15 major groups and 88 subgroups. In addition, in the 1952 revision, a third layer of classification called the "product class" was added. A product class approximates a grouping of commodities produced by a single industry or by related industries characterized by similarity of raw materials or production processes.

The index is so designed that it can be readily recomputed in accordance with any acceptable classification scheme. Each commodity is a separate cell, and these cells can be easily combined in any desired way. The general approach of flexibility is carried throughout the index, so that product classes, subgroups, and groups can also be readily added.

Sample of Commodities. The monthly index is based upon a sample of commodities, specifications, reporters, and primary-market levels of transactions, because it is neither necessary nor possible to cover all specifications, producers, markets, and buyers. Although a comparatively small list of commodities might suffice for a reliable summary all-items index, some 2,000 separate commodities have been included. This permits the development of reliable indexes for small subdivisions of the economy. For example, the prices of one type of cotton and one type of raw wool could yield general measures of the price movements of plant and animal fibers for the all-commodities index; the prices of abaca and other minot fibers are necessary to support a subindex for hard fibers, within the plant-and-animal-fibers classification, as more detail is needed, especially by business users of the index.

The commodities included in the index are not chosen by probability sampling. The selections are based upon knowledge of each industry and its important products, and are made after consultation with leading trade associations and manufacturers within each field. In general, the commodities included in the index are the most important ones in each field; some, although not important in terms of sales volume, were selected since they appear to offer good representation of price movements because of particular industry or trade characteristics.

Weights, Base Period, and Formula. The basic weights for the index are total transactions. Interplant transfers are excluded in so far as available data permit. The data for 1947 were used to establish the relationship among the groups, subgroups, and product classes. Within product classes, however, an attempt was made to approximate the most typical postwar (up to 1950) relationship between commodities within the same class. Therefore, the best information available is used for this purpose and it does not necessarily relate to 1947. For example, 1947 was a year in which the production pattern for agricultural machinery was seriously distorted by the prolonged

---

[1] Chapter 10 of BLS Bulletin 1168, *Techniques of Preparing Major BLS Statistical Series,* U.S. Department of Labor, is the source of the data in this appendix.

closing of one major plant, and industry data for 1949 were used to determine the relative weights within the product class. The relationship of agricultural machinery to total agricultural equipment and the relationship of each to construction machinery, however, are based upon the 1947 experience. In moving from individual commodities to larger groupings, any distortions which existed in 1947 become progressively less important. Moreover, any such distortions are more than offset by the advantage of having the general pattern of the index reflect a concrete time period and set of conditions—mutually consistent, marketwise and valuewise. Finally, 1947 was the only postwar year for which complete censuses for manufacturing, mining, and agriculture were available.

The base period for the wholesale price index is the average of three years, 1947, 1948, and 1949.

The index is a chain of relatives each calculated by the formula, $\Sigma p_n q_0 / (\Sigma p_0 q_0)$, where p_n and p_0 are current and base-period commodity prices and q_0 is the base-period quantity. In actual operation, the necessity for making allowance for changing specifications of individual commodities raises certain difficulties. Strict observance of the formula, using quantity weights, would require adjustments in both prices and quantities to prevent index distortion whenever there is a change in the specification of an individual commodity. To avoid this constant adjustment process the Bureau uses a modification of the formula, in which the individual commodity indexes are computed by chaining together the month-to-month price relatives (current monthly per cent change + 100) times the previous month's index, and weighting these by the values of sales, rather than using absolute prices weighted by physical quantities related to the base period. The net result is equivalent to using the previous formula and adjusting the base quantities whenever a price change results solely from a change in specification.

Limitations and Reliability. Some limitations on the use of the wholesale price index have already been mentioned. The index is designed to measure change, not absolute levels of prices, and the quotations used in the index for individual commodities do not necessarily measure the average dollars-and-cents levels of prices. The index is not

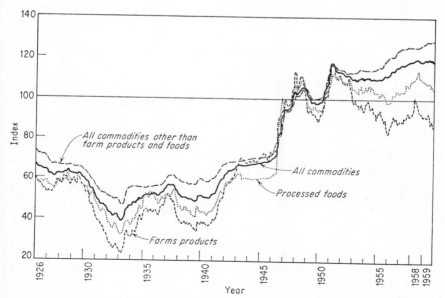

Figure 29-2. Wholesale prices (1947–1949 = 100). SOURCE: U.S. Bureau of Labor Statistics.

a true measure of the general purchasing power of the dollar—it does not include prices at retail, prices for securities, real estate, services, construction, or transportation. Even at wholesale or primary market levels, the index, while a good approximation, is not a perfect measure—since it is based on a relatively small sample of the many commodities which flow through these markets. In addition, there are some real price changes which cannot be measured—for example, some improvements in quality, hidden discounts, differences in delivery schedules, etc.

The index has not been designed for use in measuring margins between primary markets and other distributive levels. Thus, direct comparisons of the wholesale and consumer price indexes cannot be used to estimate or evaluate margins. The index does not measure prices paid by industrial consumers since it normally excludes transportation costs and similar factors affecting final prices. Finally, the index should not be used to forecast movements of the consumer price index, particularly over the short run. Many components of the wholesale price index never enter retail markets (for example, machinery); similarly, many components of the consumer price index (such as services and rents) are not covered by the wholesale price index.

The wholesale price index is based on a sample of commodities which have been purposively selected rather than chosen by random methods. The standard statistical techniques for evaluating the error in a sample are, therefore, not applicable. However, experience with the index over a long period of time suggests that the index becomes increasingly reliable as the group of prices covered is larger. That is, in most cases the reliability of a subgroup is greater than that of a product class, a group is more reliable than a subgroup, and the all-commodities index is more reliable than a group index.

Changes in the value of the wholesale price index from 1926 through 1959 are shown in Figure 29-2. In addition to the index values for all commodities, the wholesale price index values for farm products, processed foods, and all commodities other than farm products and foods are shown separately.

APPENDIX E. BLS CONSUMER PRICE INDEX

The consumer price index[1] is concerned with price changes involving retail prices of foods, clothing, housefurnishings, fuel, and other goods; fees paid to doctors and dentists; prices in barbershops and other service establishments; rents; rates charged for transportation, electricity, gas, and other utilities; etc. Prices are those charged to consumers, including sales and excise taxes. The different goods and services priced for the index are representative of the goods and services bought by city wage-earner and clerical-worker families to use, replace, and add to their possessions, as determined in a comprehensive survey of family incomes and expenditures. These families are defined as units of 2 or more persons who live in the 3,000 towns, cities, and suburbs of the United States, ranging in size from small cities of 2,500 population to the largest cities. The heads of these families are wage earners or salaried clerical workers, including craftsmen, factory workers, laborers, clerks, sales and service workers (except domestic service workers). Many of the families have two or more wage or salary workers; as a result, average family incomes are higher than average individual earnings. (Families with incomes after taxes of $10,000 or more are excluded.) The average size of the families included in the index was estimated to be about 3.3 persons, and their 1952 average family income after taxes was estimated at about $4,160. These

---

[1] "Relative Importance of CPI Components, December 1958," *Monthly Labor Review*, July, 1959, and Chapter 9 of BLS Bulletin 1168, *Techniques of Preparing Major BLS Statistical Series*, U.S. Department of Labor, are the sources of the data in this appendix.

families represent about 64 per cent of all persons living in urban places and about 40 per cent of the total United States population.

Price changes from some past reference date, in percentage terms, are averaged for the various goods and services. The resulting index number is the measure of price change from that past period (expressed as 100) to any later date. Through December, 1952, the index was calculated using the average of the 5 years 1935–1939 as a base. It was then changed to the base of 1947–1949 = 100. Prices are obtained in 46 cities so selected that their populations are representative of the entire population of the 3,000 cities in the United States. Prices in all 46 cities are then combined into the national index. Separate indexes are calculated for the 20 largest of the 46 cities— monthly for the 5 largest, and quarterly for the 15 others.

The index measures the effect of price changes on the cost of the goods and services in the family "market basket." The contents of the "market basket"—that is, the quantities and qualities of goods and services that represent what families bought in 1951–1952—is assumed to remain the same, so that the change in cost from month to month is the result of changes in prices. The index does not purport to measure the changes in spending of families that result from changes in their standards of living. It measures only the change in spending caused by changes in prices.

Index Weights and Formula. A nationwide survey of consumer expenditures was conducted in 1950 to determine what goods and services urban wage-earner and clerical-worker families buy. The representative sample of cities in this survey included all of the 12 largest urban areas with populations of more than 1,000,000 people and a sample covering 85 of the large, medium-size, and small cities. This sample was selected to account for the characteristics of different city types which affect the way families spend their money. The most important characteristics were size, climate, density of population, and level of income in the community. In each city the Bureau selected a representative sample of families from the entire population, including all family types and income classes. Interviewers visited and interviewed each family and obtained a complete record of the kinds, qualities, and amounts of foods, clothing, furniture, and all other goods and services the family bought in 1950, together with the amount spent for each item. These records for all wage-earner and clerical-worker families of two or more persons were averaged together for each city, to form the basis for index-weight determination.

The development of index weights from these survey results involved two major steps: (1) the averaging of variations in spending patterns reported by individual families, correcting the data for sampling and reporting errors and adjusting for unusually high purchases of automobiles, TV sets, and other consumer durable goods in 1950, and (2) the adjusting of survey data for price and income changes that had occurred after the survey year 1950.

The index is based on the formula $\Sigma q_\alpha p_n / \Sigma q_\alpha p_0$ where the q_α's are the average annual quantities of each item used by families of wage earners and clerical workers in 1951–1952, the base-weight year; the p_0's are the average prices for these items in the base period (1947–1949); and the p_n's the average prices in a current period. In practice, the index is calculated on a variation of this formula as a weighted average of price relatives for each item[1]

$$I_{n-1}\left[\frac{\Sigma q_\alpha p_{n-1}\,(p_n/p_{n-1})}{\Sigma q_\alpha p_{n-1}}\right]$$

where the p_{n-1}'s are the average prices of the preceding period, and I_{n-1} is the index number for the preceding period on the 1947–1949 = 100 base. Thus, the weights used in a current calculation of the index are value weights representing the cost of 1951–1952 quantities at prices prevailing in the preceding period.

---

[1] When the specification of the priced commodity changes, the formula is not a precise representation. The relative p_n/p_{n-1} would be p_n'/p_{n-1}' where n_i' is the current price of the new item and p_{i-1}' is last month's price of the new item. The price change due to the specification substitution is excluded. Only the trend of price change would affect the index.

In the process of imputing the movement of priced items to groups of the unpriced items they represent in the index, value weights—1951–1952 prices times quantities—were added together for the groups. The importance given to each item in the index, therefore, is equal to its own importance in family spending plus the importance of all the items it represents.

Limitations and Reliability. The consumer price index is not an exact measurement. It is subject to the many kinds of limitations that are always present in statistical calculations. One kind of limitation arises from sampling procedures. Expenditures for items in the "market basket" are based on interviews with about 8,000 wage-earner and clerical-worker families; price changes are based on prices of about 300 items, collected in about 2,000 food stores and 4,000 other retail stores and establishments; rents are obtained from about 30,000 tenants. Prices are collected in 46 cities, some every month, some every 3 months, and some every 4 months. Thus, the index is based on samples of families, items, stores, and cities that are only a fraction of the total. There is also a "sample" of time, since information is collected only at certain periods.

The degree of error introduced into the index through sampling depends primarily on the amount of variation in price change that exists within groups of items and between stores and cities. To gain about the same degree of accuracy throughout the index, therefore, the number of price observations obtained for any item is conditioned by its price variability and its importance in the total index. For example, prices of fresh vegetables, which are important in the family food budget, change frequently and have different seasonal patterns in different cities; they differ considerably from item to item and from store to store. To measure the average change in prices of all vegetables satisfactorily, a large number of them must be priced in a fairly large number of stores each month in every city. On the other hand, prices of men's nationally advertised brand shirts do not change often, and the same kind of shirt sells for the same price in almost all stores. These can be priced less frequently and in fewer stores, and still measure the price change satisfactorily.

Another kind of error may occur in the index because people who give information cannot always report exactly. In making surveys of consumer expenditures to determine the basic "market basket," it has been found that families can estimate very well what they spend in a year for rent, or electricity, or automobile, but not all can remember all their expenses for men's shirts or women's hose or other things that are bought frequently. Some report less than they actually bought, some more, so that these errors of recall tend to cancel out.

The index does not reflect all sales and discounts offered in retail stores nor the effect of savings the housewife may make in "shopping around." Nor does it reflect all special charges, such as tips and "under-the-counter" premium payments, that are not reported to the Bureau's price agent.

One of the principal sources of potential error in the index is in the estimation of price change for items which are important in family spending, but not included in the list of items priced. Also, failure to observe price changes in localities in which price trends differ from those in which prices are collected, introduces errors of estimation in the measurement of the national trend.

The consumer price index is specifically designed to measure the average change in prices of goods and services bought by urban wage-earner and clerical-worker families. Consequently, the index must be applied carefully when used for other purposes. The index represents all wage-earner and clerical-worker families, but not necessarily any one family or small groups of families. There are limitations on the application of the index to very-low- or very-high-income groups, to elderly couples, to single workers, or to other groups whose level or manner of living or spending are different from the average of all worker families. To the extent that these groups spend their income differently and are therefore differently affected by price changes, the index is not exactly applicable. On the other hand, when the index is applied to all city families or to the total urban population, the limitations may not be serious, since the wage-earner and clerical-worker family group represents such a large proportion (nearly two-thirds) of these populations.

The index is not designed to measure the changes in total family spending, since it measures only the effect of price change and does not take into account other factors, such as higher or lower incomes or income taxes. The index does not reflect the experience of the individual housewife, as she "shops around" to take advantage of the lowest prices, nor does it show the full effect of paying premium prices for scarce items. The index also does not reflect the change in costs experienced by families who move from one city to another or who change from renting to owning their own home.

Comparisons of city indexes show how much prices have changed in one city compared with another since the base period 1947–1949. They do not show whether prices are higher or lower in one city than in another.

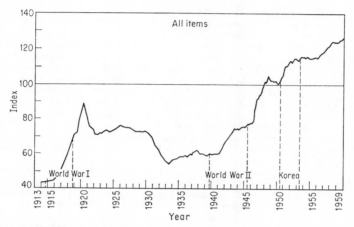

Figure 29-3. Consumer price index—for wage-earner and clerical-worker families in United States cities (1947–1949 = 100). SOURCE: U.S. Bureau of Labor Statistics.

Changes in the value of the consumer price index for all items from 1913 through 1959 are shown in Figure 29-3.

APPENDIX F. FRB INDEX OF INDUSTRIAL PRODUCTION

In the current FRB index of industrial production,[1] 207 monthly series have been grouped according to three major market sectors. In terms of total value added in 1957, the series are divided about equally between materials and final products. Consumer goods account for about two-thirds of final products and equipment, including defense, for one-third.

The major portion of all goods entering into domestic markets flows through the area covered by the industrial production index. Comparisons between industrial production measures and purchases in these markets can be fruitful in economic analysis, but in making such comparisons it is necessary to keep in mind the alternative sources of supply as well as various problems associated with the underlying data. Of particular

[1] *Industrial Production, 1959 Revision*, Board of Governors of the Federal Reserve System, July, 1960, is the source of the data in this appendix.

importance in such analysis is the treatment of agricultural production and of imports and exports of commodities.

In total, the activities covered by the index of industrial production account for about 35 per cent of total national income and product. The area represented by the index is one of central importance, for which monthly figures are available for a period of more than 40 years. The two major commodity-producing industries that are not covered by the index are agriculture and construction, which together produce 10 per cent of national income. For agriculture, extreme seasonal swings limit the significance of monthly production data, while for the construction industry, directly reported monthly output series of the type used to compile the industry production index are not available at the present time.

All other sectors of the economy are affected in some degree by developments in the industrial sector. This is partly because such a large portion of the total physical supply of commodities flows through the industries covered by the production index. Most closely related to industrial production are the freight transportation and trade sectors, in which business consists largely of conveying and distributing the materials and products of industry. These sectors account for about 20 per cent of national income. Some of the service sector is also allied to industrial production, but less directly, for example, many finance, advertising, and insurance activities. Other services are more related to government or individual consumers than to industry.

Base Period for Weights. In measuring production changes, a major problem is the selection of appropriate base periods for determining the weights used in the index. In the current index, 1957 weights are used for the period beginning with January, 1953. For the period January, 1947, through December, 1952, 1947 weights are used as they were in the old index.

The relative importance of economic activities can be measured in different ways and there is no single, unequivocal, all-purpose way. In the production index, where each of the 207 series represents changes at a stage in a flow of activities involving the process of transforming materials into final goods, the contribution of each stage to the total production flow is measured by value added in each industry. For the manufacturing and mining industries value added is calculated as a residual by subtracting the value of purchased materials, fuels, containers, and the cost of contract work from the gross value of output. For the utility industries value-added data are obtained directly by summing salaries, wages, allowances for capital consumption, and profits. Value-added data are used in preference to gross value figures because they reflect the contribution to total output made by each industry relatively free of duplication. Gross value of output, which includes material, fuel, and other purchased items, reflects the contributions already made by other producers in manufacturing, mining, or utilities.

In production indexes, value-added figures based on different weight periods will differ only if relative prices (value added per unit) in these weight periods are different. The reason is that quantities or physical output, after having been measured as accurately as feasible for each series, must be taken as given. Only the relative prices assigned to the series are subject to choice.

From 1947 to 1959 the total index shows more growth with 1947 weights than with 1957 weights. The index with 1947 weights rises 66 per cent compared with 56 per cent for the index with 1957 weights. This greater growth results in part from a larger weight given in the 1947 weighted index to industries that underwent the greatest expansion during the period, such as aircraft, television, and chemicals. Value added per unit declined after 1947 for these industries relative to most other industries. Part of the greater growth in the total with 1947 weights also stems from the larger weight given to the rapidly expanding electric and gas utilities, which grew at an annual rate three times that of manufacturing and mining. Reflecting smaller increases in prices of electricity and gas than in prices of manufactures and minerals, value added per unit for the faster growing utility industry declined from 1947 to 1957 relative to manufacturing and mining. Thus, the 1957 proportion of utilities in the total index is calculated at 6.35 per cent with 1947 weights and 4.96 per cent with 1957 weights.

The 1947 and 1957 weighted indexes were linked in January, 1953. This linking point, which is about midway between 1947 and 1957, permitted the change to a new set of price relationships after changes in these relationships had emerged. The month in which the link was made was not "abnormal" for any series nor was it in a period of marked cyclical change.

Base Period for Reference. The use of average output in the years 1947–1949 as a reference base has been continued for the revised total index and major groupings in order to facilitate comparisons with other general-purpose indexes compiled on that base. A new reference period based on the year 1957 is also used for the revised total index and its detailed components because relatives in terms of a more recent time period have advantages both for compiling current output measures and for analyzing them. Because total industrial production was about 50 per cent higher in 1957 than in 1947–1949, use of a 1957 reference base has the effect of reducing the level of the total index by about one-third. Thus, the December, 1959, level for the revised total, including utilities, is expressed as 109 instead of 165 per cent. This change, however, unlike the revisions in basic series or the change in weight base, has no effect on the percentage relationships between any two months or years in the index. The difference in scale between the 1947–1949 and the 1957 base periods for total industrial production is such that the level of 100 on the 1957 base corresponds to 152 on the 1947–1949 base, and 100 on the 1947–1949 base corresponds to 66 on the 1957 base, as shown in Figure 29-4.

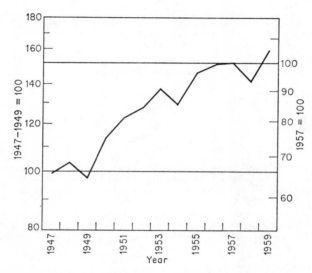

Figure 29-4. Industrial production index, 1947 to 1959, with two reference bases.

Calculation Procedure. An algebraic formulation of the procedure for calculating the production index is shown below in order to amplify the problem involved in computing points in the index beyond a link. For the period from January, 1953, on a 1957 base, the steps are as follows:

1. Multiply the relative on a 1957 base for an individual series for the given month by its 1957 weight. Symbolically, this may be represented as follows:

$$\frac{q_n}{q_{57}} (100) \frac{q_{57}p_{57}}{\Sigma q_{57}p_{57}}$$

The first ratio is the relative and the second the weight, which is value added for the series divided by total value added in industrial production in the year 1957, with value added expressed as 1957 quantity times 1957 value added per unit of quantity. Multiplying the relative by its weight gives the points for each series.

2. Total the points to obtain an aggregate for the given month, or symbolically,

$$\sum \left[\frac{q_n}{q_{57}} (100) \frac{q_{57}p_{57}}{\Sigma q_{57}p_{57}} \right]$$

3. Divide the aggregate points for the given month by the aggregate proportion in 1957, to obtain subtotal and total indexes. For a subgroup of the total index the symbolic expression is

$$\frac{\sum^* \left[\frac{q_n}{q_{57}} (100) \frac{q_{57}p_{57}}{\Sigma q_{57}p_{57}} \right]}{\frac{\Sigma^* q_{57}p_{57}}{\Sigma q_{57}p_{57}}}$$

where Σ^* represents a summation of series in the subgroup as distinct from the summation without the asterisk which includes all series in the total index. This reduces to

$$\frac{\Sigma^* q_n p_{57}}{\Sigma^* q_{57}p_{57}} (100)$$

which is the ratio of group value added in the month to the comparable value added in 1957, in value added per unit prices of 1957.

For the total index the symbolic expression is

$$\frac{\sum \left[\frac{q_n}{q_{57}} (100) \frac{q_{57}p_{57}}{\Sigma q_{57}p_{57}} \right]}{\frac{\Sigma q_{57}p_{57}}{\Sigma q_{57}p_{57}}}$$

This reduces to

$$\frac{\Sigma q_n p_{57}}{\Sigma q_{57}p_{57}} (100)$$

which is the ratio of total value added in the given month to the comparable value added in 1957, both in value added per unit prices of 1957. This is the symbolic expression of the index of total industrial production for any month of the period beginning with January, 1953.

For the pre-January, 1953, period a more complex procedure is required for each aggregate and the total index. In step 1 the relative (1947–1949 = 100) for any month is multiplied by the 1947–1949 proportion, in prices of 1947, or symbolically,

$$\frac{q_n}{q_{47-49}} (100) \frac{q_{47-49}p_{47}}{\Sigma q_{47-49}p_{47}}$$

In step 2 the points from step 1 are aggregated, in the fashion described earlier. In step 3 an index with 1947 weights is obtained, which reduces to

$$\frac{\Sigma^* q_n p_{47}}{\Sigma^* q_{47-49}p_{47}} (100)$$

The above expression is then multiplied by a ratio for January, 1953, of an index with 1957 weights to that with 1947 weights as follows:

$$\left(\frac{\Sigma^* q_n p_{47}}{\Sigma^* q_{47-49}p_{47}} \right) (100) \left[\frac{\frac{\Sigma^* q_{Jan.53}p_{57}}{\Sigma^* q_{57}p_{57}} (100)}{\frac{\Sigma^* q_{Jan.53}p_{47}}{\Sigma^* q_{47-49}p_{47}} (100)} \right]$$

The above expression indicates that indexes before January, 1953, are first calculated on a 1947–1949 base with 1947 weights, and then linked to the level in January, 1953, of the index with 1957 weights, and converted from a 1947–1949 to a 1957 base.

For the January, 1953, index, the above expression reduces to

$$\frac{\Sigma^* q_{\mathrm{Jan.\,53}} p_{57}}{\Sigma^* q_{57} p_{57}} \,(100)$$

Seasonal Adjustments. Seasonal influences on production, as well as on employment and other economic activities, result in more or less regular patterns of monthly changes within a year. These changes may be sizable and they often exceed changes arising from other forces. The amplitude of seasonal variation for a series is generally in inverse relation to the variety of products or activities which is represented. In order to measure these fluctuations in industrial production and to reveal cyclical and growth trends more clearly, 74 industry and market components of the revised index have been separately adjusted for seasonal variation. Sixty-five of these have been combined to obtain indexes for the total and for summary and major groupings in both the industry and market structures. The total number of seasonally adjusted series and subgroups published is 102.

Seasonal Computation Methods. The seasonal adjustment factors in the index are developed essentially by the ratio-to-moving-average method described in Chapter 30. However, for some series it is not feasible to use the ratio-to-moving-average method to calculate the seasonal factors. Mechanical averaging methods for determining adjustment factors have not proved suitable for series with abrupt changes in the seasonal pattern. Such changes may arise from supply or demand influences, as in the case of autos and household appliances, or from changes in the basic data underlying the series.[1]

Adjustments for Reporting Periods. Product data are converted to a daily average basis by adjusting for the number of working days in the reporting period in order to eliminate fluctuations due to differences in the length of that period. In these calculations Saturdays and/or Sundays or half days are regarded as nonworking days. No allowances for holiday shutdowns are made in the working-day adjustment and consequently the effects of holiday observances on monthly output are reflected in the indexes unadjusted for seasonal variation. A daily average computation is not required for the monthly man-hour series based on Bureau of Labor Statistics data for production workers because these data relate to the payroll period ending nearest the middle of the month and are usually little affected by calendar variations. While the procedure outlined above has generally provided satisfactory allowances for variations in working days, further adjustments have been desirable in certain series.

Changes in the values of the FRB total index from 1919 through 1959 are shown in Table 30-7.

PROBLEMS

1. Referring to the national income and product accounts of Table 29-1, does adding together the totals in the various sector accounts result in a meaningful economic measure? Explain.

2. Describe briefly the basic differences in viewpoint and account structure of the national-income and flow-of-funds accounting systems.

[1] See "Adjustment for Seasonal Variation," *Federal Reserve Bulletin*, June, 1941, pp. 518–528, for a description of the methods used in these cases.

3. A $500 million increase in the consumer sales of the motor vehicle industry and a $500 million decline in agriculture and fisheries are forecast for next year. Using Table 29-5, compute the effect of these changes on production in the iron and steel and the metalworking industries. What are the limitations of the results obtained by these computations?

4. In Table 29-23 are data on the prices and quantities of the four products (A, B, C, and D) of the Turner Corporation during 1956 through 1960. Compute index numbers to show the changes in the level of prices received by the Turner Corporation during these years using (a) a simple aggregate index, with 1956 as base year; (b) a simple average-of-relatives index, with 1956 as base year; (c) a weighted aggregate index using base-period weights, with 1956 as base year; (d) a weighted aggregate index using base-period weights, with 1958 as base year; (e) a weighted aggregate index using given-period weights, with 1956 as base year; (f) a weighted average-of-relatives index, using base-period weights, with 1956 as base year.

Table **29-23. Prices Received by the Turner Corporation, 1956 to 1960**

Year	A Price ($ per ton)	A Quan-tity (tons)	B Price ($ per unit)	B Quan-tity (units)	C Price ($ per lb)	C Quan-tity (lb)	D Price ($ per gal)	D Quan-tity (gal)
1956	$22.80	20,000	$175.00	2,000	$ 6.40	150,000	$2.10	800,000
1957	20.70	30,000	195.00	2,500	6.90	150,000	3.80	900,000
1958	18.00	25,000	190.00	3,000	7.80	180,000	2.50	800,000
1959	19.30	35,000	210.00	2,000	10.50	200,000	1.65	750,000
1960	17.50	40,000	225.00	1,500	10.00	250,000	1.40	700,000

5. What are the principal problems in the construction of index numbers?

6. What are the principal reasons that some index numbers may give misleading results?

7. Refer to the example in the text on the question of whether office salaries had kept pace with the consumer price index. How would you determine the valid answer to this question?

8. What factors need to be evaluated to decide how frequently it is desirable to change the base periods of a price index such as the wholesale price index or consumer price index?

9. The wholesale price index is widely used as a measure of the purchasing power of the dollar. Discuss the validity and reliability of its use for this purpose.

10. The consumer price index is widely used as a measure of the purchasing power of the consumer's dollar. The dollar value of wages is therefore divided by the consumer price index to obtain a measure of real wages in terms of dollars of constant consumer purchasing power. Evaluate the suitability of this procedure for the wages of (a) typists, (b) farmers, (c) surgeons, (d) machinists, (e) economists.

11. Note the statements in the text on the reliability and limitations of the consumer price index. Suggest ways in which each of the limitations could be reduced or eliminated.

12. Discuss the logic of using quantity as the weighting factor in the wholesale and consumer price indexes and value added in the industrial production index.

13. It is stated in the text that the Federal Reserve Board index of industrial production shows more growth with 1947 weights than with 1957 weights. (a) Which of these growth values is more accurate? (b) If 1947 weights give accurate results, why change to the 1957 weights? If 1957 weights give more accurate results, why not change the weights each year to the latest year for which figures are available?

14. What does Figure 29-4 indicate regarding the rate of growth of the United States economy between 1947 and 1959?

15. Do you think that a businessman who forecasts successfully on the basis of economic indicators and diffusion indexes is practicing a science or an art? Justify your answer.

16. Give logical economic reasons why you could expect each of the lead series in Table 29-20 to have lead characteristics.

30 Time-series Analysis

The primary purpose of time-series analysis is to provide assistance in forecasting the future. Emphasis needs to be placed on the word "assistance" because the results of time-series analysis cannot be mechanically applied to yield accurate results. Time-series analysis can provide assistance to good judgment, but cannot substitute for good judgment.

Time-series projections are valid in the future only if nonrecurring distortions have been removed from the projected data. In addition, unless the forces which have caused the underlying projected patterns continue into the future unchanged, supplementary analyses of causative factors and sound judgment must be applied to correct the projected patterns for changes which have occurred or will occur. It is extremely rare that the patterns underlying times series do not change. For this reason, time-series analysis can rarely be used as the sole basis for forecasting without supplementary adjustment.

A time series is a series of values of a variable that changes from one point in time to another. In a frequency distribution we classify data on the basis of the size or magnitude of the values. In a time series we classify data on the basis of time. The monthly dollar value or physical volume of sales of a company for the last eight years would constitute a time series.

Because one important interest in forecasting is the prediction of future levels of business activity or sales volume, we shall use the variation of sales over a period of time to illustrate the analysis of time series. The actual value of sales in any month can be expressed as a function of four factors:

1. Long-time trend, which we shall designate T, represents the underlying, consistent pattern of the changes in sales over a considerable period of time.

2. Cyclical variation, which we shall designate C, represents the wavelike, not generally uniform, fluctuations in sales around the trend line.

3. Seasonal variation, which we shall designate S, represents changes which occur because of conditions that vary with the time of year or the season.

4. Residual or irregular variation, which we shall designate R, represents the variation which is unexplained by the trend, cyclical, or seasonal factors.

526

Using these factors, a model of the time-series values can be constructed in a number of ways. The most commonly used model, and the one adopted in our analysis in this book, is that the factors bear a multiplicative relationship to each other. The formula expression of our model then becomes

$$\text{Actual value} = A = TCSR$$

Other models which are partially or completely additive have been used by different analysts at various times. These models have included $A = T + C + S + R$; $A = T(S + C + R)$; $A = ST(1 + CR)$.   Although good theoretical bases can be found for these other models in some cases, for most practical purposes the multiplicative model has been found to be most suitable and is most commonly used.

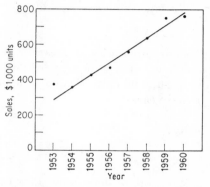

Figure 30-1. Long-term trend of Gargo Company sales—fitted by visual inspection.

Long-term Trend. The sales of the Gargo Company are shown in Table 30-1 for the years 1953 to 1960. The time series is plotted in Figure 30-1. The long-term trend of the Gargo Company's sales pattern can now be estimated by fitting a straight line by visual inspection. The straight line is designed to follow the general trend of values on the chart. This procedure is simple and is adequate for some purposes in which greater refinement of technique will not yield significantly greater accuracy.

Table 30-1. Sales of the Gargo Company

Year	Sales in units of $1,000
1953	375
1954	360
1955	425
1956	470
1957	560
1958	640
1959	750
1960	760

Least-squares Trend Line. A less subjective procedure is to fit a trend line using the method of least squares. The linear least-squares trend line has the following properties:

1. The sum of the vertical distances of the actual values from the trend-line values equals zero.[1]

[1] This is not usually true for nonlinear least-squares lines.

2. The sum of the squares of the vertical distances of the actual values from the trend-line values is a minimum (less than about any other line).

These properties of the linear least-squares trend line are analogous to the properties of the arithmetic mean of a frequency distribution: the sum of the differences between each value in the distribution and the mean equals zero; and the sum of the squares of the differences between each value and the mean is less than about any other point.

We shall demonstrate the calculation of a least-squares straight-line trend and then indicate how the procedure can be used for various kinds of nonlinear functions.

The equation of a straight line is

$$Y_T = a + bX$$

For our time-series application, Y_T equals each trend-line value for sales and X equals the number of periods before or after the base period. If we use annual data, X equals the number of years before or after the base-period year.

We can express the two properties of our least-squares line mathematically:

$$\Sigma(Y - Y_T) = 0$$
$$\Sigma(Y - Y_T)^2 = \text{a minimum}$$

We want to determine the values of a and b which will satisfy these relationships. These values are determined by two equations.[1] We obtain the first by multiplying the straight-line equation $Y = a + bX$ by the coefficient of a and summing each term. We obtain the second by multiplying by the coefficient of b and summing each term. The coefficient of a is 1. Multiplying each term by 1 and summing each term gives

$$\Sigma Y = Na + b\Sigma X$$

N is the number of actual values or years. The coefficient of b is X.

---

[1] The two equations can be derived mathematically by differentiating $\Sigma(Y - Y_T)^2$ first with respect to a and then with respect to b; and then setting the partial derivatives equal to zero to solve for the minimum point. Thus,

$$\Sigma(Y - Y_T)^2 = \Sigma(Y - a - bX)^2$$
$$\Sigma(Y - Y_T)^2 = \Sigma(Y - a - bX)^2 = \Sigma Y^2 - 2a\Sigma Y - 2b\Sigma XY + Na^2 + 2ab\Sigma X + b^2\Sigma X^2$$

$$\frac{\partial \Sigma(Y - Y_T)^2}{\partial a} = -2\sum Y + 2Na + 2b\sum X = 0$$

$$\Sigma Y = Na + b\Sigma X$$

$$\frac{\partial \Sigma(Y - Y_T)^2}{\partial b} = -2\sum XY + 2a\sum X + 2b\sum X^2 = 0$$

$$\Sigma XY = a\Sigma X + b\Sigma X^2$$

It can be shown that this least-squares line will pass through $\bar{X}$, $\bar{Y}$ and that

$$\Sigma(Y - Y_T) = 0$$

Multiplying each term by X and summing each term gives

$$\Sigma XY = a\Sigma X + b\Sigma X^2$$

To solve these two equations for a and b, we need to know ΣY, ΣX, ΣXY, and ΣX^2. X equals the number of periods from any origin we select. We select the most convenient origin to simplify our calculations. If we take our origin at the middle of the covered period, the plus and minus value of X will be equal and ΣX will equal zero. Therefore, when we have an even number of years we select the date between the two middle years as the origin. In the example of Table 30-2, December 31, 1956, or January 1, 1957, is the origin. The sales of each year are considered to be centered in the middle of each year. The X units are therefore in six-month units to avoid computations with half-year fractions. Thus, July 1, 1955, is three six-month periods prior to January 1, 1957. (When a least-squares trend line is fitted to an odd number of years, the origin for simplest computation is at July 1 of the middle year and X can be in units of a full year since the sales values of all the years are also centered on July 1.)

Substituting in the equations we obtain

$$\Sigma Y = Na + b\Sigma X$$
$$4,340 = 8a + 0$$
$$a = \tfrac{4,340}{8} = 542.5$$

$$\Sigma XY = a\Sigma X + b\Sigma X^2$$
$$5,380 = 0 + b(168)$$
$$b = \tfrac{5,380}{168} = 32.0$$

Our least-squares line is

$$Y = 542.5 + 32.0X$$

The trend values, Y_T, in Table 30-2 are computed from this equation.

Table 30-2. **Computation of Long-term Trend Values by Least-squares Method for Sales of the Gargo Company**

Year	Y, sales, in units of $1,000	X, centered at Jan. 1, 1957	X^2	XY	Y_T, Trend values
1953	375	−7	49	−2,625	318.5
1954	360	−5	25	−1,800	382.5
1955	425	−3	9	−1,275	446.5
1956	470	−1	1	− 470	510.5
1957	560	1	1	+ 560	574.5
1958	640	3	9	+1,920	638.5
1959	750	5	25	+3,750	702.5
1960	760	7	49	+5,320	766.5
Summation	4,340	0	168	+5,380	

Thus, we substitute $X = -1$ in the trend equation to compute the trend value for 1956,

$$Y_T = 542.5 + 32.0(-1) = 510.5$$

For 1953, $X = -7$ and the trend value is

$$Y_T = 542.5 + 32.0(-7) = 318.5$$

The actual sales for each year are plotted as well as the least-squares trend line in Figure 30-2.

We can easily shift the origin from which we measure X to a more convenient one in our equation. If we wish to have July 1, 1953, as our origin,

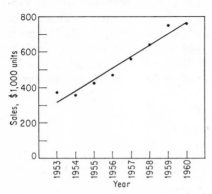

Figure 30-2. Long-term trend of Gargo Company sales—fitted by least squares.

and express X in full-year units, we make a equal to the trend value at July 1, 1953, where X will equal zero. Our new annualized b values will be twice the half-year ones. Our equation becomes

$$Y = 318.5 + 64.0X$$

Nonlinear Trend Lines. The most commonly used trend lines are straight lines both because of their simplicity and the fact that they frequently appear as logical a trend assumption as some more complicated curves. Many trends which may logically be thought to be nonlinear turn out in the long run to be linear because of the interaction of many economic forces.

A straight line may be considered a first-degree power curve of the general form $Y = a + bX + cX^2 + dX^3 + \cdots$. The second-degree power curve would be $Y = a + bX + cX^2$, commonly called a parabola. The third-degree power curve would be $Y = a + bX + cX^2 + dX^3$, which is also called a cubic. Higher-degree power curves than the cubic are rarely used for trend lines.

The normal equations for fitting higher-degree curves are derived exactly as for the straight line.[1] We multiply each term of the original equation by the coefficient of each unknown constant and sum each term. Thus, for $Y = a + bX + cX^2$, the normal equation becomes

$$\Sigma Y = Na + b\Sigma X + c\Sigma X^2$$
$$\Sigma XY = a\Sigma X + b\Sigma X^2 + c\Sigma X^3$$
$$\Sigma X^2 Y = a\Sigma X^2 + b\Sigma X^3 + c\Sigma X^4$$

---

[1] $\Sigma(Y - Y_T)$ does not usually equal 0 with a nonlinear least-squares line.

The least-square computations are similar to those for the straight line, except that they are a bit more laborious.

Exponential Trend Lines. A straight-line trend implies that the long-term trend is the addition of a uniform sum, b, per year, to the trend value (or a subtraction if it is a decreasing trend). If the underlying trend involves growth or decline at a constant rate (percentage) rather than a constant increment or decrement, an exponential equation may be appropriate. We have seen that money invested at compound interest grows exponentially. The general equation of the exponential form is

$$Y = ab^X$$

Y grows at a constant rate of b times each year.

To fit an approximate least-squares line to an exponential curve, we take the logarithm of the equation

$$\log Y = \log a + X \log b$$

Since $\log a$ and $\log b$ are constants, this curve will plot as a straight line on paper in which the Y axis is spaced logarithmically and the X axis arithmetically.

To find the least-squares line, we set up normal equations in exactly the same way as previously, using the logarithmic form of the equation.

$$\Sigma(\log Y) = N \log a + (\log b)\Sigma X$$
$$\Sigma(X \log Y) = (\log a)\Sigma X + (\log b)\Sigma X^2$$

We must now set up a table similar to Table 30-2 with the following headings:

$$Year \quad Y \quad X \quad X^2 \quad \log Y \quad X \log Y$$

Once the logarithmic form of the equation is established, the exponential form may be computed by means of antilogarithms.

Trend analysis is of primary value in long-term forecasting. For the short term, the vagaries of cyclical and residual variations, which we shall see are statistically unpredictable, will frequently cause wide variations from trend values.

Cyclical Variations. Cyclical changes in industry or company operations are wavelike oscillations. The size, length, and pattern of these oscillations need not be uniform and unchanging. They may be produced by a number of interacting causes. Variations in the general level of business activity have an effect on the particular industry or company. Industries and companies are affected by the general business cycle in different ways. A strong factor in some cases may be an equilibrium adjustment effect which is caused by reactions to forces which cause operations to go past the stable equilibrium point first in one direction and then in the opposite.

Underexpansion of facilities in an industry may produce high prices and profits which attract the construction of excess facilities which lower prices and erase profits which discourages investment in new facilities which result a number of years later in a shortage of facilities which result in high prices and profits which attract the construction of excess facilities which . . . .

Because cycle patterns are so irregular, it is not practical to forecast future cyclical behavior on the basis of a recurrence of the past pattern. Time-series analysis provides supplementary assistance to the primary tools for forecasting cyclical changes: studies of the pertinent economic factors; correlation studies such as discussed in Chapter 31; and studies of noneconomic forces, such as political considerations.

When we use annual data, seasonal changes do not produce variations in our time-series values. The variations about the trend line are therefore produced by cyclical and residual influences. Our model with annual data is

$$A = TCR$$

If we divide the actual time-series values by the trend values, $T = Y_T$, we obtain percentages representing CR, the cyclical-residual component ($A/T = CR$).

The annual sales of the Gargo Company have been divided by the trend values in Table 30-2 to obtain a cyclical and residual index, as shown in Table 30-3. The trend values are sometimes considered the normal sales,

Table 30-3. **Calculation of Cyclical and Residual Index for Sales of the Gargo Company**

Year	Annual sales A	Y_T, trend value T	Cyclical and residual index $CR = A/T$
1953	375	318.5	1.18
1954	360	382.5	0.94
1955	425	446.5	0.95
1956	470	510.5	0.92
1957	560	574.5	0.97
1958	640	638.5	1.00
1959	750	702.5	1.07
1960	760	766.5	0.99

which would occur were it not for cyclical and residual influences. The index in these cases would be considered above or below normal—when it is above or below 100 per cent. (There is, however, very little theoretical justification for considering the trend value as the normal value.) A graphic picture of the cyclical-residual index is shown in the chart of Figure 30-3.

If we were computing the cyclical-residual pattern from monthly or quarterly data, we would divide the actual values by TS, trend value times the seasonal factor, to elimi-nate the effects of both trend and seasonal factors.

Seasonal Variation. To provide monthly forecasts, or other periodic divisions of the year, we need to know the seasonal pattern of vari-ation. How can we compute a sea-sonal index?

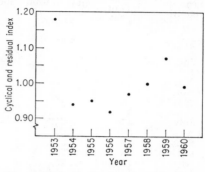

Figure 30-3. Cyclical and residual pat-tern of Gargo Company sales.

Our model is $A = TSCR$. If we can divide the actual values by a measure which represents A with S and some R removed, then only S and some R will remain in the quotient or index. The measure which represents A with S and some R removed is a 12-month moving average, which is a series of overlapping 12-month aver-ages. Since the 12-month moving average covers the entire year, all seasons are represented, the high and low values cancel each other out, and the seasonal and some residual effect is eliminated. When we divide $A = TSCR$ by this moving-average measure of A which has S and some R removed, we are left with only S and some R.

The resulting monthly seasonal indexes contain the seasonal and some residual effects. By averaging the indexes for each month over a period of years, we cancel out some of the residual, irregular variations and obtain a seasonal index.

The computation of a seasonal index is illustrated in Tables 30-4 and 30-5 for the Gargo Company. In Table 30-4 we compute a seasonal index value for each month in the time series, except the first and last six-month periods for which we do not have moving averages. In column 3 we com-pute a 12-month moving total by adding the sales for 12 months and centering the total at the mid-point of the 12-month period, between the sixth and seventh month. To obtain moving totals centered in the middle of the month in column 4, we add together the 12-month moving totals at the beginning and end of each month. The centered moving average of column 5 is obtained by dividing the moving totals of column 4 by 24, the number of months in the column 4 totals. The monthly index values are obtained by dividing the monthly sales figures of column 2 by the centered moving average of column 5 and multiplying by 100.

The centered moving average of column 5 is in reality a weighted 13-month moving average. Thus, $376,000 represents the total of the 12

Table 30-4. Computation of Monthly Seasonal Index Values for Sales of the Gargo Company

(1) Year and month	(2) Sales in units of $1,000	(3) 12-month moving total in units of $1,000	(4) Centered 24-month moving total in units of $1,000, from (3)	(5) Centered moving average in units of $1,000 (4) ÷ 24	(6) Monthly index values (2) ÷ (5) × 100
1953					
Jan.	17				
Feb.	22				
Mar.	26				
Apr.	32				
May	38				
June	41	376			
July	47	375	751	31.3	150
Aug.	56	374	749	31.2	179
Sept.	43	373	747	31.1	138
Oct.	28	372	745	31.0	90
Nov.	11	370	742	30.9	36
Dec.	15	369	739	30.8	49
1954					
Jan.	16	366	735	30.6	52
Feb.	21	361	727	30.3	69
Mar.	25	359	720	30.0	83
Apr.	31	360	719	30.0	103
May	36	360	720	30.0	120
June	40	360	720	30.0	133
July	44	362	722	30.1	146
Aug.	51	367	729	30.4	168
Sept.	41	372	739	30.8	133
Oct.	29	377	749	31.2	93
Nov.	11	384	761	31.7	35
Dec.	15	392	776	32.3	46
1955					
Jan.	18	401	793	33.0	55
Feb.	26	410	811	33.8	77
Mar.	30	417	827	34.5	87
Apr.	36	420	837	34.9	103
May	43	422	842	35.1	123
June	48	425	847	35.3	136
July	53	428	853	35.5	149
Aug.	60	430	858	35.8	168
Sept.	48	433	863	36.0	133
Oct.	32	437	870	36.2	88
Nov.	13	441	878	36.6	36
Dec.	18	446	887	37.0	49
1956					
Jan.	21	452	898	37.4	56
Feb.	28	457	909	37.9	74
Mar.	33	463	920	38.3	86
Apr.	40	466	929	38.7	103
May	47	467	933	38.9	121
June	53	470	937	39.0	136
July	59	474	944	39.3	150
Aug.	65	480	954	39.8	163
Sept.	54	487	967	40.3	134
Oct.	35	496	983	41.0	85
Nov.	14	504	1,000	41.7	34
Dec.	21	514	1,018	42.4	50

Table 30-4. **Computation of Monthly Seasonal Index Values for Sales of the Gargo Company** (*Continued*)

(1) Year and month	(2) Sales in units of $1,000	(3) 12-month moving total in units of $1,000	(4) Centered 24-month moving total in units of $1,000, from (3)	(5) Centered moving average in units of $1,000 (4) ÷ 24	(6) Monthly index values (2) ÷ (5) × 100
1957					
Jan.	25	525	1,039	43.3	58
Feb.	34	538	1,063	44.3	77
Mar.	40	548	1,086	45.3	88
Apr.	49	554	1,102	45.9	107
May	55	557	1,111	46.3	119
June	63	560	1,117	46.5	135
July	70	564	1,124	46.8	150
Aug.	78	568	1,132	47.2	165
Sept.	64	574	1,142	47.6	134
Oct.	41	580	1,154	48.1	85
Nov.	17	586	1,166	48.6	35
Dec.	24	597	1,183	49.3	49
1958					
Jan.	29	606	1,203	50.1	58
Feb.	38	617	1,223	51.0	74
Mar.	46	626	1,243	51.8	89
Apr.	55	634	1,260	52.5	105
May	61	637	1,271	53.0	115
June	74	640	1,277	53.2	139
July	79	645	1,285	53.5	148
Aug.	89	650	1,295	54.0	165
Sept.	73	659	1,309	54.5	134
Oct.	49	668	1,327	55.3	89
Nov.	20	678	1,346	56.1	36
Dec.	27	691	1,369	57.0	47
1959					
Jan.	34	706	1,397	58.2	58
Feb.	43	721	1,427	59.5	72
Mar.	55	734	1,455	60.6	91
Apr.	64	743	1,477	61.5	104
May	71	746	1,489	62.0	115
June	87	750	1,496	62.3	140
July	94	751	1,501	62.5	150
Aug.	104	752	1,503	62.6	166
Sept.	86	752	1,504	62.7	137
Oct.	58	753	1,505	62.7	92
Nov.	23	753	1,506	62.8	37
Dec.	31	753	1,506	62.8	49
1960					
Jan.	35	754	1,507	62.8	56
Feb.	44	754	1,508	62.8	70
Mar.	55	755	1,509	62.9	87
Apr.	65	757	1,512	63.0	103
May	71	758	1,515	63.1	113
June	87	760	1,518	63.2	138
July	95				
Aug.	104				
Sept.	87				
Oct.	60				
Nov.	24				
Dec.	33				

monthly sales figures from January, 1953, through December, 1953, centered between June and July, 1953. And $375,000 represents the total of the 12 monthly sales figures from February, 1953, through January, 1954, centered between July and August, 1953. Also $751,000 represents the total of these 12-month moving totals, centered at July 15, 1953. This total contains the sales of February, 1953, through December, 1953, counted twice and January, 1953, and January, 1954, counted once each. The average is thus really a 13-month moving average weighted as follows: the month in which the average is centered is weighted by 2, the 5 months prior and subsequent to the centered month are also each weighted by 2, and the 6th months prior and subsequent to the centered month are each weighted by 1. All 12 months of the year are weighted equally, but the month which is 6 months away is weighted by the values in the two adjacent years.

In Table 30-5, we first compute an average index value for each month by totaling the index values for the same month in each year and dividing by the number of years. We then adjust these average monthly index values so that they average 100 per cent (add up to 1200 per cent). We do this by multiplying each average monthly index value by 1200 divided by the sum of the average monthly index values. In this case, the adjustment factor is $\frac{1200}{1200}$. Therefore, no adjustment is required in the values of the index.

Table 30-5. Computation of Adjusted Monthly Seasonal Indexes
for Sales of the Gargo Company

Month	1953	1954	1955	1956	1957	1958	1959	1960	Total monthly index values	Average monthly index values	Adjusted seasonal indexes
Jan.	...	52	55	56	58	58	58	56	393	56	56
Feb.	...	69	77	74	77	74	72	70	513	73	73
Mar.	...	83	87	86	88	89	91	87	611	87	87
Apr.	...	103	103	103	107	105	104	103	728	104	104
May	...	120	123	121	119	115	115	113	826	118	118
June	...	133	136	136	135	139	140	138	957	137	137
July	150	146	149	150	150	148	150	...	1043	149	149
Aug.	179	168	168	163	165	165	166	...	1174	168	168
Sept.	138	133	133	134	134	134	137	...	943	135	135
Oct.	90	93	88	85	85	89	92	...	622	89	89
Nov.	36	35	36	34	35	36	37	...	249	36	36
Dec.	49	46	49	50	49	47	49	...	339	48	48

Changing Patterns of Seasonal Variation. Seasonal patterns change. When these changes occur, separate charts of the seasonal index values for each month can be useful in disclosing the changing patterns.

An example of such a chart is shown in Figure 30-4 for the month of August. A straight-line trend with a slightly declining slope has been visually fitted to the data.

In this manner, we can construct trend charts for each month. These charts provide basic information of the patterns of seasonal change. They can thus assist in forecasting future seasonal index values.

Correcting Data for Seasonal Variations. To render data more comparable and useful for analytic purposes, it is desired to eliminate the seasonal variation. For this reason, many published economic and business time series are corrected or adjusted for seasonal variation. This is accomplished by dividing the actual value by the seasonal index: $TCSR \div S = TCR$. This will deflate values for the high-season periods and raise values for the low-season periods.

Modification and Deletion of Data. When using time-series analysis for forecasting, we are interested in projecting into the future those patterns which we expect to continue or recur. We must therefore use good judgment at every stage in our analysis. We should not hesitate to be selective or to adjust data where it will improve the accuracy of our forecast.

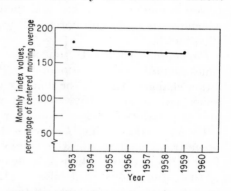

Figure 30-4. Seasonal trend for the month of August—Gargo Company.

For example, in constructing an average seasonal index from the monthly index values, the averaging process dampens the effects of some of the residual, irregular variations. However, these irregularities still influence the average seasonal index unless variations in opposite directions happen to cancel each other. For this reason, out-of-line seasonal values which are caused by factors which are not expected to occur in the future may be eliminated before computing the expected seasonal index.

Adjustments to Time-series Data. Adjustments to time-series data are sometimes desirable to improve their usefulness for time-series and correlation analysis. The three most common types of adjustments are those made to eliminate the effects of

1. Calendar variations
2. Price changes
3. Population changes

Calendar Variations. Monthly data can be corrected to reflect an average monthly value by multiplying the data for each month by the ratio of the average number of activity days per month in the year to the actual number of activity days in the month.

For sales data, every day may be considered an activity day. The January adjustment ratio would then be $\frac{365}{12} \div 31 = 0.98$. For production data, a working day may be considered an activity day. The January, 1961, adjustment ratio would then be $[249/12] \div 21 = 0.99$.

Price Changes. In many instances, dollar figures are used as the most convenient measures of sales or production volumes. However, if prices change during the period, the price changes will distort the effect of the physical volume changes. The dollar figures may be adjusted by dividing each value by an appropriate index of the price level during each period. The price-level index may be a specially constructed index measuring the price level of the items covered by the time series or may be a general price-level index such as are published by government and private groups, whichever is more appropriate. Price-index construction is discussed in Chapter 29.

Population Changes. In time-series and correlation analysis, it is sometimes helpful to adjust economic values to eliminate the effect of population changes. This can be done by dividing each value by a population index (population relative to a base year) or by working with values per unit of population. Sales volume per 100,000 persons is an example.

Using Time-series Analyses to Forecast. Our previous long-range-trend analysis for the Gargo Company developed the equation $Y = 318.5 + 64.0X$, where X is the number of years from the origin, July 1, 1953, and Y is annual sales in $1,000 units. Projecting this equation into the future, we can substitute values of X to obtain trend estimates for any year we desire. Judgment must then be applied to this estimate.

To obtain an estimate for the next year, 1961, we substitute $X = 8$ and obtain $Y_T = 830.5$. We must also take cyclical variations into account. Based upon general and industry economic analyses and forecasts as well as the Gargo Company's cyclical sales patterns, it is felt that a cyclical variation of 10 per cent below trend value would be a reasonable estimate. Forecasted sales adjusted for cyclical variation then become 90 per cent of 830.5, or 747.4.

Residual or irregular variations, by definition, cannot be forecast. However, an unusual event which is expected to affect sales may be forecast and used to modify our previous estimate.

To obtain monthly forecasts for 1961, we can adjust our trend equation as follows:

1. Compute a new a constant in terms of monthly instead of annual sales by dividing the annual value 318.5 by 12 to obtain 26.54.

2. Compute a new b constant in terms of monthly sales by dividing the annual value 64.0 by 144 (dividing by 12 twice) to obtain 0.444. (We divide by 12 twice: once to convert the data into monthly rather than annual sales and once to adjust to the fact that X increments will occur 12 times each year instead of once.)

3. To shift the origin for the annual data from July 1, 1953, to July 15, 1953, we add one-half month's value of b to a to obtain

$$a = 26.54 + \tfrac{1}{2}(0.444) = 26.76$$

Our trend equation then becomes $Y = 26.76 + 0.444X$, where X is the number of months from the origin, July 15, 1953, and Y is monthly sales in \$1,000 units.

We can now forecast the sales for October, 1961.

$$Y_T = 26.76 + 0.444(99) = 70.72 = T$$
$$S = 89$$
$$C = 90\%$$
$$TSC = 70.72 \left(\tfrac{89}{100}\right)\left(\tfrac{90}{100}\right) = 56.6$$

If monthly figures are desired for the entire year, a table can be set up to perform these calculations.

Our time-series forecast may still not represent the best judgment on what will occur next year. Time-series projections are valid only if the patterns which have occurred in the past will continue unchanged into the future. Independent correlation analysis and other methods discussed elsewhere in this volume will develop forecasts which can be used in conjunction with this time-series approach.

PROBLEMS

1. The population of the United States by decades as reported by the Bureau of the Census is listed in Table 30-6. Plot this time-series data on arithmetic graph paper. Draw a freehand nonlinear curve to indicate the trend of population growth.

2. The values of the Federal Reserve Board index of industrial production (1957 = 100) for the years 1919 to 1959 are listed in Table 30-7. Compute a linear trend line for this data using the method of least squares.

3. Plot the values of the FRB index, given in Table 30-7, on arithmetic graph paper. Draw the least-squares line computed in problem 2. Does the linear least-squares line provide a good visual fit?

4. We desire to hypothesize a constant rate of growth in industrial production rather than the constant annual increment of the straight-line trend of problems 2 and 3. We therefore want to fit an exponential equation of the form $Y = ab^x$ to the industrial production values. Compute the exponential trend line using the method of least squares.

5. Draw the exponential least-squares line computed in problem 4 on the chart of problem 3. Does the exponential least-squares line give a better visual fit than the linear one?

6. Plot the values of the FRB index, given in Table 30-7, on semilogarithmic graph paper. Draw the exponential least-squares line computed in problem 4. Does the exponential least-squares line give a good visual fit?

7. Compute a cyclical-residual index for the FRB index presented in problem 2. Plot the cyclical-residual index values on arithmetic graph paper.

Table 30-6. Population of the United States, 1800 to 1960

Year	Population (millions)	Year	Population (millions)	Year	Population (millions)
1800	5.3	1860	31.4	1920	105.7
1810	7.2	1870	38.6	1930	122.8
1820	9.6	1880	50.2	1940	131.7
1830	12.9	1890	62.9	1950	150.7
1840	17.1	1900	76.0	1960	180.7
1850	23.2	1910	92.0		

Table 30-7. Federal Reserve Board Index of Industrial Production, 1919–1959
(1957 = 100)

Year	Index	Year	Index	Year	Index	Year	Index
1919	24.8	1930	31.8	1941	56.1	1952	83.8
1920	26.0	1931	26.3	1942	68.9	1953	90.8
1921	20.0	1932	20.6	1943	82.4	1954	85.4
1922	25.4	1933	24.3	1944	81.1	1955	96.0
1923	30.3	1934	26.4	1945	70.0	1956	99.3
1924	28.4	1935	30.5	1946	59.2	1957	100.0
1925	31.3	1936	36.1	1947	65.3	1958	92.9
1926	33.1	1937	39.5	1948	68.0	1959	104.9
1927	33.1	1938	31.2	1949	64.3	1960	108.0
1928	34.5	1939	38.1	1950	74.5		
1929	38.2	1940	43.6	1951	80.8		

8. Listed in Table 30-8 are index numbers for the bottled soft drinks sector of the FRB index (1957 = 100) from 1947 to 1959. Compute seasonal indexes for this sector. (*Answer:* 75.8, 81.3, 85.2, 96.4, 109.6, 127.8, 131.9, 128.4, 108.5, 93.0, 79.8, 82.3.)

9. Refer to problem 8. Compute seasonally adjusted index numbers for the monthly values of the bottled soft drink sector of the FRB index for 1959 using the previously determined seasonal indexes.

Table 30-8. Index Numbers for the Bott'ed-soft-drinks Sector of the FRB Index of Industrial Production (1957 = 100)

Year	Jan.	Feb.	Mar.	Apr.	May	June	July	Aug.	Sept.	Oct.	Nov.	Dec.
1947	40.3	43.3	47.8	59.5	67.6	76.9	86.0	106.1	88.0	70.0	55.8	53.3
1948	49.6	58.1	62.2	77.2	79.8	95.0	102.7	97.6	84.4	65.3	58.6	57.1
1949	55.4	59.2	62.4	70.1	84.6	98.9	104.6	97.5	73.9	68.2	59.7	59.3
1950	56.4	59.6	62.5	71.4	81.2	94.2	91.8	93.0	79.2	74.0	59.9	62.0
1951	57.2	60.1	64.8	71.8	83.7	97.5	101.9	98.6	85.2	74.0	61.5	63.8
1952	62.1	65.5	68.1	77.7	88.8	115.3	113.8	104.7	89.6	75.5	68.0	67.8
1953	65.3	70.5	68.7	80.0	95.3	113.8	117.2	107.9	92.3	79.4	68.5	69.9
1954	67.3	70.8	72.2	77.3	93.7	111.3	117.1	103.0	96.8	86.2	66.0	71.2
1955	69.3	72.8	82.2	92.0	105.7	107.9	121.5	120.6	102.3	86.3	76.7	78.4
1956	74.4	81.2	85.4	92.1	105.9	124.6	118.5	120.4	100.4	91.5	81.3	89.0
1957	75.8	84.8	85.5	96.9	105.7	125.1	134.4	124.2	104.9	87.3	81.9	93.3
1958	75.7	80.8	83.0	99.2	108.9	124.7	125.1	125.7	107.6	92.9	84.2	90.6
1959	79.2	85.4	93.9	103.1	117.2	134.4	137.7	143.9	121.3	99.7	91.2	100.2

10. Refer to problem 8. Plot the seasonal index values for December from 1947 through 1958 on graph paper. (The index values for December for the twelve-year period are 73.3, 76.6, 79.9, 83.3, 80.3, 80.3, 81.5, 79.7, 82.4, 90.9, 93.4, 88.1.) Does the chart disclose any pattern of change?

31   Regression and Correlation Analysis

Regression and correlation analysis is designed to determine the nature and extent of relationships between variables. Such analysis is important for determining relationships useful in economic and business decision-making because controlled laboratory experimentation is often very difficult or impossible. Such studies can be useful in business forecasting. They can sometimes reveal the manner in which variations in the demand for products and services are caused by the interaction of various economic and technical factors.

Just as in forecasting with time series, the value of a past correlation pattern is dependent either upon the same pattern continuing into the future or upon the ability of the forecaster to modify the pattern appropriately by judgment. Regression and correlation analysis is therefore an aid to the application of good judgment. It is one of the important techniques to be used in conjunction with other approaches.

Regression and correlation studies can yield spurious as well as valid, useful relationships. A correlation, from chance causes, may sometimes be found between variables which could have no conceivable relationship to each other.

There are three principal aspects of regression and correlation analysis:

1. Determining a curve to describe the average relationship between two or more variables (frequently called the regression equation)

2. Evaluating how well this regression equation describes the relationship between the two or more variables, which is frequently done by measuring the dispersion about the regression line (standard error of the estimate) and the amount of association between the variables (coefficient of correlation)

3. Determining sampling error and confidence limits for the regression and correlation estimates of 1 and 2 above

In this chapter we shall stress the first two aspects because sampling-error and confidence-limit calculations have restricted applicability, especially when time-series data are used. We shall discuss simple linear regression and correlation, in which the relationship between two variables is represented by a straight line; multiple linear regression and correlation, in which we are concerned with the relationship among more than two variables; as well as the problem of sampling error and spurious correlations when using time-series data.

Simple Linear Regression. The Barbour Company manufactures and sells storm windows and screens to a local market. It is felt that the volume of sales is dependent to a great extent on the volume of local business payrolls. The volume of sales and of local payrolls for the years 1954 through 1959 is shown in Table 31-1.

Table **31-1. Sales of the Barbour Company and the Volume of Local Business Payrolls**

Year	Y Sales (in tens of thousands of dollars)	X Local business payroll (in tens of millions of dollars)
1954	35	48
1955	42	59
1956	48	70
1957	46	72
1958	50	75
1959	61	83

The volume of sales as a function of the size of local payrolls is shown in the scatter-diagram chart of Figure 31-1. For many purposes, drawing a freehand line which best indicates the trend of this relationship would be sufficient. In other situations, especially when the effects of a number of variables on sales are being investigated, more exact analysis may be valuable.

We can fit a least-squares line relating sales to the size of the local business payroll in the same manner as we fitted a least-squares line in the previous chapter on time-series analysis. In this case, the size of the local business payroll is the independent

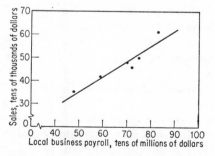

Figure 31-1. Scatter diagram showing Barbour Company sales as a function of local business payrolls.

variable (X) rather than time (the year). The dependent variable, Y, is volume of sales. We desire to determine the values for a and b in the relationship $Y = a + bX$. The coefficient b, which indicates the amount of change in Y per unit change in X, is called the regression coefficient.

Our normal equations are

$$\Sigma Y = Na + b\Sigma X$$
$$\Sigma XY = a\Sigma X + b\Sigma X^2$$

The calculations of ΣY, ΣX, ΣX^2, and ΣXY are performed in Table 31-2. We solve for a and b below.

$$282 = 6a + 407b$$
$$19,643 = 407a + 28,383b$$
$$a = 2.027$$
$$b = 0.663$$

Table 31-2. Calculation of Simple Linear Least-squares Regression

Year	Y Sales (in tens of thousands of dollars)	X Local business payrolls (in tens of millions of dollars)	X^2	XY
1954	35	48	2,304	1,680
1955	42	59	3,481	2,478
1956	48	70	4,900	3,360
1957	46	72	5,184	3,312
1958	50	75	5,625	3,750
1959	61	83	6,889	5,063
Total	282	407	28,383	19,643

Our regression equation is $Y = 2.03 + 0.663X$. This least-squares line is plotted in Figure 31-1. With a reliable forecast of next year's payroll value, we can use this equation to forecast next year's sales. For example, forecasting a total local payroll of $860,000,000 for the next year, we would estimate $Y = 2.03 + 0.663(86) = 59.05$.

Standard Error of Estimate. How good is this relationship of local payroll value as a means of forecasting the sales of the company? How good it will be in the future depends upon two factors: how good is the relationship as an explanation of past variations? will the same relationships hold true in the future as in the past?

The answer to the second question requires judgmental analysis of underlying conditions. The first question can be partially answered statistically by measuring the extent of the scatter (dispersion) of the actual values around the regression line in the past.

Just as dispersion about the mean is measured by the standard deviation, $\sigma_y = \sqrt{\Sigma(Y - \bar{Y})^2/N}$, where $\bar{Y}$ is the expected or forecast value, so dispersion or scatter about the regression line is measured by the standard error of the estimate, $S_y = \sqrt{\Sigma(Y - Y_F)^2/N}$, where Y_F is the calculated fitted or forecast value which is on the regression line. The standard error of estimate for our regression line is 2.418, as calculated in Table 31-3.

Table **31-3. Calculation of Standard Error of Estimate**

Year	Y Sales (in tens of thousands of dollars)	X Local business payroll (in tens of millions of dollars)	Y_F Fitted values	$Y - Y_F$	$(Y - Y_F)^2$
1954	35	48	33.85	+1.15	1.3225
1955	42	59	41.15	+0.85	0.7225
1956	48	70	48.44	−0.44	0.1936
1957	46	72	49.77	−3.77	14.2129
1958	50	75	51.76	−1.76	3.0976
1959	61	83	57.06	+3.94	15.5236
Total	...	...	.....	......	35.0727

$$S_y = \sqrt{\frac{\Sigma(Y - Y_F)^2}{N}} = \sqrt{\frac{35.0727}{6}} = 2.418, \text{ or } 2.42$$

$$S'_{y,\text{est}} = 2.418\sqrt{\tfrac{6}{4}} = 2.962, \text{ or } 2.96$$

The relationship between the standard error of estimate and our regression line is analogous to the one between the standard deviation and the mean. If we assume that the scatter about the regression line is produced by random variations following a normal pattern, which is approximately true in many cases, we can expect to find about 68 per cent of the sales values within a band $Y_F \pm 1S'_y$; about 95 per cent of the sales values within a band $Y_F \pm 2S'_y$; and more than 99 per cent within a band $Y_F \pm 3S'_y$. The foregoing percentages are based on the assumption that we know the standard error of estimate of the population. We do not usually know this, however. We must therefore estimate it from our sample just as we estimate σ'. We saw in Chapter 23 that $\sigma = \sqrt{\Sigma(X - \bar{X})^2/N}$, but $\sigma'_{\text{est}} = \sqrt{\Sigma(X - \bar{X})^2/(N - 1)}$. We divide by $N - 1$ for our population estimate because one degree of freedom was lost in calculating deviations from the mean: with a given $\bar{X}$ value, the last value in the sample cannot vary once the $N - 1$ values have been determined. Similarly, when dispersion about a regression line is calculated, each constant in the regression line reduces the number of degrees of freedom by one. For straight-line regression, the degrees of freedom are reduced by two, the number of constants, a and b. (If we had only two pairs of values, $N = 2$, the regression line would connect the two points and there would be no freedom for variation from the regression line.) The estimated population value of the standard error of the estimate, $S'_{y,\text{est}}$ for a straight-line regression is therefore

$S'_{y.\text{est}} = \sqrt{\Sigma(Y - Y_F)^2/(N - 2)} = S_y \sqrt{N/(N - 2)}$. For our example, $S'_{y.\text{est}} = 2.418 \sqrt{\tfrac{6}{4}} = 2.962$.

To estimate the percentage of the population falling within any given number of $S'_{y.\text{est}}$ of the regression line, we should use the Student's t distribution with $N - 2$ degrees of freedom rather than the normal distribution when our sample size is less than 30 sets of measurements.

The standard error of estimate lines for the regression of Barbour Company sales with local business payrolls is shown in Figure 31-2.[1]

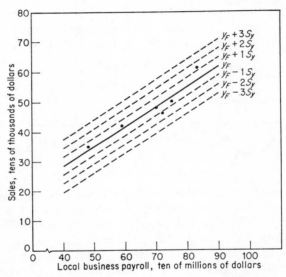

Figure 31-2. Scatter diagram showing linear regression line and standard error of estimate lines for Barbour Company sales as a function of local business payrolls.

Coefficient of Determination. The total dispersion of annual sales values over the six-year period is measured by the standard deviation of the annual sales. The square of the standard deviation, $\sigma_y{}^2$, called the variance, is a measure of the total variation of annual sales values. (σ_y is computed in Table 31-4.) The square of the standard error of estimate, $S_y{}^2$, is a measure of the total variation of annual sales values during this period not explained by the regression line. The ratio $S_y{}^2/\sigma_y{}^2$ measures the proportion of the total variation which is not explained by the regression line. $\left(S_y{}^2 = \dfrac{\Sigma(Y - Y_F)^2}{N} \right.$ and $\left. \sigma_y{}^2 = \dfrac{\Sigma(Y - \bar{Y})^2}{N} \right.$. Therefore, $\dfrac{S_y{}^2}{\sigma_y{}^2} = \dfrac{\Sigma(Y - Y_F)^2}{\Sigma(Y - \bar{Y})^2}$ equals the sum of the squares of the variations which

[1] Our discussion assumes that the distribution is homoscedastic. This means that S_y is the same regardless of the values of X.

are unexplained by the regression line divided by the sum of the squares of the total variation about the mean. This is the proportion of the total variation which is unexplained by the regression line.)

Table 31-4. **Calculation of the Standard Deviation of Barbour Company Sales**

Year	Y Sales (in tens of thousands of dollars)	Y^2
1954	35	1,225
1955	42	1,764
1956	48	2,304
1957	46	2,116
1958	50	2,500
1959	61	3,721
Total	282	13,630

$$\sigma_y = \sqrt{\frac{\Sigma Y^2}{N} - \left(\frac{\Sigma Y}{N}\right)^2} = \sqrt{\frac{13,630}{6} - \left(\frac{282}{6}\right)^2} = 7.916, \text{ or } 7.92$$

$$\sigma'_{y,\text{est}} = 7.916 \sqrt{\tfrac{6}{5}} = 8.668, \text{ or } 8.67$$

$1 - (S_y^2/\sigma_y^2)$ therefore measures the proportion of the total variation which is explained by the regression line. This proportion $1 - (S_y^2/\sigma_y^2)$ is called the coefficient of determination. For our regression line it equals $1 - [(2.418)^2/(7.916)^2] = 0.9067$. Our regression line explains 91 per cent of the variation in annual sales volume during the 1954 to 1959 period.

Coefficient of Correlation. The square root of the coefficient of determination, $\sqrt{1 - (S_y^2/\sigma_y^2)}$, is called the coefficient of correlation, designated as r. The coefficient of correlation has a value of 1 if $S_y^2 = 0$. S_y will equal zero if all the points fall on the regression line, meaning perfect correlation between the dependent and independent variables. The coefficient of correlation has a value of 0 if $S_y = \sigma_y$, meaning no correlation. The variation about the regression line is then equal to the total variation in the independent variable.

In our Barbour correlation example,

$$r = \sqrt{1 - (S_y^2/\sigma_y^2)} = \sqrt{1 - [(2.418)^2/(7.916)^2]} = 0.952$$

In actual practice, we can calculate r more directly from the following equation:

$$r = \frac{N\Sigma XY - (\Sigma X)(\Sigma Y)}{\sqrt{N\Sigma X^2 - (\Sigma X)^2} \sqrt{N\Sigma Y^2 - (\Sigma Y)^2}}$$

In our example,

$$r = \frac{6(19,643) - (407)(282)}{\sqrt{6(28,383) - (407)^2} \; \sqrt{6(13,630) - (282)^2}} = 0.952$$

Universe Values of Coefficients of Determination and Correlation. We can calculate estimates of the universe values of the coefficients of determination and correlation by using $S'_{y,\text{est}}$ and $\sigma'_{y,\text{est}}$ values:

$$(r'_{\text{est}})^2 = 1 - \frac{(S'_{y,\text{est}})^2}{(\sigma'_{y,\text{est}})^2} = 1 - \frac{(2.962)^2}{(8.668)^2} = 0.8832$$

$$r'_{\text{est}} = \sqrt{0.8832} = 0.940$$

We could also have used in this calculation the equivalent formula

$$r'_{\text{est}} = \sqrt{1 - \frac{S_y^2 \, (n-1)}{\sigma_y^2 \, (n-2)}}$$

When there is an inverse or negative correlation between two variables, the b value is negative in the regression equation. An increase in the independent variable results in a decrease in the dependent variable. The coefficient of correlation is then given a negative sign. Coefficients of correlation may thus vary from -1 to $+1$.

Meaning of a Correlation. When an apparent correlation between factors is ascertained by the regression analysis, it may be caused by random chance factors or be the effect of time-series patterns which have caused spurious results.

Even when it is not caused by the above factors, correlation does not necessarily mean that a cause-and-effect relationship exists. A correlation may involve covariation brought about by a common cause affecting both variables: e.g. the price of passenger cars and the price of trucks may show a high correlation because both will rise and fall together when the price of steel and wage costs rise and fall; the power losses and the heat generated in a power transmission line will show a high correlation because both are caused by common factors.

Correlation can also be indicative of interacting forces, such as wages and prices. An increase in wages may tend to cause prices to rise and an increase in prices may tend to pressure a rise in wages. Here it may not be very clear which is the dependent and which is the independent causative variable.

Multiple Correlation. In addition to the size of the local payroll as a determining factor of the sales volume of the Barbour Company, the change in the level of prices from year to year is also considered an important factor. We would therefore like to obtain a regression equation which relates sales volume to both the size of the local payroll and the change in prices from one year to the next. Such a regression equation would have the form

$$X_1 = a_{1.23} + b_{12.3}X_2 + b_{13.2}X_3$$

where X_1 = sales volume in tens of thousands of dollars

X_2 = size of local payroll in tens of millions of dollars

X_3 = change in price from one year to the next in units of index points

$a_{1.23}$ = constant value for the regression of 2 and 3 on 1

$b_{12.3}$ = net regression coefficient relating X_2 to X_1 taking X_3 into account

$b_{13.2}$ = net regression coefficient relating X_3 to X_1, taking X_2 into account

We determine the normal equations for solving for the values of $a_{1.23}$, $b_{12.3}$, and $b_{13.2}$ in the usual way.

$$\Sigma X_1 = Na_{1.23} + b_{12.3}\Sigma X_2 + b_{13.2}\Sigma X_3$$
$$\Sigma X_1 X_2 = a_{1.23}\Sigma X_2 + b_{12.3}\Sigma X_2{}^2 + b_{13.2}\Sigma X_2 X_3$$
$$\Sigma X_1 X_3 = a_{1.23}\Sigma X_3 + b_{12.3}\Sigma X_2 X_3 + b_{13.2}\Sigma X_3{}^2$$

Using an index of local prices, the percentage change in prices from the previous year (X_3) is shown in Table 31-5, together with sales of the Barbour Company (X_1) and the size of local payrolls (X_2) for each year from 1954 to 1959. ΣX_1, ΣX_2, ΣX_3, $\Sigma X_1 X_2$, $\Sigma X_1 X_3$, $\Sigma X_2 X_3$, $\Sigma X_1{}^2$, $\Sigma X_2{}^2$ and $\Sigma X_3{}^2$ are computed. The normal equations thus become

$$282 = 6a_{1.23} + 407b_{12.3} + 10b_{13.2}$$
$$19{,}643 = 407a_{1.23} + 28{,}383b_{12.3} + 734b_{13.2}$$
$$485 = 10a_{1.23} + 734b_{12.3} + 36b_{13.2}$$

Solving these equations, we obtain

$$a_{1.23} = -2.58$$
$$b_{12.3} = 0.7661$$
$$b_{13.2} = -1.430$$

Our regression equation is

$$X_1 = -2.58 + 0.7661X_2 - 1.430X_3$$

$\Sigma(X_1 - X_{1F})^2 = 3.6659$. Therefore, the standard error of estimate is

$$S_{1.23} = \sqrt{\frac{\Sigma(X_1 - X_{1F})^2}{N}} = \sqrt{\frac{3.6659}{6}} = 0.782$$

Our estimated standard error of estimate for the population of values is

$$S'_{1.23,\text{est}} = \sqrt{\frac{\Sigma(X_1 - X_{1F})^2}{N - 3}} = \sqrt{\frac{3.6659}{3}} = 1.105$$

Table 31-5. Calculation of Multiple Linear Least-squares Regression

Year	X_1 Sales (in tens of thousands of dollars)	X_2 Total local business payroll (in tens of millions of dollars)	X_3 Percentage change in prices from previous year (index points)	X_1^2	X_2^2	X_3^2	X_1X_2	X_1X_3	X_2X_3	X_{1p}	$(X_1 - X_{1p})$	$(X_1 - X_{1p})^2$
1954	35	48	−1	1,225	2,304	1	1,680	−35	−48	35.62	−0.62	0.3844
1955	42	59	+1	1,764	3,481	1	2,478	42	59	41.19	+0.81	0.6561
1956	48	70	+3	2,304	4,900	9	3,360	144	210	46.76	+1.24	1.5376
1957	46	72	+4	2,116	5,184	16	3,312	184	288	46.86	−0.86	0.7396
1958	50	75	+3	2,500	5,625	9	3,750	150	225	50.59	−0.59	0.3481
1959	61	83	0	3,721	6,889	0	5,063	0	0	61.01	−0.01	0.0001
Total	282	407	10	13,630	28,383	36	19,643	485	734	282.03	......	3.6659

(We have only $N - 3$ degrees of freedom in this correlation because the added constant for the extra dependent variable reduces our degrees of freedom by one more than in simple correlation.)

We note that the standard error of estimate of the multiple correlation is smaller than in the simple correlation which neglected the effect of price changes. Taking price changes into account has increased the effectiveness of our correlation. If we can anticipate price changes, it has increased our ability to forecast the future sales of the Barbour Company.

Our coefficient of multiple determination, $R^2_{1.23}$, is

$$R^2_{1.23} = 1 - \frac{S^2_{1.23}}{\sigma_1{}^2} = 1 - \left(\frac{0.782}{7.916}\right)^2 = 0.9902$$

99 per cent of the variations in sales volume are explained by the multiple-correlation equation. The coefficient of multiple correlation, $R_{1.23}$, is equal to $\sqrt{0.9902} = 0.995$.

To estimate universe values of the coefficients of multiple determination and correlation, we can use values of $S'_{1.23,est}$ and $\sigma'_{1,est}$ in the above formula or we can use the equivalent formula

$$(R'_{1.23...K,est})^2 = 1 - (1 - R^2_{1.23...K})\left(\frac{N - 1}{N - M}\right)$$

where K = number of variables in the regression equation and M = number of degrees of freedom lost in the regression equation. In this case, $K = 3$ and $M = 3$, giving

$$(R'_{1.23,est})^2 = 1 - (1 - 0.9902)\left(\frac{6 - 1}{6 - 3}\right) = 0.9837$$

In actual practice, we can calculate R^2 more directly from the following equation:

$$R^2_{1.23...K} = \frac{\left\{\begin{array}{l} b_{12.3...K}[N\Sigma X_1 X_2 - (\Sigma X_1)(\Sigma X_2)] + b_{13.2...K}[N\Sigma X_1 X_3 \\ \quad - (\Sigma X_1)(\Sigma X_3)] + \cdots + b_{1K.23...K-1}[N\Sigma X_1 X_K \\ \quad\quad - (\Sigma X_1)(\Sigma X_K)] \end{array}\right\}}{N\Sigma X_1{}^2 - (\Sigma X_1)^2}$$

In our example,

$$R^2_{1.23} = \frac{0.7661[6(19,643) - (282)(407)] - 1.430[6(485) - (282)(10)]}{6(13,630) - (282)^2}$$

$$= 0.9902$$

Partial Correlation. In multiple-correlation analysis, we frequently would like to measure the relative importance of each of the independent variables (X_2, X_3, X_4, etc.) separately in explaining variations in the dependent variable (X_1), while at the same time allowing for the variations in the other independent variable. Thus, in our previous example, we might be interested in determining the correlation of sales with total local business payroll, taking account of the percentage change in prices from previous years. This is not the same as the simple correlation of sales with total local business payroll, ignoring the percentage change in prices from previous years.

We may compute coefficients of partial determination and correlation to measure the extent to which the variation in the independent variable which was not explained by all the other dependent variables is explained by the addition of the new independent variable. Thus, $r_{12.3}$ measures the partial correlation between X_1 and X_2 after X_3 has been taken into account and $r_{13.2}$ measures the partial correlation between X_1 and X_3 after X_2 has been taken into account. $r_{12.3}^2$ and $r_{13.2}^2$ are the respective coefficients of partial determination.

In our illustrative example, we found that r_{12}^2 equaled 0.9067, indicating that local business payroll explained 90.67 per cent of the variation in Barbour Company sales. We also found that $R_{1.23}^2$ equaled 0.9902, indicating that local business payroll and percentage change in prices from the previous year together explained 99.02 per cent of the variation in Barbour Company sales. The amount of additional explanation produced by the addition of the extra independent variable, percentage change in prices from the preceding year, is thus $99.02 - 90.67 = 8.35$ per cent. The importance of this additional explanation can be determined by comparing it with the amount of unexplained variation before the extra independent variable was added, $1 - 0.9067 = 0.0933$. Dividing 0.0835 by 0.0933 gives us a coefficient of partial determination, $r_{13.2}^2 = 0.8950$. The coefficient of partial correlation is then $r_{13.2} = \sqrt{0.8950} = 0.946$.

The algebraic formulation of this calculation is

$$r_{13.2}^2 = \frac{(1 - r_{12}^2) - (1 - R_{1.23}^2)}{1 - r_{12}^2} = 1 - \frac{1 - R_{1.23}^2}{1 - r_{12}^2}$$

$$r_{13.2}^2 = 1 - \frac{1 - 0.9902}{1 - 0.9067} = 0.8950$$

$$r_{13.2} = \sqrt{0.8950} = 0.946$$

The coefficients of partial determination and correlation of sales with local business payroll, after the percentage change in prices from the previous year has been taken into account, are

$$r_{12.3}^2 = 1 - \frac{1 - R_{1.23}^2}{1 - r_{13}^2} = 1 - \frac{1 - 0.9902}{1 - 0.0310^*} = 0.9899$$

$$r_{12.3} = \sqrt{0.9899} = 0.995$$

X_2 thus appears to be of considerably greater importance than is X_3 in determining the value of X_1.

$$^* r_{13}^2 = \frac{[N\Sigma X_1 X_3 - (\Sigma X_1)(\Sigma X_3)]^2}{[N\Sigma X_1^2 - (\Sigma X_1)^2][N\Sigma X_3^2 - (\Sigma X_3)^2]} = \frac{[6(485) - (282)(10)]^2}{[6(13,630) - (282)^2][6(36) - (10)^2]}$$
$$= 0.0310$$

When we have more than two independent variables, the procedure is similar. Thus,

$$r^2_{14.23} = \frac{(1 - R^2_{1.23}) - (1 - R^2_{1.234})}{(1 - R^2_{1.23})} = 1 - \frac{1 - R^2_{1.234}}{1 - R^2_{1.23}}$$

$$r^2_{13.24} = 1 - \frac{1 - R^2_{1.234}}{1 - R^2_{1.24}}$$

And

$$r^2_{12.345} = 1 - \frac{1 - R^2_{1.2345}}{1 - R^2_{1.345}}$$

The importance of each of the individual independent variables in explaining variations in the dependent variable, allowing for the other independent variables, may also be compared using the regression coefficients in the multiple-regression equation. Thus, in our illustrative example, $b_{12.3} = 0.7661$ tells us that for each unit increase in local business payroll (expressed in tens of millions of dollars), sales will increase by 0.7661 units (expressed in tens of thousands of dollars). $b_{13.2} = -1.430$ tells us that for each unit increase in the percentage change in prices from previous years (expressed in index points), sales will decrease 1.430 units (expressed in tens of thousands of dollars). The size of these regression coefficients, $b_{12.3}$ and $b_{13.2}$, obviously depends upon the units in which X_1, X_2, and X_3 are expressed. We can make them more comparable by expressing each variable in terms of its standard deviation. They are then called beta coefficients (β) and are pure numbers whose magnitudes do not depend upon the units of measure in which they are expressed. Thus, the regression equation

$$X_1 = a_{1.23} + b_{12.3}X_2 + b_{13.2}X_3$$

becomes

$$\frac{X_1}{\sigma_1} = a'_{1.23} + \beta_{12.3}\frac{X_2}{\sigma_2} + \beta_{13.2}\frac{X_3}{\sigma_3}$$

$$X_1 = \sigma_1 a'_{1.23} + \beta_{12.3}\frac{\sigma_1}{\sigma_2}X_2 + \beta_{13.2}\frac{\sigma_1}{\sigma_3}X_3$$

Therefore, $b_{12.3} = \beta_{12.3}\dfrac{\sigma_1}{\sigma_2}$ and $b_{13.2} = \beta_{13.2}\dfrac{\sigma_1}{\sigma_3}$, and

$$\beta_{12.3} = b_{12.3}\frac{\sigma_2}{\sigma_1}$$

$$\beta_{13.2} = b_{13.2}\frac{\sigma_3}{\sigma_1}$$

For our example,[1]

$$\beta_{12.3} = 0.7661\tfrac{11.364}{7.916} = 1.0998$$
$$\beta_{13.2} = -1.430\tfrac{1.795}{7.916} = -0.3243$$

---

[1] $\sigma_2 = \sqrt{\dfrac{\Sigma X_2{}^2}{N} - \left(\dfrac{\Sigma X_2}{N}\right)^2} = \sqrt{\dfrac{28{,}383}{6} - \left(\dfrac{407}{6}\right)^2} = 11.364$

$\sigma_3 = \sqrt{\dfrac{\Sigma X_3{}^2}{N} - \left(\dfrac{\Sigma X_3}{N}\right)^2} = \sqrt{\dfrac{36}{6} - \left(\dfrac{10}{6}\right)^2} = 1.795$

X_2 thus appears to be of considerably greater importance than X_3 in determining variations in the value of X_1 when we use β coefficients, which are independent of the units of measure, for the comparison.

In our example, the beta coefficients and the coefficients of partial correlation both rank our two independent variables in the same order of importance, but not the same relative magnitude of importance, in determining the values of the dependent variable. This is not always true, but is usually the case.

In studying correlation relationships, it is important to keep in mind that intercorrelations may distort or hide the true correlation between variables. Thus, if A is negatively correlated with C and C is positively correlated with B, the correlation of A with B may be lost in a simple correlation analysis even though a positive correlation exists. Increases in C which are not noted in the simple correlation analysis will reduce the value of A while at the same time increases in B will increase the value of A, tending to cancel out the correlation. The same tendency would result if A were positively correlated with B and C, but B and C were negatively correlated. Analysis of intercorrelations is therefore advisable in many studies.

Sampling Error. We previously pointed out that it is possible to obtain a regression equation which gives a good explanation of the variation in values of a variable owing just to the random variations of sampling. Using sampling theory, various statistical procedures are available for testing the significance of these regressions, i.e. determining whether they could have been caused by chance assuming random sampling from a population of uncorrelated values as well as establishing confidence limits for the various sample values. In the case of multiple correlation, we can also test to determine whether the reduction in the dispersion from the regression-equation line when one or more additional independent variables are added is statistically significant. This is important because the use of additional independent variables in multiple correlation will usually decrease the unexplained variation even when there is no true relationship between the dependent variable and the independent variable we are studying.

However, we cannot consider that we have one single population from which we are sampling when we use time-series data. If in actual practice the underlying conditions remain relatively stable with the passage of time, this qualification may not be too important. We must therefore examine all the relevant data and environmental information to ascertain whether the population from which we have sampled was sufficiently uniform during the sample period; and whether any period into which the correlation relationship is being extrapolated is sufficiently similar to the period from which the data was drawn to justify using the originally derived relationship.

Moreover, our error formulas are based upon random-sampling theory. We have observed in a previous chapter that this means that each observation should have an equal opportunity with all others in the population to be chosen for the sample and that the values of previous observations should have no effect on the values of future ones. In time series, the values are autocorrelated (serially correlated). The succeeding values are not independent of the preceding values. And most data used in business forecasting is time-series data, even if, as in our illustrative example in this chapter, time (years) is not an explicit independent variable in the analysis.

When time-series data are used in a correlation analysis, we may sometimes obtain a spurious appearance of correlation because of the effects of similar trend, cyclical, and seasonal patterns on some of the correlated variables. This intercorrelation will tend to invalidate the error formula based upon random sampling.

One way to eliminate or reduce the effects of autocorrelation and intercorrelation of the data is to perform the correlation using first differences of all of the variables. First differences are obtained by subtracting the immediately preceding value from each observation. Autocorrelation is reduced or eliminated because the amount and direction of change of the successive values in a time series are usually not dependent, or as dependent, upon the previous amount and direction of change as are the absolute values. Thus, if the stock of an item in a warehouse was 75,000 yesterday, the stock value today can only be more or less than this 75,000 by the amount of receipts and/or deliveries during the day. Today's value is strongly influenced by the 75,000 stock yesterday. However, the increase in stock of 10,000 units which occurred yesterday would tend to have no influence on the size or direction of the change in stock today (except for the effect of possible capacity limitations in the warehouse). In a like manner, intercorrelation of time-series data because of similar trends will usually be reduced when first differences of the variable are used.

The use of first differences is illustrated in the D. B. Suits' multiple-regression determination of the demand for automobiles in Chapter 32.

When confidence-limits calculations are used in correlation studies involving time series, the limitations on the validity of these limits should be kept in mind. In correlation studies, good judgment and thorough knowledge of all the factors and their interrelationships is of greater importance than confidence-limits calculations when time-series data is used.

Nonlinear Correlation. In this chapter we have considered only linear (straight-line) correlation. This is the most frequently used relationship because it is simplest and usually well-suited to the task. The methods of least-squares fitting for several types of nonlinear curves were described in Chapter 30 for time series. These same nonlinear relationships can be used in regression and correlation analysis and these methods should be used where nonlinear correlation patterns are indicated.

The least-squares regression procedures will yield a strictly true relationship only if the assumed form of the regression equation is correct; if there is truly only one dependent variable; and if there are no errors of observation in any of the independent or dependent variables. (If there are errors of observation in the dependent variable and the errors are uncorrelated with the independent variables, the results will still be strictly true.) However, as long as the observation errors are of a generally random character and are small relative to the magnitude of the true variation, the least-squares bias will not prevent us from arriving at approximately true relationships.

PROBLEMS

Listed in Table 31-6 are index numbers (1947–1949 = 100) for per capita consumption of food, per capita disposable income, and price of food for 1922 to 1941 and 1948 to 1956, prepared by the Agricultural Marketing Service of the U.S. Department of Agriculture.

1. Referring to Table 31-6, plot per capita consumption of food as a function of per capita disposable income for the periods covered by the data. Fit a trend line by visual inspection.

2. Referring to Table 31-6, compute a linear least-squares regression equation relating per capita consumption of food to per capita disposable income.

3. Draw the least-squares line of problem 2 on the graph of problem 1 or on another graph on which the per capita consumption of food as a function of per capita disposable income has been plotted for the periods covered by the data.

4. Compute the coefficients of correlation and determination for the regression of problem 2. What is the meaning of the computed values of these coefficients? Does this correlation indicate that changes in disposable income cause changes in food consumption?

5. (a) Compute the standard error of estimate (S_y) of the regression of problem 2 using the coefficient of determination from problem 4. (b) Compute the estimated population standard error of estimate $(S'_{y,\text{est}})$ of the regression of problem 2.

6. Draw lines representing $Y_F \pm 1S'_{y,\text{est}}$, $Y_F \pm 2S'_{y,\text{est}}$ and $Y_F \pm 3S'_{y,\text{est}}$ on the

Table 31-6. Index Numbers for Price of Food, per Capita Consumption of Food, and Disposable Income

Year	Per capita consumption of food	Per capita disposable income*	Price of food*
1922	89.0	61.0	83.0
1923	90.9	68.3	84.2
1924	91.5	67.4	83.2
1925	90.9	68.5	87.7
1926	92.1	69.6	89.9
1927	90.9	70.2	88.3
1928	90.9	71.9	88.4
1929	91.1	75.2	89.5
1930	90.7	68.3	87.4
1931	90.0	64.0	79.1
1932	87.8	53.9	73.3
1933	88.0	53.2	75.2
1934	89.1	58.0	81.1
1935	87.3	63.2	84.7
1936	90.5	70.5	84.5
1937	90.4	72.5	84.9
1938	90.6	67.8	80.3
1939	93.8	73.2	79.3
1940	95.5	77.6	79.8
1941	97.5	89.5	83.0
1948	99.1	100.6	101.3
1949	98.9	100.1	98.2
1950	99.9	106.8	98.4
1951	98.1	106.6	101.4
1952	100.4	107.6	101.0
1953	101.5	110.8	98.6
1954	101.4	110.3	98.1
1955	102.8	115.5	96.9
1956	104.0	118.4	95.9

* Deflated by dividing by the Bureau of Labor Statistics consumer price index.

graph of problem 3. What percentage of the actual per capita consumption values fall within (a) $Y_F \pm 1S'_{y,\text{est}}$? (b) $Y_F \pm 2S'_{y,\text{est}}$? (c) $Y_F \pm 3S'_{y,\text{est}}$?

7. Referring to the data on food consumption in Table 31-6, compute the coefficients of correlation and determination for the regression relating the consumption of food to the price of food. What is the meaning of the computed values of these coefficients?

8. Referring to the preceding data, compute a linear multiple-regression equation by the method of least squares, relating consumption of food to per capita disposable personal income and the price of food.

9. Refer to the multiple regression of problem 8. Compute the (a) coefficient of multiple determination, (b) coefficient of multiple correlation, (c) standard error of the estimate.

10. Refer to the multiple regression of problem 8. Compute the (a) coefficients of partial determination and correlation of consumption of food with per capita disposable income, taking account of the price of food; (b) coefficients of partial determination and correlation of consumption of food with the price of food, taking account of per capita personal income. Then interpret the results of these computations.

11. Refer to the multiple-regression equation of problem 8. Compute the beta coefficients for this multiple correlation. Explain the meaning of the computed values of the beta coefficients.

12. Compare and interpret the results of the partial-correlation analyses of problems 10 and 11.

13. Compute the estimated population value of the coefficient of multiple correlation (R'_{est}) of problem 9.

32 Econometric Models, Demand Analysis, and Sales Forecasting

In previous chapters, we considered a number of subjects which are useful in general business and economic forecasting. We shall now consider more specific mathematical techniques for explaining the relationships between economic variables (econometric models), for understanding the nature of the demand for a product (demand analysis), and for forecasting the sales of a company's products and services (sales forecasting).

Fundamental to any engineering or business decision is a forecast of the future requirements for the goods or services sold by the enterprise. Future income to provide a return on investment in research or equipment or future savings to justify procurement of cost-reduction facilities are both dependent on future sales. Great accuracy in the technical and cost analyses will be of little value in assuring profitable business decisions if the sales-revenue forecast is invalid.

Sales forecasts are also required for all enterprise planning, including the economic planning of production. Short- and long-range budgeting of most of the activities in the enterprise is dependent upon short- and long-range sales forecasting.

Sales are functions of many factors: price, the price of competitive items, expected future prices, and payment terms; the relative quality of the product design, the production, and the performance; the amounts and distribution of purchasing power; the amounts and effectiveness of advertising and promotion; if a permanent product, the number and the age distribution of the items still in use; the obsolescence of the product. These are some of the more common variables. Many additional ones are important in individual instances.

There are an infinite variety of methods and combination of methods for forecasting sales. There is no one approach which will always give best results under all circumstances. Some methods are more useful under one set of conditions than under another. Each method has advantages and disadvantages which determine when it will be most useful. Many of the approaches are most useful in combination with each other.

Forecasts of the Economy. The general level of business activity will have an effect on the sales of most companies. In addition, the level of activity in various sectors of the economy has a greater effect on certain industries than on others. The machine tool industry is very sensitive to changes in the level of capital investments; the cement industry to changes in the level of construction and road-building activity; and the automobile industry to the level of disposable or supernumerary income.

We described in Chapter 29 three systems for measuring activity in our economic system: national-income accounting, flow-of-funds accounting, and input-output accounting. We also discussed the BLS wholesale and consumer price indexes, the FRB industrial production indexes, and business indicators. These and other measures can be useful in forecasting business conditions. The use of these economic measures is facilitated by the availability of forecasts of future values for these measures from governmental and private sources. The problem is not in finding these forecasts, but in establishing which of the large number of often conflicting predictions is the most valid.

Various surveys are made in attempts to measure people's expectations of future economic quantities. Survey studies of such items as capital-spending plans, consumer-buying intentions, and general-business-level expectations are made by numerous government and private organizations. Some of these, such as a survey of capital-spending plans, can be very useful in forecasting. Others, such as a survey of businessmen's own forecasts of future business levels, have more limited usefulness because they reflect the personal biases and points of view of each businessman. All surveys of this kind, including those of consumer-buying intentions, suffer from the fact that, for various reasons, people do not always report their intentions accurately and they also change their minds.

Forecasting general business conditions requires a balanced evaluation of many factors. The strategy for such forecasting should be to consider all approaches which have a potential for contributing to the accuracy of the forecast. In some cases, multiple approaches should be used to forecast the same items independently and the reasons for any differences in the independent forecasts ascertained. In other cases, the approaches are preferably used in combination with each other so that they complement each other at each stage of the forecasting procedure.

A large proportion of economic quantities and relationships change relatively slowly. Therefore, if one has the most current information on these slow-changing relationships, he will frequently not be too far off if he assumes that they will not change in the short run.

A small number of economic factors are almost completely stable on a short-term basis and, once they are known, can be used with a high degree of confidence that they will not be affected by economic developments during the period. These include such items as population, minimum wage rates prescribed by law, union contract wage rates, age distribution of many types of physical assets, productive and warehouse capacity, etc. Other factors are only slightly less stable, such as capital-budgeting plans of companies, tax rates, budget plans of government units, etc. Still other factors must, of necessity, be estimated with the possibility of large subjective bias: the effect of political elections, consumer psychology, and foreign monetary and market changes are examples of these unstable factors. The forecasted future values of these items are based to some degree upon personal opinion.

Econometric models of the economy can also be useful in this forecasting process, especially in predicting turning points and other changes in business cycles.

Econometric (Mathematical) Models of the Economy. The term "econometric model" is used to signify a mathematical representation of how economic forces operate. Many of the mathematical representations previously presented in this volume can therefore be considered econometric models. Thus, a simple mathematical representation of the theory of the firm, such as presented in Chapter 28, constitutes an econometric model. The various national accounting systems for measuring economic activity, previously discussed in Chapter 29, are also based upon models of the economy. However, they do not have the structural mathematical relationships of the formal mathematical model.

The econometric approach to mathematical model building and forecasting has the following elements:

1. Development of a satisfactory theory or theories to explain relationships between economic variables
2. Translation of the theory or theories into mathematical equations using symbols
3. Calculation of the constants in the equations based upon past data
4. Using the model to forecast future values of economic measures
5. Evaluating the usefulness (reliability and validity) of the model for explaining economic relationships and forecasting the values of economic measures

To clarify the application of econometric model building to the forecasting of general business conditions, we briefly discuss in this chapter the development of an econometric model of the whole economy of the United States. As the basis for illustrating our discussion, we shall use Klein and Goldberger's econometric model of the United States, based upon data from 1929 to 1952.[1] The Klein and Goldberger model has 20 equations with 65 variables.

The economic variables in the model are divided into two categories: exogenous and endogenous. Exogenous (independent) variables are those

[1] See L. R. Klein and A. S. Goldberger, *An Econometric Model of the United States, 1929–1952*, North-Holland Publishing Company, Amsterdam, 1955.

Table 32-1. Exogenous Variables (and Symbols) Used in Klein-Goldberger Equations

h = index of hours worked per person per year (1939 base = 100)

p_I = index of prices of imports (1939 base = 100)

t = time trend in years

F_A = index of agricultural exports (1939 base = 100)

F_E = exports of goods and services in 1939 dollars

G = government expenditures for goods and services in 1939 dollars

N = number of persons in the labor force

N_E = number of nonfarm entrepreneurs

N_F = number of farm operators

N_G = number of government employees

N_P = number of persons in the United States

R = excess reserves of banks as a percentage of total reserves

T = deflated indirect taxes less subsidies

T_A = deflated taxes less transfers associated with farm income

T_C = deflated corporate income taxes

T_P = deflated personal and corporate taxes less transfers associated with nonwage nonfarm income

T_W = deflated personal and payroll taxes less transfers associated with wage and salary income

W_2 = deflated government employee compensation

Table 32-2. Endogenous Variables (and Symbols) Used in Klein-Goldberger Equations

i_L = average yield on corporate bonds

i_S = average yield on short-term commercial paper

p = price index of gross national product (1939 base = 100)

p_A = index of agricultural prices (1939 base = 100)

w = index of hourly wages (1939 base = 122.1)

A_1 = deflated farm income

A_2 = deflated government payments to farmers

B = deflated end-of-year corporate surplus

C = consumer expenditures in 1939 dollars

D = capital consumption charges in 1939 dollars

F_I = imports of goods and services in 1939 dollars

I = gross private domestic capital formation in 1939 dollars

K = end-of-year stock of private capital in 1939 dollars

L_1 = deflated end-of-year liquid assets held by persons

L_2 = deflated end-of-year liquid assets held by enterprises

N_W = number of wage and salary earners

P = deflated nonwage nonfarm income

P_C = deflated corporate profits

S_P = deflated corporate savings

W_1 = deflated private employee compensation

Y = deflated national income

which influence the values of the endogenous variables but are themselves not influenced by factors in the system. In theory, the values of exogenous variables are completely determined by factors outside the system. Strict conformance to this definition would include only such items as weather in this category. In practice, many factors dependent upon public policy and population characteristics are considered exogenous. All other variables are endogenous (dependent and interacting) variables. The values of endogenous variables are affected by the values of the exogenous factors and other endogenous factors. Thus, we may consider that, given a set of initial conditions, the exogenous variables, plus random factors, determine the movement of the closed system of endogenous variables through time.

The exogenous variables used in the Klein-Goldberger equations and their symbols are shown in Table 32-1. The endogenous variables and their symbols are shown in Table 32-2.

The structure of each equation in the model is based upon theoretical considerations which are explicitly stipulated. Thus, the structure of the depreciation equation was developed with the following rationale.[1]

Depreciation data in our model are based on accounting records although they are revalued from accounting to current and constant prices. Most accounting estimates of depreciation charges are based on the straight-line method applied to original cost. To clarify the meaning of this remark, let us consider a homogeneous producer good, say a machine, bought in the amount of x_t during period t. The variable x_t represents gross investment. Suppose that the machine has an estimated lifetime of h periods. At the beginnning of the investment process, in period 1, we have

$$x_1 = \text{gross investment in period 1}$$

$$\frac{1}{2h}x_1 = D_1 = \text{depreciation in period 1}$$

During the first period the equipment depreciates by only half the usual periodic amount on the assumption that purchases are spread evenly throughout the period.

$$x_2 = \text{gross investment in period 2}$$

$$\frac{1}{h}x_1 + \frac{1}{2h}x_2 = D_2 = \text{depreciation in period 2}$$

The variable x_t represents money outlay during period t, and D_t represents money value of book depreciation charges during period t. If equipment prices have changed between periods 1 and 2, one component of D_2 will be at the prices of period 1 and the other component at the prices of period 2. This is the sense in which book depreciation data are valued in accounting prices.

In general, after the investment and depreciation process has been going on for several periods, we have

$$\frac{1}{2h}x_{t-h} + \frac{1}{h}x_{t-h+1} + \cdots + \frac{1}{h}x_{t-1} + \frac{1}{2h}x_t = D_t$$

The prices of the current period and the past h periods are averaged in determining the price level on which D_t is based.

By appropriate weighting of past prices in the durable goods sector of the economy, we can convert D_t from a measure in terms of accounting prices to a measure in terms of current or constant prices. In constant prices, depreciation

[1] *Ibid.*, pp. 15–16.

is a moving average of past values of gross investment measured also in constant prices. The length of the moving average is determined by the average lifetime of capital goods.

In our model we have used estimates of depreciation revalued to constant prices but do not have explicit series of gross investment prior to 1929; therefore, we did not assume depreciation to be strictly a moving average of past gross investment. Instead, we let depreciation depend on the size of the stock of capital. This gives an approximation to the mechanical aspect of depreciation, the amount of capital consumption that goes on regardless of the rate of utilization. The level of aggregate economic activity, showing the degree of utilization of capital, may also be important in inducing entrepreneurs to depart from conventional straight-line methods. Our depreciation equation [equation (5) in Table 32-4] thus takes the form

$$D_t = \epsilon_0 + \epsilon_1 \frac{K_t + K_{t-1}}{2} + \epsilon_3 (Y + T + D - W_2)_t + u_{5t}$$

$Y + T + D - W_2$ = private gross national product in 1939 dollars

Five of the equations in the model represent definitional relationships between variables. These are shown in Table 32-3.

Table 32-3. Definitional Equations of Klein-Goldberger Model

$$C_t + I_t + G_t + (F_E)_t - (F_I)_t = Y_t + T_t + D_t$$
$$(W_1)_t + (W_2)_t + P_t + (A_1)_t + (A_2)_t = Y_t$$
$$h_t \frac{w_t}{p_t} (N_W)_t = (W_1)_t + (W_2)_t$$
$$K_t - K_{t-1} = I_t - D_t$$
$$B_t - B_{t-1} = (S_P)_t$$

These equations are definitions or identities which are exactly true at all times and have no random variations in the relationships. There are therefore no constants to be estimated by statistical analysis, provided we measure all our variables in such a way that they precisely fulfill these definitional equations.

The remaining fifteen equations, shown in Table 32-4, represent mathematical expressions of a theory of the relationships among economic variables and are only approximately true at any time because of random, error variations. Some of these equations relate the behavior characteristics of different groups (consumers, investors, etc.) in the economy. Others relate to the tendency for adjustments to occur in the various markets to bring supply and demand into balance. Still others relate the technological or other constraints within which the economic system must operate.

These equations have constants (or coefficients) which must be estimated by statistical methods. The least-squares method for regression analysis, discussed in Chapter 31, is a relatively simple method of making these estimates. However, this method allows only one variable in the equation to be designated as dependent on other variables in the system. Because relationships in the Klein-Goldberger equations contain more than one endogenous variable in an equation, the simultaneous-equation method of determining the coefficients in the equations was used rather than the least-squares method and was applied in modified fashion because of computational and other limitations.

Table 32-4. Theory Equations of Klein-Goldberger Model

$$C_t = -22.26 + 0.55(W_1 + W_2 - T_W)_t + 0.41(P - T_P - S_P)_t$$
$$+ 0.34(A_1 + A_2 - T_A)_t + 0.26C_{t-1} + 0.072(L_1)_{t-1} + 0.26(N_P)_t \quad (1)$$

$$I_t = -16.71 + 0.78(P - T_P + A_1 + A_2 - T_A + D)_{t-1} - 0.073K_{t-1} + 0.14(L_2)_{t-1} \quad (2)$$

$$(S_P)_t = -3.53 + 0.72(P_C - T_C)_t + 0.076(P_C - T_C - S_P)_{t-1} - 0.028B_{t-1} \quad (3)$$

$$(P_C)_t = -7.60 + 0.68P_t \quad (4)$$

$$D_t = 7.25 + 0.10 \frac{K_t + K_{t-1}}{2} + 0.044(Y + T + D - W_2)_t \quad (5)$$

$$(W_1)_t = -1.40 + 0.24(Y + T + D - W_2)_t + 0.24(Y + T + D - W_2)_{t-1}$$
$$+ 0.29t \quad (6)$$

$$(Y + T + D - W_2)_t = -26.08 + 2.17[h(N_W - N_G) + N_E + N_F]_t$$
$$+ 0.16 \frac{K_t + K_{t-1}}{2} + 2.05t \quad (7)$$

$$w_t - w_{t-1} = 4.11 - 0.74(N - N_W - N_E - N_F)_t + 0.52(p_{t-1} - p_{t-2}) + 0.54t \quad (8)$$

$$(F_I)_t = 0.32 + 0.0060(W_1 + W_2 - T_W + P - T_P + A_1 + A_2 - T_A)_t \frac{p_t}{(p_I)_t}$$
$$+ 0.81(F_I)_{t-1} \quad (9)$$

$$(A_1)_t \frac{p_t}{(p_A)_t} = -0.36 + 0.054(W_1 + W_2 - T_W + P - T_P - S_P)_t \frac{p_t}{(p_A)_t}$$
$$- 0.007(W_1 + W_2 - T_W + P - T_P - S_P)_{t-1} \frac{p_{t-1}}{(p_A)_{t-1}} + 0.012(F_A)_t \quad (10)$$

$$(p_A)_t = -131.17 + 2.32p_t \quad (11)$$

$$(L_1)_t = 0.14(W_1 + W_2 - T_W + P - T_P - S_P + A_1 + A_2 - T_A)_t$$
$$+ 76.03(i_L - 2.0)_t^{-0.34} \quad (12)$$

$$(L_2)_t = -0.34 + 0.26(W_1)_t - 1.02(i_S)_t - 0.26(p_t - p_{t-1}) + 0.61(L_2)_{t-1} \quad (13)$$

$$i_L = 2.58 + 0.44(i_S)_{t-3} + 0.26(i_S)_{t-5} \quad (14)$$

$$100 \frac{(i_S)_t - (i_S)_{t-1}}{(i_S)_{t-1}} = 11.17 - 0.67R_t \quad (15)$$

In the simultaneous-equation method, we determine the regression of a set of endogenous (jointly dependent) variables upon a set of exogenous (independent) variables. The number of equations must equal the number of endogenous variables.

The simultaneous-equation method is generally a rather complicated, burdensome procedure compared with the least-squares method. Of course, the least-squares method will give the same answer for any equation in which only one endogenous variable is present. In general, the least-squares method will give estimates whose expected (mean) values are more biased (different from the true values) in theory than the simultaneous-equation method as the number of observations (sample size) approaches infinity. The bias of the simultaneous-equation estimates approaches zero as the sample size increases to infinity. However, the variance about the expected value (standard error) is much greater for the simultaneous-equation approach than for the least-squares approach. Thus, for any given sample size, the smaller bias of the simultaneous-equation approach may be more than offset by its large variance about this less biased estimate.

For this reason, and because of the modifications which must be used to reduce its computational complications, it appears that, in actual practice, nothing significant is gained by using the more complicated simultaneous-equation approach rather than least-squares methods.

How useful was this Klein-Goldberger model for forecasting purposes? An analysis of the accuracy of the model for forecasting economic measures in 1954 was made by C. F. Christ.[1] Klein and Goldberger had estimated the values of the predetermined variables for 1954 before the year began, or shortly thereafter, on the basis of their best guess about the government budget, etc. They then substituted these values into the equations previously presented and solved for the predicted values of the jointly dependent variables. Comparison of five predicted variables with the actual observed variables is shown in Table 32-5.

Table 32-5. **Comparison of Observed Values of Five Variables with Klein-Goldberger Model Predictions**

Variable*	Observed value	Predicted value	Error, +high, −low	Predicted direction of change	Prediction better than naïve model's
GNP...................	174.0	174.8	$+\frac{1}{2}\%$	Right	Yes
Consumption............	116.6	117.3	+ 1	Right	Yes
Gross investment........	20.3	22.7	+12	Wrong	No
Number of employees....	55.8	56.5	+ 1	Right	Yes
Price level..............	207.2	220.5	+ 6	Right	No

* All in billions of 1939 dollars, except employees in millions and wage rate and price level in indexes 1939 = 100.

The naïve model referred to in the last column of the table is a prediction based on no change from last year. In his analysis, Christ observes that the results were so good that he suspects that Klein and Goldberger had a bit of good luck with these variables in 1954.

Econometric model building can be a useful tool for establishing and forecasting economic relationships and values. Of course, it has its limitations. It is cumbersome and expensive. There is a danger of inaccurate results if good judgment is not applied in developing and using its forecasts because economic relationships may shift, the coefficients in the

[1] C. F. Christ, "Aggregate Economic Models," *American Economic Review*, vol. 46, no. 3, pp. 385–408, June, 1956.

equations may change, and new variables may assume importance with the passage of time.

Demand Analysis. The central importance of the demand function in determining the economic decisions of the firm has been noted in Chapter 28. Although a major use of demand analysis is in establishing prices, product research, advertising, and promotion programs, it is also an important technique for improving the accuracy of sales forecasts. We shall therefore consider some of the practical problems of determining demand functions for different types of products under a variety of conditions.

The word "demand" is used with two different meanings by various economists. One meaning, the classical one, is the schedule-of-demand concept of Chapter 28: how much of a commodity will be purchased at various prices. The demand varies under this concept only when the schedule changes. When the quantity which will be purchased or consumed increases because the price has been reduced, the demand or demand schedule has not changed. When more can be sold at the same price because of advertising promotion, the demand or demand schedule has changed.

The term "demand" is also commonly used to mean the total quantity purchased, sold, consumed, or demanded at a given time. In this sense the demand is a function of many variables in addition to the price of the commodity. Advertising promotion, disposable income, population, and the prices of competing products are some of these other variables.

These two meanings of the term "demand" are used somewhat interchangeably by various economists and businessmen. As long as we keep both meanings in mind, this double use of the term need not cause confusion because the intended meaning is usually evident in each case. Thus, using the term "demand" in the classical sense, we would say that changes in income, population, substitute products, and advertising expenditures will change the demand schedule for a product. Using the term "demand" in the total quantity sense, we would say that the consumption of a product is a function of many variables including prices, income, population, substitute products, advertising, etc.

When we speak of demand in either sense, it is helpful to consider the difference between the more immediate, short-run demand relationships and the longer-run relationships. Thus, a decrease in the price of a product may not have as much effect on the sales volume of the product in the short run as in the long run because it may take time for people to learn of the price reduction or to change their procurement habits. On the other hand, a decrease in price of a product may also, in the long run, induce the manufacturers of substitutes to decrease their prices and thus reduce the short-run price advantage.

When new facilities are required by the consumer to change from one product to another, differences in short- and long-run effects may be substantial. A decrease in the cost of gas may have relatively little short-run effect on gas consumption. In the long run, however, new factories and homes will be more likely to have gas-fired equipment installed than oil-fired equipment and some existing equipment will gradually be converted. Gas consumption will then rise in the long run.

There are a number of possible approaches to determining demand relationships.

1. A time-series correlation-analysis approach which uses historical data showing how sales or consumption have varied with changes in price, income, occupational and geographical status, and other factors. Several examples of this approach will be discussed in this chapter.

2. A controlled-experimentation approach, in which one variable, such as price or promotion, is changed and all other conditions are held as constant as possible. An example of the use of this type of approach in a retail department store is presented later in this chapter.

3. A market-research approach, which shows how the sales or consumption of an item or service vary with differences in price, income, occupation, geography, and other factors. An example of the use of this approach for forecasting airline demand is presented later in this chapter.

When a producer good is involved, engineering economic analyses, such as those presented in earlier sections of this book, may sometimes be used to provide the basis for estimating a demand schedule. If these engineering analyses are made in a representative sample of the different industries using the producer good and supplemented with a knowledge of the procurement procedures and plans of the companies in these industries, some useful demand relationships can be developed.

Attempts to determine demand relationships from surveys, by personal interview or by written questionnaire, are generally not too successful. The answers which people give to questions on how much they would buy under various price and other conditions are quite unreliable guides to what they will actually do.

Correlation of Price and Consumption Rate. The simplest technique for approximating demand curves is to take time-series data showing the rate of sale or consumption at various prices over the years and plot the prices (ordinate scale) as a function of the rate of sale or consumption (abscissa scale). Adjustments of the price data for the changing value of the dollar and, especially with consumer goods, adjustments of the sales or consumption data for the changing population will usually be desirable. The price data may be deflated by dividing each price expressed in current dollars by an appropriate price-level index, as illustrated in Chapter 29. The sales or consumption data may be partially corrected for population changes by reducing the quantities to a per capita basis. (The population correction may be only partial if the composition of the population, such as age distribution, has changed over the years and age distribution is a significant factor in the demand function.)

Table 32-6 shows data from 1922 to 1930 on meat consumption and meat prices.[1] Consumption has been converted to a per capita basis and prices adjusted by dividing by the BLS consumer price index. These data are plotted in Figure 32-1, on which a fitted demand curve is also shown.

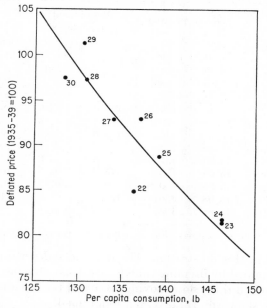

Figure 32-1. Retail meat prices and per capita consumption of meat, 1922 to 1930. SOURCE: E. J. Working, *Demand for meat*, University of Chicago Press, Chicago, 1954, p. 20.

The equation of the demand curve is $\log Y = 5.52 - 1.67 \log X$, where Y equals the deflated price and X equals the per capita consumption.[2]

Multiple Correlation of Price and Consumption Rate. Implicit in this analysis is the assumption that there was one demand function during this period. As a practical matter, we know that demand functions shift over a period of time. Therefore, if we use multiple-regression techniques to correlate price and consumption with other variables which measure changes in factors which cause the demand curve to shift, we can then hold these other factors constant at their average or any other values to see what the price-consumption rate relationship would have been if the demand schedule had not been shifting over the years.

[1] From E. J. Working, *Demand for Meat*, University of Chicago Press, Chicago, 1954.

[2] The fitted curve is a geometric mean of two least-squares regressions: the regression of logs of prices on logs of consumption and the regression of logs of consumption on logs of price.

We can illustrate this by introducing into our previous correlation only one additional variable which will take account of changes in disposable income per capita and in the values of the rent, fuel, and miscellaneous groups of the consumer price index. This additional variable is called a

Table 32-6. Consumption and Retail Price Indexes of Meat
Compared with a Demand Index

Year	Meat consumption		Retail meat price indexes*		Demand index*
	Total (billion pounds)	Per capita (pounds)	Unde-flated	Deflated	
1922	15.16	136.7	101.6	84.9	89.1
1923	16.49	146.3	99.4	81.5	100.2
1924	16.81	146.3	100.0	81.8	97.9
1925	16.22	139.1	111.3	88.8	101.4
1926	16.20	137.0	117.5	93.0	103.8
1927	16.05	134.0	115.2	92.9	103.5
1928	15.86	130.8	119.3	97.3	105.9
1929	15.98	130.4	124.1	101.3	111.4
1930	15.88	128.3	116.4	97.5	99.6

* 1935–1939 = 100. Consumers price index of the Bureau of Labor Statistics.

demand index in this illustration. The demand index values for 1922 to 1930 are determined by dividing each year's disposable income per capita by the above-noted three slow-moving groups of the consumer price index and the values shown in Table 32-6 are obtained.

Using least squares, we can now obtain an equation of the form $\log X_1 = a_{1.23} + b_{12.3} \log X_2 + b_{13.2} \log X_3$, where X_1 is price, X_2 is consumption, and X_3 is the demand index.

The equation $\log X_1 = 3.63 - 1.27 \log X_2 + 0.52 \log X_3$ was computed by a modified method and differs insignificantly from the least-squares line. We wish to estimate what the demand curve for meat would have been if the demand index had been constant at 100. We substitute $X_3 = 100$ in our multiple-correlation equation and obtain $\log X_1 = 4.67 - 1.27 \log X_2$.

Variations in the actual price of meat occurred each year because the demand index varied. We can estimate what the prices would have been if the demand index had been unchanged at 100 by multiplying the log of the difference between 100 and the actual demand index by $0.517(b_{13.2})$ and adjusting the log of the actual price. This is done in Table 32-7.

These adjusted prices as a function of per capita consumption are plotted in solid dots on Figure 32-2. The solid demand curve is the adjusted regression equation $\log X_1 = 4.67 - 1.27 \log X_2$, previously cal-

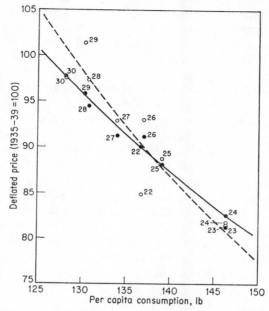

Figure 32-2. Retail meat prices, adjusted and unadjusted for a demand index. SOURCE:
E. J. Working, *Demand for Meat*, University of Chicago Press, Chicago, p. 23.

Table 32-7. Calculation of Adjusted Deflated Prices of Meat

Year	Log demand index		Adjustment (Col. 2 × .5174)	Log deflated price	Adjusted deflated price	
	Actual	Deviation from 2.0000			Logs (Col. 4 − Col. 3)	Natural No.
	(1)	(2)	(3)	(4)	(5)	(6)
1922	1.9499	− .0501	− .0259	1.9289	1.9548	90.1
1923	2.0009	+ .0009	+ .0005	1.9112	1.9107	81.4
1924	1.9907	− .0093	− .0048	1.9128	1.9176	82.7
1925	2.0060	+ .0060	+ .0031	1.9484	1.9453	88.2
1926	2.0162	+ .0162	+ .0084	1.9685	1.9601	91.2
1927	2.0149	+ .0149	+ .0077	1.9680	1.9603	91.3
1928	2.0249	+ .0249	+ .0129	1.9881	1.9752	94.5
1929	2.0469	+ .0469	+ .0243	2.0056	1.9813	95.8
1930	1.9983	− .0017	− .0009	1.9890	1.9899	97.7

SOURCE: E. J. Working, *Demand for Meat*, University of Chicago Press, Chicago,
1954.

culated. For comparative purposes, the little circles (or hollow dots) show the actual (deflated but unadjusted) prices and the dashed line shows the demand curve of Figure 32-1. We note that there is less scatter of the data about the new adjusted regression relationship which uses the demand index. The new adjusted line is less steep than the one which ignored the demand index. Presumably the steeper demand curve of the simple-correlation analysis was caused by shifts of demand which were ignored and which therefore distorted the price-consumption demand relationship.

Illustrative Demand Analyses Using Time-series Correlation Approach. We have seen that many factors may cause a demand schedule to shift during the period being studied. These shifts in the demand curve can distort a relationship which was determined without taking account of the dependency of demand on many factors. A number of examples of demand analyses which illustrate this dependency of demand on many different factors as well as the techniques and the many practical problems in measuring demand are presented in the appendixes to this chapter, in which the determination of demand for a perishable consumer product, a durable consumer product, and a durable producer good are discussed.

Perishable Consumer Product. Two studies of the demand for pork, a consumer perishable good, are presented in Appendix A. Pork is sold in competitive markets which adjust rather readily to changes in supply and demand. It is a relatively homogeneous consumer staple whose demand schedule will not be expected to change rapidly over the years.

The first of the two studies, made by the U.S. Department of Agriculture, is based upon simple-correlation analysis. Corrections are not explicitly made for shifts in the demand schedule over time. In the second study, made by the Institute of Meat Packing, multiple-correlation techniques are used to derive explicit relationships for the factors causing shifts in the demand curve.

Consumer Durable Good. Three studies of the demand for passenger automobiles, a consumer durable good, by the General Motors Corporation, by the U.S. Department of Commerce, and by the University of Michigan and Ford Motor Company are presented in Appendix B. Although the analytic techniques used in the three cases differ to such an extent that direct comparison of results is complicated, detailed examination of these three studies of automobile demand reveal many of the problems and approaches in explicitly establishing the relationships determining the sales of a consumer durable good which is sold in an imperfect market.

An elaborate study of automobile demand was made for General Motors Corporation by C. F. Roos and Victor von Szeliski. The factors affecting demand for a durable consumer good were analyzed in detail and the nature of demand relationships carefully evaluated. A summary of the study is presented in Appendix B because it reveals the more complicated methodology which must be undertaken when time is not used as a catch-all for unexplored trends.

The analysis and regression relationship in the Department of Commerce study is simpler and less sophisticated than the Roos and von Szeliski study. Nevertheless, most of the same influences are considered in both studies. The Commerce study uses real disposable income per household and its percentage change from previous years as independent variables instead of the supernumerary income (consumer income after deducting the subsistence or necessitous living costs of the consumer) of the Roos and von Szeliski study. Both studies use an index of car prices. Commerce uses average scrappage age instead of the more sophisticated replacement pressure, which is based on the application of a shifting mortality table to the age distribution of the car population. Commerce determines its regression relationship for new passenger car registrations on a per 1,000 household basis instead of Roos and von Szeliski's more sophisticated maximum ownership level, which takes into account not only the number of families but also supernumerary income and durability.

The methods used in the University of Michigan—Ford Motor Company study of automobile demand made by D. B. Suits differ from the previous two in a number of significant respects. For example, account is taken of the influence of credit conditions and the accumulation of a stock of cars. The statistical work is carried out in terms of first differences to avoid the complications of autocorrelation. A dummy variable was used to account for the special conditions of the automobile market in years of severe shortage.

Producer Durable Good. A study of the demand for steel, a producer durable good, by the United States Steel Corporation is presented in Appendix C.

The nature of the demand for producer goods differs from the demand for consumer goods in that it generally fluctuates much more violently. A producer will not usually purchase producer goods unless the investment will yield him a sufficiently high profit to make it an attractive investment. In poor times, pessimistic estimates of future sales prospects will frequently make investments look relatively unattractive. The producer will not be using much of his facilities in times of poor business, so that they will wear out more slowly. He can therefore postpone investment in new facilities more readily.

The demand for a durable producer good thus tends to be more volatile than for a consumer good. Steel is not only a nonhomogeneous, durable producer good sold on an imperfect market, but it is also a raw material which is used in the production of many widely differing kinds of producer and consumer goods. We shall therefore consider the problems in establishing a demand function for steel.

Controlled Experimentation. Controlled experimentation can be a most effective way to discover meaningful, current demand relationships. However, it is not always feasible to use controlled experimentation for determining demand relationships. The experiments are conducted by changing one variable, such as price or promotion, and holding all other conditions as constant as possible. It is difficult and in some cases impossible to do this kind of experimentation. The experimentation is costly, may cause unfavorable customer reactions, and is subject to errors because customers and competitors will react differently if they realize a price or promotion change is experimental or temporary.

A study of the methods used in determining short-run demand relationships in a department store by experimentation is given in Appendix D. This study of retail-department-store demand for R. H. Macy & Company by R. H. Whitman provides an example of the derivation of a curve for demand in an imperfect market as a function of price alone. In this study, the reaction of consumers to experimental price changes at one retail outlet was observed. This experimentation with the effect of price changes on sales in a department store over a short period of time provides an example of the type of situation in which manipulation of prices to determine short-run demand schedules is feasible.

Market Research. Market research can provide detailed information on the nature of the demand for a company's products which can be useful general background for forecasting. In addition, market research coupled with a forecast of population trends may provide a primary approach for forecasting sales.

The ultimate consumer of most of the products and services created in our economy is the population of the country (or various parts of the country). Changes in population size and characteristics are therefore important to many forecasts, especially longer-range ones. Forecasting approaches will thus frequently be concerned with predicting the number of people who will be included in one or more categories in future years.

For example, we may first determine that different segments of the population have a different demand for a product. We next forecast the sales of the product per unit population of each segment of the population. We can then multiply a forecasted total population of each segment by the forecasted demand of the product per unit population to obtain a demand forecast.

A detailed illustration of this approach is presented in Appendix E in which a demand forecast of the United States domestic-air-passenger market is developed by the Port of New York Authority. Under the market-research approach, air travel is considered essentially a commodity—one of several in competition for the buyer's dollars. This approach accepts the proposition that each trip results from a more-or-less carefully weighed decision by the traveler, made under more-or-less compelling circumstances, and tempered by the traveler's background and experience, resources, tastes and preferences, and other primarily personal considerations. The approach to the problem thus is reduced to a comprehensive, broad national marketing-research project—to determine what economic and demographic conditions seem to explain the decisions that result in air travel. Then, by applying the findings of the market analysis to the persons expected to fall under identical or similar demographic and economic groups in the future, and by assuming generally similar behavior of members of these groups with respect to air travel, it is possible to estimate the volume of air travel that the entire population would generate if the findings of the market survey were tenable.

Demand analyses, such as those discussed in this chapter, can be very useful in determining and measuring the nature of the factors which affect sales volume. They can thus help in establishing prices, planning product-research programs, and establishing promotional campaigns. They are useful aids in forecasting sales volume because they provide an understanding of underlying economic relationships.

The cautions expressed in Chapters 30 and 31 about the validity of time-series and correlation analyses for forecasting apply with equal weight to demand analyses. The value of a past demand pattern for forecasting is dependent either upon the same economic forces continuing to behave in a similar pattern in the future or upon the ability of the analyst to modify the demand function appropriately, using his judgment and knowledge of the changing economic relationships. It is extremely rare that time-series relationships do not change. Demand analysis is therefore only an aid to the application of good judgment and cannot be used as the sole basis for sales forecasting.

We must, in addition, be careful to distinguish between the demand for a company's product and the demand for the product of an entire industry. The company relationship is most significant for company sales forecasting purposes but depends a great deal upon how the other companies in the industry will react to price, promotion, and design changes; how fast they will react; as well as upon the shape of the industry demand schedule and the amount of product differentiation.

Persistence Technique. The simplest forecasting technique and, for short-term forecasting, frequently an unusually accurate method, is to forecast either

1. No change in the sales in the immediate future, or
2. No change, except for seasonal adjustments, or
3. A continuation of change, perhaps with seasonal adjustment, in the same direction and at the same rate as at present

This persistence technique has two major drawbacks: it is valid only for very short periods of time; and it will not forecast turns (changes in the direction) in the trend or cycle.

Time-series Analysis. Statistical techniques of time-series analysis were discussed in some detail in Chapter 30. These techniques for projecting trend, seasonal, and cyclical patterns into the future can provide a valuable basis for forecasting industry as well as company sales when used in conjunction with other methods. As is the case with all projections of past experience, the methods are valid only if the conditions prevailing in the past continue into the future. Therefore, the methods cannot be mechanically applied. The underlying conditions must be carefully investigated and corrections made for those conditions which are different or which are expected to be different.

A knowledge of the trend, seasonal, and cyclical patterns in the entire industry can prove very useful, especially when the company sells its product nationally. (Of course, when a company sells only in a local area, such as a power or a telephone company, national patterns have more limited significance.) In many cases, industry-wide analyses are available which have been made by trade associations, independent consulting organizations, or other firms in the industry.

In some businesses, cyclical patterns for company sales can be determined for each of its products by time-series analyses. These can be especially helpful for short-range forecasting purposes when the patterns are well established.

Correlation Techniques. If the sales of product X can be correlated with variations in the Federal Reserve Board index of industrial production, then we can use a forecast of this index as a basis for forecasting the sales of product X. We then forecast our company percentage share of product X sales based on its past historical relationships.

Why forecast the Federal Reserve index of industrial production and then use a historical correlation pattern to forecast product X sales? Why not forecast a company's sales directly? For one thing, we may be able to forecast, or obtain a forecast of, the Federal Reserve index with more accuracy than for product X directly. Data for forecasting are usually more readily and accurately available on an industry-wide rather than company-wide basis. In addition, it is useful to approach the forecast from a number of different angles. The results of following an industry-wide approach can then be compared with the results by other more direct methods and the insight gained by such comparisons can help to improve forecast accuracy. For these same reasons, we forecast industry sales first and then forecast the expected company share of this total.

We are always seeking time lags in correlation relationships. If the sales of product X were a function of the value of the Federal Reserve index of industrial production of two years previous, then we would not need to forecast the Federal Reserve index. Unfortunately, reliable time-lag correlation relationships for sales forecasting are not common.

Regression and correlation analysis is an attempt to relate causative factors to sales variations. As discussed in Chapter 31, refinements of statistical technique are helpful tools but they are not substitutes for knowledge of the pertinent economic phenomena and for good judgment. The actual forecast must be based not only on the past correlation relationships, but on an evaluation of how these relationships will behave in the future. In correlation forecasts, as in time-series forecasts, we always have the problem of determining when past and current conditions and relationships will change, so that we can correct our forecast of future relationships.

Percentage Share of Industry Sales. If we have established a reliable forecast of industry sales, we can forecast our own company's sales in this industry by forecasting the company's percentage share of the industry sales. If this percentage share has been relatively constant over the years and is expected to continue so, the constant percentage may be used as the forecast. However, it would be rare for so static a situation to exist. Forecasting this percentage may involve a time-series analysis, as illustrated by Figures 32-3 and 32-4.

In Figure 32-3, the sales of product Z by the Ardo Company are plotted as a percentage of the entire industry sales of product Z. A least-squares

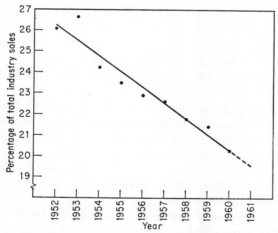

Figure 32-3. Ardo Company sales of product Z as a percentage of entire industry sales of product Z.

trend line is computed for this time series and is drawn on the chart. The trend line is extrapolated to forecast the percentage market share for the Ardo Company in future years. Thus, the forecasted percentage share for 1961 is 19.5. Similar charts would be made for each product line of the Ardo Company.

In Figure 32-4, the total sales of all products of the Neeler Company are plotted as a percentage of sales in the entire industry. A least-squares trend line is computed and it is drawn on this chart. The forecasted percentage market share for 1961 using this trend line is 13.4. When the approach of Figure 32-3 is used, forecasting separate percentage market shares for each product line, the analysis of Figure 32-4, using one per-

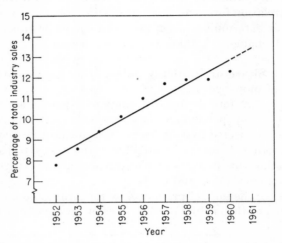

Figure 32-4. Neeler Company sales as a percentage of sales in entire industry.

centage for all product lines in the industry, may also be made for comparative purposes. The reasons for any discrepancies can then be evaluated.

The forecasting method just described or the use of a fixed percentage when no trend is present has its hazards. Changes in sales-promotion methods and expenditures can cause significant changes in trend. Moreover, a small percentage deviation may cause a high absolute error in the forecast. Thus, an error of 1 per cent, forecasting an 8 per cent share of the market instead of the correct 7 per cent, will produce an error of more than 14 per cent in the total forecast.

Composite Opinion of Company Executives. In this approach, the sales forecast is determined by asking a selected group of top company executives what they believe will be sales in a given future period. This method may be applied in a number of ways.

Each person may make estimates independently. These independent forecasts may then be reconciled by having all the estimates reviewed by a single executive (usually the president) or by a committee. The committee could be composed of the executives who made the estimates, with perhaps the addition of other executives, or might be composed entirely of other executives. A variation on this procedure is to have one executive make the initial estimates, which are then circulated for comment and suggested change among the executives. The final reconciling would be done by a committee or by the top company executive officer.

The amount of analysis and factual data used by the individuals in this method will vary widely. Some of the executives may base their estimates on various analytical procedures and facts described elsewhere in this volume.

This composite-opinion method has a number of advantages. Because it needs a minimum of statistical records and analysis, it can be done quickly, with relatively little work. When statistical data are not available, this may be the only feasible method. In all cases, it brings the different viewpoints and background of the selected top executives to bear on the sales forecast.

This procedure has a number of limitations. When used as the sole forecasting method, it substitutes opinions for the market facts underlying the company sales. Detailed breakdowns of the forecast by week or month, by product, etc., may be difficult to obtain. Where large divergences of opinion exist, reconciliation to obtain a composite may prove difficult in the absence of facts and consume much valuable executive time.

Sales-force Survey. The sales-force-survey approach is most readily applicable to shorter-term forecasts of up to one year. Each salesman is asked to estimate sales for the coming year. Sometimes sales managers are asked for independent estimates to be checked against salesmen's estimates and sometimes the salesmen's estimates are prepared in consultation with the sales managers. The estimates of different salesmen may be weighted based upon past estimating history. When sales managers are organized both regionally and product-wise, independent estimates by each group may be checked against each other and the reasons for discrepancies analyzed.

This method utilizes the judgment of the company personnel who are closest to the customers and their intentions—the salesmen and the sales managers. Detailed breakdowns by product, time period, territory, etc., can be made readily. When the total estimate is a composite of many different salesmen's estimates, a certain amount of cancellation of judgmental errors in opposite directions will take place.

The principal limitations of this method are related to the question of how good are salesmen as forecasters: do they tend to be swayed unduly by feelings of optimism and pessimism? are they aware of the economic forces shaping sales of their products in the immediate and long-range future? do the salesman and the sales manager consider the effect their estimates may have in the setting of their sales quotas? When used as the sole forecasting approach, this method substitutes opinions for analysis of the underlying economic and market facts.

Distributor or Consumer Survey. A company may survey its distributors, jobbers, etc., asking for their expectations for prospective sales.

This procedure has the advantage of obtaining objective outside estimates. However, it is rather difficult to get these outsiders interested enough to devote the necessary time to furnish accurate estimates.

Surveys of the ultimate consumer of a product will also give information which is objective. The survey can frequently be done on a sampling basis, using some of the considerations mentioned in Chapter 23 with respect to the design and size of the sample.

In forecasting sales based upon consumer intentions, errors can occur because of the inventory latitude of manufacturers in the case of a producer good and distributors, jobbers, and retailers in the case of a consumer good. Inventories tend to increase when business is good and decrease when it is bad. Thus, during periods of expanding business, consumer intentions will tend to understate factory sales demand and during periods of declining business, overstate the future sales demand.

Consumer surveys can be designed to yield much valuable information for nonforecasting purposes. Possible product-design improvements and data useful for planning future promotional and advertising efforts are examples.

The principal limitations of surveys of consumer intentions are the relatively high expense, the difficulties of interviewing and sampling, and the unreliability and changeability of expressions of intention by consumers. Planned and actual purchases by consumers may vary sharply. Short-term economic changes also cause rapid changes in consumer purchasing.

Criteria for Desirable Sales-forecasting Procedures. What characteristics are we desirous of incorporating in our sales-forecasting procedures?

Accuracy. The accuracy of the forecast is measured not only by the percentage of times it is correct, but also by how often and how closely it forecasts changes in the trend and cycle, particularly changes in direction. On a short-range basis, accuracy can be attained a large percentage of the time by relatively simple approaches. Predicting changes in direction, however, is difficult for both short- and long-range forecasts.

Ease of Comprehension. Management must understand and have confidence in the methods used in arriving at sales forecasts or it will be distrustful and not use them. This factor puts a premium on simplicity and, in some cases, seriously handicaps the use of the more complicated econometric models.

Ease of comprehension is important in improving the accuracy of the forecast because good forecasting requires good judgment. The experienced executive who has extensive knowledge of the field and good judgment finds it difficult to evaluate what the forecaster has done if he cannot understand the procedure.

Maintenance of Timeliness and Validity. An otherwise valid procedure can become useless if the maintenance of timeliness and validity is poor. The forecast should be capable of being maintained on an up-to-date basis. This has three aspects:

1. The relations underlying the procedure should be stable so that they will carry into the future for a significant amount of time.

2. Current data required to use these underlying relationships should be available on a timely basis.

3. The forecasting procedure should permit changes to be made in the relationships as they occur.

Economy. How much money and managerial effort should be allocated to obtain a high level of forecasting accuracy? The criterion here is the economic consideration of balancing the benefits from increased accuracy (value of the better planning which is possible) against the additional cost of providing the improved forecasting.

Factors Affecting Accuracy of Forecasts. The types of analytic techniques used obviously affect the accuracy of sales forecasts. However, there are a host of additional factors which are of great importance in determining the final accuracy of the forecast: the adequacy and completeness of the data being analyzed; the quality of the forecaster's judgment; the variability of sales patterns in the company and industry; the time and money spent on the forecast; and the nature of the product and the nature of the demand and market for it.

Producer goods are subject to larger variations in demand with changes in business conditions. The purchase of producer goods is based more on the relative economy of their use than is the purchase of consumer goods. The factors affecting this relative economy, such as labor rates, raw-material prices, new technological innovation, availability and cost of money, are subject to unexpected changes.

In addition, and frequently more significant, the demand for producer goods will vary much more widely with changes in general economic conditions than for consumer goods. For example, a consumer product, product C, is manufactured using a producer good, machine P. The Wyath Manufacturing Company has 100 machines P, each of which produce 10,000 products C a year, for a total production of 1,000,000 per year. The machines have an average life of 10 years, so that an average of 10 machines P are scrapped each year. If the sales rate declines 5 per cent to 950,000 units of product C per year, the company will require only 95 machines to meet this demand. On the average, it will need to replace only 5 of the 10 machines which are scrapped the first year of the declined sales. This is a 50 per cent cut. If the sales rate declined 10 per cent, it would, on the average, require no replacements during the first year.

Durable goods, whether producer or consumer, tend to have higher fluctuations with changes in business conditions than perishable goods. Producer durable goods are frequently carried in inventory. In times of declining business, producers will tend to hold back replenishing inventory as it is used up. In the case of consumer goods, the consumer usually has more freedom in timing the purchase of durable goods than perishable ones: he can more easily postpone purchasing a new car or refrigerator compared with postponing the purchase of food or clothing during times of reduced income.

When we are forecasting the sales of a few very expensive pieces of an item selling for hundreds of thousands or millions of dollars, a mistake of one item in the forecast may represent a large error in the percentage of total dollar sales. When we are forecasting the sales of relatively inexpensive units, an error of many units in the forecast may represent only a small error in the percentage of total dollar sales. Moreover, the statistical balancing out of small errors in each direction over a period of time is more difficult in the first situation.

No single procedure or combination of procedures for sales forecasting is a substitute for sound judgment. It is desirable to analyze the total situation and each of its parts from as many viewpoints as possible and then compare and reconcile the results of the different approaches. The results must be tempered by good business sense to be certain that they are reasonable.

APPENDIX A. TWO STUDIES OF THE DEMAND FOR A PERISHABLE CONSUMER PRODUCT—PORK

U.S. Department of Agriculture Study

Figure 32-5 shows a simple graphic regression between per capita consumption of pork and the price per pound of pork divided by an index of per capita disposable personal income.[1] (The war years have been omitted in this study.) We see that the demand curve for pork has been declining. The demand curves for each of the three successive periods are lower than its predecessor. Moreover, the demand curve for 1953 to 1956 is distinctly less elastic than the ones for the two earlier periods.

It will be noted that the points for 1947 and 1948 fall near the higher 1925 to 1931 demand curve. We shall note later that the 1947 and 1948 values also deviate considerably from the multiple-correlation regression line of another study.

Institute of Meat Packing Study

A large number of multiple-correlation analyses were carried out by E. J. Working to measure the way prices have changed relative to pork consumption, to consumer

[1] From F. V. Waugh, *Graphic Analysis in Agricultural Economics*, Agriculture Handbook 128, 1957.

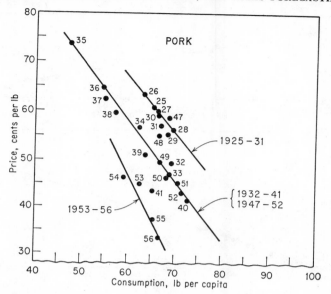

Figure 32-5. Demand for pork. SOURCE: U.S.D.A. Agricultural Marketing Service.

incomes, to total consumer expenditures, to supplies and prices of other meats, and to other factors including the passage of time.[1]

One of the analyses used the following variables:

X_1 = deflated retail price of pork, cents per pound
X_2 = consumption of pork per capita, pounds
X_3 = demand index (1935–1939 = 100) (defined in body of this chapter)
X_4 = consumption of nonpork meats per capita, pounds
X_5 = time

Using data covering the twenty-year period 1922 to 1941, the coefficient of multiple correlation was 0.9886 for the five-variable correlation. The multiple-regression equation was

$$X_1 = 36.32 - 0.353X_2 + 0.136X_3 - 0.069X_4 - 0.162X_5$$

From this it would appear that changes in the supplies of other meats as well as of pork affect pork prices.

The relationships in this multiple correlation are portrayed graphically in Figure 32-6. The plotted values of deflated price each year are the deflated values which have been adjusted for the effects of deviations of all the independent variables in the multiple-regression equation other than the one whose effects on price we are studying. Thus, in the top panel showing deflated price as a function of consumption, the plotted values have been adjusted, using the regression coefficients of the correlation equation, for deviations of the individual values of the demand index, per capita consumption of nonpork meats, and time from their respective average values. The dots therefore represent estimates of what the prices would have been if each of these variables had remained at its average value throughout the period. Correspondingly, in the next lower panel showing deflated price as a function of the demand index, adjustments were made for deviations of the per capita consumption of pork, per capita consumption of nonpork meats, and time from their respective average values.

[1] The findings of this study were adapted from Working, op. cit.

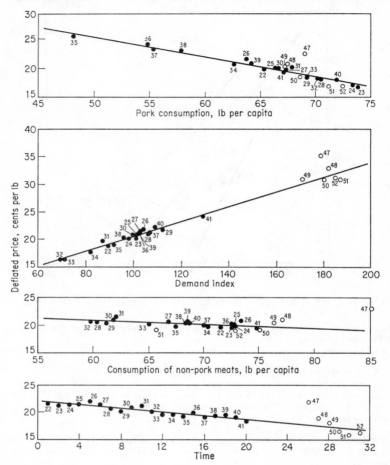

Figure 32-6. Linear regression of pork prices on related factors. SOURCE: E. J. Working, *Demand for Meat*, University of Chicago Press, Chicago, 1954, p. 71.

The solid dots represent the observations for the years included in the multiple correlations, 1922 to 1941, and the small circles show the corresponding observations for the postwar years 1947 to 1951.

A similar correlation which used logarithms of the same variables, except for time, which was in natural numbers, yielded a multiple-correlation coefficient of 0.9836. The regression equation was

$$\log X_1 = 2.196 - 1.010 \log X_2 + 0.690 \log X_3 - 0.218 \log X_4 - 0.003 X_5$$

However, this logarithmic correlation provided a poorer explanation of the postwar prices than the previous correlation equation which used natural numbers.

It was observed that for the period 1922 to 1941 the consumer price index could be used as a variable in place of time and seemed to be better from the standpoint of the resulting multiple-correlation coefficient. Thus, with X_3 = deflated disposable income per capita instead of demand index and X_5 = consumer price index instead of time, a regression equation was obtained as follows:

$$\log X_1 = 1.325 - 1.106 \log X_2 + 0.519 \log X_3 - 0.128 \log X_4 + 0.599 \log X_5$$

The multiple-correlation coefficient was 0.9913. This regression equation, when applied to the period used in the analysis, gave estimates very close to the actual prices—as might be judged from the high correlation coefficient. When applied to the postwar period, however, the results were unsatisfactory, the estimates differing much more from the actual than in the prewar period and growing steadily worse after 1948.

One of the conclusions of the study was that the short-run elasticity of demand for pork is approximately −1.0, or unit elasticity. Long-run elasticity is more difficult to approximate, but present evidence indicates it to be in the vicinity of −1.5. Both the short-run and the long-run elasticities referred to are those which result when holding other factors, including the supplies—not the prices—of competitive meats, constant. If prices of other meats are held constant, the elasticity of demand is somewhat greater than if supplies are held constant.

APPENDIX B. THREE STUDIES OF THE DEMAND FOR A CONSUMER DURABLE GOOD—PASSENGER AUTOMOBILES

General Motors Study

This study[1] of the nature of the demand for automobiles made by Roos and von Szeliski relates to retail sales of passenger cars within the United States for the years 1919 to 1938. As with all durable goods, the demand for new automobiles is derived from the demand for services which they yield. Since the automobile yields transportation services for a period from five to fifteen years, the demand for these services may be satisfied by running the old cars another year or by buying used cars instead of new cars. Thus the consumption of automobile services is disassociated from the purchases of new cars, and, as is to be expected, the former is far more stable than the latter. The number of cars in use holds up relatively well even in the trough of depressions while the sale of new cars suffers great declines.

Consumer Income. The level of consumer income is, of course, a major factor in determining the number of new car sales. When the level of income is high, sales will be high; conversely, when national income is low, car sales will be low.

A somewhat more refined analysis is possible if consumer income is adjusted by deducting necessitous expenditure. Before distributing his income among different commodities or between savings and spending, the individual consumer must first allocate a portion to meet his necessary living costs. Subsistence or necessitous living cost was estimated to have been $200 per capita for 1923 and to have varied in other years with the National Industrial Conference Board index of the cost of living. Deducting these costs from disposable consumer income, estimates of "supernumerary income" which is available for expenditures on automobiles and other goods were obtained.

Figures 32-7 relates new car sales to supernumerary income. It will be observed that for a given amount of supernumerary income the sales of automobiles were characteristically much higher when income was rising than when it was falling. The reason for this is that the demand for automobiles, as for most durable goods, depends not only on the level of income but on psychological factors, such as the state of confidence.

[1] *The Dynamics of Automobile Demand*, General Motors Corporation, New York, 1939. This presentation is adapted from TNEC Papers, United States Steel Corporation, 1940.

Declining business activity and decreasing income give rise to uncertainty and to fears that income will decline still further. As a result, even relatively high levels of income may be associated with a low volume of sales. Conversely, increasing business activity and income lead to increased confidence, and to the allocation of an increasing proportion of present and future income to automobile purchases. (The rate of change of the national income is sometimes used as an approximate, but not completely satisfactory, index of this psychological factor.)

Potential New Owners and the Maximum-ownership Level. At any given time under given economic conditions there is a maximum number of cars that will be kept in operation. In the long run, changes in this maximum-ownership level depend, of course, on the growth of population, on the development of highways, and on technical progress. From year to year, however, the level changes in response to the economic status

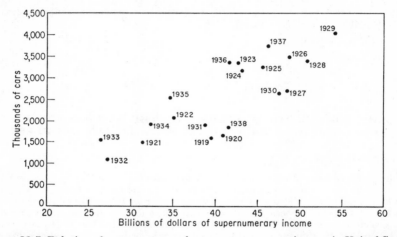

Figure 32-7. Relation of passenger car sales to supernumerary income in United States. SOURCE: *The Dynamics of Automobile Demand,* General Motors Corporation, New York, 1939.

of consumers, and to other factors, such as price and durability of the car. The number of potential new owners is equal to the difference between the maximum-ownership level and the existing consumers' stock of cars. The number of new-owner sales is proportional to the number of potential new owners, and to factors dependent on income, price, trade-in allowance, volume of installment credit, and similar factors.

Thus, the demand factors are made to enter twice in the analysis of automobile sales, first in determining the maximum-ownership level under any given set of economic conditions, and second in determining the nature of the reaction of sales to changes in the number of potential new owners. By means of these concepts, the relationship between income and automobile sales is explained. Assuming other factors to remain constant, the maximum-ownership level at any given time depends on the level of income at that time, but the stock of cars in operation depends on previous income. The number of potential new owners is the difference between the maximum-ownership level and the stock of cars in operation and depends therefore on the difference between this year's and previous years' income.

The maximum-ownership level is a potent force in determining the volume of new car sales. A sudden increase in income may increase the maximum-ownership level to a figure far above the number of cars in operation and thus lead to a very large increase in car sales. This is undoubtedly what happened in 1937. On the other hand a sudden decline in income may decrease the maximum-ownership level to a figure below the number of cars in operation. In that case there will be an actual liquidation of part of the stock of cars in operation. This is what happened during the depression years 1930 to 1932.

Replacement Demand. Not only do consumers adjust the number of cars in operation toward the maximum-ownership level, but they also adjust the quality of the cars in operation toward some optimum level by means of replacement. Replacement demand depends on the pressure for replacement and on such economic factors as price, income and trade-in allowances.

The age distribution of the cars in operation combined with experience tables for scrapping furnishes a measure of the pressure for replacement. Studies of car survival show that car life during the fifteen to twenty years prior to 1940 slowly increased. Griffin's study of 1926 shows 50 per cent of the cars surviving about seven years, whereas a study based on 1933 to 1937 registrations shows 50 per cent surviving about nine years. From these studies may be computed the percentage of an original group of cars that is scrapped after the first, second, third, etc., year of service. By application of these percentages to the figures giving the age distribution of the cars in operation in any year a measure of the replacement pressure during that year is obtained. This index represents the theoretical scrapping rate.

Theoretical scrapping, however, merely indicates normal replacement pressure. It is not equal to actual replacement since this varies with economic circumstances. In times of prosperity people scrap more cars than is indicated by theoretical scrapping. The converse is true in periods of depression. Thus in 1929 actual scrapping was about one-third higher than theoretical scrapping, whereas in 1933 it was about 60 per cent lower than the theoretical rate. Replacement sales therefore depend not only on theoretical scrapping but on income and price and other economic factors.

The Price of Automobiles. The almost continuous reduction (until 1933) of car prices undoubtedly contributed significantly to the great development of the automobile industry. The effect which price changes have on year-to-year changes in sales is, however, a more difficult question.

One of the major difficulties encountered is the fact that manufacturing specifications change so frequently. Since price changes do not occur separately but in conjunction with changes in car models, it is impossible to segregate satisfactorily the influence of price changes on car sales.

A second difficulty in analyzing the effect of price changes is the fact that there were not sufficiently wide fluctuations in car prices to warrant very reliable conclusions. A long-run decline in car prices was associated with a long-run increase in sales. But since year-to-year changes in price were not large, it was difficult to discover what effect they had on year-to-year changes in sales.

Another major problem in any statistical analysis of the effects of changes in car prices upon volume of sales is the construction of a price index. Automobiles have improved so rapidly in quality, and the changes in design and construction have been so frequent, that it is next to impossible to construct a satisfactory price index. The index used by Roos and von Szeliski is the average delivered price of the lowest-priced cars freely available in volume (Ford, Chevrolet, and Plymouth). The assumption underlying the use of this index is that this average price determines the number of cars sold, and that the prices of other cars merely determine the distribution of sales among the various makes.

It was concluded that price had not been a very important factor in determining automobile sales. It was found that the elasticity of demand was not constant but varied from year to year with changes in economic conditions, particularly with changes in income and in the maximum-ownership level. The authors point out that the elasticity was anywhere between -0.65 and -2.5, and that -1.5 was probably a good representative figure. It was noted that there had been a long-run tendency for the elasticity to increase except in periods of depression.

The factors considered above accounted for all but a small part of the annual variation in retail sales of automobiles during the period studied. There are, however, some secondary factors which are highly correlated with those we have considered and whose influence it is therefore difficult to segregate from the rest: used-car allowances, financing terms, operating costs, dealers' used-car stocks. In certain years these forces may be of particular importance in stimulating or discouraging sales.

The formula for retail sales of cars developed by Roos and von Szeliski was

$$\text{Retail sales} = j^{1.2}p^{-0.65}C[0.0254(M - C) + 0.65X]$$

In this formulation

j = ratio of supernumerary income per capita to its mean value

p = index of car prices

C = number of cars in use during year

M = maximum-ownership level, calculated using the following formula: (number of families) $(0.500 + 0.000544j)$ (durability)$^{0.3}$

X = replacement pressure, calculated by applying a shifting mortality table to the age distribution of passenger cars

Sales values calculated from this formula are graphically compared with actual ones in Figure 32-8.

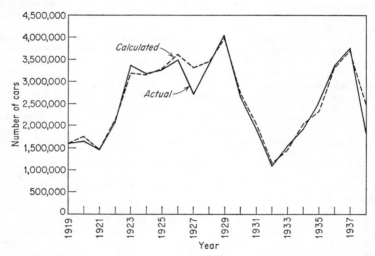

Figure 32-8. Passenger car sales, 1919 to 1938. SOURCE: *The Dynamics of Automobile Demand*, General Motors Corporation, New York, 1939, p. 60.

Department of Commerce Study

In analyzing the demand for new automobiles over a long span of years, the Department of Commerce also found a rather large number of influences which appear to be significant.[1] Only a few of the more important of these have been incorporated into the demand equation which was calculated by least-squares correlation analysis for the years 1925 to 1940. The equation is

$$Y = 0.0003239X_1{}^{2.536}X_2{}^{2.291}X_3{}^{-1.359}(0.932)^{X_4}$$

where Y = new private-passenger-car registrations per 1,000 households

X_1 = real disposable income per household in 1939 dollars

X_2 = percentage of current to preceding year in real disposable income per household in 1939 dollars

X_3 = percentage of average retail price of cars to consumers' prices

X_4 = average scrappage age

The influence of the growth in population over the period which is spanned in

[1] The results of this study are adapted from L. J. Atkinson, "Consumer Markets for Durable Goods," *Survey of Current Business*, April, 1952, pp. 19-21.

this analysis of automobile demand is exceedingly important. During this period, total population increased one-third and the number of households nearly two-thirds. Since households correspond somewhat more closely to the "primary economic unit" in so far as the demand for automobiles is concerned, income and the number of automobiles purchased are both used on a per household basis in this equation in developing the demand relation for new cars.

The most important factor affecting new automobile sales is the real purchasing power of individuals. This is measured by real disposable income. Excluding the influence of other factors, each change of 1 per cent in the level of real disposable income was associated with a change of 2.5 per cent in the same direction in new automobile sales during the base period; and each change of 1 per cent in the ratio of the current to the preceding year's income was associated with a change of 2.3 per cent in the same direction in sales.

The age at which cars are scrapped has an important though indirect influence upon new-car sales. (The influence is indirect in that three-fourths of the new-car buyers trade in their cars by the time they are five years old, but few are scrapped until they are more than twice this age.) Cars are being built more durably, and there is a secular trend toward longer useful life. This was accentuated in the years soon after the war when cars were being kept in use because of the shortage of cars available. Average scrappage age rose to a peak of 14 years in 1949, but declined to 13.5 years in 1950 and to an estimated 13 years in 1951. The latter figure is 3 years greater than the scrappage age just prior to the war. The relationship indicates that each increase in scrappage age of one year was associated with a decline in new automobile sales of about 7 per cent, other factors remaining unchanged.

The final factor used in the demand equation is the price of automobiles in relation to the consumer price index. In the first few years after the end of the war the list price of automobiles had risen about the same from the 1935 to 1939 period as consumer prices generally, and the demand for cars at this price exceeded the supply available. By 1949, there was some easing in consumer prices as a whole, but automobiles—still in short supply—advanced in price. Since that time the ratio of automobile prices to the consumer price index has been higher than in the prewar period. According to the demand equation, this has had an appreciable influence upon car sales. Aside from the influence of other factors, each 1 per cent increase in the ratio of the price of cars to the consumer price index was associated with an average decrease of $1\frac{1}{3}$ per cent in new-car sales in the base period. The price of cars includes only standard accessories. The cars sold in the postwar period have had more accessories and more deluxe features than those sold in earlier years, and as a consequence the total price paid by auto purchasers has increased somewhat more than the price indexes.

In Figure 32-9, actual new registrations of automobiles from 1925 through 1951 are compared with the amounts calculated using the least-squares regression equation.

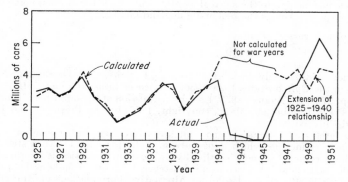

Figure 32-9. New registrations of automobiles. SOURCE: L. J. Atkinson, "Consumer Markets for Durable Goods," *Survey of Current Business*, April, 1952, p. 20.

University of Michigan—Ford Study

An analysis was made at the University of Michigan, with funds provided by the Ford Motor Company, of the demand for new automobiles in the United States from 1929 through 1956 by Suits.[1] Several differences in the methodology used in this study, as compared with the two which were previously discussed, are of interest.

In this study, the automobile market is approximately represented as a system of four equations representing (1.1) the demand for new cars by the public, (1.2) the supply of new cars by retail dealers, (1.3) the supply of used cars by retail dealers, and (1.4) the demand for used cars by the public. The variables employed in this formulation with the symbols used are as follows:

1. Retail sales of new cars (R)
2. Real disposable[2] income (Y)
3. Real retail price of new cars (P)

This third variable requires some explanation. In payment for a new car the retailer generally receives cash (or a debt instrument of cash value) and a used-car trade-in. In order to obtain the full retail cash price of the new car the dealer must then dispose of the used car, perhaps taking another in trade which in turn must be sold, etc. The net effect of these operations is to render the retail value of the new car to the dealer, although in general no single buyer pays the entire price in cash or its equivalent. The statistical problems which arise in measuring this retail price are not discussed here.[3] Conceptually, however, it may be thought of as the total receipts of new-car dealers from sales of new and used cars alike, divided by the number of new cars sold. This retail price is then converted to real terms by dividing by the consumer price index.

4. Average real price of used cars (U)
5. Average credit terms (M), the number of months the average automobile installment contract runs
6. Stock of used cars (S), the number of automobiles in existence on January 1 of the year
7. Real wholesale price of new cars (W)
8. Retailers' operating costs (T)
9. Supply of used cars to the public (R')
10. Influence of omitted factors (u_1, u_2, u_3, u_4)

The four equations then become

Demand for new cars:

$$R = a_1 \frac{(P - U)}{M} + a_2 Y + a_3 \Delta Y + a_0 + u_1 \tag{1.1}$$

The annual demand for new cars is related to the level and rate of increase in real disposable income and to the net real monthly outlay the buyer must make $(P - U)/M$. The term u_1 includes the remaining demand factors.

Supply of new cars at retail:

$$R = b_1 P + b_2 W + b_3 T + b_0 + u_2 \tag{1.2}$$

---

[1] Sections of this study are adapted from D. B. Suits, "The Demand for New Automobiles in the United States 1929–1956," *Review of Economics and Statistics*, vol. 40, no. 3, pp. 273–280, August, 1958. Used by permission of the publishers, Harvard University Press, Cambridge, Mass., copyright, 1958, by the President and Fellows of Harvard University.

[2] In a later study, Suits showed that automobile demand was more sensitive to supernumerary income (which Roos and von Szeliski had used in their study) than to disposable income. He concluded that his own demand equation is improved if about $1,500 per household is allowed as a subsistence deduction from household disposable income (see D. B. Suits, "Exploring Alternative Formulations of Automobile Demand," *Review of Economics and Statistics*, vol. 43, no. 1, pp. 66–69, February, 1961).

[3] Some aspects of Suits' procedures for determining retail prices are debatable.

The willingness of new-car dealers to sell depends on the price they obtain, the wholesale price of the car, and on dealers' costs of operations; u_2 includes the remaining factors.

Supply of used cars: $\qquad\qquad R' = c_1R + c_0 + u_3$ $\qquad\qquad\qquad$ (1.3)

This is a simple approximation equation, the supply of used cars being assumed to derive from the sale of new cars.

Demand for used cars:

$$R' = d_1 \frac{U}{M} + d_2Y + d_3\Delta Y + d_4S + d_0 + u_4 \qquad\qquad (1.4)$$

The demand for used cars depends on the monthly price of used cars (U/M) and the number of used cars in existence. Moreover it is influenced by the other factors in a way analogous to the demand for new cars.

It will be noted that we have included the existing stock of cars as a part of the used-car demand equation, but not directly as a part of new-car demand as such. This reflects the well-known fact that new-car buyers are, by and large, those who already own relatively new cars. Individuals without cars, or with old used cars, rarely go directly into the new-car market. On the other hand, the "new" supply of used cars must compete with the already existing stock. The existing stock of cars thus excercises a strong indirect influence on the new-car market via its influence on the price of used cars and hence on the net outlay required of new-car buyers.

The next step would be to confront the mathematical model with historical market data and use the appropriate statistical procedures to estimate the parameters of the equations, particularly equation (1.1). Unfortunately, the data were not adequate for this purpose. Available series of used-car prices extend back only to 1935, while reliable net outlay figures $(P - U)$ are available only since World War II. But while we cannot estimate the several equations as such, we can merge the new- and used-car demands together to obtain a composite new-car demand relation from which the unavailable variables have been eliminated. This is done by solving (1.3) and (1.4) simultaneously to obtain an expression for U/M in terms of R, Y, ΔY, and S; used-car sales, R', being eliminated in the process. Substituting this value of U/M into equation (1.1) and simplifying gives us an expression of the form

$$R = c_1 \frac{P}{M} + c_2Y + c_3\Delta Y + c_4S + c_0 + u_5 \qquad\qquad (1.5)$$

where u_5 is a linear combination of u_1, u_3, and u_4. Equation (1.5) is now an expression of the demand for new cars as a function of the total retail price (no matter how many trades are required to realize it), real disposable income, the total stock of existing cars, average credit terms, and the rate of increase in income. Put another way, (1.5) is an expression for the demand for new cars, the influence of the used-car market being implicitly taken into account.

Although the period covered by this analysis extends from 1929 through 1956, not all years could be given equal treatment. The war years 1942 to 1945 clearly had to be omitted outright, and the postwar price disequilibrium exerted such a distorting influence on the market that the years 1946 to 1948 were likewise discarded. The remaining years represent approximately normal operation of the market with the exception of 1941 (conversion) and 1952 (during which new automobile production was under government allocation and price control, and suffered from a severe steel strike). During both these years the behavior of the automobile market was distorted, but not so seriously as during 1946 to 1948. It was decided to include these years in the study but to identify them by a dummy variable (X); X has the value 0 except in 1941 and 1952 when it takes on the value 1; it is intended to act as something of a "shock absorber" and take up at least the average influence of the abnormality of these years, allowing the remaining variables to play something like their normal roles.

Like most economic functions estimated from time series, the demand for automobiles may be expected to exhibit autocorrelation of the residuals. To avoid the complications presented by this fact it was decided to conduct all analysis in terms of first differences of the variables. This also has the great advantage of suppressing the relative influence of such slowly changing factors as consumer tastes, population, etc., thus permitting a better measurement of the effect of the factors represented in the equation. The combined secular influence of the sticky factors is embodied in the constant term of the equation which represents the secular trend. The general formulation of the demand equation was thus

$$\Delta R = a_1 \Delta Y + a_2 \Delta \frac{P}{M} + a_3 \Delta S + a_4 \Delta X + a_0 \qquad (2.0)$$

The result of fitting (2.0) by least squares was

$$\Delta R = 0.106 \Delta Y - 0.234 \Delta \left(\frac{P}{M}\right) - 0.507 \Delta S - 0.827 \Delta X + 0.115 \qquad (2.1)$$
$$(0.011) \qquad (0.088) \qquad (0.086) \qquad (0.261)$$

Figures in parentheses are standard errors of the parameter estimates. In this regression, retail sales (R) and the existing stock of cars (S) are in millions of cars; real disposable income (Y) is in billions of 1947 to 1949 dollars; and the average monthly price (P/M) is obtained by dividing a retail price index by the average duration of credit contracts; ΔX is the first difference in the dummy shift variable X: $\Delta X = +1$ in 1941 and 1952; $\Delta X = -1$ in 1953; in all other years $\Delta X = 0$. It will be noted that all variables enter the regression with parameter estimates which compare very favorably with their standard errors; the omission of the rate of increase of income from the equation is due to its failure to enter significantly, as shown later. The coefficient of correlation, adjusted for degrees of freedom, is 0.93.

The close agreement between actual and calculated new-car demand is shown in Figures 32-10 and 32-11. In Figure 32-10 the first differences are compared; in Figure 32-11 the calculated difference has been added to sales of the preceding year to calcu-

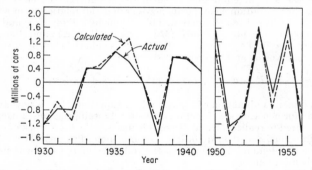

Figure 32-10. Annual changes in automobile sales, actual and calculated, 1930 to 1956. Source: D. B. Suits, "Exploring Alternative Formulations of Automobile Demand," *Review of Economics and Statistics*, vol. 43, no. 1, p. 276, February, 1961.

late total sales for the year. The real interest in form (2.1), however, lies in the fact that it includes some account of credit conditions and that the rate of change of income fails to attain significance as an explanatory variable. The statistical implications of this may be demonstrated by contrasting (2.1) with alternative formulations. To facilitate these comparisons, the regression coefficients are transformed into beta coefficients which are readily compared from equation to equation, and which, within a given equation, reflect the relative importance of the several variables. Thus transformed, (2.1) becomes

$$\Delta R = 0.919 \Delta Y - 0.578 \Delta S - 0.268 \Delta \left(\frac{P}{M}\right) - 0.317 \Delta X \qquad (2.1t)$$
$$(0.094) \qquad (0.098) \qquad (0.101) \qquad (0.100)$$

The coefficient of determination for this equation is $R^2 = 0.87$. It is readily seen that disposable income is, as would be expected, the variable of greatest importance, followed by the stock of cars on the road, and the real monthly price index.

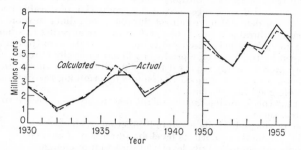

Figure 32-11. Retail sales of new passenger automobiles, actual and calculated, 1930 to 1956. SOURCE: D. B. Suits, "Exploring Alternative Formulations of Automobile Demand," *Review of Economics and Statistics*, vol. 43, no. 1, p. 276, February, 1961.

We may contrast $(2.1t)$ with the somewhat poorer result $(R^2 = 0.80)$ obtained when no account is taken of credit terms:

$$\Delta R = 1.018\Delta Y - 0.568\Delta S + 0.100\Delta P - 0.513\Delta X \qquad (2.2t)$$
$$(0.132) \qquad (0.119) \qquad (0.146) \qquad (0.167)$$

In $(2.2t)$ monthly payment, P/M, is replaced by retail price P alone. When reference to credit terms is thus omitted, the price variable no longer enters the relationship significantly and, in fact, assumes the incorrect sign.

Finally, we may compare $(2.1t)$ with the result obtained when the rate of increase in income is included along with the other variables. Where $\Delta^2 Y$ represents the second difference in income, we have

$$\Delta R = 0.843\Delta Y - 0.525\Delta S - 0.252\Delta \left(\frac{P}{M}\right) - 0.324\Delta X + 0.089\Delta^2 Y \quad (2.3t)$$

$$(0.176) \qquad (0.105) \qquad (0.106) \qquad (0.103) \qquad (0.157)$$

Inspection of $(2.3t)$ shows that the rate of increase in income is the least important of the variables in the equation, falling well below the stock of cars on the road on this score. Moreover, it fails to enter the relationships significantly. Its presence causes all standard errors to rise slightly but not enough to impugn any of the other variables In this equation $R^2 = 0.86$.

APPENDIX C. A STUDY OF THE DEMAND FOR A PRODUCER DURABLE GOOD—STEEL

A detailed study of the demand for steel was made for the United States Steel Corporation under the direction of T. Yntema in 1939.[1] Sections of this report are presented here to illustrate the economic and statistical considerations involved in the measurement of the demand for producer goods.

[1] TNEC Papers, United States Steel Corporation, 1940.

Analysis of the demand for steel is complex and presents analytical problems for a number of reasons: it is not a homogeneous commodity; it is a raw material, a producer, not a consumer, good; it is used in the production of many widely differing kinds of products made from steel; it is durable and can be stored; it is not sold in a single one-price market; and it is largely used in the production of durable goods.

The conditions of demand for producer durable goods differ in some respects from those for consumer durable goods. The types of factors affecting the demand for consumer durable goods have been discussed in our considerations of the demand for automobiles in Appendix B. However, a producer will not generally purchase a new durable good unless he can reasonably expect it to be a profitable investment. In previous sections of this book we have examined the factors determining the profitability of such producer-durable-good investments.

It was felt that the following factors might reasonably be expected to influence the quantity of steel sold:

1. The price of steel—both its level and direction of change
2. Industrial production—both its level and direction of change
3. Consumers' income—both its level and direction of change
4. Industrial profits—both its level and direction of change
5. The cost of living
6. The distribution of income among income classes
7. The stock (number of units and efficiency) of durable goods—both consumers' and producers'
8. The prices of goods and services which compete with products made from steel for the outlays of producers and consumers
9. The costs of maintaining and operating products made from steel
10. The psychological atmosphere—i.e., producers' and consumers' anticipation as to future economic conditions

Since some of these variables are very highly related to others, however, and since others tend to change slowly and smoothly from year to year, certain of them were omitted in the actual analysis. The factors which were used in the final statistical analysis were the first five listed above plus a time-trend variable. These six factors can be taken as approximately representing all of the ten previously mentioned. The period 1919 to 1938 was chosen for analysis, using annual data. However, it was found desirable to exclude the years 1919–1921 from some of the demand relations because analysis indicated that the situation in these three years was abnormal because of World War I.

Prior to the actual statistical determination of the demand for steel, it was necessary to set up an economically logical hypothesis as to the way the factors previously considered act together in determining the quantity of steel sold. The lack of information at critical points and the absence of a completely suitable body of economic theory forced recourse to what is largely an empirical determination of the demand hypothesis. Five general hypotheses as to the actual variables to be included in the demand-relation hypothesis were set up. The five general hypotheses were that the quantity of steel sold depends upon:

1. The price of steel and the volume of industrial production
2. A time-trend variable in addition to those of hypothesis 1
3. The same variables as hypothesis 2 and in addition two variables measuring respectively the rate of change in the price of steel and the rate of change in the volume of industrial production
4. The price of steel, a time trend, consumers' supernumerary income, and industrial profits
5. The same variables as 4 above and, in addition, three variables measuring respectively the rate of change in the price of steel, in supernumerary income, and in industrial profits

In 1 above it was assumed that industrial production reflected the composite effect of the most important demand factors, viz., industrial profits, consumers' income, the replacement pressure on the stock of durable goods, and, also, indirectly the psychological outlook. In 2 an additional time-trend factor was included explicitly as a variable to act as a proxy measure for all factors influencing the demand for steel which tend to change slowly and smoothly over a long period of time, such as population, the size of the stock of durable goods, and long-time changes in various price and cost levels (including the level of the prices of steel), industrial technology, and people's tastes. The anticipations of producers and consumers as to future prices, profits, income, etc., are largely determined by the rapidity and direction of change in recent and current business activity. For this reason the rate of change of industrial production was included in hypothesis 3 as a factor measuring changes in anticipations. Similarly the rate of change in the price of steel was included in 3 as a measure of steel buyers' anticipations as to the near future price of steel. In 4 and 5 industrial profits and consumers' supernumerary income and their respective rates of change have been substituted for industrial production and its rate of change to measure the composite of factors other than the price of steel influencing the demand for steel.

The next step is the formulation of a hypothesis as to the way the economic variables act together in determining the demand for steel. Each of the five general hypotheses outlined above was studied by graphical multifactor correlation techniques, in order to find out what mathematical relation seems to be the most reasonable expression of the relation between the factors and whether any of the five general hypotheses should be discarded or modified. The graphical analysis indicated that for all of the hypotheses a simple additive relation would probably give as satisfactory results as any other (such as the multiplicative or combinations of the additive and multiplicative). It was also decided from the graphical analysis to use only hypotheses 2, 4, and a modification of 3 which excluded the rate of change in the price of steel and the time trend.

Thus, four mathematical relations were formulated for further examination by statistical techniques.

$$\text{Relation I: } x_p = a_p + b_p p + c_p I + d_p t$$
$$\text{Relation II: } x_p = e_p + f_p p + g_p I + h_p I_r$$
$$\text{Relation III: } x_s = a_s + b_s p + c_s S + d_s P + e_s t$$
$$\text{Relation IV: } x_b = a_b + b_b P + c_b S + d_b P + e_b t$$

A fifth relation also was studied.

$$\text{Relation V: } x_p = A p^B I^C 10^{Dt}$$

Where x_p = quantity of production of steel ingots and castings (in thousands of gross tons)

x_b = quantity of steel bookings (in thousands of gross and net tons)

x_s = quantity of steel shipments (in thousands of gross and net tons)

p = *Iron Age* composite price of finished steel (in cents per pound)

I = index of industrial production excluding iron and steel (1923–1925 = 100)

I_r = link relatives of I

S = supernumerary income (in billions of dollars)

P = industrial profits (in billions of dollars)

t = time (in years measured from an origin depending on the period studied)

The various constants, a_p, b_p, etc., were determined by the method of least squares. The resulting statistical demand relations are shown in Table 32-8.

The same least-squares statistical procedure also gives the percentage of the total variation in the quantity of steel sold over the period studied that is accounted for by the economic factors included in the relations and the amount that can be directly attributed to the separate variations of each of the factors. These percentages are shown in Table 32-9 for relations I, II, III, and IV.

Assuming the adequacy of our economic model, two conclusions are indicated by Table 32-9: in each of the demand relations, the included factors accounted for 90 per cent or more of the observed variation in the respective measure of steel sales; over the period studied only a small fraction (10 per cent or less) of the variation in steel sales was directly attributable to variation in steel prices, while the major part of the variation was accounted for by included factors other than the price of steel. In appraising the latter conclusion, it should be kept in mind that the relative proportion

Table 32-8. **Statistical Demand Relations for Steel**

Period studied	Relation number	Equation of demand relation
1919–1938*	I[11]	$x_p = -63,800 + 7,478p + 893I - 91.1t$
1919–1938†	I[1]	$x_p = -65,200 + 8,201p + 890I$
1922–1938*	I	$x_p = -57,081 + 2,217p + 944I - 127t$
1920–1938†	II	$x_p = -71,700 + 8,605p + 857I + 87I_r$
1919–1938‡	III[1]	$x_s = 3,014 + 388p + 1,005P + 510S + 144t$
1922–1938‡	III	$x_s = 11,760 - 2,419p + 1,157P + 426S + 59t$
1919–1938‡	IV[1]	$x_b = 8,680 + 298p + 1,563P + 327S + 270t$
1922–1938‡	IV	$x_b = 33,480 - 10,254p + 1,863P + 258S + 143t$
1922–1938‡	V	$x_p = \dfrac{0.158p^{0.235}I^{2.667}}{10^{0.0020t}}$

* Origin of time variable is January 1, 1929.

† Time variable has been excluded in the equation.

‡ Origin of time variable is July 1, 1930.

Table 32-9. **Percentage of Variation in Quantity of Steel Sold Accounted for by Each Factor**

Relation number	Quantity of steel sold measured by	Variation accounted for by all factors in demand relation	Directly attributable to variation in					
			Price of steel	Industrial production	Industrial profits	Supernumerary income	Rate of change of industrial production	Time trend
I	Production of steel ingots and castings	96%	0%	88%				0%
II	Production of steel ingots and castings	96	9	81			1%	
III	Estimated steel shipments	91	1		41%	19%		0
IV	Estimated steel bookings	90	9		90	6		1

of the total variation of steel sales attributable to variation in the price of steel over any period will depend in part on the amount of variation in steel prices relative to variation in the other factors. Over the period 1922 to 1938 relative variation in steel prices was considerably less than in the other factors.

Given the statistical demand equations, it is a simple task to measure the elasticity of demand or the elasticity of the quantity of steel sold with respect to the price of steel. Let x_c be the quantity of steel sold as computed from one of the above equations. Then the elasticity of demand (E) is equal to $(\partial x_c/\partial P)\,(p/x_c)$. Thus the elasticity of demand formula for the first of the equations of Table 32-8 (relation I[11]) is:

$$E = \frac{7{,}478p}{-63{,}800 + 7{,}478p + 8931 - 91.1t}$$

The elasticity formulas for the other equations are similarly defined, except for relation V, which is directly $E = 0.235$. It is obvious therefore that, with the exception of relation V, the elasticity is not constant, but varies with the factors influencing demand.

Table 32-10 shows the values of the elasticity of demand found in the four demand relations when the values of the demand factors are at their average levels for the periods studied. The values are consistent in this very important respect: they indicate that at most a 1 per cent decrease in the price of steel would cause (other factors remaining the same) less than a 1 per cent increase in steel sales (and conversely). If this is true, and if fluctuations in the other factors continue to be as great and as important as they have been in this period, the volume of steel consumption cannot be stabilized by compensatory changes in the price of steel.

Table 32-10. Elasticity of Demand for Steel

Relation number	Elasticity
I	+0.12
II	+0.52
III	−0.21
IV	−0.88

Which of these values of the elasticity of demand is the most likely? The values obtained from relations III and IV are probably better than those from I and II for the following reasons:

1. On a priori grounds it seems reasonable that a change in the price of steel would lead to a change in the opposite direction in steel sales. Relations I and II both indicate positive relations between steel prices and sales.

2. Steel-ingot production is probably not as accurate a measure of steel sales as the estimates used in relations III and IV.

3. Industrial production (and its rate of change) is probably not as good a measure of the composite of factors other than price of steel as the combination of the two factors, industrial profits and supernumerary income.

The difference in the values obtained from relations III and IV can be due only to the difference between the estimates of steel sales used in each case, for the relations are identical in other respects. Fluctuations in the steel-bookings figures (used in relation IV) tend to lead industrial profits, while steel shipments (used in relation III) do so to a much less degree. Also accounting profit figures tend to lag behind the current profit that they supposedly measure. In the graphical analyses that were made of the various demand relations, there were clear indications that if the lags of shipments and industrial profits behind bookings were removed, relations III and IV would both give about the same results for the elasticity of demand, yielding a figure of 0.3 to 0.4.

APPENDIX D. A STUDY OF RETAIL-DEPARTMENT-STORE DEMAND AS A FUNCTION OF PRICE

The data for each of the commodities on the basis of which price-sales relationships are derived comprise the daily sales of each commodity together with the corresponding prices.[1] The period covered is 2.5 months. The commodities included are staples—carried in stock year after year—and, as far as can be determined, without violent seasonal changes in demand. These commodities are standard merchandise which can be duplicated in a number of retail stores. Partly because of this fact, price changes are more frequent than would be typical of less staple department-store merchandise.

The sales data will be subject to considerable variation independent of prices of competing commodities, etc., due to purely random causes as well as to the differing importance of various days of the week in retail selling. Rather than make minute adjustments for such variation, the daily sales for a period of constant price are averaged.

The selection of the equations to express the relationship between sales and price is simplified by the fact that quantity taken is clearly the dependent variable. A price results from certain decisions by the retailer. The customers purchase a certain amount at that price. The supply is, at least under the conditions studied, perfectly elastic at each price set. This short-cuts the problems of shifting supply curves which can plague statistical demand studies. The simplest assumption is that $Q = f(p)$, where Q is the daily sales average for each period during which price does not vary and p the price.

Since we are not concerned with other influences on sales, the only other variable which might be introduced is time. For a period of 2.5 months, time is a seasonal rather than a trend factor. Cases are selected where the seasonal variation is relatively unimportant and not likely to affect sales elasticity to any marked degree. To test the possible effect of such a factor, however, Whitman experiments with the assumption $Q = f(p,t)$, where t is the time in days from the beginning of the period.

For the specific form of the price-sales equation, only constant-elasticity equations were used because such equations fit the data very well. A straight line, $Q = a + bp$, invariably gives a poor fit to the data, while the equation $Q = Ap^a$ invariably gives a good fit. The logic of an assumption of constant elasticity can be disputed with the argument that, above a certain price, the demand for a firm's merchandise will be very elastic; below a certain price, quite inelastic. However, within the range of prices set during this study, the assumption of constant elasticity for the staple merchandise appears to be true.

The criteria of simplicity, ease of computation, and goodness of fit suggests an experiment with the following constant-elasticity equations: (a) $Q = Ap^a$ and (b) $Q = Ap^a e^{Bt}$. It will be noted that the latter equation states that, when price is fixed, the relative increment of quantity purchased per unit of time (day) is independent of the level at which price is fixed. The assumption is also made that this relative increment is constant during the period studied and that no more complex function of t is necessary to express the seasonal factor. This latter assumption does not have any a priori justification but has seemed adequate to describe the behavior of the data.

Figure 32-12 shows the average daily sales of article A plotted against corresponding prices. Using equation (a) as the form of the price-sales function, the price-sales relation is $\log Q = 4.41 - 5.95 \log P$ or $Q = 25,710p^{-5.95}$. It will be noted that the sales elasticity is high.

Table 32-11 shows the results obtained in analyzing the price-sales behavior of article A by fitting the two equations (a) and (b) described above. The coefficients of correlation are about 0.9, indicating a fairly good fit in both cases. The second equation, with time introduced as an independent variable, improves the fit only slightly. The estimates of sales elasticity obtained by both equations are similar and there is no question but that the response of sales to price is an elastic one.

Another method of studying price-sales relationships is that of link relatives. This method is useful in obtaining an over-all elasticity for a group of articles similar in nature. In many situations the price of a single item will not vary often enough to

---

[1] The findings of this study are adapted from pp. 208–221 of R. H. Whitman, "Demand Functions for Merchandise at Retail," in *Studies in Mathematical Economics and Econometrics*, edited by O. Lange, F. M. McIntyre, and T. O. Yntema, and used by permission of the University of Chicago Press, copyright 1942 by the University of Chicago Press, all rights reserved.

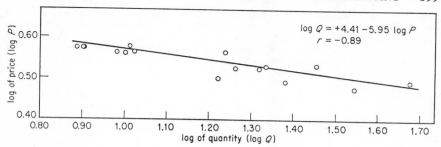

Figure 32-12. Relationship of average daily unit sales to prices, article A. SOURCE: R. H. Whitman, "Demand Functions for Merchandise at Retail," p. 214 in *Studies in Mathematical Economics and Econometrics*, edited by O. Lange, F. M. McIntyre, and T. O. Yntema, and used by permission of the University of Chicago Press, copyright 1942 by the University Press, all rights reserved.

Table 32-11. Commodity A: Characteristics of Price-Sales Relationships with Quantity as Dependent Variable for a 2.5-month Period

(Figures in parentheses are standard errors)

Q = rate of daily sale for period of constant price

p = price

t = time in days (origin at beginning of period)

Equation	Equations			Descriptive constants		
	Constant term	$\log p$	t	Elasticity of sales E	r	Coefficient of multiple correlation corrected for no. of parameters R'_{est}
(a) $\log Q$	4.41	−5.95 (0.78)		−5.95	−0.89	
(b) $\log Q$	4.47	−5.83 (0.66)	−0.0039 (0.0014)	−5.83		0.92

make it possible to derive an equation unless the analysis is extended over a longer period with the resultant introduction of the effect of changes in tastes, changes in the merchandise, etc. This greatly restricts the possibilities of analysis unless it is feasible to determine the elasticity for a "commodity" comprised of a number of similar articles. The price-sales behavior of a particular item which may be nonexistent in six months is frequently of less importance than the price-sales behavior of a commodity group. For example, suppose that ten different brands of low-priced toilet soaps in twenty different sizes are being sold. The elasticity of sales for brand C, which may not be carried another year, is less important to the retailer than the elasticity of sales for low-priced toilet soaps as a whole. The link-relative method makes it possible to generalize the price-sales behavior for all the ten brands and twenty sizes. The function will be $Q' = f(p')$, where $Q' = Q_i/Q_{(i-1)}$, and $p' = p_i/p_{(i-1)}$. Q_i and p_i are the average daily sales and price for any period of constant price, and $Q_{(i-1)}$ and $p_{(i-1)}$ are the average daily sales and price for the period immediately preceding. The equation can be fitted to all the Q', p' observations irrespective of the particular brand or size involved. The legitimacy of this procedure depends on whether sales elasticity is homogeneous for the articles included in the commodity group. This can be tested by graphic analyses or, in certain circumstances, by measuring elasticity for the individual articles. The method of analysis using link relatives is the same as previously illustrated, using Q' and p' instead of Q and p. Thus, for the assumption of constant elasticity, our model would be $Q' = A(p')^a$.

APPENDIX E. A STUDY OF DOMESTIC-AIR-PASSENGER DEMAND

Before each major phase of the development of the Port of New York Authority's regional airport program is undertaken, a long-range forecast of air traffic is prepared to guide the physical and economic planning of the airport facilities under consideration. In this connection, the Port Authority made an interesting forecast several years ago of United States domestic-air-passenger travel using a market-research approach.[1]

The Survey. The basic criteria used for this forecast were developed by analyzing the results of a market survey which provided data reflecting the effects of age, occupation, industry, income, and education upon the air travel of adults. The survey findings indicated that different types of information should be used in grouping and classifying the characteristics of the population making business trips and those making personal trips. For example, it was found unnecessary to include education as a separate factor when studying the characteristics of people making business trips, since educational level is generally implied by the person's occupation and, in part, in his industry affiliation. However, it was necessary to consider education as a separate factor in studying personal travel, since characteristics of personal travel differ between people in the same occupation, and even of the same income, but with different levels of education. For that reason, business and personal travel were analyzed separately. In studying business air travel, three major controlling components were therefore used: occupation, industry, and income. For personal travel, four components were used: age, occupation, income, and education.

Personal Travel Cells. The past, present, and future (1950, 1955, 1956, and 1975) adjusted total population was distributed into four predetermined age groups: 18–24, 25–44, 45–64, and 65 and over. The total survey population was then distributed into the five controlling occupation groups: professional, managerial, technical, and proprietor; clerical, sales, and labor; farm owners, managers, and foremen; housewives, students, and unemployed; and retired. These were then subdivided into the four predetermined income groups: (1) under $3,000, (2) $3,000–$5,999, (3) $6,000–$9,999, and (4) $10,000 and over, yielding 80 age by occupation by income cells which were further divided into the two educational groups: (1) high school graduates and (2) non-high school graduates. As the population groups over 18 years of age move forward in time, they will ordinarily maintain their present high school graduation status on the assumption that there will be no future radical change in their level of high school education. For example, that portion of the population who will be in the 45 to 64 age group in 1965 was, for the most part, in the 25 to 44 age group in 1950. Therefore, the educational level attained in 1950 by the 25 to 44 age group was applied to the 45 to 64 age group of 1965. For that portion of the population who will fall into the 18 to 24 age group of the future, estimates of their educational levels were made by adjusting the 1950 proportion of high school graduates upward according to the historically rising trend in the percentage of high school graduates to the total population of high school age. By subdividing age by occupation by income cells into their two education levels,

---

[1] The methods and results of this study are adapted and summarized from *Forecast of the United States Domestic Air Passenger Market, 1965–1975*, Port of New York Authority, New York, 1957.

160 age by occupation by income by education cells were constructed, as shown in Table 32-12.

Business Travel Cells. Since the nonemployed segment of the population was excluded from business air trips, only the employed labor force was considered in the formation of business travel cells. These were distributed into the five established occupation groups as follows: professional and technical; managerial and proprietor; sales; clerical and labor; farm owners, managers, and foremen. Because significant differences in travel characteristics were found to exist among that portion of the population in the professional, managerial, and sales occupations when they were employed in different industries, these occupations were further cross-classified under each of the 14 industrial distributions. The clerical and labor occupations were cross-classified only under the three main divisions of industry: high travel, medium travel, and low travel, since the travel characteristics of these occupations did not vary substantially within each such industry group. The farm owners, managers, and foremen required cross-classification only within the agricultural, forestry, and fishing industries. This cross-classification of the labor force by occupation and industry resulted in 46 cells, which were then further cross-classified with income distribution in each cell by the same methods used in the personal travel cells. However, the occupation by industry cells of the clerk and labor occupational groups in all industrial classifications and the professional, managerial, and sales occupational groups in the low-travel industries were not broken into the four predetermined income groups because there was no significant difference in travel in these groups that appeared to be attributable to differences in income. This cross classification of 46 occupation by industry cells by income groups resulted in the 130 occupation by industry by income cells relating to business travel.

Personal-travel-cell Frequencies. From the market survey it was possible to determine the 1955 air-travel frequency per capita of the population reported by survey respondents of each of the 160 cells. In order to forecast future volumes of air travel it was necessary to estimate the future travel frequency characteristics of each cell, which could then be applied to the future population of each of the cells to determine the number of trips made by the cell population in the estimated year. The following data derived from the survey were used to estimate future travel frequency:

1. The number of people and percentage of the total population in each cell who had never flown before the beginning of the survey year were designated as nonfliers. Included in this group, also, are those who flew for the first time during the survey year.
2. The number of personal air trips per 1,000 nonfliers.
3. The number of people and percentage of the total population in each cell who has flown prior to the survey year (designated as fliers).
4. The number of personal air trips per 1,000 fliers.

The survey indicated that the most significant reason for the constantly increasing volume of air trips recorded in the past few years has been the increase in the rate of acceptance of air as a mode of travel by former nonfliers. In order to take into account this continuing rate of acceptance and project its effect into the future, an acceptance or learning factor was developed for each cell, which measured the annual rate at which nonfliers become fliers. From the data collected in the survey it was possible to determine the proportion of each cell's population that was nonflier in 1955. This established one point on a curve used to measure the theoretical nonflier segment of the cell's population in any given year (before or after the survey year). A second point was established by going back in time to a year in which it might reasonably be assumed that 100 per cent of the cell population were nonfliers. For most of the population cells it was assumed that 1935 was such a year. (That was the initial year of operation of the first efficient commercial air carrier, the DC-3, and was also the year in which sizable increases in air travel were recorded.) Understandably, the only age group for which this assumption would not hold was the 18 to 24 age group, for most of them were born later than 1935. For this age group in 1955, the first postwar year, 1945, was chosen as the year in which 100 per cent were nonfliers. For this age group in the future population, the year of their birth was taken as the base year.

By connecting these two plotted points for each cell—the 1955 proportion of nonfliers and 100 per cent in the base year (either 1935, 1945, or year of birth)—on semi-

Table 32-12. Portion of Personal-travel-cell Population Projections

(Population of personal-travel cells: Occupation × age × income × education, 1950, 1955, 1965, 1975)

(In thousands)

Age	Education	Year	PROFESSIONAL, TECHNICAL, MANAGERIAL AND PROPRIETOR — FAMILY INCOME Under $3,000	$3,000–$5,999	$6,000–$9,999	Over $10,000	CLERICAL, SALES, LABOR — FAMILY INCOME Under $3,000	$3,000–$5,999	$6,000–$9,999	TOTAL OCCUPATION — FAMILY INCOME Under $3,000	$3,000–$5,999	$6,000–$9,999	Over $10,000	GRAND TOTAL
18–24	Non-High School Grads.	1950	298	80	6	....	5,375	963	15	10,490	1,133	26	5	11,654
		1955	168	166	24	....	2,920	2,777	325	5,128	4,956	422	218	10,724
		1965	242	229	54	20	3,067	3,497	824	5,668	6,093	1,039	807	15,607
		1975	289	252	83	45	3,551	4,084	1,804	6,472	6,850	2,164	1,919	17,405
	High School Grads.	1950	356	86	7	2	608	122	2	2,140	224	10	4	2,378
		1955	223	173	32	14	398	452	91	1,203	1,008	208	57	2,476
		1965	363	274	82	36	767	929	321	1,994	1,868	593	239	4,694
		1975	472	334	136	89	1,122	1,361	849	2,797	2,576	1,346	776	7,495
25–44	Non-High School Grads.	1950	881	1,133	267	111	9,963	6,776	462	25,475	8,517	849	214	35,055
		1955	346	1,106	692	278	3,487	10,699	3,151	9,956	17,535	5,155	1,163	33,809
		1965	256	884	927	601	2,174	8,071	4,862	6,775	13,870	7,388	3,004	31,037
		1975	214	759	1,181	1,088	1,506	5,762	7,402	5,557	11,442	10,635	5,545	33,179
TOTAL—Over 18	TOTAL Non-High School Grads.	1950	2,155	2,111	628	335	22,452	12,277	961	64,508	15,959	1,932	595	82,994
		1955	894	2,120	1,513	825	8,932	20,740	6,693	29,328	36,469	12,909	3,347	82,053
		1965	723	1,640	1,906	1,596	7,343	18,659	11,946	25,025	32,804	19,473	8,146	85,448
		1975	671	1,417	2,184	2,600	6,584	14,974	17,684	24,109	28,522	27,334	14,998	94,963
	TOTAL High School Grads.	1950	1,625	1,912	772	458	1,829	1,347	221	8,280	3,514	1,064	573	13,431
		1955	740	2,073	2,005	1,130	778	2,586	2,103	3,696	8,750	6,464	2,287	21,197
		1965	906	1,867	2,756	2,566	1,238	3,047	3,937	5,486	8,662	11,628	6,697	32,473
		1975	969	1,663	3,065	4,131	1,663	3,549	5,798	6,571	8,361	15,961	12,650	43,543
	GRAND TOTAL (Survey Population)	1950	3,780	4,023	1,400	793	24,281	13,624	1,182	72,788	19,473	2,996	1,168	96,425
		1955	1,634	4,193	3,518	1,955	9,710	23,326	8,796	33,024	45,219	19,373	5,634	103,250
		1965	1,629	3,507	4,662	4,162	8,581	21,706	15,883	30,511	41,466	31,101	14,843	117,921
		1975	1,640	3,080	5,249	6,731	8,247	18,523	23,482	30,680	36,883	43,295	27,648	138,506

logarithmic graph paper and extending this assumed growth curve into the future to 1975, it was possible to estimate from the chart the proportion of the population in each cell that would be nonfliers at any future or past point in time. The difference between the percentage of nonfliers at any date and 100 per cent, therefore, would be the estimated percentage of the cell population who were fliers on that date. This technique assumes that the nonflier proportion of the population in each cell decreases at a constant rate from the first year of their exposure to commercial aviation to the year 1955 when the survey was completed and will so continue to some future point in time when (by arbitrary limitations) only 10 per cent of the population in any cell may still remain nonfliers. For example, the survey indicated that in 1955, 35 per cent of the professional and managerial group, aged 25 to 44, earning between $6,000 and $9,999, high school graduates, were nonfliers (or conversely 65 per cent were fliers). By 1965, based on the acceptance curve plotted for this cell, 22 per cent of the population will not have flown (or 78 per cent will be fliers) and by 1975 only 12 per cent will still be nonfliers.

Business-travel-cell Frequencies. The survey results indicated that the business traveler had apparently already completed the learning process by 1955 since only a relatively few of the business travelers had taken their first air trip during the survey year. Therefore, no distinction was made between the business-air-travel characteristics of fliers and nonfliers. The 1955 business-air-travel frequency characteristics were ascertained for the total population of each business cell by computing the average number of business air trips during 1955 per 1,000 population of the cell. Although no learning factor was applied to business travel it was assumed that the frequency of air travel per 1,000 population in each cell would nevertheless continue to increase at an arithmetic rate equal to the average annual rate of growth during the period 1935 to 1955. This rate of increase was determined by assuming that during the base year of 1935, the first business trips were taken. Connecting this zero point in 1935 and the point representing the average number of business trips per 1,000 found in 1955 yielded a trend describing the estimated rate of change in the frequency of business air travel per capita for the cell. For example, in 1955, professionals in the manufacturing industry earning between $3,000 and $5,999 took 600 trips per 1,000. On the basis of the above estimate, they made 450 trips per 1,000 in 1950 and are expected to make 900 trips per 1,000 by 1965 and 1,200 per 1,000 by 1975.

Personal-travel Forecast. After developing the proportion of fliers and nonfliers in each cell, the population of each cell falling into each of these categories was computed for 1965 and 1975. That portion of the cell population estimated to be fliers in the future year was assumed to have the same traveling frequency per capita as did the fliers found in the market survey in 1955. The total number of air trips per cell, therefore, was calculated by adding

Trips by fliers = number of fliers times the average number of trips per flier

plus

Trips by nonfliers = number of nonfliers times the average number of trips per non-flier

Business-travel Forecast. As explained previously, no acceptance factor for business travelers was estimated; it was assumed that those who must make business trips had learned to fly by 1955. Therefore, to estimate future business air trips it was necessary only to multiply the population of each cell by the trips per capita determined for that cell in 1955, as increased for the forecast year in accordance with the estimated arithmetic rate of growth in frequency of trips per capita indicated during the past 20 years.

Total Forecast. By summarizing the estimated future air trips calculated for each of the personal and business cells, estimated by the methods outlined above, a forecast of air trips by the survey population is obtained. Since the resulting estimates of air trips refer to the survey population only, they explicitly exclude trips made by those components of the population that were excluded from the survey: children under 18; armed forces living on post; persons living in hotels, boarding houses, schools and other institutions; foreigners traveling in the United States; and other special groups. In order to estimate total future trips made by the total future population, the forecast obtained from the survey population was expanded by using the comparisons between enplaned passengers in 1950 and 1955 as reported by the Civil Aeronautics Administration and estimated trips accounted for by the survey population in those years. The forecast for 1965 and 1975 was obtained as follows.

	1965	1975
Estimated round trips by survey population:		
Personal....................................	15,100,000	25,207,000
Business....................................	19,941,000	39,764,000
Total round trips.........................	35,041,000	64,971,000
Total trips by survey population (round trips doubled)....................................	70,082,000	129,942,000
Forecast (128.3% of total trips by survey population)..	90,000,000	167,000,000

PROBLEMS

1. The concluding sentence of the text discussion of econometric models states that there is a danger of inaccurate results if good judgment is not applied. If this is so, why not avoid the expensive and time-consuming model-building procedure and apply the judgment directly to the economic variable being forecast?

2. When the businessman uses the word "demand," to which of the two meanings mentioned in the text is he usually referring?

3. Refer to Figure 32-5, which shows the demand for pork based upon a simple graphical regression. (a) Has the demand for pork been increasing or decreasing during the period 1925 through 1956? (b) Estimate an approximate range for the percentage change in the demand for pork between the 1925 to 1931 period and the 1932 to 1941, 1947 to 1952 period. (c) Estimate an approximate range for the percentage change in the demand between the 1932 to 1941, 1947 to 1952 period, and the 1953 to 1956 period. (d) What is the approximate elasticity of demand for pork for the 1953 to 1956 period?

4. Refer to discussion in the text of Working's multiple-correlation studies of the demand for pork. Can you suggest a possible reason that the correlation using the consumer price index instead of time gave unsatisfactory results postwar, compared with its extremely high correlation prewar?

5. What is the logic of using supernumerary income rather than disposable income in studying automobile demand in the Roos–von Szeliski (General Motors) study of automobile demand?

6. Compare the three studies of automobile demand described in the text (General Motors, Department of Commerce, University of Michigan) on the basis of (a) the variables used, and (b) the analytic methods and techniques.

7. Since steel is a producer rather than a consumer good, different types of variables enter its demand function than for the previously considered durable good, automobiles, which is primarily a consumer item. Which variables were considered in the U.S. Steel study and not the automobile studies?

8. Derive the formula for the elasticity of demand for relation II of the U.S. Steel study.

9. Refer to the study by Whitman presented in the text of retail-department-store demand as a function of price. In what ways could the results of this type of demand study be useful in department-store management decision-making?

10. Discuss the validity of the method for estimating the number of fliers in future personal-travel cells in the Port of New York Authority air-travel forecast. Can you justify the arbitrary limitation of nonfliers in any population cell to no less than 10 per cent of the population? Can you suggest improvements or a better method?

11. Accuracy was presented in the text as one of the criteria of desirable sales-forecasting procedure. (a) Is the ability to be correct a high percentage of time more important than ability to predict changes in cycle? (b) Analyze, with respect to the two aspects of accuracy mentioned in (a), the strength and weakness of the following forecasting approaches presented in the text: (1) persistence technique, (2) demand analysis and market research, (3) time-series analysis.

33 Short-run Cost Relationships

Short-run cost relationships refer to cost variations which are associated with short-run rate-of-output adaptations of the enterprise to market and production conditions. Thus, in the short run, the size of the plant, the production techniques, the prices for materials, labor rates, managerial procedures, quality of management, etc., are all considered constant. The short-run cost analysis is concerned with variations in total cost caused by changes in the rate of production using existing facilities. It measures cost changes caused by variations in the utilization of fixed facilities. The analysis of costs into fixed and variable elements is based on short-run cost concepts.

Fixed and Variable Costs. The expenses of operating any enterprise may be divided into two groups: those which do not vary with changes in the volume of activity (called fixed costs); and those which vary in direct proportion with the volume of operations (called variable costs). In general terms, it may be stated that the fixed costs are derived from the fact that a business needs to have in readiness the capacity to produce a certain volume of goods or services regardless of the exact status of the orders on hand at any time. The fixed costs are thus "possession and readiness" costs occasioned by the necessity to provide capacity for production. Variable costs are the additional expenses, roughly proportionate to the volume of output, required to supplement the "possession and readiness" expenses to enable production of the goods or services. The conventional profit and loss statement does not make this differentiation between fixed and variable costs.

Fixed expenses vary with time. Variable expenses vary with production or sales performance (volume). Some expenses have a proportion varying with time (fixed portion) and a proportion varying with volume (variable portion).

This concept of fixed and variable costs is based on a consideration of total costs during a period of time. If unit or average costs are considered rather than total costs, then the situation is reversed: the fixed total costs are variable when expressed as unit or average costs and the variable total costs are fixed when expressed as unit or average costs.

These facts are illustrated by the cost data in Table 33-1. The data of this table are plotted in Figures 33-1 and 33-2. The fixed portion of the total costs, $100, becomes the variable portion of the unit costs on the chart of average costs, Figure 33-2. The variable portion of the total costs

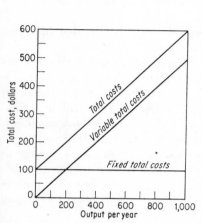

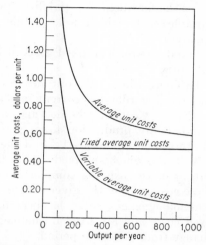

Figure 33-1. Total-cost variation with volume.

Figure 33-2. Average unit-cost variation with volume.

becomes the fixed portion of the average costs, $0.50, on this same chart.

The concept of fixed and variable costs which we shall use will be based on total costs: fixed expenses being a function of time; variable expenses being a function of operational volume.

Table 33-1. Illustration of Differences between Fixed and Variable Total Costs and Fixed and Variable Unit Costs

(1)	(2)	(3)	(4)	(5)	(6)	(7)
No. of units per year	Total costs (3) + (4)	Fixed portion of total costs	Variable portion of total costs	Average unit costs (2) ÷ (1)	Fixed portion of unit average costs (4) ÷ (1)	Variable portion of unit average costs (3) ÷ (1)
100	$150.00	$100	$ 50	$1.50	$0.50	$1.00
200	200.00	100	100	1.00	0.50	0.50
300	250.00	100	150	0.83	0.50	0.33
400	300.00	100	200	0.75	0.50	0.25
500	350.00	100	250	0.70	0.50	0.20
600	400.00	100	300	0.67	0.50	0.17
700	450.00	100	350	0.64	0.50	0.14
800	500.00	100	400	0.63	0.50	0.13
900	550.00	100	450	0.61	0.50	0.11
1,000	600.00	100	500	0.60	0.50	0.10

Just as costs are not inherently direct or indirect, but acquire these characteristics as a result of managerial and accounting decision, so costs are not inherently fixed or variable. Managerial policy affects and determines the fixedness or variability of costs. In the delineations of fixed and variable costs which follow, this element of managerial decision is apparent.

Fixed Costs. The fixed costs of operations may be divided into two categories:

1. Those which will continue to occur provided the business does not dissolve, regardless of current managerial policy, of how drastically volume may vary, of whether any particular products are produced, of whether any production takes place at all—these items will be called pure-fixed costs and are beyond the control of the current management.

2. Those which are fixed only in the sense that variations in volume or output of the existing complement of products will cause no change in these costs during the given budget or planning period in which the current management policy has been fixed—these costs will be called policy-fixed costs and are fixed by managerial policy in each period and may change from period to period.

Pure-fixed costs, as defined above, may include items such as interest costs on mortgages, depreciation charges, property taxes, certain insurance expenses, rentals, certain executive salary expenses, etc. These costs are beyond the immediate control of the current management and will continue even if production is completely discontinued. Over a period of time, of course, the management can exercise some control by not replacing equipment, by reorganizing its corporate executive structure, by selling a plant, by renegotiating taxes. (If a long enough period of time is considered, no costs in the enterprise are fixed.)

Policy-fixed costs may include such items as contract advertising expense, supervisory salary expenses, general management expense, plant management expense, sales management expense, certain utility costs, plant protection expenses, etc. These costs are fixed in the sense that, based on present managerial policy as expressed in the current budget, the costs will not change with limited variations in volume of operations.

Variable Costs. Variable costs may include such items as direct labor, direct material, certain supplies, certain types of depreciation, etc. Variable costs include all items which change in a manner proportionate to volume. Managerial policy is, of course, a determining factor in the classification of these costs as variable. Thus, direct labor is a variable cost—i.e., varies in proportion with volume—only when the company management establishes and enforces procedures whereby, by dismissals and hirings, the labor force is decreased with decreasing volume and increased with increasing volume. However, a company may decide to keep its direct-labor payroll intact over what appears to be a temporary recession to maintain worker morale and save costs associated with dismissals, hirings, and retrainings. In such cases, then, some labor costs will become fixed expenses.

Controllability of variable costs is dependent upon the intensity of management's insistence on efficiency. This varies with the state of the economy and the prosperity of the firm. Variable costs remain variable only as long as management has effective control of these operating costs and insists that variable costs actually vary down as well as up.

Thus, depending upon the relative ability of management to adjust costs to conform with the changing requirements of different operating volumes, business costs may be classified as (1) pure-fixed, (2) policy-fixed, (3) variable.

Universality of Fixed and Variable Costs. The examples of pure-fixed, policy-fixed, and variable costs previously mentioned are not universally valid. An item that is variable in one company will be found to have fixed elements in another. In a processing company, the number of employees required to operate the equipment may not vary with volume because a definite-sized crew is required regardless of the volume of material going through the equipment. Direct labor, which is frequently a variable cost, is a fixed cost for this company.

The requirements of union contracts are tending to make direct-labor costs much more fixed than they have been in the past. The cost of labor which is a variable expense in one company may be a fixed expense in another company if the labor contract impairs management's ability to adjust the size of the labor force.

It is sometimes necessary to examine the validity of accounting methods when they affect the determination of whether a cost is fixed or variable. If the depreciation of equipment is charged on the usual straight-line basis, it is a fixed cost because the size of the total charge in any period does not vary with the output volume. If the depreciation is charged on the basis of units of production, then it is a variable cost because the size of the total change in any period varies in direct proportion with the output volume. The straight-line method is valid if the life of the equipment is determined primarily by factors which are a function of time, e.g., obsolescence and supersession. The units-of-production method is the more proper one if the life of the equipment is determined primarily by factors which are a function of use, e.g., wear and tear or depletion.

Shape of the Short-run Total-cost Line. The shape of a company's total-cost line depends upon the values of its fixed and variable cost elements.

Fixed Costs. Fixed costs are not always completely fixed. For example, the salary of the timekeeper in a plant may be considered a fixed cost because, regardless of variations in the size of the labor force, the one timekeeper is required. Let the number of men employed in the plant go over some figure, however, and a second timekeeper will be required. The fixed costs will have jumped from one level to another. Figure 33-3 shows the fixed costs jumping to successively higher levels in this manner. Such a situation may also occur when additional volume of production requires the use of additional units of equipment. At those points where the additional equipment is required, abrupt jumps in fixed equipment costs will occur.

The fixed cost with changing levels, shown in Figure 33-3, contains some elements of variability. When many of these fixed costs with vari-

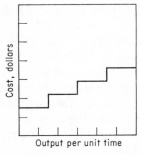

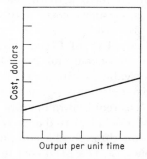

Figure 33-3. Fixed costs with changing levels.

Figure 33-4. Summation of fixed costs with changing levels.

able stages are added together, the cumulative effect of adding steps which occur at many different output volumes will frequently give a rather smooth line sloping upward to the right, as shown in Figure 33-4.

Variable Costs. Variable costs are not necessarily constant per unit of output, as shown in Figure 33-1. They may curve downward in certain sections and upward in other sections. Thus, when output is near zero, the increments of cost per additional output volume may be high because short-order production methods are used. As volume gets into the normal operating range, where more efficient processes, material handling, etc., can be used, the incremental or variable costs settle down to a lower per unit figure. In the rare case where production volume may be extended past the economic capacity of the facility, the incremental or variable cost per unit will tend to go up again. In mechanical or assembly operations, overcrowding of workers will result in labor inefficiencies. In a process or chemical plant, yields on raw materials and product recoveries will fall off and maintenance charges will increase at a more rapid rate when a facility is overloaded. The shape of the resultant variable costs curve is illustrated in Figure 33-5.

When many different variable costs are added together, we find that a straight line, such as in Figure 33-6, is frequently approximated even when many of the individual costs have curves approximating Figure

33-5. The concavities of some of the cost elements will occur at the same output volume as the convexities of other cost elements.

Fixed Plus Variable Costs. Combining each of the pictures of fixed costs (Figures 33-3 and 33-4) with each of the pictures of variable costs (Figures 33-5 and 33-6), we obtain four total-cost curves. The four shapes are illus-

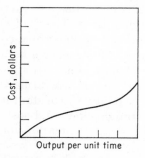

Figure 33-5. Variable costs.

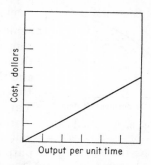

Figure 33-6. Summation of variable costs.

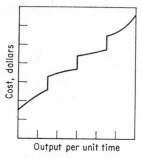

Figure 33-7. Total-cost curve, discontinuous function—A.

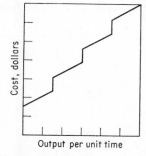

Figure 33-8. Total-cost curve, discontinuous function—B.

trated in Figures 33-1 and 33-7 to 33-9. Figures 33-7 and 33-8, made by combining the fixed-cost function of Figure 33-3 with each of the two variable-cost charts (Figures 33-5 and 33-6), give us discontinuous cost functions. These are sometimes of importance in specialized applications. Figure 33-9, made by combining the fixed-cost function of Figure 33-4 with the variable-cost function of Figure 33-5, gives us the shape of the classical cost curve which we used in the economic analyses of Chapter 28. Combining the fixed-cost function of Figure 33-4 with the variable-cost function of Figure 33-6 gives us a straight-line total-cost curve, such as Figure 33-1. We are most concerned with these last two curves because they are the kinds which are usually present in economic decisions.

The Short-run Cost Line in Economic Analysis. You will recall that we developed the U-shaped marginal- and average-cost curves in our discussions of economic theory of the firm in Chapter 28. These U-shaped curves are derived from the slanted S-shaped curve type of Figure 33-9.

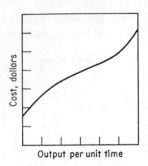

Figure 33-9. Total-cost curve.

Yet, in most practical economic problems we use a straight-line short-run cost function, despite the theoretical validity of the slanted S-shaped curve. How do we justify this?

The usual straight-line total-cost curves assume constant marginal costs. This is often substantially true. In other cases, marginal costs do theoretically decrease at first, reach a minimum, and then increase with increasing output volume. However, within the normal operating ranges, marginal costs will be relatively constant in most of these cases. A straight-line total-cost curve will then give a good approximation for most purposes.

Table 33-2 shows total, marginal, and average costs for the Haring Company. The total costs of this company are plotted in Figure 33-10. The marginal- and average-cost curves are plotted in Figure 33-11 and

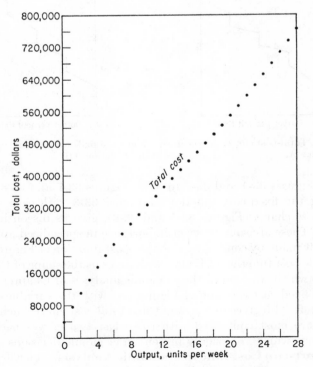

Figure 33-10. Total-cost curve of Haring Company.

have the classical U shape. Yet within the output range from 7 to 20 the total-cost function is essentially a straight line. Considering the errors involved in estimating this function in actual practice, a straight line will even approximate the true cost function outside this range well enough for most purposes.

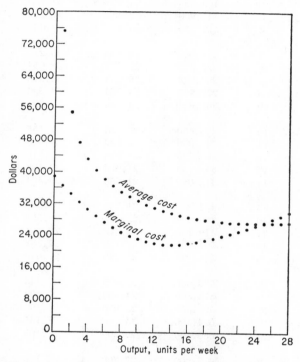

Figure 33-11. Average- and marginal-cost curves of Haring Company.

Studies of short-run costs by economists, accountants, and engineers have shown that marginal costs are constant within the normal range of output. Thus, a straight-line total-cost curve in the normal output ranges is usually appropriate even when very real variations in marginal cost are present if the entire range of possible operations is considered.

Unit of Measurement of Output Volume. Our discussions of short-run cost variation have presupposed the measurement of output volume of a facility or firm without specification of what units of measure may be appropriate.

In a single-product company—relatively rare these days—the problem of finding a suitable measure of output volume is simple. A physical unit can be employed. Measures such as number of units, pounds, or cubic feet for a given period of time will provide a satisfactory result.

Table 33-2. Haring Company Costs

Output	Total cost	Marginal cost	Average cost
0	$ 38,750	$38,750	
1	75,200	36,450	$75,200
2	109,500	34,300	54,750
3	141,800	32,300	47,267
4	172,250	30,450	43,063
5	201,050	28,800	40,210
6	228,325	27,275	38,054
7	254,225	25,900	36,318
8	278,925	24,700	34,866
9	302,625	23,700	33,625
10	325,550	22,925	32,555
11	347,850	22,300	31,623
12	369,725	21,875	30,810
13	391,400	21,675	30,108
14	413,050	21,650	29,504
15	434,800	21,750	28,987
16	456,800	22,000	28,550
17	479,125	22,325	28,184
18	501,875	22,750	27,882
19	525,125	23,250	27,638
20	548,900	23,775	27,445
21	573,300	24,400	27,300
22	598,350	25,050	27,198
23	624,100	25,750	27,135
24	650,600	26,500	27,108
25	677,900	27,300	27,116
26	706,075	28,175	27,157
27	735,075	29,000	27,225
28	764,975	29,900	27,321

For the usual multiproduct company, however, no completely satisfactory composite measure of output is available. It is rather difficult, in most cases, to find a single satisfactory physical unit to serve as a measure of the volume of all activities in the enterprise. A satisfactory measure of volume, aside from being simple to understand and easy to apply, should reflect changes in those activities which cause costs to vary and should not be appreciably affected by variations other than volume changes. These criteria are difficult to satisfy.

Output Factor. One solution to the problem of measuring the output of a variety of products is to construct a weighted index of the unit outputs of the various products. The number of each different item produced is weighted by its importance as determined by one or more significant variables, such as the relative sizes, areas, or weights of the different products. If the importance weights are valid (related to the cost characteristics of the products) and the index is easily understood, it can be a most satisfactory measure of output.

Sales Dollars. A common procedure is to use sales dollars, with no adjustment for changing values. This is an easily calculated output measure. In effect, it weights the outputs in proportion to sales prices of the various products. The amount of distortion in the cost-output relationship which is produced by this kind of measure depends upon the similarity of the cost and price characteristics of the various products. A decrease in the selling price of a product will change the cost-volume relationship, for price changes will produce changes in the dollar sales volume even though physical volume and costs have not changed. In some cases, indexes of sales in which the various products are weighted in accordance with their relative importance are used. However, such indexes are sometimes complicated and not easily understood by management. They should not be used if other more familiar measures can be found.

Input Factor. Output volume may sometimes be measured most satisfactorily by the input volume of a significant production ingredient. Output volume in a refinery may be measured by the volume of crude oil processed. In some mechanical industries, direct-labor hours is a suitable measure. This is a particularly good measure when the other production costs, such as material and equipment, are used in the various products in about the same ratio as the direct labor. In other cases, machine-hours may be suitable. Direct-labor dollars can also be used instead of direct-labor hours. However, variation in wage rates may produce some distortion in the cost-volume relationship in such cases. These input procedures are most satisfactory when the input ingredient is used in the manufacture of a number of products whose proportionate shares in the total production can be varied over a fairly wide range.

Indexes of weighted input factors may sometimes be most suitable from the technical cost variation point of view, but, as in the case of indexes of sales, they are not always easily understood.

Percentage of Capacity. Use of percentage of capacity as a measure of production volume is sometimes favored because it is an easily understood concept. It furnishes a common unit in which to express the output of many multiproduct firms. It also furnishes a basis for comparing changes in profit performance and in the break-even point as a percentage of capacity over a period of time.

However, there are some practical problems and limitations on the use of the capacity concept. It is usually very difficult, if not impossible in some cases, to determine physical capacity accurately. (Economic capacity—the optimum operating rate for lowest average unit cost—is usually below the physical capacity.) And the measurement of the proportion of the capacity utilized by each product is also difficult: the output must be measured in some unit before it can be converted into a percentage of capacity.

Conversion Cost. In a company manufacturing several product lines using common facilities, conversion cost (direct labor plus overhead cost) may sometimes be a good capacity as well as input measure. The number of workers that can be accommodated in the factory building and the capacity of the installed machinery are the principal factors limiting the plant capacity. Conversion cost may be a convenient common denominator for expressing and measuring this capacity.

The factory cost of the product contains three principal elements: direct labor, direct materials, and factory overhead. The amount of direct labor and overhead cost which a given plant can carry is determined by its worker and machine capacity. This direct-labor-plus-overhead cost is called factory-conversion cost. (Together with the sales, distribution, and administrative costs, the direct-labor-plus-overhead costs which are used to measure capacity constitute a measure of the value added by the company's activities to the materials and components which were purchased.) The materials cost of the products may vary widely without affecting the plant capacity or conversion cost, although variations in materials cost will affect the total cost of sales. Thus, the factory cost of converting these materials into the company's products may sometimes be a convenient capacity measure to express output volume.

Time Interval or Period. Volume or output may be measured in units per week, per month, per quarter, per year. Which time interval should be used?

The shorter the observation interval, the greater the probability of obtaining many readings covering a wide range of output. This is important when historical data are used as the primary basis for estimating the fixed and variable components of operating costs. When longer time intervals are used, fluctuations in operating rate within the interval may not be apparent because they are lost in the averaging of the high and low rates within the period.

Also, the same number of observations can be obtained within a much shorter period of time when the shorter intervals are used. This will reduce the possible distorting effects on the cost-output relationship of changes in methods and technology, size and price relationship, managerial efficiency, etc. Other things being equal, the shorter the over-all span of the study, the smaller the likelihood of these changes being significant.

However, when the interval is very short, the problems of arbitrary assignments of costs to individual periods and of insuring that costs are assigned to the time intervals in which the product is completed are more difficult. Maintenance and repairs and depreciation costs are especially important in this connection. When maintenance and repairs can be postponed during periods of tight expense control, adjustments to correctly match the cost with the output periods may be necessary.

In addition, seasonal effects may distort the cost-volume relationships when weekly, monthly, or quarterly data are used.

Determination of Short-run Cost Functions. How do we determine the short-run cost function of a company?

This problem has no easy solution. There is no highly accurate or exact procedure for determining the amounts of fixed and variable costs which is also inexpensive. For most practical purposes, however, reasonably accurate results may be obtained by the use of the simpler approaches described in this section. Great precision in estimating these costs is frequently uneconomical.

There are numerous approaches to this problem of estimating short-run cost functions. It is frequently desirable to use several independent approaches to provide checks on the reliability of the procedures and thus assist in obtaining more accurate results. The principal approaches to the determination of short-run cost functions use one or a combination of the following techniques:

1. Judgmental decision as to the variability of the various cost items or groups of cost items.

2. Statistical analysis of historical cost data to ascertain the effects of output changes on cost. This analysis will sometimes involve multiple-correlation techniques to isolate and measure the effects and interactions of all significant factors, such as seasonal variations, size of production job, output variability, etc.

3. Engineering analysis to estimate the physical relationships of input and output which are then converted into dollars at prospective prices to obtain an estimated cost relationship.

We shall discuss here the following approaches which may be used to estimate short-run cost-volume relationships:

1. Classification analysis of the operating accounts into fixed and variable elements

2. Historical-statement analysis, usually on a graphic basis, without detailed adjustments

3. Statistical analysis of historical statements, adjusting the data for changes in prices, technology, etc., which occurred during the period under study

4. Multiple-correlation analysis of historical cost and operating data

5. Engineering analysis based upon scientific knowledge of physical and operational relationships which can be converted into cost relationships

These various approaches do not constitute completely independent methods of analysis but rather differences in emphasis. We will see that some aspects of all three techniques are used in each approach.

Classification Analysis of the Operating Accounts. This approach is the simplest and cheapest. It should, therefore, be used wherever applicable. Even when it is not the principal approach, it is valuable as a check on the results obtained by more sophisticated techniques.

Table 33-3. **Analysis of Expenses for Producing 20,000 Units Annually**

	Fixed	Variable	Total
Direct material................	....	$100,000	$100,000
Direct labor....................	....	50,000	50,000
Factory overhead..............	$ 30,000	20,000	50,000
Administration................	20,000	15,000	35,000
Advertising and selling.........	15,000	30,000	45,000
Interest and other items........	35,000	....	35,000
Total......................	$100,000	$215,000	$315,000

In this approach, the accounting records of the company are analyzed to classify each type of expense as either fixed, variable, or partially fixed and partially variable. This classification is made on the basis of the judgment of the analysts who should be familiar with the business's

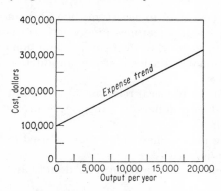

Figure 33-12. Expense trend line.

operations and how costs change with short-run changes in operating volume. The detail of this classification will depend on two principal factors: how large and complex is the business; how careful and thoroughgoing an analysis is being made.

The analysis may consist of no more than a rough classification of the principal categories of expense, such as is shown in Table 33-3.

The chart of Figure 33-12 can then be drawn, plotting total costs of $100,000 at zero output and $315,000 at 20,000 units per year, and drawing a straight line through the two plotted points. The expense trend line is

Costs = $100,000 + $\frac{215,000}{20,000}$ (units per year)

$\qquad$ = $100,000 + $10.75 (units per year)

For greater accuracy, more detailed review of each account in the chart of accounts would be made. Each account would be classified as either fixed or variable or a definite proportion of fixed and variable. Engineering estimates of how certain costs will change may be made, especially where new or changed processes are involved. Statistical analysis may be used to supplement and check judgment where desirable.

One of the important dangers in the analysis of accounting data for the determination of short-run costs is that the costs used will not always be relevant. The accountant is accustomed to deal in the past—what have the costs and revenues been? The analyst must keep reminding himself that he is interested in estimating the future and that the past and present merely provide assistance in determining what the future holds.

This procedure has a large element of judgment. The reliability of the results is, therefore, greatly influenced by the personal qualifications of the persons making the study as well as the care and thoroughness with which the study is conducted.

Historical-statement Analysis. The historical-statement-analysis approach to determine costs in relation to output volume involves the use of the data contained in the profit and loss statements of the company over a period of years. One of the simplest examples of this approach is presented for Allen Manufacturing Company.

The operating figures for the Allen Manufacturing Company for the years 1956 through 1960 are shown in Table 33-4. Using this data, the chart of Figure 33-13 has been drawn. The scale on the horizontal axis

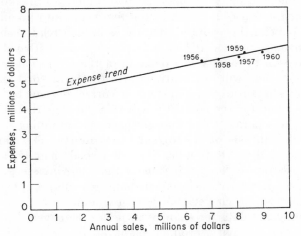

Figure 33-13. Allen Manufacturing Company expense trend.

is sales in dollars. The vertical scale shows expenses in dollars. The total operating expense each year was plotted as a function of the sales for the year. The expense trend line was fitted by inspection through the plotted expense points.

Table 33-4. **Allen Manufacturing Company Total Sales and Operating Expenses, 1956 to 1960**

Year	Total sales	Total operating expense
1956	$6,650,000	$5,900,000
1957	8,100,000	6,050,000
1958	7,300,000	5,950,000
1959	8,300,000	6,200,000
1960	9,000,000	6,250,000

The equation of the expense trend line is

$$\text{Costs} = \$4,450,000 + \frac{\$2,100,000}{\$10,000,000} \text{ (annual sales dollars)}$$
$$= 4,450,000 + 0.21 \text{ (annual sales dollars)}$$

In this case, all operating expenses were grouped together and changes in the business and economic environment over the years were ignored because they were not considered important enough to affect the results significantly. The trend line was fitted by inspection rather than by any more refined statistical technique, such as the method of least squares.

We can refine our analysis somewhat by obtaining a breakdown of the total operating expenses for each of the five years into broad groupings of expense. We can then obtain separate estimated relationships of how each more homogeneous category of expense varies with volume. If we have good reason to modify one or more of these relationships because of past biases which will not continue into the future or because of expected changes in future relationships, a correction can be made. The expense trend line for the company will then be constructed by adding together all the separate trend lines for each cost grouping.

Statistical Analysis of Historical Statements. The simple historical-statement-analysis techniques just described may be refined and made more accurate by a combination of the following steps:

1. Breaking down the costs into more homogeneous groupings and independently analyzing their variability with volume

2. Correcting the data for changes in prices, managerial policy, technology, taxes, productivity, product, plant, etc.

3. Using more accurate statistical techniques (such as the method of least squares) in computing the expense trend line

It is necessary to have cost and operating data available covering a long enough period of activity with sufficient variability in output volume to obtain good coverage of the range in which we are interested. This approach is aided by having supplementary data available in addition to the profit and loss statements which comprise the principal source of information.

To eliminate possible distortion of the cost-volume relationship, the cost data are adjusted so that wage rates and prices of materials, etc., are held constant at base-period rates or some standard rates. Cost data must also be adjusted for changes in product, plant size, technology, operating methods, equipment, size and variability of production orders, management efficiency, etc. Thus, the fewer the significant changes which have occurred in the factors affecting cost performance during the period covered by the study, the simpler will be the statistical analysis.

Certain other conditions will simplify the statistical problems. The smaller the number of different products, the easier it will be to construct a meaningful measure of output. The shorter the production time cycles (the length of time from the start of the production process to the time of completion of the finished product), the simpler will be the problem of making sure that costs are in the same period as the outputs which caused them. The more uniform the production methods and facilities, the easier it will be to eliminate cost variations caused by variations in the efficiency of the methods and equipment used.

A study of short-run cost relationships made by the United States Steel Corporation under the direction of T. O. Yntema in connection with hearings before the Temporary National Economic Committee provides an excellent example of the use of this more refined technique. An outline of the steps in this study is presented in Appendix A to this chapter. The methods for statistical analysis of historical statements illustrated in this study are applicable to a wide variety of industrial situations. The data required are normally available in the records and reports of most enterprises and the analytic techniques are not unusually complex. For these reasons, this approach is very useful for determining short-run cost functions.

Multiple-correlation Analysis. The approach of statistically analyzing historical statements, which has just been described, involves the analysis and adjustment of the raw historical data to correct for changes in conditions during the period under study. The multiple-correlation approach refines the analysis further by explicitly relating cost variations not only to output variations but also to other independent variables which influence behavior of the costs. In this manner, not only is the accuracy of the cost-output relations improved, but additional information is obtained which is useful in evaluating the patterns of cost variations for improved decision-making as well as for flexible budgetary control.

Thus, the multiple-correlation procedures provide us with separate measures of the relationship of cost and each independent variable (including output volume), taking account of the effects of the other independent variables. They also provide us with means of evaluating the degree to which cost variations are accounted for by each of these variables.

The multiple-correlation approach is most likely to yield successful results when a plant making a small number of uniform, homogeneous products has been operating over a long enough period of time with detailed records to furnish sufficient data. It is desirable that there be a rather wide range in operating volumes between periods, that no major changes in methods or technology have taken place during the periods being studied, and that all the facilities used be of fairly consistent efficiency (not some very modern efficient equipment and some old, inefficient equipment being used only to meet high output requirements).

The application of multiple-correlation techniques to the determination of the relationship of cost to output cannot be used very widely both because of the relatively high costs and time involved as well as the limited suitability of many plants for this type of study. In many cases, however, some applications of these techniques on a partial basis may yield valuable results in obtaining and verifying relationships for use with other approaches.

An example of this multiple-regression approach is provided by an analysis made by J. Dean of a leather belt shop. The results of this study are briefly summarized in Appendix B to this chapter.

Engineering Analysis. Engineering analysis as a means of determining costs as a function of volume of output utilizes scientific and engineering knowledge and operational data regarding the processes, equipment, operating efficiencies, etc. It may be the most effective method to determine cost-output relationships when the variabilities in the operation can be analyzed completely on a theoretical basis.

However, where engineering experimentation and research have not yet determined the so-called design laws or formulas, the analytical cost-output relationship is more difficult to determine by engineering approximations. Nevertheless, the engineering approach may still be the primary one if the lack of historical records and experience precludes the use of other methods.

In some cases, the engineering approach may provide a valuable means of checking and supplementing all or a portion of the results obtained using other approaches.

An example of a rather elaborate but effective use of engineering analysis to develop a cost function for airline fuel consumption is given by A. R. Ferguson.[1] Based upon the principles of thermodynamics and aerodynamics, the basic physical determinants of fuel requirements are set down in equations which indicate the interrelationships in relatively pre-

---

[1] A. R. Ferguson, "Empirical Determination of a Multidimensional Marginal Cost Function," *Econometrica*, vol. 18, no. 3, pp 217–235, July, 1950.

cise terms. These equations relate marginal fuel costs (in physical units) to variations in the quantity of output, quality of output, and techniques of production and take account of technological change as well as changes in operating conditions. Dr. Ferguson shows that the equations yield reasonably accurate results when data from Northeast Airlines are utilized to demonstrate the practicality of using the equations. An analysis of total airline costs would require similar analyses of all input factors as well as analysis of the effects of factor-price interrelationships upon the combination of factors which will be used.

As Dr. Ferguson points out, the limitations of an approach as elaborate as the one he uses are self-evident: the amount of effort and expense is very great; and the method cannot be applied in many fields in which engineering theory does not provide adequate postulates for the physical relationships.

Variable Budgets and Short-run Cost-volume Relationships. Variable budgets give a picture of how costs should vary with changes in output volume in accordance with current managerial plans. They are the basis for management planning and control of expenditures.

Variations from planned or budgeted expenditures occur. The size of these differences will depend upon two factors: how accurately has the budget been prepared; and how effectively does management control costs in accordance with the budgetary plan.

The accuracy of the budget preparation is dependent upon the methods which are used to determine the short-run cost-volume relationship for each organizational unit and activity. Resort should usually be made to one or several of the approaches mentioned in this chapter. The procedure should provide for systematic studies of the materials, facilities, labor, overhead, administration, and other items required at various output volumes.

The variable budget procedure is concerned with controlling costs of the various functions and departments. The bases for measuring output or activity rate may therefore differ in the various functions and departments. For this reason, it may not be possible to simply add the budgeted cost figures at various output volumes to obtain a short-run cost function for the company. It may be necessary first to solve the problem of converting the activity measures to a common output measure before the cost elements of the functions and departments can be added together.

APPENDIX A. A STUDY OF THE SHORT-RUN COST-VOLUME RELATIONSHIP FOR STEEL PRODUCTION

In this study of the short-run cost relationships of the United States Steel Corporation,[1] which was conducted under the direction of T. O. Yntema, weighted tons of products shipped (weighted by average cost) is used as the output volume measure. Costs were broken down for each of the years under study (1927 to 1938) into the following categories: (1) taxes other than Federal income and profits taxes and social security, (2) interest, (3) depreciation and depletion, (4) payroll, (5) pensions, (6) social security taxes, and (7) other expenses (including goods and services purchased from others). The variation of each of these categories of cost with volume over the period studied was analyzed separately. Federal income taxes were excluded because they are a function of profits, not of costs or volume of business.

Some duplication would result if these cost components were simply added together from the profit and loss statement figures because the statement figures included transactions between the subsidiary companies of United States Steel Corporation. Since the intercompany sales of any one company constitute the costs of the other, and since intercompany profits are eliminated from inventory valuations in making inventory adjustments, both costs and sales and revenues are inflated, from a consolidated viewpoint, by the amount of the intercompany items, but the profit shown is unaffected by this method of handling. These intercompany transactions are segregated in the accounts of the corporation and its subsidiaries and in the annual reports as far as the sales of products and some of the miscellaneous operations are concerned, but the accounting systems of the common-carrier transportation companies make no provision for this segregation. Consequently, the intercompany business done by the common-carrier transportation companies must be estimated. Estimates of the net sales and operating revenues with all of the intercompany items eliminated had already been prepared by the comptroller's department of the corporation. By subtracting these net sales and operating revenues derived from outside sources from the total of net sales and operating revenues shown in the profit and loss statements, the estimated amount of all intercompany items was ascertained. Since the relationship between the physical volume of outside business and the cost of doing all outside business was what was desired, the intercompany items had to be deducted from the costs.

The output measure used in this analysis is tons of products shipped. However, it is necessary to make some adjustment for changes in the proportions of high- and low-cost products constituting the total. For instance, if the shipment figures showed that in each of two years 10 million tons had been shipped, the total costs would be greater in the year in which costly products, such as sheets and tin plates, constituted most of the tonnage than in the year when lower-cost products, such as rails and heavy plates, predominated. Adjustment for such a condition has been made by letting each ton of rolled and finished steel product, which is of a type whose 1933 to 1937 average mill cost was less than the average cost of all rolled and finished steel products, count proportionately less than a full ton, while tons of products of a class which is on the average more costly than the average cost of rolled and finished steel products, have been made to count proportionately more than a full ton. By weighting in this way the number of tons of all tonnage products shipped each year has been converted into equivalent tons of average-cost rolled and finished steel products. Thus in any years in which the 1933 to 1937 average proportions of high- and low-cost products were sold the actual tonnage is the same as the weighted tonnage, while the total tonnage for years having an abnormal proportion of high- or low-cost products has been converted to a tonnage figure that is comparable to the normal years from a cost standpoint.

---

[1] This material is adapted from the United States Steel Corporation TNEC Papers, published by the United States Steel Corporation. Some of the techniques used in this study have been criticized by a few economists as introducing various types of biases. The linearity of the cost function has been especially disturbing to some.

By a similar weighting process, the total tonnage of rolled and finished products shipped has been further adjusted to include the equivalent tons of steel represented by the products other than steel which are sold on a tonnage basis by the corporation's subsidiaries.

Since the relationships between costs and volume under 1938 conditions were desired, the cost figures for each of the years prior to 1938 were adjusted. Adjusted cost figures were calculated for each of the years from 1927 to 1938, adjusted to 1938 interest, tax, pension, and wage rates; to 1938 price levels; as well as to 1938 general efficiency. This latter efficiency adjustment was necessary because a gradual increase in efficiency over the eleven years preceding 1938 was associated with a total drop in costs roughly equal to 4.32 per cent of average costs.

Two of the components, interest and pensions, are in no way dependent upon the volume of business performed. These items are completely fixed. Hence, to convert to 1938 conditions, all that had to be done was to substitute in each year the 1938 amount of interest and pensions paid.

Since tax rates have changed considerably over the period under consideration, it is clear that some adjustment in the tax figures was necessary. Taxes, other than social security and Federal income and profits taxes, are compared with the weighted tons of products shipped by plotting taxes against shipments as shown on Figure 33-14.

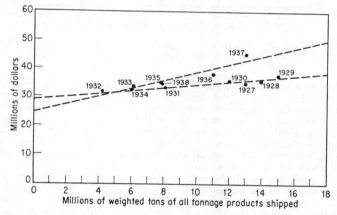

Figure 33-14. Taxes and volume of business, U.S. Steel Corporation and subsidiaries. (Taxes include all taxes except Social Security and Federal income and profits taxes.)

An inspection of the chart shows that the points for 1927 to 1931 fall approximately along one line, while the points for 1932 to 1938 fall along another. The simplest estimate of what the taxes would be at various rates of operation under 1938 conditions was to compute the average relationship, by the least-squares method, for the period 1932 to 1938. It will be noted that the 1938 taxes fall very close to the line and very close to the points for other years when volume was about the same. Hence it is evident that the tax rates which affect the corporation with regard to taxes other than Federal income and social security taxes were not materially altered throughout the 1932 to 1938 period. The taxes paid from 1927 to 1931, however, are clearly much below what would be paid at the same operating rates. For this reason in this study the actual taxes paid for each of the years 1932 to 1938 have been used in computing the estimated total costs under 1938 conditions, but the taxes for the years prior to 1932 have been estimated on the basis of the average 1932 to 1938 tax-volume relationship. This relationship indicates that total taxes, other than Federal income and social security, amount to $24,217,000, plus $1.43 for each weighted ton of product sold.

Wage rates increased considerably from the low point of the depression and even from the prosperity year of 1929. Hence, the need for adjustment of the payroll figures to 1938 conditions is obvious. The payrolls for each of the respective years are multiplied by the ratio of the 1938 average hourly earnings to the average hourly wage prevailing in the year of the payrolls. Figure 33-15 shows the relation to volume of

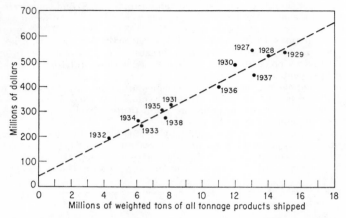

Figure 33-15. Payroll adjusted to 1938 wage rates and related to volume of business, U.S. Steel Corporation and subsidiaries (construction payrolls excluded).

the payrolls for each of the respective years adjusted to 1938 wage rates. A line of average relationship has been constructed by the least-squares method. An inspection of the chart shows that, in general, payrolls for the later years are lower than what they would have been for the earlier years if 1938 hourly rates had prevailed. This indicates that, to some extent at least, the increases in hourly wage costs have been offset by increased productivity per man-hour. Adjustment for this factor has been taken care of, however, by the adjustment for long-term trend in the cost-volume relationship which will be discussed later.

Costs of depreciation and depletion, social security taxes, and other expenses (including goods and services purchased from others) were similarly analyzed and adjustments made where necessary. The adjustment for changing prices of materials and services purchased was made on the basis of the Bureau of Labor Statistics index of wholesale commodity prices other than farm and food products. Since many of the things which are purchased did not change in price during the period, only one-half of the "other expense" items were adjusted by multiplying them by the ratio of the 1938 index to the index prevailing in the year in which the "other expenses" were incurred.

The various components of cost for each of the respective years adjusted to 1938 interest, tax, pension and wage rates and to 1938 price levels were added together to give total-cost figures. These total-cost figures represent what would have been the cost for the volume sold in each of the respective years if 1938 conditions of wages, interest, taxes, pensions, and prices had prevailed. These total costs, however, do not take into consideration the long-term downward trend of costs in relation to volume due to changes in methods of production within the industry itself and hence do not quite represent what the cost would have been if the same volume had been sold in 1938. An instance of this was referred to in connection with the adjustment of payrolls where it was seen that the payrolls for earlier years would have been greater in relation to volume produced than present-day payrolls if present-day hourly rates were paid. Hence it became necessary to make a further adjustment of total costs for any general increase in efficiency and other changes in operating conditions that may have taken place during the period.

In Figure 33-16, the total costs adjusted to 1938 interest, tax, pension, and wage

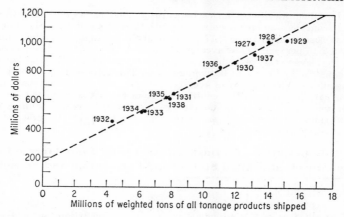

Figure 33-16. Total costs adjusted to 1938 interest, tax, pension, and wage rates and 1938 price levels, but unadjusted for changed operating conditions related to volume of business, U.S. Steel Corporation and subsidiaries.

rates and 1938 price levels are plotted against the number of weighted tons shipped. The line of average relationship computed by the least-squares method has been drawn upon the graph. In Table 33-5 have been set forth the actual adjusted costs and next to them have been placed what those total costs would have amounted to for the same volume if they were actually located on the line. In the fifth column, the deviations or differences between the two are set down, and in the sixth column, the deviations are reduced to percentages of the average cost for the volume in question as indicated by the line of average relationship. These percentage deviations are plotted by years on Figure 33-17. An inspection of this chart will show that many of the deviations are

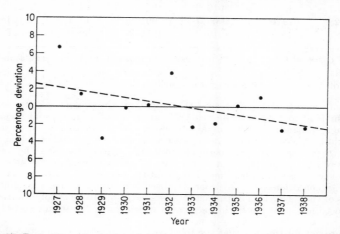

Figure 33-17. Percentage deviations from average—total costs adjusted to 1938 interest, tax, pension, and wage rates and 1938 price level, but unadjusted for changed operating conditions, U.S. Steel Corporation and subsidiaries.

more or less at random, but that to a certain extent costs in later years tend to be lower than average, while costs in earlier years tend to be higher. This general trend, computed mathematically by the least-squares method, shows the extent to which the deviations from the average are correlated with the passage of time. The computation shows that costs tended to be 2.17 per cent above average at the beginning of the period and 2.15 per cent below average at the end. Thus the gradual increase in efficiency in the eleven years preceding 1938 has been associated with a total drop in costs roughly equal to 4.32 per cent of average costs. This represents an average decrease in costs equal to 0.393 per cent of average costs per year. Thus, the costs under 1938 conditions can be estimated by subtracting from the actual adjusted costs for any particular year the amount of the average cost for that year's volume multiplied by 0.00393 times the number of years intervening between the year in which the costs were incurred and 1938.

Table 33-5. **Deviation of Adjusted Total Costs* from Average Costs for Volume Involved, United States Steel Corporation and Subsidiaries**

Year	Millions of weighted tons of products shipped	Actual adjusted costs	Average adjusted costs for volume†	Deviation	Deviation as percentage of average cost
1932	4.4	$ 446.1	$ 429.7	+16.4	+3.8%
1934	6.1	518.3	529.1	−10.8	−2.0
1933	6.2	522.5	535.0	−12.5	−2.3
1935	7.6	617.6	616.8	+ 0.8	+0.1
1938	7.8	614.3	628.5	−14.2	−2.3
1931	8.1	646.7	646.1	+ 0.6	+0.1
1936	11.0	824.6	815.6	+ 9.0	+1.1
1930	11.9	866.1	868.2	− 2.1	−0.2
1927	13.0	994.8	932.5	+62.3	+6.7
1937	13.2	919.9	944.2	−24.3	−2.6
1928	14.0	1005.1	991.0	+14.1	+1.4
1929	15.1	1016.3	1055.3	−39.0	−3.7

* Total costs adjusted to 1938 interest, tax, pension, and wage rates and to 1938 price levels.

† As indicated by line of average relationship.

The resulting adjusted-cost figures thus represent the original cost for each of the years from 1927 to 1938, adjusted to 1938 interest, tax, pension, and wage rates, to 1938 price levels and to 1938 general efficiency. (The final adjusted figure for 1938 is, as it should be, the same as the unadjusted figure for that year, except that the social security taxes allocable to construction payroll have been eliminated.) These are plotted on Figure 33-18. A computation of the line of average relationship fitted to these points by the least-squares method shows that the normal relation of costs to volume under 1938 conditions is $55.73 per weighted ton shipped, plus $182,100,000. The smallness of the deviations of the actual costs, adjusted to 1938 conditions, from the normal cost line shows the faithfulness with which the corporation's costs follow this pattern.

If it were not for the fact that the total costs obtained by adding together the adjusted components of cost that were developed in connection with the derivation of the total-cost pattern had to be adjusted for the gradual increase in efficiency and other changes in conditions over the period, it would be possible to obtain a breakdown of the fixed and variable total costs simply by listing the fixed and variable elements of the various adjusted components. Since the total costs were adjusted for these changes in operating conditions as indicated by the long-term trend in the cost-volume relationship, an approximate breakdown could be made only by making a similar adjustment for time trend for each of the individual components in which a time trend exists.

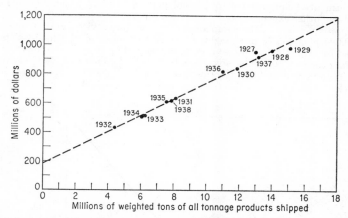

Figure 33-18. Relationship between total costs of operation and volume of business, 1938 conditions, U.S. Steel Corporation and subsidiaries. (Total costs adjusted to 1938 interest, tax, pension, and wage rates; to 1938 price levels; and to 1938 efficiency.)

Since the 1938 amounts of interest and pensions were used for all volumes, no time-trend adjustment had to be made with regard to these items. An inspection of the movement of taxes and of depreciation and depletion with increases in volume reveals that no appreciable time trend exists with regard to these items. The social security taxes will vary directly with any adjustments that are made in the payroll figure. It is apparent that the bulk of the adjustment made in the total-cost figures for time trend arose from the time trends involved in the payroll and "other expense" items. Clearly, then, it was these two items which had to be adjusted for time trend in order to obtain an approximate breakdown of total costs.

Payroll costs and "other expenses" under 1938 efficiency conditions were estimated in the same manner as was done for total costs: the deviations of cost as a percentage of average cost were plotted; a general trend computed using the method of least squares; and costs under 1938 conditions estimated by subtracting from each year's actual adjusted costs an amount to compensate for the gradual increase in efficiency over the years.

Adding together the fixed and variable elements of the payroll costs and "other expenses," adjusted for the time (efficiency) trend, and the adjusted figures previously determined for the other components of cost, we obtain total costs of $185,200,000 + $55.46 per ton. This is substantially the same as the results previously obtained by adjusting total costs instead of the components for time trend.

It would seem that the time-trend adjustment made with respect to total costs would represent the more accurate figure of the two. First of all, it includes any slight time trends that may exist with regard to the other components. Second, the payroll figures are not comparable with shipments to the extent that production is greater or less than shipments. Consequently some of the deviations on which the payroll time trend was estimated may be the result of inventory fluctuations. Similarly, since the "other expense" classification was simply the residual amount after deducting from total costs the other components of cost, the amount of this item for each year has been overstated to the same extent that payroll has been understated, or vice versa, because of inventory fluctuations, and some of the deviations on which the "other expense" time trend was computed may also have been the result of the inventory situation. Since total costs were extracted from the profit and loss statements and represent the sum of any offsetting errors in "other expenses" and payroll, they are comparable with shipments and the deviations cannot be attributed to inventory fluctuations, except to the minute extent that the situation just described resulted in payroll adjustments being applied to a small portion of costs which should have been classified as "other expense," and vice versa.

The approximations of the components are therefore revised so that total costs are $182,100,000 plus $55.73 per weighted ton of product shipped, which was previously developed by adjusting total costs for time trend. The entire adjustment is made in the "other expense" figures because the adjustment does not involve a relatively large amount in any event and because the "other expense" classification represents a conglomeration of items and is also the least accurate classification. Figure 33-19 graph-

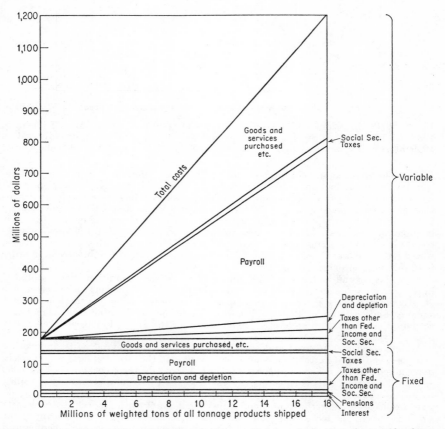

Figure 33-19. Composition of total costs of operation in relation to volume of business, U.S. Steel Corporation and subsidiaries. (1927 to 1938 experience adjusted to 1938 conditions.)

ically portrays the relation of the various elements of cost to volume. The differences between the two estimates of fixed and variable costs previously discussed are so small that the graphing of either upon the chart would show the same result. The "other expense" item has been labeled "goods and services purchased, etc." on the chart to indicate its general nature.

APPENDIX B. A STUDY OF THE SHORT-RUN COST-VOLUME RELATIONSHIP IN A LEATHER BELT SHOP

This study by J. Dean[1] of leather belt shop costs covered the period from January 1, 1935, to June 1, 1938. Output rate and other cost determinants varied over a sufficiently wide range; and plant, equipment, and technical methods of production were unchanged during this period. The four-week accounting period used by the company on its cost records was used as the observation time unit.

Expenses arbitrarily allocated to the leather belt shop that bore no relationship to its operating conditions, such as certain head office administrative expenses, were excluded. The recording of the cost of machinery repairs, supplies, and cement was subject to time lags which needed correction. Thus, operating executives estimated that about one-fifth of machinery repair expenditures were for minor replacements necessitated by current production and likely to be recorded in the same period. The larger fraction, however, was caused primarily by past production and could be allocated to output approximately three months earlier. Accordingly, machinery repair costs were corrected so that they were composed of one-fifth of the current figure and four-fifths of the cost three months later. The costs of supplies, in contrast to machinery repairs, are recorded in advance, and were corrected by a similar device. The distortion caused by the lag in cement cost was recognized, but could not be removed.

Direct and indirect labor, salaries, and cement costs were adjusted by deflating the recorded expenditures to rates and prices of the base period. Leather cost, depreciation, insurance, and taxes were adjusted by charging them to production at an average rate for the entire period.

In the multiple-correlation analysis of the adjusted data, preliminary studies using graphical methods were made of the effects on costs of nine operating variables: output, weight of belting, width of belting, magnitude and direction of change of output from preceding month, percentage of single-ply belting in total output, variability of rate of output in period, size of manufacturing lot, proportion of special orders, and rate of labor turnover. From an evaluation of these studies, it was concluded that only two were suitable independent variables for the formal least-squares multiple-regression analysis of total cost: output (measured by square feet of single-ply equivalent belting); and weight (average weight per square foot of single-ply equivalent belting). (In the analysis of overhead cost variations, the magnitude and direction of change of output from the preceding month was also included as a significant variable.)

The multiple-regression equation for total combined cost, derived by least-squares analysis, was

$$X_1 = -60{,}178 + 0.770X_2 + 70{,}181X_3$$

where X_1 = combined cost in dollars
  X_2 = output in square feet of single-ply equivalent belting
  X_3 = average weight in pounds per square foot
To determine the partial regression equation of total combined cost, corrected for average weight, on output, the average of the average weight in pounds per square foot ($\bar{X}_3 = 0.8998$) is inserted in the regression equation,

$$X_1 = -60{,}178 + 0.770X_2 + 70{,}181(0.8998)$$
$$= 2{,}971 + 0.770X_2$$

The regression curves of total, average, and marginal cost on output are shown in Figure 33-20. The cost observations shown in the charts were corrected for deviations from average weight. Thus, if a total-cost observation was based on belting having an average weight 0.02 lb per square foot more than the average average weight ($\bar{X}_3$), $0.02(70{,}181) = \$1{,}404$ was subtracted from the total-cost observation.

[1] Adapted from J. Dean, *The Relation of Cost of Output for a Leather Belt Shop*, National Bureau of Economic Research, Technical Paper 2, December, 1941.

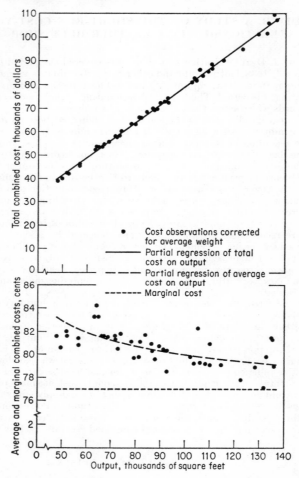

Figure 33-20. Partial regressions of total, average, and marginal combined cost on output. SOURCE: J. Dean, *The Relation of Cost of Output for a Leather Belt Shop*, National Bureau of Economic Research, Technical Paper 2, December, 1941, p. 27.

PROBLEMS

1. Illustrate each of the following statements by examples: (*a*) "Costs which are fixed from a total-cost point of view are variable from a unit-cost point of view and those which are variable from a total-cost point of view are fixed from a unit-cost point of view." (*b*) "The same costs may be fixed or variable,

depending upon current managerial policy." (c) "All costs are variable if a long enough period of time is considered."

2. Propose a suitable unit of measurement of output volume for each of the following and justify briefly: (a) TV receiver manufacturer, 25 models; (b) Drug manufacturer, 50 products, from aspirin to antibiotics to polio vaccine; (c) Paper manufacturer, 8 types of paper; (d) Metal parts supplier to automobile and electronic industries, fabricating thousands of metal parts to meet the custom specifications of the purchaser; (e) Steel producer.

3. Rank the five approaches to the determination of short-run cost functions as to (a) the degree to which subjective judgment will generally influence the results, (b) the general applicability of the method, (c) the costliness of the approach.

4. Under what conditions would it be preferable to use the classification analysis rather than the simple historical-statement-analysis method of determining a company's short-run cost function? Under what conditions would the converse be true?

5. Under what conditions would it be preferable to use the statistical-analysis-of-historical-statements approach rather than the multiple-correlation approach? Under what conditions would the converse be true?

6. Under what conditions must primary dependence be placed on the engineering approach to the determination of short-run cost functions?

34 Break-even Analysis for Profit Planning

Break-even analysis is a method of organizing and presenting some of the static, short-run economic relationships of a business. The break-even chart shows how costs, revenues, and profits will vary with output changes, other things being equal. The break-even relations are static: they use short-run costs and revenue functions which are valid only under one given set of conditions which are completely valid at only one point in time.

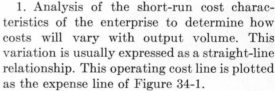

Figure 34-1. Break-even chart.

Break-even analysis involves the following steps:

1. Analysis of the short-run cost characteristics of the enterprise to determine how costs will vary with output volume. This variation is usually expressed as a straight-line relationship. This operating cost line is plotted as the expense line of Figure 34-1.

2. Expression of the short-run revenue of the enterprise as a linear function of operating volume. This revenue line is plotted as the sales line of Figure 34-1.

3. Forecasting the output volume of the enterprise. The break-even chart then makes possible a forecast of profits.

4. Controlling cost expenditures. The expense line on the break-even chart is the forecast of how these costs should vary with changes in operating volume.

5. Constructing modifications of the break-even chart to determine the effects of proposals and alternative business decisions on the static profit characteristics of the company.

The break-even technique thus provides a focal point for tying together the short-run sales-forecasting, expense-control, and profit-planning functions of an enterprise.

In this chapter, we shall examine some uses of the break-even technique as well as its limitations and the dangers of its misuse. Break-even analysis can be a very useful tool for assisting economic decision-making on a large variety of problems in the firm. However, a clear understanding of the limitations which are presented in our discussions is important to avoid errors in application and interpretation.

Construction of a Break-even Chart. To construct a break-even chart, the operating expenses of the enterprise are divided into two groups: fixed costs and variable costs. Fixed costs consist of those items, such as depreciation, interest, certain administration costs, etc., which are of constant value and do not vary with the volume of production. Variable costs consist of those items, such as direct labor, direct material, etc., which vary in direct proportion with the volume of operations. Many cost items are partly fixed and partly variable, with differing proportions of fixed and variable costs. (Detailed discussions of the nature and classification of costs and of short-run cost relationships were presented in Chapters 3, 4, and 33.)

The Badger Chemical Company makes and sells by the pound a chemical known as R-N. This is the sole product of the company, which is presently selling 200,000 lb of R-N per month at $1.60 a pound. Capacity production with present facilities is about 250,000 lb per month. Each of the costs of manufacturing is analyzed and the proportion of fixed and variable costs is ascertained. For example, it is determined that, of the monthly power cost of $10,500, $2,000 is a fixed cost which does not depend on the volume of operations and $8,500 is a variable cost proportional to operating volume. All of the direct-material cost of $18,000 is determined as variable. Analyzing all the manufacturing costs and totaling the fixed and variable amounts as determined in the above manner, it is found that $92,000 of the monthly manufacturing costs are fixed and $108,000 are variable. Similarly, the administrative and sales expenses are analyzed. The breakdown of the total monthly costs of these latter items is determined as $84,000 fixed and $14,000 variable costs. The total monthly costs of the company are thus $176,000 of fixed items and $122,000 of variable items, or a total of $298,000 per month to produce and sell 200,000 lb of product R-N.

Using this analysis of the current cost structure of the Badger Chemical Company, we can now construct a break-even chart. The horizontal scale of Figure 34-2 is labeled "product per month, thousands of pounds" and the vertical scale is labeled "expenses and sales, dollars."

To draw the expense line, we locate one point at $298,000 of monthly expenses for an output of 200,000 lb. The second point on the expense line is at zero rate of production or output, where the total expenses is equal to the total of fixed costs, $176,000. By connecting these two points with a straight line, we locate the expense line. We locate the sales line as follows: at zero output, total sales income is zero; at output of 200,000 lb, the income equals 200,000 times the current market price of $1.60, or

$320,000. The sales line is then drawn by connecting these two points with a straight line.

Profit Forecast. What does this chart now reveal? It tells the company management that to make a profit selling its product at $1.60 a pound, it must sell more than 178,000 lb per month. Also, based on its present cost structure, if the company were to increase its sales by 10 per cent

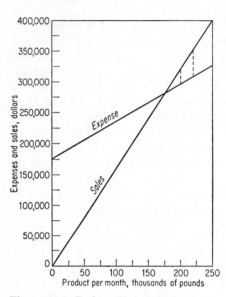

Figure 34-2. Badger Chemical Company break-even chart.

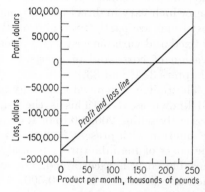

Figure 34-3. Alternative design of Badger Chemical Company break-even chart.

to 220,000 lb per month, it would almost double its profits of $22,000 per month. These profits are indicated by dashed lines on Figure 34-2.

Alternative Break-even "Profit" Chart. An alternative, more direct method of charting profit variations of the Badger Chemical Company with changes in sales volume is shown in Figure 34-3. On this chart, the changing profit picture can be read more easily. The distance above the zero horizontal base line represents profit and the distance below this zero line represents loss. On the previously constructed chart, it was necessary to subtract the sales-revenue-line value from the expense-line value to get the profit figure.

However, for purposes of analyzing the cost and revenue structure of the enterprise, this oversimplified chart is not as valuable as the break-even chart showing separate cost and sales lines. The effects of several possible alternative courses of action cannot be demonstrated as clearly and simply on this chart as on the one showing both sales and expense lines.

Comparison of the Badger Chemical Company and the Monago Company. The Monago Company makes R-N by a somewhat different process than does the Badger Chemical Company. The Monago product is almost the same as the Badger product and sells for $1.50 per pound. Analysis of the costs of the Monago Company reveals the following data:

Monthly production rate............	350,000 lb
Monthly fixed expense..............	$425,000
Monthly variable expense..........	$ 87,500

The Monago Company has a capacity of about 500,000 lb per month.

With this information, a break-even chart, Figure 34-4 is constructed. Comparing this break-even chart of the Monago Company with the

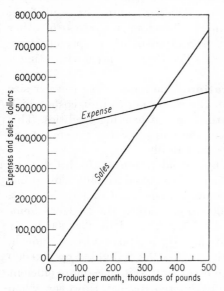

Figure 34-4. The Monago Company break-even chart.

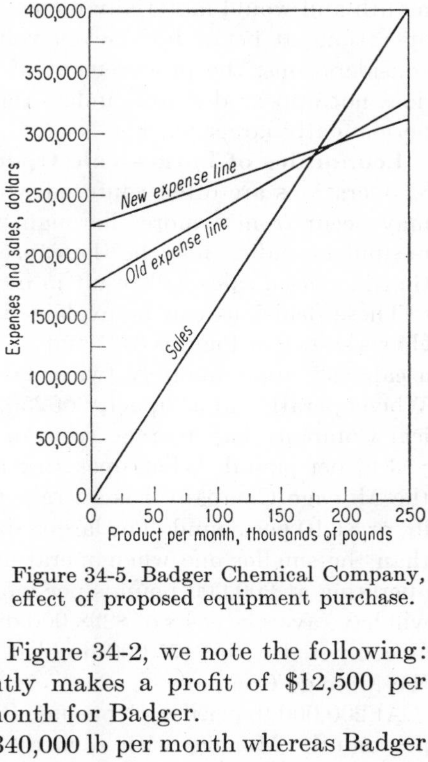

Figure 34-5. Badger Chemical Company, effect of proposed equipment purchase.

Badger Chemical Company chart of Figure 34-2, we note the following:

1. The Monago Company currently makes a profit of $12,500 per month compared with $22,000 per month for Badger.

2. Monago breaks even at sales of 340,000 lb per month whereas Badger needs only 178,000 lb per month.

3. Monago's profits will more than quadruple to $56,250 if sales are increased 10 per cent whereas Badger only about doubles its profits (from $22,000 to $41,800) by a 10 per cent increase in sales.

4. With its present facilities, Monago's potential profits if it can utilize its idle capacity are close to $200,000 per month compared with a Badger potential of only about $72,000.

Evaluating Equipment Program. The Badger Chemical Company has been considering for some time the purchase of new equipment which will save 26 cents a pound on material and labor costs but will raise the fixed costs for space, depreciation, interest, insurance, taxes, etc., to $225,000 per month. To see how the purchase would affect the static break-even picture, a new cost line is constructed in Figure 34-5. At zero output, the costs now total $225,000. At 200,000 lb per month of output, the costs now total $295,000 ($225,000 of fixed costs plus the former variable cost, $122,000, minus the 200,000 lb times the 26 cents of variable cost which is saved). The new cost line does not go below the original one until output exceeds almost 200,000 lb per month. The new cost structure would raise the break-even production by several thousand pounds per month and would materially increase the deficit which might result from operations at below break-even volumes. Therefore, regardless of other considerations, the procurement of this equipment at the present time does not appear desirable unless there is good reason for anticipating a permanently larger market.

Economics of Large-scale Operation. The economies of larger size of operations are often confused with the reduction of unit costs which may occur from a more thorough utilization of existing facilities. This misunderstanding may be the cause of the many incorrect assumptions that increased sales will result in increased profits.

These delusions can be explained by consideration of the break-even charts shown in Figures 34-4 and 34-5. The Monago Company's plant has a capacity approximately twice the Badger Chemical Company's plant. When operating at a capacity of 250,000 lb per month, the Badger Chemical Company has average costs of $328,500 divided by 250,000 lb, or $1.314 per pound. When operating at capacity of 500,000 lb per month, the Monago Company has average costs of $550,000 divided by 500,000 lb, or $1.10 per pound. The larger-size plant is, in this case, more efficient than the smaller one when operating at design capacity. However, when operating at 200,000 pounds per month, the Badger Chemical Company will have average costs of $298,000 divided by 200,000, or $1.49 per pound as compared with $475,000 divided by 200,000, or $2.375 per pound for the Monago Company.

At 200,000 lb per month output, Badger currently has profits of $22,000 per month. Monago with a current production rate of 350,000 lb per month has a profit of $12,500 per month. The sales department of each company proposes that output be raised 100,000 pounds per month for sale in foreign markets at no additional sales expense and at regular domestic prices, f.o.b. the factory. For the Monago Company, the answer is simple. Increasing output and sales 100,000 lb per month will result in monthly profits of $137,500, an increase of $125,000. For Badger Chemical Company, however, the problem is more complex. If the company increases output only 50,000 lb per month, monthly profits will be $72,000, an increase of $50,000. To increase output another 50,000 lb per month will require the construction of additional facilities. If only 50,000 lb of additional capacity is constructed, engineering analysis discloses that the break-even characteristics of the company will be as shown in Figure 34-6. If a larger, more economical additional unit to add 250,000 lb of additional capacity is constructed, the break-even chart of the company will be as shown in Figure 34-7.

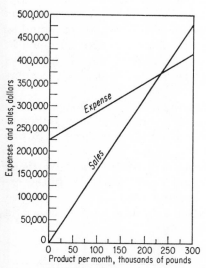

Figure 34-6. Badger Chemical Company, with 50,000 lb of additional capacity.

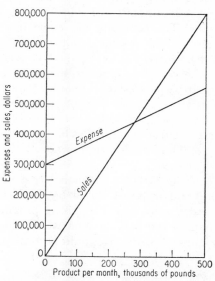

Figure 34-7. Badger Chemical Company, with 250,000 lb of additional capacity.

The smaller addition will result in just about no increase in profits over $72,000 per month even if the additional 50,000-lb capacity is entirely used. Moreover, it will lower profits if the entire capacity is not sold and will raise the break-even point of the company from 178,000 lb per month to about 235,000 lb per month.

The doubling of capacity by adding a $250,000 facility, shown in Figure 34-7, will reduce profits to $24,000 per month if only the forecasted 50,000 lb of this additional capacity is used. However, if sales can be expanded further so that 100,000 lb or more of this additional capacity is utilized, the additional construction will result in increased profits over the $72,000 possible with existing facilities and operating methods. At 350,000 lb per month, profits will be about $78,000 per month. If sales can be developed to utilize the full new capacity, the potential profit is about $240,000 per month. Of course, the break-even point of the company would be raised to 278,000 lb per month.

Evaluating Price Cuts and Promotions. After quite a number of years have passed, the Badger Chemical Company has begun to feel the effects of the competition of some other manufacturers who are selling substitutes at lower prices. (The cost and revenue structure of the company has changed considerably since the previous charts were made and new analyses and charts are prepared. For the sake of simplicity in our illustration, however, we shall use the old operating figures.) Unless new prices and/or promotion policies are adopted, it is estimated that sales will fall to about 175,000 lb per month, which is below the break-even point. The company has come to the conclusion that, to maintain its present sales volume, it must cut its price for R-N to $1.50 per pound or it must increase its sales and advertising expenditures by $20,000 a month. If the company were to adopt both policies, it is estimated that sales could be increased to about 235,000 lb per month. Which of the alternatives would prove most profitable?

Considering just the effect of decreasing the price to $1.50 a pound, we can construct a new sales line on the break-even chart, as shown in Figure 34-8. This new chart shows that the profits would be reduced to $2,000 per month.

Of the $20,000 additional cost of an expanded sales and advertising program, $18,000 would be fixed costs and $2,000 variable. If the expanded sales and advertising program were adopted without any price change, the expense line would be revised to the condition shown in Figure 34-9. Profits would be $2,000 per month.

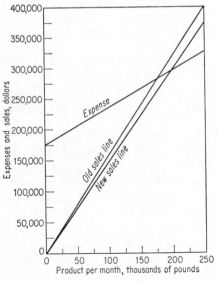

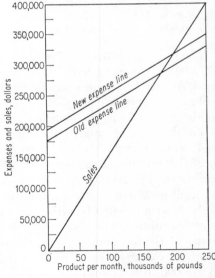

Figure 34-8. Badger Chemical Company, effect of proposed price cut.

Figure 34-9. Badger Chemical Company, effect of proposed sales and advertising program.

If at the same time that the enlarged sales and advertising program were adopted the price were also reduced to $1.50, the resultant effect is shown in Figure 34-10. Approximately $13,000 profits per month are anticipated as shown by the dashed line.

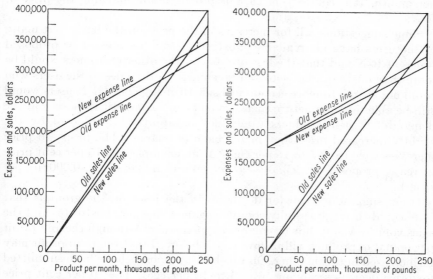

Figure 34-10. Badger Chemical Company, combined effect of proposed price cut and sales and advertising program.

Figure 34-11. Badger Chemical Company, effect of proposed quality change.

It would thus appear that other things being equal, the best policy would be to lower the price at the same time that the sales and advertising program are expanded. However, this policy raises the break-even point considerably, with the possibility of relatively large losses if the high-volume sales fail to materialize.

Evaluating a Quality Change. The Badger Chemical Company has also been considering for some time a reduction in the quality of its product by using a cheaper raw material. (This is not meant to imply that use of a cheaper raw material necessarily or usually reduces the quality of finished products.) The price would then be reduced to $1.40 per pound. It is expected that sales under these conditions could now be maintained at 250,000 lb without the additional promotion and advertising previously discussed. Would this be preferable to the alternative just mentioned? The cheaper raw material would lower variable costs 6 cents a pound. The new expense and sales curves are drawn in Figure 34-11. The profit expectation of more than $36,000 per month in this case compares with $13,000 in the best previously considered alternative. Moreover, the break-even point is lower in this case than in the best previously evaluated alternative. However, the long-run effect of reducing the quality of the product must also receive serious consideration.

Evaluating Effects of Price Changes on Sales Requirements. The Badger Chemical Company is currently making a profit of $22,000 per month. It is considering various proposals for changing the price of R-N.

Some suggestions call for increases in the price on the basis that many of the users have no available substitutes near the present or proposed prices of R-N and that the loss of a few of the other customers would be more than offset by the increased revenue from the sales to the users who could not switch to more economical substitutes. (These R-N users would still be able to manufacture their products on a competitive basis and the demand for their products would not be appreciably affected by the slightly increased price they might have to charge.) The proposed price increases vary from 5 to 15 per cent. As an example, the 15 per cent price increase proposal anticipates a reduction in sales of 50,000 lb per month.

Other suggestions call for decreases in the price on the grounds that R-N could then successfully compete against cheaper substitutes and the sales volume would thus be enlarged appreciably. Although the unit profit per pound of product will be lower, it is believed that the total profit may be increased in this manner. On this basis, proposals have been submitted for price decreases ranging from 5 to 10 per cent. The 10 per cent price decrease proposal is based on an anticipated sales increase of 45,000 lb per month.

As a basis for considering these proposals, a modification of the previously constructed break-even chart is made to indicate the sales volumes which are required to maintain the present profit of $22,000 assuming various price levels for the product R-N. This chart is shown in Figure 34-12.

The various lines on this chart were constructed in the following manner. The expense plus present profit line is parallel to the expense line and above it by the amount of present profits. The various sales lines are obtained by drawing straight lines between zero dollars of sales at zero pounds per month and the total sales dollars at any other pounds per month using the increased and the reduced prices. Thus, this second point on the 10 per cent price increase sales line might be at 200,000 lb per month and $352,000 of sales (200,000 lb times $1.76 per pound equals $352,000.)

The points of intersection of the expense plus present profit line with the various sales lines indicate the volume of monthly product sales which are required to maintain profits at the present level if the price changes are made. Thus, a 15 per cent increase in price will be desirable only if the sales volume can be maintained in excess of 161,000 lb per month.

Otherwise profits will be no greater than they are at present. If a 10 per cent reduction in price will not result in an increase of sales beyond 238,000 lb per month, profits will not be increased by this proposal. In fact, if the sales do not increase to this volume, profits will be lower.

Assuming that the sales estimates previously mentioned for the 15 per cent price increase and 10 per cent price decrease proposals are valid,

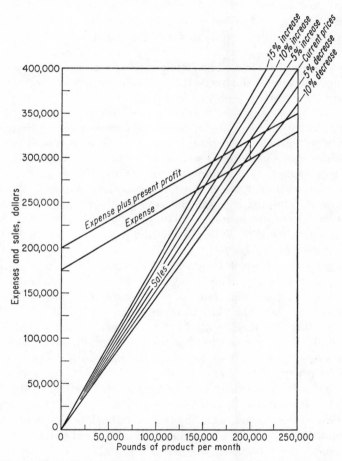

Figure 34-12. Badger Chemical Company, pricing break-even chart.

we can readily see on the chart that the 15 per cent price increase proposal is not a good proposal but that the 10 per cent price decrease proposal appears to be desirable.

The magnitude of the expected increase or decrease of profits under any of these alternatives is indicated by the distance between the sales line and the expense plus present profit line. Thus, the 15 per cent price increase would involve an expected reduction in sales of 50,000, to 150,000 lb per month. The distance between the expense plus present profit line and the 15 per cent increase sales line, or about $14,000, is the expected reduction in profits. The 10 per cent price decrease will increase sales by 45,000 to 245,000 lb per month. The distance between the 10 per cent decrease sales line and the expense plus present profit line, or about $5,000, is the expected increase in monthly profits.

Changes in price concessions from list price can be treated the same as sales price changes and their effects analyzed in an analogous manner.

Price Discrimination. The break-even chart can be very useful in presenting a picture of the over-all effects of contemplated price discriminations on the company's economic position.[1]

One form of price discrimination sometimes practiced is known as "dumping." Dumping can take a variety of forms. A product may be sold on the foreign market at a lower price than the usual domestic price. (The possible danger of the material sold at a cheaper price in foreign countries finding its way back to the domestic market and interfering with regular domestic sales at higher prices must be properly evaluated.) A variation of this form of dumping is to sell the same product on the domestic market at two different prices under two different brand names. Another form of dumping practice is the sale of a stylized product at successively lower prices as it goes out of style.

The break-even chart of Figure 34-13 illustrates this type of price discrimination. In this case, the Bab Company would lose money were it not for the price discrimination. At the $75 standard price it charges in the domestic market, the Bab Company can expect to sell only 1,200 equipments. The distance A–A', $5,000, represents the loss which would occur if the business were entirely at the standard domestic price. B indicates the break-even point (1,200 units per month) if no price discrimination were practiced.

It has been determined by competent research and analysis that 800 additional units per month could be sold at $50 per equipment with no possibility of the equipments finding their way back to the regular market. The distance A'–A", $6,000, represents the additional fixed costs of operating in the second lower-priced market. C indicates the total volume (1,830 units per month)—regular and lower-priced—required to break even, assuming 1,200 units of regular business at the standard price. D–D', $3,000 per month, represents the profits of the combined operation. E (the point of intersection of the total expense line with a line drawn parallel to the sales line and above it by the fixed loss of $5,000 which would occur if there were no price discrimination) represents the volume (1,540 equipments) required to make the price discrimination pay for itself. If

[1] Certain forms of price discrimination are contrary to Federal and local laws.

the total volume will not exceed 1,540 units per month, then the company would be better off without the dumping.

The location of the break-even points will vary with changes in the volume of regular priced business being transacted. The larger the proportion of regular priced business, the lower is the break-even point.

Dumping is most profitable with flat cost curves. The higher the proportion of fixed costs, the greater the discount from standard which it is possible to make and still increase profits.

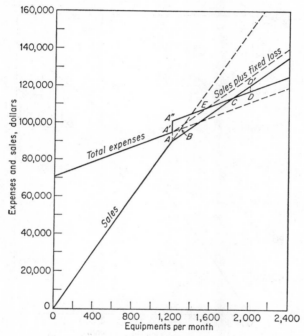

Figure 34-13. Bab Company, effect of price discrimination.

Figure 34-14 illustrates the application of dumping to the Pud Company, which is already operating profitably, but is considering price discrimination to further increase profits. If price discrimination will result in additional sales of more than 1,075 units over and above the current 3,350 units per month, thus bringing sales past D (point of intersection of the total expenses line with a line drawn parallel to the sales line and below it by the profit of $47,000 which would occur if there were no price discrimination), then price discrimination would be profitable.

A–A' represents the profits of $47,000 per month without price discrimination. A'–A'' is the additional fixed costs of $20,000 per month which must be expended if the price-discriminated market is to be entered. B indicates the break-even point of 2,330 units per month. Profits of the combined standard and price-discriminated operation are represented by the difference between the sales and total expenses lines. Based on the predicted sale of 2,000 equipments at the reduced price, total monthly profits would be $65,000, represented by C–C′ at output of 5,350 units per month.

Multiproduct Companies. Very few businesses are single-product companies. The vast majority have several to a large assortment of products. This poses additional problems requiring managerial decision: which

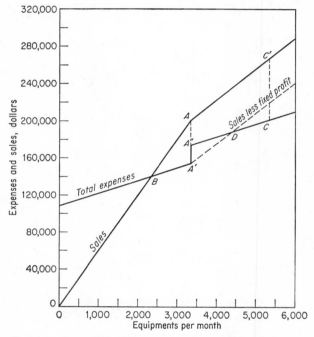

Figure 34-14. Pud Company, effect of price discrimination.

products should receive additional emphasis and which should, perhaps be dropped; should we raise the prices on a certain product?

For a multiproduct company, it is not usually convenient to use physical units as the measure of business volume. Each of the various products usually has different costs and usually sells for different prices. One common denominator to measure total output is dollars. (Measures of output were discussed in Chapter 33.)

The Charles Company, Inc., manufactures four different products, which we shall call W, X, Y, and Z. These products are manufactured using the same types of equipment and labor. Analysis of the total monthly operating costs of the Charles Company reveals the following picture:

Sales.......................	$800,000
Costs:	
Fixed............. $300,000	
Variable.......... 450,000	
Total..................	750,000
Profit.......................	$ 50,000

With this information, the break-even chart shown in Figure 34-15 is constructed. The total cost line is drawn by connecting the following two

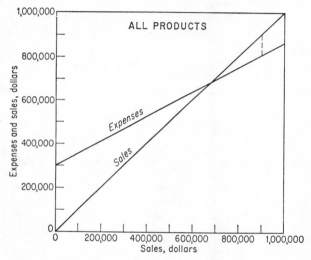

Figure 34-15. Charles Company, Inc., break-even chart.

points: total expense of $750,000 at $800,000 total sales; total expense of $300,000 at zero sales. The sales line is drawn by connecting total sales of $800,000 at $800,000 total sales; total sales of zero dollars at zero total sales.

Figure 34-15 indicates that sales in excess of $687,000 are necessary if this business is to make a profit under present price relationships. What would be the profit if sales were expanded to $900,000? Reading from the chart, the expected monthly profit would be in excess of $94,000 and is indicated by the dashed line.

Product Mix. This estimate—and all other estimates using this chart —is made on the assumption that the product mix of the company remains substantially the same. If the proportions of the total business volumes in products W, X, Y, and Z change appreciably, then the cost-revenue relationship will also change. If the company's business in its most profitable lines increased in comparison with its less profitable ones, then it is obvious that its profit position will have improved. Yet the break-even chart just depicted will not show this improvement. According to this chart, the profit expectancy from an increase in the dollar volume of the least profitable lines is the same as the profit expectancy from an increase in the most profitable products. This is a serious limitation of the chart and can cause errors of interpretation.

Product Break-even Charts. One approach to this product-mix problem is to compare separately the revenues and costs from each product. To make this comparison, all the fixed-, variable-, and mixed-cost items of the company are carefully analyzed and a proportion of each cost is assigned to the products which are responsible for the cost. For example, building costs may be distributed on the basis of the square-foot usage of building space. The actual cost of direct labor and material may be directly assignable to the using products. (Allocation of indirect costs is discussed in Chapter 3.)

Analyzing the costs of the Charles Company, the following results were obtained.

	Product				
	W	X	Y	Z	Total
Sales............	$300,000	$200,000	$125,000	$175,000	$800,000
Costs:					
Fixed..........	80,000	120,000	40,000	60,000	300,000
Variable.......	195,000	85,000	75,000	95,000	450,000
Total........	$275,000	$205,000	$115,000	$155,000	$750,000
Profit............	$ 25,000	$ −5,000	$ 10,000	$ 20,000	$ 50,000

These results were then used to construct separate break-even charts for each product line. On examining these charts, as shown in Figures

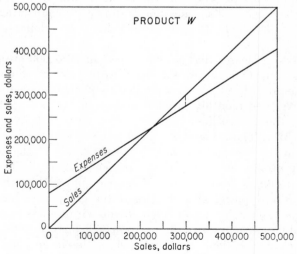

Figure 34-16. Charles Company, Inc., break-even chart.

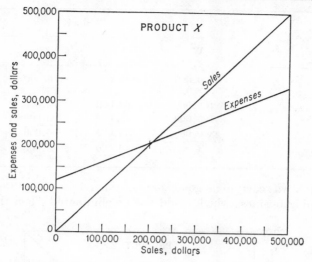

Figure 34-17. Charles Company, Inc., break-even chart.

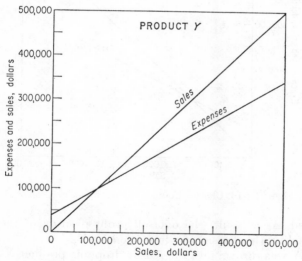

Figure 34-18. Charles Company, Inc., break-even chart.

34-16, 34-17, 34-18, and 34-19, the company president said, "If we cannot immediately bring product X out of the red, if we cannot increase the sales of this product to exceed the break-even volume of about $209,000, then let us discontinue the line completely and save the $5,000 a month this product is losing."

After product X was discontinued, the operating cost analysis showed the following.

	Product			
	W	Y	Z	Total
Sales....................	$300,000	$ 125,000	$175,000	$600,000
Costs:				
Fixed.................	105,000	60,000	75,000	240,000
Variable..............	195,000	75,000	95,000	365,000
Total..............	$300,000	$ 135,000	$170,000	$605,000
Profit...................	0	$ − 10,000	$ 5,000	$ − 5,000

Product X was carrying a good share of the overhead and the allocated costs of doing business which could not be eliminated when the product

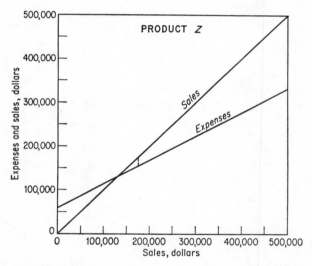

Figure 34-19. Charles Company, Inc., break-even chart.

was dropped. As a result, the over-all profit position of the enterprise was impaired by the decision to drop Product X.

Product Y was thrown into the red by dropping product X. If product Y is now dropped, products W and Z will go very deeply into the red and the enterprise will suffer further losses.

Pure-fixed and Policy-fixed Costs. To attempt a more realistic approach to multiproduct break-even analysis, a refinement in the analysis of the fixed costs of the business must be made. We have defined fixed costs or expenses as those charges which do not vary with changes in the volume of operations of the enterprise. We noted in Chapter 33 that two categories of fixed costs can be distinguished. The interest cost on mortgages is a fixed cost of the business, which must be met regardless of the output of the products produced; however the salary of the product W manager is a fixed cost only if product W is produced. Some or all of the depreciation costs of the business will occur regardless of operations; but the fixed expense of the existing advertising policy may be changed by a new managerial program. Two broad categories of fixed costs may be established: those fixed costs which will continue to occur regardless of current managerial policy, regardless of how drastically volume may vary, regardless of whether any particular products are produced, regardless of whether any production takes place at all; and those fixed costs which are fixed only in the sense that variations in volume or output of the existing complement of products will cause no change in these costs during the given budget or planning period in which the managerial policy has been fixed. We call the first category pure-fixed costs, and the second category policy-fixed costs.

Our cost analysis is now refined to segregate the two types of fixed costs. For the Charles Company the following revised statement was secured.

| | Product | | | | |
	W	X	Y	Z	Total
Sales............	$300,000	$200,000	$125,000	$175,000	$800,000
Costs:					
Pure-fixed......	35,000	60,000	30,000	20,000	145,000
Policy-fixed.....	45,000	60,000	10,000	40,000	155,000
Variable........	195,000	85,000	75,000	95,000	450,000
Total........	$275,000	$205,000	$115,000	$155,000	$750,000
Profit...........	$ 25,000	$ -5,000	$ 10,000	$ 20,000	$ 50,000

Contribution Break-even Charts. A new set of break-even charts can now be constructed, as shown in Figures 34-20 to 34-23. Three parallel cost lines are plotted along with the sales line. If the slope of the variable cost line for any product were steeper than the revenue line, then at all volumes the product would lose money for the enterprise—and the larger the output, the greater would be this loss. The immediate managerial decision would then be to eliminate the product unless changes in the cost structure or market were anticipated or it was desirable to sell the product at a loss for some reason.

The intersection of the sales line with the variable plus policy-fixed costs gives a contribution break-even point. If operating volume is below this point, then total profits of the enterprise would be greater if the product were eliminated. If the operating volume is greater than the contri-

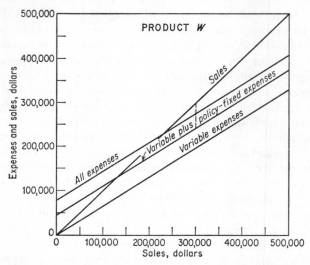

Figure 34-20. Charles Company, Inc., contribution break-even chart.

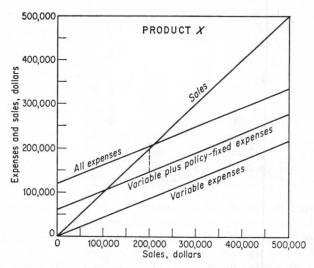

Figure 34-21. Charles Company, Inc., contribution break-even chart.

bution break-even volume, then, despite the possible indication of a product loss, the product is carrying a share of the pure-fixed overhead. It is thus contributing to the total profits of the enterprise.

Contribution Profit. The difference between the sales revenue and the variable plus policy-fixed costs is termed contribution profit. If positive, it represents the additional revenue contributed to the profitableness of the enterprise by the continued production and sales of the product or services. The contribution profits for current sales volumes are indicated by dashed lines in the charts of Figures 34-20 to 34-23. A comparison of these values gives a better picture of the performance of each product.

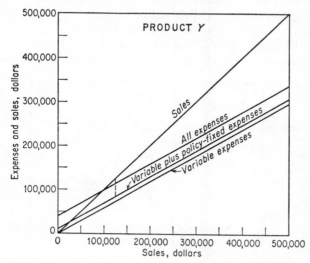

Figure 34-22. Charles Company, Inc., contribution break-even chart.

For the data just analyzed, the following contribution profits at the current sales volumes are obtained from the charts:

Product W	$ 60,000
Product X	55,000
Product Y	40,000
Product Z	40,000
Total	$195,000

These figures indicate that, despite the apparent profitableness of products Y and Z and apparent unprofitableness of product X, the elimination of either products Y or Z would not have reduced the total profits as much as the elimination of product X. Moreover, this analysis shows that the elimination of any of the products will reduce profits.

When the products use common facilities and plant capacity considerations are significant, a plant-capacity measure of output volume, such as conversion cost, may be more desirable than sales dollars as the independent variable in the break-even charts. Examination of the slopes of the different product-cost lines furnishes some guidance as to which products may be pushed and promoted most profitably. Other things being equal, an increase in the dollar volume of those products having the steepest revenue and flattest cost lines with lowest break-even points will result in the greatest profit advantage.

Analyses similar to those which were made for a one-product company can be made with the break-even charts for each product of a multiproduct company. The cost and revenue curves are subject to the same general type of manipulation to ascertain the effects of changes in production, pricing, promotion and market conditions. However, care must be exercised not to misinterpret the meanings of these static cost and revenue lines. When the proportions of the business devoted to the various products change significantly, the allocation of the pure-fixed costs of the

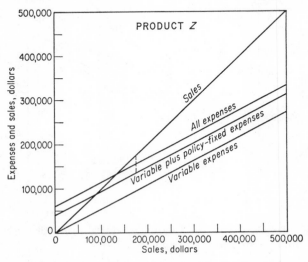

Figure 34-23. Charles Company, Inc., contribution break-even chart.

enterprise will also change. This will affect the product profit and loss statement but not the contribution profit.

Multiproduct Profit Graph. An adaptation of the profit graph shown earlier may be useful in shedding some light on the relative revenue contributions of various products, assuming given sales volumes.

Figure 34-24 is constructed by plotting fixed costs as a loss at zero sales volume. (Theoretically, at zero output, there would be no income and only fixed costs.) The slope of the line segment for each product shows the amount contributed by the sales of each product toward carrying this fixed cost and earning a profit.

Thus, the selling of $300,000 of product W adds $300,000 less the variable costs of $195,000, or $105,000, toward the fixed costs and profits of the company. Product W volume reduces the starting fixed-cost loss by $105,000 to $195,000. The product W line segment rises from $300,000 loss at zero sales to $195,000 loss at $300,000 sales. The selling of $200,000 of product X adds $200,000 less the variable cost of $85,000, or $115,000, toward the fixed costs and profits of the company. Product X volume reduces the loss from $195,000 at $300,000 sales to $80,000 at $500,000 sales.

In the case of the Charles Company, the revenue from each of the products exceeds the variable cost. Each product therefore contributes something toward carrying the fixed costs of the enterprise and earning a profit. Of course, we might have a situation where the revenue just equaled the variable cost. The line segment for that product would then be horizontal. Increases or decreases in the sales of this product have no

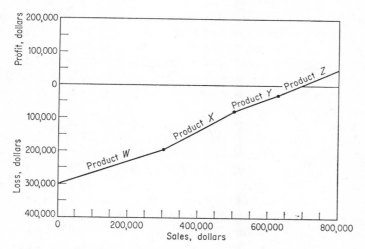

Figure 34-24. Charles Company, Inc., multiproduct profit graph.

effect on profits. The additional costs of additional units equals the price received for them. Still worse, we might have a situation in which the revenue from a product was less than variable cost. The line segment for this product would be declining. Then increases in sales of this product would reduce profits and decreases in sales would increase profits.

Price and Product Emphasis Policies. Cost-plus pricing, percentage markups, or other methods of pricing which are based solely on costs fail to consider the market or demand for the product. As illustrated in some of our previous examples, the pricing policy should relate costs with the market for the product to be effective in promoting the welfare of the enterprise. To price products and to plan production most effectively, estimates of the price demand for the products are of prime importance: how much can be sold at each of a series of prices. Knowing this as well as our costs, we can determine whether to lower prices, raise them, or leave them the same on each of our products.

Successful price setting, of course, involves consideration and forecasting of many tangible and intangible factors. Among these are the following:

1. The present and forecasted market demands for the product and the relationships of these demands to the demands for other products

2. Existing and future distribution channels

3. Company long-range policy with respect to market share, quality goals, etc.

4. The economics of the affected industries

5. The cost relationships resulting from the current and prospective technology and managerial methods

The relative importance of the various factors in determining prices will depend on the circumstances and economic characteristics of the industry. Thus, in some cases, cost relationships may furnish a floor below which price quotations would not be made: it would rarely be advisable to charge less than the out-of-pocket variable cost for long periods of time. Market conditions might furnish a ceiling above which they might not rise: there is frequently a price above which very few consumers will buy your product.

In our analyses of various pricing and product-emphasis problems, we have taken the position that there is no rule of thumb, no universal formula which can be applied to every situation. Each pricing problem must be handled on its own merits. Our line of reasoning has developed the following general concepts:

1. Each product should be sold at a price which will recover at least the cost which would be saved were it not produced, i.e., variable plus policy-fixed costs. If it cannot be sold at that price in the long run, it is preferable to eliminate it, other things being equal.

2. If any of the plant facilities are used to capacity or very near to it, then, in addition to recovering the incremental costs mentioned in paragraph 1, the price should also include a contribution toward the general overhead expense and profit of the enterprise as large as the contribution made by any other products with which it competes for use of the limited facilities, i.e., the marginal profit contribution per unit of capacity used should be as large as that of any product competing for use of the facilities.

3. If the plant facilities are not used very near to capacity—if sales capacity is smaller than plant capacity—then the goal is to recover the incremental costs of paragraph 1 plus as much additional as possible toward general overhead expense and profit.

There are quite a number of questions which are not covered by the above. Is it desirable to carry an unprofitable product to have a complete line of products? Is it desirable to carry an unprofitable product because the demand will grow or unit costs will decrease in the long run so that it can be sold more profitably? Should the product quality be increased rather than the price reduced to maintain or increase sales volume? In pricing a new product, should short-run profits be sacrificed and the price kept low to obtain the long-run benefits of high market penetration? Or should the initial price be high and lowered in several stages to obtain the short-run benefits of price discrimination?

Multiplant Break-even Charts. Many companies operate several plants and in some cases make the same products in some or all of them. These plants may differ considerably from each other with respect to size, technical equipment and production methods, wage rates, material prices, and access to natural resources and consumer markets. The costs of operations in each of these plants will vary depending on these factors. At any given company-wide output rate, the total cost line will be the sum of the operating costs at each of these plants. Among the factors in determining how the desired production is allocated amongst the plants is the proximity of the consumers to the plants, the relative efficiencies and capacities of these plants, and the market situation in the different geographic areas. Because the distribution of production among the company's plants at higher outputs may not be in the same proportions as at lower outputs, a composite break-even chart for the entire operation at all the plants of the company may give misleading results.

If the differences in the cost functions at the various plants are significant, it is necessary to construct separate break-even charts for each plant. Having separate analyses of the economic characteristics of each unit will aid in allocating production so as to make the most effective over-all use of the company's facilities.

Accounting Cost Categories. Accounting statements generally break down costs into three principal groupings:

1. Manufacturing expenses
2. Selling expenses
3. Administrative expenses

Other more refined breakdowns are also used. Break-even charts incorporating these groupings by category of costs or broad areas of responsibility are shown in Figures 34-25 and 34-26. Figure 34-26 will separately reveal the sales volumes required to cover all manufacturing expenses (A); or to cover all manufacturing and selling expenses (B); or to cover all manufacturing, selling, and administrative expenses (the break-even volume) (C). These separate intersection points are identified on the chart and the output volumes are labeled successively A, B, and C.

Importance of Fixed Costs. Some insight into the significance of the differentiation of costs into fixed and variable elements may be gained by a comparison of the break-even charts of four hypothetical companies shown in Figure 34-27.

Chart A shows a company in which all costs are variable. In this case, the company makes a constant amount of money on each unit of sales regardless of the volume of operations. The break-even point does not exist, but is theoretically at zero volume of operations. A company with all costs variable might also lose a constant amount of money on each unit.

Chart B shows a company which has a relatively small proportion of fixed costs and Chart C shows one with a relatively large proportion of fixed costs.

Chart D pictures a hypothetical company in which all costs are fixed. In this case, the total of all receipts from sales beyond the break-even volume comprises the profit from operations. If the break-even point is

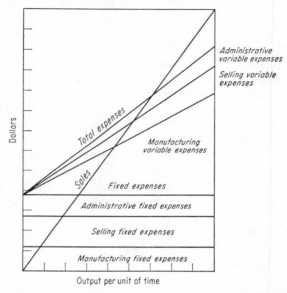

Figure 34-25. Break-even chart with costs categorized, Type I.

not reached, then the loss is equal to the difference between the break-even sales volume and the actual sales volume for the period.

These graphs illustrate the following facts:

1. With a given price structure, fixed costs are largely responsible for the position and significance of the break-even point.

2. Other things being equal, the larger the proportion of the costs which are fixed, the further to the right is the break-even point and the higher the sales volume required before the company will make money.

3. When investments resulting in fixed costs are properly and wisely made, the companies with the higher fixed costs have greater profit potentialities if they can achieve the required volume of sales beyond the break-even point.

Industrial and technological progress has frequently produced increases in the proportion of fixed costs. Investments in laborsaving machinery may result in reduced amounts of direct-labor (usually variable) costs and increased amounts of depreciation (usually fixed) costs. Improved prod-

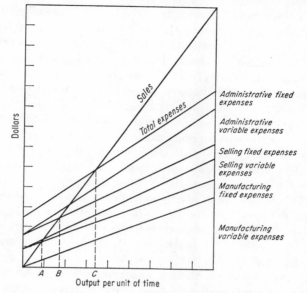

Figure 34-26. Break-even chart with costs categorized, Type II.

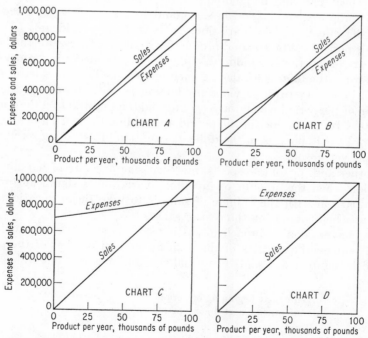

Figure 34-27. Break-even charts. Chart A—company with no fixed costs. Chart B—company with relatively small proportion of fixed costs. Chart C—company with relatively large proportion of fixed costs. Chart D—company with no variable costs.

uct designs reduce material (usually variable) costs as well as direct labor (usually variable). As a result of these trends, the break-even points of some companies in the United States have been moving toward the right especially when prices are weak. This is producing a situation in these companies in which relatively small variations in volume of operations will make the difference between a large, healthy profit and a painfully large loss. To some extent, then, this situation is introducing an element of inflexibility into our industrial structure as well as into the operations of the companies: these companies cannot adjust themselves as readily to profitable operations over a wide sales volume range.

Sales and Production Volumes. In our previous break-even analyses, we have tacitly assumed that sales volume and production volume were the same. This, quite obviously, is not always true. Inventories may be increased or depleted, depending upon production, market, and other factors. When the size of inventories changes in any appreciable amount, the change will cause a difference between the production and the sales figures for that period.

In many cases, however, the size of inventories is small in comparison with production and sales, so that even relatively large variations in the size of the inventory will have small effect on the total sales figure. The problem can thus be ignored in a large percentage of studies.

When the analysis period is short and inventory changes large, the distorting effect of these variations is likely to be significant. (A short analysis period will mean total production and sales figures for the period which are proportionally reduced.) One way to provide for inventory variations would be to adjust sales for each period to eliminate sales of items held in inventory from previous production periods and to add the production of the period which was as yet unsold (i.e., subtracting the opening inventory from the sales of the period and adding the closing inventory). This, of course, puts us in the difficult situation of assuming receipts for items as yet unsold.

Another and, in some respects, more satisfactory way of handling the situation when the amount of inventory variation is significantly large in comparison with the volume of sales is to take these variations into account when computing the cost of sales.

The conventional approach to costing sales is to charge the material, labor, and overhead costs of the item to the cost of sales of the period in which the item was sold. The usual accounting statement will read as follows:

Inventory at beginning of period...........	$100,000
Manufacturing cost during period..........	800,000
Total.................................	$900,000
Inventory at end of period...............	150,000
Cost of sales............................	$750,000

The inventory values in this statement usually include all manufacturing costs, both fixed and variable.

For the purposes of our short-term cost-volume relationship, we will want to charge to this period all the fixed expenses because they are a function of time and not of volume. Regardless of whether we had produced more or less during the period and had thus increased or decreased the inventory, these costs would have been incurred.[1] For our analysis, then, we will not include fixed factory overhead costs in inventory valuations. We will consider these costs as charges to that period's operations. The variable costs, of course, would not have been incurred if the additional units were not produced for inventory and should, therefore, not be charged to the period's operations but are held in the inventory asset account.

Thus, if $10,000 of the $100,000 opening inventory and $20,000 of the $150,000 closing inventory represented fixed overhead costs, the statement for break-even analysis purposes would read:

Inventory at beginning of period	$ 90,000
Manufacturing cost during period	800,000
Total	$890,000
Inventory at end of period	130,000
Cost of sales	$760,000

The additional $10,000 in the computed value of the cost of sales is caused by the fact that the $10,000 of the fixed cost associated with the additional inventory remains a charge to the period rather than being held in the inventory valuation. There was $20,000 of fixed cost in the closing inventory based on conventional accounting procedure. Subtracting the $10,000 which was in the opening inventory using conventional methods gives us the $10,000 of fixed cost which is excluded from inventory valuation and added to cost of sales for this period.

Accuracy of Cost Lines. In the construction of our break-even charts, we use straight lines to indicate how costs vary with volume of production. This implies that unit variable costs are perfectly constant and that fixed costs are perfectly fixed regardless of volume. Neither of these is completely true. Although many variable costs are directly proportional to

---

[1] There are a number of factors other than those involved in break-even analysis which favor the exclusion of fixed factory overhead from inventories for accounting purposes. Excluding fixed factory overhead results in an improved operating statement from many points of view. When inventories are increasing and fixed overhead costs are being accumulated in inventories instead of being charged to operations, operations are not carrying the normal amount of fixed overhead chargeable to the period. When inventories are decreasing, operations will be charged with a normal amount of fixed overhead plus the fixed overhead in the old inventories which are charged into cost of sales. This procedure thus overstates profits (or understates losses) in times of inventory accumulation and understates profits (or overstates losses) in times of inventory decline.

the output volume, others are correlated with other activity factors which are related to output in somewhat different patterns. With increasing volume of production, it is sometimes possible to use more efficient processes which will lower unit variable costs. With larger operating volumes, fixed costs may also increase somewhat.

If correctly understood, however, these facts are not too disturbing to our analysis. The tendencies at higher volumes toward slightly lower unit variable costs and slightly higher fixed costs will tend to counteract each other at the most usual operating volumes. We also noted in Chapter 33 that short-run total costs tend to be linear in the normal operating ranges of most companies even if the theoretical curves covering all possible output volumes are curvilinear.

A source of error in break-even analyses is the possible inaccuracy of the short-run cost line. These inaccuracies occur because of the limitations of the firm's accounting system as well as inadequacy in the methods of determining the cost line. Methods of measuring and accounting for costs and profits, together with some of their limitations and inaccuracies were discussed in Chapters 3, 4, and 7. Many of the sources of bias and inaccuracy in determining the short-run cost line are discussed in Chapter 33 and methods of correcting some of them are suggested. However, it is frequently not economic to refine the break-even analysis to eliminate all distortions which could be corrected.

Revenue as a Linear Function of Volume. The revenue or sales line of the break-even chart is based on the assumption of a fixed price regardless of sales volume. From a dynamic charting point of view—considering how prices will change with volume over a period of time—this concept is valid only if a purely competitive condition exists in the industry so that all the production of the enterprise can be disposed of at the prevailing price. In most industries, an imperfect competition prevails in which the quantity that can be sold at any time varies inversely with the price in some sort of relatively complicated relationship which is difficult to ascertain accurately. Moreover, for an unregulated monopoly firm there is a definite, inverse relationship between the price charged and the volume of product which can be sold, other things being equal.

Thus, for many companies, the dynamic total-revenue line is not a straight line. The larger the output, the lower is the unit price obtainable. However, in the static break-even chart analysis, price is constant. If a lowering of price to increase volume is being considered, a new break-even chart to convey a picture of the effects of the new price conditions must be drawn to help evaluate the desirability of the proposed change.

Algebra of Break-even Analysis. For those inclined to a formula presentation of break-even analysis, a brief explanation of several simple algebraic approaches to some of the graphic presentations in the previous sections is presented here.

The symbols used in this section are as follows:

P = profit

R = revenue or sales

Q = price per unit

C = total cost

F = fixed cost

V = variable cost per unit

N = number of units or volume

B = break-even volume

Then,

$$P = R - C$$
$$R = NQ$$
$$C = F + NV$$

Therefore,

$$P = NQ - F - NV$$

The break-even point occurs at the point at which profits are zero Thus, to find the break-even volume,

$$0 = NQ - F - NV$$

and solving for $B = N$,

$$N(Q - V) = F$$
$$N = \frac{F}{Q - V} = B$$

Maintaining Present Profits—Changes in Cost. A common question when cost increases are imminent or proposed is: What total sales volume do we need to maintain our present profits if we do not increase our prices?

Let us assume that fixed costs are increased by ΔF and variable costs per unit by ΔV. Profits under these new conditions will be called P_1. The total sales volume required to keep profits the same as at present will be called N_1.

Under present conditions,

$$P = NQ - F - NV \quad \text{and} \quad P + F = NQ - NV$$

Under the new conditions,

$$P_1 = N_1Q - (F + \Delta F) - N_1(V + \Delta V)$$
$$P_1 = N_1Q - F - \Delta F - N_1V - N_1\Delta V$$

If the same profit is to be maintained,

$$P = P_1$$
$$NQ - F - NV = N_1Q - F - \Delta F - N_1V - N_1\Delta V$$

Canceling the F values and dividing both sides of the equation by N,

$$Q - V = \frac{N_1}{N}Q - \frac{N_1}{N}V - \frac{N_1}{N}\Delta V - \frac{\Delta F}{N}$$
$$\frac{N_1}{N}(Q - V - \Delta V) = Q - V + \frac{\Delta F}{N}$$
$$\frac{N_1}{N} = \frac{Q - V + (\Delta F/N)}{Q - V - \Delta V}$$

To express this another way, we can multiply numerator and denominator by N,

$$\frac{N_1}{N} = \frac{NQ - NV + \Delta F}{NQ - NV - N\Delta V}$$

Then, since,

$$P + F = NQ - NV$$

$$\frac{N_1}{N} = \frac{P + F + \Delta F}{P + F - N\Delta V}$$

$$N_1 = N \left(\frac{P + F + \Delta F}{P + F - N\Delta V} \right)$$

Maintaining Present Profits—Changes in Sales Price. If changes in selling price are being considered, the equation is similar. How much can sales volume decline before it will wipe out the potentially profitable effects of a price increase? Let ΔQ stand for the increase in sale price. Under the present conditions,

$$P = NQ - F - NV$$

Under the new conditions,

$$P_1 = N_1(Q + \Delta Q) - F - N_1 V$$

$$P_1 = N_1 Q + N_1 \Delta Q - F - N_1 V$$

$$P = P_1$$

$$NQ - F - NV = N_1 Q + N_1 \Delta Q - F - N_1 V$$

$$Q - V = \frac{N_1}{N} Q + \frac{N_1}{N} \Delta Q - \frac{N_1}{N} V$$

$$\frac{N_1}{N} = \frac{Q - V}{Q - V + \Delta Q}$$

Since $P + F = NQ - NV$ and $\dfrac{N_1}{N} = \dfrac{NQ - NV}{NQ - NV + N\Delta Q}$,

$$\frac{N_1}{N} = \frac{P + F}{P + F + N\Delta Q}$$

$$N_1 = N \left(\frac{P + F}{P + F + N\Delta Q} \right)$$

Increasing or Decreasing Profits. What sales volume is necessary to double profits? What price increases are required to raise profits 50 per cent? How much will profits be reduced by increased costs?

The previously presented equations can be adapted to answer these questions. Let us call the change in profits ΔP and, for the simplest case, assume no changes in costs.

Under present conditions,

$$P = NQ - F - NV$$

Under the new conditions,

$$P + \Delta P = N_1 Q - F - N_1 V$$
$$P = N_1 Q - F - N_1 V - \Delta P$$

The P values in each equation are equal to each other.

$$NQ - F - NV = N_1 Q - F - N_1 V - \Delta P$$
$$N_1 Q - N_1 V = NQ - NV + \Delta P$$
$$\frac{N_1}{N} = \frac{Q - V + \dfrac{\Delta P}{N}}{Q - V}$$

Multiplying numerator and denominator of the right side of the equation by N,

$$\frac{N_1}{N} = \frac{NQ - NV + \Delta P}{NQ - NV}$$

Since $P + F = NQ - NV$,

$$\frac{N_1}{N} = \frac{P + F + \Delta P}{P + F}$$
$$N_1 = N \left(\frac{P + F + \Delta P}{P + F} \right)$$

The break-even charts presented in this chapter answer profit questions graphically, whereas these equations answer them algebraically. The graphic presentation is frequently the preferable one because of the greater ease of comprehension of the relationships.

Historical Break-even Chart. The break-even analyses thus far presented have been based upon a static concept of costs and revenues. When historical data are used to estimate fixed and variable costs, they are corrected when necessary for changes in methods, prices, facilities, etc. In the historical break-even chart, however, the effects of these changes are not excluded from the profit function.

In Chapter 33, we established an expense trend line using unadjusted cost data for the Allen Manufacturing Company. A historical break-even chart using this trend line is shown in Figure 34-28.

When substantial changes in market or manufacturing methods have taken place, when additions to the plant have been constructed, when the price structures of the company's products have changed considerably, this trend analysis may furnish a generalized picture of the effects of these changes. For example, let us consider the operating statements of the Allen Manufacturing Company back to 1950, as shown in Table 34-1.

Adding this additional data on a historical break-even chart, Figure 34-29, we find two separate expense trend lines: one for operations up to 1956 and one for operations from 1956. We can see here very clearly the

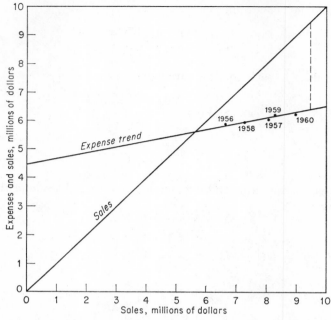

Figure 34-28. Allen Manufacturing Company, historical break-even chart (1956–1960).

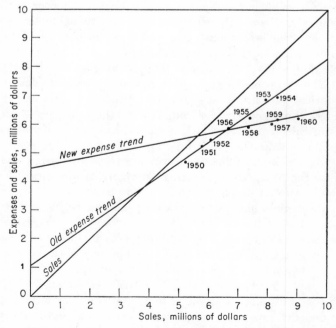

Figure 34-29. Allen Manufacturing Company, historical break-even chart (1950–1960).

Table 34-1. Allen Manufacturing Company

Year	Total sales	Total operating expense	Operating profit
1950	$5,200,000	$4,700,000	$ 500,000
1951	5,750,000	5,250,000	500,000
1952	6,050,000	5,500,000	550,000
1953	7,900,000	6,900,000	1,000,000
1954	8,260,000	6,980,000	1,280,000
1955	7,350,000	6,250,000	1,100,000

general effect of some significant changes in the company's picture. It is evident that the company must operate at a considerably higher volume to make a profit under present conditions as compared with the earlier period. We also see, however, that if the company can maintain this higher volume, it will make a considerably greater total profit under the new conditions.

Meaningfulness of Expense Trend. The expense trends of many companies show linear relationships with only a moderate scatter. Historical break-even charts can then be useful devices. It must be remembered, however, that the historical chart may not indicate present cost-revenue-volume relationships. The apparent cost-volume relationship may be developed by the tendency of both sales dollars and costs to rise during inflationary periods and decline during deflationary periods. When prices are determined by cost-plus pricing (any formula which estimates costs and then adds profits), this tendency will be accentuated.

When a company's fixed costs have increased during a period of expansion, the historical chart may tend to overstate the variability of the expense trend, producing a break-even point which is too low from a short-range and possibly from a long-range point of view as well. A consideration of the operating figures of the Hall Company will illustrate this situation. Table 34-2 gives break-even data compiled by the comptroller's

Table 34-2. The Hall Company

Year	Sales	Total expenses	Fixed expenses	Variable expenses
1954	$45,200	$42,800	$22,000	$20,800
1955	51,400	47,600	23,000	24,600
1956	56,200	51,700	24,300	27,400
1957	66,800	56,300	27,900	28,400
1958	73,200	62,800	28,900	33,900
1959	75,100	65,100	29,200	35,900
1960	79,400	63,800	29,200	34,600

staff of the company. (Under the usual circumstances in which the historical approach is used, these figures may not be available.) These data are plotted in Figure 34-30 and a composite break-even chart constructed.

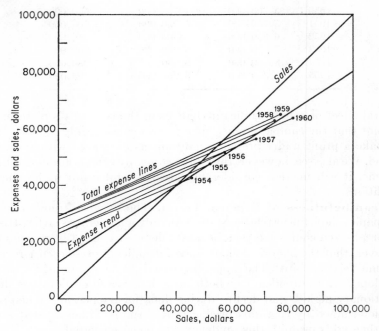

Figure 34-30. Hall Company, composite break-even chart.

In addition to the historical expense trend line, the estimated static short-run expense lines are shown for each year based upon the comptroller's breakdown of costs into fixed and variable elements.

We now see that there was a rise in fixed costs during the period under consideration. The break-even point was increasing steadily in a manner not apparent from the historical trend line. The break-even volume increased from $40,000 to $56,000 from 1954 to 1959 and decreased to $54,000 in 1960.

These factors which distort the expense trend line tend to become more pronounced as the data goes back farther into past years. We therefore try to use data which reflect current conditions as much as possible, going back only enough years to obtain wide enough output-volume fluctuations to produce a satisfactory trend line.

PROBLEMS

1. (*a*) What are the principal assumptions underlying the usual types of break-even analysis? (*b*) What are the principal limitations of break-even analysis for short-term profit planning?

2. The Roscoe Manufacturing Company analyzed its past performance, making adjustments for important past, current, or prospective changes, and estimated the following.

	Fixed costs	Variable costs (percentage of sales)
Direct material..................		34.9%
Direct labor.....................		21.6
Expenses:		
Factory.......................	$62,850	10.5
Selling and shipping...........	6,900	4.2
General and administrative.....	18,600	0.7

Forecasted sales for next year are $500,000.
(*a*) Prepare a break-even chart for the Roscoe Manufacturing Company.
(*b*) What is the break-even sales volume for the company?
(*c*) What is the profit at the $500,000 forecasted sales volume?
(*d*) If the actual sales volume is $50,000 below or above the forecasted volume, what are the respective profits?

3. Refer to Figure 34-2, showing the break-even chart for the Badger Chemical Company. The Badger Chemical Company is subject to Federal and state income taxes at the following rates on annual profits: 33 per cent on the first $25,000 and 56 per cent on all amounts over $25,000. Redraw the break-even chart with two expense lines: expense before income taxes and expense after income taxes. Label the profit-after-income-taxes area.

4. Refer to the illustration in the text of the use of a break-even chart in the evaluation of an equipment program. Does this type of break-even study supersede or complement the analytic procedures on evaluation of alternatives discussed in earlier chapters? Explain.

5. If all of a firm's products make a contribution profit, does this insure that the firm is profitable? Explain.

6. Is there a conflict between the theory presented in the discussion of the economics of the firm, Chapter 28, and the use of break-even charts in evaluating pricing alternatives discussed in this chapter? Explain.

7. It is suggested in the text that, when sales and production volumes differ significantly, we cannot ignore this difference in measuring output volume, but must adjust either the sales or the cost figures. Comment on the relative desirability of each of these alternatives.

8. Obtain sales and cost statistics on a selected manufacturing corporation listed in a financial guide available in your library (such as Moody's or Standard & Poor's). (a) Plot a historical break-even chart for the company. (b) What does this chart indicate regarding the operating characteristics of the business? (c) What are the limitations of the chart? In what ways can it be misleading?

9. Compare the relationship between cost and output in the break-even models of this chapter with the relationship between cost and output in the input-output accounting model of the economy described in Chapter 29.

35 Long-run Cost Variations (Scale of Operations)

Whereas short-run cost variations are predicated on a given set of facilities, production techniques, etc., that cannot be changed on short notice, long-run cost variations are designed to show the variations of cost which occur when the period of time is long enough to allow all the factors affecting costs and output to be changed. In effect, all costs are variable in this kind of long-run analysis.

A long-run cost function describing the relationship between size of plant (measured in output rate) and cost of production can be visualized conceptually as the envelope of a large number of short-run average-cost curves. The short-run average-cost curves were, of course, established with the previously mentioned assumptions of constancy of technological development, prices of material, wage rates, quality of management, etc. This theoretical model of long-run cost curves is pictured in Figure 35-1.

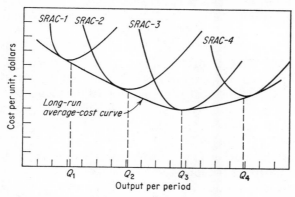

Figure 35-1. Long-run average-cost curve (envelope of short-run average-cost curves).

The long-run average-cost curve shows the average cost of producing a given output, assuming that the correct size of facility for producing that output has been chosen. If we know what output we desire from a facility, we can design one which will give the lowest possible costs at

671

that output. The average cost for this minimum-cost facility is shown as one point on the long-run average-cost curve. Each point on the long-run cost curve represents a different-size facility. The average cost shown for each output rate is the average cost which will occur when using the best size of facility for that output volume.

Each facility can, of course, operate at other output levels. It will, therefore, have its short-run average-cost curve describing how its costs will vary over its operating range. Only one point on this short-run curve is shown on the long-run curve.

In the short run, adjustments in output as demand increases are made by moving to the right on the short-run average-cost (SRAC) curve. This is done by increasing the input of variable items, by employing more labor, and by using more materials. As an example in Figure 35-1, if we were operating on SRAC-1, we may move our operations to the right on this curve, past its intersection with SRAC-2. We could then operate with lower costs if we invested in a larger plant or facility to give us a short-run cost curve farther to the right, similar to SRAC-2.

As demand increases, larger and larger amounts of investment in larger facilities will appear desirable to obtain short-run average-cost curves with lower average costs. Depending upon the state of technology and costs at any given time, there is an optimum size of facility which will give us the lowest short-run average-cost curve. The short-run cost curve for this optimum-size plant is shown on our diagram as SRAC-3. Plants beyond this in size will have higher short-run cost curves. Of course, for a given output volume, the average costs may be lower in plants larger than the optimum size. This is easily seen in our diagram if we compare the average costs on SRAC-3 and SRAC-4 at outputs above the intersection of the two curves.

Thus, in Figure 35-1 we have drawn four short-run average-cost curves, SRAC-1, SRAC-2, SRAC-3, and SRAC-4, which are tangent to the long-run average-cost curve. Theoretically, we could draw an infinite number of SRAC curves if the range of possible plant sizes is continuous. If only a limited number of sizes is possible, the long-run average-cost curve will be scalloped, following the possible SRAC curves to each intersection with the adjacent SRAC curves.

If I were establishing a facility which was expected to operate at a given output shown on the long-run cost curve, I would choose that size of the facility which would give me a short-run cost curve which is tangent to the given output in the long-run curve. As can be seen in Figure 35-1, this point of tangency occurs to the left of the short-run minimum-average-cost point for those outputs to the left of the long-run lowest-cost point. The point occurs to the right of the short-run minimum-cost point for those outputs that are to the right of the long-run lowest-cost point. For the optimum-sized facility, the point of tangency coincides with both the short-run minimum-cost as well as the long-run minimum-cost point. Thus, for outputs below the long-run minimum-cost point, it is more economical to underutilize a slightly larger facility than to operate a smaller facility at its minimum-cost point. For outputs above the long-run minimum-cost point, it is more economical to overutilize a slightly smaller facility than to operate a larger facility at its minimum-cost point. Only when plant is designed to produce the long-run optimum output (the optimum-size plant for the current state of technology) will it be most economical to operate at the short-run minimum-cost point.

Variations of Facility and Firm Size. The size of a facility may vary for several reasons:

1. Because of the depth of its operation, analogous to its vertical integration. An electronic computer plant manufacturing its own parts has more depth than one that assembles parts that are purchased.

2. Because of the width of its operation, analogous to horizontal integration. A plant operating its own marketing, distributing, and district warehousing organization has more width than one that markets through selling agents.

3. Because of the output volume it is capable of handling.

In long-run cost analysis, we are interested in the manner in which variations in facility size for the third reason affect costs. We should, therefore, carefully define the extent (depth and width) of the facility whose long-range cost-output variations we are measuring.

We must also be certain not to confuse size of facility with size of the firm. Because of the number of individual plants or facilities included in its organization, a firm with separate, but smaller, assembly plants in each section of the country, may be larger in total output capacity than a firm with a single larger plant. A firm may be vertically integrated, but its plants may not be vertically integrated: the electronic computer plant may receive its parts from a separate parts manufacturing plant also owned and operated by the firm.

A Planning Curve. Knowledge of long-run cost functions is valuable to management to assist in establishing long-range plans for plant size and location as well as for the development of all types of operational performance standards. Because of its usefulness in planning for capital expenditures and growth over long periods, the long-range average-cost curve is sometimes called a planning curve. It is useful in assisting management in determining the best scale of operations for its various facilities.

Long-run cost curves are sometimes not as useful by themselves as they are in conjunction with the analysis of the short-run cost variations which must be considered in the statistical development of the long-run curves. In determining the most desirable facility size, we are usually interested in how costs will vary when the plant is not operated at its design or optimum output volume. To improve ability to manage and control operations and costs in a multifacility firm, we are interested in knowing the kinds of short-term cost variations we can expect in the different sizes of facilities we operate.

The long-run cost curve indicates the relative economy of different sizes of plant or facility or economic operation at a given time under one set of technological and economic conditions. With new developments in equipment design and in production and operating methods, and with changes in prices and wage levels, new curves must be developed.

Determination of Long-run Cost Function. How do we determine the long-run cost function of a company?

We can study the relationship of costs to the size of the facility using numerous approaches. All of these use one or more of the following techniques which are analogous to those used in short-run cost determinations:

1. Judgmental evaluation of how each cost factor will vary with size of facility.

2. Engineering analysis to estimate the variation of physical inputs with size of facility. The physical input estimates are then converted to dollar costs to obtain the cost-size relationship.

3. Statistical analysis, including multiple-correlation techniques, to isolate the cost-size relationship.

Using these techniques, many approaches are possible. When more than one approach can be followed independently in all or part of the analysis, it is valuable to do so and have checks to improve accuracy.

The judgmental technique places great emphasis on intuitive analysis of how and why costs varied as they did in the past to ascertain the effects of facility size on costs. Cost accounting, budget, and other records are used to assist in this judgmental process. Intuitive evaluations of how and why costs have changed as facilities have been expanded in the past as well as experience with costs in different sizes of facilities in the same or different companies will be important factors in this technique.

In the engineering technique, intuitive judgment is supplemented by knowledge of physical laws and relationships. This knowledge is used to assist in estimating how costs vary with different sizes of facilities.

When the statistical technique can be used, additional rigor and accuracy can be brought into the determination of the cost-size relationship. Different approaches are suitable under various conditions and availability of data.

The most difficult, and least used, approach is to make a detailed statistical analysis of the changes in costs which occurred as a facility was expanded over a period of time. First of all, many firms expand by increasing the number, rather than the size, of their facilities. Second, the required data covering the years of expansion is seldom available. Finally, the problems of making statistical corrections and allowances for changes in product, technology, accounting and management procedure, prices of materials, labor, services, etc., may be insurmountable even when the data are available.

For these reasons, the most practical statistical approach is to analyze differences in the costs of different-sized facilities which are operated at the same time. These facilities may be owned by one company or they may be owned by different companies. When the facilities are not owned by one company, the cost-size relationship may be more difficult to determine because of the greater likelihood that adjustments will have to be made for differences in accounting and management procedures, technology, prices of materials, labor, etc.

The most common approach in industry is to use a combination of the engineering and judgmental technique. The statistical-analysis technique cannot be used in many instances because the required data are not available. Because it is much more expensive than the engineering and judgmental techniques, it is not economic to use it for many problems.

Two illustrations of the determination of long-run cost functions are presented in appendixes to this chapter: one is a study of warehousing costs using primarily multiple-correlation techniques; the second is a study of butter-nonfat dry milk plant costs determined primarily from accounting data and engineering relationships.

An analysis of the long-run costs of the warehouses of a New England manufacturer made by Bowman and Stewart, presented in Appendix A, illustrates some of the technical problems involved in the use of a multiple-correlation approach to building a cost model of a distribution facility, as well as some of the potential benefits from such a study. The study showed that the company's actual branch warehouse areas ranged from about 95 to 150 per cent of the individually computed optimum areas. This disclosed that most of the branch warehouse areas were too large and that, therefore, there were not enough warehouses in outlying districts.

A study of butter-nonfat dry milk plant costs by Walker, Preston, and Nelson, presented in Appendix B, illustrates the derivation of long-run costs as the envelope of short-run cost curves and the added utility of knowing the short-run cost function when making scale-of-operation decisions. In this study, the models were built by piecing together costs established from accounting data and engineering relationships. Although all the detailed findings in this study were too numerous to be summarized in a few sentences, the principal conclusions were as follows:

1. Within a given plant the efficiency of the plant increases, but at a declining rate, as volume of milk processed increases up to and including the assumed practical capacity of the plant. (This capacity is less than absolute technical capacity but approximates the concept of capacity generally held in the industry.)

2. Unit costs decline as scale of operations increases. Under existing

technical processes, butter-powder manufacturing appears to be a decreasing-cost industry. The relative decline in unit costs progressively decreases from a high rate among small-scale plants to a lower rate among the larger plants.

3. The implications of these conclusions for the industry is that with declining average costs and low-marginal costs relative to average costs, there are real economic incentives for owners and managers of butter-powder plants to expand plant operations. Similarly, the long-run industry cost curves provide the basis for understanding the long-run trend in the dairy manufacturing industry toward concentration of manufacturing operations into fewer but larger plants.

APPENDIX A. A STUDY OF THE
LONG-RUN COSTS OF WAREHOUSING

The company studied by Bowman and Stewart[1] had acquired more than a dozen warehouses in the five states served from its manufacturing plant. Warehouses had been added in some areas and discontinued in others as changing conditions seemed to dictate. The problem was, How large a territory should be served by a warehouse to result in a minimum total cost for warehousing, trucking between plant and warehouses, and delivery from warehouse to customers?

The measure of effectiveness chosen, after examination of warehouse operations, was cost (within the warehouse district) per dollar's worth of goods distributed. It was this cost which should be minimized. Available data were obtained from the company's records. Examination of these data revealed that the cost of material handled in each warehouse district appeared to be primarily dependent upon two opposing factors: the volume of business passing through the warehouse and the area served by the warehouse. The greater the volume handled, the smaller would be the cost per dollar's worth of goods distributed. However, the greater the area served, the greater would be the cost per dollar's worth of goods distributed.

Many other variables in this situation could affect the measure of effectiveness. For instance, the price paid for gasoline in each warehouse area would affect the cost of operations in the area and undoubtedly varies throughout the New England states. The particular design of the warehouse, for example, whether the loading platform was at tailgate level of trucks or on the ground, might also affect these costs. However, since it was desirable to keep the analysis fairly simple, only the two factors considered most important were included.

Warehousing costs per dollar of goods handled tend to decrease with increasing volume: costs of supervision and other overhead are spread over more units, labor can usually be used with a lower proportion of idle time, etc. Since distance traveled would be the main factor determining costs associated with area, it followed that this cost would tend to vary approximately with the square root of the area. (Radius and diameter vary with the square root of the area of a circle.) As concentric rings of equal area are added, rings rapidly become narrower; that is, additional distance traveled becomes smaller.

[1] This presentation is adapted from E. H. Bowman and J. B. Stewart, "A Model for Scale of Operations," *Journal of Marketing*, national quarterly publication of the American Marketing Association, vol. 20, pp. 242–247, January, 1956.

Thus, the cost per dollar's worth of goods distributed was equal to certain costs (warehousing) which vary inversely with the volume plus certain (delivery) costs which vary directly with the square root of the area plus certain costs which were affected by neither of these variables. Putting this last factor first, these variables arranged as a mathematical expression are as follows:

$$C = a + \frac{b}{V} + c\sqrt{A}$$

where C = cost (within the warehouse district) per dollar's worth of goods distributed —the measure of effectiveness

V = volume of goods in dollars handled by the warehouse per unit of time

A = area in square miles served by the warehouse

a = cost per dollar's worth of goods distributed independent of either the warehouse's volume handled or the area served (variable cost)

b = costs for the warehouse per unit of time, which divided by the volume will yield the appropriate cost per dollar's worth distributed (fixed cost)

c = cost of the distribution which depends upon the square root of the area; that is, costs associated with miles covered within the warehouse district, such as gasoline, truck repairs, driver hours, etc. (fixed cost)

It was possible to determine for each warehouse the cost per dollar's worth of goods distributed (C), the volume of goods handled by the warehouse (V), and the area served by the warehouse (A). Then, by least-squares multiple regression, the values of the coefficients or parameters a, b, and c were determined. The correlation coefficient was found to be 0.89, indicating a fairly high degree of correlation.

Having determined this long-run cost, we now desired an expression which will make the cost a minimum. To do this, it was necessary to express cost as a function of only one unknown (area). A relationship was found between volume and area for each section of New England. This sales density (K), expressed in dollar volume per square mile of area, is

$$K = \frac{V}{A}$$

Therefore, $V = KA$, and it is possible to substitute this expression for V in the original model, giving

$$C = a + \frac{b}{KA} + c\sqrt{A}$$

where a, b, and c are now specific figures determined from the multiple-regression calculation. To find the minimum C, we differentiate.

$$\frac{dC}{dA} = -\frac{b}{KA^2} + \frac{c}{2\sqrt{A}} = 0$$

Solving for A,

$$A = \left(\frac{2b}{cK}\right)^{\frac{2}{3}}$$

This expression for the area A indicates that area which would yield a minimum cost and is a function of b and c (costs calculated from the data) and K (the sales density of the area in question).

The cost which is minimized is the explicit cost within the warehouse district. The implicit cost, interest on investment in inventory and equipment, was analyzed and demonstrated to be insignificant for the purposes of this study. The costs also did not include the cost of loading semitrailer trucks at the plant and transporting them to the branch warehouses, since—as long as goods are handled from a branch warehouse—these costs will be incurred and will not be affected by volume handled or area served by each branch warehouse.

APPENDIX B. A STUDY OF THE LONG- AND SHORT-RUN COSTS OF BUTTER-NONFAT DRY MILK PLANTS

The principal objective of this study by Walker, Preston, and Nelson[1] was to determine existing relationships in specialized butter-powder plants between scale of operations and efficiency of use of labor, equipment, and other resources. Other important objectives included (1) determination of physical and monetary costs of manufacturing butter and nonfat-dry milk solids, and (2) development of cost standards which may be used by plant managers in measuring efficiencies of their plants and in making decisions relative to altering plant operations.

Twelve butter-powder plants located in Washington, Oregon, and Idaho were studied intensively. Detailed information on the facilities and operations of these plants was obtained from their records, by observation, by physical measurement, and by interview. Both physical and monetary data were obtained for the two years of 1948 and 1949. No data were obtained on the procurement or distribution (and selling) operations of these plants. The study is limited to an analysis of processing costs from the moment milk is received at the plant up to and including the operation of loading out the finished butter and powder.

Processing costs were obtained for each of 17 functions in 4 broad categories:
1. Overhead
   a. Office
   b. Boiler
   c. Shop
   d. Refrigeration
   e. Water and sewage
   f. Miscellaneous
2. Joint
   a. Milk receiving
   b. Laboratory
   c. Separating
3. Butter manufacturing
   a. Cream processing
   b. Butter making
   c. Packing and storing
   d. Loading
4. Powder manufacturing
   a. Skim-milk processing
      (1) Storing and evaporation in spray-process plants
      (2) Storing and preheating in roller-process plants
   b. Drying
   c. Packing and storing
   d. Loading

These 17 functions comprise the basic production processes necessary to the production of butter and nonfat dry milk. These basic data were divided into three cost elements, namely, capital, labor, and supplies. This minute breakdown of the manufacturing processes was necessary inasmuch as the observed plants as complete units were heterogeneous. This unlikeness was due to the diversion of whole milk, cream, and nonfat milk to other plants. However, each of the 17 functions and their cost elements contributed to the production process in the same way, except for the difference between the two types of production—spray- and roller-processed powder. The plants differed greatly with respect to seasonality of milk receipts, volume output in relation to the capacity of the plant facilities, and individual institution factors. However, the plants were relatively homogeneous with respect to each of the 17 functions.

---

[1] This presentation is adapted from S. H. Walker, H. J. Preston, and G. T. Nelson, *An Economic Analysis of Butter-nonfat Dry Milk Plants*, University of Idaho Agricultural Experiment Station, Research Bulletin 20, June, 1953.

This functional analysis permitted interplant comparisons and the development of costs in relation to the volumes processed in each function.

Three average-cost figures were computed for each plant and each function. These are designated as observed, adjusted, and standard costs. The observed costs were based on data obtained for the most part from plant records. The adjusted expenses are the observed costs altered by use of common rates of payment for resources, e.g., the wage rate used in the model plants for all plants for a given type of labor. Therefore, the adjusted expenses eliminate cost differences among plants resulting from differences in rates of payment for resources but they continue to reflect differences among the plants in physical rates of resource use. The standard costs that are discussed later in this report were developed from the model plants. In essence, these costs are the costs which probably would exist with the least-cost combinations of capital, labor, and other resources of the model plants at uniform rates of payment for resource inputs and adjusted to the operating conditions, especially for the diversions of milk from the butter and powder operations, of the observed plants.

Actual plants commonly differ in so many minor respects as to obscure their more fundamental differences in structure and operation. Models, in contrast, can be constructed to show clearly and vividly the total structure and operation of their prototypes under standardized plant operating conditions which probably cannot be duplicated in the real world.

Twelve models of specialized butter-powder plants were constructed. Five of them are models of roller-process plants and seven are spray-process models.[1] The number of models equals the number of observed plants, both in total and by type of drying process, because most of the data essential to construction of the models could be obtained only from analysis of the observed plants. However, additional information was obtained from equipment manufacturers, engineers, architects, and other sources of technical information. Common practices and conventions of the industry were also considered in developing the models.

Although these models were developed in the main from the data and functional relationships obtained through analysis of the observed plants, none of the 12 models is an exact copy of its prototype. The models resemble the observed plants but do not possess the latter's peculiarities, details, and special problems. The models possess, however, all essential elements of plant structure, operation, and production relationships.

The model plants were synthesized from the functional relationships of the observed plants. Each function was constructed so as to be in balance with all other functions in each model plant. Also, many of the features of the model plants are common to all model plants. Difficulties of analysis were thus reduced considerably and the fundamental nature of the relationships existing between volumes of milk processed and efficiency in use of productive resources could be seen more clearly. Realism was achieved by basing the models on typical or efficient conditions found among the observed plants and in the dairy industry generally.

The principal general assumptions underlying the development of the models are listed below:

1. Techniques of processing are essentially the same in all plants, except for the assumed differences between groups of plants in methods of drying skim milk.

2. All plants produce a single, high quality of butter and the qualities of powder produced are high and fully comparable between and within the groups of plants.

3. All prices paid for productive resources of a given kind and quality are equal for all plants: e.g., wage rates are the same in all plants for a given kind of labor.

4. All labor is hired for full shifts of 8 hr per day except office, laboratory, and supervisory employees. The office and laboratory personnel are employed 44 hours per week.

5. Milk received by all plants averages 4 per cent butterfat.

6. Yields of butter and powder are equal for all plants at 4.92 and 8.28 per cent of the pounds of milk received.

7. All plants operate at their rated full capacity (as defined in this study) in June and at uniformly varying percentages of this volume in other months. That is, seasonal

---

[1] The five roller-process model plants are numbered 1 through 5 and the seven spray-process model plants are numbered I through VII.

patterns of milk receipts are the same for all plants in a relative sense even though absolute volumes differ.

8. Average daily milk receipts per farmer are the same for all plants at any given time and the average annual weight of milk received per can is 60 lb.

9. The type of ownership of the plants, while not specified, is assumed to be the same for all plants.

10. The quality of resources used (labor, buildings, etc.) is assumed to be the same for all plants with the exception that frequently within the dairy industry the larger plants' buildings are of a slightly higher quality.

Average total costs per 1,000 lb of milk processed were computed for each of the 12 model plants for all 12 monthly average daily milk volumes assumed for each plant. This process was repeated for all months and all plants. The costs vary within each plant as its volume changes, producing the short-run cost curves of Figure 35-2. The

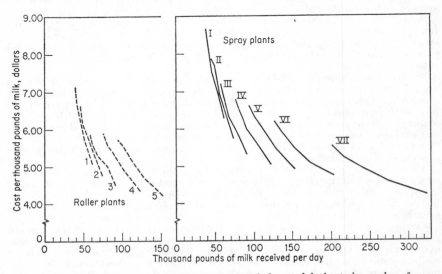

Figure 35-2. Short-run average-unit-cost curves of the model plants by scales of operation. SOURCE: S. H. Walker, H. J. Preston, and G. T. Nelson, *An Economic Analysis of Butter-nonfat Dry Milk*, University of Idaho Agricultural Experiment Station, Research Bulletin 20, June, 1953.

short-run cost curves indicate that plants of different scales will operate at the same volume of output. Thus, the larger plant during the low seasonal flow of milk and the smaller at its peak process the same quantity of milk. Three different plants of each type can each process 60,000 lb of milk per day, but in each of these plants—six in all—there are different average unit costs at this volume. This indicates that the production function of the individual plants differ and a different combination of the factors of production is required for each of the plants when it is processing this volume.

However, each of the plants is operating at a different level of capacity because of the seasonal variation of milk production at the farm level. This seasonality of production causes plants to have plant facilities greater than their average annual volume in order to market the farmer's production. For example, the average annual production for Plants 2 and II is 57,208 lb. Plants 1 and I have the plant capacity to process 60,900 lb per day, but due to the seasonality of production, they process only an average of 47,596 lb per day. The same condition applies to other plant sizes. The average annual costs of Plants 2 and II are $5.56 and $6.84 per 1,000 lb of milk. These same volumes, with no seasonal variation, could have been processed in Plants 1 and I at a cost of $5.45 and $6.62 per unit. This means that the seasonality of production costs 11 cents and 22 cents per unit under the conditions depicted in these model plants. This cost is approximately $2,300 and $4,600 annually.

The long-run cost curves of Figure 35-3 show the relationships between average

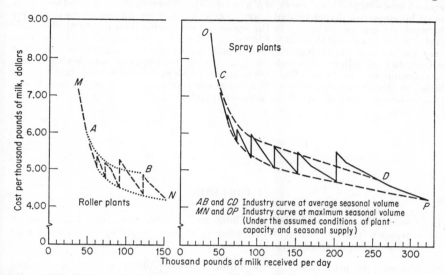

Figure 35-3. Long-run industry cost curves for butter-nonfat dry milk manufacturing plants. SOURCE: S. H. Walker, H. J. Preston, and G. T. Nelson, *An Economic Analysis of Butter-nonfat Dry Milk,* University of Idaho Agricultural Experiment Station, Research Bulletin 20, June, 1953.

costs and scale of operations. The shape of the industry curve will be affected by the interpretation of the number of plants that can be constructed. For this study seven spray and five roller-plants were selected. If it is assumed that only these plants can be constructed, the planning curve will be the irregular line *OP* for the spray process and the line *MN* for the roller process. This is not a rigid condition because other combinations of equipment and labor are possible. In this study, the volume is selected by the size of observed churns and by assuming an 8-hour shift in the butter-making function. Further, it is assumed that when two or more churns are employed, they will be of the same size. These assumptions are consistent with observed conditions but they are not necessary. On the other hand, it is possible to assume that by varying equipment and working periods slightly, more plants of each type can be constructed. With this assumption the smooth line *OP* represents the industry curve for spray process and the smooth line *MN* for roller process. Since only decreasing costs are depicted, the least-cost point for each plant curve becames the most important point on the plant curve for constructing the industry curve. The least-cost points on the plant curves are developed from the assumptions used in this study. Since changing any of the assumptions would change the least-cost point on the curve, the validity of the least-cost point is applicable only to the extent that the assumptions are applicable. Changes in the operating levels of the plants and changes in the price of labor and capital will affect the least-cost points.

A further ramification of the least-cost concept is the effect of operating at less than capacity during most of the year because of the seasonal pattern of milk receipts. Each plant operates at many levels along the plant curve during each year. For the year, this results in an average unit cost higher than the annual average daily volume would indicate if compared directly to the plant curve. A line connecting these points of average annual unit costs for a series of plant curves indicates the average annual long-run industry curve. This is the line CD for spray and AB for roller process.

This method of long-run plant selection and planning poses the question of whether the average annual cost curves AB and CD have important differences from the smooth long-run planning curves MN and OP. The difference between the two curves must be measured perpendicularly, and, when this is done, an important difference between the curves is evident in the spray-process plants. The plants at the small scales of operation and those at the large scales have less vertical differences between these curves than have the medium-scale plants. (Inasmuch as larger plants were not constructed for roller-type plants, it is impossible to determine whether this same relationship would exist in roller-process plants.) This may be by chance, but if not, it indicates that seasonality affects the average costs more adversely in the middle-size plants than in either the small- or large-size plants.

PROBLEMS

1. Discuss the relationship between long-run cost functions and management decisions relating to (*a*) facility expansion, (*b*) plant location, (*c*) expense budgeting in multiplant operations.

2. "For outputs below the long-run minimum-cost point, it is more economical to underutilize a slightly larger facility than to operate a smaller facility at its minimum cost." Explain the reason for the phenomenon expressed by this quotation from the text.

3. Refer to the warehouse cost problem presented in the text. (*a*) Would it not have been simpler and equally useful if, instead of making the formal correlation analysis illustrated, the accounting department had prepared a tabulation showing for each of the company's warehouses the cost per dollar's worth of goods distributed, the volume of goods handled by the warehouse, and the area served by each warehouse during the past year or two? Could we not then more easily determine the optimum-sized area and volume for a warehouse? Explain. (*b*) Would cost per pound of goods distributed have been a better or a poorer criterion measure than cost per dollar of goods distributed? Explain.

4. Refer to the butter-nonfat dry milk plant study in Appendix B. (*a*) Suggest possible reasons for seasonality having a greater effect on the average costs of the middle-size plants than on the small or large-size ones. (*b*) Would you have expected this industry to have declining costs as the scale of operations increased? Do you think that the long-run cost curve will decline indefinitely as you increase the size of the operation? Explain. (*c*) How could the results of this study be useful to management in making decisions relative to altering plant operations?

Appendix

Table 1. $\frac{1}{2}\%$ Interest Factors

Period n	Single-payment compound-amount (SPCA) Future value of $1 $(1 + i)^n$	Single-payment present-worth (SPPW) Present value of $1 $\dfrac{1}{(1 + i)^n}$	Uniform-series compound-amount (USCA) Future value of uniform series of $1 $\dfrac{(1 + i)^n - 1}{i}$	Sinking-fund payment (SFP) Uniform series whose future value is $1 $\dfrac{i}{(1 + i)^n - 1}$	Capital recovery (CR) Uniform series with present value of $1 $\dfrac{i(1 + i)^n}{(1 + i)^n - 1}$	Uniform-series present-worth (USPW) Present value of uniform series of $1 $\dfrac{(1 + i)^n - 1}{i(1 + i)^n}$
1	1.005	0.9950	1.000	1.00000	1.00500	0.995
2	1.010	0.9901	2.005	0.49875	0.50375	1.985
3	1.015	0.9851	3.015	0.33167	0.33667	2.970
4	1.020	0.9802	4.030	0.24813	0.25313	3.950
5	1.025	0.9754	5.050	0.19801	0.20301	4.926
6	1.030	0.9705	6.076	0.16460	0.16960	5.896
7	1.036	0.9657	7.106	0.14073	0.14573	6.862
8	1.041	0.9609	8.141	0.12283	0.12783	7.823
9	1.046	0.9561	9.182	0.10891	0.11391	8.779
10	1.051	0.9513	10.228	0.09777	0.10277	9.730
11	1.056	0.9466	11.279	0.08866	0.09366	10.677
12	1.062	0.9419	12.336	0.08107	0.08607	11.619
13	1.067	0.9372	13.397	0.07464	0.07964	12.556
14	1.072	0.9326	14.464	0.06914	0.07414	13.489
15	1.078	0.9279	15.537	0.06436	0.06936	14.417
16	1.083	0.9233	16.614	0.06019	0.06519	15.340
17	1.088	0.9187	17.697	0.05651	0.06151	16.259
18	1.094	0.9141	18.786	0.05323	0.05823	17.173
19	1.099	0.9096	19.880	0.05030	0.05530	18.082
20	1.105	0.9051	20.979	0.04767	0.05267	18.987
21	1.110	0.9006	22.084	0.04528	0.05028	19.888
22	1.116	0.8961	23.194	0.04311	0.04811	20.784
23	1.122	0.8916	24.310	0.04113	0.04613	21.676
24	1.127	0.8872	25.432	0.03932	0.04432	22.563
25	1.133	0.8828	26.559	0.03765	0.04265	23.446
26	1.138	0.8784	27.692	0.03611	0.04111	24.324
27	1.144	0.8740	28.830	0.03469	0.03969	25.198
28	1.150	0.8697	29.975	0.03336	0.03836	26.068
29	1.156	0.8653	31.124	0.03213	0.03713	26.933
30	1.161	0.8610	32.280	0.03098	0.03598	27.794
35	1.191	0.8398	38.145	0.02622	0.03122	32.035
40	1.221	0.8191	44.159	0.02265	0.02765	36.172
45	1.252	0.7990	50.324	0.01987	0.02487	40.207
50	1.283	0.7793	56.645	0.01765	0.02265	44.143
55	1.316	0.7601	63.126	0.01584	0.02084	47.981
60	1.349	0.7414	69.770	0.01433	0.01933	51.726
65	1.383	0.7231	76.582	0.01306	0.01806	55.377
70	1.418	0.7053	83.566	0.01197	0.01697	58.939
75	1.454	0.6879	90.727	0.01102	0.01602	62.414
80	1.490	0.6710	98.068	0.01020	0.01520	65.802
85	1.528	0.6545	105.594	0.00947	0.01447	69.108
90	1.567	0.6383	113.311	0.00883	0.01383	72.331
95	1.606	0.6226	121.222	0.00825	0.01325	75.476
100	1.647	0.6073	129.334	0.00773	0.01273	78.543

Table 2. 1% Interest Factors

Period n	Single-payment compound-amount (SPCA)	Single-payment present-worth (SPPW)	Uniform-series compound-amount (USCA)	Sinking-fund payment (SFP)	Capital recovery (CR)	Uniform-series present-worth (USPW)
Given → Find	P → S	S → P	R → S	S → R	P → R	R → P
	Future value of $1 $(1+i)^n$	Present value of $1 $\dfrac{1}{(1+i)^n}$	Future value of uniform series of $1 $\dfrac{(1+i)^n-1}{i}$	Uniform series whose future value is $1 $\dfrac{i}{(1+i)^n-1}$	Uniform series with present value of $1 $\dfrac{i(1+i)^n}{(1+i)^n-1}$	Present value of uniform series of $1 $\dfrac{(1+i)^n-1}{i(1+i)^n}$
1	1.010	0.9901	1.000	1.00000	1.01000	0.990
2	1.020	0.9803	2.010	0.49751	0.50751	1.970
3	1.030	0.9706	3.030	0.33002	0.34002	2.941
4	1.041	0.9610	4.060	0.24628	0.25628	3.902
5	1.051	0.9515	5.101	0.19604	0.20604	4.853
6	1.062	0.9420	6.152	0.16255	0.17255	5.795
7	1.072	0.9327	7.214	0.13863	0.14863	6.728
8	1.088	0.9235	8.286	0.12069	0.13069	7.652
9	1.094	0.9143	9.369	0.10674	0.11674	8.566
10	1.105	0.9053	10.462	0.09558	0.10558	9.471
11	1.116	0.8963	11.567	0.08645	0.09645	10.368
12	1.127	0.8874	12.683	0.07885	0.08885	11.255
13	1.138	0.8787	13.809	0.07241	0.08241	12.134
14	1.149	0.8700	14.947	0.06690	0.07690	13.004
15	1.161	0.8613	16.097	0.06212	0.07212	13.865
16	1.173	0.8528	17.258	0.05794	0.06794	14.718
17	1.184	0.8444	18.430	0.05426	0.06426	15.562
18	1.196	0.8360	19.615	0.05098	0.06098	16.398
19	1.208	0.8277	20.811	0.04805	0.05805	17.226
20	1.220	0.8195	22.019	0.04542	0.05542	18.046
21	1.232	0.8114	23.239	0.04303	0.05303	18.857
22	1.245	0.8034	24.472	0.04086	0.05086	19.660
23	1.257	0.7954	25.716	0.03889	0.04889	20.456
24	1.270	0.7876	26.973	0.03707	0.04707	21.243
25	1.282	0.7798	28.243	0.03541	0.04541	22.023
26	1.295	0.7720	29.526	0.03387	0.04387	22.795
27	1.308	0.7644	30.821	0.03245	0.04245	23.560
28	1.321	0.7568	32.129	0.03112	0.04112	24.316
29	1.335	0.7493	33.450	0.02990	0.03990	25.066
30	1.348	0.7419	34.785	0.02875	0.03875	25.808
35	1.417	0.7059	41.660	0.02400	−0.03400	29.409
40	1.489	0.6717	48.886	0.02046	0.03046	32.835
45	1.565	0.6391	56.481	0.01771	0.02771	36.095
50	1.645	0.6080	64.463	0.01551	0.02551	39.196
55	1.729	0.5785	72.852	0.01373	0.02373	42.147
60	1.817	0.5504	81.670	0.01224	0.02224	44.955
65	1.909	0.5237	90.937	0.01100	0.02100	47.627
70	2.007	0.4983	100.676	0.00993	0.01993	50.169
75	2.109	0.4741	110.913	0.00902	0.01902	52.587
80	2.217	0.4511	121.672	0.00822	0.01822	54.888
85	2.330	0.4292	132.979	0.00752	0.01752	57.078
90	2.449	0.4084	144.863	0.00690	0.01690	59.161
95	2.574	0.3886	157.354	0.00636	0.01636	61.143
100	2.705	0.3697	170.481	0.00587	0.01587	63.029

Table 3. 2% Interest Factors

Period n	Single-payment compound-amount (SPCA) Future value of $1 $(1 + i)^n$	Single-payment present-worth (SPPW) Present value of $1 $\dfrac{1}{(1+i)^n}$	Uniform-series compound-amount (USCA) Future value of uniform series of $1 $\dfrac{(1+i)^n - 1}{i}$	Sinking-fund payment (SFP) Uniform series whose future value is $1 $\dfrac{i}{(1+i)^n - 1}$	Capital recovery (CR) Uniform series with present value of $1 $\dfrac{i(1+i)^n}{(1+i)^n - 1}$	Uniform-series present-worth (USPW) Present value of uniform series of $1 $\dfrac{(1+i)^n - 1}{i(1+i)^n}$
1	1.020	0.9804	1.000	1.00000	1.02000	0.980
2	1.040	0.9612	2.020	0.49505	0.51505	1.942
3	1.061	0.9423	3.060	0.32675	0.34675	2.884
4	1.082	0.9238	4.122	0.24262	0.26262	3.808
5	1.104	0.9057	5.204	0.19216	0.21216	4.713
6	1.126	0.8880	6.308	0.15853	0.17853	5.601
7	1.149	0.8706	7.434	0.13451	0.15451	6.472
8	1.172	0.8535	8.583	0.11651	0.13651	7.325
9	1.195	0.8368	9.755	0.10252	0.12252	8.162
10	1.219	0.8203	10.950	0.09133	0.11133	8.983
11	1.243	0.8043	12.169	0.08218	0.10218	9.787
12	1.268	0.7885	13.412	0.07456	0.09456	10.575
13	1.294	0.7730	14.680	0.06812	0.08812	11.348
14	1.319	0.7579	15.974	0.06260	0.08260	12.106
15	1.346	0.7430	17.293	0.05783	0.07783	12.849
16	1.373	0.7284	18.639	0.05365	0.07365	13.578
17	1.400	0.7142	20.012	0.04997	0.06997	14.292
18	1.428	0.7002	21.412	0.04670	0.06670	14.992
19	1.457	0.6864	22.841	0.04378	0.06378	15.678
20	1.486	0.6730	24.297	0.04116	0.06116	16.351
21	1.516	0.6598	25.783	0.03878	0.05878	17.011
22	1.546	0.6468	27.299	0.03663	0.05663	17.658
23	1.577	0.6342	28.845	0.03467	0.05467	18.292
24	1.608	0.6217	30.422	0.03287	0.05287	18.914
25	1.641	0.6095	32.030	0.03122	0.05122	19.523
26	1.673	0.5976	33.671	0.02970	0.04970	20.121
27	1.707	0.5859	35.344	0.02829	0.04829	20.707
28	1.741	0.5744	37.051	0.02699	0.04699	21.281
29	1.776	0.5631	38.792	0.02578	0.04578	21.844
30	1.811	0.5521	40.568	0.02465	0.04465	22.396
35	2.000	0.5000	49.994	0.02000	0.04000	24.999
40	2.208	0.4529	60.402	0.01656	0.03656	27.355
45	2.438	0.4102	71.893	0.01391	0.03391	29.490
50	2.692	0.3715	84.579	0.01182	0.03182	31.424
55	2.972	0.3365	98.587	0.01014	0.03014	33.175
60	3.281	0.3048	114.052	0.00877	0.02877	34.761
65	3.623	0.2761	131.126	0.00763	0.02763	36.197
70	4.000	0.2500	149.978	0.00667	0.02667	37.499
75	4.416	0.2265	170.792	0.00586	0.02586	38.677
80	4.875	0.2051	193.772	0.00516	0.02516	39.745
85	5.383	0.1858	219.144	0.00456	0.02456	40.711
90	5.943	0.1683	247.157	0.00405	0.02405	41.587
95	6.562	0.1524	278.085	0.00360	0.02360	42.380
100	7.245	0.1380	312.232	0.00320	0.02320	43.098

Table 4.   3% Interest Factors

Period Given Find	Single-payment compound-amount (SPCA) $\dfrac{P}{S}$ Future value of $1 $(1 + i)^n$	Single-payment present-worth (SPPW) $\dfrac{S}{P}$ Present value of $1 $\dfrac{1}{(1+i)^n}$	Uniform-series compound-amount (USCA) $\dfrac{R}{S}$ Future value of uniform series of $1 $\dfrac{(1+i)^n - 1}{i}$	Sinking-fund payment (SFP) $\dfrac{S}{R}$ Uniform series whose future value is $1 $\dfrac{i}{(1+i)^n - 1}$	Capital recovery (CR) $\dfrac{P}{R}$ Uniform series with present value of $1 $\dfrac{i(1+i)^n}{(1+i)^n - 1}$	Uniform-series present-worth (USPW) $\dfrac{R}{P}$ Present value of uniform series of $1 $\dfrac{(1+i)^n - 1}{i(1+i)^n}$
1	1.030	0.9709	1.000	1.00000	1.03000	0.971
2	1.061	0.9426	2.030	0.49261	0.52261	1.913
3	1.093	0.9151	3.091	0.32353	0.35353	2.829
4	1.126	0.8885	4.184	0.23903	0.26903	3.717
5	1.159	0.8626	5.309	0.18835	0.21835	4.580
6	1.194	0.8375	6.468	0.15460	0.18460	5.417
7	1.230	0.8131	7.662	0.13051	0.16051	6.230
8	1.267	0.7894	8.892	0.11246	0.14246	7.020
9	1.305	0.7664	10.159	0.09843	0.12843	7.786
10	1.344	0.7441	11.464	0.08723	0.11723	8.530
11	1.384	0.7224	12.808	0.07808	0.10808	9.253
12	1.426	0.7014	14.192	0.07046	0.10046	9.954
13	1.469	0.6810	15.618	0.06403	0.09403	10.635
14	1.513	0.6611	17.086	0.05853	0.08853	11.296
15	1.558	0.6419	18.599	0.05377	0.08377	11.938
16	1.605	0.6232	20.157	0.04961	0.07961	12.561
17	1.653	0.6050	21.762	0.04595	0.07595	13.166
18	1.702	0.5874	23.414	0.04271	0.07271	13.754
19	1.754	0.5703	25.117	0.03981	0.06981	14.324
20	1.806	0.5537	26.870	0.03722	0.06722	14.877
21	1.860	0.5375	28.676	0.03487	0.06487	15.415
22	1.916	0.5219	30.537	0.03275	0.06275	15.937
23	1.974	0.5067	32.453	0.03081	0.06081	16.444
24	2.033	0.4919	34.426	0.02905	0.05905	16.936
25	2.094	0.4776	36.459	0.02743	0.05743	17.413
26	2.157	0.4637	38.553	0.02594	0.05594	17.877
27	2.221	0.4502	40.710	0.02456	0.05456	18.327
28	2.288	0.4371	42.931	0.02329	0.05329	18.764
29	2.357	0.4243	45.219	0.02211	0.05211	19.188
30	2.427	0.4120	47.575	0.02102	0.05102	19.600
35	2.814	0.3554	60.462	0.01654	0.04654	21.487
40	3.262	0.3066	75.401	0.01326	0.04326	23.115
45	3.782	0.2644	92.720	0.01079	0.04079	24.519
50	4.384	0.2281	112.797	0.00887	0.03887	25.730
55	5.082	0.1968	136.072	0.00735	0.03735	26.774
60	5.892	0.1697	163.053	0.00613	0.03613	27.676
65	6.830	0.1464	194.333	0.00515	0.03515	28.453
70	7.918	0.1263	230.594	0.00434	0.03434	29.123
75	9.179	0.1089	272.631	0.00367	0.03367	29.702
80	10.641	0.0940	321.363	0.00311	0.03311	30.201
85	12.336	0.0811	377.857	0.00265	0.03265	30.631
90	14.300	0.0699	443.349	0.00226	0.03226	31.002
95	16.578	0.0603	519.272	0.00193	0.03193	31.323
100	19.219	0.0520	607.288	0.00165	0.03165	31.599

Table 5.   4% Interest Factors

(Handwritten annotations at left: "Given" with "P, S, R, S, P, R" over columns; "Period" / "Find" with "S, P, S, R, R, P")

Period	Single-payment compound-amount (SPCA) — Future value of $1 $(1+i)^n$	Single-payment present-worth (SPPW) — Present value of $1 $\frac{1}{(1+i)^n}$	Uniform-series compound-amount (USCA) — Future value of uniform series of $1 $\frac{(1+i)^n-1}{i}$	Sinking-fund payment (SFP) — Uniform series whose future value is $1 $\frac{i}{(1+i)^n-1}$	Capital recovery (CR) — Uniform series with present value of $1 $\frac{i(1+i)^n}{(1+i)^n-1}$	Uniform-series present-worth (USPW) — Present value of uniform series of $1 $\frac{(1+i)^n-1}{i(1+i)^n}$
1	1.040	0.9615	1.000	1.00000	1.04000	0.962
2	1.082	0.9246	2.040	0.49020	0.53020	1.886
3	1.125	0.8890	3.122	0.32035	0.36035	2.775
4	1.170	0.8548	4.246	0.23549	0.27549	3.630
5	1.217	0.8219	5.416	0.18463	0.22463	4.452
6	1.265	0.7903	6.633	0.15076	0.19076	5.242
7	1.316	0.7599	7.898	0.12661	0.16661	6.002
8	1.369	0.7307	9.214	0.10853	0.14853	6.733
9	1.423	0.7026	10.583	0.09449	0.13449	7.435
10	1.480	0.6756	12.006	0.08329	0.12329	8.111
11	1.539	0.6496	13.486	0.07415	0.11415	8.760
12	1.601	0.6246	15.026	0.06655	0.10655	9.385
13	1.665	0.6006	16.627	0.06014	0.10014	9.986
14	1.732	0.5775	18.292	0.05467	0.09467	10.563
15	1.801	0.5553	20.024	0.04994	0.08994	11.118
16	1.873	0.5339	21.825	0.04582	0.08582	11.652
17	1.948	0.5134	23.698	0.04220	0.08220	12.166
18	2.026	0.4936	25.645	0.03899	0.07899	12.659
19	2.107	0.4746	27.671	0.03614	0.07614	13.134
20	2.191	0.4564	29.778	0.03358	0.07358	13.590
21	2.279	0.4388	31.969	0.03128	0.07128	14.029
22	2.370	0.4220	34.248	0.02920	0.06920	14.451
23	2.465	0.4057	36.618	0.02731	0.06731	14.857
24	2.563	0.3901	39.083	0.02559	0.06559	15.247
25	2.666	0.3751	41.646	0.02401	0.06401	15.622
26	2.772	0.3607	44.312	0.02257	0.06257	15.983
27	2.883	0.3468	47.084	0.02124	0.06124	16.330
28	2.999	0.3335	49.968	0.02001	0.06001	16.663
29	3.119	0.3207	52.966	0.01888	0.05888	16.984
30	3.243	0.3083	56.085	0.01783	0.05783	17.292
35	3.946	0.2534	73.652	0.01358	0.05358	18.665
40	4.801	0.2083	95.026	0.01052	0.05052	19.793
45	5.841	0.1712	121.029	0.00826	0.04826	20.720
50	7.107	0.1407	152.667	0.00655	0.04655	21.482
55	8.646	0.1157	191.159	0.00523	0.04523	22.109
60	10.520	0.0951	237.991	0.00420	0.04420	22.623
65	12.799	0.0781	294.968	0.00339	0.04339	23.047
70	15.572	0.0642	364.290	0.00275	0.04275	23.395
75	18.945	0.0528	448.631	0.00223	0.04223	23.680
80	23.050	0.0434	551.245	0.00181	0.04181	23.915
85	28.044	0.0357	676.090	0.00148	0.04148	24.109
90	34.119	0.0293	827.983	0.00121	0.04121	24.267
95	41.511	0.0241	1012.785	0.00099	0.04099	24.398
100	50.505	0.0198	1237.624	0.00081	0.04081	24.505

Table 6. 5% Interest Factors

Given Period Find	Single-payment compound-amount (SPCA) $\dfrac{P}{S}$ Future value of $1 $(1+i)^n$	Single-payment present-worth (SPPW) $\dfrac{S}{P}$ Present value of $1 $\dfrac{1}{(1+i)^n}$	Uniform-series compound-amount (USCA) $\dfrac{R}{S}$ Future value of uniform series of $1 $\dfrac{(1+i)^n-1}{i}$	Sinking-fund payment (SFP) $\dfrac{S}{R}$ Uniform series whose future value is $1 $\dfrac{i}{(1+i)^n-1}$	Capital recovery (CR) $\dfrac{P}{R}$ Uniform series with present value of $1 $\dfrac{i(1+i)^n}{(1+i)^n-1}$	Uniform-series present-worth (USPW) $\dfrac{R}{P}$ Present value of uniform series of $1 $\dfrac{(1+i)^n-1}{i(1+i)^n}$
1	1.050	0.9524	1.000	1.00000	1.05000	0.952
2	1.103	0.9070	2.050	0.48780	0.53780	1.859
3	1.158	0.8638	3.153	0.31721	0.36721	2.723
4	1.216	0.8227	4.310	0.23201	0.28201	3.546
5	1.276	0.7835	5.526	0.18097	0.23097	4.329
6	1.340	0.7462	6.802	0.14702	0.19702	5.076
7	1.407	0.7107	8.142	0.12282	0.17282	5.786
8	1.477	0.6768	9.549	0.10472	0.15472	6.463
9	1.551	0.6446	11.027	0.09069	0.14069	7.108
10	1.629	0.6139	12.578	0.07950	0.12950	7.722
11	1.710	0.5847	14.207	0.07039	0.12039	8.306
12	1.796	0.5568	15.917	0.06283	0.11283	8.863
13	1.886	0.5303	17.713	0.05646	0.10646	9.394
14	1.980	0.5051	19.599	0.05102	0.10102	9.899
15	2.079	0.4810	21.579	0.04634	0.09634	10.380
16	2.183	0.4581	23.657	0.04227	0.09227	10.838
17	2.292	0.4363	25.840	0.03870	0.08870	11.274
18	2.407	0.4155	28.132	0.03555	0.08555	11.690
19	2.527	0.3957	30.539	0.03275	0.08275	12.085
20	2.653	0.3769	33.066	0.03024	0.08024	12.462
21	2.786	0.3589	35.719	0.02800	0.07800	12.821
22	2.925	0.3418	38.505	0.02597	0.07597	13.163
23	3.072	0.3256	41.430	0.02414	0.07414	13.489
24	3.225	0.3101	44.502	0.02247	0.07247	13.799
25	3.386	0.2953	47.727	0.02095	0.07095	14.094
26	3.556	0.2812	51.113	0.01956	0.06956	14.375
27	3.733	0.2678	54.669	0.01829	0.06829	14.643
28	3.920	0.2551	58.403	0.01712	0.06712	14.898
29	4.116	0.2429	62.323	0.01605	0.06605	15.141
30	4.322	0.2314	66.439	0.01505	0.06505	15.372
35	5.516	0.1813	90.320	0.01107	0.06107	16.374
40	7.040	0.1420	120.800	0.00828	0.05828	17.159
45	8.985	0.1113	159.700	0.00626	0.05626	17.774
50	11.467	0.0872	209.348	0.00478	0.05478	18.256
55	14.636	0.0683	272.713	0.00367	0.05367	18.633
60	18.679	0.0535	353.584	0.00283	0.05283	18.929
65	23.840	0.0419	456.798	0.00219	0.05219	19.161
70	30.426	0.0329	588.529	0.00170	0.05170	19.343
75	38.833	0.0258	756.654	0.00132	0.05132	19.485
80	49.561	0.0202	971.229	0.00103	0.05103	19.596
85	63.254	0.0158	1245.087	0.00080	0.05080	19.684
90	80.730	0.0124	1594.607	0.00063	0.05063	19.752
95	103.035	0.0097	2040.694	0.00049	0.05049	19.806
100	131.501	0.0076	2610.025	0.00038	0.05038	19.848

Table 7. 6% Interest Factors

Given *n* Find	Single-payment compound-amount (SPCA) Future value of $1 $(1 + i)^n$	Single-payment present-worth (SPPW) Present value of $1 $\dfrac{1}{(1 + i)^n}$	Uniform-series compound-amount (USCA) Future value of uniform series of $1 $\dfrac{(1 + i)^n - 1}{i}$	Sinking-fund payment (SFP) Uniform series whose future value is $1 $\dfrac{i}{(1 + i)^n - 1}$	Capital recovery (CR) Uniform series with present value of $1 $\dfrac{i(1 + i)^n}{(1 + i)^n - 1}$	Uniform-series present-worth (USPW) Present value of uniform series of $1 $\dfrac{(1 + i)^n - 1}{i(1 + i)^n}$
1	1.060	0.9434	1.000	1.00000	1.06000	0.943
2	1.124	0.8900	2.060	0.48544	0.54544	1.833
3	1.191	0.8396	3.184	0.31411	0.37411	2.673
4	1.262	0.7921	4.375	0.22859	0.28859	3.465
5	1.338	0.7473	5.637	0.17740	0.23740	4.212
6	1.419	0.7050	6.975	0.14336	0.20336	4.917
7	1.504	0.6651	8.394	0.11914	0.17914	5.582
8	1.594	0.6274	9.897	0.10104	0.16104	6.210
9	1.689	0.5919	11.491	0.08702	0.14702	6.802
10	1.791	0.5584	13.181	0.07587	0.13587	7.360
11	1.898	0.5268	14.972	0.06679	0.12679	7.887
12	2.012	0.4970	16.870	0.05928	0.11928	8.384
13	2.133	0.4688	18.882	0.05296	0.11296	8.853
14	2.261	0.4423	21.015	0.04758	0.10758	9.295
15	2.397	0.4173	23.276	0.04296	0.10296	9.712
16	2.540	0.3936	25.673	0.03895	0.09895	10.106
17	2.693	0.3714	28.213	0.03544	0.09544	10.477
18	2.854	0.3503	30.906	0.03236	0.09236	10.828
19	3.026	0.3305	33.760	0.02962	0.08962	11.158
20	3.207	0.3118	36.786	0.02718	0.08718	11.470
21	3.400	0.2942	39.993	0.02500	0.08500	11.764
22	3.604	0.2775	43.392	0.02305	0.08305	12.042
23	3.820	0.2618	46.996	0.02128	0.08128	12.303
24	4.049	0.2470	50.816	0.01968	0.07968	12.550
25	4.292	0.2330	54.865	0.01823	0.07823	12.783
26	4.549	0.2198	59.156	0.01690	0.07690	13.003
27	4.822	0.2074	63.706	0.01570	0.07570	13.211
28	5.112	0.1956	68.528	0.01459	0.07459	13.406
29	5.418	0.1846	73.640	0.01358	0.07358	13.591
30	5.743	0.1741	79.058	0.01265	0.07265	13.765
35	7.686	0.1301	111.435	0.00897	0.06897	14.498
40	10.286	0.0972	154.762	0.00646	0.06646	15.046
45	13.765	0.0727	212.744	0.00470	0.06470	15.456
50	18.420	0.0543	290.336	0.00344	0.06344	15.762
55	24.650	0.0406	394.172	0.00254	0.06254	15.991
60	32.988	0.0303	533.128	0.00188	0.06188	16.161
65	44.145	0.0227	719.083	0.00139	0.06139	16.289
70	59.076	0.0169	967.932	0.00103	0.06103	16.385
75	79.057	0.0126	1300.949	0.00077	0.06077	16.456
80	105.796	0.0095	1746.600	0.00057	0.06057	16.509
85	141.579	0.0071	2342.982	0.00043	0.06043	16.549
90	189.465	0.0053	3141.075	0.00032	0.06032	16.579
95	253.546	0.0039	4209.104	0.00024	0.06024	16.601
100	339.302	0.0029	5638.368	0.00018	0.06018	16.618

Table 8. 8% Interest Factors

Period	Single-payment compound-amount (SPCA) $\frac{P}{S}$ Future value of $1 $(1 + i)^n$	Single-payment present-worth (SPPW) $\frac{S}{P}$ Present value of $1 $\frac{1}{(1 + i)^n}$	Uniform-series compound-amount (USCA) $\frac{R}{S}$ Future value of uniform series of $1 $\frac{(1 + i)^n - 1}{i}$	Sinking-fund payment (SFP) $\frac{S}{R}$ Uniform series whose future value is $1 $\frac{i}{(1 + i)^n - 1}$	Capital recovery (CR) $\frac{P}{R}$ Uniform series with present value of $1 $\frac{i(1 + i)^n}{(1 + i)^n - 1}$	Uniform-series present-worth (USPW) $\frac{R}{P}$ Present value of uniform series of $1 $\frac{(1 + i)^n - 1}{i(1 + i)^n}$
1	1.080	0.9259	1.000	1.00000	1.08000	0.926
2	1.166	0.8573	2.080	0.48077	0.56077	1.783
3	1.260	0.7938	3.246	0.30803	0.38803	2.577
4	1.360	0.7350	4.506	0.22192	0.30192	3.312
5	1.469	0.6806	5.867	0.17046	0.25046	3.993
6	1.587	0.6302	7.336	0.13632	0.21632	4.623
7	1.714	0.5835	8.923	0.11207	0.19207	5.206
8	1.851	0.5403	10.637	0.09401	0.17401	5.747
9	1.999	0.5002	12.488	0.08008	0.16008	6.247
10	2.159	0.4632	14.487	0.06903	0.14903	6.710
11	2.332	0.4289	16.645	0.06008	0.14008	7.139
12	2.518	0.3971	18.977	0.05270	0.13270	7.536
13	2.720	0.3677	21.495	0.04652	0.12652	7.904
14	2.937	0.3405	24.215	0.04130	0.12130	8.244
15	3.172	0.3152	27.152	0.03683	0.11683	8.559
16	3.426	0.2919	30.324	0.03298	0.11298	8.851
17	3.700	0.2703	33.750	0.02963	0.10963	9.122
18	3.996	0.2502	37.450	0.02670	0.10670	9.372
19	4.316	0.2317	41.446	0.02413	0.10413	9.604
20	4.661	0.2145	45.762	0.02185	0.10185	9.818
21	5.034	0.1987	50.423	0.01983	0.09983	10.017
22	5.437	0.1839	55.457	0.01803	0.09803	10.201
23	5.871	0.1703	60.893	0.01642	0.09642	10.371
24	6.341	0.1577	66.765	0.01498	0.09498	10.529
25	6.848	0.1460	73.106	0.01368	0.09368	10.675
26	7.396	0.1352	79.954	0.01251	0.09251	10.810
27	7.988	0.1252	87.351	0.01145	0.09145	10.935
28	8.627	0.1159	95.339	0.01049	0.09049	11.051
29	9.317	0.1073	103.966	0.00962	0.08962	11.158
30	10.063	0.0994	113.283	0.00883	0.08883	11.258
35	14.785	0.0676	172.317	0.00580	0.08580	11.655
40	21.725	0.0460	259.057	0.00386	0.08386	11.925
45	31.920	0.0313	386.506	0.00259	0.08259	12.108
50	46.902	0.0213	573.770	0.00174	0.08174	12.233
55	68.914	0.0145	848.923	0.00118	0.08118	12.319
60	101.257	0.0099	1253.213	0.00080	0.08080	12.377
65	148.780	0.0067	1847.248	0.00054	0.08054	12.416
70	218.606	0.0046	2720.080	0.00037	0.08037	12.443
75	321.205	0.0031	4002.557	0.00025	0.08025	12.461
80	471.955	0.0021	5886.935	0.00017	0.08017	12.474
85	693.456	0.0014	8655.706	0.00012	0.08012	12.482
90	1018.915	0.0010	12723.939	0.00008	0.08008	12.488
95	1497.121	0.0007	18701.507	0.00005	0.08005	12.492
100	2199.761	0.0005	27484.516	0.00004	0.08004	12.494

Table 9. 10% Interest Factors

Period n (Given / Find)	Single-payment compound-amount (SPCA) Given P, Find S: Future value of \$1 $(1+i)^n$	Single-payment present-worth (SPPW) Given S, Find P: Present value of \$1 $\frac{1}{(1+i)^n}$	Uniform-series compound-amount (USCA) Given R, Find S: Future value of uniform series of \$1 $\frac{(1+i)^n - 1}{i}$	Sinking-fund payment (SFP) Given S, Find R: Uniform series whose future value is \$1 $\frac{i}{(1+i)^n - 1}$	Capital recovery (CR) Given P, Find R: Uniform series with present value of \$1 $\frac{i(1+i)^n}{(1+i)^n - 1}$	Uniform-series present-worth (USPW) Given R, Find P: Present value of uniform series of \$1 $\frac{(1+i)^n - 1}{i(1+i)^n}$
1	1.100	0.9091	1.000	1.00000	1.10000	0.909
2	1.210	0.8264	2.100	0.47619	0.57619	1.736
3	1.331	0.7513	3.310	0.30211	0.40211	2.487
4	1.464	0.6830	4.641	0.21547	0.31547	3.170
5	1.611	0.6209	6.105	0.16380	0.26380	3.791
6	1.772	0.5645	7.716	0.12961	0.22961	4.355
7	1.949	0.5132	9.487	0.10541	0.20541	4.868
8	2.144	0.4665	11.436	0.08744	0.18744	5.335
9	2.358	0.4241	13.579	0.07364	0.17364	5.759
10	2.594	0.3855	15.937	0.06275	0.16275	6.144
11	2.853	0.3505	18.531	0.05396	0.15396	6.495
12	3.138	0.3186	21.384	0.04676	0.14676	6.814
13	3.452	0.2897	24.523	0.04078	0.14078	7.103
14	3.797	0.2633	27.975	0.03575	0.13575	7.367
15	4.177	0.2394	31.772	0.03147	0.13147	7.606
16	4.595	0.2176	35.950	0.02782	0.12782	7.824
17	5.054	0.1978	40.545	0.02466	0.12466	8.022
18	5.560	0.1799	45.599	0.02193	0.12193	8.201
19	6.116	0.1635	51.159	0.01955	0.11955	8.365
20	6.727	0.1486	57.275	0.01746	0.11746	8.514
21	7.400	0.1351	64.002	0.01562	0.11562	8.649
22	8.140	0.1228	71.403	0.01401	0.11401	8.772
23	8.954	0.1117	79.543	0.01257	0.11257	8.883
24	9.850	0.1015	88.497	0.01130	0.11130	8.985
25	10.835	0.0923	98.347	0.01017	0.11017	9.077
26	11.918	0.0839	109.182	0.00916	0.10916	9.161
27	13.110	0.0763	121.100	0.00826	0.10826	9.237
28	14.421	0.0693	134.210	0.00745	0.10745	9.307
29	15.863	0.0630	148.631	0.00673	0.10673	9.370
30	17.449	0.0573	164.494	0.00608	0.10608	9.427
35	28.102	0.0356	271.024	0.00369	0.10369	9.644
40	45.259	0.0221	442.593	0.00226	0.10226	9.779
45	72.890	0.0137	718.905	0.00139	0.10139	9.863
50	117.391	0.0085	1163.909	0.00086	0.10086	9.915
55	189.059	0.0053	1880.591	0.00053	0.10053	9.947
60	304.482	0.0033	3034.816	0.00033	0.10033	9.967
65	490.371	0.0020	4893.707	0.00020	0.10020	9.980
70	789.747	0.0013	7887.470	0.00013	0.10013	9.987
75	1271.895	0.0008	12708.954	0.00008	0.10008	9.992
80	2048.400	0.0005	20474.002	0.00005	0.10005	9.995
85	3298.969	0.0003	32979.690	0.00003	0.10003	9.997
90	5313.023	0.0002	53120.226	0.00002	0.10002	9.998
95	8556.676	0.0001	85556.760	0.00001	0.10001	9.999

Table 10. 12% Interest Factors

Period n	Single-payment compound-amount (SPCA)	Single-payment present-worth (SPPW)	Uniform-series compound-amount (USCA)	Sinking-fund payment (SFP)	Capital recovery (CR)	Uniform-series present-worth (USPW)
Given	P	S	R	S	P	R
Find	S	P	S	R	R	P
	Future value of \$1 $(1+i)^n$	Present value of \$1 $\frac{1}{(1+i)^n}$	Future value of uniform series of \$1 $\frac{(1+i)^n-1}{i}$	Uniform series whose future value is \$1 $\frac{i}{(1+i)^n-1}$	Uniform series with present value of \$1 $\frac{i(1+i)^n}{(1+i)^n-1}$	Present value of uniform series of \$1 $\frac{(1+i)^n-1}{i(1+i)^n}$
1	1.120	0.8929	1.000	1.00000	1.12000	0.893
2	1.254	0.7972	2.120	0.47170	0.59170	1.690
3	1.405	0.7118	3.374	0.29635	0.41635	2.402
4	1.574	0.6355	4.779	0.20923	0.32923	3.037
5	1.762	0.5674	6.353	0.15741	0.27741	3.605
6	1.974	0.5066	8.115	0.12323	0.24323	4.111
7	2.211	0.4523	10.089	0.09912	0.21912	4.564
8	2.476	0.4039	12.300	0.08130	0.20130	4.968
9	2.773	0.3606	14.776	0.06768	0.18768	5.328
10	3.106	0.3220	17.549	0.05698	0.17698	5.650
11	3.479	0.2875	20.655	0.04842	0.16842	5.938
12	3.896	0.2567	24.133	0.04144	0.16144	6.194
13	4.363	0.2292	28.029	0.03568	0.15568	6.424
14	4.887	0.2046	32.393	0.03087	0.15087	6.628
15	5.474	0.1827	37.280	0.02682	0.14682	6.811
16	6.130	0.1631	42.753	0.02339	0.14339	6.974
17	6.866	0.1456	48.884	0.02046	0.14046	7.120
18	7.690	0.1300	55.750	0.01794	0.13794	7.250
19	8.613	0.1161	63.440	0.01576	0.13576	7.366
20	9.646	0.1037	72.052	0.01388	0.13388	7.469
21	10.804	0.0926	81.699	0.01224	0.13224	7.562
22	12.100	0.0826	92.503	0.01081	0.13081	7.645
23	13.552	0.0738	104.603	0.00956	0.12956	7.718
24	15.179	0.0659	118.155	0.00846	0.12846	7.784
25	17.000	0.0588	133.334	0.00750	0.12750	7.843
26	19.040	0.0525	150.334	0.00665	0.12665	7.896
27	21.325	0.0469	169.374	0.00590	0.12590	7.943
28	23.884	0.0419	190.699	0.00524	0.12524	7.984
29	26.750	0.0374	214.583	0.00466	0.12466	8.022
30	29.960	0.0334	241.333	0.00414	0.12414	8.055
35	52.800	0.0189	431.663	0.00232	0.12232	8.176
40	93.051	0.0107	767.091	0.00130	0.12130	8.244
45	163.988	0.0061	1358.230	0.00074	0.12074	8.283
50	289.002	0.0035	2400.018	0.00042	0.12042	8.304
55	509.321	0.0020	4236.005	0.00024	0.12024	8.317
60	897.597	0.0011	7471.641	0.00013	0.12013	8.324
65	1581.872	0.0006	13173.937	0.00008	0.12008	8.328
70	2787.800	0.0004	23223.332	0.00004	0.12004	8.330
75	4913.056	0.0002	40933.799	0.00002	0.12002	8.332
80	8658.483	0.0001	72145.692	0.00001	0.12001	8.332

Table 11.   15% Interest Factors

Given Period Fixed	Single-payment compound-amount (SPCA) $\dfrac{P}{S}$ Future value of $1 $(1 + i)^n$	Single-payment present-worth (SPPW) $\dfrac{S}{P}$ Present value of $1 $\dfrac{1}{(1 + i)^n}$	Uniform-series compound-amount (USCA) $\dfrac{R}{S}$ Future value of uniform series of $1 $\dfrac{(1 + i)^n - 1}{i}$	Sinking-fund payment (SFP) $\dfrac{S}{R}$ Uniform series whose future value is $1 $\dfrac{i}{(1 + i)^n - 1}$	Capital recovery (CR) $\dfrac{P}{R}$ Uniform series with present value of $1 $\dfrac{i(1 + i)^n}{(1 + i)^n - 1}$	Uniform-series present-worth (USPW) $\dfrac{R}{P}$ Present value of uniform series of $1 $\dfrac{(1 + i)^n - 1}{i(1 + i)^n}$
1	1.150	0.8696	1.000	1.00000	1.15000	0.870
2	1.322	0.7561	2.150	0.46512	0.61512	1.626
3	1.521	0.6575	3.472	0.28798	0.43798	2.283
4	1.749	0.5718	4.993	0.20027	0.35027	2.855
5	2.011	0.4972	6.742	0.14832	0.29832	3.352
6	2.313	0.4323	8.754	0.11424	0.26424	3.784
7	2.660	0.3759	11.067	0.09036	0.24036	4.160
8	3.059	0.3269	13.727	0.07285	0.22285	4.487
9	3.518	0.2843	16.786	0.05957	0.20957	4.772
10	4.046	0.2472	20.304	0.04925	0.19925	5.019
11	4.652	0.2149	24.349	0.04107	0.19107	5.234
12	5.350	0.1869	29.002	0.03448	0.18448	5.421
13	6.153	0.1625	34.352	0.02911	0.17911	5.583
14	7.076	0.1413	40.505	0.02469	0.17469	5.724
15	8.137	0.1229	47.580	0.02102	0.17102	5.847
16	9.358	0.1069	55.717	0.01795	0.16795	5.954
17	10.761	0.0929	65.075	0.01537	0.16537	6.047
18	12.375	0.0808	75.836	0.01319	0.16319	6.128
19	14.232	0.0703	88.212	0.01134	0.16134	6.198
20	16.367	0.0611	102.444	0.00976	0.15976	6.259
21	18.822	0.0531	118.810	0.00842	0.15842	6.312
22	21.645	0.0462	137.632	0.00727	0.15727	6.359
23	24.891	0.0402	159.276	0.00628	0.15628	6.399
24	28.625	0.0349	184.168	0.00543	0.15543	6.434
25	32.919	0.0304	212.793	0.00470	0.15470	6.464
26	37.857	0.0264	245.712	0.00407	0.15407	6.491
27	43.535	0.0230	283.569	0.00353	0.15353	6.514
28	50.066	0.0200	327.104	0.00306	0.15306	6.534
29	57.575	0.0174	377.170	0.00265	0.15265	6.551
30	66.212	0.0151	434.745	0.00230	0.15230	6.566
35	133.176	0.0075	881.170	0.00113	0.15113	6.617
40	267.864	0.0037	1779.090	0.00056	0.15056	6.642
45	538.769	0.0019	3585.128	0.00028	0.15028	6.654
50	1083.657	0.0009	7217.716	0.00014	0.15014	6.661
55	2179.622	0.0005	14524.148	0.00007	0.15007	6.664
60	4383.999	0.0002	29219.992	0.00003	0.15003	6.665
65	8817.787	0.0001	58778.583	0.00002	0.15002	6.666

Table 12.   20% Interest Factors

Period	Single-payment compound-amount (SPCA) $\dfrac{P}{S}$ Future value of $1 $(1+i)^n$	Single-payment present-worth (SPPW) $\dfrac{S}{P}$ Present value of $1 $\dfrac{1}{(1+i)^n}$	Uniform-series compound-amount (USCA) $\dfrac{R}{S}$ Future value of uniform series of $1 $\dfrac{(1+i)^n-1}{i}$	Sinking-fund payment (SFP) $\dfrac{S}{R}$ Uniform series whose future value is $1 $\dfrac{i}{(1+i)^n-1}$	Capital recovery (CR) $\dfrac{P}{R}$ Uniform series with present value of $1 $\dfrac{i(1+i)^n}{(1+i)^n-1}$	Uniform-series present-worth (USPW) $\dfrac{R}{P}$ Present value of uniform series of $1 $\dfrac{(1+i)^n-1}{i(1+i)^n}$
1	1.200	0.8333	1.000	1.00000	1.20000	0.833
2	1.440	0.6944	2.200	0.45455	0.65455	1.528
3	1.728	0.5787	3.640	0.27473	0.47473	2.106
4	2.074	0.4823	5.368	0.18629	0.38629	2.589
5	2.488	0.4019	7.442	0.13438	0.33438	2.991
6	2.986	0.3349	9.930	0.10071	0.30071	3.326
7	3.583	0.2791	12.916	0.07742	0.27742	3.605
8	4.300	0.2326	16.499	0.06061	0.26061	3.837
9	5.160	0.1938	20.799	0.04808	0.24808	4.031
10	6.192	0.1615	25.959	0.03852	0.23852	4.192
11	7.430	0.1346	32.150	0.03110	0.23110	4.327
12	8.916	0.1122	39.581	0.02526	0.22526	4.439
13	10.699	0.0935	48.497	0.02062	0.22062	4.533
14	12.839	0.0779	59.196	0.01689	0.21689	4.611
15	15.407	0.0649	72.035	0.01388	0.21388	4.675
16	18.488	0.0541	87.442	0.01144	0.21144	4.730
17	22.186	0.0451	105.931	0.00944	0.20944	4.775
18	26.623	0.0376	128.117	0.00781	0.20781	4.812
19	31.948	0.0313	154.740	0.00646	0.20646	4.843
20	38.338	0.0261	186.688	0.00536	0.20536	4.870
21	46.005	0.0217	225.026	0.00444	0.20444	4.891
22	55.206	0.0181	271.031	0.00369	0.20369	4.909
23	66.247	0.0151	326.237	0.00307	0.20307	4.925
24	79.497	0.0126	392.484	0.00255	0.20255	4.937
25	95.396	0.0105	471.981	0.00212	0.20212	4.948
26	114.475	0.0087	567.377	0.00176	0.20176	4.956
27	137.371	0.0073	681.853	0.00147	0.20147	4.964
28	164.845	0.0061	819.223	0.00122	0.20122	4.970
29	197.814	0.0051	984.068	0.00102	0.20102	4.975
30	237.376	0.0042	1181.882	0.00085	0.20085	4.979
35	590.668	0.0017	2948.341	0.00034	0.20034	4.992
40	1469.772	0.0007	7343.858	0.00014	0.20014	4.997
45	3657.262	0.0003	18281.310	0.00005	0.20005	4.999
50	9100.438	0.0001	45497.191	0.00002	0.20002	4.999

Table 13. 25% Interest Factors

Period	Single-payment compound-amount (SPCA) $\dfrac{P}{S}$ Future value of $1 $(1 + i)^n$	Single-payment present-worth (SPPW) $\dfrac{S}{P}$ Present value of $1 $\dfrac{1}{(1 + i)^n}$	Uniform-series compound amount (USCA) $\dfrac{R}{S}$ Future value of uniform series of $1 $\dfrac{(1 + i)^n - 1}{i}$	Sinking-fund payment (SFP) $\dfrac{S}{R}$ Uniform series whose future value is $1 $\dfrac{i}{(1 + i)^n - 1}$	Capital recovery (CR) $\dfrac{P}{R}$ Uniform series with present value of $1 $\dfrac{i(1 + i)^n}{(1 + i)^n - 1}$	Uniform-series present-worth (USPW) $\dfrac{R}{P}$ Present value of uniform series of $1 $\dfrac{(1 + i)^n - 1}{i(1 + i)^n}$
1	1.250	0.8000	1.000	1.00000	1.25000	0.800
2	1.562	0.6400	2.250	0.44444	0.69444	1.440
3	1.953	0.5120	3.812	0.26230	0.51230	1.952
4	2.441	0.4096	5.766	0.17344	0.42344	2.362
5	3.052	0.3277	8.207	0.12185	0.37185	2.689
6	3.815	0.2621	11.259	0.08882	0.33882	2.951
7	4.768	0.2097	15.073	0.06634	0.31634	3.161
8	5.960	0.1678	19.842	0.05040	0.30040	3.329
9	7.451	0.1342	25.802	0.03876	0.28876	3.463
10	9.313	0.1074	33.253	0.03007	0.28007	3.571
11	11.642	0.0859	42.566	0.02349	0.27349	3.656
12	14.552	0.0687	54.208	0.01845	0.26845	3.725
13	18.190	0.0550	68.760	0.01454	0.26454	3.780
14	22.737	0.0440	86.949	0.01150	0.26150	3.824
15	28.422	0.0352	109.687	0.00912	0.25912	3.859
16	35.527	0.0281	138.109	0.00724	0.25724	3.887
17	44.409	0.0225	173.636	0.00576	0.25576	3.910
18	55.511	0.0180	218.045	0.00459	0.25459	3.928
19	69.389	0.0144	273.556	0.00366	0.25366	3.942
20	86.736	0.0115	342.945	0.00292	0.25292	3.954
21	108.420	0.0092	429.681	0.00233	0.25233	3.963
22	135.525	0.0074	538.101	0.00186	0.25186	3.970
23	169.407	0.0059	673.626	0.00148	0.25148	3.976
24	211.758	0.0047	843.033	0.00119	0.25119	3.981
25	264.698	0.0038	1054.791	0.00095	0.25095	3.985
26	330.872	0.0030	1319.489	0.00076	0.25076	3.988
27	413.590	0.0024	1650.361	0.00061	0.25061	3.990
28	516.988	0.0019	2063.952	0.00048	0.25048	3.992
29	646.235	0.0015	2580.939	0.00039	0.25039	3.994
30	807.794	0.0012	3227.174	0.00031	0.25031	3.995
35	2465.190	0.0004	9856.761	0.00010	0.25010	3.998
40	7523.164	0.0001	30088.655	0.00003	0.25003	3.999

(handwritten annotations at left: "Given" above Period; "Find" below Period; column ratio symbols P/S, S/P, R/S, S/R, P/R, R/P)

Table 14.   30% **Interest Factors**

Given Period Final	Single- payment compound- amount (SPCA) $\dfrac{P}{S}$ Future value of \$1 $(1+i)^n$	Single- payment present- worth (SPPW) $\dfrac{S}{P}$ Present value of \$1 $\dfrac{1}{(1+i)^n}$	Uniform- series compound- amount (USCA) $\dfrac{R}{S}$ Future value of uniform series of \$1 $\dfrac{(1+i)^n-1}{i}$	Sinking-fund payment (SFP) $\dfrac{S}{R}$ Uniform series whose future value is \$1 $\dfrac{i}{(1+i)^n-1}$	Capital recovery (CR) $\dfrac{P}{R}$ Uniform series with present value of \$1 $\dfrac{i(1+i)^n}{(1+i)^n-1}$	Uniform- series present- worth (USPW) $\dfrac{R}{P}$ Present value of uniform series of \$1 $\dfrac{(1+i)^n-1}{i(1+i)^n}$
1	1.300	0.7692	1.000	1.00000	1.30000	0.769
2	1.690	0.5917	2.300	0.43478	0.73478	1.361
3	2.197	0.4552	3.990	0.25063	0.55063	1.816
4	2.856	0.3501	6.187	0.16163	0.46163	2.166
5	3.713	0.2693	9.043	0.11058	0.41058	2.436
6	4.827	0.2072	12.756	0.07839	0.37839	2.643
7	6.275	0.1594	17.583	0.05687	0.35687	2.802
8	8.157	0.1226	23.858	0.04192	0.34192	2.925
9	10.604	0.0943	32.015	0.03124	0.33124	3.019
10	13.786	0.0725	42.619	0.02346	0.32346	3.092
11	17.922	0.0558	56.405	0.01773	0.31773	3.147
12	23.298	0.0429	74.327	0.01345	0.31345	3.190
13	30.288	0.0330	97.625	0.01024	0.31024	3.223
14	39.374	0.0254	127.913	0.00782	0.30782	3.249
15	51.186	0.0195	167.286	0.00598	0.30598	3.268
16	66.542	0.0150	218.472	0.00458	0.30458	3.283
17	86.504	0.0116	285.014	0.00351	0.30351	3.295
18	112.455	0.0089	371.518	0.00269	0.30269	3.304
19	146.192	0.0068	483.973	0.00207	0.30207	3.311
20	190.050	0.0053	630.165	0.00159	0.30159	3.316
21	247.065	0.0040	820.215	0.00122	0.30122	3.320
22	321.184	0.0031	1067.280	0.00094	0.30094	3.323
23	417.539	0.0024	1388.464	0.00072	0.30072	3.325
24	542.801	0.0018	1806.003	0.00055	0.30055	3.327
25	705.641	0.0014	2348.803	0.00043	0.30043	3.329
26	917.333	0.0011	3054.444	0.00033	0.30033	3.330
27	1192.533	0.0008	3971.778	0.00025	0.30025	3.331
28	1550.293	0.0006	5164.311	0.00019	0.30019	3.331
29	2015.381	0.0005	6714.604	0.00015	0.30015	3.332
30	2619.996	0.0004	8729.985	0.00011	0.30011	3.332
35	9727.860	0.0001	32422.868	0.00003	0.30003	3.333

Table 15. 40% Interest Factors

Given → Period / Find → n	Single-payment compound-amount (SPCA) $\dfrac{P}{S}$ Future value of \$1 $(1+i)^n$	Single-payment present-worth (SPPW) $\dfrac{S}{P}$ Present value of \$1 $\dfrac{1}{(1+i)^n}$	Uniform-series compound-amount (USCA) $\dfrac{R}{S}$ Future value of uniform series of \$1 $\dfrac{(1+i)^n-1}{i}$	Sinking-fund payment (SFP) $\dfrac{S}{R}$ Uniform series whose future value is \$1 $\dfrac{i}{(1+i)^n-1}$	Capital recovery (CR) $\dfrac{P}{R}$ Uniform series with present value of \$1 $\dfrac{i(1+i)^n}{(1+i)^n-1}$	Uniform-series present-worth (USPW) $\dfrac{R}{P}$ Present value of uniform series of \$1 $\dfrac{(1+i)^n-1}{i(1+i)^n}$
1	1.400	0.7143	1.000	1.00000	1.40000	0.714
2	1.960	0.5102	2.400	0.41667	0.81667	1.224
3	2.744	0.3644	4.360	0.22936	0.62936	1.589
4	3.842	0.2603	7.104	0.14077	0.54077	1.849
5	5.378	0.1859	10.946	0.09136	0.49136	2.035
6	7.530	0.1328	16.324	0.06126	0.46126	2.168
7	10.541	0.0949	23.853	0.04192	0.44192	2.263
8	14.758	0.0678	34.395	0.02907	0.42907	2.331
9	20.661	0.0484	49.153	0.02034	0.42034	2.379
10	28.925	0.0346	69.814	0.01432	0.41432	2.414
11	40.496	0.0247	98.739	0.01013	0.41013	2.438
12	56.694	0.0176	139.235	0.00718	0.40718	2.456
13	79.371	0.0126	195.929	0.00510	0.40510	2.469
14	111.120	0.0090	275.300	0.00363	0.40363	2.478
15	155.568	0.0064	386.420	0.00259	0.40259	2.484
16	217.795	0.0046	541.988	0.00185	0.40185	2.489
17	304.913	0.0033	759.784	0.00132	0.40132	2.492
18	426.879	0.0023	1064.697	0.00094	0.40094	2.494
19	597.630	0.0017	1491.576	0.00067	0.40067	2.496
20	836.683	0.0012	2089.206	0.00048	0.40048	2.497
21	1171.356	0.0009	2925.889	0.00034	0.40034	2.498
22	1639.898	0.0006	4097.245	0.00024	0.40024	2.498
23	2295.857	0.0004	5737.142	0.00017	0.40017	2.499
24	3214.200	0.0003	8032.999	0.00012	0.40012	2.499
25	4499.880	0.0002	11247.199	0.00009	0.40009	2.499
26	6299.831	0.0002	15747.079	0.00006	0.40006	2.500
27	8819.764	0.0001	22046.910	0.00005	0.40005	2.500

Table 16.   50% Interest Factors

Period Find	Single-payment compound-amount (SPCA) $\dfrac{P}{S}$ Future value of $1 $(1+i)^n$	Single-payment present-worth (SPPW) $\dfrac{S}{P}$ Present value of $1 $\dfrac{1}{(1+i)^n}$	Uniform-series compound-amount (USCA) $\dfrac{R}{S}$ Future value of uniform series of $1 $\dfrac{(1+i)^n-1}{i}$	Sinking-fund payment (SFP) $\dfrac{S}{R}$ Uniform series whose future value is $1 $\dfrac{i}{(1+i)^n-1}$	Capital recovery (CR) $\dfrac{P}{R}$ Uniform series with present value of $1 $\dfrac{i(1+i)^n}{(1+i)^n-1}$	Uniform-series present-worth (USPW) $\dfrac{R}{P}$ Present value of uniform series of $1 $\dfrac{(1+i)^n-1}{i(1+i)^n}$
1	1.500	0.6667	1.000	1.00000	1.50000	0.667
2	2.250	0.4444	2.500	0.40000	0.90000	1.111
3	3.375	0.2963	4.750	0.21053	0.71053	1.407
4	5.062	0.1975	8.125	0.12308	0.62308	1.605
5	7.594	0.1317	13.188	0.07583	0.57583	1.737
6	11.391	0.0878	20.781	0.04812	0.54812	1.824
7	17.086	0.0585	32.172	0.03108	0.53108	1.883
8	25.629	0.0390	49.258	0.02030	0.52030	1.922
9	38.443	0.0260	74.887	0.01335	0.51335	1.948
10	57.665	0.0173	113.330	0.00882	0.50882	1.965
11	86.498	0.0116	170.995	0.00585	0.50585	1.977
12	129.746	0.0077	257.493	0.00388	0.50388	1.985
13	194.620	0.0051	387.239	0.00258	0.50258	1.990
14	291.929	0.0034	581.859	0.00172	0.50172	1.993
15	437.894	0.0023	873.788	0.00114	0.50114	1.995
16	656.841	0.0015	1311.682	0.00076	0.50076	1.997
17	985.261	0.0010	1968.523	0.00051	0.50051	1.998
18	1477.892	0.0007	2953.784	0.00034	0.50034	1.999
19	2216.838	0.0005	4431.676	0.00023	0.50023	1.999
20	3325.257	0.0003	6648.513	0.00015	0.50015	1.999
21	4987.885	0.0002	9973.770	0.00010	0.50010	2.000
22	7481.828	0.0001	14961.655	0.00007	0.50007	2.000

Table 17. Uniform-gradient Conversion Factors
Values of factors to convert a uniform gradient, *g*, to an
equivalent uniform payment, *R*

$$\text{UGC} = \left[\frac{1}{i} - \frac{n}{(1+i)^n - 1}\right]$$

n	Interest rate (i)										
	2%	4%	6%	8%	10%	15%	20%	25%	30%	40%	50%
1	0.00	0.00	0.00	0.00	0.00	0.00	0.00	0.00	0.00	0.00	0.00
2	0.50	0.49	0.49	0.48	0.48	0.47	0.45	0.44	0.43	0.42	0.40
3	0.99	0.97	0.96	0.95	0.94	0.91	0.88	0.85	0.83	0.78	0.74
4	1.48	1.45	1.43	1.40	1.38	1.33	1.27	1.22	1.18	1.09	1.02
5	1.96	1.92	1.88	1.85	1.81	1.72	1.64	1.56	1.49	1.36	1.24
6	2.44	2.39	2.33	2.28	2.22	2.10	1.98	1.87	1.77	1.58	1.42
7	2.92	2.84	2.77	2.69	2.62	2.45	2.29	2.14	2.01	1.77	1.56
8	3.40	3.29	3.20	3.10	3.00	2.78	2.58	2.39	2.22	1.92	1.68
9	3.87	3.74	3.61	3.49	3.37	3.09	2.84	2.60	2.40	2.04	1.76
10	4.34	4.18	4.02	3.87	3.73	3.38	3.07	2.80	2.55	2.14	1.82
11	4.80	4.61	4.42	4.24	4.06	3.65	3.29	2.97	2.68	2.22	1.87
12	5.26	5.03	4.81	4.60	4.39	3.91	3.48	3.11	2.80	2.28	1.91
13	5.72	5.45	5.19	4.94	4.70	4.14	3.66	3.24	2.89	2.33	1.93
14	6.18	5.87	5.56	5.27	5.00	4.36	3.82	3.36	2.97	2.37	1.95
15	6.63	6.27	5.93	5.59	5.28	4.56	3.96	3.45	3.03	2.40	1.97
16	7.08	6.67	6.28	5.90	5.55	4.75	4.09	3.54	3.09	2.43	1.98
17	7.53	7.07	6.62	6.20	5.81	4.93	4.20	3.61	3.13	2.44	1.98
18	7.97	7.45	6.96	6.49	6.05	5.08	4.30	3.67	3.17	2.46	1.99
19	8.41	7.83	7.29	6.77	6.29	5.23	4.39	3.72	3.20	2.47	1.99
20	8.84	8.21	7.61	7.04	6.51	5.37	4.46	3.77	3.23	2.48	1.99
21	9.28	8.58	7.92	7.29	6.72	5.49	4.53	3.80	3.25	2.48	2.00
22	9.71	8.94	8.22	7.54	6.92	5.60	4.59	3.84	3.26	2.49	2.00
23	10.13	9.30	8.51	7.78	7.11	5.70	4.65	3.86	3.28	2.49	
24	10.55	9.65	8.80	8.01	7.29	5.80	4.69	3.89	3.29	2.49	
25	10.97	9.99	9.07	8.23	7.46	5.88	4.74	3.91	3.30	2.49	
26	11.39	10.33	9.34	8.44	7.62	5.96	4.77	3.92	3.30	2.50	
27	11.80	10.66	9.60	8.64	7.77	6.03	4.80	3.93	3.31	2.50	
28	12.21	10.99	9.86	8.83	7.91	6.10	4.83	3.95	3.32		
29	12.62	11.31	10.10	9.01	8.05	6.15	4.85	3.96	3.32		
30	13.02	11.63	10.34	9.19	8.18	6.21	4.87	3.96	3.32		
35	15.00	13.12	11.43	9.96	8.71	6.40	4.94	3.99	3.33		
40	16.89	14.48	12.36	10.57	9.10	6.52	4.97	4.00			
45	18.70	15.70	13.14	11.04	9.37	6.58	4.99				
50	20.44	16.81	13.80	11.41	9.57	6.62	4.99				

Table 18. Areas under the Normal Curve*

Fractional parts of the total area (1.000) under the normal curve between the mean and a perpendicular erected at various numbers of standard deviations from the mean, $(X - \bar{X})/\sigma$. To illustrate the use of the table, 39.065 per cent of the total area under the curve will lie between the mean and a perpendicular erected at a distance of 1.23σ from the mean. The values in the table represent the shaded area in the normal distribution shown at the right. Each figure in the body of the table is preceded by a decimal point.

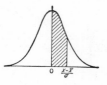

$\dfrac{(X - \bar{X})}{\sigma}$	.00	.01	.02	.03	.04	.05	.06	.07	.08	.09
0.0	00000	00399	00798	01197	01595	01994	02392	02790	03188	03586
0.1	03983	04380	04776	05172	05567	05962	06356	06749	07142	07535
0.2	07926	08317	08706	09095	09483	09871	10257	10642	11026	11409
0.3	11791	12172	12552	12930	13307	13683	14058	14431	14803	15173
0.4	15554	15910	16276	16640	17003	17364	17724	18082	18439	18793
0.5	19146	19497	19847	20194	20450	20884	21226	21566	21904	22240
0.6	22575	22907	23237	23565	23891	24215	24537	24857	25175	25490
0.7	25804	26115	26424	26730	27035	27337	27637	27935	28230	28524
0.8	28814	29103	29389	29673	29955	30234	30511	30785	31057	31327
0.9	31594	31859	32121	32381	32639	32894	33147	33398	33646	33891
1.0	34134	34375	34614	34850	35083	35313	35543	35769	35993	36214
1.1	36433	36650	36864	37076	37286	37493	37698	37900	38100	38298
1.2	38493	38686	38877	39065	39251	39435	39617	39796	39973	40147
1.3	40320	40490	40658	40824	40988	41149	41308	41466	41621	41774
1.4	41924	42073	42220	42364	42507	42647	42786	42922	43056	43189
1.5	43319	43448	43574	43699	43822	43943	44062	44179	44295	44408
1.6	44520	44630	44738	44845	44950	45053	45154	45254	45352	45449
1.7	45543	45637	45728	45818	45907	45994	46080	46164	46246	46327
1.8	46407	46485	46562	46638	46712	46784	46856	46926	46995	47062
1.9	47128	47193	47257	47320	47381	47441	47500	47558	47615	47670
2.0	47725	47778	47831	47882	47932	47982	48030	48077	48124	48169
2.1	48214	48257	48300	48341	48382	48422	48461	48500	48537	48574
2.2	48610	48645	48679	48713	48745	48778	48809	48840	48870	48899
2.3	48928	48956	48983	49010	49036	49061	49086	49111	49134	49158
2.4	49180	49202	49224	49245	49266	49286	49305	49324	49343	49361
2.5	49379	49396	49413	49430	49446	49461	49477	49492	49506	49520
2.6	49534	49547	49560	49573	49585	49598	49609	49621	49632	49643
2.7	49653	49664	49674	49683	49693	49702	49711	49720	49728	49736
2.8	49744	49752	49760	49767	49774	49781	49788	49795	49801	49807
2.9	49813	49819	49825	49831	49836	49841	49846	49851	49856	49861
3.0	49865									
3.5	4997674									
4.0	4999683									
4.5	4999966									
5.0	4999997133									

* Adapted from F. C. Kent, *Elements of Statistics*, McGraw-Hill Book Company, Inc., New York, 1924.

Table 19. Student's *t* Distribution*

The body of the table indicates the number of standard error unit deviations from the mean. The probability headings on the columns refer to the proportion of the area of the distribution which is outside these deviations from the mean (on both sides). The probability includes both tails, as indicated by the shadings on the right. For example, with 15 degrees of freedom, there is a probability of 0.10 that a sample value will deviate 1.753 standard errors or more above or below the mean value.

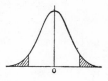

Degrees of freedom	Probability							
	0.90	0.80	0.50	0.20	0.10	0.05	0.01	0.001
1	0.158	0.325	1.000	3.078	6.314	12.706	63.657	636.619
2	0.142	0.289	0.816	1.886	2.920	4.303	9.925	31.598
3	0.137	0.277	0.765	1.638	2.353	3.182	5.841	12.941
4	0.134	0.271	0.741	1.533	2.132	2.776	4.604	8.610
5	0.132	0.267	0.727	1.476	2.015	2.571	4.032	6.859
6	0.131	0.265	0.718	1.440	1.943	2.447	3.707	5.959
7	0.130	0.263	0.711	1.415	1.895	2.365	3.499	5.405
8	0.130	0.262	0.706	1.397	1.860	2.306	3.355	5.041
9	0.129	0.261	0.703	1.383	1.833	2.262	3.250	4.781
10	0.129	0.260	0.700	1.372	1.812	2.228	3.169	4.587
11	0.129	0.260	0.697	1.363	1.796	2.201	3.106	4.437
12	0.128	0.259	0.695	1.356	1.782	2.179	3.055	4.318
13	0.128	0.258	0.694	1.350	1.771	2.160	3.012	4.221
14	0.128	0.258	0.692	1.345	1.761	2.145	2.977	4.140
15	0.128	0.258	0.691	1.341	1.753	2.131	2.947	4.073
16	0.128	0.257	0.690	1.337	1.746	2.120	2.921	4.015
17	0.128	0.257	0.689	1.333	1.740	2.110	2.898	3.965
18	0.127	0.257	0.688	1.330	1.734	2.101	2.878	3.922
19	0.127	0.257	0.688	1.328	1.729	2.093	2.861	3.883
20	0.127	0.257	0.687	1.325	1.725	2.086	2.845	3.850
21	0.127	0.257	0.686	1.323	1.721	2.080	2.831	3.819
22	0.127	0.256	0.686	1.321	1.717	2.074	2.819	3.792
23	0.127	0.256	0.685	1.319	1.714	2.069	2.807	3.767
24	0.127	0.256	0.685	1.318	1.711	2.064	2.797	3.745
25	0.127	0.256	0.684	1.316	1.708	2.060	2.787	3.725
26	0.127	0.256	0.684	1.315	1.706	2.056	2.779	3.707
27	0.127	0.256	0.684	1.314	1.703	2.052	2.771	3.690
28	0.127	0.256	0.683	1.313	1.701	2.048	2.763	3.674
29	0.127	0.256	0.683	1.311	1.699	2.045	2.756	3.659
30	0.127	0.256	0.683	1.310	1.697	2.042	2.750	3.646
∞	0.126	0.253	0.674	1.282	1.645	1.960	2.576	3.291

* R. A. Fisher, *Statistical Methods for Research Workers*, Oliver & Boyd, Ltd., Edinburgh and London, and abridged from Table III of R. A. Fisher and F. Yates, *Statistical Tables for Biological, Agricultural and Medical Research*, published by Oliver & Boyd, Ltd., Edinburgh and London, and used by permission of the authors and publishers.

Table 20. Random Digits*

48867	33971	29678	13151	56644	49193	93469	43252	14006	47173
32267	69746	00113	51336	36551	56310	85793	53453	09744	64346
27435	03196	33877	35032	98054	48358	21788	98862	67491	42221
55753	05256	51557	90419	40716	64589	90398	37070	78318	02918
93142	50675	04507	44001	06365	77897	84566	99600	67985	49133
98658	86583	97433	10733	80495	62709	61357	66903	76730	79355
68216	94830	41248	50712	46878	87317	80545	31484	03195	14755
17901	30815	78360	78260	67866	42304	07293	61290	61301	04815
88124	21868	14942	25893	72695	56231	18918	72534	86737	77792
83464	36749	22336	50443	83576	19238	91730	39507	22717	94719
91310	99003	25704	55581	00729	22024	61319	66162	20933	67713
32739	38352	91256	77744	75080	01492	90984	63090	53087	41301
07751	66724	03290	56386	06070	67105	64219	48192	70478	84722
55228	64156	90480	97774	08055	04435	26999	42039	16589	06757
89013	51781	81116	24383	95569	97247	44437	36293	29967	16088
51828	81819	81038	89146	39192	89470	76331	56420	14527	34828
59783	85454	93327	06078	64924	07271	77563	92710	42183	12380
80267	47103	90556	16128	41490	07996	78454	47929	81586	67024
82919	44210	61607	93001	26314	26865	26714	43793	94937	28439
77019	77417	19466	14967	75521	49967	74065	09746	27881	01070
66225	61832	06242	40093	40800	76849	29929	18988	10888	40344
98534	12777	84601	56336	00034	85939	32438	09549	01855	40550
63175	70789	51345	43723	06995	11186	38615	56646	54320	39632
92362	73011	09115	78303	38901	58107	95366	17226	74626	78208
61831	44794	65079	97130	94289	73502	04857	68855	47045	06309
42502	01646	88493	48207	01283	16474	08864	68322	92454	19287
89733	86230	04903	55015	11811	98185	32014	84761	80926	14509
01336	66633	26015	66768	24846	00321	73118	15802	13549	41335
72623	56083	65799	88934	87274	19417	84897	90877	76472	52145
74004	68388	04090	35239	49379	04456	07642	68642	01026	43810
09388	54633	27684	47117	67583	42496	20703	68579	65883	10729
51771	92019	39791	60400	08585	60680	28841	09921	00520	73135
69796	30304	79836	20631	10743	00246	24979	35707	75283	39211
98417	33403	63448	90462	91645	24919	73609	26663	09380	30515
56150	18324	43011	02660	86574	86097	49399	21249	90380	94375
76199	75692	09063	72999	94672	69128	39046	15379	98450	09159
74978	98693	21433	34676	97603	48534	59205	66265	03561	83075
85769	92530	04407	53725	96963	19395	16193	51018	70333	12094
63819	65669	38960	74631	39650	39419	93707	61365	46302	26134
18892	43143	19619	43200	49613	50904	73502	19519	11667	53294
32855	17190	61587	80411	22827	38852	51952	47785	34952	93574
29435	96277	53583	92804	05027	19736	54918	66396	96547	00351
36211	67263	82064	41624	49826	17566	02476	79368	28831	02805
73514	00176	41638	01420	31850	41380	11643	06787	09011	88924
90895	93099	27850	29423	98693	71762	39928	35268	59359	20674
69719	90656	62186	50435	77015	29661	94698	56057	04388	33381
94982	81453	87162	28248	37921	21143	62673	81224	38972	92988
84136	04221	72790	04719	34914	95609	88695	60180	58790	12802
58515	80581	88442	65727	72121	40481	06001	13159	55324	93591
20861	59164	75797	08928	68381	12616	97487	84803	92457	88847

* Reproduced with permission from the Rand Corporation, *A million Random Numbers*, Free Press, Glencoe, Ill., 1955.

Table 21. Random Normal Numbers*
(Gaussian deviates)

1.102	− .944	.401	.226	1.396	−1.030	−1.723	− .368	2.170	.393
.148	−1.140	.492	−1.210	− .998	.573	.893	− .855	−2.209	− .267
2.372	1.353	− .900	− .554	− .343	.470	−1.033	−1.026	2.172	.195
− .145	.466	.854	− .282	−1.504	.431	− .060	.952	− .343	.735
.104	.732	.604	− .016	− .266	1.372	− .925	−1.594	−2.004	1.925
1.419	−1.853	− .347	.155	−1.078	.623	− .024	.498	.466	.049
.069	− .411	− .661	− .037	.703	.532	− .177	.395	− .278	.240
.797	.488	−1.070	− .721	−1.412	− .976	−1.953	− .206	1.848	.632
− .393	− .351	.222	.557	−1.094	1.403	.173	− .113	.806	.939
− .874	−1.336	.523	.848	.304	− .202	−1.279	.501	.396	.859
.125	−1.170	− .192	1.387	2.291	− .959	.090	1.031	.180	−1.389
−1.091	− .649	− .514	− .232	−1.198	.822	.240	.951	−1.736	.270
2.304	.481	− .987	−1.222	.549	−1.056	.277	− .919	.148	1.517
− .961	2.057	− .546	− .896	.165	− .343	.696	.628	− .929	− .965
− .783	.854	− .139	1.087	.515	− .876	− .448	.485	.589	− .804
.487	.557	.327	1.280	−1.731	− .339	.295	− .724	.720	.331
− .299	.979	− .924	− .649	.574	1.407	− .292	− .775	− .511	.026
1.831	− .937	−1.321	−1.734	1.677	−1.393	−1.187	− .079	− .181	− .844
.243	.466	−1.330	1.078	−1.102	1.123	− .421	− .674	2.951	− .743
−2.181	−1.854	−1.059	− .478	−1.119	.272	− .800	.841	− .061	2.261
.154	− .333	1.011	−1.565	1.261	.776	1.130	1.552	− .563	.558
−1.065	1.610	.463	.062	− .086	.021	1.633	1.788	.480	2.824
1.083	− .760	− .012	.183	.155	.676	−1.315	.067	.213	2.380
.615	− .594	− .028	− .506	− .054	3.173	.817	.210	1.699	1.950
.178	− .500	1.100	1.613	1.048	2.323	− .174	− .033	2.220	− .661
− .507	−1.273	.596	.690	−1.724	−1.689	.163	− .199	− .450	.244
.362	− .588	−1.386	.072	.778	− .591	.365	.465	2.472	1.049
.775	1.546	.217	−1.012	.778	.246	1.055	1.071	.447	− .585
.818	.561	−1.024	2.105	− .868	.060	− .385	1.089	.017	− .873
.014	.240	− .632	− .225	− .844	.448	1.651	1.423	.425	.252
−1.236	−1.045	−1.628	.687	.983	− .840	−1.835	−1.864	1.327	− .408
− .567	−1.161	.010	− .853	.111	1.145	1.015	.056	.141	1.471
.278	−1.783	.170	− .358	.705	− .054	1.098	.707	− .585	− .305
− .959	− .497	.688	− .268	−1.431	− .791	− .727	.958	.237	.092
1.249	.037	.497	.579	− .227	.860	.349	2.355	2.184	−1.744
− .915	− .164	−1.166	1.529	.008	.636	−1.080	− .688	2.444	−1.316
.132	2.809	−1.918	−1.083	− .642	− .179	.339	.637	.063	− .079
− .156	−1.664	1.140	.295	1.086	−2.546	− .002	− .672	.205	− .039
.538	−1.143	− .390	.165	− .160	.457	−1.307	.273	− .670	− .988
.027	− .057	.742	− .149	− .801	1.702	− .346	− .053	.892	−1.181
.023	.423	1.051	− .831	− .325	− .795	−1.129	− .287	.172	− .793
− .196	−1.457	1.060	.557	− .190	− .891	− .768	.282	−1.432	− .447
.133	.577	− .332	−1.932	.220	.189	−1.521	.896	− .781	− .899
.020	− .217	− .856	.605	.072	.520	1.222	− .181	− .266	−1.222
1.405	1.065	1.350	1.353	−2.289	−1.003	.375	1.621	−1.126	.937
.178	−1.237	− .520	− .603	−1.615	− .358	.605	− .407	−2.579	−1.811
−1.438	.104	−1.821	− .390	− .630	1.294	1.470	.991	− .355	−1.285
1.768	− .175	− .450	.915	− .221	− .019	1.864	.038	.058	1.212
.099	1.076	2.348	−1.550	.458	.147	−1.223	.994	−1.657	1.264
.951	.252	−1.261	− .963	.221	− .036	− .395	− .252	−1.379	1.885

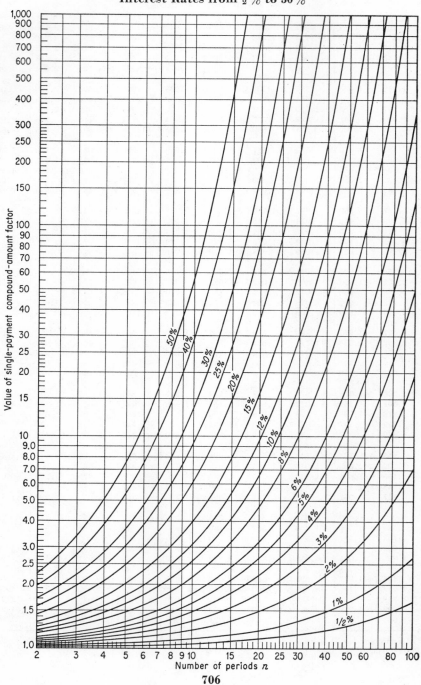

Chart 2. Single-payment Present-worth Factors for Various Interest Rates from $\frac{1}{2}\%$ to 50%

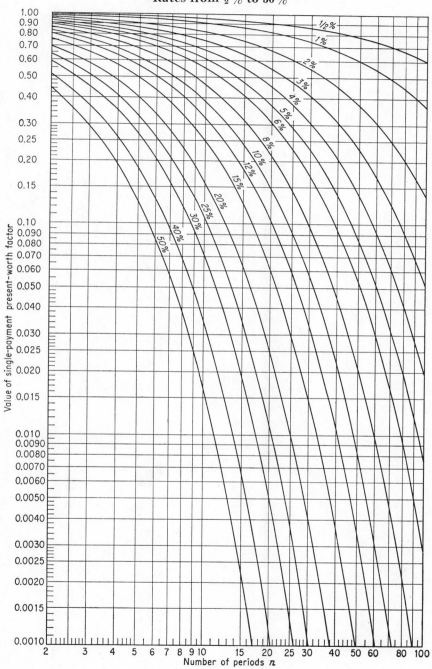

Chart 3. Uniform-series Compound-amount Factors for Various
Interest Rates from $\frac{1}{2}$% to 50%

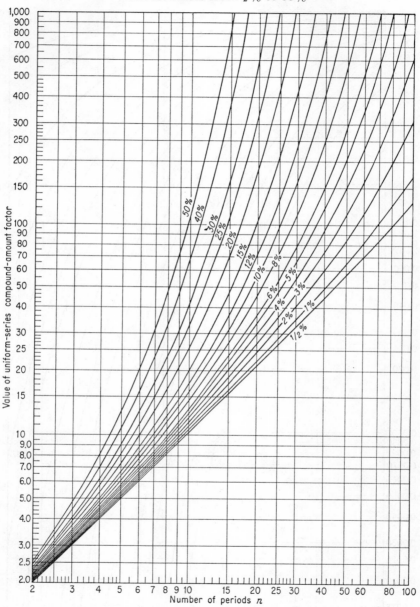

Chart 4. **Sinking-fund-payment Factors for Various Interest Rates**
from $\frac{1}{2}\%$ to 50%

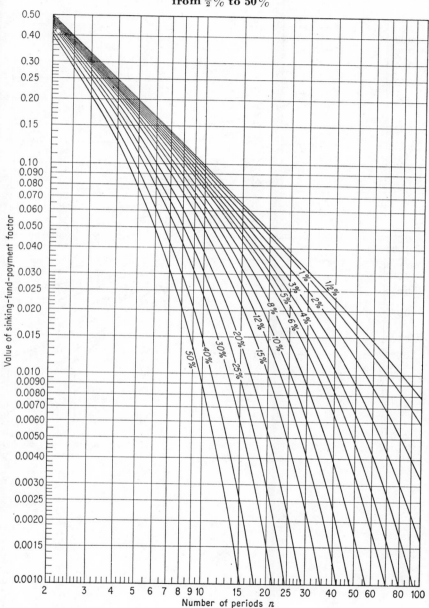

Chart 5. **Capital-recovery Factors for Various Interest Rates from $\frac{1}{2}\%$ to 50%**

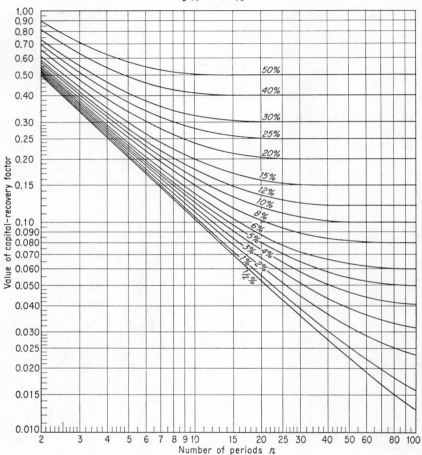

Chart 6. Uniform-series Present-worth Factors for Various Interest Rates from $\frac{1}{2}\%$ to 50%

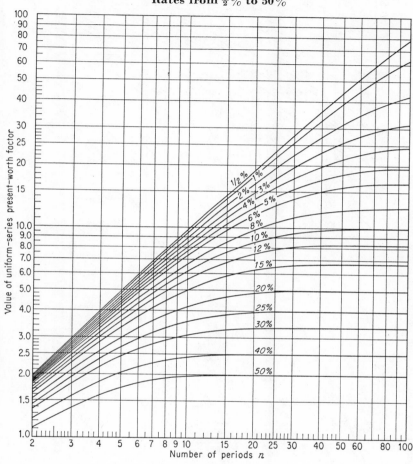

Chart 7. Curves for Determining Probability of Observing *d* or Less Poisson Occurrences in a Sample Selected from a Population Having an Average of *c* Occurrences Per Unit of Space or Time

(Reproduced, with slight modifications, from Dodge and Romig, *Sampling Inspection Tables,* John Wiley & Sons, Inc., New York, 1944.)

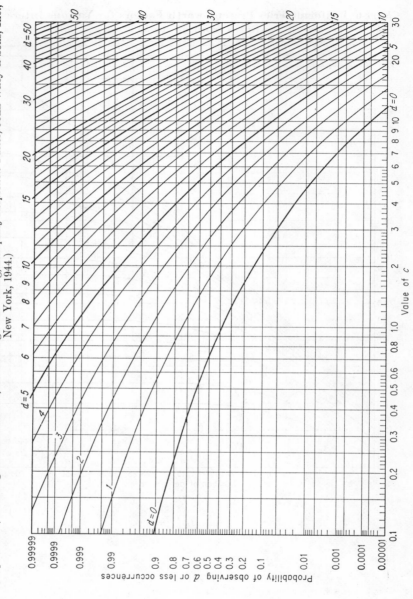

Selected Bibliography

BOOKS

General

Barish, N. N., *Systems Analysis for Effective Administration*, Funk & Wagnalls Company, New York, 1951.

Bowman, E. H., and R. B. Fetter, *Analysis for Production Management*, Richard D. Irwin, Inc., Homewood, Ill., 1957.

Buffa, E. S., *Modern Production Management*, John Wiley & Sons, Inc., New York, 1961.

Cabell, R. W., and A. Phillips, *Problems in Basic Operations Research Methods for Management*, John Wiley & Sons, Inc., New York, 1961.

Carson, G. B. (ed.), *Production Handbook*, The Ronald Press Company, New York, 1958.

Chapin, N., *An Introduction to Automatic Computers*, D. Van Nostrand Company, Princeton, N.J., 1957.

Churchman, C. W., R. L. Ackoff, and E. L. Arnoff, *Introduction to Operations Research*, John Wiley & Sons, Inc., New York, 1957.

Dean, J., *Managerial Economics*, Prentice-Hall, Inc., Englewood Cliffs, N.J., 1951.

Goetz, B. E., *Management Planning and Control*, McGraw-Hill Book Company, Inc., New York, 1949.

Goode, H. H., and R. E. Machol, *System Engineering*, McGraw-Hill Book Company, Inc., New York, 1957.

Ireson, W. G., and E. L. Grant (eds.), *Handbook of Industrial Engineering and Management*, Prentice-Hall, Inc., Englewood Cliffs, N.J., 1955.

Juran, J. M. (ed.), *Quality Control Handbook*, McGraw-Hill Book Company, Inc., New York, 1951.

——— and N. N. Barish, *Case Studies in Industrial Management*, McGraw-Hill Book Company, Inc., New York, 1955.

Manne, A. S., *Economic Analysis for Business Decisions*, McGraw-Hill Book Company, Inc., New York, 1961.

March, J. G., and H. A. Simon, *Organizations*, John Wiley & Sons, Inc., New York, 1958.

Maynard, H. B. (ed.), *Industrial Engineering Handbook*, McGraw-Hill Book Company, Inc., New York, 1956.

McCloskey, J. F., and F. N. Trefethen, *Operations Research for Management*, Johns Hopkins Press, Baltimore, Md., Vol. I, 1955, Vol. II ,1956.

McKean, R. W., *Efficiency in Government through Systems Analysis*, John Wiley & Sons, Inc., New York, 1958.

Miller, D. W., and M. K. Starr, *Executive Decisions and Operations Research*, Prentice-Hall, Inc., Englewood Cliffs, N.J., 1960.

Morris, W. T., *Engineering Economy*, Richard D. Irwin, Inc., Homewood, Ill., 1960.

Morse, P. M., *Queues, Inventory, and Maintenance*, John Wiley & Sons, Inc., New York, 1958.

——— and G. E. Kimball, *Methods of Operations Research*, Technology Press, M.I.T., Cambridge, Mass, 1951.

Saaty, T. L., *Mathematical Methods of Operations Research*, McGraw-Hill Book Company, Inc., New York, 1959.

SASIENI, M., A. YASPAN, and L. FRIEDMAN, *Operations Research Methods and Problems*, John Wiley & Sons, Inc., New York, 1959.

SHUBIN, J. A., *Managerial and Industrial Economics*, The Ronald Press Company, New York, 1961.

SIMON, H. A., *Administrative Behavior*, The Macmillan Company, New York, 1957.

SPENCER, M. H., and L. SIEGELMAN, *Managerial Economics*, Richard D. Irwin, Inc., Homewood, Ill., 1959.

VILLERS, R., *Dynamic Management in Industry*, Prentice-Hall, Inc., Englewood Cliffs, N.J., 1960.

Costs

ANTHONY, R. N., *Management Accounting*, Richard D., Irwin, Inc., Homewood, Ill., 1960.

BARDES, P., J. J. MAHON, Jr., J. McCULLOUGH, and M. E. RICHARDSON (eds.), *Montgomery's Federal Taxes*, The Ronald Press Company, New York, 1958.

GRANT, E. L., *Basic Accounting and Cost Accounting*, McGraw-Hill Book Company, Inc., New York, 1956.

——— and P. T. NORTON, *Depreciation*, The Ronald Press Company, New York, 1955.

HILL, T. H., and M. J. GORDON, *Accounting—A Management Approach*, Richard D. Irwin, Inc., Homewood, Ill., 1959.

SMITH, C. A., and J. G. ASHBURNE, *Financial and Administrative Accounting*, 2d ed., McGraw-Hill Book Company, Inc., New York, 1960.

STELSON, H. E., *Mathematics of Finance*, D. Van Nostrand Company, Inc., Princeton, N.J., 1957.

U.S. Master Tax Guide, Commerce Clearing House, Inc., Chicago, Ill., Published annually.

Tangible Engineering Economic Evaluation

BULLINGER, C. E., *Engineering Economy*, 3d ed., McGraw-Hill Book Company, Inc., New York, 1958.

DE GARMO, E. P., *Introduction to Engineering Economy*, The Macmillan Company, New York, 1960.

GRANT, E. L., and W. G. IRESON, *Principles of Engineering Economy*, The Ronald Press Company, New York, 1960.

HAPPEL, J., *Chemical Process Economics*, John Wiley & Sons, Inc., New York, 1958.

HUR, J. J. (ed.), *Chemical Process Economics in Practice*, Reinhold Publishing Corporation, New York, 1956.

MARSTON, A., R. WINFREY, and J. C. HEMPSTEAD, *Engineering Valuation and Depreciation*, McGraw-Hill Book Company, Inc., New York, 1953.

OSBURN, J. O., and K. KAMMERMEYER, *Money and the Chemical Engineer*, Prentice-Hall, Inc., Englewood Cliffs, N.J., 1958.

PETERS, M. S., *Plant Design and Economics for Chemical Engineers*, McGraw-Hill Book Company, Inc., New York, 1958.

SCHWEYER, H. E., *Process Engineering Economics*, McGraw-Hill Book Company, Inc., New York, 1955.

STEINBERG, M. J., and W. GLENDINNING, *Engineering Economics and Practice*, W. Glendinning, Bayside, N.Y., 1949.

THUESEN, H. G., *Engineering Economy*, Prentice-Hall, Inc., Englewood Cliffs, N.J., 1957.

TYLER, C., and C. H. WINTER, JR., *Chemical Engineering Economics*, 4th ed., McGraw-Hill Book Company, Inc., New York, 1959.

Capital Management

BIERMAN, H., and S. SMIDT, *The Capital Budgeting Decision*, The Macmillan Company, New York, 1960.

DEAN, J., *Capital Budgeting*, Columbia University Press, New York, 1951.

EISNER, R., *Determinants of Capital Expenditures*, University of Illinois Bulletin, University of Illinois Press, Urbana, Ill., 1956.

FOULKE, R. A., *Practical Financial Statement Analysis*, 4th ed., McGraw-Hill Book Company, Inc., New York, 1957.

LESSER, A. (ed.), "Planning and Justifying Capital Expenditures," *The Engineering Economist*, Stevens Institute of Technology, Hoboken, N.J., 1959.

MEYER, J. R., and E. KUH, *The Investment Decision: An Empirical Study*, Harvard University Press, Cambridge, Mass., 1957.

TERBORGH, G., *Business Investment Policy*, Machinery and Allied Products Institute, Washington, D.C., 1958.

————, *Dynamic Equipment Policy*, McGraw-Hill Book Company, Inc., New York, 1949.

Inventory Models and Linear Programming

CHARNES, A., W. W. COOPER, and A. HENDERSON, *An Introduction to Linear Programming*, John Wiley & Sons, Inc., New York, 1953.

GASS, S. I., *Linear Programming*, McGraw-Hill Book Company, Inc., New York, 1958.

HOLT, C. C., F. MODIGLIANI, J. F. MUTH, and H. A. SIMON, *Planning Production, Inventories, and Work Force*, Prentice-Hall, Inc., Englewood Cliffs, N.J., 1960.

KOOPMANS, T. C. (ed.), *Activity Analysis of Production and Allocation*, John Wiley & Sons, Inc., New York, 1951.

MAGEE, J. F., *Production Planning and Inventory Control*, McGraw-Hill Book Company, Inc., New York, 1958.

MOORE, F. G., *Production Control*, 2d ed., McGraw-Hill Book Company, Inc., New York, 1959.

SYMONDS, G. H., *Linear Programming: The Solution of Refinery Problems*, Esso Standard Oil Company, New York, 1955.

WHITIN, T. M., *The Theory of Inventory Management*, Princeton University Press, Princeton, N.J., 1953.

Decision Theory

ARROW, K. J., *Social Choice and Individual Values*, John Wiley & Sons, Inc., New York, 1951.

BROSS, I. D. J., *Design for Decision*, The Macmillan Company, New York, 1953.

CARTER, C. F., G. P. MEREDITH, and G. L. S. SHACKLE (eds.), *Uncertainty and Business Decisions*, The University Press Liverpool, 1954.

CHERNOFF, H., and L. E. MOSES, *Elementary Decision Theory*, John Wiley & Sons, Inc., New York, 1959.

CHURCHMAN, C. W., *Prediction and Optimal Decision*, Prentice-Hall, Inc., Englewood Cliffs, N.J., 1961.

LUCE, R. D., and H. RAIFFA, *Games and Decisions*, John Wiley & Sons, Inc., New York, 1958.

THRALL, R. M., C. H. COOMBS, and R. L. DAVIS (eds.), *Decision Processes*, John Wiley & Sons, Inc., New York, 1954.

Probability and Statistics

BROWNLEE, K. A., *Statistical Theory and Methodology in Science and Engineering*, John Wiley & Sons, Inc., New York, 1960.

DEMING, W. E., *Sampling Design in Business Research*, John Wiley & Sons, Inc., New York, 1960.

DERMAN, C., and M. KLEIN, *Probability and Statistical Inference for Engineers*, Oxford University Press, New York, 1959.

DUNCAN, A. J., *Quality Control and Industrial Statistics*, Richard D. Irwin, Inc., Homewood, Ill., 1959.

EZEKIEL, M., and K. A. FOX, *Methods of Correlation and Regression Analysis*, John Wiley & Sons, Inc., New York, 1959.

FISHER, R. A., *Statistical Methods for Research Workers*, Hafner Publishing Company, New York, 1948.

GRANT, E. L., *Statistical Quality Control*, 2d ed., McGraw-Hill Book Company, Inc., New York, 1952.

HALD, A., *Statistical Theory with Engineering Applications*, John Wiley & Sons, Inc., New York, 1952.

HOEL, P. G., *Introduction to Mathematical Statistics*, John Wiley & Sons, Inc., New York, 1954.

KENDALL, M. G., *The Advanced Theory of Statistics*, Vols. 1 and 2, Charles Griffin & Co., Ltd., London, 1952.

KURNOW, E., G. J. GLASSER, and F. R. OTTMAN, *Statistics for Business Decisions*, Richard D. Irwin, Inc., Homewood, Ill., 1959.

PARZEN, E., *Modern Probability and Its Applications*, John Wiley & Sons, Inc., New York, 1960.

SAVAGE, L. J., *The Foundations of Statistics*, John Wiley & Sons, Inc., New York, 1954.

SCHLAIFER, R., *Probability and Statistics for Business Decisions*, McGraw-Hill Book Company, Inc., New York, 1959.

WILKS, S. S., *Elementary Statistical Analysis*, Princeton University Press, Princeton, N.J., 1948.

———, *Mathematical Statistics*, Princeton University Press, Princeton, N.J., 1946.

Economics, Econometrics, and Forecasting

ALLEN, R. G. D., *Mathematical Economics*, St. Martin's Press, Inc., New York, 1956.

BASSIE, V. L., *Economic Forecasting*, McGraw-Hill Book Company, Inc., New York, 1958.

BAUMOL, W. J., *Economic Theory and Operations Analysis*, Prentice-Hall, Inc., Englewood, N.J., 1961.

BEACH, E. F., *Economic Models: An Exposition*, John Wiley & Sons, Inc., New York, 1957.

BODENHORN, D., *Intermediate Price Theory*, McGraw-Hill Book Company, Inc., New York, 1961.

BRATT, E., *Business Cycles and Forecasting*, Richard D. Irwin, Inc., Homewood, Ill., 1959.

CHAMBERLIN, E. H., *Theory of Monopolistic Competition*, Harvard University Press, Cambridge, Mass., 1956.

COLBERG, M. R., W. C. BRADFORD, and R. M. ALT, *Business Economics*, Richard D. Irwin, Inc., Homewood, Ill., 1957.

COPPOCK, J. D., *Economics of the Business Firm*, McGraw-Hill Book Company, Inc., New York, 1959.

DAVIDSON, R. K., V. L. SMITH, and J. W. WILEY, *Economics: An Analytical Approach*, Richard D. Irwin, Inc., Homewood, Ill., 1958.

DORFMAN, R., P. A. SAMUELSON, and R. M. SOLOW, *Linear Programming and Economic Analysis*, McGraw-Hill Book Company, Inc., New York, 1958.

DOYLE, L. A., *Economics of Business Enterprise*, McGraw-Hill Book Company, Inc., New York, 1952.

KLEIN, L. R., *A Textbook of Econometrics*, Row, Peterson & Company, Evanston, Ill., 1953.

——— and A. S. GOLDBERGER, *An Econometric Model of the United States 1929–1952*, North-Holland Publishing Company, Amsterdam, 1955.

LEWIS, J. P., *Business Conditions Analysis*, McGraw-Hill Book Company, Inc., New York, 1959.

NEWBURY, F. D., *Business Forecasting*, McGraw-Hill Book Company, Inc., New York, 1952.

SAMUELSON, P. A., *Economics: An Introductory Analysis*, 5th ed., McGraw-Hill Book Company, Inc., New York, 1961.

Short-term Economic Forecasting, National Bureau of Economic Research, Studies in Income and Wealth, Vol. 17, Princeton University Press, Princeton, N.J., 1955.

SHUBIK, M., *Strategy and Market Structure*, John Wiley & Sons, Inc., New York, 1959.

TINTNER, G., *Econometrics*, John Wiley & Sons, Inc., New York, 1952.

VALAVANIS, S., *Econometrics*, McGraw-Hill Book Company, Inc., New York, 1959.

JOURNALS

The American Economic Review, published five times a year at Menasha, Wisc., by the American Economic Association

Econometrica, published quarterly at the North-Holland Publishing Company, Amsterdam, by the Econometric Society

The Engineering Economist, a quarterly journal devoted to the problems of capital investment, published at Stevens Institute of Technology, Hoboken, New Jersey, by the Engineering Economy Division of the American Society for Engineering Education

The Journal of Industrial Engineering, published bimonthly at Atlanta, Georgia, by the American Institute of Industrial Engineers

Management Science, published quarterly at Baltimore, Md., by the Institute of Management Sciences

Operations Research, published bimonthly at Baltimore, Md., by the Operations Research Society of America

BIBLIOGRAPHIES

CARPENTER, R. N., *Guidelist for Marketing Research and Economic Forecasting,* Research Study 50, American Management Association, New York, 1961.

DISNEY, R. L., "A Review of Inventory Control Theory," *The Engineering Economist,* vol. 6, no. 4, pp. 1–33, Summer, 1961.

EDWARDS, W., "The Theory of Decision Making," *Psychological Bulletin,* vol. 51, no. 4, pp. 380–417, July, 1954.

MALCOLM, D. G., "Bibliography on the Use of Simulation in Management Analysis," *Operations Research,* vol. 8, no. 2, pp. 169–177, March–April, 1960.

NEWBERRY, T. L., "A Classification of Inventory Control Theory," *Journal of Industrial Engineering,* vol. 11, no. 5, pp. 391–397, September–October, 1960.

Operations Research Group, Case Institute of Technology, *A Comprehensive Bibliography on Operations Research,* John Wiley & Sons, Inc., New York, 1958.

SWALM, R., "Economics of Machine Selection and Replacement—A Bibliography," *The Engineering Economist,* vol. 6, no. 3, pp. 51–57, Spring, 1961.

WASSERMAN, P., with F. S. SILANDER, *Decision-making: An Annotated Bibliography,* Graduate School of Business and Public Administration, Cornell University, Ithaca, N.Y., 1958.

Index